THE LAITY IN CHRISTIAN HISTORY AND TODAY

KENNETH HYLSON-SMITH

*This book is dedicated to my son Simon
with great affection and respect*

First published in Great Britain in 2008

Society for Promoting Christian Knowledge
36 Causton Street
London SW1P 4ST

Copyright © Kenneth Hylson-Smith 2008

All rights reserved. No part of this book may be reproduced or transmitted in any form or by any means, electronic or mechanical, including photocopying, recording, or by any information storage and retrieval system, without permission in writing from the publisher.

SPCK does not necessarily endorse the individual views contained in its publications.

Unless otherwise noted, Scripture quotations are taken from the New Revised Standard Version of the Bible, Anglicized Edition, copyright © 1989, 1995 by the Division of Christian Education of the National Council of the Churches of Christ in the USA. Used by permission. All rights reserved.

British Library Cataloguing-in-Publication Data
A catalogue record for this book is available from the British Library

ISBN 978–0–281–06074–0

1 3 5 7 9 10 8 6 4 2

Typeset by Graphicraft Ltd, Hong Kong
Printed in Great Britain by Ashford Colour Press

Produced on paper from sustainable forests

Contents

About the author		iv
Preface		v
Abbreviations		vii
Introduction		ix
1	From apostolic times to AD 313	1
2	From AD 313 to the beginning of the medieval period	25
3	From the eleventh century to the late fourteenth century	44
4	From the late fourteenth century to the mid-seventeenth century	68
5	The laity and the birth of the modern age	87
6	The laity in worldwide nineteenth-century Christianity	107
7	The laity in twentieth-century Christianity	129
8	The laity in the Orthodox Church	147
9	The contemporary lay scene in worldwide Christianity	163
Notes		184
Bibliography		200
Index		209

About the author

Dr Hylson-Smith is a former Bursar and Fellow of St Cross College, Oxford, and the author of ten previous books on Church history, including the three-volume works *The Churches in England from Elizabeth I to Elizabeth II* (SCM Press, 1996, 1997, 1998) and *Christianity in England from Roman Times to the Reformation* (SCM Press, 1999, 2000, 2001) and *To the Ends of the Earth: The Globalization of Christianity* (Paternoster Press, 2007).

Preface

In 1963 a highly distinguished team of academics wrote a series of essays, edited by Stephen Neill and Hans-Ruedi Weber, under the title, *The Layman in Christian History*.[1] Recently a major new multi-volume publication, again with contributions by prominent scholars, called *A People's History of Christianity* was launched.[2] Both were pioneer works. This present book addresses the same topic, but it has the advantage of being by one author, thus giving coherence and unity to what is said, and it also gains from being restricted to one quite slender volume.

It is remarkable that it has taken so long for such historical accounts of the church to appear. After all, it is the laity who together give the fullest and most tangible expression to the whole concept of the church as being the body of Christ on earth. Not only so, but they have become ever more prominent in the post-Reformation church, and are currently a key element in global Christianity. And yet, despite their undoubted and increasing importance, their story, and an analysis of their role in contemporary world Christianity, has been almost totally neglected other than in the works just cited.

And now is an opportune moment to issue this book. In addition to the much-increased worldwide lay participation in church matters during the last two hundred years or so, other developments have highlighted the centrality of the laity in the life of the universal church. Among the most noteworthy of these have been the emergence and staggering growth of Pentecostalism as an almost totally lay movement; the proliferation of indigenous independent churches, especially in sub-Saharan Africa, that often stress the importance of the laity; the multiplication of Christian lay organizations that act as agencies for evangelism, pastoral work and a vast range of relief and welfare works; and the enhanced prominence of lay women in church life.

Inevitably, the wide-ranging nature of the present study means that it rests almost completely on secondary sources. The bibliography and the notes attest to the author's utter dependence on the work of others. He is also aware that he has leant heavily on some of his previous publications, simply because they deliberately tried to give due weight and importance to the laity. These are listed in the bibliography.

Preface

In the writing of this book, I am especially indebted to all the decision-making bodies of SPCK, to the staff involved, and especially to Simon Kingston, the General Secretary, Rebecca Mulhearn, Hannah Ward, Neil Whyte, Louise Clairmonte, and other members of the SPCK Editorial and Production teams. All concerned have been unfailing in their encouragement, support and assistance.

Abbreviations

AJPH	Australian Journal of Politics and History
EHR	English Historical Review
H	History
HJ	Historical Journal
JBAA	Journal of the British Archaeological Association
JBL	Journal of Biblical Literature
JBS	Journal of British Studies
JEH	Journal of Ecclesiastical History
JIH	Journal of Interdisciplinary History
MS	Mediaeval Studies
P&P	Past and Present
S	Speculum
SCH	Studies in Church History
TBGAS	Transactions of the Bristol and Gloucestershire Archaeological Society
Trad	Traditio
TRHS	Transactions of the Royal Historical Society
TS	Theological Studies

Introduction

This book is ambitious in what it attempts to do. It tries to break through the conventional historical approach, at least in the Western world, of focusing attention very largely on the foremost public personalities, events, movements and group activities of any age, while, at the same time, allocating only a minor role in the drama of history to the rest of humanity. 'Traditionally, history has been regarded, from Classical times onwards, as an account of the doings of the great.'[1]

Fortunately, there has been a recent corrective trend to balance such a 'view from above' by at least some attempt at 'history from below'. Changes have been taking place during the last few decades. A new methodology is emerging. The concern of the historians who are adopting this new perspective is to take full account of the part played in the historical process by ordinary people; their experiences, opinions and contributions are reckoned as important. Some political, economic and social historians, and a few historians of the Christian church, have moved in this quite revolutionary direction, although the new approach is in its infancy.[2]

In the case of church history, the long-established, traditional 'paradigm' which gives priority to the lives, careers, policies, beliefs and philosophies of the most prominent church leaders, and to the leading political and other personalities who have seemingly had the greatest impact on the course of events in the life of the church, is still pre-eminent. Paramount attention is likewise given to the major theological or other relevant movements that have helped to shape the history of the church. This is perfectly understandable. It is fully justified to slant accounts of the past in this way, in order to provide a picture of the dominant features of the religious landscape at any one moment or over a period of time. The problem lies in the fact that up to the mid-twentieth century, and to a large extent beyond that time, there has been an almost complete preoccupation with these macro matters to the virtual total neglect of what was happening at the grass roots. Regrettably, 'until a relatively recent date, the history of the Church was too often limited to the history of its hierarchy and its clergy, leaving the Christian masses in the shadows, as if they were somehow disreputable'.[3] It is only in the last half century or so that changes have started to appear.

In parallel with this tentative introduction of a more comprehensive attitude to church history, there has been the development of other associated disciplines. This has encouraged historians to collaborate with fellow academics to a degree that was not typical in the past. Cooperation with sociologists, social anthropologists, economists, literary critics, psychologists and others, has become more common, or historians have at least taken note of pertinent works in these relevant disciplines. Church historians do not, to anything like the same extent as in the past, pursue their studies in isolation.

Even so, there is a need to probe still further into the lives, activities and outlook of ordinary people than has so far been the practice. It is undeniable that they have always made up the vast majority of the church. In many respects they have always and everywhere been the most important part of the church. And this is not merely a matter of counting heads. As will be seen time and time again, the laity have been in the vanguard of church expansion, and then pivotal in establishing and consolidating local churches.

Of course, strictly speaking, all Christians, including ordained clergy and ministers, are laity in the sense that they are part of the *laos* of God of which the church is the collective entity. Nonetheless, 'there is a case for the separate study, both historical and theological, of the laity in the Church. The distinction between ordained and lay, between those whose sphere of service is primarily the Church and those whose sphere of service is primarily the world, is a real one.'[4] Of course, the church is in and is part of 'the world', and the terms 'church' and 'world' as just used can only be justified if 'church' is reckoned as the institutional, organized and structured body of believers, and the 'world' is taken as the sphere of life beyond and outside such a corporate expression of the faith. In this sense, 'it is mainly through its laity that the Church enters into contact with the world'.[5] Also, in every age, and especially in the modern era, some of the laity have been much more involved in the life of the institutional church than has typically been the norm in past centuries, and there have been worker-priests and others who somewhat blur the distinction between the two categories of *laos*, but this does not negate the differentiation. As a general rule, there is a valid distinction between the clergy and members of religious orders (of whom a number, although technically lay people, nevertheless receive their material support from the church), and those who rely solely on the generation of income from secular activities.

It has to be acknowledged at the outset that many and great difficulties surround any history of the laity so defined. For one thing, they are an elusive category of church membership, with very scant primary or secondary documentation to chart their history, and very little evidence of their attitudes, beliefs, practices and achievements. Clearly, this does not apply,

Introduction

at least to the same extent, to socially or politically prominent laity such as kings and nobles who have engaged in high-level matters of ecclesiastical policy-making and issues to do with religion and the state, as well as being patrons of cathedrals, abbeys, monasteries, churches and other Christian institutions and foundations. Such exalted members of society have received the attention of historians almost exactly in proportion to their importance on the social and political map of their day and generation, and to the extent that information on them is readily accessible. But the ordinary, local lay people have not been given the attention accorded to their more prominent and illustrious fellow laity. They just got on with their lives. For most of the two thousand years of church history they have truly been the submerged majority.

The hazard of over-simplified summaries and blanket generalizations is fully appreciated. Locally, nationally, regionally and, of course, universally, Christians have never been one undifferentiated body of socially identical believers. They have always been enormously varied from every point of view. And this complexity increased with the passage of time, as the number of Christians massively multiplied, and as the range of their social origins, and of their status and standing in society expanded. What Colin Morris said of the laity in the early years of the second millennium in the West is of wider relevance. He writes:

> There was not one lay culture, but many: the expression of a great noble's religion was very different from that of a citizen or a peasant, while peasant cultures were locally rooted and varied very much across the face of Europe. Worse than that, the concept [of lay Christianity] suggests that there was a distinctive type of religion characteristic of the laity, and this is broadly untrue. The *populus* does not appear as an autonomous cultural group, but as the recipients, eager or reluctant, of ideas handed down by their social and spiritual superiors.'[6]

The diversity of the laity must at all times be acknowledged, and differences identified. Nonetheless, as will be seen, it is still possible to discern overall patterns, and to comment on trends and general characteristics.

The present work also has high aspirations in that it attempts to cover the full gambit of Christian history from Roman times to the present day, and to encompass all the continents. This inevitably means much selection and many omissions. Despite its limitations and the pitfalls, however, a two-millennium time span, and a global picture is useful, and may help to stimulate further and fuller studies on particular times or places.

It needs to be made emphatically and unambiguously plain at the outset of this book that the present work is in no way an anti-clerical diatribe. It is not to be interpreted as a treatise exalting the laity at the expense of the clergy and ordained ministers. It in no way claims, or even implies, that the laity are more important than fellow Christians who are ordained; neither does it attempt to drive a wedge between the laity and 'full-time Christian workers'. It is not intended as an extended essay that champions full lay involvement in the life of the church either as a whole, or in the context of individual churches in particular, at the expense of clerical engagement. Far from it, for it appears that Christianity has had the greatest cutting edge, and been most dynamic and effective, when there has been a fruitful partnership between ordained and lay Christians. As will be seen, the church seems to have been most true to the New Testament pattern set for it, and to have been most impressively acting as salt and light, and as a vehicle for the propagation of the Christian faith by word and life, when the laity as well as the clergy and ministers have been mobilized, equipped and motivated for the task of faithfully serving as a vital part of the true *laos* of God.

1

From apostolic times to AD 313

The apostolic era – an all-member ministry

From the day of Pentecost to at least the end of the first century AD, Christianity was essentially a lay movement. As the faith spread from Jerusalem outwards, the converts gathered together in non-hierarchical groups in the homes of their members. There they enjoyed fellowship, prayed together, and shared in worship. The homes in which they met may have incorporated a small chapel, but they typically showed little evidence of any architectural elaboration or decoration, and would usually have been used for family and social purposes when not acting as a venue for the Christians. In a few cases, where the community felt secure and not threatened, they may have adorned one room in an overtly Christian manner. Whether this was so or not, the Christian groups would always have been small in number, but with all the sense of vibrancy and excitement that must have characterized companies of ordinary people who had enthusiastically accepted a new life-giving and life-transforming faith. Spontaneity and improvisation were evident in all that they did. Together, the believers explored their recently acquired faith, learning 'theology and practice' as they went along. Here were new, closely knit and highly charged communities of those who were launching out on uncharted waters.

This goes a long way to explaining how, despite the indebtedness of Christian worship to Jewish practices, there rapidly developed 'a distinctly Christian worship and fellowship from the very first days of the apostolic age',[1] and why Paul and other Christian writers paid such great attention to family life. In these Christian cells, the early church had the means of giving intimate fellowship to the converts. The house churches provided the basis for a Christian polity. They supplied a training ground for the laity as a whole, and for the leaders in particular. They were a potent factor in the building up of the early Christians in their faith, in welding them together, and in making them a powerful force in spreading the faith.

The laity, as distinct from any specially educated, trained or set-apart category of 'ordained' Christians, were central to the life, witness and work of the church as depicted in the New Testament, and this continued to be so for a considerable time. The apostles had a peculiarly prominent status and standing, not only, with the exception of Paul, as the personal friends and companions of Christ in his earthly ministry, but as the fathers in Christ of many of the converts; and their writings were of paramount importance in guiding the early church in its theology, liturgy and conduct. 'The intense missionary activity of Paul was, so far as is known, unique in the ancient world.'[2] Nonetheless, hugely important as the apostles and other itinerant evangelists were in providing the main initial missionary thrust to the Jesus movement, they did not exercise any controlling rights over local Christian fellowships. To the members of these unstructured, autonomous bodies fell the task of being Christ's ambassadors mostly, but not entirely, in urban areas, in an ever-widening circle. The first, quite small but nevertheless dramatic and significant, victories of the new faith were accomplished by a mixed array of believers, not many of whom were outstanding either socially or in terms of their talents and abilities.

The New Testament teaching and its practice

The New Testament makes it clear that all Christians have a calling to some form of ministry in the church. Chapter 12 of Paul's epistle to the Christians in Rome, and chapter 12 of his first epistle to the Corinthian believers are especially explicit and unambiguous on this point.[3] These and other New Testament passages leave no doubt that Christian believers are all to be viewed as *doulos*, slaves, of Christ, devoted to his service; all are exhorted to place themselves at God's disposal for service, as described in Acts 13.1ff. Every one of them, including the apostles, were designated as *diakonos*: those who were required to serve others, often in menial tasks. There is no hint that such devotion to God, and such service, is in any way to be the prerogative of a limited range of people, except for the precise, well-defined and particular appointment of deacons in the special situation arising at Jerusalem (see Acts 6.1–6).

The New Testament makes it plain that all Christians should regard themselves, and should be seen as members, one of another. The gifts given to each and every one of them should be used for the good of the whole, and for the promotion of the work of God. Paul uses the term *charisma*, not in the sense of extraordinary qualities that make a person remarkable, as expounded by the German sociologist Max Weber,[4] but as God-given abilities and talents which all the believers possess in varying forms. Romans chapter 12 mentions prophecy, serving others, teaching, exhortation, giving, leadership and showing compassion. Chapter 12 of

1 Corinthians identifies the utterance of wisdom, the utterance of knowledge, faith, the gift of healing, the working of miracles, prophecy, discernment of spirits, speaking in tongues and the interpretation of tongues. Ephesians 4.11–12 draws attention to different roles and responsibilities: apostles, prophets, evangelists, pastors and teachers. All such gifts and callings should be exercised and undertaken with love, which is the bond uniting all the believers as they individually apply themselves to one or more of the diverse and particular duties allotted to them. By and through such love, and by the working of the Holy Spirit in their midst, they are welded together into one harmonious and healthy body.

For the New Testament writers and for the Christians in the pioneering days of the first century, any suggested distinction between 'clergymen' and 'laity' would have sounded meaningless and absurd. They neither taught nor advocated any differentiation between two categories of Christians; between what in later parlance were described and perceived as the professionals, and the amateurs. Such a division, it seems, would have been alien to their view of the nature of the church, and even anathema to them. The gifts and tasks that were subsequently regarded as the perquisites of the clergy were not distinguished from those that were later to be seen as appropriate for the laity. All were part and parcel of a total mix and range of attributes required for the wholeness of the church. Every member of every church had something to contribute, and they were urged to play their part by doing what they were best able to do. There was not even a pecking order to distinguish who were more important than others. Perhaps the reverse, for Paul stressed how some of the members of the body 'that seem to be weaker are indispensable'.[5] It was all the Christian 'exiles of the Dispersion in Pontus, Galatia, Cappadocia, Asia and Bithynia', without exception, that the apostle Peter described in 1 Peter 2.9 as 'a chosen race, a royal priesthood, a holy nation, God's own people', brought to faith in order that they might 'proclaim the mighty acts of him who' had called them 'out of darkness into his marvellous light'. The status of the *laos* of God could hardly have been pitched at a higher level.

A number of well-known terms are used in the New Testament in reference to the various ministries that the early Christians fulfilled, but they are used in ways that are now unfamiliar. The three that are of most relevance to the present study are *episkopos*, meaning overseer, or bishop, *presbuteros*, meaning elder, or presbyter, and *diakanos*, meaning minister, or deacon.[6] A close look at these will help in appreciating the extent and way in which an original every-member ministry by the *laos* was first of all modified, and then radically altered, as changes took place in the leadership of the local churches.

In the first stage, the apostles exercised oversight over the small number of scattered believers and house churches that then existed.[7] Some people in some places seem to have used *episkopoi* to describe the local leaders. The collective term *presbuteroi* does not seem to have been used in this very early period. As the house churches multiplied, and as the various household leaders acted collectively, the word was applied to them. In the third stage, represented by the pastoral epistles of the New Testament and the writings of Ignatius, when the local churches had been deprived of apostolic oversight and were threatened with disunity and dissent, *episkopos* came to refer to the overall leader of a group of house churches in a town. The use of these two terms, together with *diakanos*, therefore appears to have been flexible, with changing connotations as the church developed and spread. But, always, everywhere and consistently, the terms were applied to lay Christians who were not distinguished from fellow believers in any way other than by their particular roles.

In almost every local situation the house church probably met in the home of a member who could provide the largest and most suitable venue. Such a householder naturally assumed some prominence. There was a great contrast between the comfortable and spacious houses of prosperous members of the trading and administrative classes, and the often adjacent or nearby relatively squalid living quarters of the more poverty-stricken members of society. Because they were able to offer sufficiently large and congenial accommodation for a local group of Christians, this alone helped to enhance the standing of some individuals within the fellowship.

In the Pauline churches, and probably in others as well, despite the members being equal, with no hierarchy, certain differences were apparent. Thus, in writing to the Christians at Thessalonica, Paul asked the believers to respect those who laboured among them, had charge of them in the Lord and admonished them, and to 'esteem them very highly in love because of their work'.[8] Such leaders were given no official title, largely because there was none to use, but these leaders stood out among the rest as *primus inter pares*.

Although the term deacon had a general meaning, it also had a more specific reference to a distinctive category of Christians; and, interestingly, this primitive diaconate included women. It is clear from Romans 16.1 that Phoebe held some official position, and she is described as *diakonos* of the church at Cenchreae. Women played a more significant part in early Christianity in general than was the case in any other religion. The declaration in Galatians 3.28 that 'there is no longer male and female' was exemplified by the fact that it was to women that the resurrected Christ first appeared, and it was to them that he entrusted the first proclamation of his resurrection to the disciples. The women were among the gathering of Christians praying together (Acts 1.14), and awaiting the promised outpouring of the Spirit. Some of the houses that were used for the meeting together and the worship of Christians were owned by women (see, for example, Acts 12.12; Acts 16.14; Rom. 16.11; and Col. 4.15), and women such as Mary and Tryphaena are mentioned as being engaged in Christian work.

It has been claimed that 'women were active evangelists, co-workers, patrons, even apostles in the early Pauline churches'.[9] Whatever the exact extent and scope there may have been for them to exercise a varied ministry, there certainly seems to have been an opening up of possibilities. There appears to have been fluidity and variation in the degree to which women were given freedom to speak and to act in a largely male-dominated environment. It is understandable that the moves to find roles for women were tentative and exploratory. 'Gender roles were under discussion and debate in Roman society',[10] and the thinking and practice of the young church was probably influenced by such reappraisals.

There have been various interpretations of the New Testament evidence for the part played by women in the life of the early church. Some scholars have asserted that they were 'subordinated within the Christian movement' rather 'than emancipated by it', and that the 'women of the Pauline church achieved brief visibility, and then respectable anonymity'.[11] This may be a somewhat harsh and cynical interpretation, as almost every believer, both male and female, appears and disappears in the same way in the New Testament writings, and some of the women are given as much extended attention as some of the men.

Nonetheless, it has to be said, that the degree of female emancipation, and the opportunity for service that was available to women in the apostolic and sub-apostolic era, are very much open to debate. And there remains the problematical exhortation of Paul in 1 Timothy 2.12, in which he states, without qualification, that a woman should 'learn in silence with full submission'. This apparent clamping down on the 'rights' of women in the church is seemingly further emphasized in the same passage, where the apostolic injunction is apparently clear and precise: that no woman is 'to teach or to have authority over a man'; but was rather 'to keep silent'. Scholars continue to argue over the appropriate exegesis of this passage. Some suggest that such a restriction applied to a peculiar situation in which there had been female abuse of legitimate authority, or that it made reference only to marital situations, with 'woman' being interpreted more accurately as 'wife', and 'man' as 'husband'. It must, anyhow, be said that the possible implications of a few verses in the pastoral epistles should not swamp 'the stronger witness of the apostolic churches as a whole that women and men initially acted as co-workers in the gospel of Christ'.[12]

Taking the scene in its entirety,

> [It] is clear that women were active in the expansion and shaping of the Church in the first centuries: they were apostles, prophets, teachers, presbyters, enrolled widows, deacons, bishops and stewards. They preached the Gospel, they spoke prophetically and in tongues, they went on mission, they prayed, they presided over the Lord's supper, they broke the bread and gave the cup, they baptized, they taught, they created theology, they were active in care of the poor and the sick, and they were administrators and managers of burial places.[13]

The overall picture regarding both lay men and lay women is incontestable. There was a noble and lofty concept of the church and of local churches. 'The letters of the Pauline circle are rich in words and phrases that speak of the Christians as a very special group and of the relations between them in terms charged with emotion.'[14] They are called 'saints' or 'holy ones'; they are the 'elect', 'called' by God, and 'known' by him; they are an extended family of believers, who can address each other as 'brother' or 'sister', because of their common salvation and adoption by God as his people, and they can greet one another with a 'holy kiss' (Rom. 16.16; 1 Cor. 16.20; 2 Cor. 13.12; 1 Thess. 5.26). In their fellowship, they strove to respect differences of race, social standing or sex, and to regard themselves as 'one in Christ Jesus' (Gal. 3.28). They even, as in Jerusalem at least, so cared for one another and were so concerned to express their unity in Christ that they shared their possessions (Acts 2.44; 4.32). The new religious community to which the believers belonged is described as 'the Way' (Acts 9.2; 19.9, 23; 22.4; 24.14, 22), and as a household of faith (Gal. 6.10). It is a new *ecclesia*, or 'assembly', whose members were united by their belief in the risen Jesus, and who confessed 'one Lord, one faith, one baptism' (Eph. 4.5). They are collectively called by this Lord to be 'holy and distinctive, an alternative society in the midst of a corrupt world'.[15] The believers entered into a new fellowship (*koinonia*) united by love (*agape*) for one another. All the terms used to describe the members of this fraternity are exalted and uplifting; and every person is equally qualified and responsible for making their individual contributions to the life and welfare of the whole body.

The depth and dynamism of the fellowship into which the converts entered helped in a process of re-socializing in which the individual's identity was 'revised and knit together with the identity of the group'; and this was made even more potent and effective when it was also 'accompanied by special terms for "the outsiders", and for the "world".[16] The Christians were taught to conceive of only two classes of humanity: themselves and the outsiders, many of whom were perceived as hostile to the beliefs and practices of the believers.

In addition to these designations of individuals and local Christian fellowships, the term *ecclesia*, or church, was used to cover Christian groups everywhere, considered either severally or as a whole. Thus, Paul spoke of the church of a province, such as Galatia, Asia, Macedonia or Judaea (1 Cor. 16.1; 16.19; Gal. 1.2; 2 Cor. 8.1; 1 Thess. 2.14), the church of the Gentiles (Rom. 16.4), and 'all the churches of Christ' (Rom. 16.16) or 'the churches of God' (1 Cor. 11.16, 22; 2 Thess. 1.4). Indeed, Paul and other leaders of the Christian mission stressed the notion of a universal brotherhood and sisterhood of the believers.

The emphasis on equality within the Christian fellowship applied despite differences in social standing. Paul says of the Christians in Corinth that not many of them 'were wise by human standards, not many were powerful, not many were of noble birth', but 'God chose what' was 'foolish in the world to shame the wise; God chose what' was 'weak in the world to shame the strong; God chose what' was 'low and despised in the world, things that' were 'not, to reduce to nothing things that' were, 'so that no one might boast in the presence of God'.[17] This probably applied to all the other local fellowships of Christians at the time. It implies that the great majority of the converts were quite low on the educational and social ladder, but in his description of the Corinthian believers, Paul repeatedly said 'not many', rather than 'none'. There appear to have been a very wide range of social strata represented within each local church, with some of the members able to read, and others, as attested by early Christian literature, able to write as well, which would place them in the top 2 per cent of Roman society.[18] Even so, 'there were no significant numbers of Roman elites in their ranks until Constantine'.[19]

It seems that the majority of these early believers were 'in the middle levels (but not as a middle class), between the elites and those of no status at all'.[20] Although there was no 'class' concept in that age and culture, it can be said with confidence that the bulk of the Christians were neither from the higher ranks of society, nor from the more populous lower, underprivileged or servile sections of the population. There were individuals from the higher echelons of society, such as people 'in Caesar's household', and Erastus in Corinth, who was the 'steward of the city'. One member of the exclusive Athenian Areopagus paid respectful attention to the preaching of Paul, and the 'first man of Malta' listened with respect to what the apostle had to say. 'Asiarchs' in Ephesus, who were at the summit of provincial society, gave him friendly advice, and the Roman governor of Cyprus was impressed by a miracle that was performed in his presence. At the other extreme, the Christian converts included slaves, and those in Macedonia who lived in deep, abysmal poverty. It can be said of the believers at the end of the first century, that, as stated by Pliny in a letter to Trajan in about 110, they were people of 'every rank, age and sex'.

Taking the churches as a whole, the most typical believer was 'likely to be an artisan, small trader; or skilled manual worker'. Some of these were of reasonable wealth. This was probably so with the tentmakers Priscilla and Aquila, who were free to move from city to city and act as patrons for both local believers and visiting evangelists (Rom. 16.3–4). Lydia, who was the first convert in Europe, was a merchant dealing in luxury purple fabrics, and her residence in Philippi was sufficiently large to accommodate Paul, Silas and their friends (Acts 16.13–15). 'The majority, however, were probably of more modest means – small-scale merchants, shopkeepers, and trades-people', but 'usually not people of significance or prestige within their society'.[21]

'Ordained' and 'lay'

There is thus an unambiguous and uncompromising picture presented in the New Testament of an all-member ministry, with each believer playing his or her part in the life of the nascent fellowships. In addition, there was no distinction made between full-time and part-time ministry. Paul and at least a few of his companions worked with their hands at certain times in order to help provide for their personal needs, and there is little evidence of a firm divide between those who may be said to have exercised official ministries and those who can be regarded as having served the church in less formal ways. Neither can a precise distinction be drawn between local leaders and itinerants.

Even so, this does not exclude the possibility that there was what would today be recognized as an ordained ministry. There is evidence that in some cases bishops, presbyters or deacons were set apart for their work with prayer and the laying on of hands. Acts 9.17 and 14.23, 2 Corinthians 8.19, 1 Timothy 4.14, 2 Timothy 1.6 and Hebrews 6.1–2 all point to this. The public recognition by the Christian community of the gift of leadership represented by such a commissioning suggests that there was some difference between 'ordained' and 'lay' believers. 'The sequence of apostles, then those whom the apostles in turn instructed, whether designated as "elders", "deacons", or something else', also points to 'a certain implicit order of spiritual and practical authority'.[22] But these are the only hints of such a differentiation, and the every-member ministry is the dominant and prevailing pattern that emerges both from the writings and the practice of the primitive church. Even when the beginnings of a more formal ministerial organization are indicated, as in the so-called pastoral epistles, 1 and 2 Timothy and Titus, with some identified and specified local church leaders whose authority was deemed to have derived from an apostolic commission, the ministry in its various manifestations seems to have been shared by a wide range of ordinary lay believers.

Thus, although the leading of worship was soon viewed as a function of the specialized ministry, there was no suggestion that it should be restricted to them. It was accepted that any member of the congregation had the freedom to speak out with some teaching, 'prophecy', choice of a psalm, or contribution by an utterance in tongues, provided everything was done in an orderly and edifying manner, as stated in 1 Corinthians 14.26, 40. And such diffused sharing in the conduct of services seems to have extended to the administration of the sacraments. Nowhere in the New Testament is it stated who should baptize and who should preside at the Lord's Supper. 'It apparently never occurred to the first generation of Christians that these actions hung together as a specific area into which no "layman" might trespass.'[23]

This house-church, lay form of corporate Christian life was to be found universally in the 42 cities of the Roman Empire where churches have been identified as established by the end of the first century.[24] The majority of such cities were in the Roman provinces that constitute modern Turkey, but they were scattered from Rome to Edessa in the Syrian East, and from Philippi in Macedonia to Cyrene in Libya. Arranged alphabetically, these territories included Achaia, Asia, Bithynia, Cappadocia, Cilicia, Crete, Cyprus, Dalmatia, Egypt, Galatia, Illyricum, Italy, Macedonia, Mysia, Pamphylia, Phrygia, Pisidia, Pontus and Syria, as well as the coastal areas of Palestine and Samaria.[25]

But there were limits on the extent of departure from the accepted normal structures and type of social life entailed in becoming a Christian. Although the early Christian fellowship members had an intense and profound sense of camaraderie, there is no evidence that the Pauline communities, let alone the later local churches, demonstrated 'the eschatological and enthusiastic form of sharing goods which we assume to have been practised by the earliest community in Jerusalem'.[26] The Jerusalem model appears to have been unique. Other churches did not imitate it.

> The reason for this is first, that the tension of the expectation of an imminent end was relaxed in favour of the task of world-wide mission, and

secondly, that in the long run the form of 'love communism' practised in Jerusalem was just not possible. It was impossible to maintain a sharing of goods in a free form, without the kind of fixed organization and common production we find, say, at Qumran.[27]

It was not, however, their corporate mode of living, whatever form it took, that was a problem in the relationship of the early Christians to the Roman authorities. The primary cause of stress between them and the state was not so much their conduct as their beliefs. The Romans were both very religious and yet tolerant of all faiths. Their only stipulation was that no religion should present a threat to Roman political and social values or Roman lordship. They were not so much theorists as practical men of action. They were quite prepared to condone numerous gods in their polytheistic societies; so that Christianity in this respect was no problem for them.

The trouble came for the Christians as a result of their exclusiveness; as a consequence of their assertion that their faith demanded full and unreserved allegiance; and by virtue of the fact that they could not compromise this by any acknowledgement of a competing deity or any yielding to a counter-claim on their devotion. This was the rub. To the Romans, the emperor was an embodiment of the unity of the empire, and was accorded honour that at times amounted to deification. State religion was not concerned with implanting personal faith, but was intended to reinforce the loyalty of subjects to the empire. The gods, so it was believed, would protect the state if the necessary rituals were performed; and any individual or corporate nonconformity detracted from and even put in peril the fulfilment of the divine side of the transaction. The worship of the Capitoline Triad of Jupiter Optimus Maximus, Juno and Minerva was therefore given high priority in the army and in the officially founded Roman towns, where most of the Christians resided. There was consequently a conflict on occasions between the Christian acknowledgement of the Lordship of Christ and the Roman insistence that all the people should pay at least lip service to the imperial cult, of which a central plank was the recognition of the divinity of the emperor. It was a dilemma that, in the second century, was to result in a number of martyrdoms.

The second century

By AD 200, the expansion of Christianity was still, as at the beginning, largely confined to urban areas. There were but few Christian communities in rural districts and smaller towns or villages. The largest cities involved were Rome, with an estimated population of 650,000, Ephesus (200,000),

Antioch (150,000), Corinth (100,000), Damascus (45,000) and Athens (30,000).[28] Eventually, churches in these and other cities became catalysts and resource centres in spreading the gospel and in establishing further churches in neighbouring towns and rural areas.

Of course, the power, drive and vibrancy that was evident in the first years of the life of the church could not be replicated exactly in subsequent generations. 'By the time of Hadrian, most Christians were born into the faith rather than converts.'[29] Even so, there was a persistent universally impressive level of dedication and energetic Christian witness during the second century, and the laity continued to play the major part in promoting the faith.

> The Christian community had no organizing centre, no missionary task force, no specially trained clergy. It spread through a network of family, friendship, business contacts, through the migration of its members, at times through the scattering effect of persecution, through the striking moral example its members offered – especially when persecuted – and through the impact of its rapidly increasing body of literature.[30]

As far as the latter channel of presenting the Christian faith is concerned, the 'lay' input was impressive. Although the general level of literacy among the laity was not high, there were a few notable exceptions, including those who increasingly contributed to the literary presentation and defence of the Christian faith. They were the primary authors of the works called *apologiae*. It is known that some of the apologists, such as Melito, Bishop of Sardis, and Apollonaris, Bishop of Hierapolis, were members of the ecclesiastical hierarchy, but 'the lack of any clear indication of the status of others probably means that they were simply members of the lay community'.[31]

The most outstanding among these so-called apologists[32] was Justin, who was martyred during the reign of Marcus Aurelius, in about 165. Despite the fact that he was the foremost of the apologists, he had no great philosophical or writing skill. But he was the first Christian thinker to attempt to reconcile the claims of faith and reason. He allowed that traces of the truth were to be found in the pagan thinkers, since all of humankind shared in the 'generative' or 'germinative' Word; but he set forth Christianity as the only truly rational creed. The Word became incarnate in order to teach people the truth and to redeem them from the power of demons.

However, despite the persisting centrality of the laity in evangelism and in the upholding of the faith, there was a slow but perceptible increase in the distinction made between them and the leaders of the church. The laying on of hands, and the commissioning of some for special ministry, which was a feature of the apostolic church, was sufficient to allow the idea of a distinction between 'ordained' and 'lay' to enter gradually into the thinking and practice of the believers and to become ever more firmly embedded and consolidated. It was the first sign of a moving away from the primitive conviction that all Christians were equally called to serve, and no one individual or group was superior to another. The seeds of a firm entrenchment of the threefold Christian ministry of bishop, priest and deacon were being sown. It was an order of ministry that was to become a hallmark of the church before alternative patterns were introduced from the sixteenth century onwards, and it came about as a response to changing circumstances, as the church grew in numbers and enlarged its geographical boundaries.

Nevertheless, the adaptations came about slowly. There was no rapid transition from one largely informal, non-hierarchical, unstructured pattern to another more rigid pattern involving greater differentiation. Thus, 'in the second century both women and men were active as prophets', and 'we find reference to the prophetic speech of individuals'.[33]

Three relics of the oldest Christian literature, the *Didache*, or the *Teaching of the Twelve Apostles*, certain literary fragments that constitute the *Apostolic Canons*, and the *Letters of Ignatius of Antioch*, all apparently written between AD 100 and 180, give a good idea of the changes that were introduced affecting the place of the laity in the life of the church.

Even as late as the middle of the second century, Justin, in his *Apology* (1:65), refers to the celebrant at the Lord's Supper simply as 'the president', and the *Didache* makes it clear that such an official was not invariably one particular type or category of person. What became increasingly evident, however, was the widespread, if not total, adoption of a more uniform and to a degree more rigid system of church administration. Each church began to have a recognized pastor or bishop, and the congregation was required to appoint at least two elders or presbyters. Every church was obliged to have at least three deacons, who were to minister to the people in their private and home life. They were charged to report on any unseemly conduct that might call for disciplinary action by the elders. Each church was also under obligation to have three women, called widows, to assist the sick women of the congregation, and to exercise a ministry of prayer. Finally, each congregation was expected to appoint a Reader, whose task was to read the Scriptures during the church services with a good voice and a clear delivery.

Taking the church as a whole, although there was no common, invariable, development, there was an increasing formalization. The letters of Ignatius to the western Asia Minor churches in the very early years of the second century portray the bishop 'as a chief minister, flanked by a group of presbyters and assisted by deacons, but it is also clear that such a three-fold ministry of bishops, presbyters, and deacons, did not exist everywhere'.[34] The letters of Ignatius were all addressed to named bishops. This suggests that in those cases at least, as at Antioch, there was already a system in which one person had come to assume overall responsibility for the life of the local church. Here can be traced the tap root of what would eventually blossom into a uniform system of monarchical bishops.

In spite of this measure of institutionalization and uniformity, however, the local church was still regarded as essentially an independent fellowship of believers, with a large degree of involvement of every member in its pastoral and evangelistic activity, and without an excessive amount of control either from the leaders or from without. 'For one thing, it seems clear that whatever the authority of the bishop may have been, it did not extend beyond his own church or congregation.'[35] He administered the finances of the church; he had moral oversight of the whole congregation, and he was the president of the court of discipline: he was empowered to call, and presumably to preside over, the congregational meetings; and to him was given the sole regulation of the sacraments. But this was all within the context of a local church and the self-government of each congregation.

Various other changes took place within the Christian communities, which likewise were gradual, but of considerable importance. One of these was an evolving, fuller and more complex pattern of initiation. In apostolic times, and up to the end of the first century, great care was taken to ensure that those who sought baptism understood the basic tenets of the faith and were resolved to abide by Christian moral standards. Baptism had mostly followed soon after a profession of faith. But as the number of converts from pagan backgrounds increased, it became more necessary to elaborate on the elementary instruction that had previously been found sufficient. The *Didache* reveals that it had become the common practice by the late first or early second century to require converts to pass through a period as catechumens, or 'those under instruction' (Greek *catechumenoi*), as a prelude to full admission into church membership. Whether the period of such instruction was a few days or weeks or as long as two or three years, it was undertaken with great seriousness both by the catechumen and by the spiritual leaders, primarily bishops, who took responsibility for the theological, liturgical, ritual and moral teaching entailed. And the candidates were not just treated as a group. They were examined individually in order to ascertain their progress, and what they especially required. The culminating baptism service itself was given great prominence. It was a solemn affair, preceded by fasting and followed by much rejoicing.

Worship – public and private

The worship of the lay Christian communities also altered considerably throughout the first two centuries of the Christian era. Within twenty years of the death of Christ, it had become the widespread practice to treat 'the first day of the week' (Acts 20.7; 1 Cor. 16.2) as the special time for Christian worship, commemorating the day on which the Lord had risen from the dead. Although the Jewish Sabbath was probably maintained as well by Jewish believers, by the beginning of the second century Sunday had replaced it for the vast majority of Christians. Nonetheless, it was not until the fourth century that it was formally sanctioned as a day of rest; and in the interim it remained for most of the Christians a regular working day.

It was during the later first century that the Eucharist became separated from the *agape* – the former being generally held on a Sunday morning, and the latter in the evening. By the middle of the second century, the *agape* had become only an occasional event, and by the third century it had almost ceased to be held at all, having become a charity supper for the needy rather than a fellowship meal for regular worshippers.[36]

What persisted throughout these early centuries was the practice of holding the Eucharist several times in the week or even, as stated in Acts 2.46, daily. The range of venues for such celebrations expanded in the second century. Social circumstances and the measure of freedom to worship were crucial variables. The normal location for the services remained the home of one of the believers but, especially during the times of persecution, the celebration was sometimes conducted in somewhat hidden and obscure places such as cemeteries, prisons and the tombs of martyrs or revered saints.

Alongside communal worship, the believers practised fasting and private prayer. The *Didache*, which was the oldest ecclesiastical manual, directed that Wednesdays and Fridays should be observed as Christian fast days, to dovetail into the Jewish fast days on Mondays and Thursdays.[37] Daily prayer continued to be regarded as an essential commitment of believers, and by the third century the usual three times for such prayer were the third, sixth and ninth hours of the day, that is, about 9 a.m., 12 noon and 3 p.m., which correlated with the prevailing divisions of the Roman working day. Prayer, Bible reading and singing, especially of the Psalms, were systematized into what became known as a daily 'office', used particularly when people were at home or with their families.

Prophecy

It was the almost total demise of the prophetic lay ministry that was of special significance in the corporate life of Christian worship. This had been a notable feature of the apostolic and immediate sub-apostolic times. 'Every prophet', the *Didache* pronounced, 'who speaketh in the Spirit, ye shall neither try nor judge; for every sin shall be forgiven, but that sin shall not be forgiven.'[38] But somewhat later, near the end of the second century, Bishop Irenaeus expressed very different sentiments. 'Wretched men', he says, 'who wish to be false prophets . . . holding aloof from the communion of the brethren.' And the litmus test of being in communion with the brethren was not to hearken to the prophets, but 'to obey the elders who are in the Church.'[39]

This move away from a key feature of the first-century church was one of those pivotal moments in the history of the laity:

> The change between the time when the prophet was not to be judged, but to be obeyed, and when disobedience to his commands was believed to be 'an unpardonable sin'; and the time when the test of a true prophet was obedience to the office-bearers of the local church, whose superior he had once been, amounted to a revolution.

The 'overthrow of the supremacy of the prophetic ministry rent the Church'.[40]

What it heralded was the ominous emergence of dissenting movements, in which Christians sought a greater 'freedom of the Spirit' as an alternative to the existing churches. The most prominent, divisive and momentous example of such a move in the first few centuries of Christianity, and no doubt the one which led Irenaeus to speak with such passion on the matter, was the sudden and devastating appearance of Montanism.

Montanism was both one of the causes and one of the results of the clamping down on the spontaneous prophetic elements in the churches, and the ever more pronounced formalization and non-participatory nature of Christian worship. There seems to have been a yearning after a lost empowerment; a feature of church life that was to reoccur with dramatic and on occasions devastatingly divisive consequences throughout Christian history, first in Europe then, from the eighteenth century onwards, in North America as well, and finally, from the nineteenth century to the present day, in the southern regions of the world, most notably in sub-Saharan Africa. Both in the early church and in later centuries, it was, on the one hand, a sign of vitality, enthusiasm, energy,

Christian zeal and earnestness, but, on the other hand, a major factor that helped to stimulate unhealthy schismatic tendencies. From the point of view of the present work, Montanism and the countless other such movements in the course of the following almost two thousand years are of particular interest because they have always been predominantly lay uprisings, albeit in many instances led by ordained men and women.

The Montanist standard of revolt was raised in the mountainous region of Phrygia, in Asia Minor, probably in 172. The territory was as much peopled by Christians as any part of the Roman Empire. It had also experienced outstanding examples of Christian prophecy. 'The daughters of Philip had lived in the great city of Hierapolis. The Christian prophets Quadratus and Ammia had belonged to Philadelphia.'[41] Attalus of Pergamos had been taught in visions.[42] Polycarp, the most distinguished Christian of the whole of Asia, was a prophet. Ignatius had exhibited his prophetic gifts in Philadelphia.[43] At the same time, if the territory had produced many Christian prophets, its churches had also been among the earliest to organize themselves under the threefold ministry. The prophetic and the local ministries confronted each other there as they did nowhere else.[44]

Two prophetesses, Priscilla (or Prisca, as Tertullian called her) and Maximilla, joined the Phrygian prophet Montanus, and the three declared that they were prophesying under the direct inspiration of the Paraclete. Unlike the traditional prophecy of earlier Christianity, which took the form of declaring the revealed word of God in the third person ('Thus says the Lord . . .'), they claimed to be the Holy Spirit's actual mouthpiece. Their utterances were probably accompanied by speaking in tongues and other open manifestations of fervour. They declared that the end of the world was near, they lived in expectation of the imminent outpouring of the Holy Spirit on the church, and they declared that the heavenly Jerusalem would soon descend near Pepuza in Phrygia. The movement spread rapidly from its original rural backwater to most parts of Asia Minor, and to urban as well as country districts.

Among its distinctive features was the sense of power and authority that it gave to a wide social range of lay men and, to the consternation of some mainline church leaders, to lay women as well. The 'New Prophecy', as it was termed, 'seemed to give at least some women a status that challenged conventional cultural assumptions about the overall primacy of male leadership, not to say the established structures of family life in which the man was head'.[45]

Lay Christians in society

By the end of the second century, Christians throughout the Roman Empire were still a small minority group. But they had grown considerably in numbers and they were more widely distributed. This enhanced and intensified their influence sufficiently to make them marked people in many places. Their beliefs and practices excited curiosity and interest, but also a degree of annoyance on the part of the authorities that was greater than in the first century. They were regarded at best as an irritant, and at worse they were quite often viewed as a threat, and detested. They met in secret, worshipped a triune God, and held to belief in a Saviour who claimed to be the exclusive way, truth and life – the only source of eternal life. Because of this, they stood out in contrast to the other religions which, as formerly, were far more tolerant, more open and public, less mysterious, and, in polytheistic Roman societies throughout the Empire, represented no threat to the imperial cult. The Christians, by what they believed and practised jeopardized the maintenance of the *pax decorum*, the peace of the gods. Understandably, they were on occasions hated and vilified because of this.

Many regarded the refusal of these upstart religious enthusiasts to indulge in the imperial cult, which frequently disqualified them for military service, as a dereliction of civil duty. The distancing of Christians from a wide range of social activities, associations, festivals and feasts, as well as trade guilds or social clubs, because of the link between all of these and traditional Roman religious values, 'must often have been resented by neighbours, relatives, and acquaintances as expressions of self-righteousness, and their apparent concentration on their own spiritual preoccupations must often have seemed like an obnoxious resistance to the patterns and practices of normal social life'.[46]

The discomfort and tension for ordinary Christian believers in attempting to hold to their faith must have been intense. Wherever they may have been living, such stress was continuous and relentless. It was a daily struggle for many of them simply to understand and to live out their faith in the midst of societies that were dominated by values that were so frequently anti-pathetic to what they held dear. This was perhaps especially so when such Christians lived in one of the outposts of the Empire, far away from the main centres of the Christian faith. It needs little imagination to picture individual believers, or small groups of Christians, wrestling with all the issues that confronted them; trying to grasp the essentials of the faith, and to grow in spiritual understanding in the context of an overwhelmingly pagan environment. Indeed, many if not most of the converts themselves must have had personal experience of one form or another of the various pagan cults before they became Christians; and the beliefs and practices of generations of ancestors were not readily discarded. It must have been an uphill struggle for those early Christians, and in many ways debilitating and enervating for them, to maintain their distinctive faith and to put it into practice day by day, year in, year out.

In addition, a high proportion of them in the second and third centuries, and to a lesser extent in the fourth and early fifth centuries, would probably not have totally abandoned their belief in the pagan gods and their powers. They had come to accept and to put their trust in the one they were convinced was the true God, and had found salvation in and through Jesus Christ. The pagan gods they had once worshipped were no longer regarded as true gods, but they had not ceased to exist in the belief and in the memory of the recent Christian converts. For these erstwhile pagans the age-old struggle between the forces of good and evil was compounded by the struggle to abandon deep-seated non-Christian beliefs that had, until very recently, been so powerful in their lives. 'Their own God would inevitably be victorious but the hostile powers were not to be treated lightly.'[47]

It was such Christians, weak, tremulous and all too aware of their own vulnerability, who, on occasions, were confronted with fearful persecution. The Christian martyrs were not, for the most part, exceptional, hardy, brave and fearless super men and women, but ordinary, frail, lay Christians, with a simple but sincere faith, which was focused on a personal, and for them very real, relationship with their Saviour, Jesus Christ. It was the strength that they found in and through their union with Christ, and the enabling that they were convinced was imparted to them by God the Holy Spirit, that allowed a host of 'ordinary' believers to face untold trials, tortures and death in a spirit that in so many instances seems to have been devoid of bitterness or hostility. Rather, there appears so often to have been a transparent sense of triumph and victory in the midst of pain and suffering. There was no active and prolonged hounding and persecution of Christians, and martyrdoms were few and far apart; but their effectiveness in both strengthening the resolve and dedication of the Christians as a whole, and as a means of witness to the faith, was considerable, and out of all proportion to the numbers who underwent such trials.

The Christian apologists also continued to play a powerful part in the promotion of the faith. Their works were not widely read, but their very existence was a proof that Christianity was becoming more intellectually respectable. By the later second century, Christianity had established itself 'as a teaching to which people of rank could respond'. What Christians believed 'could now be heard from educated people, not stray Galilean missionaries, and as converts began to be won in higher places', an ever-increasing number of non-Christians 'could hear of the faith from people to whom they could relate'.[48] As with the home or marketplace 'gossiping of the gospel', this was a slow, almost unobserved, process, but nonetheless pervasive and of great consequence. By the written and the verbal testimony of Christians, and by the quality of their lives, Christianity was making noteworthy strides forward.

The third century

By the beginning of the third century, Christianity was still an urban rather than a rural religion, although there is evidence that it was spreading out from the towns to many quite remote places. For example, by the year 200, 'there were more than 130 North African bishops, each presiding over a separate Church, sometimes hardly ten miles apart'.[49] The church was certainly not stagnant, and the lay members were undoubtedly active in both upholding the faith and in spreading it.

By the end of the century Christianity had advanced substantially in both its geographical coverage and in the number of followers: 'no other cult in the Empire grew at anything like the same speed'.[50] Despite remaining a small body in any one place, it was beginning to make its presence felt in society in a far more telling way than before. It was becoming deep-rooted, and it was about to receive official recognition by the emperor.[51] There were perhaps at least five purpose-built churches in Britain; Spain had almost sixty; in France and Germany there seem to have been almost one hundred; as well as more than one hundred in Roman North Africa, as just noted. There was also the considerable growth of the church in Italy, Egypt and Roman Turkey, which remained as the greatest concentrations of Christians in the world at the time. Finally, Christians had travelled east at an early stage, and by the beginning of the third century they were well established in Persia (the modern Iraq and Iran), were present in Nisibis (Syria), and had penetrated to the modern Indian province of Kerala.

For much of the third century, despite occasional and sometimes fierce persecution, the church existed in the open. The house churches continued to be the main feature of congregational life, but opportunities for the construction of more permanent meeting places were multiplying. Although the houses still used for the corporate life of the Christians remained as first and foremost domestic residences, their physical structure was increasingly altered to provide one or more dedicated rooms for long-term Christian fellowship and worship.

The social composition of the churches had undergone some modification since the pioneer days. As in former times, 'their centre of gravity lay with the humbler free classes, not with the slaves, whom they did little to evangelise'. There were Christians in the army and also in the imperial household, but it seems that there were 'no more than one, perhaps two, Christian senators. Women of all ranks were conspicuous and there was a notable presence in some churches of women of high status.'[52]

Christians were also beginning to participate in a greater diversity of work and leisure-time activities. They 'took a growing part in public life and a greater share of office', and by so doing they were confronted by the traditional celebrations surrounding public life with all that this implied for their religious loyalty to an exclusive faith. But there was an increasingly strong attempt to circumvent this problem by means of 'de-valuing the religious significance of traditional civic celebrations'. A case was made 'for treating these as no more than secular in nature'; as events that 'could be celebrated without the stain of idolatry'.[53]

Organizational, leadership and other changes

With the growth in the number of Christians, their greater dispersion, and the increased range of their social backgrounds, an ever more comprehensive and rational church structure and organization emerged.

First, there were changes among the laity themselves. By the third century there was a quite widespread acknowledgement of a two-tier laity: 'those who lived an ordinary Christian life in sincere commitment to the teaching of Jesus and the traditions of their community, and those who were pledged to a still nobler path, destined for spiritual perfection'.[54] There are indications of persisting prophetic activity, but this was exceptional, and not given much prominence or value. More store was placed on the style of life and the witness of Christians.

The universally recognized pinnacle in the attainment of discipleship perfection continued to be martyrdom, but short of this there were many ways to achieve greater self-sacrifice, all of which demonstrated and were tokens of the pursuit of ever greater Christlikeness and commitment to Christian ideals. These included poverty, chastity and the much emphasized preservation of virginity. The believers who adopted and abided by such ways of life were often reckoned to possess special intercessory powers. At times this attribution of higher spiritual status to such individuals had the regrettable consequence of denigrating ordinary believers who, in extreme cases, were hardly thought to be genuine followers of Christ at all.

Martyrs were even more the recipients of honour and adulation than in the past, and there is no doubt that they were remarkable. 'Their constancy and steadfast devotion were truly amazing. No passage of time, no change of circumstances can dim their glory.'[55] Behind their horrific suffering and death lay the whole theology of martyrdom in the early church. They and their fellow believers viewed their ordeals as a following, in some small measure, in the footsteps of Christ. 'Love of Christ and hope of salvation through Christ alone was their inspiration and the essence of their faith.'[56]

It is perhaps of little wonder, therefore, that from the second century, if not earlier, the veneration of the relics of those who had been martyred, or who for whatever reason were recognized as saints, was widespread and intense. Not only so, but there was a growing belief that miracles were in some cases associated with the bodily remains or other relics of saints.[57] This was a conviction that mushroomed during the fourth century, especially after 313, when Constantine declared Christianity to be a tolerated, and indeed favoured, religion.

Because the attainment of a higher spiritual status and standing, either as a result of martyrdom or for some other reason, was open to all Christians, both lay and ordained, it helped to blur the distinction between these two categories of Christians, and gave a greater measure of fluidity to this relationship.[58] But in general, and despite this levelling factor, in most local church situations there was a hardening and reinforcing rather than a lessening of the differences between the laity and, by the fourth century, what may be referred to as the clergy.

During the third century there were clear, if initially hesitant, moves towards what was later deemed to be a mediating priesthood, in which the ordained priest stood between the people and God as a sort of intermediary. Gradually it came about that teachers imparted and people received, priests interceded and sinners were pardoned through their intercession and, both in the acts of worship and in the life of the local church, rulers commanded and subjects obeyed. The laity was becoming the subordinate and subjected majority, and the leaders the dominant minority. It was a move that was to become ever more pronounced during the next thirteen hundred years.

Slowly, and at the time almost imperceptibly, a loose and flexible structure was replaced by a more rigid federation of local churches that was bound together by shared beliefs, hammered out at important councils that consisted almost entirely of bishops or other ordained Christians.

Such official creedal statements were then given confirmed authenticity by legitimate secular rulers, and were, for the most part, meekly received with unquestioning compliance by the laity. 'Authority in the church was being exercised collegially everywhere', and 'the effective, worldwide range of that authority'[59] was becoming very evident. By the middle of the third century, tests of orthodoxy that were contained in documents arising out of the large and important synods and councils, were supplemented by statements of belief issued by many of the major communities.

With all of this, went an augmentation of the authority of the bishop as head of the local church, to whom the local laity were expected to yield implicit obedience. 'Apart from presiding over the liturgy, ordaining clergy, and preaching, the bishop's life in the mid-third century was a busy one.' There was 'a continuous round of negotiations with authorities, of organizing charity and relief, theological debate, disciplining errant subordinates, as well as action on major questions affecting relations with other important sees'.[60] It was this new, more authoritarian federation of churches, under the bishops, that decided who were to be deemed as heretics and rebels, and that then went to work excluding from the church those so labelled. The church was to an extent, whether consciously or not, starting to be modelled on the organization of the Roman imperial cult. This was exemplified in the title of *Pontifex Maximus*, applied at first in scorn by Tertullian at the beginning of the third century to what he regarded as an overweening Bishop of Rome. It was an attribution that was then deliberately appropriated by the Bishop of the capital city. And it remained, with all that it powerfully implied of a claim to be the Christian ruler over the whole of the Christian church as then constituted.

One of the consequences of this much greater formalization, centralization, comprehensiveness and rigidity of structure was a multiplication of subordinate ecclesiastical offices. In both the East and the West, there was a notable increase in the number and diversity of lower-order clergy. It was a trend that was purposely set and led mainly by the Roman church, and implemented by the organizational genius of that ever more efficient international body. The process began in the fourth decade of the third century and, in the West, the minor orders had been almost completely instituted and established by the beginning of the fourth century. In addition to the bishops, elders and deacons, there were sub-deacons, readers, exorcists, acolytes, door-keepers and grave-diggers, with the readers and exorcists essentially representing the old prophetic ministry, and the acolytes and the door-keepers being reminiscent of the officials in the state temples.

Many of the lesser officers and personnel in what was becoming a formidable civil service headed by the bishops were not ordained, but the general drift was clearly in the direction of increased clericalization. This was emphasized in the way that the liturgy was becoming more rigid and the penitential system more exact, with both becoming a clerical preserve. At the beginning of the third century, the lay people in many places were still expected to take an active part in the services of worship, as at Carthage, where they prophesied or sang something they had composed. In that church, and possibly also at other places including Rome, the laity could also baptize. But by the mid-third century this had changed. There is little or no reference from then onwards to baptism services conducted by laity, and the celebration of the mysteries had become the responsibility of priests alone.

The church and the laity at the opening of the fourth century

As the fourth century opened, Christianity had been planted, or in many cases had become well established, in a wide swathe of the then known world. And, wherever one looks, its expansion, its taking root and its growth had relied not on military force or political influence, but upon the zeal, the dedication and the often patient and gentle witness and work of ordinary lay Christians as well as ordained Christian leaders. As in previous centuries, in all areas 'Christianity spread informally between individuals'.[61] Other religions and religious movements, both old and new, had been plentiful and pluralism was a fact of life, but this one faith had blossomed and become a remarkably powerful force as none other had done. Within the Roman Empire itself, it has been reckoned that by the early fourth century 10 per cent or more of the population called themselves Christian.

In parallel with this, and partly as a result of the triumphant march of Christianity, there had been a pronounced decline in the popularity of pagan cults and regional deities by the first decade of the fourth century. This helps to account for the fact that even before the 313 Edict of Milan, the Christian community had attracted more wealthy and high-status individuals than in former years, including, at least in the case of the church at Rome, ladies of high social standing (*matronae*) and civil servants (*Caesariani*) who had their own slaves. The core element among the believers continued to be those in the middle ranks of the social strata, but the drift was upwards socially rather than downwards. This is attested by the art, writing and ethical code of the late third-century and early fourth-century Christians.

As a facet of these shifts in religious alignment, the life of local churches had become more open and visible.

> Christians still often met in private houses, but in many places their meeting rooms were officially recognized as church property, their clergy were publicly accepted as leaders, and their rituals, teachings, and patterns of organization were witnessed routinely by society at large.[62]

Of course, Christianity was far from being a phenomenon of widespread interest and attention. The majority of the people in places where there were Christians were uninterested, unconcerned and unmoved by what was seen or what was rumoured to be the odd behaviour and beliefs of these followers of the Way. But it was not easy to ignore them or escape from the effects of their enthusiasm in the closely knit, intimate, face-to-face conditions of ancient urban society, or the small, compact, environment of rural settlements. In any case, they were far too prolific to be totally disregarded.

The unwillingness of Christians to engage in social activities that they considered unacceptable did not mean that they stood aloof from the societies in which they resided. From the first century, they had been taught to participate in public life, so long as they remained untainted by pagan beliefs and practices, and in so far as they did not compromise their faith and its ethical and moral standards. They were not to be a 'withdrawn' community, like the contemporary Essenes and Therapeutai communities. 'It was not social "status" (*klesis*) but the call to seek the welfare of the city both physically and spiritually that was to be the focus of the Christian community.'[63]

On the eve of great changes

As Christianity entered the fourth century it unknowingly faced some dramatic changes. The apostolic and sub-apostolic era of all-member, lay-focused church life had been greatly modified by the early fourth century; but it was about to be transformed beyond all recognition.

2

From AD 313 to the beginning of the medieval period

The big divide

The Edict of Milan in 313, the 'Peace of the Church', was a pivotal and epoch-making event in Christian history. It permanently transformed the role of the Christian laity both within the church and in terms of their standing as a corporate body in the society in which they were placed. It revolutionized the status of Christianity as a religion. It greatly reinforced the changes in the relationship between the laity and the clergy that have already been observed, and helped to establish what had come to pass in a form that was to be perpetuated and consolidated throughout the following twelve hundred years and more. But the changes it effected and which it heralded were not as dramatic and as sudden as was once thought. Modern research and academic debate, especially since the 1980s, has revealed that the process of change from an essentially pagan empire to one more fully, if not completely, dominated by Christianity and permeated by Christian values, was slower and more painful than previously rather taken for granted. There was not an overnight transformation from a 'Roman' to a 'Christian' empire. Nor can it be said that 'with the new foundation of Constantinople as a Christian capital, the ancient world was over and done with, the Middle Ages had begun; likewise the Byzantine era had begun'.[1] The process of change was not as simple as that. Paganism was not slain; killed at a stroke. It was not stopped dead in its tracks, or eliminated for ever. Christianity did not suddenly have all things its own way. It continued to interact with the still very evident paganism in its various guises, and it had a fight on its hands to a far greater degree, and for a more extended period, than was once believed.

New battle lines were indeed well and truly drawn up, and the forces of Christianity and paganism confronted each other soon after Constantine's momentous declaration in a more public and obvious manner than before. The new imperial policy of destroying pagan temples and outlawing non-Christian acts of worship, combined with assistance in erecting churches, and the bestowal of many gifts upon the newly liberated church, did not result in either the undoubted victory of the church nor the total suppression of paganism. Although both Constantius and Constans pursued an actively anti-pagan policy, taking measures to close pagan shrines and to discontinue some pagan rituals, the whole thrust of pro-Christian actions was suddenly and traumatically brought to a halt, and for a time reversed, when Julian 'The Apostate' became emperor in 361. Even before this explicit assault on Christianity, there had, understandably, been much resentment regarding the favour conferred on what to many non-Christians was a bizarre religion. This was especially so 'among traditionally minded aristocrats, and many conventional religious observances and pagan festivals and holidays were still widely kept'.[2] Paganism had a firm hold on the affections and emotions of the people in much of the countryside in the empire, and especially in Italy and Gaul. Areas such as North Africa and parts of the Nile Valley were the exception to the general rule in being so dominated by Christianity that paganism was more fully squeezed out, but even there the Christians wrestled with a strong residue of alien, and often aggressive, counter-beliefs. Christians, indeed, were not made comfortable and free from embattlement overnight in any area. They still faced a prolonged struggle to consolidate what gains had been granted, and to make further inroads into what were still fundamentally non-Christian cultures.

Julian, in his short time as emperor from 361 to 363, showed that the security of the Christians was fragile and liable to reversal. His efforts to restore paganism included intellectual attacks on the faith, restrictions on Christians as teachers, and the toleration of rival doctrinal positions within churches. He introduced religious toleration designed to allow for the revival of pagan cults, with an accompanying reversal of the privileges extended to Christianity. He repaired pagan temples and altars throughout the East and the West and built new ones; and he reorganized pagan priesthoods. The emperor himself observed daily animal sacrifices, and enthusiastically consulted soothsayers and pagan oracles, showing a deep fascination for augury, divination and astrology. The policy must have had adverse effects on the lives of lay Christians, at least in making them more vulnerable to verbal and perhaps physical attack, and it reintroduced some of the previous emotional pressures on the believers. It certainly showed that the Christians could not take state favour for granted.

This is not to say that there were not immediate and marked improvements in the situation from a Christian point of view after 313. Despite the short-lived efforts of Julian, the overall transformation of mood was clear. 'Christians, who had formerly constituted a threatened and beleaguered minority' had come 'to define their identity in a changed context of religious respectability in which their faith had become a source of privilege and power'.³ The legislation undeniably made life easier for Christians most of the time and in most places, although harassment and persecutions were still quite common. Christianity certainly became more popular, and attracted many more adherents. The church grew 'in membership, in acceptance within surrounding communities, and in the breadth of its distribution across the empire'.⁴

There was a fairly quick increase in the prestige of Christianity, and the profession of Christian faith could result in social, economic or professional advantages. This quite rapidly resulted in an unprecedented interest in what Christianity had to offer. People started to accept the label of Christian for mixed, and in some cases entirely wrong, motives. 'While some were won over by genuine intellectual and spiritual conviction, others had more pragmatic reasons for aligning themselves to the Christian cause.'⁵ Both pagan and Christian spokesmen drew attention to the fact that

> conversion under pressure was unlikely to reach very far down into the mind. Prudential considerations, to curry favour or gain a rich wife, or not to lose one's job or one's life, diminished the meaning of conversion. Everything encouraged a sense of triumph and conviction among the crowds attending church; but everything also encouraged hypocrisy.⁶

This means that the counting of Christian heads becomes more difficult and hazardous. By the end of the fourth century Christianity had drawn into its fold perhaps half of the population. This sudden accretion of new members was fine as a sign of the wider propagation of the faith, but it demanded a clear spelling out of the theological and moral standards and requirements of the faith. And, to its credit, the church on the whole greatly elaborated and tightened its programme of catechesis, renunciation and scrutiny that had been evolving over the previous two centuries. The process of initiation into the church became stricter and more thorough.

Of one thing there is little doubt. With the arrival of state approval, those previous trends already noted, whereby the laity became less central in the active life of churches, were accelerated and made more explicit. The process of formalization, institutionalization and bureaucratization went ahead with greatly reinforced momentum.

The clericalization of the ecclesiastical organization, which had been steadily evolving in the course of two centuries, and which, in the third century, became very evident, was further developed. The ministerial arrangements were made more rigid, authoritarian and complex in the fourth century. The function of lay men and women as close collaborators with the ordained leaders, which in the third century had begun to disappear, was circumscribed even further. The distinctive lay tasks of writing apologias, and of propagating the faith, which lay men had undertaken on the basis of equality with the clergy, in the third century 'began to be undertaken exclusively by the members of the hierarchy, or at least under their direct control',[7] and in the fourth century were almost totally confined to them and eliminated as spheres of lay engagement. The distinction between the clergy and the laity, which had originally not been a feature of the church, but which had become more obvious over the years, in the fourth century became so clearly enunciated and put into practice that it was recognized by the state and by the public at large.

An essential element in the demarcation of the two categories, lay and clerical, and in the increasingly evident classification of orders within the clerical ranks, was the degree to which the holders of any particular office were licensed to engage in sacramental activity. This became a key benchmark in defining the authority and status of any office-holder. Thus, the laity widely believed that the highest offices of bishop and presbyter gained their authority and status largely because the occupants of such posts could carry out sacerdotal functions, and especially the consecration of the bread and wine in the Eucharist; these were rights that were denied to lay people. Deacons and sub-deacons likewise achieved their authority from their close association with and participation in the administration of the eucharistic liturgy, although they could not actually consecrate the bread and wine.

This clerical–lay distinction was even expressed in the structural and architectural features of the new purpose-built churches. The apse was reserved for the clergy, and at its centre was a raised throne on which the bishop sat. Permanent stone altars or tables in front of the apse became an almost universal feature, where the Eucharist was conducted, and beneath them saints' relics were often housed. The bishop and his attendants processed from the apse to that area, and would then preside while the congregation listened and observed. Catechumens, baptismal candidates and penitents preparing for reconciliation were not allowed to go beyond the narthex or porch area at the rear of the nave. In some of the churches the separation of the clergy from the laity was further accentuated, as at St Peter's in Rome, by means of a transverse hall or transept which crossed the church between the nave and the apse.

Within the ever more rigid ministerial structure, as well as among the laity, women were increasingly marginalized. During the second and third centuries, they 'had come to exercise far less visible roles in ministry than had been the case in apostolic times, and in the fourth century and beyond the official face of the churches was overwhelmingly male.[8] There are instances, few and far between, where women engaged in tasks such as preaching or the administration of the Eucharist, but such actions were regarded, even by the laity as a whole, as irregular or as valid only in distinctly limited and well-defined situations, such as communities of other women. Although women continued to serve as deacons, especially in the churches of the East, the commission to undertake such work was not viewed as comparable to ordination to the male diaconate. These women deacons were sometimes looked upon with suspicion, and as usurpers of the male prerogatives in ministry, and this attitude was reinforced as a result of a number of cases where they clearly did exceed their designated authority. The title 'deaconess' was only introduced in the fourth century, and the special diaconate that it represented declined in importance as a result of its reluctant acceptance and the occasional misuse of the powers it conferred. The acceptance of women in such a role had, in any case, been much slower to develop in the West than in the East, and the sixth-century councils in Gaul abolished the office of female deacon altogether. All of this must have undermined the status of lay women within a laity that was anyhow by then severely restricted in its rights and in its ability to contribute to the life of the church.

Local church life in the immediate post-313 years

A depiction of the churches and what went on within them gives a good idea of what it meant in the fourth century to be an ordinary lay person. It to some extent draws back the curtain on that far off age.

With the Edict of Milan, Christians started as never before to meet openly in purpose-built churches. Constantine undertook an ambitious and extensive building programme that stretched to almost every quarter of the empire. It was an attempt to make up fully or in part for the losses that had been sustained in the persecutions, and it was a tangible and highly visible demonstration that the faith enjoyed imperial patronage.

The most common structures were of the basilican form, which comprised a rectangular hall and an apse or rectangular area at the east end, which provided the focus of the building. Many of them had a central nave and side aisles, divided from the nave by columns that supported a number of windows. There may also have been windows built in to the main walls of the church. The rural churches were frequently rectangular rather than basilican in design. Such was the case in England, as seen at Icklingham, Suffolk and also, possibly, at Brean Down on the Bristol Channel, at Nettleton in Wiltshire and at Maiden Castle. Some of the churches were located at military sites, as at Richborough in Kent, and Vindolanda and Housesteads along Hadrian's Wall.[9]

Many of the basilicas, either established as a direct result of imperial beneficence, or influenced by that development, were lavishly decorated on the inside. Murals on the walls vividly portrayed biblical themes. These served both as attractive forms of ornamentation, and as visual aids to inculcate biblical stories and teaching to the laity, many of whom were illiterate or semi-literate.

The more public nature of the Christian faith in the fourth century was made clear with the construction of detached baptisteries. From the latter part of the second century, if not earlier, young children as well as adults were baptized. Despite opposition to this from within the church, the practice of paedobaptism, as it was later called, was widespread in the third century, especially in North Africa and other parts of the West, and the custom was greatly extended in the fourth century. There were considerable variations in the age at which children were accepted for the rite, ranging from a few days old to nine years of age or more. The universally high level of infant mortality massively increased the pressure upon the church to offer very early baptism.

After they had been baptized, the new church members would be entitled to participate in the foremost act of worship, the *eucharistia*, or thanksgiving, a term that by the fourth century was largely used as a replacement for the more primitive 'breaking of bread' or 'Lord's Supper'. The churches were mostly disciplined in only admitting the baptized to the sacred meal.

Attendance at the Eucharist every Sunday was considered obligatory for all believers, despite the dangers that this might entail in the few times of persecution. Constantine promoted the setting apart of Sunday as a special day of the week. In 321, he closed the imperial law courts on that day, for all purposes except the emancipation of slaves, and he enjoined an abstention from work on Sundays, with the exception of farm labourers. Although his motive in making these enactments was respect for the sun, of which he continued to regard himself as a comrade, and for which he maintained veneration, rather than specifically and solely the facilitating of Christian worship, it was the first official recognition of the day as being special. And it encouraged and promoted the increasing regard for Sunday as the particular day of corporate Christian worship, a time away from the normal secular pursuits of the other days of the week.

Many churches started using greatly enriched ornaments and vessels in worship; although liturgical elaboration proceeded at a slower pace in the West than in the East. Overall, however, with the congregations no longer being made up entirely or even primarily of the truly committed, there was more need to emphasize the majesty of the occasion.

> [The] Eucharist increasingly came to be presented as a mysterious sacred drama, and styles of liturgical action were developed to emphasize the seriousness and profundity of what was taking place. Such notes had of course been sounded since early times, but in the fourth century they became more necessary than ever before.[10]

These refinements of the liturgy helped to give a boost to the use of song in worship. This had always been important to the laity, as it bolstered a sense of corporate adoration and reinforced an awareness of unity in the faith, but it became more widespread and more highly appreciated in the fourth century. Psalms continued to be cherished as in former times, but other expressions of praise came to be valued, and to be an accepted component of worship.[11] These included the *Gloria in Excelsis* ('Glory to God in the highest') and the *Gloria Patri* ('Glory be to the Father . . .'). The *Magnificat* ('My soul magnifies the Lord . . .'), the *Benedictus* ('Blessed be the Lord . . .'), the *Nunc Dimittis* ('Now let your servant depart . . .') and the *Benedicite* ('Bless the Lord . . .'). Alongside such universal expressions of belief and praise, however, hymns of other kinds were common as both acts of worship and as a means for communicating doctrinal instruction. Among these, the most celebrated was the Latin hymn, the *Te Deum*.

In addition to changes in the content and mode of Christian worship, the fourth century was notable for a marked expansion of the cult of the saints. And among the saints the Virgin Mary was especially prominent. She commanded an adoration and exalted status that was especially evident from the fourth century. Popular piety found in her a source of comfort, help and companionship that no other saint could equal. By the following, fifth, century the extent to which she was widely and ardently venerated is indicated by the passions aroused over the use of the title *Theotokos* ('The God-bearer') to describe her.

The concept of sainthood, and all that it represented, was especially precious to lay people, who were embroiled in the hard and demanding life of that coarse and in many ways brutal age. Those who had little to relieve the monotony, drudgery and grind of work and home life, with its almost totally predictable diet of wearisome labour and few things out of the ordinary, would doubtless have found immense attraction in the colourful and elevated lives of the saints. The world of miracles, remarkable dedication and holiness exhibited by the saints would have appealed to people who struggled to maintain reasonable moral standards amid the multitude of pressures placed upon them to conform to practices and values that fell far below what was their ideal. In a world without penicillin or any of the amenities that have given material comfort to modern men and women, when pain and discomfort were the everyday lot of all the people, but especially those outside the small coterie of the rich and privileged elite, there was a predisposition to accept anything that offered solace and the hope of better things. 'Beyond all question men believed in miracles. The bones of holy men brought healing to the sick. Food was provided for travellers in strange deserted lands. Fires were extinguished. The dead were restored to life.'[12]

It is to the fourth century that we can look for the origins of popular pilgrimages. 'Before Constantine the Great pilgrimage was rare and individual; groups would have attracted a lot of dangerous attention.'[13] The holy places that began to be favoured in the fourth century as pilgrim destinations were from the start those associated with the life, works and miraculous powers of Christ himself, or of a recognized saint. 'The ancient Church did not think particular places (or stones, springs, or trees) numinous in separation from the holy men and women who had said or done things there or whose bones were there located.'[14] As pilgrimages multiplied in the West, the shrines of Peter and Paul in Rome became especially powerful magnets for pilgrims.

A new form of lay political sponsoring of Christianity

Taking the church as a whole, a landmark in the relationship between lay rulers and the official, institutional church can be traced to the year 457, from which date in the empire of Constantinople, 'a ceremony of coronation by the Patriarch had become a necessary part of the act of elevation to the Imperial throne'.[15]

In the West, from the end of the fifth century through to and beyond the start of the medieval period, perhaps the greatest contribution of lay Christians to the promotion of Christianity took the form of political initiatives and assistance at the highest level. A key date was 499. Seven years before this, the Frankish King Clovis had married the Burgundian Christian princess Clotilde. But in 499 he underwent an experience similar to that of Constantine, when he accepted the Christian faith as a result of victory in battle. He apparently vowed to become a Christian if he was successful in defeating the Alamanni, and he kept his word when this came about. He was baptized in about the same year, together with as many as three thousand of his soldiers. 'The event is said to have been the first mass conversion of a Germanic group to the catholic faith.'[16]

Of course, this did not mean that a large number of people in his kingdom accepted the Christian faith and committed themselves to it. As with a series of other such events that were to follow throughout the West in particular, perhaps only a handful of the Franks were converted to Christianity in any deep and meaningful way. There was much nominal acceptance of Christianity, and the true and genuine coming over to the Christian faith was confined largely to some leaders rather than extending to the people in general. Likewise, the moral character of the country was not suddenly and markedly changed; it continued to be characterized by violence, intrigue and brutality. But the conversion of the head of state, and his personal promotion of Christianity, with the support of some of his main and most powerful companions, was hugely and potently symbolic of a change in religious allegiance, and it typically presaged a more fundamental and deep-rooted move towards establishing a Christian state.

A massive impulse was given to this type of Christian thrust forward with the accession of Justinian I as Roman emperor in 527. He was the most energetic of the early Byzantine emperors, and he had a consuming passion to restore the political and religious unity of the empire of the East and the West. He constructed many basilican churches in Constantinople, with Santa Sophia being outstanding, in Ravenna and in a host of other places. He greatly favoured ornate and impressive statues, icons and pictures representing Christ or some Christian saint or topic, and from then onwards these became an increasingly common and yet imposing feature of popular piety, especially, but not by any means exclusively, in the East.[17]

The centrality and significance of lay political leadership in the sponsorship and in the furthering of the work of the church from the end of the sixth century onwards is well illustrated by the process of re-establishing the church in Britain, after it had undergone quite serious decline following the end of the Roman occupation. It is a story that graphically illuminates the imperative part played by kings and other leading lay men in various parts of the Western world in those centuries, whereby whole kingdoms were turned to the Christian faith; and it is therefore worth recounting in some detail.

When St Augustine landed in Thanet in 597, sent on a mission to Britain by Pope Gregory I,[18] he immediately despatched an envoy to Ethelbert, the powerful king of Kent.

Kent was unique among the southern kingdoms of Britain in having already been a kingdom-state, long before the advent of the Saxons. It had been a Celtic Iron Age principality, and subsequently a Romano-British *civitas* with its capital at Canterbury, which was the focus of the Roman roads system for the area.[19] By the time Augustine set his feet upon Kentish soil most of southern Britain except Devon, Cornwall and Wales was subject to Anglo-Saxon political control, and the former British dynasties and aristocracies had been destroyed. It had been a gradual process over about two centuries. A number of kingdoms were founded, but a certain degree of unity was imparted most notably in periods when one ruler, a bretwalda, or over-king, exercised a large measure of control over much of the territory south of the Humber. Ethelbert was such a monarch.

There was the further propitious circumstance from the Christian point of view, that the kingdom of Kent already had some contact with Christianity. The king had for some time been married to Bertha, who was a Frankish Christian princess. She was a great-granddaughter of Clovis, and she was the daughter of King Charibert of Paris and his wife Ingoberg. This influential lay woman had been resolute in maintaining her Christian faith in the midst of what appears to have been a predominantly pagan society. She had been permitted to bring a bishop named Liuhard with her to Canterbury, where the king and queen resided. Not only so, but Bertha and Liuhard had been able to worship in the church of St Martin outside the city walls.[20] By the time Augustine appeared on the scene Ethelbert had known the close company of Christians for a decade or more.

Since the fall of Ceawlin of Wessex in 592, Ethelbert had become what Bede reckoned as the third of the Anglo-Saxon bretwaldas, with authority to summon other kings to join him in battle, and to command their forces.

> The God of gods venerated by the most powerful overlord of the day would be adopted by those rulers who sought or needed his favour. The support and protection of a powerful overlord was a potential advantage that no early medieval mission could afford to neglect.[21]

The place was right as well. Because it was the nearest English kingdom to the continent, and because it was not surrounded by other potentially hostile pagan kingdoms, Kent was ideal as a base from which to launch a mission, with the aim of extending the message proclaimed throughout the whole land.

Augustine was well received. He made an initial good impression, and the Roman mission continued to be successful. There were conversions, and most notably the king came to believe for himself and was baptized. In a letter to the patriarch of Alexandria, Pope Gregory states that on Christmas Day 597 Augustine had baptized more than ten thousand converts to the faith. From this it can be reasonably concluded that the king was converted in 597. Perhaps the number of converts quoted was an exaggeration, but it at least shows that the people were responding to the gospel on a large scale.

With the conversion of Ethelbert the way was opened to extend the mission to other parts of Kent and perhaps other kingdoms that came under the king's influence.

In the meantime, other kings in the north of Britain were also helping to promote the Christian faith. St Columba (*c.* 521–97) established a monastery on the island of Iona off the west coast of Scotland. By the time of his death, he seems to have founded one or more monastic institutions, and thereby obtained a Christian foothold, in the nearby Scottish mainland region of Dal Riata. The monks from these communities were about to be the key players in a missionary thrust from their remote vantage point, via Northumbria into the heartland of Britain. It was to be one arm of an unplanned pincer movement, complementing the concurrent Roman mission in the south.

King Edwin of Deira, or Northumberland, publicly accepted the gospel. He renounced idolatry and confessed his faith in Christ. Of course there may have been mixed motives that finally persuaded him to embrace the Christian faith, but there does appear to have been a genuine change of heart. A great number of people responded and became Christians, were baptized and forsook their paganism.

Edwin's successor, Oswald, was converted while in exile among the Irish. It was therefore natural that when he became king in 635 he applied to the monastery of Iona for a bishop who would propagate and strengthen Christianity in his kingdom. His 'action contributed, in a perceptible way, to the subsequent history of north-east England'.[22] The bishop who finally came was Aidan, 'a man of outstanding gentleness, devotion, and moderation',[23] who was also zealous and, as seen from his ministry in Northumbria, courageous yet discreet. The king gave him a place for his episcopal cathedra on the island of Lindisfarne, and there he established a monastery as a base for his activities. Oswald was clearly a convinced Christian, 'a man of faith and prayer; and he used his position to promote the conversion of his people, assisting his bishop in a way which associated him intimately with the work of evangelisation'.[24]

Here was another fine case of lay and clerical cooperation in a joint and fruitful undertaking. With the example of the king, and with the aid of many Christians, chiefly monks from Iona and perhaps Ireland as well, the work prospered. People came to faith, churches were built, and large numbers of the population met in public places to hear what was being proclaimed. The king also provided land and property for the establishment of monasteries.

A model of king and bishop working together had been established, which was followed by others. Oswy succeeded Oswald as king of Northumbria; and the new king was largely the means of bringing Paeda, king of the Middle Angles,[25] to Christian faith and baptism. The same happened with Sigbert, the king of the East Saxons who, after his conversion, was sent a bishop, Cedd, and another priest, who proved to be very effective in converting people and building up Christian churches. When Sigbert was murdered by two kinsmen, his successor, Swithhelm, was baptized, and the work of the church in East Anglia continued to thrive. Cedd retained his links with Northumbria, and he founded the monastery of Lastingham in Yorkshire on land provided for him by Othelwald, king of Deira, who was the son of Oswald.

In the eighth century, there was an innovation of immense importance in this cooperative relationship between lay ruler and prelates. This was the introduction of a specifically Christian ceremony to mark the assumption of kingly powers. The pivotal event in this development was the anointing of King Pippin by Archbishop Boniface in 751. It was the first act of its kind in the West of which there is a reliable record. 'From this moment religion and secular power became inextricably interwoven in Western Europe.'[26] Although, as already noted, such a service had been introduced in the empire of Constantinople in the fifth century, this was a first for the West. Other examples followed, all undoubtedly based on a conscious copying of the Old Testament account of Samuel's anointing of King David, whereby 'the Spirit of the Lord came upon David'.[27] It was a major divide in church–state affairs.

> From this time forward, and in virtue of this ceremony, the rulers of the Franks and soon those of the English could take the title, so pregnant with mysterious meaning, and assume the position of *Christus Domini*, the Lord's anointed. During the following centuries, contrary to what is often thought, the religious adulation of the lay ruler went further in the West than in Byzantium itself, and though curbed in the eleventh century it was always ready to break out into new life.[28]

Once anointed, the Christian role of the monarch then began. He was expected to care for the churches and work for the promotion of Christianity. This entailed the choice of suitable pastors and the provision of means whereby such Christians were supported financially and in other ways. It also included the calling of councils as necessary for the settling of problems and the dissipation of heresy. These two requirements were onerous, but they established the king as a key figure in the life of the church.

> In virtue of this dual responsibility, he was frequently referred to as both *rex* and *sacerdos*, and the example of Melchisedech was quoted to support the amalgamation of kingly and priestly functions. Of course, no one supposed that the lay ruler was *sacerdos* in the sense that he could administer the sacraments. Even such an exalted personage as the king was regarded as exempt from what was deemed a clearly clerical privilege. But the phrase did express an almost universal conviction that the ruler was, so to speak, enveloped in a sacerdotal aura.[29]

Such politico-religious advances as these meant that by the eighth century Christianity had made remarkable strides towards capturing the hearts and minds of many lay people throughout Europe. Even so, it had not to any great extent infiltrated the lower ranks of society; and that was just where paganism was most fully ingrained. During the seventh and eighth centuries, however, major victories were gained over the ever-diminishing force of paganism. Christian rulers, church leaders, other clergy and, to a very limited extent, ordinary lay men and women, were responsible for what was a golden age in the process of Christianization. The faith became so well founded and diffused in a few places that it was virtually immovable, and the process irreversible. Nonetheless, for many pockets and some large regions it was still only superficially introduced, and in such lands its future remained uncertain.

Local church life from the eighth to the tenth centuries

Most people in the West in the eighth century lived in the countryside. Although the towns and cities were the focus of regional or national political, economic and social life, they only accounted for a minority of the population in the various provinces of Europe, and in a large proportion of territories such urban centres were mostly very small. This mismatch between where the bulk of the people lived and where the political, social and economic elite lived meant that in a vast number of small and scattered villages and hamlets there was still no purpose-built place of worship or, indeed, any provision for Christian witness or worship. It was only by a slow and uneven process that the religious life of all or most of these rural inhabitants became focused on a church building with a resident priest. This was the age before the parish and the parish church as we know it. Even by the late eighth century these defects and shortcomings had not been remedied. It was symptomatic of a church that was still in a pioneering mode and needed to be built up and thoroughly grounded. Everything was on a small scale and much hinged on the opinions, influence and actions of a select company of high-status individuals and groups.

Having said that, there were a number of what in Britain have been called 'mother' churches or minsters. It seems that in the seventh century there was a large lay population in Britain whose lives were profoundly affected by their dependence on these large churches that were served by a team of clergy. It has been said that 'the conversion of the English kingdoms was effected largely through the agency of the minsters or *monasteria*',[30] and this may well be so. The land was almost certainly peppered with them. Once again, however, such a provision for pastoral care and for the further extension of Christianity left little place for the laity to act as witnesses to their faith to non-believers, or to participate in the life of Christian communities. There was little scope for the laity to make their valid and valuable contribution to the functioning of local church life. What was done was done for them not by them, or indeed in any way with their involvement. They remained the largely passive recipients of spiritual beneficence.

But they could, and they did, provide various forms of financial and material help. Throughout the West, there were many somewhat differing systems for eliciting such lay assistance, mainly for the upkeep of churches and priests. In Britain there was, from the seventh century, the church-scot and the soul-scot. The former was a tax imposed by authority, which consisted of a penny payable within a fortnight after Easter in respect of each plough-team working in a parish. By slow degrees the tithe, a levy of 10 per cent on all produce and income, came to replace this as the basis of parochial financial support for the parish. The soul-scot was a voluntary offering of a proportion of a dead person's goods given for the welfare of his or her soul. At the open grave at the time of burial it was handed to the priest of the deceased person's local church. Such ecclesiastical dues, with different names, and with variations in their form from one region of the West to another, amounted to a serious charge on the peasantry, and became an impossible burden in hard times of famine or war. But it was part of a concerted effort by the church in the seventh and eighth centuries to provide and sustain an effective and comprehensive form of pastoral oversight.

Christianity in Europe was undoubtedly, if slowly and patchily, marching forward. It was winning victories and gaining ground. Progress was being made. It is, for example, a measure of the advance and greater maturity of the churches in the eighth century that Christians in all countries and regions were finding themselves ever more firmly drawn into the task of international evangelism. Thus, for instance, it is a testimony to the health and non-parochialism of at least some sections of the English church at that time that it made a massive and telling contribution to mission work on the continent.[31]

The ninth to the eleventh centuries

Despite such encouraging advances, even the more well-developed and mature European churches still had to face trials and testing. One of these took the form of pagan invasions. From the late eighth century onwards, there were quite frequent barbarian incursions into Christian Europe. It was fortunate for the churches that the attackers were aggressively non-Christian rather than anti-Christian. Religion was not the motivation that drove them from their homelands; or at least it played a minor part in the various enterprises involved. Those who troubled to leave their mother countries to seek new opportunities in other regions were driven by the lure of wealth, and by the understanding that in the territories they intended to invade political weakness and consequent military ineptitude made the risks entailed worth taking. Those who embarked on such predatory expeditions were apparently for the most part young and energetic, and they had an eye to the bounty that would result from their foraging. Monasteries had to shoulder much of the sometimes devastating consequences of invasion and pillaging, because of the treasures to be found in them. Then, as ever larger war bands caused widespread havoc, churches also were often particular targets, not again because of their religious significance, but because of the possibility of loot. Gradually, however, periodic raids turned into permanent settlement, and then the question of possible conversion to Christianity confronted and challenged the host country churches and local Christians.

The scattered local church communities that encountered these hardy adventurers soon discovered, after they had settled among them, that the newcomers were incontestably polytheistic. The natural world of the Vikings and others was filled with a multitude of gods and goddesses, and nature worship was axiomatic to peoples who lived so close to fountains, groves and streams, and who earned their living from work on land or sea. To the fore in the Northern pantheon were Odin (Woden), Thor and Frey, of whom Thor gradually assumed a predominant place.

The occupation of lands by these foreign assailants must have greatly tested the evangelistic and pastoral effectiveness of the local churches. And this was so throughout much of Europe in the last two centuries of the first millennium and the immediate succeeding period. Although there is known to have been a severe breakdown of clerical pastoral care in some places, most of the European churches survived and continued to function as fellowships of believers. Indeed, during the following two hundred years, there was development and growth. Thus, in Britain at the time of the Domesday Book (1086) there were 2,000 churches serving 13,000 settlements – a pointer to the fact that the major part of the nationwide church provision remained intact despite the Danish crisis, or was able to recover from dislocation soon after the raids lessened or ceased, and after the Danes had settled down to peaceful community life with their native British neighbours.

This speaks well for the tenacity and quiet witness to their faith of the local British Christians, and it is a story that was, no doubt, replicated in many other regions of Europe. The fact that after a while there was no apparent major religious or indeed any other form of tension between those who made England their new home and the existing native population was a credit to both parties. But, beyond this, it seems that the Vikings quite readily conformed to Christian customs and even to Christian belief once they had settled in the host society – a good indication that the lay Christians were commending their faith by word and conduct. For example, as with the Anglo-Saxons in a previous age, the new settlers appear to have 'respected Christian burial grounds and used them for the disposal of their own dead'. They seem to have 'reacted quickly to their Christian surroundings and were soon adapting their burial customs to those of the Anglo-Saxon population'.[32] And this change of burial custom may be reckoned as related to a more general change of religious belief.

All of this testifies to the important role of the ordinary laity in transmitting the Christian faith, when given the opportunity to do so. But there was still very much a place for kings to have a massive and lasting influence as well. Until the 870s in England, no king among the Danish invaders or settlers had abjured paganism and personally accepted the Christian faith. It was therefore an historic moment when Guthrum and his chief followers accepted baptism in 878 as the price of a treaty with King Alfred. Once more, as on former occasions, and as in similar circumstances throughout Europe, the sincerity and depth of the individual faith of those concerned is, of course, open to question, and even cynicism. But such acts were, at the very least, highly symbolic. And, in the English example, the embracing of Christianity was not limited to that small band of Vikings. Guthfrith, the first known king of Danish Northumbria, who died in 895, was a Christian. The Christian tide was perhaps beginning to turn; and at the centre of all that was happening in England and elsewhere in those critical last three decades of the ninth century was not a high-placed ecclesiastic, but a king, in this case Alfred.

The laity in the church at the beginning of the second millennium

During the tenth and eleventh centuries Christianity made further progress. A great number of local, purpose-built, mostly stone, churches were impressively provided, so that by the mid-eleventh century they were a valued element in the life of almost all cities, towns, villages and hamlets of mainland Europe and Britain, and they were widely, although not universally, appreciated by the residents as never before. The extent of church building works varied considerably from one country to another, and within countries between different districts. Thus, in England, the construction of dedicated churches was particularly great in those parts known as the Danelaw.

> Typically, a lone priest served in these new, lay-founded churches, usually a man of relatively low origin who had a rudimentary education, was isolated from the church hierarchy and the large collegiate minsters, and was called upon to meet the daily, practical needs of an agricultural population. In this environment, and through this kind of clerical agency interacting with local folk culture and domestic life, popular religion was formed.[33]

And this kind of effective local ministry was to be found in various forms throughout continental Europe.

The upper-middle social order of Christians played an especially crucial part in the promotion of Christianity in that age of Christian consolidation. Such was the proliferation of local churches that by the eleventh century, in England as elsewhere, 'the possession of a church was looked upon as one of the attributes of thegnly rank, along with a cookhouse, a fortified gatehouse, and five hides of land'.[34] And the advantages of owning a church went far beyond the prospect of higher social status. The builder of the church and his heirs possessed and retained the right to appoint the priest who would serve it, the so-called advowson, and they enjoyed an interest in the tithes, offerings and the oblations. 'In effect, the village church was both essential to the status of the Late Saxon thegn and a part of his capital worth. Like his estate, his hall, and his weapons of war, it was a necessary element in his equipment.'[35]

By the opening of the second millennium, Christian values and beliefs pervaded every sphere of life for a considerable proportion of the people of continental Europe and Britain. It was the same for the institutions and the corporate life of the people. Most of the lay guilds, and other such bodies, had a spiritual aspect. A substratum of Christian presuppositions had been established in many European countries and communities that provided a bedrock for individual and social life. The clergy could generally rely on a widespread concern among their flock for matters of Christian belief and conduct. Surviving homilies, written largely by monks, provide a window into the teaching which was being set before the people, and which, presumably, represented the essence of lay belief at that time. Taken as a whole, the theology that was proclaimed was sober, and issues of morality and Christian conduct were to the fore. The miraculous did not feature as prominently as in earlier times. The Trinity was expounded carefully. Baptism was held in high esteem, but confirmation was hardly mentioned. Fasting and abstinence from carnal relations during Lent were emphasized; but the fast most pleasing to God was the avoidance of sin.

Of course, all of what has just been said should not imply that Christianity either held a monopolistic place in Western societies at the dawn of a new millennium, or that the societies of that time were filled with pious and totally dedicated Christians. This was far from being so. There was much folklore, superstition, hypocrisy and downright cynicism or disbelief. Mingled with genuine and deep-rooted faith there was a residue of the paganism that non-Christian peoples had brought with them in their quite recent campaigns of conquest and settlement. Such non-Christian perspectives remained as a kind of subterranean remnant of former potent influences in the lives of ethnically and culturally mixed populations. The West was a complex of many and varied faiths, forms of magic, religious indifference and decidedly non-Christian or even anti-Christian philosophies or beliefs. But the Christian faith had emerged supreme in many countries; and in these places it had become so ingrained consciously and subconsciously, corporately and in the lives of individuals, that it was in effect the overriding, authoritative, largely unchallenged determinant of communal and personal religious beliefs and moral standards. It had established itself as the main, but by no means the sole, source of those largely unuttered presuppositions that undergirded individual and societal life and thinking. Christianity was in effect quite well on its way to becoming an almost universally regarded ethical and religious measuring rod and standard in at least a number of Western countries. Its progress in this respect was definite and staggering. It had a long, uphill and arduous climb ahead before it was pre-eminent, but it was advancing decisively.

It was also making a remarkable contribution to the growing sense of nationhood in regions that were slowly being welded into recognizable and self-conscious units, each with its sense of single identity. Of course, other factors were necessary to determine how the particular countries developed a more sophisticated awareness of their separateness and of their distinctiveness as a nation. But in all cases the Christian faith was helping all the laity, as well as the clergy, to recognize common interests that bound them together. 'Men were made aware of their group unity in the religious and linguistic fields long before the political.'[36]

In addition to, and beyond, national boundaries, there was also a developing, although still somewhat hazy, collective as well as individual sense of 'Christendom' as an amalgam and embodiment of identifiable political, social, cultural and philosophic, as well as more especially religious, factors, values and general orientation. This was to manifest itself in various ways in the ensuing centuries as a sort of common element over and above national differences. With the passage of time, at both the national and supra-national levels, and after countless occasions of conflict and antagonism, there was a certain drawing together of ecclesiastical and political interests and objectives. There was not total concord, or anything approaching this, but there was an acknowledgement by all concerned that there were shared purposes, and common deep matters of ultimate meaning and importance, that transcended all the lesser drives and motivations that impregnated societies. By the mid-eleventh century Christianity was the single most potent force moulding the thinking and the behaviour of countless lay men and women in many Western lands. In the course of the following medieval period, its powerful religious and moral grip on the minds and hearts of people, on institutions and on societies as a whole was to be tightened even further.

3

From the eleventh century to the late fourteenth century

For most lay people on the European mainland and in England during the period from the eleventh century to the late fourteenth century there was a readiness to be quiescent, conformist and uncomplaining, and to take for granted a religious landscape that had all the appearance of being the natural order required and ordained by God. It seemed to most people that a community of men, women and children who had been baptized and who worshipped according to a Catholic liturgy was by virtue of those facts alone a Christian community. 'Prayer was a communal activity according to set forms, and private prayer was no more than an overflow of communal worship.'[1] The almost complete silence in the sources about the weekly devotions of ordinary people is probably a powerful mute testimony to the fact that such regular acts of corporate piety were commonplace and uncontroversial, and so accepted as part of the rhythm of life that they did not seem worth mentioning and describing. But there is sufficient evidence to provide clues as to what went on within the various places of worship, and to gauge quite accurately what were the beliefs and practices of the laity in the medieval period. The surviving data also gives an insight into the changing place of Christianity in society at large, and the part that lay people were playing in this unfolding drama.

The great churches

Although, as seen in the last chapter, there had been great churches in the past, such as the larger Roman basilicas, the greater Carolingian abbeys and the English minster churches, there had never been the number or size of churches that now began to be constructed. Prominent among these was Monte Cassino, which was completed in 1071, the abbey churches and cathedrals of Norman England, and the reconstructed monastic complex of Cluny in Burgundy. Here, in mortar and stone, were majestic testimonies to the piety and the imperial ambitions of kings and princes. The architectural landscape was changed for ever by these new and imposing structures, and lay people throughout Europe stood in wonder as such monuments to a triumphant faith were erected. To the millions of peasants and lowly workers on the land and in the towns and cities, these witnesses to an ever more influential and apparently omnipresent faith must have been enormously impressive and reassuring. They also fostered a sense of the unity of the faith, as pilgrims went from one magnificent church to another on such great pilgrim roads as that which led from France to Spain and terminated at the shrine of St James of Compostela.

For the laity as a whole, as in the past with minster churches and the like, these great churches were more of a stimulus and a boost to faith than places of worship. Most of them were probably open to the laity, at least for the main festivals, but they did not play much part in the life of the vast majority of the populations in the countries where they were constructed. They were not intended to hold large congregations. They were there to provide houses of prayer for the few, and places of inspiration for the many. They were also depositories for relics, so that the crowds went to them on pilgrimages, and on patronal festivals. In addition, the spacious naves allowed for grand processions at High Mass when, quite commonly, the people were only allowed in to the galleries or to a westward extension where they stood in such a way that they did not impede the ceremony taking place. 'In a sense, the church was conceived as a theatre.'[2] But what an effective theatre! Soaring above the mostly mean houses in their neighbourhoods, on a scale that dwarfed any other building, and with their awesome array of external and internal features, these massive and highly visible expressions of the Christian faith must have had an incredible impact on those who saw and who visited them. And, of course, such stupendous buildings greatly bolstered the prestige of the clergy who served in them.

During the medieval period there was, in fact, a steady increase in the status and standing of the clergy generally.

> With the conspicuous exception of the monastic movement, and especially the appearance of the mendicant friars in the early years of the thirteenth century, the Middle Ages saw clerical theory elevated to such a degree that any concept of a wider priesthood was virtually obscured. Even the Franciscans were compelled to turn away from their lay roots in spite of their founder's innovative realization of the wider priesthood in 1221 in the founding of the lay brotherhood known as the Tertiaries.[3]

It was in fact the Franciscans who represented what was arguably the boldest and most imaginative attempt in the medieval centuries to provide an outlet for dedicated lay service.

> Unfortunately, the subsequent institutionalisation of the Franciscans was a sign that the Church was not prepared to pay a sufficiently high price to retain the allegiance of the masses, i.e., a religious order with a predominantly lay character. After 1242 no lay brother could be appointed to offices in the order.[4]

It was but one more step in the segregation of the laity from the clergy, in the clamping down on lay initiatives, and in the seemingly unstoppable advance of clericalism.

This moving apart of the clergy and the laity was once again emphasized structurally and architecturally in the plans and layout of churches. In northern Europe, and particularly in England, the previous separation of the choir or *schola cantorum* from the laity by a low enclosure was made much more conspicuous by a more substantial and more pronounced division. A massive screen or *pulpitum* was built across the church, usually to the west of the tower crossing. Prominent examples were at Beverley, where it was introduced in the 1060s, and at Canterbury, where it was constructed in Lanfranc's time (1070–89). This *pulpitum* soon quite commonly became a heavy stone barrier, which allowed no access to the choir area except through side doors that led into the aisles of the choir.

The celebration of the Mass in these stunningly constructed and elaborately decorated centres of worship expressed and demonstrated this dichotomy between the clergy and the laity. It took place at the high altar that was often located far away from the nearest member of the congregation. Such a distancing of the celebrant and the other clergy from the congregation of laity was yet further emphasized by the addition of a huge veil suspended within the sanctuary during Lent and on weekdays.

The laity seem to have accepted that the separation of clergy and laity in both life and worship, with the clergy acting as the spiritual elite, was the normal; and for the most part they meekly concurred and acknowledged that such was the way things should be. The contention of Abbo of Fleury just before 1100 that within the body of the church 'there are three grades or orders, of which the first is of laymen, the second of clerks, and the third of monks', and that of these grades 'the first is good, the second better and the third best',[5] appears to have been treated as self-evident by the laity of the day. It is significant that one of the few lay reforming movements in the eleventh and twelfth centuries, the *Patarini* of Milan, demanded not greater lay participation, but greater clerical purity. The church authorities throughout the medieval period appear to have been largely concerned to maintain the status quo. They seemed to have been excessively anxious to guard, enhance and magnify the status and the standing of the clergy. Any questioning of their authority, and of the honour and respect accorded to them must be prevented. The submissiveness of the laity should be fostered, and any sign of non-compliance with what the church taught should be promptly and ruthlessly stamped upon. 'The laity in their "simplicity" should keep to their place and not try to tackle issues beyond their mental capacities.'[6] As one observer said in reference to thirteenth-century France, 'The laity ought not to rise up to look into the secrets of the faith . . . but adhere to them implicitly.'[7]

But there was a further division. The Catholic Church regarded men and women differently. 'Men controlled the institutional church and men dispensed the sacraments.' Women had no part in this most sacred of functions. A wide gulf was set between men and women by virtue of their gender. All women were always and at all times to display meek obedience. It was their sexual nature that had in some way to be overcome if they were to achieve full holiness.

> Virginity was preferable to marriage. Woman's nature was sexual, and she represented a constant danger to herself as well as to men because her sexuality inclined her to sin. A woman was polluted during menstruation and by childbirth. Furthermore, her nature rendered her particularly vulnerable to the wiles of the devil. Just as Eve had fallen, and with her the whole human race, so women represented a continuing danger after the Fall.[8]

Local churches

During the medieval period, the people as a whole lived in a world that was small and severely circumscribed: 'Villagers shared values and ideas which found expression in organizations and occasions involving a wide spectrum of the community.'[9] Nowhere was the closeness and intimacy of community life more apparent to the people than in their religious lives. The villagers 'attended services in church or chapel by compulsion, but from their participation in other voluntary parish activities' they

> clearly identified with the church as both a religious and social focus. They joined parish guilds which supplemented rather than rivalled the parish; they were involved in the great drinking sessions at church ales organised by the churchwardens as fund-raising events; they took part in processions, some of which, like the perambulation of the parish on rogation days, served a practical function in preserving memory of boundaries.[10]

And all of these activities were part and parcel of a wide range of secular festivals, leisure-time events and sports, such as summer games that very frequently brought the village folk together. Christianity was very much integrated with the totality of both individual and corporate life, and the ministrations of the church were welcomed and endorsed by almost everyone in the community.

Of course, this whole ordering of life meant that there was a degree of openness and sharing that left little room for confidentialities and hidden secrets. 'Dignity and privacy were not concepts dear to the hearts of mediaeval men, who conducted their communal lives on the unspoken assumption that the sins of one were the business of all.'[11] And the parish was a tight-knit, inward-looking community that, largely as a result of its intense self-awareness, encouraged such a highly charged sense of corporate frankness. The parishes that were emerging in the eleventh and twelfth centuries had well-defined frontiers, especially in rural areas, with all the inhabitants belonging to a single church.

> The parishioner 'belonged' in a very real sense to his church, and lived his whole life under its shadow. There, and there alone, he was baptized and married, attended Sunday Mass, paid his tithe and offerings, and there he was buried when he died.[12]

The parish church was even made into a closed society, restricted to local lay people. The statutes of the church stated that no one might receive the sacraments in any church but his or her own. Pierre de Collemieu, Archbishop of Rouen, 'required parish priests to keep a list of their parishioners, and to eject any strangers they found in their churches on Sundays, except for noblemen and beggars'.[13] The Lateran Council of 1215 decreed that lay confessions of sins should be made to the local parish priest, and to no one else.

Between the tenth and twelfth centuries in England, as in many other regions in the West, there was a rapid increase in the provision of local or private churches, each with a resident priest. There was a remarkable leap forward in the construction of stone churches that reached a pinnacle during the eleventh and twelfth centuries, with approximately two thousand being built between about 1075 and about 1125 alone.[14] The old minsters were ceasing to be the means of local church provision during the eleventh century, and the division of their parishes between local churches, with the accompanying crystallization of the modern parochial system, was completed by the thirteenth century.[15]

This pattern of local church development, and the chronology of its evolution, was not uniform throughout the Western world. The basic network of local churches in France was largely provided during the Carolingian period of the late eighth and early ninth centuries, while in many parts of northern Italy minster churches or *pievi* continued to exercise a baptismal monopoly up to and even beyond the fourteenth century. The increased provision of local churches throughout much of the West may in part have been a consequence of lay demand for easier access to the sacraments. Indeed, in some regions under Germanic law, there were collective lay efforts that led to 'communally owned churches' (*genossenschaftliche Gemeindekirchen*). Nevertheless, whatever the timescale, whatever the particular impulses that propelled the movement forward in any region, and however the details of the resulting church provision may have differed, the common factor was an escalation in the number of local churches. Some towns of England were in the vanguard of such expansion numerically. This had become evident by the sixteenth century in the remarkable profusion of local priests compared with the provision on the European mainland. 'While Braunschweig, Rostock, and Hamburg each contained four, Cologne 12, and Toledo in Castile 28, York possessed 40, Norwich 46, and London 110.'[16] The variation between countries is highlighted by the more ample supply of clergy in relation to the number of local inhabitants, with England once again in the forefront. 'In the pre-Reformation diocese of Geneva, there may have been 50 households per secular priest, in sixteenth-century Castile over 40, but in England just 22.'[17]

Although by the mid-eleventh century the abundance of local churches was especially evident in northern France, in Italy, in the southern half of England, and in many of the Mediterranean lands,[18] there were considerable variations in how these were administered. For example, in addition to the 'communally owned churches', there was a system to be found in Norway, which was similar to the Germanic arrangement, whereby, from about 1000,

> every legal district erected one central church, often on an old pagan site, and several neighbourhood churches, all under communal government. Besides providing furnishings, ornaments, and bells the inhabitants also built the churchyard wall, administered the tithe, and even elected the priest.[19]

In some regions of continental Europe, however, the provision of churches was much more haphazard. In the eastern part of Europe there were a number of comparatively underdeveloped regions where churches were few and far between or non-existent. There was no church at all in the Fichtelgebirge on the eastern border of Germany until the twelfth century, and even as far west as central southern Germany there were very few. Silesia had to wait for the large-scale German settlement in the thirteenth century before it was provided with purpose-built churches.

In the towns it was quite normal for a small number of churches to form one ecclesiastical unit in which the provost of the major churches appointed clergy to serve at the others. In the twelfth century, in some cities, including Paris, such urban churches proliferated astonishingly. This meant that the laity were better supplied with places of worship than ever before, and with clergy to minister to them.

Throughout central and western Europe the laity shared with the clergy in the upkeep and maintenance of church buildings.[20] The exact nature of this evolved in a somewhat random and unclear manner, but arrangements seem to have become more standardized and formalized in the early and mid-medieval years.[21] Various English thirteenth-century synodical statutes pronounced on the division of responsibility, with the rector assigned the chancel and the laity the nave and the churchyard. But although these became nationwide guidelines, local custom varied, and there was plenty of scope for conflict. Even so, and whatever the officially declared statutory or canonical situation, the lay responsibility in this matter persisted throughout western and central Europe during the Middle Ages, but in an ever more defined manner. Most German communities introduced special fabric boxes, so that patrons and tithe-owners could readily make contributions where the money so provided was insufficient to meet the demands. A similar system emerged in France, where the rectors normally maintained the chancel and the parish community the nave, although this was not made official until the seventeenth century, and other arrangements coexisted with this core division of responsibility.

The laity in most European countries and in England were additionally responsible for providing ornaments and liturgical books; a duty enshrined in English canon law from about 1250 and also, for example, in the statutes of the Council of Rouen of 1335.

A by-product of this enlarged lay responsibility was the desire of parishioners to keep the newly established communal funds firmly under their control, and well outside the incumbent's grasp. As money, land and tenements were increasingly offered as endowments for Masses, anniversaries, lights and chantries, thus enlarging the lay area of material support for the church, so there was an ever greater demand for independent wardens or lay representatives to supervise what were becoming complex administrative matters. Such officials were common by the mid-fourteenth century, after which they assumed duties other than those connected with the fabric and started to administer a common purse rather than a specific fund. Once established, in England the lay officers became known from 1386 as church-reeves, from 1429 as kirkmasters, and finally from at least 1466 as churchwardens. It is of note that those who served in this capacity were mostly neither from the very top nor from the bottom layers of local society; they were mostly from the broad middling social band, the layer of society that had formed the core of church membership for many centuries.

The office of churchwarden, or its equivalent in continental countries, gave a rare opportunity for lay men of modest income and little formal education, but with an established reputation for being among the more solid and dependable members of the local community and the church, to play a responsible and dignified part in the life of the village, or in the life of an urban parochial area.

Despite these moves to laicize and democratize church administration, however, the problem of communicating the faith to the mass of the population remained. After all, most of them were unable to read, and even if semi-literate all of them except the rich were denied access to books. Then, when they went to a church service, they found that the liturgy was celebrated in a language that was incomprehensible to them, except, perhaps, in Italy. Such barriers to understanding the faith and responding to it meant that familiarity with church rituals, regularity of liturgical forms, a set calendar of saints' days, and visual aids of various types became essential. The major ceremonies of the church, including festivals associated with particular saints, the adoration of the cross on Good Friday, and the kindling of the new fire on Easter Day, which in some areas was taken into the homes of each parishioner, were all useful in inculcating an awareness of the main teaching of the church and the main tenets of the faith.

In fact, the liturgy was at the very centre of lay Christian life in the Middle Ages.

> Within that great seasonal cycle of fast and festival, of ritual observance and symbolic gesture, lay Christians found the paradigms and the stories which shaped their perception of the world and their place in it. Within the liturgy birth, copulation, and death, journeying and homecoming, guilt and forgiveness, the blessing of homely things and the call to pass beyond them were all located, tested, and sanctioned. In the liturgy and in the sacramental celebrations which were its central moments, medieval people found the key to the meaning and purpose of their lives.[22]

More specifically, it was the Mass that was the one most powerful and pervasive Christian influence in communicating the faith to the lay population as a whole.

The liturgy lay at the heart of medieval religion, and the Mass lay at the heart of the liturgy. In the Mass the redemption of the world, wrought on Good Friday once and for all, was renewed and made fruitful for all who believed. Christ himself, immolated on the altar of the cross, became present on the altar of the parish church, body, soul, and divinity, and his blood flowed once again, to nourish and renew Church and world. As kneeling congregations raised their eyes to see the Host held high above the priest's head at the sacring, they were transported to Calvary itself, and gathered not only into the passion and resurrection of Christ, but into the full sweep of salvation history as a whole.[23]

Even those not present in the church could and did pause wherever they may have been, and in the midst of whatever they may have been doing, in the fields or in other places of work, in their homes, in the middle of private prayer, as, just before the sacring in every mass, a bell was rung to alert all the people to look up. As the chimes sounded, all knew that the moment of consecration and the raising of the Host was near. The laity almost to a person passionately believed that hearing the Mass and seeing the Host conferred precious benefits for body and soul. Here was to be found an assurance of safe delivery for a pregnant mother, safe arrival at their destination for travellers, good digestion for the eaters and drinkers, and the merciful and loving hand of God upon all in their daily lives.

The churches also helpfully provided visual aids for the largely unlearned laity in the form of images of various types. Many of these were simple and unembellished, but some were covered with precious metal. In the course of the eleventh century simple wooden statues gained in popularity. They were often painted in natural colours, so that they appeared to the worshippers to be very lifelike, and even evoked a belief that they occasionally showed signs of animation. The most common of the images was that of the Virgin and Child. The crucifix had always been a central feature in churches, but it gained in importance as a result of its focal incorporation into the great rood that became the most prominent item in the furnishing of the churches in northern Europe in the period from 1050 to 1200.

In the twelfth century stone sculpture, which was very rare before 1100, rapidly became common in the great churches. Profusely painted sculptural themes on the capitals of the arcades and on the west front powerfully conveyed aspects of Christianity. And these devices were once more, at least in part, an attempt to instruct the laity, in accordance with the dictum of Gregory the Great that 'what writing presents to the literate, pictures do to the ignorant who see them'.

As far as the spoken word is concerned, the laity did not benefit greatly from preaching in the medieval centuries. Although the twelfth century was a golden age for learned preaching, this was in Latin, 'and while individual preachers could have dramatic effects they could have contributed almost nothing to the general level of instruction in the population as a whole'.[24] There is an almost total absence of sermons that were clearly directed to a lay audience, although there are scraps of evidence to indicate that this sort of provision was made in some places. Where, exceptionally, and as a matter of some rarity, it was the custom to do so, it seems that the preaching was in the congregation's own language. 'Latin was the language of record, but sermons for the "illiterate", that is those without Latin, were delivered in the common language.'[25] As a rule, such valiant efforts to communicate the Christian gospel were restricted to a few of the great urban churches, and confined to a tiny proportion of the population. The vast majority of the laity was dependent on their country priest, and it is not even clear whether he was supposed to preach. The overwhelming view was that preaching was an episcopal prerogative. All members of the church were obliged to know the Creed and the Lord's Prayer, and the local priest typically seems to have restricted his teaching to what was contained in these foundation Christian texts. Of course this was a very circumscribed basis for understanding Christianity, and it raises the question of the extent to which such laity had anything more than an elementary knowledge of the faith.

Nonetheless, as the medieval period progressed, there were moves to increase the extent and effectiveness of preaching and of pastoral care. During the twelfth century there was an increased concern to make preaching more common, to make better use of the confessional and to provide better guidance on practical ethics. The Fourth Lateran Council, convoked by Pope Innocent III in 1215, took the reforms further. Bishops were instructed to provide competent men to preach, to hear confessions, and to give penance. Every adult was commanded to make his or her confession once a year, to perform the penance that the church enjoined, and to receive the sacrament of the Eucharist at Easter. This implies that prior to the early thirteenth century, annual confession and communion were not generally practised or observed, and the requirement that the new dictates should be published frequently and enforced, with the pain of suspended admission to the church, and prohibition of Christian burial, for non-compliance, strengthens the impression that new habits were being inculcated. Laudable as all this was, it is perhaps of little surprise that these decrees in no way envisaged the possibility of a radical new lay spirituality. The concern was that the laity should be more disciplined in their church lives, and better instructed in right belief and right behaviour through sermons, the confessional, and other means. There was no thought of raising them from their essentially subservient and submissive status and giving them a more central and active role in the life of the church.

Even so, there was little protest from the laity. There is scant evidence of discontent among the populace of Europe as a whole in medieval times concerning what the church provided and taught. The incidents of anti-clericalism and movements offering alternative expressions of the faith were few and far between. And when they did occur they were not widely supported. Humble compliance with church requirements and conformity to church dictates remained the norm.

None of what has been said should be taken as implying that attendance at church for most of the laity was merely mechanical and lacking in content or seriousness. There seems to have been widespread deep reverence. Behind and underpinning the corporate religious drama of the liturgy was often the very sincere and earnest, if frequently very simple, personal religion of medieval men and women. It is apparent from the many surviving prayers, 'jotted in the margins or flyleaves of books, collected into professionally commissioned or home-made prayer-rolls, devotional manuals, and commonplace books, above all gathered into the primers or Books of Hours (*Horae*)',[26] as well from the related collections of prayers, that private prayer was widespread, genuine, and of great significance to a vast number of the laity. For many of them, the liturgy was the public expression of what was a deep-seated personal faith. This was also made apparent in the guilds, confraternities and charities of this highly religious era.

Guilds, confraternities and charities

The opportunities for the laity to express their faith in acts of charity were not confined to the local church and the diligence or otherwise of the priest and laity acting in concert. There were also the guilds, confraternities or charities. These provided support for sick and needy members, arranged funerals and offered prayers for the departed, gave financial assistance to the local church, and often had their own altar in the parish church, which they maintained. In the twelfth century these traditional bodies were supplemented or replaced by ones with a strong commitment to a range of practical works of charity, or organizations devoted to particular trades or professions.

There are extant statutes for a number of tenth- and eleventh-century English guilds. Although the activity of each of them was focused upon a minster, 'the motivation to form a society appears to have come in every case from among the laity, who moreover comprised a preponderance of the membership'.[27] Not surprisingly, all was not sober and earnest with such corporate expressions of local lay piety. There were, for instance, communal feasts, when those involved broke through their usual constraints. 'Members solemnly undertook to provide the wherewithal on these occasions to render the company drunk as lords.'[28] But such conviviality, which often caused a scandal, did not dictate the character of the guilds, or divert them from their main, and somewhat more respectable and commendable, objectives.

One of these was responsibility for arranging and then attending special Masses in their local minster or church. Such services were separate from, and additional to, those celebrated at the parish altar. They took place on weekdays rather than Sundays, they were held at special nave altars rather than at the high altar, and they had their own furnishings and their own peace rituals.

The guilds were a crucial part of the strong emphasis on the communal nature of lay religion, which was so evident in the medieval period. Lay men and lay women seldom acted individually or in isolation in serving the church in practical ways. The guilds additionally served to reinforce the lay sense of unity and corporate identity by their devotion to one particular saint.

Monks, nuns and friars

The many documents describing the foundation of monasteries and nunneries, especially in their heyday from the late tenth century to the early twelfth century, but also later, show clearly how great and sustained was the lay involvement.

> The initiative generally lay with a great baron who gave the site, provided an endowment of land and revenues, granted jurisdictional immunities, decided the affiliations of his monastery and regulated the future relations of his family to the community. But close on the heels of the baron came his vassals: they also contributed lands and rights, and claimed a share in the spiritual benefits of the monastery.[29]

As already noted, the establishment of religious foundations in the so-called Carolingian age of the eighth and ninth centuries, had almost entirely relied on the munificence of kings or members of a royal household.

> But the strength of the later monasteries, like the strength of the new social order itself, lay in their widespread and intricate connection with the countryside; their possessions were scattered, generally in small parcels, among the lands of the neighbouring aristocracy to whom they owed their origin. Like the society which produced them, these monasteries were intensely local in their interests and independent in their government.[30]

The laity as a whole increasingly looked to the monastery in their vicinity as the source of inspiration for holy living, and quite often as the means for educational advance. This was especially so for any lay person who aspired to a standard of Christian life higher than the ordinary.

Then there were the friars. Francesco Bernardone of Assisi, Francis of Assisi, may be regarded as the first friar, the forerunner of many, and the outstanding model for what was entailed in being a friar. Most significantly from the perspective of the present book, he and his followers were initially lay men starting a lay movement. He was indeed one of the most influential lay men of the Middle Ages.

He was the son of a wealthy cloth merchant, and was born in 1181. He gave up a comfortable life, and he set out without shoes on his feet, and dressed only in a simple grey tunic tied with a cord, to preach and to serve people in whatever way he thought right. By their lifestyle, and by what they did, he, and his band of Friars Minor, or Grey Friars as they became known, served as an example of simple, uncomplicated Christian devotion. They were renowned for their unselfconscious, wholehearted dedication. They expressed their faith in countless acts of charity, and by straightforward but sincere preaching.

Pilgrimages, saints and relics

In the eleventh and twelfth centuries there was a notable escalation in the scale of pilgrimages, and a distinctive upgrading of the value attributed to participation in them. What had been an important element in the lives of many lay people over many centuries, quite suddenly became even more significant as an expression of Christian devotion. This was supplemented by a much greater perceived benefit accruing from participation in one of them. The pilgrim acquired a special, enhanced, status in the eyes of the churches. Masses for pilgrims; the liturgical blessing of pilgrim staffs and wallets; emblems issued by the great shrines that pilgrims could wear to show that they had completed the journey; and the imposition of excommunication on all those who stole from pilgrims, all attest to the increasing emphasis placed upon pilgrimages as a valid activity for all the laity whatever their social standing.[31] Pilgrimages were also great occasions for communal bonding.

> Villages would organize a pilgrimage together led by a cantor, with the sick carried with them on carts. News of miracles spread from one group of pilgrims to another; we have several cases of people who set out for one shrine but were 'captured' by news of a good miracle at another. Healings were greeted enthusiastically by the crowds.

Prayers at the shrine 'were both communal and crude'.[32]

The purpose of pilgrimages was also extended. 'The notion that a pilgrim had only to go to a particular shrine to be pardoned is scarcely found before the ninth century and did not command universal acceptance until the eleventh.'[33] Linked with this was the use of pilgrimages by the church hierarchy as part of the procedures available for disciplining the laity. 'Bishops and confessors only now begin to impose specific pilgrimages on penitents. Rome was the usual destination.'[34]

But it by no means stood alone. Throughout the Middle Ages pilgrimage destinations fell into three categories: those which were associated in one way or another with the earthly life and death of Christ; those that commemorated the Virgin Mary; and those that chiefly honoured one of a galaxy of saints recognized by the church.

The Virgin Mary had always elicited the greatest enthusiasm from Christians in general. But it was not until the later medieval period that the adoration of the mother of Christ became a pronounced feature in 'official' church promulgations. 'Mariology, as it is sometimes called, was a movement guided by the church from above but welcomed, too, by the ranks of the laity for whom religion was becoming a more directly personal matter.'[35]

A measure of the centrality of saints in the life of the medieval laity is the fact that images of some of them were painted on or attached to the dados or loft-fronts of rood-screens. The saints literally stood under the cross, and this spoke of their dependence on and mediation of the benefits of Christ's passion, and their perceived role as intercessors for the worshippers both in the present and at the last day.

> The saints were often portrayed as embodying precisely those elements of tenderness and compassionate humanity which were the distinguishing marks of late medieval devotion to the name and person of Jesus. Like their master and exemplar, the saints were gentle, loving, merciful.[36]

Whether the destination of the pilgrims was one of the major magnets for Westerners, such as Rome, Jerusalem and Santiago de Compostela, a leading local Christian centre, or one of the countless churches, cathedrals and abbeys, relics of Mary, of one of the canonized saints or even of Christ himself, were an essential provision for those who came seeking special consolation and blessing. These were material objects, open to the gaze of pilgrims, and they acted as a focal point for the pilgrims. They were invariably associated with miracles of healing, which was a continuous indicator in authenticating and corroborating the power and authority of the saint. 'The conviction that the saints, who inhabited both the earthly and the celestial realms, were especially responsive to prayers uttered in the vicinity of their relics, was one of the dominant themes of popular religion in the Middle Ages.'[37]

The crusades

The crusades were in some respects akin to pilgrimages. In both, it was lay people who were mostly involved in what were essentially corporate enterprises focused on sacred Christian shrines. The crusaders were certainly inspired by a desire to champion the cause of Christ as the participants and the supporters viewed it, despite the fact that in many cases such a purpose was mingled with less worthy motives. The one overriding, enormous and tragic difference, however, was the fact that the crusades entailed suffering, death and destruction on a massive scale and over a prolonged period, and left a disastrous legacy of bitterness, resentment and a fraught relationship between Islam and Christianity. Despite all the good intentions, the pious talk, and the many acts of chivalry, they must be accounted as among the most horrific episodes in the history of the laity in Christianity. They left a stain on that history that is irremovable. They were an almost unmitigated tragedy.

From the start, the crusades assumed a central place in the thinking, emotions and, in a minority of cases, the active lives of medieval men and women. The first, launched in 1095 by Pope Urban II at the Council of Clermont, has even been described as 'the central event in the history of mediaeval Christianity'.[38] The Pope painted a sombre picture of a dire situation. Islamic forces were conquering the Holy Land. And he then made his great appeal. Western Christendom, and that largely meant the laity, should march to the rescue of the East. 'Rich and poor alike should go.' The need for action was urgent. 'There must be no delay. Let them be ready to set out when the summer had come, with God to be their guide.'[39] The response was immediate and sensational. The Pope had lit a torch that was not to be finally extinguished for three hundred years and more.[40]

Such was the mainly lay fervour generated that the Council decided to grant to all those who, with pious intentions, took part in the holy war, remission of the temporal penalties due for their sins; and it was guaranteed that all the worldly possessions of the crusaders would be protected by the church during their absence. Each participant was to wear a cross of red material on the shoulder of his surcoat as a symbol of dedicated service. Thousands upon thousands of lay people enlisted in one or more of the crusades.

The attraction of the appeals being made may have lain in the sense of service in the world that was being offered to laity as complementary to service in the monasteries for the monks. The monks were engaged in a battle with the devil using spiritual weapons. Lay men were to fight the heathen in the flesh. Service as a monk in a monastery was viewed at the time as the pinnacle of individual spiritual attainment. The monks were accorded a high status in societies that gave a central place in personal, local and national life to Christian belief, values and practices. The crusaders were now being offered all the kudos, the sense of personal achievement, and the assurance of spiritual merit, that attached to a combination of Christian pilgrim and soldier of Christ. Seen in this light, crusading may have unconsciously paved the way for the eventual substitution of Christian withdrawal from the world as the ultimate and supremely honoured path of Christian discipleship, for the Protestant alternative of fighting the good fight of faith within the world. And, taken further still, it is also possible to discern in this greater entanglement of Christians with secular matters one of the major moves towards the so-called secularization of society: a process that has occupied the attention of many sociologists.[41]

Whatever the explanation of the astounding response to the call to participate in a crusade, it has to be acknowledged that the sudden and sustained welling up of intense emotion was not the result of cool and calm calculation at the time; it came from the hearts rather than the heads of those involved. The preaching of a crusade at that particular time caught the mood of Christian Europe; it was 'a high tide in the perpetual flow of the spiritual life'.[42] A deep and strong sense of Christian commitment, and obligation to Christian service, together with an intense concern about personal salvation, clearly loomed large in the outlook of many if not the vast majority of the people of western Europe. And the crusades drew upon such strong emotions. There was a powerful Christian element also in the corporate aspect of such profound feelings; in what may be called the collective consciousness.

By the end of the thirteenth century the crusades had become such an established feature of continental European and English religious life that regular appeals for money, special church services, processions and prayers incorporated into the liturgy, frequent grants of indulgences, taxation and the near permanent presence of collection chests for them in many parish churches had become accepted and largely unquestioned features of everyday life for the entire population.

The surest sign of deep-rooted lay opinion on any issue in any age is the degree to which the genuine and heartfelt support and prayers of ordinary people of quite low social status and standing were generated for it, as expressed in obscure gatherings far from the public gaze. The pious, charitable and commercial guilds of fourteenth-century Europe provided the opportunity for such practical and intercessory support. It is clear that without any apparent pressure or hope of reward, they spontaneously yet in a persistent way typically accumulated special funds for pilgrims, and particularly for those travelling to Jerusalem, and they prayed regularly for the crusaders and for the patriarch of Jerusalem. Their devotion to the welfare of the Holy Land is impressive, and they supply convincing evidence that such concern lasted until the latter part of the fourteenth century.

'Heretical' movements

The support for the crusades came from within the institutional church, from lay members who appear to have been thoroughly at one with the church in what it taught, and in what it undertook. They were the stalwart conformists.

Some laity in the Middle Ages, however, were not prepared to conform to all the Catholic beliefs and practices that have been discussed so far in this chapter. Such non-conformity resulted in a number of remarkable movements, all of which the Catholic Church dubbed as 'heretical'. Examples of these can be found throughout the four hundred and fifty years from the end of the eleventh century to the first half of the sixteenth century. They were mostly separate and uncoordinated. They were all largely composed of, and quite often led by, lay people; and they arose as a result of the shared, similar concerns, of all those involved. A

> reaction against the impersonal and institutional framework of Carolingian religious observance and towards the search for a personal link between creature and creator, away from the unquestioning acceptance of the revealed truth as it was expounded by the church towards commitment to the inner light which might beckon a man from his own conscience, manifested itself both within and outside the church.[43]

There were repeated, and mostly vehement, affirmations that sacraments administered by degenerate priests were worthless; and baptism was of no avail when it involved infants who were too young to understand its meaning. But more fundamentally and devastatingly, there was the implication, if not the explicit declaration, that the claim of the Catholic Church to be the only refuge for the soul in its search for salvation was both unscriptural and inconsistent with the evident imperfection of its priests and with the whole conduct of the church.

Although the overall message of all the dissentients was clear, the doctrinal and organizational alternatives to the contemporary church they offered varied from one individual or group to another. Some of the movements were more socially exclusive and more radical than others. The more extreme were often apocalyptic and millenarian in theology, and exuberant in their life and behaviour. In many cases there were also but partially hidden non-theological agendas. There were indications that theological protestations may have masked social aspirations. Demands for social or economic reform were frequently implicit, if not explicit. During the entire medieval period, repeatedly, 'the desire of the poor to improve the material conditions of their lives became transfused with fantasies of a new Paradise on earth, a world purged of suffering and sin, a Kingdom of the Saints'.[44] To all appearances most of these movements were solely religious in intent, but they also contributed to the story of how, again and again, 'apocalyptic lore became charged with social aspirations, animosities and anxieties to which it in turn gave a new and peculiar dynamic'.[45] It has been suggested by many commentators that these largely lay movements were variously 'a revolt of the urban poor against nascent capitalism, of the rural poor against the elaboration of seigniorial control and exploitation, of women against the growing domination of men, or laymen against ecclesiastical control of their activities and communities'.[46]

Characteristically, whatever the wellsprings of their appearance, and despite the almost unbounded enthusiasm of their adherents, one after another of these movements quite rapidly disappeared. Even so, they were an important component in the religious, and in the more specifically lay religious, life of medieval Europe. In particular, they added to the radical tide that was plainly flowing not so far beneath the surface of European society.

Of special note, however, were two somewhat new types of 'heresy', the Cathars and the Waldensians, both of which were distinguished by their concern to propagate their views within the framework of the church. They called for radical changes both among the clergy and in the relationship between the church and society; and they demanded a collective facing up to the social implications of the gospel. This new type of movement offered almost unlimited opportunity for lay participation. It was socially inclusive, appealing to every social group.

Catharist influences spread widely from the eleventh to the thirteenth centuries, being especially strong in northern Italy and southern France.[47] Theologically, they were particularly condemned for the belief of many, although not all, of their members, that two equal and opposite principles of good and evil operated in the world. This dualism was a variation of the ancient heresy of Manichaeism, and as such it was said to deny and discard foundational mainline Christian monotheism. It is of little wonder that this movement, more than any other heretical group, aroused alarm and hostility. In fact, it was the ferocious response of the Catholic Church to the Cathars that was responsible for the establishment and development of the Inquisition.

As with all the schismatic movements, sects and cults of medieval times, the Cathar membership was almost entirely made up of laity. In Italy, as elsewhere, the Cathars were mostly based in the cities. There was some support from the nobility, leading city men, and even from the upper privileged clergy on occasions.[48] But the bulk of the followers came from the suburbs, from working-class areas, and the small-scale traders and feudality of the Midi also became adherents en masse.

From 1300 onwards, the Cathars played little part in the history of the Western Church. But this was not so with the Waldensians.[49] They were small in number, but they survived to have some influence on the Protestant Reformers of the sixteenth century; and they still exist as a community of believers in Piedmont. It was Peter Valdes, a rich merchant, who, in the late twelfth century, became an itinerant, mendicant preacher, and soon gathered a group of both men and women followers who were united in their assault on what they regarded as the worldliness of the clergy, and bound together in opposition to the dualist heresy of the Cathars. Despite receiving the approval of Pope Alexander III for his vow of voluntary poverty, Valdes and his companions were forbidden to preach except when invited to do so by a clergyman. Clearly, there were quite strict reservations about what the laity would be permitted by the clergy to do on their own initiative. It is, perhaps, little wonder that Valdes soon ceased to obey this prohibition.

In about 1179–80 he made a meticulous profession of his orthodoxy, but nevertheless the Council of Verona in 1184 placed the poor men of Lyons under the ban of excommunication along with the Cathars. A wedge was being driven between the Waldensians and the church of which they were only too prepared to reckon themselves a part, and the followers of Valdes increasingly organized themselves as a body, separate from the official church. They ignored the decrees and sanctions of the Catholic Church, and appointed their own ministers. They were inclined to doubt the validity of sacraments when they were administered by unworthy ministers, and they shunned such practices as prayers for the dead and the veneration of saints and relics as being unscriptural. More than anything else, they insisted on the right and duty of preaching. As a final tenet of belief, they vehemently disapproved of either judicial or military killing.

The Waldensians were cast in the role of a body set apart from their mother church, and from the ethos and life of the lay society of which they were members. It is therefore perhaps surprising, and indicative of latent feelings among the laity of the Catholic Church, that they grew rapidly in numbers, especially among the lower and middling classes. They extended their reach, most notably in southern France and Spain, and subsequently in Germany, Piedmont and Lombardy. They were a small but robust Christian fellowship and ginger group. After the death of their leader, they shunned any centralized leadership or formal organization, but persisted as a number of local, largely unstructured, communities, united by informal connections and common, strongly held beliefs.

The Catholic Church's attitude and policy towards the Waldensians reached a climax around 1200, by which time 'the balance in the battle between heretical minorities and ecclesiastical authority had definitely swung against the Church'.[50] At that stage, Pope Innocent III tried by peaceful persuasion to woo them back into the Catholic fold, but with little success. With the growth of the Inquisition, they underwent severe trials, and their numbers dwindled. But they were not annihilated, and they lived on, most remarkably in Italy. They later also expanded into Bohemia, Poland and Hungary.

The church and the laity at the end of the fourteenth century

By the end of the fourteenth century, the church in the West was firmly established as the second power in most countries after the Crown or whatever other form of secular political authority held sway. In most of the lands it was also arguably without equal in the comprehensiveness and complexity of its institutional organization and, of course, it was part of an international body that extended to most of the known world of the day.

Superficially, all seemed quite well. There was as yet neither doubt nor questioning of either the beliefs or the practices of the Catholic Church, at least on anything other than an occasional individual or very small-scale basis.[51] Such submissiveness mainly resulted from fear: the church held the keys of heaven and hell, and it took a brave person to criticize and oppose such an august body.

Indeed, there was a considerable emphasis throughout the medieval period on death, which some have seen as an obsession. And this may have reached a pinnacle of preoccupation by the end of the fourteenth century. It may be true that 'no other epoch has laid so much stress as the expiring Middle Ages on the thought of death'. And that in those years an 'everlasting call of *memento mori*'[52] sounded through life. Certainly, there was an unavoidable and overwhelming lay and clerical concern, from peasant to monarch, and from local priest to pontiff, with the safe transition of the soul from this world to the next.

The fear of eternal damnation and the desire for eternal bliss haunted the laity as well as the clergy. It can be seen as the foundation upon which the whole vast edifice of the medieval church was constructed.[53] That is why the medieval laity accepted so readily Christ's promise of pardon to the repentant sinner, even if there were many times when the individual fell back into sin, and even if it was left to a deathbed repentance to snatch a soul from the jaws of hell. It also accounts for the vivid belief in purgatory, where souls not yet fit for the everlasting riches of heaven could spend a time of waiting, which earnest supplication on earth, and special grants from the pope, might shorten or end. It was a dominant topic of 'lay awareness, and provided the rationale underlying the immense elaboration of the late medieval cult of intercession for the dead. The whole structure of mortuary provision of Masses, alms, pilgrimage, and the adornment of churches and images' which, was to 'characterize almost all the wills of fifteenth- and sixteenth-century English men and women, was raised on the belief that such largesse would hasten the soul's passage through the pains of Purgatory'.[54] Fear of Purgatory and of eternal damnation, and rejoicing at the prospect of endless heavenly rapture, were the most important motivations for the many and often massive benedictions of the lay rich. Land was given, and money was paid, with this eternal destiny in mind, and chantries were built in order that prayers should be offered for the soul of the benefactor and the souls of his or her family members.

The ubiquitous cult of the dead did not, however, mean that medieval religion in general, and that of the late medieval period in particular, was morbid or doom-laden. There was much joviality and celebration among the clergy and laity alike. Medieval Catholicism was a religion 'where shouts of laughter as well as roars of rage were common in church, where the clergy waged a constant if perhaps sometimes half-hearted battle against the invasion of fun, entertainment and commerce into their church building'.[55] Such freedom for the full and corporate expression of human emotions meant that there was much contentment among the laity in late medieval Christendom. Until the last quarter of the fourteenth century, there was no major discarding of mainline Catholicism in favour of an alternative version of Christianity.

Few would have been willing to break ranks, and to jeopardize their eternal destiny by standing up against the awesome medieval church. There was anti-clericalism and anti-papalism, but these did not entail a wholesale rejection of the teaching and conduct of the church as such. Nonetheless, it was soon to come, as will be seen in the next chapter. The first stirrings involving lay as well as clerical church members were evident before the end of the fourteenth century. And the mounting volume and intensity of discontent was partly a result of greater and more universal education.

Although it may be an exaggeration to talk of a literate laity towards the end of the fourteenth century, it is certainly legitimate to speak of a laity that was better informed and more articulate than a century earlier. It was a laity that had been given access to some of the sources of their faith through literacy and translation. It was a laity that was encouraged to view the clergy and the church with greater independence and growing impatience, largely as a result of what they had come to appreciate for themselves through their new literary explorations. And it was a laity that had moved a long way along the path of enfranchisement from their former spiritual servility and complacency.[56] Of course it was probably no more than a small minority who were advancing educationally in this way, and who were viewing church matters with more openness than in any previous age, but it was a greater and more widespread move forward than societies had ever undergone before. And it was the clergy as well as the laity who were gaining in literacy and learning.[57] This had enormous implications, not only in terms of the kind of ministry required, but also in the way that there were quite suddenly, and increasingly, far more enquiring minds, with new vernacular literature on which to feed their hunger. It was to this new type of lay person that John Wyclif and John Hus were able to appeal with devastating short, medium and long-term effect.

Nonetheless, prior to the Lollards and the Hussites there was little sign of lay protest or rebellion, and certainly no lock, stock and barrel rejection of the existing ecclesiastical system and clerical apparatus. The laity, especially in rural areas, which accounted for most of the people, was innately conservative.

From about the middle of the thirteenth century, however, changes were afoot in the rudimentary ways of teaching the faith that were pointers to what lay ahead. The religious plays, which had been performed in the church and had been under the guiding hand of the incumbent, were increasingly taken over by the laity and presented in guildhalls or in the open air. The language used changed from Latin to native tongues, and the dramas enacted became less liturgical, and more didactic and geared to popular taste. These 'miracle' plays introduced new themes such as the 'Harrowing of Hell', and the passion became a widely adopted subject. By the early fourteenth century municipalities and guilds were organizing such vernacular plays in a considerable number of places. The new, secular, settings encouraged more adventurous productions, and long pageants were presented that traced the story of humanity's redemption from the fall of Lucifer to the Day of Judgement. They were put on most frequently at Whitsuntide, or at the feast of Corpus Christi, which was instituted in 1311. Later on came the morality plays. It was a remarkable enlargement of Christian communication. The illiterate or semi-literate laity were becoming better informed. These moves literally brought the Christian message, and all that it entailed, out of the church and into the marketplace.

Alongside these changes, there was also a flood of small treatises in simple language, together with substantial and erudite works, to help the more literate members of the public in town and country to understand and to live out their faith in their daily lives. Geoffrey Chaucer, William Langland, John Gower, and later Dante Alighieri, were able to write what they did because a reading public was emerging that was ready to receive such high-quality literature. This development of reading ability and availability of works to satisfy a growing literary hunger together proved to be revolutionary both for the church at the time, and as a preparation for future events. In the course of the fourteenth century, the increasing literacy and professionalism among the laity introduced what was at first a quiet and restrained challenge to the existing beliefs and practices of the church, and criticism of its more blatant shortcomings and failures. But lay boldness slowly increased. The growth in the number of literate lay people, and the emergence of many lawyers, judges, stewards, bailiffs and others with professional skill and knowledge, to an extent broke through the barrier of awe and unquestioned acceptance of the clergy and what they asserted. There was a new, still only tentative, tendency to regard the clergy as only one profession among others, and to be jealous of their claim to special and extensive legal and economic rights.[58]

Cracks were appearing as never before, most notably in relation to the status and standing of the laity. The people of many countries reached the year 1400 far more restless and critical of the institutional church and its abuses than at any other previous time, despite the fact that the fundamental Christian view of the world and the world to come remained essentially intact.

4

From the late fourteenth century to the mid-seventeenth century

New religious movements

The church internationally and institutionally was in a sorry state in the last quarter of the fourteenth century. It was beset with problems. Throughout Christendom there were wars, conflicts and tensions between nations, and between nations and the papacy, unfulfilled ecclesiastical hopes, a church very publicly at odds with itself, and widespread evidence of mass discontent with the ecclesiastical authorities and with many features of contemporary Christianity.

Calamitous developments in the history of the papacy had dire consequences for the whole of the Christian world. 'A new epoch in the history of the western Church opened inauspiciously when the disturbed condition of Italy led Pope Clement V (1305–14) to take up residence at Avignon.'[1] The popes of the Babylonian Captivity, as the period of papal exile in Avignon between 1309 and 1377 is called, made financial and other demands on the European churches and nations that caused much resentment. Then there was the shameful papal schism (the Great Schism) in 1378 when the election of Pope Urban VI was declared null and void soon after he had taken up office, because of discontent with him, and a second nominee was declared pope under the title of Clement VII. Immediately the different states of Europe declared their allegiance to one or other of the rival popes, according to their dynastic interests, and there was an unseemly period of hostility between the two camps. The schism was a tragedy of monumental proportions. Both rival claimants could only crush their opponents by the use of military force, which meant that they abandoned their proper task of mediation and actually encouraged war. This subjected them to further deserved criticism, and brought additional dishonour upon the church.

Late medieval men and women were 'easily attracted to charismatic figures who claimed to be prophets with a special word from God and who sometimes posed a serious threat to the church and to social order'.[2] A number of examples of such religious excitement and social disruption caused by a popular prophet could be cited. One will suffice. It was ignited when a cowherd named Hans Boehm appeared in the German village of Niklashausen in 1476, claiming to have had a vision of the Virgin Mary, in which he had been commanded to proclaim a message. What this 'Drummer of Niklashausen' declared was provocative and inflammatory.

> He preached violently against the government and the clergy, and against pointed shoes, slashed sleeves, and long hair. He also claimed that water, pasture, and wood ought to be held in common by all and that tolls and export payments should be abolished. The whole country, he said, was mired in sin and wantonness and, unless . . . [the] people were ready to do penance and change their wicked ways, God would let all Germany go to destruction.[3]

The effect of his reported vision and his aggressive teaching was immediate and astonishing. People came from near and far. They confessed their sins and took the appropriate sartorial action regarding their shoes and other attire. When the drummer was cast into prison, his followers attacked the jail crying out that the Virgin Mary would protect them from harm. But their expectations were thwarted when the soldiers fired on the crowd, killing and wounding many. Boehm and three others were burnt at the stake.

The unsettled theological state of affairs of which this is but one, late example, was not confined to such popular, lay agitations. Even within the exalted circles of the academic elite, the hundred and fifty years before the outbreak of the Reformation was a time when the theological waters were uncomfortably disturbed. Few areas of life, and no sectors of the population, seem to have been totally immune to the impact of the unrest. All, in varying degrees, either directly or indirectly, felt the effect of the fourteenth- and fifteenth-century agitation and questionings, and the theological disturbance certainly penetrated the walls of the universities. It was, however, when new thinking within the confines of Oxford breached the closed circle of that imposing institution and infiltrated the wider realm of English society in the late fourteenth century that the cat was really among the pigeons.

By the time that John Wyclif and John Hus appeared on the scene, their task of spreading a new message was greatly facilitated not only by the increased literacy, already noted, but also by linguistic developments. In England, French had ceased to be the dominant language.

> For the first time since the Conquest all Englishmen enjoyed a common language, and the linguistic barriers between different orders in lay society had been broken. Nothing now prevented any layman who could read from access to books in the vernacular.[4]

This was a crucial factor in giving a new homogeneity to English society. Such increased sense of oneness,

> combined with the extension of literacy, popular enthusiasm for austere religious movements and the perennial jealousy of the wealth of the Church, all help to explain how the esoteric writings of an Oxford theologian could become the basis for an outburst of radical questioning of the Church which for a time found wide-scale support.[5]

John Wyclif and the Lollards, and John Hus and the Hussites

John Wyclif (c. 1330–84) was an eminent Oxford don who late in his life and career started to place great stress on the Bible.[6] He made 'constant appeal to the Scriptures as the primary and absolute authority'.[7] He became the first English academic since Stephen Langton (d. 1228) to comment on the whole of the Bible when he delivered his lectures. To Wyclif, the Bible was 'the source of all genuine human knowledge; the logic of Scripture was the only and all sufficient logic';[8] and he reaffirmed scripture as 'the true basis for doctrine in the Church'.[9]

Such an emphasis on the Bible was revolutionary. Wyclif used the Bible and its teaching to reassess all matters. He blamed all the ills of the church and of society on a refusal to submit to its authority.

Action to remedy what he regarded as a disastrous departure from the very fundamentals of a true church had to be taken at the local level. A radical change was needed in the relationship between the church and the government in order to correct blatant and manifold deviations from true Christianity. The king of England and other temporal lords should be given the final control over the temporal property of the church and, in the absence of good bishops, the monarch and his aides should superintend many purely ecclesiastical matters in the church as part of their feudal jurisdiction. This indeed was strong meat.

The relationship between John Wyclif and Lollardy is obscure.[10] He does not appear to have headed up a movement, but he may have been happy with much that was declared by the Lollards.

Outside of Oxford, in the country as a whole, the followers of Wyclif were few, and they were scattered, so that there was little concentration of them in any one place. Nevertheless, those who proclaimed the Lollard message were sufficiently forthright to attract the attention of the church authorities, and to be dubbed by their enemies and detractors with their collective name, with its meaning of mumblers who talked nonsense.[11]

Too much can be made of the attraction of Wyclif's teaching for the ordinary, often poor, people as a consequence of their deprived or hard social circumstances. Even so, enthusiastic itinerant preaching, and the vibrant declaration of the gospel by Lollards who remained in one place for many years, was probably effective in its appeal to the kind of people who supported or joined in the 1381 Peasants' Revolt. It is perfectly reasonable to surmise that the socially and economically disadvantaged members of society who enlisted for, or at least hailed, the one with gladness, may also have sought comfort and salvation in what was offered by the other a few years later.

Those lay people who responded most fervently to the Lollard teaching and who embraced it with such vehemence often demonstrated remarkable dedication and zeal. Such, for example, was the Leicester blacksmith William Smith. He is reported to have been illiterate, and a man of despicable and deformed appearance. Yet as part of the profession of his new calling he learnt both to read and to write, and then spent eight years copying English translations of the Gospels, the Epistles and works of the early fathers.

There were many lay men and lay women like William, who resolutely applied themselves to solitary study, who wrestled with their own inadequacies as readers, and who tried to come to grips with the problems of textual comprehension. Such private study was complemented by expositions of the Bible at Lollard gatherings, and by various forms of domestic worship and instruction, with servants reading to masters, husbands to wives, fathers to families, and in-laws to in-laws. The Lollard movement in those days demonstrates the validity of the claim of one of its early members that 'the lewed people crieth after Holy Writ, to kunne it and keep it'.[12]

What the Lollards set forth was also highly relevant to the emerging socially mobile members of society.

> Wyclif's appeal lay to no small extent in the expression which he gave to the frustrations of the underprivileged who were increasingly aware of their condition. He conferred self-respect on men and women who, although outside the spiritual elite of the religious orders and lacking the status and authority of priests and prelates, were yet gaining ambition in the wake of literacy, freedom, land and prosperity.[13]

This was especially novel with regard to the status, standing and prospects offered to women. In fact, the presence of women among the active Lollards caused particular alarm in church circles. And there was precedence for such fears.

> From the earliest days of Christianity, the church fathers had commented adversely upon the attraction of women to heresy. Female support for the Cathar and Waldensian heresies of the fourteenth and fifteenth centuries in Europe was marked, and there were women preachers.[14]

So it is understandable that the teaching of Wyclif in this respect, and the expectations or possibilities he raised, produced apprehension. By reducing the distinction between the clergy and the laity, he offered encouragement to women, whose sex debarred them from the priesthood. There is evidence that women were not only preachers in the formative early stage of the movement, but that claims were made for them to be eligible for the priesthood. It was even rumoured that women offered the sacrament to believers.[15]

One of the most momentous results of Wyclif's teaching was the part it played in precipitating an allied and triumphant dissenting movement in the far-off kingdom of Bohemia.[16] Wyclif's distinctively biblical approach came to the attention of Jan Hus, the Dean of the Philosophical Faculty at Prague University, and it promptly helped to give greater shape and precision to his growing dissatisfaction with the contemporary church; a reappraisal that was shared by other leading Czech churchmen. What Hus had to say resonated with the Czech people from the royal family to the ordinary citizen, who were at one in asserting Czech identity. His sermons, in which he stressed the need for church reform, and in particular the need to correct the corruption and worldliness of the clergy, were immensely popular in the city, and his position and influence were greatly enhanced in 1409 when a royal decree gave control of the university to the Czech people. It soon became a stronghold of Wyclifite doctrines, with Hus as Rector. He expressed and promulgated the new teaching 'so effectively that the significance of the movement ceased to be merely local and became as wide as Latin Christendom'.[17]

In 1414, Hus responded to a summons to attend a General Council of the Catholic Church at Konstanz in order to explain his teaching and acts of rebellion, and he relied on the safe-conduct provision from the Holy Roman Emperor Sigismund. But the Council ignored this, seized him and put him on trial for heresy. He was condemned and burnt at the stake in 1415, showing great fortitude in his suffering. But this was not the end of the story. Back in Bohemia, he was hailed as a national hero; his university declared him to be a martyr, and his feast was fixed for the day of his death. The sense of outrage at what had happened was widespread and heartfelt in the country, and within five years a Czech rebellion resulted in the establishment of a Hussite Church in Bohemia that was independent of Rome. 'For the first time – and a full century before Luther – a nation challenged the authority of the Church as represented by pope and council.'[18]

Such a revolution in central Europe was a huge embarrassment for the Roman Catholic Church. Although the changes introduced in Bohemia did not amount to a formal break with the Church of Rome, and were conceived by their authors as reforms within the church designed to win over the church as a whole, the movement in effect entailed at least a snub to the church authorities. They had to stand by helplessly, while the new church slipped out of the control of its leaders and was taken over by its more radical, largely lay, elements. A bitter civil war ensued as the existing political as well as religious hierarchy was opposed, with no outside power able to destroy the revolution despite attempts to do so. And through all this upheaval the Hussite Church survived. In the process it gave greater freedom and rights to the laity. This was contentiously and publicly made evident in the use in worship of Czech, the language of the people, rather than Latin, and in the practice of administering the wine as well as bread to the worshippers at the Eucharist.[19]

This series of events also reverberated through Europe and remained as a reminder of what could happen. The Czech example could be repeated, and next time it might be far more extensive or revolutionary. The Roman Catholic authorities must also have been particularly aware from the fourteenth century onwards that a breaking-forth of some protest movement was an ever-present possibility. Rebellion or dissent, whether predominantly religious, or mainly social, but with a large religious component, was not far from the surface.

The dissident laity on the eve of the Reformation

The theology and outlook of the sixteenth-century Protestant reformers had much in common with that of the Lollards. 'At the heart of both faiths lay the conviction that Scripture alone enshrined all religious truth, and that to every layman belonged the right to find that truth for himself.'[20] The whole paraphernalia of Catholicism, including confession, penance and pardons, whereby 'the clergy held the laity in thrall',[21] was placed under the microscope of the Bible and its teaching.

The more widespread literacy of the laity was now harnessed to a greater general intellectual curiosity aroused by the Renaissance.[22] The Wyclif Bible and other Christian works became increasingly available and influential, especially after the revolution of movable print in the eighth decade of the fifteenth century. The impact of the Renaissance was especially powerful among the prosperous and well-educated merchants, gentry, lawyers and others who were just the kind of people to be touched by the impending Protestant message. The lay people were able and prepared as in no previous age to think and decide for themselves on matters that had literally been a closed book to them in former centuries, rather than meekly and unquestioningly accepting what the priests, pope and others in authority told them they should believe. And literacy was seeping down the social scale, as well as to some extent to women. Although much of this newly aroused curiosity, especially in its humanistic form, was to turn people against the Christian faith altogether, it also undoubtedly prepared the ground for the new Protestant seed that was about to be sown.

Of particular importance was the translation of the New Testament into the vernacular, and the dissemination of its teaching to a host of people ranging from those of high status to the ploughman and the farm labourer. Desiderius Erasmus's 1516 edition of the New Testament, with its accompanying commentary, was especially inspirational to many aspiring Protestant reformers, most notably as a result of its bold retranslated version of some familiar passages. Matthew 3.2, in which John the Baptist's cry in the wilderness was *metanoeite*, is an example. The long-accepted official translation by Jerome of this word was *poenitentiam agite*, 'do penance', and the medieval church had built its whole theology and practice of the sacrament of penance on that interpretation. In contrast Erasmus presented the message of John the Baptist as a call to inward, individual change of heart, of repentance, and he translated the demand of the Baptiser into Latin as *resipiscite* (revive, recover, come to one's senses). It was in such ways, and by such means, that the reformers were further emboldened to challenge the teaching of the church. Through what Erasmus and others taught, they were encouraged in their efforts to persuade the people to work out their salvation with fear and trembling, and then to walk in holiness, with the Bible to guide them.

The pre-Reformation laity in traditional Catholicism

It was not, however, a single type of message that emerged out of the advent of printing in the 1470s, whereby books could be multiplied 'with a speed, an accuracy, and a cheapness hitherto inconceivable'.[23] The Catholic Church was in on the act, and took advantage of this new medium for promoting its ideas.[24] A new battle to win the allegiance of the people had begun, and it is not easy to decide, in retrospect, which side at the time was best placed to win the titanic struggle.

Among the Catholics there were various new expressions of deep Christian commitment and dedication in which, to a great extent, lay people took the lead. The pre-eminent style of late fourteenth-century and fifteenth-century lay as well as clerical Catholic piety was epitomized by the Brethren of the Common Life, founded by Gerard Groote (1340–84), and dubbed the modern devotion, or *Devotio Moderna*. It was the best known of a number of 'lay associations founded for the purpose of spiritual renewal, whose strength lay in their potential to enhance the spiritual lives of individuals and bring reform to the wider church through Christians who had experienced renewal'.[25] Groote 'gathered around him laymen and clerics who desired to live a common life but not separate themselves from the world. Living like monks, they kept a common household, involving physical and menial work as well as regular prayer, but they did not take vows'.[26] And, with its typically 'intense, introspective and creative mode of reaching out to God',[27] it appealed to numberless men, women and children, to single people and to entire families. It was an all-embracing pattern of life that touched the innermost thoughts and emotions, as well as every facet of daily conduct; and its overarching purpose was summed up in the title of Thomas à Kempis's famous and highly influential devotional treatise, *The Imitation of Christ*. The movement, as with the book, gave much weight to private prayer and moral self-renewal. The *Devotio Moderna* was not linked in any way to the emergence and subsequent activities of the Lollards and the Hussites, but it had in common with those movements a stress on the teaching of the Bible, and it provided a means whereby lay people could enter into a truly spiritual style of life.

It was likewise, to some extent, with mysticism, especially as this was propounded by the fourteenth-century Dominican friars Johann Tauler and Henry Suso. They propagated a form of it throughout the Rhineland that was associated with the former Dominican friar Johannes Eckhart, who had helped to take Christianity out of the cloister and into the daily lives of people as a whole.

The mystics inspired a yet further, largely lay, movement, the Friends of God, which originated in Switzerland in the fourteenth century and spread down the Rhine Valley to the Netherlands. The central concern was to encourage a spiritual quest by individuals in fellowship with others of like mind, although there were also fierce attacks on what was viewed as the corruption of the church.

All these movements remained within the framework of the Catholic Church, and they strengthened it immeasurably. Undoubtedly, traditional Catholic religion was still very much alive and, in most respects, well for the vast proportion of the lay people of the fifteenth century and the early sixteenth century.[28]

There is no evidence on the eve of the Reformation of a mass loss of confidence in the old ways of church life, no sign of wholesale disenchantment.

> Much, but not all, of late medieval Catholicism may have been mechanical and ill informed. Beneath the official life and teaching of the institutional Church there may have lain much popular religion that was shot through with semi-pagan survivals, sub-Christian folklore and magic. As events were to prove, pre-Reformation Catholicism was vulnerable. But there is little sign of growing popular hostility towards it.[29]

And, of course, it could command the allegiance of lay men of the calibre of Sir Thomas More (1478–1535).

Pre-Reformation changes in the role of the Catholic laity

Nonetheless, despite the firm grip that traditional Catholicism still had upon the people as a whole in pre-Reformation Europe, there were changes taking place, in addition to those already mentioned, which were slowly but surely bringing the laity more definitely into the frame. For one thing, the churches in Europe were becoming organizationally more complex and expensive to maintain, and this highlighted the greater need for the support of the laity, both financially and as a source of enhanced administrative assistance. Such bureaucratic growth and increased intricacy made more evident the urgent requirement for a committed and cooperating laity. The wholehearted support of the laity was more than ever vital in order to ensure the good health of the church. The local church in many regions of the West, and more particularly the laity in those churches, needed to be given additional responsibilities in order to relieve some of the pressure on diocesan or other officials. The use of volunteers in various capacities became increasingly necessary as a means of avoiding the employment of extra paid employees, with all the costs that entailed.

In the late medieval period there was also a gradual but notable further democratization and social broadening of church patronage. Switzerland was a forerunner of what became a European-wide practice when it introduced a procedure whereby 'local communities eroded seigneurial patronage and acquired not only presentation rights (backed up by papal bulls), but the administration of tithes and even a share of ecclesiastical jurisdiction'.[30] As in the Tyrol and certain French parishes, priests were obliged to sign detailed contracts before being entrusted with the cure of souls.

In many cases such agreements covered only a year or two, and the failure of the priest to come up to expectation resulted in peremptory sacking. Such appointment of incumbents by parishioners was exceptional, and it depended on relatively weak lordship. Nevertheless, there were widespread examples of it among Italian *pievi*, in some French parishes, in churches in the Pyrenees and the Basque Provinces, and also in German urban and rural communities such as Dithmarschen in Lower Saxony, in the almost lordship-free areas of Frisia, and in such towns as Braunschweig and Cologne.[31]

Greater lay engagement in church affairs additionally came about with the fuller use of the churches for an ever-expanding range of activities. Although the medieval church had always been the scene of 'secular' as well as 'sacred' activities, changes took place in the fifteenth century and in the early sixteenth century that greatly extended such events, so that there was a sort of quantum leap forward in this aspect of local church life. All such blurring of the territorial demarcations between secular and religious activities and life helped to make the local church less obviously and exclusively the unchallenged stronghold of the priest.

Related to this was the escalating tendency for religious assemblies themselves to address strictly non-church matters. It seems, for example, to have been more common than in previous times for the French *curé*, as with his English and Italian counterparts, to use the Sunday Mass for the proclamation of seigneurial or state regulations, and it was not uncommon for secular dignitaries to be elected in churches.

What has been said makes it clear that the late medieval church was going on its way as a recognized and accepted part of local, regional and national life in most parts of the West. Its problem on the eve of the Reformation was not primarily one of decay and decadence, although there were highly questionable, if not downright objectionable, practices such as those associated with the sale of indulgences. The church was not particularly degenerate or depraved; it was not so much corrupt and moribund as stuffy. The most obvious internal problem for the Western Church in the first quarter of the sixteenth century was, in fact, 'complacency born of success'.[32]

Even so, issues such as the form and conduct of the Mass[33] continued to concern an increasing number of lay people and, in addition, there was a growing measure of lay annoyance concerning other specific problems that seemed to demand action, but which were left to fester. For over a century there had been calls for church reform, and some people were frustrated that there had been no substantial response, and no signs that the church leaders were prepared to address the matters causing concern.

There was no evidence that they were genuinely determined to put their house in order. Even when some of the chief issues that caused most aggravation had been debated at the Council of Constance (1414–18) and the Council of Basle (1431–39), nothing of substance had been agreed. No remedial measures of any note were proposed. And there were no more such general councils of the church for the next hundred years. Then the Fifth Lateran Council (1512–17) failed to achieve any reform. By that time, the Reformation hour was at hand, for it was in the same year that the Council came to an end that Luther nailed his thesis to the door of the Wittenberg church and set the whole of Christendom ablaze.

It is highly significant that the various new movements that arose in late medieval Christendom were 'largely directed towards the laity',[34] and the Reformation was to a great extent to be a lay movement, despite the fact that most of the prominent actors in the drama were ordained men. It was in essence a mass movement, depending for its progress on unnumbered lay men and lay women.

It must therefore be stressed that the Reformation was not the work of one man, or even of a handful of men, nor solely the consequence of a theological struggle which was won by one side because of the superior merit of what it had to offer, important though the individuals and the theological battle were. It was created as a combination of 'politics, force and the power of new ideas',[35] but these were embodied and expressed in large measure by the laity.

The laity in the Reformation

'It has become a commonplace of historians that the Reformation was in large measure "the layman's reformation".'[36] In a manner unknown since the early centuries lay men and a small minority of lay women came forward to take up responsibility in the life of the church, to exercise what they saw as their rights, and to find undreamt of opportunities for service.

From the start, Luther recognized the centrality of the laity as theologically undeniable, and as one of the foundation principles of the new church tradition that was rapidly emerging. In 'the first of his three great Reformation tracts of 1520', he, 'with characteristic forthrightness, undid the neglect of centuries and restored to the centre of Christian thought the biblical doctrine of the priesthood of all believers'. And he concluded that 'whoever comes out of the water of baptism can boast that he is already consecrated priest, bishop and pope'.[37]

Although Luther, Philipp Melanchthon, John Calvin, Ulrich Zwingli, Thomas Cranmer and other ordained men occupied centre stage, especially in the first formative years of the Reformation, a host of lay men and lay women, from kings and princes to students, scholars and men and women of humble social standing, soon assumed their indispensable roles in the unfolding saga. Indeed, even in its initial phase some lay men, such as Friedrich 'the Wise', the Elector of Saxony and protector of Luther, and Landgraf Philipp of Hesse, who as early as the 1520s brought his territories into the Protestant fold, and who 'was to prove the ablest, most politically competent and resolute princely defender of the evangelical cause in Germany',[38] were to the fore. And King Henry VIII, the architect of the political revolution in England that went in tandem with the religious Reformation headed by Archbishop Thomas Cranmer, was cast in a similar role, in his case perhaps somewhat reluctantly, in the front line of the new movement.

The principle of *cuius regio eius religio*, as first proposed in 1526 at the Diet of Speyer, was a clear acknowledgement that the leadership of the Reformation in the Holy Roman Empire was to be assigned to its lay rulers. As the Reformation became established, there were a number of outstanding lay monarchs who, in their own distinctive ways, fervently supported it, and applied its principles to the ordering of ecclesiastical and secular affairs in their own territories in the way they saw fit. Among the foremost were Maurice of Saxony (1521–53), Ottheinrich of the Palatine (1502–59), and, in England, Edward VI (1537–53) and Elizabeth I (1533–1603). The seventeenth century produced other sovereigns of similar calibre, of whom perhaps the most brilliant example was Gustavus Adolphus, King of Sweden (1594–1632), who was the champion of German Protestantism in the Thirty Years' War. And in England there was the Lord Protector, Oliver Cromwell (1599–1658). Although these, and other national leaders, are the personalities who capture the headlines, the Reformation also brought into the limelight a host of other lay men and lay women to an extent seldom if ever known since the age of the apostles. 'That the layman has no mere walk-on part in the drama of the Reformation is self-evident.'[39]

In the first few years of the Reformation students and recent graduates were prominent. There were, for instance, a handful of them in Oxford and Cambridge who received and welcomed the teaching of Luther.[40] It was then not long before there was an underworld of Evangelicals in London. City merchants and others joined clerics who had been won to the new doctrines at the universities in a fellowship that was made more intense and firm as a result of persecution and the sense of unity in a common cause that such trials produce. 'The faithful were fired and organized to proselytize, and they made London the storm-centre of their mission.'

London offered the largest concentration of potential converts in the country. 'To the reformers, preaching was the way whereby the Word might be illuminated for the people, and though risk was acute, preach they did.'[41] And a similar pattern can be discerned in selected continental towns. This enthusiastic engagement of laity in direct pastoral and evangelistic work was to be one of the trademarks of the Reformation.

The printed word also proved invaluable as a Protestant evangelistic tool. It has been found that the buyers of the cheap religious pamphlets of various kinds that abounded, especially in the late sixteenth century and early seventeenth century, were not so much the minority of godly 'elect' but 'the ordinary parishioners. If the sermon was soporific, and the old images of saints no longer worked, the godly ballads and chapbooks caught the attention of some of the audience which gathered around the pedlar in the churchyard or marketplace.'[42]

None of what has been said so far should be reckoned to indicate a widespread, let alone a universal, interest in the Christian faith in its new guise. Far more common than such enthusiasm, and far more undermining for those seeking to win others to their faith, were those twin features found in varying degrees in every age: worldliness and apathy. Indeed, one historian has identified the Elizabethan period in English history as 'the age of the greatest religious indifference before the twentieth century'.[43] Despite the fact that 'this may seem an exaggeration it is certain that a substantial proportion of the population regarded organized religion with an attitude which varied from cold indifference to frank hostility'.[44]

Nonetheless, many people were won to the new Protestant view of Christianity, and once they were incorporated into the new church, they discovered a form of religious life that contrasted markedly with that of only a few decades before. As Protestantism became established, the local or parish church

> was no longer a place in which the visual senses were focussed on the elevation of the host at mass and enriched by an abundance of painted symbols and images filling corners, chapels, and aisles. It had become an open space in which the minds of a pew-seated congregation were fixed on the pulpit and cerebrally engaged by biblical texts on whitewashed walls.[45]

It was the same in most places where Protestantism in one form or another assumed a prominent place.

Many and quite startling changes soon became evident in the attitudes and behaviour of the new Protestant laity compared with their Catholic predecessors. 'The priest was no longer set apart from the laity by the ritual condition of celibacy, and he was no longer capable of working the miracle of the Mass.'⁴⁶ The Reformation robbed the priest of many of his former functions.

> His powers of exorcism were taken away, and his formulae of benediction and consecration much reduced. The end of the belief in transubstantiation, the discarding of Catholic vestments, and the abolition of clerical celibacy, cumulatively diminished the mystique of the clergyman within the parish. At the same time the growth of facilities for lay education weakened the clergy's monopoly of learning, which, even before the Reformation, had been crumbling away.⁴⁷

It all represented a revolution in terms of the status and standing of the laity. 'By depreciating the miracle-working aspects of religion and elevating the importance of the individual's faith in God, the Protestant Reformation helped to form a new concept of religion itself.'⁴⁸ And in this new concept the laity suddenly and increasingly assumed a more central role in the life and work of the churches.

Even so,

> the contrast can be drawn too extremely. In the new order there were practices preserved from the old, rituals that survived even if transformed, a moral vigour that tapped into an earlier tradition. There were pious practices in the new order that a parishioner, faced with change but brought up in an older faith, recognized and ultimately accepted.⁴⁹

The conservatism of the laity varied greatly from one region to another. In England, for instance, in the south-west, 'the Reformation unquestionably entailed a dramatic decline of support for traditional religion',⁵⁰ and this came in a rush after 1570, whereas, in other areas, for instance Yorkshire, adherence to old-style Roman Catholicism lingered. Also, the majority of the Protestants were to be found in urban communities; and overall there were more men than women.

The lay Protestant converts, wherever they lived, and especially in the earlier phases of the movement, were marked men and women. They were the ones who bore the brunt of any opposition to the new religious traditions that were emerging. 'Although many clergy suffered, an overall picture of the persecution of Protestants in the sixteenth century, including the Anabaptists, shows that the great majority of martyrs were laymen and women, many of them of humble station.'⁵¹ Of the 43 London Protestant martyrs who died during the reign of Mary Tudor, only 8 were known to be priests or in orders. All the rest were lay people from a range of social classes and occupations, with a great number being what may be described as artisans.⁵² The five thousand Huguenots and other Protestants slaughtered, together with the mutilation of many others, in Paris and other cities of France on St Bartholomew's Day, Sunday 24 August 1572, and the English martyrs during the reign of Mary Tudor, were but the most prominent of such trials endured by Protestant laity. It is a testimony to the rapidity and profundity of the impact of the new faith that so many ordinary people were prepared to suffer and die rather than to deny the faith they had embraced.

But the role of the Protestant laity must not be overstated. Although the new Protestant lay men and even lay women were given an important role in the life of the church, nevertheless the oversight of the clergy was considered to be essential, at least in the early stages of the Reformation. Within the new mainline Protestant churches, there was no frenetic anti-clericalism. It was likewise with the respect that each of the main Protestant churches expected from its members towards the lay magistrate and ruler. There was no toleration of anti-authoritarianism or political nonconformity. The lay people were expected to play their part as elders, deacons, churchwardens, and in the various other tasks open to them according to the somewhat different traditions that soon developed, but such new powers were to be used circumspectly and in conformity with the responsibly devised systems of church government.

Each of the mainline Protestant churches that emerged in the sixteenth century tried to keep the balance between quite radical change in the direction of giving the laity access to the chief sources of their faith and supremely the Bible, and all that flowed from that, and the often expressed need to retain what were seen as the treasures and commendable features of the old faith. Thus, it was the common practice in the new Protestant regions to place copies of the vernacular Bible in the churches, and hymns in the local language were introduced. But both the Bible and the hymns were used in a measured and responsible manner, so that there was not an unseemly departure from traditional forms of worship or other practices that were rightly viewed as of secondary importance. Gradually, what were considered as unintelligible rites were suppressed, but many of the well-established and widely valued practices were retained, such as the elevation of the Host and the use of traditional vestments, and it was quite usual for the ornate medieval reredoses with all that they symbolized, to be left unmolested. The policy of the reformers was not to found new churches, but to purify the Catholic Church, by purging it of certain abuses that had crept in to corrupt and defile it. And even those second-generation reformers or Protestant secular leaders who were confronted with the fait accompli of separation from the Catholic Church were concerned that there should not be a wild and unnecessarily violent Protestant swing away from the familiar and much appreciated beliefs and patterns of behaviour that had nurtured countless generations of laity. Thus, as one example, the Elizabethan Settlement in England was a careful and well planned and structured *via media*.

Given this cautious approach, it was understandably horrific for the Protestant leaders, and especially for Luther, to encounter fiercely rebellious and dissident groups from an early stage of the Reformation. It was a severe shock to him when, so soon after having tasted the new wine of what he regarded as a purified and elevated Christian faith and system of belief, worship and lifestyle, fellow Protestants should break ranks and go their own ways, often in a highly bizarre fashion.

Messianic, millenarian and apocalyptic groups

The part played by the laity in nascent Protestantism was not of course all glorious and unblemished. There were a number of regrettable instances that did great dishonour to the new movement. These were mostly associated with the so-called Radical Reformation. The Magisterial Reformation, as it came to be known, was carried out with the cooperation of the established authorities or magistrates. The Radical Reformation, on the other hand, involved a number of spontaneous, often peculiar, and not infrequently militant, movements that quite typically splintered into many small sects with differing theologies and attitudes to reform. Although there were great variations between the groups, from those that were fairly pacific to the more aggressive and sometimes apocalyptic or millenarian examples, it is the latter that attracted most attention at the time and since, and which so harmfully stained the Reformation record.

Each of the radical groups was convinced that it was a special, select company of believers, uniquely favoured and called by God for such a time as that to be separate and distinctive. Among the more abnormal examples of those that harboured peculiar doctrines, and that indulged in excessive and unruly behaviour were the so-called Zwichau prophets, of the early 1520s, and the various Anabaptist groups, of which the most notorious were led by Thomas Müntzer, Jan Matthys (Mattijszoon) and John of Leyden.

Of course, these movements were eye-catching because of their dramatic nature. But the vast majority of lay Protestant support was to be found in the mainline Lutheran, Calvinist or Church of England bodies. The scene only started to change substantially and permanently towards the end of the sixteenth century and at the beginning of the seventeenth century. It was at that time, and largely in England, that Protestantism started seriously to fragment, with hugely important and lasting consequences for lay church people.

Late sixteenth-century and early seventeenth-century Puritan separatism

The introduction into Christianity in the sixteenth and seventeenth centuries of the notion of 'the gathered church' of true believers, and its outworking, in the form of the Presbyterian, the Congregational and the Baptist Churches, was revolutionary in the history of the laity in Christianity. It was transformational. It became an accepted principle not only for the various dissenting bodies concerned, and later for the Nonconformist or Free Churches as a whole, but it had its effect on the thinking of the mainline 'established' or national churches, such as the Lutheran Church, the Church of England, and later the Anglican Communion. In the twentieth century it was to be given a new, enlarged meaning and dimension by the Pentecostals, with remarkable global consequences. It represented a major and permanent move away from the theology of church governance that had underpinned the Catholic Church of the West and, in a different but equally firm way, the Orthodox Church of the East, for a thousand years and more.

In the system of church governance that was approved by John Calvin, the ministry of the church was to be shared between pastors, doctors, elders and deacons, or at least these four functions were to be accommodated and expressed in some form.[53] This opened a floodgate for the possible incorporation of lay men, and even lay women, into the central governance, management and ministry of churches locally, regionally and nationally.

As the ideas of Calvin and others were applied and developed in various areas, and more especially in France, the Netherlands and Scotland, the new systems were far more genuinely representative of the laity than was so in either Roman Catholicism or in the other main Protestant traditions. In the Calvinist and Presbyterian Churches the congregation, along with the minister, decided who would be an elder in the consistory; and in the consistory, where there might have been between one and two dozen elders, the voice of the laity was a real check on the danger of clerical monopoly in decision-making. Such a system restored to the laity some of the powers and functions within the church that the abolition of the guilds had removed. And the same was true for the other Dissenting churches as they adopted their somewhat differing theologies and church practices. The end result can be seen as a yet further phase in the transformation of the church landscape.

By the fourth decade of the seventeenth century the West was far removed from the medieval unity of Catholicism, in which there had been but occasional 'heretics' disturbing the peace. It had become a patchwork of Roman Catholicism, a wide range of Protestant churches and, of course, the continuance of those various religious beliefs and practices subsumed under the titles of folklore, witchcraft and astrology.[54] It was a market situation, in which the laity could choose what best fitted their needs. It was a complex scene, and it provided the setting for an extended period of hostility between the Catholics and the Protestants, in which the laity were the main sufferers.

North America

In 1620, a section of the Separitist church that had been established in Amsterdam under the leadership of William Brewster sailed to the New World. They were subsequently renowned as the Pilgrim Fathers.

After a disastrous start at Cape Cod in Massachusetts, in which a savage winter and the ravages of disease resulted in half of them dying, the remainder gradually established two new towns, Scituate and Duxbury. 'By 1650 there were ten towns, with a total population of about 2,500. In each town a church was gathered; in Scituate, because of controversy, there were two.'[55] There was a considerable influx of Puritans to Massachusetts Bay in the 1630s, which did much to set the tone of the region. The life in New England gave great scope for lay men and women whose talents had been stultified in their English and mainland European homelands to undertake new and exciting tasks. Assisted by some very able men, the settlers were equipped to explore the application of what they regarded as biblical teaching to the various spheres of family, church and state life. In practice, the schools they quickly founded, the legal system they established, and the way they conducted themselves in their varied occupations, followed closely the patterns that they had known back in their countries of origin but, of course, with much enlarged opportunities to put their ideals to the test.

A massive immigration of Europeans during the rest of the century, chiefly from England, and mainly from among the lesser gentry and the yeoman classes, with a significant proportion that did not share to the full the Puritan convictions of the founders, was a challenge to those who were anxious to preserve the special character of the colony as envisioned by the Pilgrim Fathers. In order to do this, at least to some degree, 'the "company" was changed from an open corporation to a closed commonwealth by limiting the franchise to church members. The elect saints, a minority of the population, were in control of both church and state.'[56] This does not mean that the Bay colony was technically a theocracy, for the ministers did not exercise civil power. Church and state were looked upon as separate but cooperating and co-ordinated spheres. The church had its own specific area of activity, but the Christian faith, as mediated by the churches, strengthened and helped to guide the hands of the civil authorities. The magistrates

> were charged with seeing that the Ten Commandments were observed, and with putting down such things as idolatry, blasphemy, heresy, Sabbath-breaking, and the disruption of worship. The laws of the colony were to be informed by the laws of God as those were made known through the Scriptures.[57]

Religious conflict within a divided Europe

From the second decade of the seventeenth century onwards for thirty years and more, a fierce and protracted battle ensued between Protestants and Catholics for possession of large slabs of the Continent. The laity of the churches fought with great vehemence and ferocity to achieve territorial advantage. It has been calculated that within the German lands between 15 and 40 per cent of the population met an early death as a consequence of the military operations or the associated famine and disease.[58] The bitterness engendered was intense and lasted well beyond the end of military hostilities. The Peace of Westphalia, which brought the carnage to an official end on 24 October 1648, did not heal the seared memories of the peoples of Europe, nor did it prevent a long-lasting and deeply felt legacy of hatred and resentment. Although dynastic rivalry had played an important part in igniting this protracted conflict, it was regrettably religion that lay at the heart of the causes and the course of the war. The sack and virtually total destruction of Magdeburg by an imperial army in 1631, in which the majority of the city's twenty thousand, mostly Protestant, inhabitants perished either killed by the sword or burned alive in the fires that reduced the city to a wasteland, although exceptional in scale and brutality, was but an extreme example of unbridled aggression that scarred the Protestant imagination for many generations. It was matched in ferocity by Oliver Cromwell's campaign of death and destruction in Ireland. That venomous onslaught likewise left the Roman Catholics with inerasable and soured recollections. There were also more localized conflicts that had largely religious origins, and that resulted in even further religious division, in all of which the laity played a dominant part. It was all most unfortunate, and indeed scandalous, abhorrent and highly reprehensible.

5
The laity and the birth of the modern age

Now is the moment in this present study to adopt an enlarged geographical perspective. Attention must be given not, as has been the case primarily up to this point, to Western Christianity alone, but to the world scene. The period from the late fifteenth century to the early nineteenth century saw the first tentative beginnings of the modern globalization of Christianity.[1]

But it needs to be emphasized that this exciting and dramatic expansion of Christianity was not a novelty, initiated and carried out by the Christian West in an outreach to the non-Christian world. It was mostly a story of recovery (see Table 5.1), and of consolidating and then greatly extending what had previously existed for many centuries but had largely disappeared. What went on from the sixteenth century to the early twenty-first century was in many respects and in many cases a massive reconversion phenomenon; but alongside and in addition to this there was an unprecedented encounter of Christianity with non-Christian cultures. From the late eighteenth century onwards, the new centre of gravity for the history of the laity in Christianity changes, at first slowly and almost imperceptibly, then in a more pronounced way, and finally, in the twentieth century, rapidly and astoundingly in a gigantic and revolutionary way.

Table 5.1 Distribution of Christians (in millions) in ancient and medieval times

Continent	Year			
	500	1000	1200	1500
Africa	8	5	2.5	1.3
Asia	21.2	16.8	21	3.4
Europe/Russia	14.2	28.6	46.6	76.3

Source David B. Barrett, *World Christian Encyclopedia*, Nairobi, Kenya: Oxford University Press, 1982, p. 796, quoted in Jenkins, *The Next Christendom*, p. 24.

The spread of Christianity up to the sixteenth century

It has been a Western convention at all levels, from the teaching at schools to that at postgraduate colleges, and also a popular view of church history, that for at least fifteen hundred years the Christian faith was almost exclusively confined to Europe and the Mediterranean seaboard, with Palestine at the extreme eastern end of this geographical region.[2] The Christian lands have typically been depicted as almost entirely coterminous with the Roman Empire in the first era of Christianity, and then, after the Muslim conquests from the seventh century onwards, as having their focal point ever further west, embracing, in addition to Italy, territories that were later to become Britain, France, Spain, Germany and the other countries of northern Europe. But this is a serious distortion of the actual situation.

By as early as the fourth century, Christianity had its major foci beyond the area just delineated. Of the five ancient patriarchates, one, Alexandria, was in Africa, three, Constantinople, Antioch and Jerusalem, were in Asia, and only one, Rome, in Europe. In the fifth century, the Christian faith was well established, and to a great degree thriving, in Tunisia, Ethiopia and Armenia, and in the latter two regions it survived, with a rich literary, musical and architectural culture, right up to the present day.

Although historical demography is a hazardous and uncertain science, the picture presented by David Barrett (see Table 5.1) is indicative of the situation, and may well err on the low side for Africa at least, where the number may have been double that quoted for 1200, and possibly likewise for Asia. At least what he, on good evidence, postulates helps to demolish the myth of an almost totally predominant pre-sixteenth-century Western Christianity.

It seems highly probable that during the time that Christian Europe was preoccupied with the earlier crusades, the more representative lay Christian was not a European knight, an English yeoman or a French artisan, but a Syrian peasant, a Mesopotamian town-dweller or an Ethiopian farmhand; an Asian or an African and not a European. The account of the laity in Christianity given so far has concentrated on Europe rather than these other territories, not because it was more important, but mainly because of the unavailability of information for the development of the faith in non-European regions up to the sixteenth century. In the present state of knowledge, an account of the laity in sub-Saharan Africa, South America and Asia prior to the sixteenth century is therefore not possible. One day such a massive gap, and such neglect, may well be correctable.

The numerical decline in Africa and Asia was variously the result of the advance of Islam, epitomized in a number of jihads, local hostility, as in the case of the aggression of the Ming dynasty rulers from 1368 onwards in China, and the internal loss of Christian vibrancy. It was in the sixteenth century, at a time when the numbers of Christians outside Europe and Russia had shrunk to an alarming level, that the West started on its missionary endeavour that was to produce such startling results in the course of the following four centuries. And at all stages in the kaleidoscopic world scene, in whatever place considered, with but few exceptions, the laity were to the fore, either as a result of their numerical preponderance only, or as a consequence of this plus their crucial part in promoting Christian expansion, and in the subsequent nurturing of Christians.

The Roman Catholic missionary outreach

In the immediate pre-Reformation period, the Roman Catholic Church attempted to convert indigenous people in scattered areas of the world, and most notably in Central and South America. Spain and Portugal were in the forefront of this effort, as they began their global enterprises ostensibly in the name of Christianity, but with political and economic objectives clearly of paramount concern. By the end of the sixteenth century they could claim great successes in Asia, Africa and the Americas. For the first time, the Roman Catholic Church started to have the appearance of a global institution. By the 1520s, there were eight bishoprics in the Antilles, and for the first time sees were established in Mexico. An impressive array of bishoprics was provided to cover what would later be the nations of Peru, Ecuador, Bolivia and Chile. The Philippines was granted an archdiocesan see by 1595. This vast enterprise was reinforced by the missionary endeavours of the Jesuit order, which was granted papal approval in 1534. Such an array of achievements seemed to be of monumental importance for the move towards global Christianity. But a closer look at what actually happened largely pricks that seemingly glowing bubble.

Masses of lay people accepted some form of Christianity. Nevertheless, in almost every region this response to the Christian faith was achieved under duress, by dubious means, and with the knowledge that the 'Christian' conquerors were also perpetrators of horrific cruelty on a massive scale. When the new faith was embraced, it was heavily mixed with local non-Christian beliefs, and was often of questionable authenticity and dubious depth. The fact that native converts were only granted admission to communion on the rarest of occasions appears to substantiate the impression that conversions were often shallow. The almost total non-admission of natives to the ordained ministry points in the same direction.

Catholic lay men and lay women in these vast new areas were certainly not outstanding either in the depth of their Christian commitment or in the quality of their Christian lives; and the fault rested not so much with them as with their European masters.

The same pattern persisted into the seventeenth century and up to the end of the eighteenth century. Until that time, 'large-scale missionary efforts were strictly the preserve of the Catholic powers'.[3] But by then, the Protestants had come on the scene, and were soon to be the dominant force; and in that story the profile assumed by the laity in both the evangelistic and the pastoral life of the existing mainline churches, and in those new churches that emerged, was pronounced.

The laity in the transatlantic Evangelical revival

Although the eighteenth-century transatlantic Evangelical revival is commonly regarded as having originated in the 1730s, its shared roots lay further back, and more particularly in the emergence on the European mainland of Pietism and Moravianism. Both of these expressions of religious belief and practice were distinguished by their strong emphasis on the crucial role of the laity in promoting Christianity, and in providing pastoral care.

These two Christian movements were critical in kick-starting one of the most astonishing series of events in modern church history: the Evangelical British and continental European revivals, and the North American, and more especially New England, awakenings that persisted for many decades. In each of the regions concerned, there were periods when there was a sudden, largely spontaneous, marked increase in the extent and intensity of the commitment of a number of individuals in particular churches to the beliefs and practices of their faith, accompanied by a sudden increase in the number of conversions from among nominal church members or from among those almost entirely outside the church membership and sphere of activity. The prolonged revivals also gave birth on both sides of the Atlantic to a new and sustained missionary impulse, and to an amazing growth in charitable works. It was a movement without parallel in the modern era in the West, and only to be rivalled, and perhaps outdone in magnitude and range, by what was to occur in the nineteenth and twentieth centuries in sub-Saharan Africa, South America and parts of Asia. And in all these examples of vibrant Christianity, which were central to the growth of the worldwide church throughout the last two hundred years, the laity were the one most significant and indispensable element. It is an astonishing saga that must receive close attention.

The laity and the birth of the modern age

The typical account of the Evangelical revival of the eighteenth century gives pride of place, and often almost exclusive attention to the foremost ordained leaders involved.

It was, however, ordinary lay people who were converted and who then became the main driving force of the movement as it grew in numbers and in the depth of its corporate life. It was largely unlettered or semi-literate people who formed the army of converts. They sought to spread the good news as they had received it in what became a great international crusade, the effect of which had untold repercussions and consequences.

As a result of the ingathering of lay people on both sides of the Atlantic, the opportunities for lay service were legion. From its early days Methodism depended very much upon the laity. The leaders of the small Methodist groups, called classes and bands, and the majority of those involved in the management and control of the societies were lay men. 'Save for the distant control of Wesley and his few clerical coadjutors, the Methodist cadres were entirely in lay and often plebeian hands.'[4] This gave opportunities to those with the appropriate talents to use their gifts in a way that would probably not have been possible for them in any other sphere of their lives. It was an indispensable element in Methodism 'that societies should act as a training school for lay religious leadership and for the promotion of lay spiritual "gifts"',[5] and this included an ever-expanding place for women to use their talents.[6]

Among the women who distinguished themselves as Evangelicals of special note was Selina, Countess of Huntingdon.[7] She was a particular supporter of George Whitefield, whose Calvinistic doctrines she favoured rather than the Arminianism of the Wesley brothers. She did much to bring the revival message to the attention of fellow members of the aristocracy. She established a number of chapels throughout the country for this purpose. As a consequence of a combination of circumstances, and much to her regret, these were eventually declared to be dissident and separatist, and she was pressurized into organizing them into the independent Countess of Huntingdon's Connexion.

One of the most interesting and, from the point of view of the present work most significant, innovations in early Methodism was the employment of lay preachers. Even in the first few years of the revival an urgent need for extra manpower for evangelism and pastoral care had arisen because of the excessive pressures upon Whitefield and the Wesleys. They were moving from one part of the country to another, and they did not remain long enough in any one place to be able to offer the kind of high-quality, intense and sustained local leadership that was necessary if the work was to be consolidated and extended. In the case of Whitefield, there was also the pressing demand made upon him as a result of his ministry in the North American colonies. The greater use of lay assistants was, however, controversial.

Methodism was central to the eighteenth-century revival, but it did not monopolize the scene. From soon after the revival in England began, Evangelicalism in the Church of England was a vital part of the total movement. There was much common ground between the Evangelicals in the Established Church and the Methodists, but there were also differences in outlook and practice that created a wedge between the two. Of major importance was the evident clericalism of the former in contrast to the ever-growing lay character of Methodism, with the lay preachers as its chief agents. Many Church of England Evangelicals were suspicious of, if not hostile to, this Methodist tactic and to some other 'irregularities' adopted by the Methodists, not primarily because they were innovations or necessarily objectionable in themselves, but because of their inherent potential threat to church order.

The eighteenth-century climax to this parting of the ways came in 1784 when Wesley ordained two lay preachers, and set Dr Thomas Coke apart as the superintendent of the Methodist work in North America. This was an affront to many Evangelicals, and there was an outcry from them. Not only were lay leaders by this action being given the authority and functions reserved for duly ordained Church of England clergy, but the status of ordination itself was seen as thereby being compromised. It was viewed as being diluted and denigrated.

And, of course, non-Evangelical churchmen were even more aggressive in condemning the use of lay people in 'ministry'. In this respect, the revival was a most important dividing line, for it implicitly challenged conformist churches to reconsider the status and standing of their laity. The theory and theology for such a development had been present in the separatist churches for some time, and especially among the Presbyterians, but it was given an unprecedented importance and prominence, and was applied, as never before on such a scale with the advent of the Methodists. The effects of this new, extensive and obviously effective use of the laity in the decision-making, the administration, the evangelistic work and the pastoral ministry of the church were transformational for the churches as a whole. The repercussions were widespread and revolutionary.

The 'age of the common man'

The last three decades of the eighteenth century and the first two of the nineteenth century saw the inauguration in all its essentials of the modern phase of English, European and North American history, and the first cautious steps in the modern globalization of Christianity. What took place during those fifty years or so helped to set in motion a major process of transmutation in Christian life for sub-Saharan Africa and parts of Asia, with the clear potential for the extension of that process to other regions, including South America. In addition, there was an accelerated laicization of churches, sometimes by accident rather than by deliberate action based on conviction, but nonetheless with the same end result. The laity in the home churches soon came into their own in a quite astounding way, and a high level of lay participation in church life became a benchmark of the new churches in much of the southern part of the world. It was manifestly a momentous and pivotal era.

The implantation of new thinking and the process of radical change in every aspect of Western human life was the result of a series of revolutions and revolutionary movements. The American revolution was not restricted to a transfer of territory and sovereignty from the British monarchy and government to the North Americans. It was even more fundamental than that. It was a traumatic rebellion against the whole principle and practice of authority being imposed on a people, and it was an assertion of the rights of the people themselves to self-determination, liberty and the pursuit of happiness. Such new ideas and ideals could not be confined to one country. The concept of 'democracy' was in the air; and it was bound to spread. The *ancien régimes* of Europe could not be insulated from such questioning theories and aspirations, or shielded from the implications of their enactment. A new dimension had been added to the whole outlook of the reformers and the potential radicals; and a new hope of success in achieving change had been engendered.

In North America, the Puritans could readily identify with this new thinking. After all, they had originally fled from what they justifiably regarded as the tyrannical regimes of oppressive rulers. They were 'watchful lest hard-won rights and freedoms' would 'be jeopardized by Episcopal aggressiveness'. Among the Anglicans, there was a deeply ingrained sense of loyalty to the English throne, but the new ideals of the colonists were even more powerful. Overall, taking all the colonies together, the balance of episcopal opinion was pro-independence. 'Probably two-thirds of those who signed the Declaration of Independence were affiliated with the Church of England.'[8]

Among the non-episcopal laity, there was likewise a strong sense of divided loyalty, even if the stress this created was not generally as great. The balance was tilted by the fact that Methodism was mainly in the hands of native lay preachers, and they strongly tended to favour independence.

They used their undoubtedly great influence to guide the societies under their care in that direction. This was countered to some extent when John Wesley finally declared his opposition to the Revolution. But even his great influence was not decisive. It was not enough to overrule the strong belief of the Methodist colonists, and especially their local lay leaders, in passionately held values that were regarded as fundamental in order to build a new society in a new land. The Lutherans of the middle colonies rejoiced in the toleration that had been shown to them by the British, and they at first remained neutral, although a majority eventually supported the American cause. The Quakers, Moravians, Mennonites and the German Baptist Brethren, known as Dunkers, adhered to their traditional anti-war stance of neutralism and non-resistance, and often suffered harsh indignities as a consequence, even including murder. The churches of the Reformed or Calvinist tradition were predominantly supporters of the cause of independence, largely as a result of their emphasis on obeying God rather than man. Their leaders proclaimed it their right to resist tyranny, and a 'very important contribution to the shaping of the revolutionary spirit was made by those strongly influenced by Calvinist political philosophy'.[9]

Then, of course, there was the traumatic French Revolution, with its watchwords, Liberty, Equality and Fraternity.

The combined effect of these two momentous political transformations on attitudes relating to the place of the laity in the life of the churches was undoubtedly great, especially as it coincided with the industrial and agricultural revolutions, an incredibly rapid and massive urbanization and a great increase in populations, as well as the Romantic movement. All of these epoch-making developments were crucial in generating a pro-laity view. And such a reconstruction of opinion was permanent. The churches could not be immune to the forces at work in 'the age of the common man'; and, indeed, the Evangelical revival itself contributed to the remarkable transmutations that occurred. In both Europe and North America it is not fanciful to describe what happened from the era of the eighteenth-century revivals to the third quarter of the nineteenth century as a 'religious revolution', along with the other revolutions.

As well as the unquestionably great, specifically religious, phenomenon of revivalism, there were also a number of unintended consequences resulting from such a powerful stirring-up of human emotions. One of these was political. 'By stressing the universality of sin, and the possibility that any person might find salvation, and by elevating the place of the common man in church and society', the revival on both sides of the Atlantic contributed 'to the spread of the democratic ideal'. In addition to the other forces at work, 'the undergirding of democratic tendencies by evangelical religion' was 'a major part of the whole story'.[10] The enlarged scope of the laity in church life was but part of the fuller process of democratization. The 'new styles of piety and fresh patterns of religious organization' that were introduced were part and parcel of the consequences of the transatlantic revival that 'extended well beyond the churches and are woven into the fabric of American' and European 'history'.[11]

William Wilberforce and the 'Clapham Sect'

Rather than rest contented with generalized statements about this new era of realized lay potential, three specific examples will be far more effective in conveying an awareness of what actually happened – the life and works of William Wilberforce and the activities of the 'Clapham Sect'; the achievements of the 'Hackney Phalanx'; and the contribution of both these bodies to world mission.

The first causes to attract William Wilberforce,[12] those that were to occupy him most fully for the rest of his life, and those that gave him his major opportunity to show forth the fruit of his Evangelical convictions, were the movement for the abolition of the slave trade and that for the ending of slavery in all British territories. From 1787 onwards his life, and that of a small company of lay Evangelicals who worked with him, was dedicated to what John Wesley in a letter to Wilberforce described as a 'glorious enterprise', namely, the cessation of the slave trade, as well as to other aims of national and international importance consistent with, and expressive of their Evangelical faith. An inner band of them lived in the same neighbourhood of London, and they consequently became known as the 'Clapham Sect'; a few were Members of Parliament, where they were collectively identified as 'the Saints'. They were a distinguished fraternity of Christians.

The Thornton family had long been connected with Clapham. In 1792, Henry Thornton, the son of the philanthropist John Thornton, arranged for Wilberforce to share his residence, Battersea Rise House; and in the next ten years they were joined in Clapham by Charles Grant, John Shore, the first Baron Teignmouth, Granville Sharp, Zachary Macaulay and James Stephen. All of them were intimately associated with the Evangelical movement, and they had as their rector the Evangelical John Venn. It was an outstanding group, which was about to achieve great things.[13] Here were men of distinction, who had held high office, who gave away as much as six-sevenths of their income, and who dedicated all the time they could spare to campaigns on behalf of especially needy people.[14]

Of those lay men and women who did not reside in Clapham, but who were closely identified with the thinking and action of the Clapham Sect, special mention should be made of Hannah More.[15] Her most astounding literary works took the form of *Cheap Repository Tracts* issued during the 1790s. By 1795, 700,000 copies had been sold. They set before the people the anti-slavery issue, as well as providing moral and religious instruction for the poor. In these works, and in her *Village Politics*, which was intended as an antidote to what she and fellow Evangelicals regarded as the poison of Thomas Paine's *Rights of Man*, she broke new ground for she adopted not only the style of the 'lively stories and ballads for community singing as supplied by chap-book and broad-sheet, but their format also, and by under-selling the hawkers and pedlars' she 'beat them at their own game'.[16]

In addition to her literary works, she expressed her faith in a very practical manner when she and her sisters set up, and subsequently laboured tirelessly running, a number of schools in the Mendip Hills. These provided elementary education for about twenty thousand socially and educationally deprived children over a period of twenty-five years.

In the parliamentary arena, the Clapham Sect Members of Parliament were part of a wide coterie of Evangelicals. Political and religious affiliations in the Commons were complex,[17] and the 112 or more Members between 1784 and 1832 who can be reckoned as Evangelicals did not belong to one political 'party' or always vote in the same way. Although the majority of them were Tories, a core body of Saints, whose numbers varied, but averaged about thirty, were determined and unshakeable in their resolve to repudiate all party alignments and to maintain absolute independence.

After a slight pause following the 1807 abolition of the slave trade, a new crusade led by the Evangelical Thomas Fowell Buxton culminated in governmental approval for the abolition of slavery itself in 1833.[18] Of course there were many others who played their part,[19] but the Church of England lay Christians represented the consistent and persistent nucleus of the campaigns. They were the storm troopers, and at the very centre of the crusading movements, giving them the inspiration, determination and organizational efficiency without which what was attained would not have been possible, at least within the time span in which the tasks were in fact successfully brought to triumphant conclusions. And both of the campaigns were titanic struggles.

Nonetheless, it is clear that the Saints, the Clapham Sect, and its backers, were not one- or two-measure groups. They had an important and impressive agenda of other concerns for the alleviation of need and for the granting of assistance to the disadvantaged. Although, as children of their time, they acquiesced in domestic legislation that would now be considered repressive, even one of their severest critics concedes that they 'were more liberal in their attitudes and activities than most historians have acknowledged'.[20] Not only did nearly every Evangelical Member of Parliament fully participate in the crusades against the slave trade and colonial slavery, when this represented advanced liberal thinking, but collectively they 'emerge as a group of highly active and liberally inclined Christian politicians, committed to bringing about reforms on a wide variety of fronts'.[21] They were more questioning, and more willing to introduce change, than most of their peers in church and state, who were largely paralysed by fear of radicalism and Jacobinism.

The Evangelicals did as much as any other group in their generation to meet the promptings of their own consciences. As early as 1786 Wilberforce carried through the Commons a small measure of penal reform, and subsequently supported Sir Samuel Romilly in his various attempts to abolish the death penalty for a range of offences. The Clapham Sect advocated the abolition of the press gang, improvement in the conditions of asylums and madhouses, the relief of climbing boys, and the regulation of factory conditions. Wilberforce united with Sir Robert Peel in introducing the first Factory Act in 1802, but protested that it did not go far enough. In 1805 he took up the cause of the Yorkshire weavers; and in 1818 he supported Peel in a further extension of the Factory Act. The liberal Sir James Mackintosh judged Wilberforce to be a Tory by predilection, but by his actions 'liberal and reforming'.[22] It was a judgement that could justifiably be applied to most, if not all, of the other Evangelicals associated in some way with him and his circle in their extensive and far-reaching efforts to bring about change.

High Church laity and the Hackney Phalanx

The Evangelicals were not alone in bringing Christian laity to the fore in the life of the English church. In the age of the French Revolution and the Napoleonic Wars, lay High Churchmen in England 'had an enthusiasm of their own which gave their utterances a zeal unmatched by the Orthodox Establishment'. It was not the same as the zeal that motivated the Evangelicals, but they had their own passionate objectives. 'For them the *status quo* was no matter of mere utility; it was sacred. The preservation of order was a divine commandment, and not a human expedient.'[23] What they wrote and said was certainly suffused with a sincere desire for personal piety, but more specifically it was impelled by a deep and consuming concern for the preservation of the existing authority of the church, and also the state. At a time when such authority was under severe threat, in an age of iconoclasm, and with pressures for reform or revolution in all and every aspect of national life, they steadfastly championed conservatism in its non-political connotation.

Their unyielding determination to remain faithful to what they perceived as a God-given purpose gave them their own brand of intensity, which bears comparison with the differently motivated intensity of the contemporary Evangelicals. They also were engaged in a crusade, convinced in the midst of much shaking of the traditional Christian foundations in Europe and North America, and threats to the existing social and religious system from the advocates of revolutionary change, that they were right in holding to the orthodox Church of England views concerning belief, establishment, continuity of structures and the retention of the order of bishops, priests and deacons. And these dedicated lay people communicated their convictions in a way that was far more virile, and far less in the style of eighteenth-century decorum, moderation and dry formality, than has commonly been acknowledged. They were a power in the church and in the land.

The High Church equivalent to the Evangelical Clapham Sect was the so-called Hackney Phalanx, or Clapton Sect, named after the parts of London where many of the leaders lived. It became the powerhouse of another remarkable Christian pressure group. The history of the Hackney Phalanx is bound up with the personal history of Joshua Watson.[24] He joined his father's very prosperous business, but as he became increasingly rich, he became more and more convinced 'that he was entangled and ensnared in business when the divine command and the needs of men required him to use his abilities and his wealth in the service of God and his fellows'.[25] Neither his faith, nor his decision in 1814 to abandon his business life and give himself to new tasks, was the result of a sudden and climacteric experience. He abhorred introspection, and his change in life was calmly undertaken, with no drama, but with 'all the inevitability of a duty gladly accepted'.[26]

During the remainder of his life he continued to give away over half of his income for charitable purposes, and by what he did and what he accomplished he made a contribution to the life of the Church of England that places him among a select band of lay men of all time. He was instrumental in shaping and executing key features in the policy of the Church of England. And, like his contemporary William Wilberforce, he demonstrated what a wealthy man, dedicated to the service of God, could achieve. He was not a charismatic leader like his Evangelical counterpart, able to arouse the enthusiasm of a crowd. He was more at home on a committee than in the vanguard of a crusade; but it was committees that were needed then, and Watson was highly regarded for his ability, tirelessness, dedication, clear headedness and integrity. From the time of the battle of Trafalgar in 1806 to the time of the Reform Bill in 1832, much of the creative work in the church was inspired and organized by Watson and his friends.

The Hackney Phalanx, like the Clapham Sect, was a tightly knit group of lay Christian friends that combined scope for individuality with fellowship and a common purpose. There was a useful variety and complementarity of talents among the believers, so that each member was able to make his or her distinctive contribution to the collective work. In addition to Joshua Watson, William Stevens was in the forefront, but there were between fifty and one hundred lay men and clergy who either counted themselves part of the Phalanx or worked in close association with its members to achieve its objectives.

The first of these aims was educational reform, for elementary education seemed to them to be one of the greatest needs of the age. An inner group of the Phalanx immediately set to work on a project that resulted in the inauguration in 1811 of The National Society for Promoting the Education of the Poor in the Principles of the Established Church, more commonly known as The National Society. As a result of the initiative and energetic leadership of these core Phalanx members, property and funds were acquired within a few months, so that a school could be started in London. A vigorous campaign was initiated to encourage the formation of local parish schools throughout the land, and requests for schoolmasters, books and advice were received not only from parishes but also from overseas dioceses, the Army and Navy and others who wanted to run classes or organize schools. By 1815 every diocese in England was consulting the Society, and one hundred thousand children were in its schools – a number that rose to almost one million twenty years later.

The Phalanx had effectively and successfully conducted an impressive mass literacy crusade. They pioneered popular elementary education, ensured that education in England would be Christian and not secular for the foreseeable future, and enabled the national church to exercise direct control over at least some of the schools as a prelude to the dual system introduced in 1870. These were not mean achievements. But there were others.

The members of the Phalanx were acutely and painfully aware of the condition of the Church of England in the newly emergent industrial areas. This was perhaps the thing that most heavily weighed on their minds. Christian schools, Christian missions and Christian charity were of secondary importance in their scale of values if England was becoming increasingly pagan. The church needed to be strengthened, especially in the new industrial towns. An Incorporated Church Building Society was founded, and its considerable success was mainly due to the drive and hard work of Joshua Watson and another Phalanx member, John Bowdler.

All the efforts bore fruit. In 1818 the House of Commons voted £1 million for church-building, to be administered by a Commission on which Watson served, and this was supplemented in 1824 by a further £0.5 million, to which was added over £200,000 in subscriptions. In was a central tenet of the Commission's strategy that the churches built should help to meet the current pressing needs, and they were constructed with this in mind, with simple, rather than refined or intricate, designs. Watson was a key figure in the wise management of the government grants and in raising large voluntary donations during the twenty years after 1818, and the work involved taxed his abilities to the full. 'The building programme depended upon him more than any other single man.'[27]

Having done a gigantic work on the provision of new churches, Watson and a small group of colleagues turned to the equally urgent task of providing extra curates to assist the desperately overworked and burdened urban clergy. In 1837, Watson, Sir Robert Inglis MP and Benjamin Harrison founded the Additional Curates Society, which was pledged to work through the bishops. Watson gave a lump sum of £500, and £100 each year for the rest of his life. He also drew up the Society's constitution and served as joint Honorary Treasurer.

The Clapham Sect and the Hackney Phalanx and world mission

Both the Clapham Sect and the Hackney Phalanx made major contributions to the modern global missionary movement in its early phase.

By the end of the eighteenth century the churches in England and, indeed, generally throughout Europe and North America, were still blinkered in their outlook, despite the noble efforts of a few individuals. Notwithstanding many centuries of Catholic activity in various regions of the world, and over two hundred years of colonial penetration into North and South America and Asia, as well as parts of Africa and other regions of the world, Christianity remained a predominantly European religion. No European Protestant country had embarked on a systematic programme of overseas mission, or even made much effort to confront non-Christian people, lands and cultures with the Christian gospel. 'In 1800 it was still by no means certain that Christianity would be successful in turning itself into a universal religion.'[28] Those who were engaged in colonial expansion had done little to propagate the Christian message in the lands they so colonized, and the churches were almost completely unresponsive to the opportunities for mission that had been fortuitously opened up. The cross had not followed the flag to any great extent. The fact that North America, 'together with the West Indies, had become a white man's world' was of little relevance to the task of making inroads into non-Christian lands and among non-Christian people. 'The dominance of his religion and his civilization in those areas provided no answer to the question whether Christianity could make itself permanently at home in the lands of the great and ancient non-Christian civilizations.'[29]

There was, however, considerable progress made in the 1790s. The main landmarks are clear. In 1792, the lay cobbler, William Carey, published a work entitled *An Enquiry into the Obligation of Christians to Use Means for the Conversion of the Heathen*. In it he argued that the Great Commission of Christ to go and preach the gospel to all nations was still binding on Christians. In the same year, he was instrumental in establishing the Baptist Missionary Society, 'the first foreign mission to spring from the revival'.[30] By the following year he was pioneering its operation in India. It was the 'first British missionary society designed exclusively to convert the heathen',[31] and as such it was a significant step forward in world mission. A further advance was made in 1795 with the founding of the largely Nonconformist London Missionary Society.

But it was within the Church of England that the greatest efforts were made. After much protestation and lobbying, an Act of Parliament was passed which enabled the Church of England to commence its colonial and missionary episcopate. But even this fell very far short of meeting the needs of those vast overseas territories where there was no Christian witness. Such a shortcoming and evangelistic failure was of particular concern to members of the Clapham Sect, and they took steps to remedy the deficiency in some small measure. They pressed for the introduction of a provision in the Charter of the East India Company that would promote the religious and moral improvement of the inhabitants of India; and more specifically, that would empower and require the Company to send out fit and proper persons to act as schoolmasters and missionaries. They failed to achieve their objective in 1793, but they applied persistent pressure so that twenty years later, in 1813, the Charter was adapted to guarantee liberty to propagate the Christian faith. It was a major step forward. William Wilberforce was convinced that the foundation stone had been laid 'of the greatest edifice that ever was raised in Asia'.[32]

In its concern for the church worldwide, the Clapham Sect also engaged in attempts to open up new regions to Western Christian influence, and to improve the lot of countless disadvantaged groups and societies in various parts of the world, and especially in sub-Saharan Africa and certain countries of Asia. Wilberforce was one of the early members of the African Association, which was founded in 1788 to send out explorers. Within less than three weeks of the passing of the Abolition Bill in 1807, the men of Clapham founded the African Institution. As the slave trade did not cease with its official abolition, this new body soon concentrated on trying to curb such illegal activity.

It is also to the credit of the Clapham Sect that they took practical steps to help freed slaves. As early as 1787, Granville Sharp had been concerned to assist London's 'black poor' – the freed slaves and unemployed black people formerly employed as servants. With Treasury help, he shipped some of them to form a self-governing community at the abandoned trading stations of the small mountainous peninsular that formed Sierra Leone in West Africa. It was to be a 'Province of Freedom' in which peaceful commerce replaced the slave trade. It had a chequered history. The little community had to weather many trials. The capital, Granville Town, was torched by the local chieftain in revenge for an outrage perpetrated by some unruly settlers. The French invaded the colony, burned the houses, destroyed all that they could lay their hands on, robbed the colonists of their possessions and wrecked the contents of the church. And there were serious tensions and difficulties among the members of the settlement itself. Nevertheless, the colony survived; one more testimony to the unremitting endeavour of the Clapham Sect.

In the meantime, almost all the Clapham Sect members were engaged in an initiative that was to have untold and lasting worldwide importance: the founding, on 12 April 1799, of the Society for Missions in Africa and the East, later to be renamed the Church Missionary Society. It was to become the largest missionary organization in the world.[33]

For many years members of the Hackney Phalanx also played a leading part in arousing missionary concern at home, and in promoting missions abroad. In their case, they focused their attention on the two long-established Church of England missionary societies, the Society for Promoting Christian Knowledge (SPCK) and the Society for the Propagation of the Gospel (SPG). On the initiative of the Phalanx, a committee was set up in 1810 to help revive the somewhat drooping SPCK, largely by means of organizing local diocesan committees, with the sanction and under the direction of the bishops. In 1814 Watson became Treasurer of the SPCK. He also laboured energetically for the SPG, and strove to link the two societies together as closely as possible. Like the SPCK, the SPG was in urgent need of new men and new ideas: it had degenerated into a board for holding various trust funds. Its total income was only about £8,000, of which less than £500 came from donations or subscriptions. By the time of Watson's death in 1855, this had increased to more than £82,000, mainly due to an enormous increase in subscriptions, and to frequent collections in churches.[34]

Phalanx members kept fully informed about the church overseas, so that they were well placed to respond to varied calls for personnel or money. They recognized the need to provide assistance to dioceses throughout the world, while at the same time encouraging and fostering their independence and self-sufficiency.

It was in the realm of world mission that the extent of common ground between the Clapham Sect and the Hackney Phalanx was perhaps most clearly evident and most fully demonstrated.[35] As a consequence of their united efforts Parliament authorized the sending of missionaries to India and created a small establishment of one bishop and three archdeacons.

It was to the lasting credit of the Phalanx members that, in addition to educational and social issues, they were instrumental in placing mission well and truly on the agenda of every bishop, as well as on the list of priorities of every aspiring and would-be bishop. And this achievement was complementary to the somewhat different approach adopted by the Evangelicals.

The laity in the American revolutionary period

While all of this was going on in England, and in continental Europe, momentous developments were taking place in North America. And these were not confined to the military and political spheres associated with the achievement of independence. It is to that birth period and early life of the new republic that some of the most important national character-forming events and trends can be traced, two of the foremost features of which were the centrality of Christianity in the life of the country, and the strength of lay influence.

It was the earnest belief of the majority of the people, whatever cause they espoused, that the guiding philosophy and the moral standards that underlay most of the official pronouncements, and what was enacted or taken on board as policy for the new nation, should be firmly and unequivocally based on the Christian faith and, more particularly, on the teaching of the Bible. There were, understandably, a few prominent dissidents who did not share this conviction, but they were in a very small minority, and the constitution, the laws passed and the many decisions made were impregnated with Christian perspectives.

And this continued to be so as the new nation forged ahead and started to assume its own identity. In the process of political, constitutional, economic and social evolution, the Christianity of the nascent country was both moulded to a great extent by the drift of events and itself helped to determine the essential nature of all that was being created. There was a generally healthy and creative interplay and interrelationship between the political and the religious spheres of life in the new nation. And, by dint of their sheer weight of numbers, let alone anything else, the laity were extremely effective in both embodying the Christian beliefs and norms, and in applying the pressure to ensure that biblical perspectives and values determined the dominant points of departure and the frame of reference of the newly formed republic at both the national and local levels of its corporate life.

In the early years of the nineteenth century, the churches received a yet further renewal of their life and popularity, and an enhancement of their influence. This was manifested most dramatically in the course of opening up the western frontier of the new country. The new Evangelical fervour was remarkably and spectacularly demonstrated, and made extremely public, in what became known as camp meetings. Of these, the one at Cane Ridge, Kentucky in August 1801 was especially sensational. Over a period of several days, a mixed array of Presbyterian, Baptist and Methodist black and white preachers fervently proclaimed the gospel, and thousands responded in one way or another. There were countless conversions.

The same format for camp meetings as at Cane Ridge was adopted in a host of other places with widespread success, and the membership of churches, including that of the Presbyterians, soared in the Southern states.

> By comparison, however, Presbyterian efforts paled beside the accomplishments of the Methodists and the Baptists. Methodist circuit riders and Baptist farmer-preachers fanned out through the South and the opening West in unprecedented numbers. By the 1830s these groups had replaced the Congregationalists and Presbyterians as the largest denominations, not only in the South but in the whole of the United States.[36]

An important aspect of the changing lay Christian scene was the growth in the number of conversions among the black people. Although slaveholders did little to promote the evangelization of black people at any stage, some slaves and those who were free had embraced the faith by the time of the Revolution. In the period just after the Revolution, when there was much spoken about freedom, and when the rapid rise of the Methodists and the Baptists, with their stress on reaching out to the less privileged members of society was to the fore, this adherence of black people notably increased. The widespread teaching of these two denominations, and in particular their stress on the supreme importance of a personal experience of God's grace, had a great appeal. This was especially so in the 1780s and 1790s when, for a few years, such a message was accompanied by a notably egalitarian attitude, and even the occasional protest against slavery itself. Soon the activities of white itinerant preachers were supplemented by the preaching of black people to black congregations, and the number of African Americans in the churches between the 1770s and the 1830s mounted. Most of these new lay believers were formally attached to white congregations and denominations, but they quite commonly gathered together in informal, exclusively black, meetings that provided them with their deepest and most appreciated spiritual sustenance.

It was at that stage that a few of the more able black leaders formed independent churches for their fellow black people. Richard Allen was one example. He was a slave from birth who was converted by Methodists at the age of 17. He quite promptly began to preach, initially to his family, then to his master, and after that to blacks and whites throughout the region around his Delaware plantation. After many problems, he succeeded in establishing the Bethel Church for negro Methodists in 1793. Finally, in 1814, his congregation, together with other black Methodist churches, organized their own denomination, the African Methodist Episcopal Church.

It was a story that in essence was to be repeated many times during the nineteenth and twentieth centuries. The camp meetings helped to set in motion a powerful new trend. 'The new Awakenings precipitated significant shifts, schisms, and realignments in the denominational patterns of American life.'[37] There was both a meteoric increase in the number of Christian laity and a marked diversification in their individual and corporate Christian lifestyles.

As in Britain and continental Europe, one sign of the resurgence of vibrant Christianity was the emergence of a missionary consciousness. Missionary societies were organized throughout the young republic for both home and overseas evangelistic work. Two examples will suffice. First, the New York Missionary Society was founded in 1796. It was interdenominational, and received support from Presbyterian, Reformed and Baptist bodies. Second, in 1798, the General Association of Connecticut elected to become the Missionary Society of Connecticut. In that capacity, it sent out ministers on short-term duty to frontier regions to labour among the estimated 250,000 Indians.

There was even a measure of help from the Government for the initiatives taken to evangelize the Indians. This came about largely because both the new missionary societies and the political authorities shared the hope that, along with the more explicitly religious consequences arising from such missionary outreach, there would be a 'civilizing' influence. 'For the missionary movement, conversion and civilizing were seen as parts of one process, and conversion meant a transformation of native existence into accommodation to Western ways.'[38] Unfortunately, this somewhat rigid linkage of religious and cultural concerns was to complicate and mar some of the valiant and well-intentioned work of the missionaries. The frequently very evident, and often narrow, cultural identity and cultural imperialism was a hindrance to the more specifically Christian work that was being attempted, especially when it was accompanied by a lack of understanding or sympathy for native cultures. It was, however, much more regrettable that the rush to the border regions of land-hungry settlers, bent on the acquisition and exploitation of land, quite frequently involved the sweeping aside of treaties that had been made with the indigenous peoples. Invariably the 'white man' appeared hypocritical as he proclaimed a message of love. The blatant greed and brutal pursuit of self-interest by ruthless and ambitious pioneers intent on material gain to a great extent nullified the noble intentions of the missionaries, who were essentially humane, despite many shortcomings. The good works of many missionaries were largely overridden and swamped as 'new tragic chapters were added to the story of conquest and displacement'.[39]

The new missionary impulse was not, however, confined to the homeland. An enthusiasm for global mission work can be traced to a revival at Williams College that spilled over into the student body of Andover Theological Seminary, the nation's first fully fledged school for theological education. A certain Samuel J. Mills Jr experienced both these events and, in 1810, together with friends, he helped to found the American Board of Commissioners for Foreign Missions. Within two years this new organization had dispatched the first American missionaries to India and the Far East. A new field of possible service had been opened up to American lay men and women.

6

The laity in worldwide nineteenth-century Christianity

A new era dawns

The sudden coming into prominence of lay groups in the late eighteenth century and early nineteenth century on both sides of the Atlantic, and the steps taken to launch the modern missionary movement, heralded the dawn of a new age. As will be seen in the following two chapters, what happened then was not just a temporary phenomenon. It was symptomatic and foundational. In both Europe and North America, but also increasingly in other parts of the world, the laity were at the heart of all the new and exciting developments that took place. A new era was opening up for lay people worldwide. With the benefit of hindsight, it is evident that almost everything almost everywhere was in the melting pot. And as the 'secular' world underwent a transformation of colossal proportions, so also did the purpose, function and status of lay Christians in most territories. It is to that astounding story that most of the remaining chapters of this book are devoted.

In some respects the nineteenth century was the heyday of lay initiatives and contributions to a robust Christianity in England, continental Europe and North America. It was to a great extent lay men and women who were the prime movers and driving force in creating the kind of vibrant Christianity that characterized so many countries and areas of the Western world. And it was such a dynamic Christianity that was able to inaugurate and sustain an escalating nineteenth-century missionary movement covering a variety of far-flung regions of the world. Countless Western Christian agencies emerged that both provided the motivation, workforce and financial support for a host of 'home-based' charitable, evangelistic and pastoral works, and that also resourced an unprecedented missionary outreach to other lands.

The laicization of Christian social action

In England, as in other regions of the Western world, Christians, and especially the Evangelicals, were the main initiators and providers of nineteenth-century charitable works. Despite the widely held view that Evangelicals were preoccupied with preaching, evangelism and doctrinal matters, they are in fact as much if not better 'remembered for what they did rather than for their theology'.[1] Their good works, as it were, followed them, and cannot be gainsaid. Their means to that most worthy end was the founding of innumerable specialist societies. It is generally true that 'Evangelicalism in the nineteenth century was in its practical outworkings, a religion which functioned largely through an extensive network of societies.'[2]

The single most inspirational and influential Evangelical in this demonstration of 'religion in action' was undoubtedly the eminent lay man, Lord Shaftesbury.[3] He embraced a staggering breadth and comprehensiveness of activities on behalf of deprived, underprivileged and downcast human beings. It encompassed factory reform, public health legislation, ragged schools, orphanages, homes for the crippled, the care of homeless families, relief for destitute incurables, the provision of assistance for the mentally ill, for the blind, for cabmen in need, for needlewomen, members of the merchant service, and many others.

But he did not stand alone, nor was he one of a small band of active Christian philanthropists, benefactors and labourers in undertaking charitable tasks. There was a veritable army of lay Christians who started and then continued the work of numberless nineteenth-century societies and organizations to help relieve an incredible volume and diversity of personal and social hardships in England and North America in particular, but also in parts of continental Europe. There were large national or city-wide organizations, and innumerable smaller, more localized missions and societies covering almost every conceivable area of human need or suffering; and the reach of these bodies extended to animals as well. Not only did these voluntary organizations deal in a practical way with the most heinous and offensive nineteenth-century social problems, but they also established principles and set the pattern for future social welfare work.

It was also lay Christians who were mainly responsible for founding and then staffing and continuing a host of large-scale enterprises that encompassed whole countries. Some of these had originated in the eighteenth century; and almost all of them became part of the very fabric of the societies in which they operated. A noteworthy example of this was the Sunday school system. This provided religious instruction, but also elementary education to countless thousands of children who, without such a facility, would have had no means of learning to read or write or even to grasp the basics of arithmetic.

The nineteenth-century lay Christians involved in charitable works were often not given much credit for their efforts by contemporary, and more particularly subsequent, critics. Derision rather than praise quite frequently greeted such an outpouring of concern and such practical expressions of social compassion. The providers of these services have been accused by some of being dispensers of first aid when what was needed was major surgery. They have been reprimanded for a lack of social policy and of being content to deal with the fruit of social evil rather than with its root. They have been censured for accepting the prevailing class structure, and for being concerned with palliatives rather than with radical social change; of dealing with failures in the political, economic and social system of countries rather than providing a more fundamental appraisal, and being prepared to advocate more 'root and branch' solutions to specific social problems than they did. There is some truth in such a critique. Nevertheless, even though they were essentially conservative, accepting the status quo, bowing to the prevailing political and social philosophies and norms of their age, with little if any questioning of the social framework and political regime, credit must be given to them for being pragmatic and for taking action that few others even contemplated. They had neither the time nor the inclination to be serious social analysts. Too many urgent immediate matters awaited their attention. In any case, there were other Christians who did attempt to address the underlying malaise that produced the seemingly boundless social problems of the age.

The Christian Socialists

Although he was to a great extent overshadowed by his colleagues, F. D. Maurice and Charles Kingsley, a French lay man, J. M. Ludlow, was the real founder of the Christian Socialist movement.[4]

The small company of mostly lay pioneer Christian Socialists were acutely and painfully aware of the threat to the Christian faith of the secular spirit, which they regarded as peculiarly powerful in their day, and they warned the church about it. They were desperately concerned, in the name of Christianity, to establish a more humane and caring social order, so that social suffering in its various manifestations was lessened. They, and particularly Ludlow, did much to prevent the antagonism between the churches and Socialism that was to be found in most countries from spreading to other nations.

The Christian Socialists were appalled by what they regarded as the nineteenth-century attempts to restrict religion to a narrow moralism and pietism. They were aghast at what they viewed as an excessive if not exclusive anxiety about personal ethics and personal religion. They emphasized the concept of the Kingdom of God, which it was envisaged must embrace nothing less than the whole of God's creation. Religion must concern itself intimately, and as a matter of urgency, if not priority, with the fate of all humankind, and with the condition of the secular world in which men and women live. Nevertheless, in spite of this genuine concern to address the live issues confronting ordinary people in their daily lives, the Christian Socialists were first and foremost theoreticians.

Lay-founded international social service bodies

How different were the impulses and motivations underpinning the foundation and subsequent onward march of both the Salvation Army and the Church Army. All those involved in these two organizations from the beginning and ever afterwards were consumed with a sincere desire to address the actual and hard circumstances and problems that deprived and disadvantaged members of society had to endure. The concern was to proclaim the gospel to sections of society largely ignored or neglected by the churches and, in tandem with that, to express the faith in deeds as well as with words. The founders and members of these two lay armies were men and women of action.

Nonetheless, despite their different theological stance, William and Catherine Booth, the founders of the Salvation Army,[5] and Wilson Carlyle, the founder of the Church Army,[6] gave tangible form to the essence of what the Christian Socialists were proclaiming. They and all the lay members of their armies passionately sought to 'earth' Christianity; and they instituted an astonishing range of works in their grave concern to help down-and-outs, and others in desperate need, and to make the gospel known to them.

Lay women

One of the consequences of so many and such a wide range of Christian charitable works that were so central to the alleviating of distress in nineteenth-century England and North America in particular, but also in some continental European countries as well, was the increasing opportunity provided for the involvement of lay women, sometimes at very senior levels. In fact, the expanded role of women in philanthropic work generally, and this included explicitly Christian work, and the greatly increased scope for the undertaking of responsible tasks that was opened up for women, went ahead of the generally accepted norms of society. 'As the conditions of daily life changed the gap widened between what the conventional wisdom expected of women and what was their real status. Industrial and demographic change was working to complicate and reshape the relations between the sexes.'[7] A vastly increased number of women helpers were required to make all the new projects operationally viable. And such valuable, compassionate, self-sacrificing contributions to the benevolent empire that was emerging could be fitted into household routines. Lay women found that they had ways to assist in the care of the young, the sick, the elderly, the poor and the deprived, while at the same time fulfilling their domestic duties and enriching their own lives. In many cases they were inspirational in what they achieved. And, as far as the churches were concerned, there was the discovery of a largely untapped, or at least grossly underused, lay resource that could be mobilized for new, worthwhile and exciting welfare ventures.

Women were additionally able to take part in the overseas missionary enterprises that assumed ever greater prominence in the British, European and North American Christian scene as the nineteenth century progressed. Not only did they go abroad as missionaries, first as the wives of missionaries and then in their own right, but they were active in giving home financial and other support. Auxiliaries were established by women within little over a decade of the launching of the modern Protestant missionary movement. It seems that the first of these may have been the Female Missionary Society in Northampton, which contributed 10s.6d. to the Baptist Missionary Society in 1805.[8] Similar auxiliaries organized by and for women appeared in Aberdeen in 1809, to assist the Edinburgh Bible Society, and, perhaps most effectively in the sense of spreading the auxiliary idea, in London in 1811, where they helped to promote and fund the British and Foreign Bible Society. The London Society for Promoting Christianity among the Jews provided a parallel funding device when it started penny societies for ladies and children. By the 1840s, the concept of branches or auxiliaries to uphold and further the work of charities and missionary societies had become extremely popular. The laity had found yet another avenue for service, with women very much a part of it. And the women involved continued to discharge all these highly valuable duties despite much opposition and derision. They were mocked and verbally abused for undertaking tasks that were claimed to be inappropriate for their sex, that were said to divert them from their domestic duties, and that were deemed by many to be characterized by feverishness and enthusiasm that was unfeminine and smacked of vanity.

Some of the societies, even if they welcomed such female help, were cautious in progressing too quickly. The Church Missionary Society excluded women from its annual meeting until 1813; and the Bible Society delayed such permission to attend until 1831.

Concurrently, with this flowering of lay Christian engagement in charitable works, two other incalculably important developments were taking place: the proliferation of new lay-centred Christian sects and denominations, and the hazardous launching out on the modern global expansion of Christianity.

A multiplication of lay-centred denominations and movements

Among the most influential of the new lay-centred denominations was the Catholic Apostolic Church, which has the distinction of being the first modern institutionalization of 'the gifts of the Spirit', and can thus claim to be the precursor of the Pentecostal churches and the charismatic movement, which, jointly, were to transform global Christianity in the twentieth century. Another new church, the Brethren, like the Catholic Apostolic Church, gave considerable stress to an expected millennium. The Church of Jesus Christ of Latter-Day Saints, or the Mormons, as they are generally known, were also prominent among the Christian and quasi-Christian groups that arrived on the scene in the first half of the nineteenth century. Then there was the Seventh-Day Adventist Church, and the energetically proselytizing Jehovah's Witnesses. To add to the mix, there were new churches such as Christian Science and the Spiritualist churches of various kinds that were more marginal to mainline Protestant orthodoxy.

The end result of greatly augmenting the already confusing range of options open to the laity was to create an even more crowded and complex Christian scene. This had the advantage of offering vastly enlarged alternatives to meet a massive range of demands and personal predilections and needs, but the disadvantages of confusion and the appearance of unhealthy divisiveness.

The laity and the birth of the modern Western missionary movement

The inauguration of missionary bodies in England in the 1790s was not accompanied by a surge of lay Christian concern for the vast areas of the world that were dominated by non-Christian religions, where there were no, or very few, Christians. The awakened missionary zeal of that time was limited to a quite small number of the bolder and more visionary members of the denominations involved in the nascent missionary organizations. There was no wave of enthusiasm that engulfed Western Christendom, as is sometimes implied. Such a great event as the departure of William Carey for India in 1793 was only seen to be momentous many years later. At the time, the 'consecrated cobbler' was mostly the subject of sneers or indifference.

In its first years, the Church Missionary Society faced daunting difficulties and received little support. It encountered much initial discouragement: the glamour of it as an adventurous and imaginative pioneer enterprise came only in retrospect, after it had acquired great stature. For many years no bishop identified himself with it and no British missionaries, clerical or lay, could be found. The only suitable candidate who offered his services, and who would have been joyfully accepted, was the brilliant Senior Wrangler of St John's College, Cambridge, Henry Martyn, but he chose to go to India as an East India Company chaplain because of difficulties and restrictions to which a professed missionary would have been subject. By the time the Society was ten years old, it had sent out only five missionaries, all Germans, of whom one was dead, one had been dismissed and three were still at work. As the number of new, mainly lay, recruits gradually increased, there were quite often tragedies, much hardship and not infrequent loss of life, as in 1823. In that year, of seven schoolmasters and five wives who had landed at Sierra Leone in the previous eighteen months, ten died, and there were also three deaths among other missionaries, as well as the deaths of two chaplains and their wives. Even so, despite the innumerable setbacks, and the continuing problems, the work of the Society progressed in varying degrees in India, Sierra Leone and New Zealand, and new mission fields were opened, including Ceylon (1818), Egypt (1826), British Guiana (1827) and Abyssinia (1830).

A by-product of the missionary thrust was its small but important contribution to the breaking down of denominational barriers. The London Missionary Society was notable as 'the first interdenominational society and the first to make a large-scale bid for public support'.[9] In addition there were the two non-denominational bodies: the Religious Tract Society, started in 1799, and the British and Foreign Bible Society, inaugurated in 1804. And in all of these, lay Christians were very much involved both in the initial concept, in getting the bodies off the ground, and in keeping them going and expanding.

Contributions to the birth and growth of the early modern Western missionary movement were made by a variety of countries. A host of prayer cells focusing largely on the as yet unevangelized regions of the world were, by 1814, operating in Holland, Switzerland, Germany, Britain and in the newly created independent American republic, in India and in Africa. And missionary societies were founded in many countries, often with the initiative being taken by lay people. In continental Europe, Switzerland led the way with the Basel Mission in 1815. Other countries followed: Denmark in 1822, France in 1822, Germany, with the Berlin Mission Society, in 1824, then Sweden (1835) and Norway (1842). Thereafter the list began to grow steadily until, by the end of the century, every nominal Christian country and almost every denomination had joined the missionary cause.

The movement began when it did largely because the revival of the eighteenth century had sparked it off. By the end of that century, and for much of the following century, there was a reservoir of enthusiastic lay men and women that owed its existence chiefly to the direct or indirect effect of the preceding Evangelical revival, and subsequent revivals. These powerful outpourings of transformational Christianity resulted in a large number of converts, whose sons and daughters in so many cases also found faith. Such people had an inner drive as a result of their life-changing experiences that made them willing to take part in and support missionary enterprises. The revivals also coincided with, or were followed by, a momentous 'opening-up' of new territories for trade and, in some instances, for the founding of colonies. Such a fortuitous combination of circumstances facilitated the spreading of Christianity. Lay Christians were given the potential for service on a grand scale, and in ways and forms perhaps never available before, as a direct result of the sequence of religious, entrepreneurial and political events. And a massive and increasing number of them responded with keenness, prepared and eager to take advantage of the opportunities afforded, either by giving the necessary 'home support' in their own countries or by serving in one of the ever-growing number of areas around the world where Western missionaries were being sent, or where Christians were taking up secular posts.

The laity in nineteenth-century North America

In a young country such as America, there was much going on, and many demands were being made on the people. There was an expanding frontier, with all the toil, sweat and stress that were entailed for the adventurous trail-blazing pioneers in order just to carve out a living in a difficult working and living environment. The Americans, who were venturing ever further westward, faced a range of hazards and frequent unexpected suffering or death. They were often separated from other members of their families by immense distances and had to cope with all the unpredictable forces of nature and of life in what was for them an alien land. Those who were sedentary, remaining in the already settled territories, often had a hard daily struggle trying to forge a living. Almost all the people, wherever they were or whatever they were doing, were preoccupied with mere survival and the overcoming of mountainous obstacles, or were vigorously attempting to improve their lot.

This varied and severe draining of the time and energy of people left little room for church attendance or for commitment to the Christian faith in anything but a very superficial manner. A high proportion of the population had little opportunity for extended periods of reflection or for altruistic thoughts and actions. Life was rigorous and enervating, and all a person's strength and efforts were frequently required just to provide for individual and family needs. In view of such circumstances, it was therefore highly commendable that churches, and dedicated lay Christians, were so active and effective in undertaking evangelistic and pastoral ministries, in providing welfare work and in supporting overseas missions. The fully committed Christians were men and women of considerable calibre. It is little wonder that with such widespread and sacrificial service being offered, the Christian laity made a superlative contribution to all aspects of the life of the new nation.

Among the most conspicuous national agencies for the promotion and consolidation of Christianity at home and abroad that emerged in the early nineteenth century, in great measure as an expression of revival faith in action, were the already mentioned American Board of Commissioners for Foreign Missions, founded in 1810, the American Education Society (1815) and the American Bible Society (1816). A little later there were the American Colonization Society (1817), the American Sunday School Union (1824), the American Tract Society (1825), the American Temperance Society (1826), the American Home Missionary Society (1826), the American Peace Society (1828), and the American Anti-Slavery Society (1833). All of these, and a great number of others, relied on the active involvement of a host of prominent lay men, and a few lay women, as well as some of the foremost clergymen and ministers of their day and generation. Such Christians served on the boards of the multitudinous societies, and undertook the innumerable tasks involved, both in the homeland and increasingly in other countries, with astounding energy, enthusiasm and resolve. 'Interlocking directorates' controlled this comprehensive network of agencies. The lay people engaged in the varied tasks were from every social stratum. They included a mainly eastern group of well-educated, well-placed men, among whom the wealthy New York Presbyterian merchants Arthur and Lewis Tappan were conspicuous. What they undertook, and what they achieved, was most noteworthy, and it had long-term consequences.

A glance at a few of the areas of homeland community service will indicate something of the breadth of Christian, and it must be said mostly lay, activity of a novel and stirring nature, which helped to meet some of the most pressing social and welfare needs of that emerging, yet still youthful, country. In many of the enterprises, and perhaps most obviously in the first two of these, education and the temperance campaign, there were conspicuous likenesses with what was taking place on the other side of the Atlantic. It was almost as if they were two expressions of one movement, with but slight variations because of the peculiar local circumstances.

Clearly, education was absolutely basic to the needs of the new republic.[10] And the Christians were the single most important group in helping to create and establish an educational system.

The American Sunday School Union was crucial as a sort of foundation block for all other developments. In keeping with the policy adopted by many of the societies at that time, its first efforts were directed at frontier regions, but at the same time this was but part of a national strategy. It initially resolved to establish 'a Sunday school in every destitute place where it is practicable, throughout the Valley of the Mississippi'.[11] Soon, however, Arthur Tappan called for 'a Sabbath school . . . in every town' of the country. The Union provided materials for the weekly lessons and helped to mobilize a large body of helpers in every quarter of the nation. With assistance from a number of other voluntary societies, it was not long before the Union had started a countless number of Sunday schools stretching from the Alleghenes to the Rockies. Although some of the denominations established their own Sunday schools, the movement retained a semi-autonomous character for a considerable time.

It was the Sunday schools that were the major suppliers of elementary education for lower- and middle-class boys and girls in an age before the introduction of mass public education. For many decades they were a source of religious instruction, with the spin-off that they taught the fundamentals of writing, reading and arithmetic. 'In a number of localities the Sunday schools served as surrogates for common schools until the latter could be established.'[12] Some of the workers responsible for the inauguration of these schools were astonishingly successful; most notably the self-educated lay man Stephen Paxson, who founded an incredible twelve hundred of them.

The Sunday School Union was given a new lease of life near the end of the century when the wealthy Chicago Christian, B. E. Jacobs, joined its ranks. He introduced a uniform lesson plan whereby Sunday school teachers from various denominations in a locality would gather together during the preceding week to prepare for the next Sunday's Bible lesson. The founding of seventy thousand new Sunday schools by the Union in the course of the nineteenth century is a measure of its impact throughout the land.

The work of Christians in the sphere of college education was on a far smaller scale, but vital none the less. There were only a few state colleges by the end of the eighteenth century, and the noteworthy expansion of such institutions did not take place until after the Civil War (1861–65). In the meantime, however, most of the mainline Protestant denominations made invaluable contributions to this critical sphere of educational provision, with almost 70 per cent of colleges being sponsored by Congregationalists, Presbyterians or Episcopalians in the period up to 1820. By the time of the Civil War, and for the period thereafter, Methodists and Baptists were staffing a third of the country's institutions of higher education; the other three large denominations just mentioned accounted for a further third, with the remaining religious groups responsible for staffing another 10 per cent. A high proportion of the colleges that had been founded by about 1875 owed their existence, and their continued operation, either to Protestant Evangelicals or to Roman Catholics. Only rarely, in cases such as Harvard, did institutions drift away from earlier Christian sponsorship and control and adopt a broader and less explicitly Christian character.

Then there was moral reform. 'Essentially the same premises and methods that informed the missionary, tract and education societies also guided those which conducted reforming crusades – and they envisioned the same goal for a Christian America.'[13] The movement was launched organizationally when the Connecticut Moral Society was founded in 1813. It did not take long for other similar bodies to appear across the land. Each had local objectives, but they also had wider and more all-embracing aims, and they were ambitious in what they sought. 'The full christianisation of America seemed possible, within the framework of religious freedom.'[14] It was not a totally unrealistic dream in view of the way the nation developed with a high regard for Christian principles, and with an eye very much to Christian teaching.

Of the many reform issues that attracted the attention of active Christians, it was the cause of temperance that commanded the greatest following in North America, as in Britain and continental Europe. The American Temperance Society spearheaded a movement in which, especially in the

1830s, there was a blitz made on church and chapel congregations and the non-churchgoing public, alerting all and sundry in the nation to the peril of excessive alcohol consumption. This quite frequently entailed the uncompromising advocacy of total abstinence.

The prohibitionists were remarkably successful, as seen in the extent to which they were able to introduce changes in state laws. During the 1840s and 1850s the crusade successfully secured the passage of legislation in Massachusetts and Maine that restricted access to drink. And after the Civil War there was a further advance as the movement 'carried the ideals of rural and small-town America into the cities, where large populations and the expansion of merchandising had made the trade in drink a major feature of the environment'.[15]

This was but one facet of the Christian reforming impulse that extended to the nation's rapidly growing cities. Other outstanding components of a comprehensive programme in this moral and ethical forward thrust were championed with the arrival from Britain of the Salvation Army in 1880, and with the teachings of the informal, loosely organized but influential Social Gospel movement, which became a force from about the same time.

A distinctive feature of the prohibition movement was the immense scope it gave to women to exercise a fruitful ministry. And, once more, the American experience almost exactly replicated what was evolving in Britain and continental Europe at about the same time. In both, women were in the forefront. Indeed, one of the most forceful, persuasive and active groups in the whole temperance enterprise was the Women's Christian Temperance Union. This was led by the highly able Methodist, Frances Willard, who was extremely successful in broadening the concern of the movement to cover the general protection of the family. Towards the end of the century, the WCTU united with other more distinctly political organizations, so that in 1895 it became possible to found the American Anti-Saloon League. Protestants and Roman Catholics, conservative Christians and liberals were able to present a united front in promoting moral reform.

And the prohibition movement was not alone in attracting and giving scope for the participation of lay women. They played a crucial part in a number of campaigns, such as that for prison reform. They also made their mark in the controversial crusade against slavery.

In the course of the eighteenth century an anti-slavery view had emerged in the thinking of Christians in both New England and the south. The Congregationalist Samuel Hopkins made the first public anti-slavery statement in New England, and it reverberated through the churches for the rest of the century, as a kind of agenda-setting declaration. The antagonism to slavery that he expressed was also widespread in the south at that time. 'All the revivalistic religious bodies in the southern colonies developed strong anti-slavery views and, by the close of the War of Independence, manumission of slaves had become increasingly common, particularly among those people who had been religiously awakened.'[16] The revival had touched the lives of many negroes, and a great number of slaves were received into the churches. In the 1780s it was especially the Presbyterians, Baptists and Methodists who took a resolute anti-slavery stance, and translated that into action. Such a strongly pronounced sentiment continued to be reiterated on countless occasions in the early nineteenth century. David Price, the father of Presbyterianism in Kentucky, David Barrow, a well-known Virginian Baptist preacher, and many others, were convinced that slavery was contrary to the laws of God and nature and inconsistent with republican forms of government, and they were vehement advocates of slave emancipation.

But this unmistakable, uncompromising and strong body of Christian opinion in opposition to slavery did not persist. It failed to gather momentum, and to become an ever more accepted policy of the mainline churches as the nineteenth century unfolded. The situation became increasingly complex and blurred as a variety of opinions were articulated. In fact, it is difficult to do justice to the complicated ramifications of the Christian anti-slavery efforts in the north and the south throughout the nineteenth century. Although, for some, the practice of slavery undeniably struck at the very heart of the ideals and aspirations of the new nation, there were many who took issue with such a view. The opponents of slavery 'focussed insistently on the disparity between the American profession of freedom and democracy and the demonstrable facts of human bondage', but others dissented, often quite fiercely, from such an interpretation of the situation. The differences between the two camps were deep-seated and produced pronounced tensions and even animosity.

It is unquestionable that the issue of slavery 'was a major factor in precipitating the Civil War in 1861'.[17] Although it exposed basic differences in attitude among the churches, and among individual lay Christians, it is again difficult to make generalizations that fairly summarize the variety of views propounded. There were so many twists and turns, so many statements and resolutions passed, and so much campaigning, let alone variations in attitude and policy within the churches from one area to another, that it is problematic to discern the main nuances and subtle features of what was being taught and practised. Even so, the outline picture is reasonably clear.

In the opening quarter of the nineteenth century a number of anti-slavery movements carried on the campaigns of the previous century.[18] In 1807 the anti-slavery Baptists in Kentucky inaugurated the Friends of Humanity Association. It brought together anti-slavery Baptist churches, and was based on what was known as Tarrant's Rules. The first of these declared that no person was to be admitted to any of the churches comprising the Association if he or she appeared to be in favour of perpetual slavery. In no circumstances was a member to purchase a slave except to rescue the negroe concerned from perpetual slavery, and even then this was to be done in a way that was approved by the member churches. Branches of the Association were later found in Illinois and Missouri, all pledged to the same anti-slavery principles.

In theory, there was considerable, but not total, agreement among the churches. Such near unanimity sometimes surfaced, as in the exceptionally strong statement by the General Assembly of the Presbyterian Church in the early part of the century, which was approved unanimously in a vote by southern as well as northern commissioners. It declared slavery to be 'utterly inconsistent with the law of God'. But even so, despite what appears to have been a comprehensive and unambiguous denunciation of the notion and the practice of slavery, the report of the General Assembly went on to state that instant emancipation would result in great hardship to both masters and slaves. The Presbyterian declaration, which represented a large body of opinion both within and beyond that denomination, assumed that the slave system would continue for several generations. In the meantime, in accordance with this gradualist approach, religious instruction should be provided for the slaves and every effort should be made to prevent any form of cruelty in the treatment of slaves, especially that involved in separating family members. In other words, expediency had triumphed over principle.

As a sort of palliative in the midst of this twisting and turning, the American Colonization Society strove hard and with much publicity, but with little success, to arrange for the voluntary return of freed black people to Africa. Most black people objected in principle to being sundered from their brothers in bondage, and only twelve thousand accepted the offer and were settled in Africa, mainly in Liberia.

In the meantime, the strong opposition to slavery, which had been at the forefront of many denominational policies in the early years of the nineteenth century, began to reassert itself. The pendulum began to swing once more in that direction in the second quarter of the century. By the early 1830s, a new, radical and militant movement, headed by William Lloyd Garrison, was demanding immediate abolition, and it propagated its message in the columns of an unyielding, caustic and bitter newspaper, the *Liberator*, which commenced publication in 1831. The gradualist abolitionists were alarmed. A slave rebellion in Virginia in the same year, led by Nat Turner, in which many lives were lost, turned apprehension to fear and panic.

In the north, where, by 1830, slavery had ceased to exist, the pressure for immediate nationwide abolition mounted. It was spurred on by the British ending of slavery in the West Indies in 1833. In that year, the American Anti-Slavery Society was started in Philadelphia, with many free black people engaged in it, including half a dozen who served on its board of managers. But even this body was rent by differences of opinion that resulted in a split, and in the founding in 1840 of the American and Foreign Anti-Slavery Society, with its dual concern to eliminate slavery and to elevate freemen.

The campaign against slavery attracted the support of a number of extremely able lay women. Among these, special mention should be made of Harriet Beecher Stowe, largely because of her immensely influential novel *Uncle Tom's Cabin* (1852), the powerfulness and potency of which resulted, at least in part, from its 'forceful summation of Christian revivalism, Christian domesticity, and Christian abolition'.[19]

Another perspective on the whole matter of slavery and freed black people is gained by a brief consideration of Christianity within the black community itself. It appears that 'the number of Christians among the black people more than doubled in the period from the turn of the century to the Civil War, from an estimated 5 per cent' of the total population of the country of approximately one million, 'to somewhere between 12–15 per cent of an estimated four and a half million, of which about four million were slaves'.[20]

Almost all the slaves were illiterate, because they were denied education, and many never had the opportunity to hear the gospel. And, of course, any proclamation of the Christian message by the whites was quite often considered grossly and offensively inconsistent in view of the treatment meted out to the slaves. On the other hand, the essentials of the Christian gospel, with its portrayal of the suffering Christ, 'despised and rejected of men', dying to set men and women free from the bondage of sin, and offering new and abundant life to those who accepted what he accomplished in and through his crucifixion and resurrection, greatly and poignantly resonated with the slaves. This was made evident in the negro spirituals, where there was often an elemental religiosity expressed. They gave utterance to obviously intense personal Christian experiences that were movingly relevant to their agonies, their sufferings and their deprivations. The gospel spoke most powerfully to them, to their deep yearning for liberation in this world, and to their hope for what the world beyond death had in store.

Black people preaching to black congregations was a particularly effective channel of communication. Here was a sense of rapport, with the preachers able in a lot of cases to make the Bible come alive in an extraordinary way. Whether it was in the context of recognized institutional worship or in secret gatherings of slaves, these preachers were greatly appreciated. By such means, many black people heard about and received biblical faith.[21] Alongside this, denominations were becoming more adept in ministering to the slaves, and this was especially so with the Methodists[22] and the Baptists. At the time of the Civil War, in excess of 200,000 slaves were Methodists and approximately 175,000 were Baptists. In the north some free black people took advantage of their liberty to develop their own congregations.

The missionary impulse in America

With the founding of the various missionary societies and missionary boards in the late eighteenth century and first two decades of the nineteenth century, America entered the lists in the early modern phase of Christian global evangelization. This meant that United States Protestants were committing themselves to an organized, multinational effort to spread the Christian faith throughout the world. And in America, as in other countries, this entailed the engagement of the laity in a new sphere of service; a process that was at first hesitant and stuttering, and slow to gain pace, but which accelerated as the century progressed.

The work of D. L. Moody was of particular significance in the intensification of foreign missionary interest in the last few decades of the century. And the most important avenues for the recruitment of lay people for such service were the international denominational and non-denominational societies, and in particular the YMCA and YWCA branches on college campuses. A recruitment leap forward was made with the formal organization in 1888 of the Student Volunteer Movement for Foreign Missions. With its motto, 'the evangelisation of the world in this generation', it inspired an immeasurable multitude of students to offer themselves for service abroad. Indeed, by the end of the century, the change was quite remarkable. 'The resurgence of missionary interest in the evangelical churches was heightened as the century drew to a close by a growing feeling that Protestant Christianity was rapidly becoming the most important religious force in the world.'[23] There were many contemporary expressions of this sense of a triumphant advance. In 1890, for instance, a Congregational theologian declared:

> Today Christianity is the power which is moulding the destinies of the world. The Christian nations are in the ascendant. Just in proportion to the purity of Christianity as it exists in the various nations of Christendom is the influence they are exerting upon the world's destiny. The future of the world seems to be in the hands of the three great Protestant powers – England, Germany, and the United States. The old promise is being fulfilled; the followers of the true God are inheriting the world.[24]

However excessive this analysis and prediction may have been, it reflects a mood of almost unbounded optimism and expectation that undoubtedly characterized many transatlantic churches, Christian organizations and other Christian groups in the generations prior to the First World War. The extent to which this was justified and fulfilled will become more evident as the twentieth century is surveyed in the following chapter. What is undoubtedly true is the noble part played by the USA throughout the nineteenth century in helping to take the Christian message to almost every region of the world.

The laity in Africa, in parts of Asia and in South America

The thrilling story of the at first slow but then accelerating growth of Christianity in territories throughout the world, beyond the shores of Britain, Europe and North America, in modern times since the late eighteenth century is replete with the heroic deeds of the laity. In fact, it is largely a lay saga; and certainly far more so than is often appreciated. Take sub-Saharan Africa as a start.

West Africa, and more particularly Sierra Leone, was the first territory in Africa to experience the impact of the modern Western missionary awakening. And virtually all the Nova Scotians and the other pioneer settlers in the area, and in Freetown in particular, in the first half of the nineteenth century, were thoroughly committed lay Christians, as also were the British and European white people who went there, so that the town and the settlement as a whole was emphatically Christian from the beginning. The lay black men and women were the core element in the life of the church, and in the proclamation and expansion of Christianity to neighbouring and nearby areas. This was partly because the weather, the diseases and the poor supply of drugs or lack of knowledge about them and how to survive meant that a high proportion of the whites died within a few years of arrival. In contrast, the blacks were more able to cope, and they had the great additional benefit of having originated in the tropical regions that were being newly infiltrated by Christianity. This gave them a rapport with indigenous peoples, and therefore a head start in recommending the Christian faith.

> As clerk, railwayman, mechanic, and above all as trader, the Sierra Leonean penetrated everywhere the British did, and often further. And where he went, he took his Bible, his hymn singing, and his family prayers. In area after area, well into the twentieth century, the first contact of African peoples with the Christian faith was through an itinerant or immigrant Sierra Leonean. And the mission to Yorubaland, which marked a turning point in bringing about a well-grounded church in inland Africa, came about because Sierra Leoneans had made their way back as traders over hundreds of miles to the places from whence they had once been taken as slaves.[25]

And what was true for West Africa regarding the centrality and indispensability of black lay Christians applied to other territories in sub-Saharan Africa.

Many of the Westerners who explored the continent, and who helped to open up the continent to commerce and Christianity, and most notably David Livingstone and H. M. Stanley, were also Christian lay men. Together with such entrepreneurial pioneers as Cecil Rhodes, they helped to provide the necessary geographical knowledge, and the aids to travel such as roads and railways, that carved out a pathway for the bearers of the gospel. But even so, in the end it still needed the courage, the spirit of daring and adventure, and the boldness of testimony of countless individual Christians and companies of believers, for the faith to be established in remote regions. The modern penetration of sub-Saharan Africa by ambassadors of the gospel was an almost totally African lay enterprise. And this advance of Christianity was achieved at great human cost, with the lay Africans bearing the brunt of the hostility and suffering. Two examples will help to illustrate this.

Most of the two hundred Christians who were 'speared, smothered or burned to death, poisoned, hurled from cliffs or boiled alive in rice pits'[26] in Madagascar in the 1850s, when the Protestant faith was being established in that country, were lay Africans.

It was likewise in East-Central Africa. Shortly after the Nyanza Mission had been founded in 1875, with the objective of undertaking pioneer missionary work in Buganda, a small missionary band had entered the territory. One of them returned to England because of ill health; porters deserted, and the medical doctor among them died of fever before they even reached the country. And soon after the arrival of the survivors in

Buganda, two of the party were murdered. But by 1882, the first Protestant baptism had taken place. Two years later, in 1884, James Hannington arrived as the first Bishop of Eastern Equatorial Africa, but he was slaughtered before he could reach Buganda.

In the meantime, the young Bugandan church was facing great trials. Native lay Christians were exiled and imprisoned. Three of them were hacked with knives and then thrown on a large fire. Other suffering and death followed. Some of the most outstanding converts were burnt or tortured to death in ghastly ways. One member of the church council was brutally clubbed and thrown into the flames; and another had his limbs cut off one by one and roasted before his eyes. Thirty-two of the African Christians were burnt on one huge pyre. About two hundred in all perished in the severe persecution. But, as in so many cases, the blood of the martyrs proved to be the seed of the church. By the end of the century there were thousands of Christians in Buganda, with their own churches, clergy and teachers; and this was in no small way due to such faithful witness of lay Christians.

These instances of the intense agonies and horrific deaths endured by Christians have been taken as indicative of the extent to which ordinary lay men and women were in the front line of the Christian church in newly evangelized areas. They graphically show the depth of commitment and the willingness of African Christians to bear testimony to their faith, come what may. Such believers were in the vanguard of the expansion of the church, and they were pillars in the churches that were established.

The same pre-eminence of lay Christians in the establishment and propagation of the Christian faith is repeated for many parts of Asia and, to a lesser extent in the nineteenth century, in South America. A few examples from some of the main countries of those regions will once more serve to underline the key role of the laity in establishing and consolidating churches.

India was the scene of the first of the modern Western Protestant attempts to spread Christianity in a predominantly non-Christian region that was dominated religiously by one of the other major world faiths.

When the lay man William Carey arrived in Bengal in 1793, he was determined to head up a vigorous crusade to convert the country. Soon after his arrival, but seemingly unconnected with his activities, there was the first Protestant mass movement of conversions in India. This took place among the hardy and energetic, but almost totally illiterate, community in the neighbourhood of Cape Comorin. 'Between 1795 and 1805, the Tanjore missionaries and their Indian colleagues baptized upwards of

5,000 people'.[27] It meant that from the outset, a host of dedicated native Indian lay Christians became the backbone of the young church.

Carey and his colleagues undertook much valuable translation work, and in the succeeding decades many lay missionaries engaged in hospital and teaching tasks. Gradually a considerable number of Indians were won to the faith, and between 1851 and 1901 the Protestant community in India increased tenfold. This was to a marked extent due to further mass movements, mainly in a substantial number of the 750,000 villages of the country. The greatest number of these movements occurred among the downtrodden, underprivileged castes, although higher caste members were also brought into the Christian fold.

In the modern era, China has been a remarkable illustration of the potential for lay evangelism, lay pastoral concern and social action and lay leadership. Despite efforts by Western missionaries to penetrate the interior of the country, by 1865 there was not one missionary to be found in 11 of the 18 provinces; and in the 7 that had a Christian presence, the advance was confined to zones not far from the coast, with the exception of a number of stations in the Yangtze valley. Christian work was a perpetual struggle. 'Missionary progress up to the very end of the nineteenth century was punctuated by insult, riot, and bloodshed.'[28]

In the midst of a not very promising situation for Christianity in China, there entered one of those exceptional laymen who have been able to transform the whole trend of events and set in motion a new and fruitful movement. James Hudson Taylor played a 'role of unique importance in the task of evangelising the millions of China'.[29] In 1865 he started the China Inland Mission, which for a time became the largest mission in the world. It was, moreover, the first and, until 1950, the largest of what are called 'faith missions', making no direct appeal for funds. It was an immediate success in its ability to recruit almost entirely lay missionaries, and in what was achieved in a short time, so that by 1882 all the provinces had been visited, and there were missionaries resident in all but three of them. By 1885, there were 641 of these ambassadors for Christ, all of them attired in Chinese dress as a symbol of their identification with the Chinese people, with most of them remaining true to their calling. And the concentration of effort and attempts at outreach were not confined to the central regions of China, massive though that task was, and incredibly demanding. Work was started among the aboriginal peoples in the far west of China, and missionaries laboured in Sinkiang (Chinese Turkestan) and on the borders of Tibet.

The Western missionaries had to contend with much serious anti-foreign rioting and uprisings. These sometimes involved physical assaults and the murder of some of them, as in the Hupeh province in 1891 and 1893. And ten members of the CMS were also slaughtered in 1895 in the Kucheng massacre in Fukien province. A total of 28 Protestants were martyred before the climax of such rebellions was reached in 1900 with the Boxer uprising. By then, there were about half a million lay Chinese Christian adherents, of whom almost eighty thousand were communicants. These believers formed the core of a church, both Protestant and Catholic, that in the twentieth century and early twenty-first century, as will be seen in the next chapter, was to endure great suffering and deprivation, but which finally underwent an astounding resurrection.

The small country of Korea will serve as a final illustration of lay Christianity in nineteenth-century Asia, not so much because of what happened then but because the seeds were sown at that time for what was to be one of the most astonishing examples of late twentieth- and early twenty-first-century lay Christianity in the world.

In an amazing way, and as a result of reading Christian literature, a group of Korean students in the late eighteenth century accepted Christianity and spread their faith.[30] These were predominantly, if not entirely, Roman Catholic. Despite a series of persecutions, in which a number of priests sent to minister to the Christians were martyred, the lay believers remained steadfast and others were added to their number. By 1886, there were reckoned to be twenty-five thousand believers, and a Catholic Church hierarchy was established. But further and more severe persecution resulted in the killing of two bishops, seven priests and at least eight thousand lay Korean Christians. A treaty between Korea and the United States in 1882 started to open the door to Westerners, including a number of Protestants, and the scene was set for the twentieth-century lay Christian expansion.

Finally, the story of the laity in the Christianity of South America hinges in many respects on the impact of one lay man: Allen Gardiner. Prior to the mid-nineteenth century, there were comparatively few lay Christians in that massive region. The efforts of Protestant and Roman Catholic missionaries alike to propagate Christianity in the eighteenth century and the first half of the nineteenth century had been piecemeal and sporadic. Then came the change, with the founding of the South American Missionary Society.

The new society was born out of tragedy. Gardiner experienced an evangelical conversion while serving as a Commander in the British Navy. In 1834, at the age of 40, he resigned his commission and became a missionary. A series of failures followed as he engaged in abortive missionary efforts in Natal, New Guinea, Paraguay and Bolivia, in the course of which he saw not a single convert during 17 years, or any evidence of fruit from all that he did. Then, in 1850, with six companions, he went to Tierra del Fuego, the desolate archipelago that forms the southernmost tip of South America, and one of the bleakest and most tempestuous regions in the world. The group was stranded and, without any aid arriving, they all died of starvation. Gardiner's diary was discovered in which he had written: 'Poor and weak as we are, our boat is a very Bethel to our souls, for we feel and know that God is here. Asleep or awake, I am, beyond the power of expression, happy.'[31]

The reporting of his death, and his last message, spread far and wide, and there was a spontaneous stirring of interest in South America. The South American Missionary Society and other such bodies sprang up. Mostly lay missionaries spread the gospel to many parts, and Protestant work was established in all the republics, often at the cost of much pain and sometimes death. Even so, by the end of the century there were probably no more than 500,000 Protestants in Latin America, including those in Central America, Mexico and the main islands of the Caribbean, with the other regions being widely Roman Catholic, as they had been, with various swings of fortune, for centuries. But the Christian scene was to change beyond recognition within the following 100 years, with lay Christians playing a vital part in the remarkable transformation.

7
The laity in twentieth-century Christianity

The twentieth century witnessed an astonishing change in the global Christian centre of gravity. At the beginning of the century, the supreme political and economic power was located in the Old and New Worlds of the so-called West. This was accompanied by an overriding sense of cultural and social superiority that was innate in the people of the Western nations, and to a great extent accepted by much of the lesser developed lands and their inhabitants. At the end of the century, this was far from true. By then new independent nations had emerged, new economies had been forged, and new cultures were well advanced, building on their own ancient civilizations and the new Western influences. Many of the peoples outside the Western world were still poor and underprivileged, lacking in many of the health, welfare and educational facilities so richly enjoyed by the citizens of the Western nations. And they were devoid of, or deficient in, so many of the advantages that a fully exploited and applied technology could provide. But, despite all these inadequacies, a catching-up process was well on its way. Some of the non-Western countries had either assumed a place at the table of leading world powers, or were on the brink of doing so. Even the less privileged nations had high aspirations, and were reaching out, with varying success, for further all-round development and maturity.

And along with this general, fascinating process of re-formation went a total change in the world Christian configuration. The 'old' world of the North, with the exception of North America, witnessed an alarming, if often overstated, marginalization of institutional Christianity, whereas much of the South saw a staggering Christian growth and vitality. In both cases, the situation of the laity in Christianity altered massively.

There are therefore two tales to tell: one covering the 'Western' world, and the other covering the lands of the South, and more especially sub-Saharan Africa, Asia and South America. They represent contrasts more than similarities, with two major exceptions: Pentecostalism, and neo-Pentecostalism, more familiarly known as the charismatic movement, appeared and blossomed in both zones. In fact, many of the most outstanding changes in the history of the laity throughout the world, both in the Western and non-Western regions, were bound up with the amazing growth and impact of these two exceptional, vibrant and transforming movements. In the Western world they helped to bolster and revivify often weary and flagging churches, and thereby imparted a greater measure of hope for the future. In the non-Western world there was the exciting process of indigenization, and the establishment of lively local, independent churches, where Pentecostalism and the charismatic movement were part of an often encouragingly healthy Christian growth in numbers, robustness and dedication. In both cases, Pentecostalism and neo-Pentecostalism were unrivalled in their importance in the life of all Protestant denominations and in the Roman Catholic Church. It is reasonable, therefore, to start a review of the laity in that incredible century for universal Christianity with an account of these two, very largely lay, movements.

Pentecostalism

Pentecostalism introduced a whole new dynamic and dimension to worldwide church life. It was a mighty and awesome force.[1]

It is, indeed, arguable that Pentecostalism has been the single most important lay movement in the entire history of Christianity. After all, there were no Pentecostals as such in 1900, although various scattered groups and individuals had claimed Pentecostal-like experiences before then, but by the year 2000 there were approximately 500 million of them throughout the world, or one in four of all Christian believers. By the end of the first millennium, Pentecostalism was a recognized branch of world Christianity with a vast number of churches in most countries. It, and the associated charismatic movement, had revolutionized Christianity in every region of the world, and had contributed more than any other factor in not only adding immensely to Christian numbers but in giving the laity a prominence hitherto unknown except in the apostolic age.

The origins of the Pentecostal movement can be traced to no one founder, nor to one place. Conventionally, its roots have been located in the United States of America but, as will be seen, it sprouted independently and at about the same time in other parts of the world. Not only so, but various individuals and movements preceded it, which gave it different pedigrees according to the territories concerned.

In the Western world, in spite of such preparatory influences as the evangelistic campaigns of Charles Finney, D. L. Moody and R. A. Torrey, and incidents of glossolalia and other 'gifts of the Spirit' on both sides of the Atlantic, including the so-called Holiness Movement, it is from 1901 that a continuous flow can be identified of what was clearly a single stream of ever-growing magnitude. It was in the winter of that year, and in response to prayer and the laying on of hands, that a student at Charles F. Parham's Bethel Bible College, in Topeka, Kansas City, is said to have spoken in tongues. Subsequently, Parham had the same experience, as did many of the other students. He publicly declared that speaking in tongues was a gift available to all believers, and that it was evidence of baptism in the Holy Spirit. He founded a second Bible School, at Houston, Texas; and it was one of the students from there, named William J. Seymour, who in 1906 held meetings in an abandoned warehouse at 312 Azusa Street in Los Angeles, with devastating effect and momentous repercussions. The address 'became internationally known as the cradle of the Pentecostal movement in America'.[2]

Here was a new power let loose in the churches of America, and soon in Britain and Europe. Speaking in tongues and healing were not only demonstrated as still available Christian experiences, but they were shown to be accessible to all and every Christian. A new depth of fellowship was created which helped to abolish barriers of colour and class, and a new empowerment was given to every member of local churches. Prophecy slowly became a recognized part of worship, with all the members of any congregation being free to utter a prophetic word or revelation. A new meaning was imparted to the concept of the 'gathered church', and a new and bold reliance on the power of God was introduced that brought release to many and strengthened the ability of believers to proclaim the gospel.

And this enrichment of fellowship and renewal for service rekindled a lay zeal for the proclamation of the gospel. Personal evangelism became a priority, and this was supplemented by a deep concern to spread the faith throughout the world. In 1909, even before such Pentecostal bodies as the Elim Church, the Assemblies of God and the Apostolic Church had emerged, a Missionary Union was formed and missionaries started to go abroad, taking the Pentecostal message to Africa, China, India and elsewhere. This remarkably rapid action in launching out, even to the extent of penetrating non-Christian cultures, was a powerful indicator of things to come. And the lay men and women who adventurously and courageously embarked on these exploits did so more often than not without any special training or preparation, other than that provided for the few in the Missionary Training School of the Pentecostal Missionary Union. In most cases the individual who felt called to serve abroad had to rely on his or her inner drive, and on a spontaneous, heartfelt desire to spread the faith. Organized efforts were rare, and there was often very slender financial support from a local church for any missionary. It was astonishing that so many lay men and women were so moved with the desire to serve as missionaries that they fought against all these obstacles and allowed nothing to prevent them from going forth.

Even with such scattered examples of heroic dedication, the initial Pentecostal growth was not especially noteworthy. The various Pentecostal churches expanded steadily although not sensationally in the first two decades of the century. But then the expansion became more pronounced. For example, in 1920 the Apostolic Church claimed a mere 50 assemblies; but by 1930 this number had risen to about 150 in Britain, with a further 50 elsewhere. By 1947, there were 1,250 assemblies throughout the world, and by 1962 this total was well over 2,000.[3]

By the 1980s, Pentecostalism had become a strong component of global Christianity, and one of the leading examples of lay-centred Christianity. There had been great gains in Britain, but these were far exceeded by the progress in Scandinavia generally, and especially in Norway and Sweden, where Pentecostalism was stronger than any other denomination. There were notable advances in other countries of Europe, and in the USSR the success was outstanding, due in large part to the efforts and courage of Ivan Voronaer during the 1920s.[4] It has been estimated that by the 1980s there were about 200,000 Pentecostals in the Soviet Union, of which 20,000 were seeking emigration.

Pentecostalism had, by that time, become firmly rooted in all the continents.[5] The Indian Pentecostal Church was founded in 1923, and by the last quarter of the twentieth century the number of Pentecostals in that nation had risen to 100,000, a not unimpressive number in a country dominated by Hinduism and Islam. The Pentecostals had gone as missionaries to Japan, the Pacific Islands, New Guinea and elsewhere in the Antipodes, and Pentecostalism was well established in large areas of Africa. But the pre-eminent example of Pentecostal penetration outside the Western world was South America. In Chile, one in seven of the population of 7 million were Pentecostals, and, most strikingly, the growth in the number of Pentecostals in Brazil in the last two decades of the century was bewildering. By 1991, 12,567,992 Protestants were enumerated for Latin America, of which 8,179,708 were Pentecostals.[6]

In Africa, as in South America, Pentecostalism originated and subsequently underwent amazing expansion, as a local and indigenous phenomenon. It was, in most cases, a home-grown product. African Pentecostalism was

> essentially of *African* origin with roots in a marginalized and underprivileged society struggling to find dignity and identity. It expanded initially

among oppressed African people who were neglected, misunderstood, and deprived of anything but token leadership by their white ecclesiastical 'masters'. But fundamentally, it was the ability of African Pentecostalism to adapt to and fulfil African *religious* aspirations that was its main strength.[7]

And this was likewise true for those parts of Asia where Pentecostalism emerged as a surpassing force. It was a critical part of its astonishing 'success' that it had so manifestly arisen out of the local soil and culture and was so in harmony with local modes of thought, norms and mores. It clearly owed its core characteristics and forms of expression to native mindsets and dispositions. It was not an alien import foisted on a reluctant and unsympathetic people.

Regrettably, the earnestness, enthusiasm and dedication of the Pentecostals proved to be a contributory factor in a most unfortunate fissiparous inclination. As in innumerable cases throughout history, but at no time on such a scale as with Pentecostalism, a price had to be paid for the highly charged, often highly emotional, faith and lives of those who claimed to have been touched in a very special way in their individual and corporate experiences by the power of God. Intensity of faith had not in many situations been balanced by an equal concern for order, restraint, discipline and a determination to hold the faith in the unity of peace. Pride and intolerance had too often overridden humility. The fine balance between strong and resolute personal and corporate commitment and faithfulness to dearly held beliefs on the one hand, and a willingness to compromise on inessentials when such rigidity and vehemence threatened unity, on the other hand, had never been easy to achieve. It was a problem at the end of the twentieth century, and continued to be so as a new millennium began.

The charismatic movement

The charismatic movement was, in a nutshell, the appearance of Pentecostal features within existing non-Pentecostal denominations, which then remained and became a fully recognized part of the life of those churches. It first manifested itself in Protestant circles in 1955 and 1956, and assumed the characteristics and proportions of a fully fledged movement in the following decade. Although there had been sporadic and isolated instances of Pentecostal-type experiences within the Roman Catholic Church, this only became identifiable as a movement when a group of lay men met at Duquesne University in Pittsburgh in 1966. From there, it spread in the following year to the University of Notre-Dame, Indiana.[8]

Among the first to undergo a Pentecostal experience in the Protestant Episcopal Church of the USA was David Bennett, the Rector of the fashionable St Mark's Church, Van Nuys, California. Much to the surprise of his congregation, on Passion Sunday, 1960, he related from the pulpit how he had been filled with the Holy Spirit and had spoken in tongues.[9] The ripples from this one incident, and from what followed, were felt far and wide on both sides of the Atlantic, helped by Bennett's subsequent itinerant ministry. In the 1960s, the charismatic movement started to infiltrate churches in Europe and other areas, but, for the most part, in an initially quiet and not very spectacular manner.

During the third quarter of the twentieth century, both in the Western and the non-Western regions of the world, there was, however, a shift of considerable importance in the whole structure and character of the charismatic movement. It became a global force in its own right, separate from but clearly related in many manifestations of its power and influence to Pentecostalism.

But, of course, the story of Christianity, and more especially of the laity within the churches, in the twentieth century went far beyond these two, albeit sensational, movements. And this saga is best approached regionally, as was done in the last chapter with reference to the nineteenth century.

The Western world

In order to simplify the picture, and contain it within reasonable bounds, the review of the so-called Western world in the twentieth century will once more be confined to Britain, continental Europe and the USA. And here the contrast between the first two regions taken together and the last is pronounced. In the former there was an apparently woeful story of numerical decline in church membership, and a series of rearguard actions by churches conscious that they were battling for survival. In the latter, there was a persistence of buoyancy and even evidence of the increased influence of the churches and of the Christian laity in the life of the nation.

Statistics for church membership and numbers of communicants, together with observations on church attendances and involvement in church activities, point in one direction only for many Western countries. They show clearly that the churches were not thriving numerically. Nonetheless, throughout Europe, including Britain, such obvious institutional decline was accompanied by a remarkable retention among the various populations of certain basic beliefs, even allowing for the fact that what was said in answer to questionnaires was arguably without much depth of conviction. It appears that there was probably a widespread, ill-defined and seldom articulated religious disposition among the population at large that was not translated into church attendance. In a rather diffuse way, there was a measure of 'believing without belonging'.

Even so, the overall situation was somewhat dire and distressing from the Christian point of view, not least of all for the laity. This becomes more apparent when compared with Christianity in the United States, where the churches more than held their own during the twentieth century. There were obviously peaks and troughs, but the overall resurgence was pronounced, most notably as the third millennium approached.

In the last half of the twentieth century in particular, America received as citizens a vast number of people from innumerable countries. Among these, however, there were strikingly few who adhered to non-Christian religions. It has been plausibly estimated that the combined numbers of American Jews, Buddhists, Muslims and Hindus at the end of the century amounted to a mere 4 or 5 per cent or so of the total population. By the year 2000, in numerical terms at least, America was still substantially a Christian country, as it had always been. And within that seemingly healthy Christian environment, the laity constituted an extremely powerful force, with women becoming ever more significant in the life and witness of the churches.

At the heart of the late twentieth-century reinvigorated churches was a spectacular growth of conservative Protestantism. This was triggered off in the 1950s, which was a boom decade for the mainline churches as a whole. Some of them made vigorous efforts to win converts and attract new members. The Southern Baptists were particularly successful with a thrust forward under the slogan 'A Million More in Fifty-Four'. And the staggering progress that they made provoked other denominations to be more outward-looking and pro-active in striving for growth. Thus, as but one example, the Assemblies of God increased their lay membership by 71 per cent between 1973 and 1983.

The new zeal that was generated had manifold ramifications. Among these was the astounding and very public influence exerted by the churches on the political life of the nation. Jimmy Carter was an avowed Southern Baptist, and the backing of the Evangelicals was of considerable assistance to Ronald Regan both in his campaign for election to the presidency and in his tenure of that high office. Such Evangelical politico-religious organizations as Christian Voice and Religious Roundtable, but more especially Jerry Falwell's Moral Majority, had high profiles and were remarkably effective in achieving their religious, political and social objectives. And, to underscore the revived Evangelical involvement in political matters, the renowned television evangelist Pat Robertson campaigned in an effort to win the Republican Party nomination for the presidency of the United States. It is clear that the churches in the USA as a whole entered the twenty-first century in a buoyant mood.

Worldwide lay Christianity

The twentieth century was the time when the potential for Christian expansion on a global scale, which had been created in the nineteenth century, was realized to an impressive degree. And one of the outstanding characteristics of the millions of new and embryonic churches in Africa, Asia and Latin America was the eminent part played by the laity in helping to create and then to sustain them. New generations of Christian laity in their billions formed a worldwide Christian resource of amazing possible influence; and this latent force for evangelism, pastoral and charitable work was frequently geared up and mustered for action. In a remarkable number of instances, in places as far apart as Nigeria, East-Central Africa, China, Korea, Brazil and Argentina, great things were achieved as clergy, ministers and lay people worked together.

The sheer volume of additional lay Christians globally was startling. It hugely exceeded any previous expansion of Christianity. By the year 2000 the total number of Christians had soared to about 2 billion, which represented one person in three of the entire world population. And of these, almost 60 per cent were to be found in South America, sub-Saharan Africa and Asia.

In the latter half of the twentieth century in particular,

> millions of new members poured into the churches. It was precisely as Western colonialism ended that Christianity began a period of explosive growth that still continues unchecked, above all in Africa. Just since 1965, the Christian population of Africa has risen from around a quarter of the continental total to about 46 per cent.[10]

Such a statistic alone reveals one of the most stunning rates of escalation in the size of a Christian community in any one region in the whole of Christian history. And at the end of the century, there was no sign of the rate of growth slowing down. This is attested by the carefully presented facts of the 2001 edition of the *World Christian Encyclopedia* with reference to Africa. 'The present net increase on that continent', it reported, 'is 8.4 million new Christians a year (23,000 a day) of which 1.5 million are net new converts (converts minus defections or apostasies).' And en-route various historic landmarks were passed, as in the 1960s, when 'Christians first outnumbered Muslims in Africa'.[11]

The involvement of the laity in establishing and sustaining churches

One outstanding feature of the multiplying and mushrooming churches of the twentieth century in South America, Africa and parts of Asia was the active engagement of the laity in every aspect of their life. Clerical or ministerial dominance was exceptional. Lay passivity was exceptional. Vigorous lay involvement was the norm. A few examples will give some insight into this often heroic lay testimony and activity.

In South America, special mention should be made of the base communities (CEBs – *Comunidades Eclesiasticas de Base*, in Portuguese *Comunidades Eclesiais de Base*). The CEBs, which started to appear in the 1960s, were a widespread and outstanding example of the attempt by the Roman Catholics to more fully engage the laity in the life of the churches. They were a response to the expressed Roman Catholic Church's need to remedy the severe shortage of priests and other personnel in part at least by training lay people to become more fully involved in religious and catechistic functions. But they soon extended their role. They often became, in various respects, radical and revolutionary: a kind of specific and particular example of liberation theology expressed in action. Even so, the type of CEB that propounded this type of theology or attempted to practise such radicalism was not typical. In most cases these cells of lay Christians were not so political and left wing, and many, but by no means all, bishops and priests encouraged the creation of CEBs or similar bodies, which devoted themselves to a wide range of less extreme, more conservative, and therefore more acceptable, activities.

Indeed, the CEBs did not emerge spontaneously among the poor, but were the result of initiatives taken by authorized, official, Roman Catholic pastoral agents. Such instigators and catalysts for the establishment of CEBs, and also subsequent members of the cells so created, were a mixture of seminarians, nuns and lay people. Although some of the participants in CEB activity had poor origins and resided in the communities in which they worked, that was the exception rather than the rule. In the majority of cases, the workers involved were from outside the areas where they were employed, and they were of a somewhat higher socio-economic status than the people among whom they worked. They had typically moved from their home towns and had improved their standard of education and their social standing as a consequence of their work and personal efforts to improve themselves. In fact, most of them were college students or graduates; and the poor people in the districts concerned did not completely understand or accept the CEBs in the form that was proposed by the 'sending' agents.[12] Nevertheless, in spite of these shortcomings, they were impressive.

There were significant variations in the reasons for establishing the groups, and in the main functions and focus they adopted. In a number of examples, the members were largely intent on helping the local rural and urban poor. As a means to such an end, and in order to be of assistance, the CEB members gave a lead in organizing such underprivileged citizens into self-help cells dedicated to improving the lot of their fellow citizens by tackling some of the main problems that blighted their lives. This was especially necessary and fruitful when there was suffering entailed as a result of land conflicts and invasions, and when there was a need for peasant organization in order to confront and overcome some particular combination of adverse or oppressive circumstances. In such cases, the base communities enabled 'the poor to assert their civil rights as active participants in society and church'. When they fulfilled this particular role, 'the internal dynamic of the base communities' generated 'a phenomenon of enormous importance, the inbreaking of the word or, better, the discovery of a voice'. It was, 'without any doubt, a cell-by-cell process of breaking down isolation which ... [made] it possible for the poor to assert their civil rights. The experience of community ... [enabled] the poor to become conscious of their dignity and worth as active participants in society.' It was 'an experience which was felt as a personal enrichment'.[13]

In other instances the groups were less socially active and concentrated on Bible study and fellowship. In still further cases, the CEBs were a part of the parish and diocesan decision-making structure. And finally, there were a few examples where the leaders and members looked upon themselves as a nucleus for a 'People's church' that would ultimately displace the authority of the hierarchy.

The characteristic that was common to most CEBs was their community involvement, and their identity with the life and spirit of the community, rather than their regulation and control by the Roman Catholic Church. And, of course, this independence and self-regulation had its dangers. Foremost among these was the possibility that any one such group, or a cluster of them in a particular region, might become identified with political or social causes to such an extent that they almost lost sight of their fundamental religious purpose and motivation. And this is exactly what happened in some instances to a degree that was found unacceptable by the church authorities. Such political entanglement reached a pinnacle of affront to the official Roman Catholic Church, and aroused the maximum opposition from critics, when the 'People's Church' became identified with the Sandinista government in Nicaragua, with the FMLN

The laity in twentieth-century Christianity

revolutionary army in El Salvador and with the revolutionary Poor People's Guerrilla Army in the bloody conflict in Guatemala. Although such support for militant rebellious movements entailed mostly priests, lay people were also involved.

Nevertheless, such political and military engagement was rare and should not be allowed to distort the general picture regarding CEBs. Most of them were dedicated to the discussion of matters relating to personal morality, to charitable works and to Bible study and participation in religious festivals. In such ways, they fulfilled a time-honoured function of lay organizations. They achieved much as agents for valuable religious and social works that were greatly appreciated by the beneficiaries. And in the process, and as a sort of by-product, they confirmed individuals in their deep-seated aspirations for social status and social mobility. They gave lay people opportunities to use their talents in constructive and fulfilling ways. And in some circumstances they enabled their members to identify with, and to some extent to partially replace, the figure of the local priest, whereby they acquired a measure of recognition as role-players in local parish life.

Whatever their particular format and function within the local church and within society, by the 1990s, in Brazil especially, they had become 'one of the most important factors in the shaping of a new vision of the Church'. They had by then played 'a key part in realizing the goal of creating a Church of the poor'.[14] They demonstrated the church's preferential love for the common, often downtrodden people, and they enabled the church to unearth and to bring into play the evangelizing potential of the poor. Although they often gave great stress to social and even political matters, they seldom lost sight of the overriding Christian component in their raison d'être.

This same pattern of small lay groups being prominent in the church of the South can be seen in Asia and Africa as well. Take Singapore as an example.

In the last decades of the twentieth century, first Bishop Chiu Ban and then Bishop Moses Tay were passionately concerned to develop the spiritual life of the diocese to the full, and to encourage evangelism and mission as central to such an objective. In order to achieve these aims, they established and extended home cells, which supplemented, but did not supplant, the regular Sunday worship of the churches. Such home-based fellowships became a vital part of the whole strategy of the diocese. The idea, and its implementation, was simple, but highly effective.

> Small groups of a dozen or so, meeting weekly in homes, were led by lay men or women, normally those who had gone through the entire Diocesan

Lay Training Programme. These cells proved invaluable in many ways. They cut down on backsliding, since all church members were encouraged to belong to one. They developed leadership skills. They were a natural and easy vehicle for evangelism, for many who would never go near a church were happy enough to go along to a home group when invited by a good friend. They alerted members to the social needs in their immediate vicinity, which they tried to meet. They were ideal for building up young Christians and in due course for supporting missionary ventures into other countries.[15]

Such cells became one of the main ways the Christian faith was spread throughout Singapore and the surrounding regions. By 2000 they had become so prolific, effective and essential to the life and outreach of the churches in Singapore that it was planned and anticipated that there would soon be a cell in every street and every high-rise block.

In Africa, as in so many places, the massive engagement of the laity in the life of churches was often associated with the immense impact of the charismatic movement. Its emergence in that continent in the early 1970s signalled not only the onset of a substantial Christian awakening, but also a new period of lay Christian innovation and activity within all age groups and across the entire social spectrum, but most notably among young people. 'In fact, in no period since the missionary enterprises of the nineteenth century have youths been actively involved in evangelism to the extent apparent in the 1970s and 1980s.'[16] And this renewal very frequently resulted in varied forms and expressions of social concern. New, invigorated spiritual life often led on to new or renewed efforts to assist the needy.

By 1985, the charismatic movement was the fastest-growing element in the churches in West Africa, and in East and Central African countries such as Kenya, Tanzania, Zambia and Zimbabwe. Although the total number of charismatics throughout Africa was only about 8 million, which was small compared with the entire population of the continent, the laity compensated for their lack of numbers by their vigorous activity and by their commitment. And the scale of some charismatic church ministries was quite often staggering, as with the Deeper Life Bible Church in Lagos, Nigeria, which, prior to decentralization in 1990, claimed a congregation of 40,000 for its Sunday services.

It was also of considerable importance that 'the leadership and a substantial percentage of membership of the movements' were 'educated elites – the college students, the school leavers and the university and college graduates. This class of people, though small in number', had 'immeasurable influence in African society'. They possessed a 'transformative potential based on cohesiveness and a strong sense of self-identity'.[17]

The laity in twentieth-century Christianity

There were two fairly distinct phases in the emerging structure of the sub-Saharan charismatic organizations and in the whole evolving character of the charismatic movement in that region. In the early years, from about 1970 to about 1982, the lay people involved mostly continued to attend their mainline churches, with charismatic meetings being held only on weekdays, and they were linked together only by a very loose and informal network. During those years the teachings, practices and techniques of the few existing organizations were geared to sustaining that arrangement, and their evangelistic efforts relied on person-to-person witness and tract distribution. It was only from about 1983 that some of the organizations began to exhibit independent denominational tendencies. In each phase, however, the movement was predominantly lay in both leadership and, of course, membership, with a great stress being laid on the 'every member' principle in all aspects of the worship, witness and internal life of the fellowships concerned.

At every stage in the evolution of the charismatic movement in sub-Saharan Africa, the ministry of care to the poor and needy in society was not neglected. There was an impressive marrying of evangelistic, missionary and social concern. The social concern was underlined by the prompt founding of the Christian Evangelical Social Movement in 1977, and the missionary concern by the establishment of the Christian Missionary Foundation in 1981. By 1986, the latter had undertaken work in Ivory Coast, Gambia, Liberia, Kenya, Uganda, Cameroon, Benin and Zimbabwe, as well as in its first mission field, Nigeria.

It is of note that while all these changes were taking place, the Roman Catholic Church in Africa, as in most other regions of the world, still struggled with its rigid clerical authority structure. In the mid-1990s, a well-informed commentator bemoaned this:

> Lay men and women in Africa ... [were] far from exercising their rightful role in the Christian community. Although Catholic social teaching visualizes the creation of participatory institutions in which Africans can set their own agenda for the socio-economic recovery and development of their continent, such principles have scarcely been applied to the Church itself.[18]

Attempts were made to remedy such a deficiency. The Second Vatican Council exerted a considerable influence in trying to bring about change. It was a 'major catalyst', and it 'provided both the inspiration and the theology for lay engagement rooted in the baptism common to all rather than in any delegation from Church authority'.[19] It was likewise with Pope John Paul II's post-synodal exhortation of 1988, entitled *Christifideles Laici*, in which he called upon the lay faithful 'to take an active, conscientious and responsible part in the mission of the Church'.

Thus, even with the papal and conciliar encouragement for the laity to play their full part in the life and witness of the Roman Catholic Church, with greater opportunities for lay initiatives, and with more varied avenues of service, the move forward in practice had still been very hesitant and lacking in boldness right up to the beginning of a new century. And the church authorities were nervous even about the little progress that seemed to have been made. The entrusting of greater responsibility to the laity was treated with great caution. There was widespread and not well-hidden fear and trepidation about the consequences of offering too much scope for innovation and new ideas too soon. Most of the moves in that direction tended to be tentative and restrained. Some observers at the end of the twentieth century noted that even in those few lay communities that were set up, 'their free-floating relationship to the church's structures' did 'not always appeal to the clerical establishment, and in many other parts of Africa there' was 'only a half-hearted response towards' the promotion of such communities. 'Roman Catholic authoritarianism' was 'a serious handicap for the Church in sharing in the socio-political aspirations of ordinary Africans and in generating African creativity in Church and State'.[20]

This tension between centralized authority and local lay liberty to 'do their own thing' was widespread and by no means restricted to the Roman Catholic Church, although it may have been more evident in that communion than in other, less rigid, hierarchical and authoritarian Christian churches.

In the meantime, while these attempts by the churches to make the Christian faith meaningful and pertinent to ordinary lay people were going on, large numbers of Christians throughout much of the world were finding how costly it could be to remain true to their faith.

Martyrs

In the minds of many people, Christian martyrs are typically associated with times in the far distant past: with the Roman arena and death from wild animals, with ghastly experiences of torture and final slaughter in the first four centuries of the Christian era, and with the stake, beheading or being hung, drawn and quartered in the Reformation or immediate post-Reformation era. But the age of martyrdom had not passed as the churches entered the modern age. Indeed, there were probably more Christians who suffered or died for their faith, often cruelly and in unimaginably horrid ways, in the twentieth century than in all the previous centuries combined.

Just to list some of the places where Christians have suffered greatly and have died for their faith in the twentieth century is more than merely to provide a catalogue of martyrdom. It gives some measure of the comprehensiveness of the worldwide persecution that took place, and the price that was paid by the victims who, inevitably, were mostly lay Christians. The methods of inflicting pain have to an extent changed over the centuries, with modern devices for submitting the sufferers to intolerable agonies; and the final taking of life has taken new forms, with modern methods of bringing life to an end. But martyrs there have been in abundance. The countries involved include China, Manchuria, Japan, Korea, Thailand, Vietnam, Laos, Cambodia, Tibet, India, Bangladesh, Pakistan, Nepal, Sri Lanka, Burma, Indonesia, Papua and surrounding islands, Malaysia and Singapore, Taiwan, the Philippines, Germany, Russia, Lithuania, Latvia, Estonia, Bulgaria, Hungary, Czechoslovakia, Poland, Yugoslavia, Albania, Armenia, Lebanon, Syria, Egypt, Jordan, Israel, the Sudan, Ethiopia, Somalia, Chad, Mali, the Republic of Guinea, the People's Republic of Congo, the Malagasy Republic, the Central African Empire, the Kingdom of Benin, Liberia, Nigeria, Ghana, Sierra Leone, Cameroon, Mozambique, Angola, Tanzania, Kenya, Uganda, Zimbabwe, Zambia, Malawi, South Africa, Namibia, Burundi and Rwanda, Zaire, Cuba, Haiti, the Dominican Republic, Mexico, Central America, Brazil, Uruguay, Argentina, Chile, Paraguay, Bolivia, Peru, Ecuador and Colombia.[21]

But, to return to the witness of Christians in life as well as in death, the last half of the twentieth century witnessed a range of new efforts to express the love of God in both theory and action. Confronted with poverty, disease and intense human need and suffering of many kinds, and on an unimaginable scale, Christians struggled to find ways of making the Christian faith more relevant to actual, on-the-ground human situations. Liberation theology was one of the results of such efforts.

Liberation theology and its implementation

Many lay people were engaged in the theology of liberation that emerged in the late 1960s and flowered in the following decade. It represented a radical approach to the pressing question of Christian mission to the downcast, disadvantaged, destitute and deprived members of society, whom the church so often seemed powerless to help or influence. Here was an audacious attempt to respond to Jesus' Messianic programme, 'to bring good news to the poor', to 'proclaim release to the captives and recovery of sight to the blind, to let the oppressed go free, to proclaim the year of the Lord's favour' (Luke 4.18–19). The liberation theologians were anxious to take heed of the words of Christ that 'anyone who resolves to do the will of God will know whether the teaching is from God'.[22] This specifically New Testament-based teaching was adopted alongside and in union with the dictum of Karl Marx that the object of all true attempts to bring relief to people was not to understand society but to change it. Action among the poor would lead to reflection; and theology and practice needed to be integrated. This whole approach went counter to the traditional academic 'neutrality' of the Western universities. It was infused with an intense Christian desire to serve others.

Among those who thought and wrote in this manner was the Peruvian priest and theologian Gustavo Gutiérrez, who laboured among the poor of Lima. His agonized pondering on the plight of the people to whom he sought to minister the consolations of the gospel, who had to endure severe deprivation and pain, led to a radical conclusion. In his *Theology of Liberation*, he declared that what was needed was not the failed way of development, but liberation, by means of a 'profound transformation of the private property system, access to power of the exploited class and a social revolution'.[23]

Essentially, liberation theology was concerned with love of God and solidarity with the poor. It may have arisen when it did, partly because of a local sense of Christian impotence when confronted with the overwhelming social problems of Latin America, and partly because of the vacuum in radical theological speculation that was created in the immediate aftermath of Vatican II. Among those most concerned to minister to the needs of the marginalized groups in society, this dual reason for inactivity was frustrating in the extreme. It went far to explain 'the almost desperate recourse to the language of liberation'.[24]

Inroads into many spheres of social life

Liberation theology had the poor and needy in its sights, and the groups that were established as a direct or indirect result of it generally consisted of lay men and women from the less privileged sectors of society. This was, however, but one consequence of the incredible impact of Christianity on people from all socio-economic groups and the engagement of lay Christians in an ever-enlarged arena of activity. As Christians increased in numbers and expanded to embrace all social strata, in many countries they enlarged their range of political, social and cultural interests, and their focus of attention broadened. In South America the penetration of Protestants in particular into politics, the media and sport was increasing in the last quarter of the twentieth century. Thus, as but one example, 'seven of the

22 Brazilian football squad that won the 1994 World Cup were evangelicals who held high profile meetings throughout the tournament and were responsible for the scene after the final, in which the whole team huddled together on the pitch and prayed'.[25]

In developing countries especially, where all facets of national life were important in the forging of national identity, such infiltration of society by Christians was a key feature in the Christian witness. And, of course, almost all the Christians involved were lay men or women who were simply living out their Christian lives as well as they could, taking their faith into the 'real world' of everyday life. It was a highly potent and promising aspect of lay Christianity at the end of the twentieth century.

And with this came the adoption of lifestyles that had previously been frowned upon by Christians in general and Evangelicals in particular. Social, entertainment and leisure-time activities, previously regarded with some measure of suspicion if not hostility, became not only more acceptable but were embraced with enthusiasm and used as channels for the presentation and communication of the faith. The new era was typified by the launching of Christian rock, funk and rap musical productions as well as the Christian promotion of Brazilian idioms such as samba, pagode and baiao. The whole character of Evangelicalism in particular seemed to be undergoing radical change. Although, in the course of undertaking these new forms of outreach, the foundation beliefs of those involved do not seem to have been compromised in the vast proportion of cases, there was an openness to adventurous forays into hitherto forbidden or little explored aspects of popular culture that was indicative of a seismic change in outlook.

Such daring initiatives were but symptoms of a more general and more fundamental realignment of Christian thinking and action. They reflected what in effect was a rapid and remarkable redefinition of what was entailed in lay Christians being 'in the world but not of the world'. The kind of breaking loose from previous conventions just indicated helped to heighten even further an awareness of the complementary worlds inhabited on the one hand by the laity, and on the other hand by the ordained, set-apart clergy and ministers. It also brought into relief the remarkable contrast between the world Christian scene in 1900 and that on the eve of the third millennium. It was astonishing what changes had taken place in 100 years.

By the end of the twentieth century, not only were new Christian lifestyles and methods of evangelism and worship well on the way to remoulding the face of Christianity, but issues previously under wraps, or only considered hesitantly and nervously, were beginning to surface. Such a shift brought to light in a new and painful way the ever-widening gap between the characteristically evangelical and dogmatic stance of many churches in the Southern part of the world, compared with the more inclusive and mixed theological and ecclesiological situation in much of the Western world. It highlighted differences of view on specific issues such as homosexuality, same-sex marriages, the ordination of women and the consequential associated matter of women bishops. By the turn of the century, the potential for severe and serious divisiveness was becoming agonizingly evident.

Aside from these irritating domestic matters, there were such stupendous issues as the Christian response to world poverty, malnutrition, health problems, and more especially AIDS. There were grievous matters that demanded some sort of Christian response, including international slavery that operated on a massive scale and was to be found in various forms in a vast number of countries, the death and destruction caused by internecine strife, the fearful consequences of tyrannical regimes, sometimes including ethnic cleansing, constant civil rights issues, and the potentially catastrophic results of global warming and other environmental problems. The future agenda for worldwide Christianity on the one hand was full of promise, but on the other hand was awesome and daunting in the extreme.

8

The laity in the Orthodox Church

The Eastern Churches up to the mid-fifteenth century

The Orthodox Church did not come into existence in 1054, at the time of the so-called Great Schism, as is often implied or stated categorically. Rather, it emerged in the centuries before this, and only assumed a more definite form in the mid-eleventh century.

The churches of the West and the East shared a common origin and early life. Both traditions look to the three hundred years after the death and resurrection of Christ as a formative time, and they only identify a slow process of going their own ways after the Edict of Milan in 313.

In order to appreciate the Orthodox view of their status and standing in the Christian world, and the evolving European perspective on the life of Eastern Christianity, the year 330 must be reckoned as pivotal.[1] It was then that the Roman Emperor Constantine established a second, 'new' Rome on the site of the ancient city of Byzantium and named it Constantinople. 'From that moment onwards the peoples under the sway of these great centres of power, Rome and Constantinople, moved steadily apart and elaborated two very distinctive and different cultures.'[2]

Even in these early centuries of the Christian era in the East, a unique place was accorded to one supreme lay man:

> At the heart of the Christian polity of Byzantium was the Emperor, who was no ordinary ruler, but God's representative on earth. If Byzantium was an icon of the heavenly Jerusalem, then the earthly monarchy of the Emperor was an image or icon of the monarchy of God in heaven; in church people prostrated themselves before the icon of Christ, and in the palace before God's living icon – the Emperor.[3]

It was a pattern of church–state relations that was to be a hallmark of Eastern Orthodoxy throughout its history.

The laity in the Eastern Churches up to the mid-fifteenth century

'The line between things spiritual and things temporal, between religious and secular, was never very precisely drawn in the Byzantine world.'[4] In this regard, what has been said about the changes in the role of the laity in the Western Church does not apply to the Eastern Church. There was far more flexibility and fluidity in the opportunities for lay men to participate actively in the life of the church in the East than in the West. There was no stage at which there was such a pronounced development of clericalism, and the clerical monopoly of both theological expertise and ministerial practice, in the East as in the West. The distinctions between clerical and lay roles in the church were more blurred. The opportunities for able lay men to make a theological contribution, or to exercise what in the West at the time were considered as prerogatives of the clergy in church ministry, were enormous.

> It was not unusual that a man of affairs should be an erudite theologian, that a priest should be a married man with a family, that a holy man should remain unordained, or that a layman should be appointed as Patriarch of Constantinople. Thirteen of the 122 Byzantine patriarchs were elevated from the laity, four of them in the eighth and ninth centuries.[5]

There are examples of high-ranking civil servants and scholars who trod that path, much to the indignation of the popes. But this did not restrain the Byzantines, who saw nothing odd or objectionable in the practice. 'They continued, from time to time, to appoint a layman rather than a priest to the highest office in their Church.'[6]

And the top-ranking lay man in society, the lay ruler or person in command, acquired a special position and status in the eyes of the church, which went well beyond the acknowledgement of his standing as the head of state, for he played a central part in the life of the church.[7] The emperor was charged with the onerous responsibility of protecting the church, while not interfering in its internal affairs. He did not just call ecumenical councils, or rubber-stamp church legislation. By examining and approving the laws, or by personally issuing laws affecting the life of the church, he either ensured that they became state law or that they were withheld from such implementation. And, in practice, he was not always a neutral, non-participant in domestic theological matters. On a number of occasions the Christian prince directly engaged in theological debates and attempted to swing church opinion in favour of his view. This was particularly noticeable when matters of heresy were at stake, or when questions of schism and the unity of the church were under consideration. In some cases, the ruler forced a patriarch or bishop to resign, and then filled the vacancy with a person of his own choosing. In all these ways, the lay ruler was undoubtedly powerful, with an influence that was more wide-ranging and all-embracing than was usual for Western rulers.

And it was not just at the highest levels that the principle of lay participation in the theology and ministry of the church operated. In the pre-eleventh-century world, as now, all baptized members belonged to the class of laity, and this automatically conferred on them certain rights and privileges, as well as duties and responsibilities. The sacrament of ordination through the laying on of hands was then as now viewed as conferring a special charisma, and the ordained person was thereby 'entitled to the right and duty of church administration, sanctification of the faithful and preaching of the Word of God'.[8] But lay people had their part to play. They were active in the realm of church organization. Although the lay Byzantine emperor convened every ecumenical council, and these constituted the highest authority in the ordering of church affairs, and although he was present in some sessions of these high-status bodies, he was often represented by his lay delegates throughout all the sessions. There were also other lay men, besides state officials, who took part in the synods and in related activities. Many were theologians, and many were members of special church assemblies that were called for the purpose of selecting new bishops and patriarchs. Lay men were also directly or indirectly involved in the election and appointment of the clergy.

Most importantly, however, it was open to lay people to achieve the quality of life that conferred on them the status of sainthood. 'Throughout the centuries sainthood found its expression', in a number of ways, through 'a life full of obedience to God'.[9] Before the fourth century, many of the recognized saints, both clerical and lay, were martyrs who suffered and died as a result of persecution, but others were members of the laity who displayed an exceptionally high quality of life, and possibly exhibited unusual spiritual powers, such as the ability to confer healing.

From the fourth century onwards, monasticism additionally offered a much respected and honourable way for lay men and lay women to renounce the world and to find a means of sanctification, and even to attain recognition of sainthood. And monasticism, from the very beginning, was not an ecclesiastical institution, but a distinctly lay movement. Within it, the taking of holy orders was deliberately and definitely discouraged. It occurred sometimes by special dictate from superiors, but even abbots were frequently lay men. The life of obedience and penitence, which was at the very centre of monastic life, was regarded as hardly compatible with the dignity and authority that was commonly associated with priesthood. To a great extent, monasticism cut across the distinction between clergy and laity.

By the fourteenth century, this essentially lay character of monasticism was revealed in a new way, as monks started to assume a prominent place in the life of the 'secular' church. In fact,

> the highest office in the church became a prerogative of monks. That did not mean that the religious had triumphed over the secular, because, still, as in former times, most Byzantine monks were never ordained. There were, of course, the *hieromonachi* or priest monks, who dispensed the sacraments. But the majority were always laymen.[10]

The laity and the Divine Liturgy

The Orthodox Church believed and taught that the importance, and the status and standing, of the laity were bestowed on them. They were gifts of God. 'By means of its sacraments, or mysteries as they were called, special graces were conferred.'[11] There was not a rigid pinning down of the sacraments to the seven recognized in the Latin Church, although this was the usually accepted number. Of these, baptism was fundamental, as it marked the infant's entry into the church. Such was its importance that it was often accompanied by elaborate ceremonial, and was invariably regarded by parents and all concerned as a most solemn and inspiring occasion. It was closely associated with confirmation or *chrismation*, in which the person concerned was anointed with chrism or oil. Baptism made the person concerned a full member of the church who could henceforth receive the consecrated bread and wine in the sacrament of the Eucharist.

The Divine Liturgy, as this sacrament was known in the Orthodox Church,[12] was at the heart of Christian life for all the laity; the humble peasants and urban poor as well as and alongside the high-ranking members of society. All members of the laity were intimately engaged in the worship of the church; and most notably in the celebration of the Holy Eucharist. Even during the medieval period, when in the West the lay people were virtually passive observers at such acts of worship, this was not the pattern to be found in the Orthodox liturgy. The canons of the church declared that the Holy Liturgy might not be performed in the absence of laity. The Holy Eucharist was not conceived and conducted as a service distant in space and comprehension from the laity, but was understood as 'the corporate worship of the whole Church inclusive of the lay people, wherein every member' had 'his appropriate liturgy to perform. In the offering of the holy elements, 'and throughout the Liturgy' the priest always used 'the expression "we" instead of "I", as the officer who' spoke 'in the name of the congregation and not of himself. Throughout the centuries, the Orthodox Church has never known an alienation of the laity from their liturgical functions during the celebration of the sacraments, of the kind which happened in the West.'[13]

And it is difficult to overstate what the Divine Liturgy meant for the laity as a whole. 'This is the final mystery,' said St Nicholas Kabasilas (c. 1322–c. 1391), 'beyond this it is not possible to go, nor can anything be added to it.'[14] From the earliest times after the Edict of Milan, the Divine Liturgy, together with the church building in which it was celebrated, was viewed as a foretaste of heaven. It was an ever-recurring theme and notion in Byzantine and Slavonic sources. 'The visitor's mind', Prokopios wrote in the 530s as his response to visiting the newly restored Hagia Sophia in Constantinople, 'is lifted up to God and soars aloft, thinking that he cannot be far away, but must especially love to dwell in this place that he himself has chosen.'[15] It is a sentiment that was reiterated by countless others, including Photios in his homily delivered at Constantinople in about 864.[16] And it applied to the humble local churches as well. Week by week, the worshippers found them to be the very gate of heaven.

The Eastern Church Eucharist did not consist entirely of liturgy. The sermon played a more central part in it, and in the teaching imparted to the laity, than has often been recognized. Surviving manuscripts indicate that 'sermons represented one of the most popular genres in the Byzantine world'.[17] It appears that a greater number of ordinary people understood them, and to a far greater extent, than has sometimes been assumed. Although illiteracy in the general sense of not being able to read or write was prevalent, a distinction must be made between everyday use of language and the language of worship.

> We must remember that church-going Byzantines probably understood Biblical and liturgical language, even if they were unable to read it. A number of lay people and probably most monks would have attended at least elementary school and learned sections of the Psalms and the New Testament by heart.[18]

The Byzantines lived in a world where verbal communication was far more important than the written word. By frequent immersion in the liturgy, the language of the homilies would have been partially, if not fully, comprehensible to people who were accustomed to hearing the scriptures read, and this familiarity would also have applied to the 'texts of the liturgy, the offices, and the growing corpus of hymns, whose words were at least as important as their musical settings'.[19]

Of course, the importance of the liturgy in the lives of simple folk who were bent on earning a living and keeping a family can be overstated and overgeneralized. For a considerable number of those lay people, the experience of attending their local church was undoubtedly less profound, and far more mundane than has so far been indicated. Even so, in their services of worship there appears to have been a general sense of the numinous, and a quite deep awareness of fellowship with fellow worshippers, with the universal company of believers and with those believers who had departed this life. And this was an experience that was central to the lives of countless lay people. It provided a mainstay and an anchor for the majority of them. In varying degrees, they were made conscious that during the Divine Liturgy there was a uniting of the earthly and the heavenly realms, and this helped to strengthen and uphold them in what for most of the laity were tough, toilsome and short lives.

And the times of worship were usually enjoyable and fulfilling for the participants. For the mostly simple, uneducated and not very sophisticated lay men and women, worship was not all sombre and overwhelmingly sacred and other-worldly. In addition to the awesomeness, there was also a sense of homeliness and relaxed informality that was characteristic of family life.[20] It is almost certain that, as in contemporary Orthodoxy, there was not an ordered, formal and highly regimented timetable of worship, but rather a certain diversity and spontaneity in which people arrived late, often talked vociferously among themselves and casually lit candles and venerated icons. 'Here in church', Chrysostom complained, 'there is great disturbance and confusion, and it is as bad as a tavern. There is so much laughter and tumult, with everyone chattering and making a noise, just as they do at the baths or the market.'[21] Emotions were not hidden. Opinions on a variety of topics were exchanged in a buzz of animated conversations, and the congregation was lively and vocal as the assembled people made known their views of the sermon.

There was also a certain physicality and almost domestic materiality in the worship. In the Eucharist, for example, the bread was always leavened and the wine always red; and baptism, except in situations of emergency, was by immersion. The link between the liturgical rites and the daily round of life was emphasized by the acknowledged divine significance of the other sacraments, marriage, holy orders, penance and the anointing of the sick, as well, of course, as the final rite surrounding the death of the Orthodox Church member. And it was not just lip service that was paid to them; their relevance was deeply ingrained in the psyche of all Orthodox believers. All of these rites of passage were, by their very nature, to do with the pivotal experiences in life for all people, irrespective of social status and standing. And the all-embracing relevance of liturgical rites was made apparent as it was also extended to cover the blessing of streams, rivers and the sea. Such comprehensiveness ensured that the sacramental ministry of the church enveloped the whole of life. It touched not only on the profoundest moments, but also upon all matters both great and small. It also engendered a deep-rooted sense of religious life being corporate and reaching far back into ancient times.

Although the stress laid by all the Orthodox on the centrality in life of prayer and praise to God was focused on the worship that was offered regularly and frequently in cathedrals and churches, it was perhaps supremely exhibited in the life of the monasteries. The services, or offices, in monasteries gave a 24-hour framework for such acts of devotion. There were seven or eight of these, depending on whether the one at midnight was counted separately or linked with the orthros that immediately followed it. These were midnight, orthros, prime (which took place about 6 a.m., but was variable according to the season of the year), terce, sext, none, vespers and compline. The greatest importance was given to orthros and vespers, and they were conducted with extremely elaborate ceremonial.

Both these services, as with the other acts of worship, changed little during the entire history of the Orthodox Church. Their essentially unaltered format and content amply demonstrates the fundamental conservatism of life in general in cultures dominated by the Orthodox Church, and in the church itself in particular. But certain modifications also make it clear that this core of continuity 'was tempered by creativeness and change'.[22] The basic components of both orthros and vespers consistently remained the psalms, readings from the Bible, prayers, and versicles and responses, together with appropriate commemorations of saints' lives. But there were changes introduced in the medieval period, most notably the introduction of splendid hymnody. At its best this was distinguished by a high poetic quality and spiritual content, indissolubly bound up with the accompanying music. And, throughout the centuries, icons and pictures, painted scenes in mosaic, frescoes on the walls and the various depictions of the saints stimulated the sense that the faithful departed were at one with the contemporary congregation as it met together.

The whole history of salvation and the sense of the communion of the faithful throughout time and space were portrayed visually. The present church members were stimulated to think of the mighty acts of God in the past.

> Within the church everything symbolized some aspect of the Divine economy. The altar was Christ's tomb; the sanctuary stood for the unseen

heavenly sanctuary; the bishop's throne in the apse behind the altar was where Christ sat with the apostles and it prefigured his coming again in glory (the *parousia*).[23]

Such an evocative environment, and

> the drama of the rite, the music and responses added over the years, all had their place in conveying to the faithful however unlettered the events of the Christian dispensation, and an awareness of their participation in the 'mystery of the faith' and in the cosmic unity of all believers.[24]

But the worship and adoration of God was not confined by space or restricted to corporate liturgies. Anyone could practise the presence of God, anywhere and at any time. Spiritual discipline and submission to the will of God in prayer and thanksgiving was open to all. Although there were differences of emphasis and variations over time in what was stressed as necessary or best for the personal promotion of holiness, in general there was agreement on the core requirements.

> [The] body must be brought under control by constant fasting and prayer, by mourning, repentance, and tears, thus inducing a state of *apatheia* which was not simply the elimination of passions, but an active state of charity and perpetual turning towards God.[25]

In the attempt to practise prayer without ceasing, various invocations of the name of 'Jesus' or 'Lord Jesus' were advocated, which were similar to the later standard form of the 'Jesus prayer', 'Lord Jesus Christ, Son of God, have mercy on me'. Once the state of *apatheia* had been attained, it was maintained by withdrawal into holy quiet or *hesychia*: 'This spiritual silence, this peace of heart, was in its highest form a state of wordless prayer.'[26]

For such a spiritual journey, no hierarchy or mediator was needed. In Byzantium, as in other places and at other times, the holy person, who was possibly ordained but usually not, was specially revered and had a charisma that was unquestioned. Holiness and sanctification were ever-present possibilities for all the faithful. Any person who yearned to achieve sainthood as understood by the Orthodox Church needed motivation and discipline of a high order, but the goal was attainable by all believers.

The extent to which this high calling was realized, or even approached by lay people as a whole, is difficult, if not impossible, to assess. There is much evidence of sins and omissions, there was a widespread survival of pagan rites, and magic was prevalent. Superstition was powerfully present, and Christian beliefs and practices were undoubtedly tinged with non-Christian views and influences. Nonetheless, the church did make considerable efforts to inculcate orthodox opinions, and to implant a desire to follow after righteousness. Children were typically well instructed, either as the offspring of the owners or the servants on country estates, or the residents in the towns and villages. The rites of passage brought the laity into contact with the church, and in the large cities like Constantinople, there were often crowded services, as in Hagia Sophia. Both the cities and the villages had their panegyria, when there may have been spectacular festivities. In the midst of these, the thronging crowds would, at least to some extent, have been touched by the transcendental spirituality of the liturgy. There was a genuine desire by most of those involved in organizing such public acts of celebration to testify to events or saints remembered by the church with gratitude, and the accompanying liturgy and special chants appropriate to the day were introduced as a reinforcement of this intention. The aura of reverence and devotion that was invariably generated was no doubt transmitted to many of the inarticulate majority of the local populace, as well as to the many foreign visitors who were typically present.

The Eastern Churches from the mid-fifteenth century to the nineteenth century

The fall of Constantinople in 1453 ushered in 350 years of isolation and oppression for the Eastern Church. It was deprived of much of its territory, or it was hemmed in on many fronts, in the wake of an advancing Islam. The power and rule of Islam was relentlessly extended.

Wherever they went, the Muslims obliged the subjugated people to adapt their religious and cultural life to accord with the new regime. The lay Orthodox Christians, together with the Jews, were allowed to practise their religion, but they were excluded from citizenship. And the lay Christians suffered acutely. There were no new churches constructed; no church was allowed to ring its bells or display a cross; the systematic training of the clergy was ended, higher education was made impossible, and the schooling of children was cut back to a few rudiments. And, most tragically and calamitously, Christians were obliged to supply the Sultan with slaves from among their boys. The loss of so many of the most vigorous males was a major reason for the evident stagnation of the church in the Christian East.

Russia was to a great extent an exception to this overall gloomy picture. In 1480, she was liberated from the tyrannical rule of the Tartars. She immediately began to flourish, and 'this growth of political power was accompanied by a sense of special vocation associated with the belief in Moscow as the third and last Rome'. At the heart of such a conviction was the belief of the Russian people that they were 'guardians of unpolluted orthodoxy. Linking their history with the glories of antiquity they felt called to world-wide service, failure in which duty would entail divine rejection and punishment'.[27] A monk, Philothey, graphically captured these thoughts in an epistle to Basil III, Grand Prince of Moscow (1505–33):

> The Church of old Rome fell for its heresy; the gates of the second Rome, Constantinople, were hewn down by the axes of the infidel Turks; but the Church of Moscow, the new Rome, shines brighter than the sun over the whole universe. Thou art the ecumenical sovereign, thou shouldst hold the reins of government in awe of God; fear Him who has committed them to thee. Two Romes have fallen, but the third stands fast; a fourth there cannot be. Thy Christian Kingdom shall not be given to any other ruler.[28]

Although by the end of the eighteenth century the Eastern Church was arguably at a very low point in terms of vitality and general health, as the nineteenth century progressed, there were signs of new zeal. The new vigour imparted to the church was made evident in various ways. For one thing, there was the appearance of new Christian role models such as St Serafim of Sarov (1759–1832), and the frail and shy, but saintly and highly intelligent Philaret Drozdov, the Metropolitan of Moscow from 1821 to 1867.

But the real heart of the spirituality of the Russians during the nineteenth century lay with 'the Russian peasantry, those who described themselves as "the dark people" on account of their illiteracy. It was of them that Metropolitan Filaret [Philaret] said, "They have much warmth but little light".'[29] In the delicate task of trying 'to trace the spiritual strand that runs through the warm, "dark" traditions of the Russian people during the century preceding the Bolshevik revolution',[30] due weight should be given to such faithful, almost hidden, and certainly not trumpeted, believers.

The nineteenth century also saw the emergence of national autocephalous churches in the Balkans, and most notably in Greece, Rumania and Bulgaria, as well as in Austria-Hungary.

The twentieth century

In the early years of the twentieth century there was a surge and swirl of new philosophies in the main regions where the Orthodox Church held sway or exercised a considerable influence. Occultism and theosophy and various cosmologies, as well as Marxist ideas, captured many hearts and minds. Each of them created a wide appeal and won many followers. The more intellectually alert and theologically aware lay Orthodox members found themselves amid a welter of competing world-views. Poets such as

Alexander Blok (1880–1921), Andrey Biely (1880–1935), Viacheslav Ivanov (1886–1949), writers like Dimitry Merezhkovsky (1865–1941), Vasily Rozanov (1856–1919), composers including Alexander Scriabin (1871–1915), and painters such as Mikhail Vrubel (1856–1910), Viktor Vasnetsov (1848–1942), Mikhail Nesterov (1862–1942), Nikolay Reirih (1874–1947) and Vasily Kandinsky (1866–1944) were all preoccupied with religious matters. And, among the many intellectuals who wrestled with questions of atheism and Christian belief, four ex-Marxists, Piotr Struve (1870–1944), Sergey Bulgakov (1871–1944), Nikolay Berdiaev (1874–1948) and Simeon Frank (1877–1950) caused a great stir when they were converted to Christianity from materialism and atheism, and joined the Orthodox Church.[31]

The revolution of 1917, and the subsequent attack on the Christians by the new regime, sent shock waves through the whole Orthodox world. Lenin's materialism and belief in historical determinism initially led him to the view that the clergy were merely serving in the church for material benefit, and the laity were simply deluded because of ignorance and as a result of their obsessions and fears. Because of this, the self-evident truth of his teaching would, he and like-minded fellow revolutionaries believed, ensure the demise of the church. So he permitted both religious and anti-religious teaching and propaganda.

The central coterie of Communists were shocked that such a policy utterly failed. Their expectation that the sudden, forceful and violent appearance of a new materialistic and atheistic ideology would instantly and completely destroy the church was not realized. So Lenin and his co-revolutionists resorted to a vicious programme of persecution. It was a traumatic time for a church that had by then become firmly embedded in the Russian culture. But it proved to be a period of renewed strength rather than decline and of greater vigour rather than deterioration and death for the church. The profanation of churches, the murder of several bishops and priests, as well as lay men and women, and the various anti-Christian decrees, strengthened the church by providing martyrs and purged it of unstable or nominal members. It was consolidated and imbued with greater vitality and power. It underwent a revival.

Another Communist ploy was also unsuccessful in putting an end to the church. The authorities hoped that the church would be mortally divided and undermined as a result of a Communist-sponsored so-called 'Living Church Movement', which lasted from 1922 to 1926. The new organization managed to attract a number of ambitious bishops and priests who were lured by the prospect of securing control of the church with the assistance of the Party. But the vast majority of both the clergy and the laity remained faithful to the Patriarch, and 'The Living Church' shrivelled to nothing even with state assistance and protection. The lay people as a whole were adept at distinguishing the genuinely spiritual and authentic faith from that which was spurious. The fiercest assault on the church in those inter-World War years was launched in 1937–39, but others were made after the Second World War had ended.

In spite of all its trials and persecutions, however, the Orthodox Church continued to attract a large number of laity. By the 1960s, the Eastern wing of Christendom amounted to roughly 180 million. All of them had a sense of being members of one church community and tradition, with a pronounced awareness of unbroken historical continuity and a close kinship with former saints, martyrs and teachers.

The value placed on the saints of the past has been misunderstood. These treasured examples of godliness were then, in the 1960s, and have remained, teachers and friends of the faithful, who prayed with the contemporary believers. But they were then, and still are, not regarded as mediators. Despite the fact that some misguided people in every age have had a mistaken attitude to the saints, these exemplary Christians have always been viewed as fellow believers who are able to inspire and uplift the less saintly Christians in their daily search for holiness. Such a looking back to models of belief and conduct has, for the Orthodox, always been part of a life of humble seeking for, and then following, the path of righteousness. It has never detracted in any way from the redemptive and mediatorial role of Christ, except for those who have wrongly understood the place of the saints in the Orthodox religion.

It is the same with worship, and supremely the Eucharist. In fact, there has always been a close link between the cult of the saints and the corporate worship of the Orthodox. It is because of their great sense of the unity in one vast fellowship of all contemporary Orthodox believers with those who have gone before that those distant but not forgotten believers are seen in a very real way as leading the prayers of congregations. For the Orthodox there has been a consistent and persistent stress on the merging of one's own life with that of the whole body of believers, living and deceased, and this is most clearly manifested in corporate acts of worship. Of course, throughout history, this has been supplemented by private devotions, and the Orthodox laity have been taught to pray every morning and evening at home, with a selection of prayers being recommended for this purpose, which have been contained in readily available manuals. But the services in the local churches have always been treasured and supported with a quiet, undemonstrative enthusiasm, as something special. In participating in the liturgy, the laity are made aware that they are guests at a banquet, at which the saints have the place of honour; hence the many icons.

The Orthodox clergy and laity during the whole course of the twentieth century and into the twenty-first century have typically hesitated to define too closely what to them has been the mystery of how and when the bread and the wine are changed into the body and the blood of the Saviour. They have characteristically made little or no attempt to arrive at precise statements, but have been satisfied to receive the gift of the elements as a mystery, as with much else in life. This contrasts with the more rational, more abstract and more authoritarian theology of the West, whether Catholic or Protestant. For the Eastern Christian, whether ordained or lay, whether erudite or illiterate, God, and much to do with the divine, has always been beyond exact human understanding and speculations. The spiritual life on offer has to be received and enjoyed, not analysed and dissected.

The life of worship and prayer has, for more than a thousand years, been exemplified most notably and most famously in the monastic life of Mount Athos. There, many generations of monks have withdrawn from the secular world, with its problems, pressures and entanglements, in order to find peace, space for contemplation, scope for the development of personal spirituality, and an opportunity for unimpeded intercession. Of course, such an environment and way of life is exceptional. The believers in the countless Orthodox churches throughout the world have historically been acutely aware that human salvation takes place within community, and that they are called to be light and salt in the world, relating their faith to their mundane everyday life. They have ideally made their ethical and moral conduct, their care for others, and their attempt to live at peace and unity with their neighbours, an extension of the reconciliation, mutual forgiveness and recognition of their responsibility for each other that the regular liturgy and ritual inside the church building is supposed to inculcate. The one is an expression of the other, and the two are intimately interrelated. Nonetheless, in the Orthodox spiritual economy there is a much honoured and revered place for Mount Athos and all that it represents. There is a universal acceptance by Orthodox Christians that such a set-apart life is the genuine and special vocation for some of their fellow believers. It is perhaps unanimously considered by the Orthodox clergy and laity that the church worldwide, both Orthodox and non-Orthodox, and the secular world (although, of course, it does not know or acknowledge it) would be very much the poorer but for the holy and intercessory lives of these monks in their remote locations.

In view of the long history, and the deep-seated nature of Orthodoxy and its ingrained character in the lives of countless ordinary people throughout many centuries, and bearing in mind the Orthodox holistic conception of the Christian faith as pervasive and powerful in every aspect of life, it is perhaps not surprising that the church proved to be irrepressible despite the Communist efforts to put an end to it. And these attempts to crush it continued in the last three decades of the twentieth century.

The harassment and persecution of the Russian Orthodox Church in the latter part of the twentieth century was both subtle and blatant.[32] The Communist repression continued almost unabated up to the 1990s. Indeed, penetration of the hierarchy seems to have intensified during the Brezhnev-Andropov era. The police clampdown on religious activists persisted.

And this was not restricted to the hierarchy and to the larger, mostly urban churches. Vigilantes were infiltrated into smaller local congregations during divine services. And if any evidence of what was seen as excessive zeal was discovered, pressure was promptly put upon the parish council to dismiss the offending clergy. By such means, the lay people were deprived of the ministry of the more ardent priests. All these measures represented a frontal attack on the churches. But the result once again was not defeat for the churches, but a veritable blossoming of Christianity. There was also the first example in the country of ecumenical cooperation as Christians from six denominations joined in June 1976 to appeal to the Soviet authorities and to the World Council of Churches for an end to state interference and discrimination. And the signatories included many famous Orthodox activists.

Even so, after a few years there was further repression. The 1980s and 1990s saw swings of the pendulum in the government policy towards the churches. Although Gorbachev took the familiar aggressive stance against religion and religious expression, he appreciated the gains to be had from using the goodwill of the laity in order to further perestroika. Freedom of conscience was finally enshrined in law in 1990. In this transition period, parish life slowly revived. In 1988 alone the authorities registered 1,610 new religious communities, 1,244 of which were Russian Orthodox, bringing their total parishes to 6,893, over 4,000 of which were in the Ukraine.

At the end of the twentieth century, the Orthodox Churches of Russia and Eastern Europe represented by far the largest of the five major clusters of world Orthodoxy. In addition to Russia, this included the churches of Serbia, Romania, Bulgaria, Georgia, Poland, Albania and Czechoslovakia, and in total amounted to in excess of 85 per cent of the entire global membership of the Orthodox Church.

The Orthodox Church in Western Europe and the USA

So far, the concentration has been on Eastern Europe, Russia and adjacent regions that may legitimately be regarded as the homelands of the Orthodox Church. Western Europe and the USA provide interesting examples of the problems encountered when such a Christian tradition, that has, to a great extent, been bound up with particular ethnic groups and cultures, attempts to take root and to flourish in a totally different setting. They are both regions outside what can be viewed as the 'natural habitat' of the Orthodox Church.

Western Europe is to a great extent a special, and indeed unique, case. For many centuries it was in touch with the Orthodox Church. Because of its geographical proximity to the territories that from the beginning were the centres for 'Eastern', 'Russian' or 'Greek' Orthodoxy, and because of the chequered relationship between the Orthodox Church and the Roman Catholic Church, Western Europe had some, albeit very limited, links with the Orthodox world. For a long period of time there were even minority Orthodox groups in some Western European countries. And, with the increasing ease of travel in the eighteenth and nineteenth centuries, there was a measure of intercommunication made possible for those wishing to venture further east than was customary on the grand tour. In the course of the twentieth century, this process of interconnection and interaction was greatly increased in extent and depth, and contact, arising out of 'holidays abroad', and through business and other channels, was extended to all classes and groups within Western societies.

Much of this was rather superficial, but it broke the ice, and helped to prepare individuals and groups for deeper and more lasting relationships. The links were further strengthened when large ethnic groups of Orthodox believers started to take up residence in Western countries. Local churches were established, and they became a valued part of the life of the exiles in their countries of settlement. And there was a measure of contact between the Orthodox settlers and host society Christians. In addition, and for a combination of possible reasons too complex and unfathomable to attempt to unravel at present, there has been a recent and mounting tendency for a small number of students, or other intelligent young Western people, to become interested in Orthodoxy.

The USA is not in quite the same situation, largely because the distinctive geographical and ecclesiastical factors just mentioned for Western Europe do not apply, but also because of the special circumstances of that massive country. From the early days of European settlement, but much more noticeably in the nineteenth and twentieth centuries, Orthodox believers, in their attempts to establish a strong presence in America, had to grapple 'with a bewildering array of ethnic divisions complicated by ambiguous ties to European homelands'.[33]

Russian Orthodox monks were active in North America, in what is now Alaska, as early as the 1790s, working sporadically among the Eskaleutian tribes. Then, in the late nineteenth century, there was a large influx of Orthodox believers, with the consequent establishment of many new Orthodox congregations, at first in certain large port cities and then in other major urban areas. In 1905, Bishop Tikhon Bellavin transferred his see from San Francisco to New York in order to minister more effectively to the centres of Russian settlement, which were largely in the east. He encouraged greater lay participation in the councils of the church, and in the following year he convened the first All-American Council, as an initial step in a move to consolidate and increase cooperation among the Orthodox in North America.

To an extent, these worthy efforts to produce unity were thwarted by the Russian Revolution of 1917. The American Russian Orthodox Christians rapidly became divided. There were those who were fiercely anti-Communist and tenaciously ethnic, who continued to adhere to the Russian Orthodox Church in its traditional form. And there was another group, the Patriarchal Exarchate, which was totally loyal to the Patriarch of Moscow. But he, in his turn, was compelled to tow the line dictated by the Kremlin. The third and largest group, which became known as the Metropolia, had a somewhat ambiguous allegiance to the Patriarchy of Moscow. It, more than any other of the Orthodox bodies, adapted to the cultural values and norms of American life. In 1970, the Patriarch of Moscow granted it an independent status (autocephaly), and it quite readily changed its name to the Orthodox Church in America. It later tried valiantly to provide a spiritual home for Orthodox believers who were outside the Russian immigrant community.

It was mainly due to the strenuous efforts of the Greek Bishop Meletios Metaxakes, who itinerated in the USA from 1918 to 1921, and to the ministry of Athenagoras Sperou, the head of the Greek Orthodox Church in the United States from 1930 to 1949, that the huge Archdiocese of North and South America came into existence. By the 1980s it numbered about 2 million and was the largest Orthodox body in the Americas. Although, in common with other Orthodox Churches, this membership represented ethnic identification rather than active participation in church life for many of those listed, the statistic is impressive, and gives a measure of the lay loyalty the church commanded.

9

The contemporary lay scene in worldwide Christianity

In making an assessment of the contemporary role and function of the laity in global Christianity, and the potential for constructive and useful change and development, it is helpful to distinguish four separate but inter-related church situations and spheres of operation. There are, first, those churches that are in a somewhat unhealthy state, most notably in continental Europe and Britain, where a greater involvement of the laity in church life could be regarded as desirable, or even as a life-saving necessity. Then, second, there is the deeply rooted, pervasive and still highly influential Christianity of the USA. Third, there are the churches in the Southern regions of the world, and especially in Latin America, sub-Saharan Africa and certain countries of Asia, where Christianity is well and truly on the move, where there is outstanding Christian energy displayed, and where there are sure signs of spiritual vitality. But even in the midst of such spiritual buoyancy there remain questions concerning the extent and type of lay contributions to the life of churches that are actually being made, and what changes may reinforce and enhance even further what the laity is already doing. Fourth, there is the impact of Pentecostalism and the charismatic movement worldwide, with its distinctive views on 'every-member' ministry. And, last, there is the question of how far, in all regions of the world, lay Christians are being equipped for witness and appropriate Christian conduct, not only within the institutional churches, but also, and perhaps most importantly, in the home, among relatives and friends, in the neighbourhood and in places of work.

The laity in regions where the churches are in decline

Christianity in Europe and in Britain both gains and suffers from its long history, and from the culture it has nurtured, or that has accompanied its emergence. The gains are obvious. There is the unbelievably rich inheritance of cathedrals, abbeys, minsters, churches, chapels and other places of worship. There are all the inexpressibly magnificent works of art, music and literature that have been inspired and moulded to such a great extent by Christianity and, in so many cases, owe their very existence, and their form and content, to the Christian faith of their creators. And there is the unutterable splendour of the accumulated musical compositions and Christian writings, which are so readily available to the current generation of people. All these assets are priceless and irreplaceable. They are individually and collectively an invaluable legacy. They can touch deeply the minds and hearts of contemporary men and women, and even children, and can plumb the depths of human emotions and sensibilities. They can powerfully stimulate and promote an awareness of the divine dimension in life; and they have a great ability to convey what Christianity has to offer. But there is a down side.

The institutional church, which is to a great degree the most obvious and prominent guardian of these gifts from the past, can so easily be viewed by non-church 'outsiders' as caught up in a time warp, in a world whose beliefs and values have passed away. The present forms of worship, the language used, the dress of the clergy and the whole paraphernalia and ethos of the churches, and more especially the mainline, historical, territorial, 'conformist' churches, can so readily be a barrier to those who are searching for the true meaning of the faith. The relevance of the churches to such outsiders, who live in the new age of computers, other forms of technology and space exploration, and who are accustomed to lifestyles that conform to ever-changing attitudes, can be undermined and lessened rather than promoted and strengthened by these various iconic items from the distant past. The stranger to Christianity can be deterred from consideration of the faith and its personal relevance by what often has the appearance of a deliberate and obvious emphasis on expressions of the faith that originated in a time long ago and that has an inherent 'feel' of the past about it. The current proclamation of Christianity can be hindered rather than helped by such a Christian public face. The medium can so readily be the message; and the form and setting for the declaration of the Christian faith can be an obstacle rather than an effective channel in conveying what is intended. At a time of rapid and stupendous change in all spheres of life, when flexibility and adaptability are so widely conceived as necessary for a full and fulfilling life, that which appears to be static, archaic and stuffy can readily be decried and discounted.

There are also, more specifically, the large number of manual workers and others, whose origin can be traced to the so-called industrial and agricultural revolutions of the eighteenth and nineteenth centuries, who have never been drawn into the life of the churches and chapels. Institutional Christianity in the overwhelming majority of cases has not lost contact with this huge section of society; it has never established a meaningful connection and rapport with it in the first place or at any stage. Formalized Christianity has rarely been an integral part of the life of the vast majority of residents in the 'down-town' areas of the massive industrial conurbations and cities of the land. The inhabitants of such uncongenial places have never had much involvement with 'the church', or indeed 'the chapel', and only very few of them have ever been actively engaged in its life and witness. And it is still so today. For most of them, church and chapel life is something unknown and remote. Only a very small minority of them ever step across the threshold of a place of worship except, perhaps, on the occasion of a funeral. Even the other rites of passage that might, until quite recently, have brought them into contact with a place of worship have to a marked degree been squeezed out of their lives. Baptisms are becoming ever less common, and weddings are rapidly being 'secularized', without any meaningful reference to Christianity or any involvement of a church.

From the Christian point of view, the remarkable advance of atheism and agnosticism has also helped to worsen this unsatisfactory situation. The history of these two philosophies is too complex to be summarized in the context of the present book. It is sufficient to draw attention to the increased acceptance in modern times of both as either vague, often unarticulated orientations that help to colour outlooks on life, or as more precise guides to be embraced as personal creeds. Some of the most brilliant scholars of the past two centuries, and an untold host of lesser academics, together with countless men and women from every strata of society in every country of the Western world, have based their lives on such ideologies and have propagated their beliefs with increasing effectiveness. The result is that the atheistic or agnostic outlook on the world and on life now commands considerable respect and widespread acceptance. It permeates the contemporary Western world; it helps to form attitudes and opinions, to an astonishing degree; and it tends to encourage a widespread disregard for Christianity, or at any rate the institutional expression of that faith.

Within the churches themselves, there has been a great transformation in the role and function of the Christian clergy and ministers. Increasingly during the last 150 years, their place and purpose within society has become less well defined, until now, when it is very obscure. This is a result of two connected developments. First, the churches themselves have become less accepted and respected bodies in society. This means that the clergy and ministers are no longer regarded locally or nationally as having the same status as the representatives of individual and societal beliefs, values and conduct, as was once the case. Second, the state, local authorities, the social services and an abundance of voluntary charitable and other bodies have taken over many of the former spheres of clergy activity. This has helped to marginalize both clergy and ministers as authoritative figures in society and as fulfillers of needed or valued functions. Their accepted place in society has shrivelled to an alarming degree. Their role has been greatly diminished. It has, to a great extent, become restricted to 'church' or 'chapel' activities, such as the conducting of services. And this is where lay men and women come into the frame.

A corollary to the erosion of the role and function of the clergy and ministers is that far too often those who are ordained, or set apart, for the 'full-time ministry' cling, at times almost desperately, to what appears to them to be the remaining authority and control they possess, and in doing so they try to keep the reins securely in their own hands. In a quite high proportion of cases they seem to exert what influence they still retain, by monopolizing the main strategy and policy-making responsibilities of the local church or chapel and the decision-making in reference to important ministerial matters. They then all too frequently think they have fully co-operated with the laity and engaged them in church activities, when they have assigned to some of them duties concerned with money, management and maintenance, rather than with mission or pastoral care in any explicit organizational or strategic form. There is often an appearance of sharing with the laity in the devising of a policy and strategy in reference to evangelism, pastoral ministry and social action; but in effect this far too commonly cloaks the actual exercise of control by the incumbent or minister. In too many instances mere lip service is given to full lay participation. As part of the clinging-on process, clergy and ministers all too typically appear to be over-cautious in sharing true leadership with the lay people or in giving them full and unfettered independence, and even fearful to do so. They tend more characteristically to allocate only somewhat routine matters to lay men and lay women, which smacks over much of 'keeping them in their place', however much this restrictive practice is disguised. Such apprehension is fully understandable. There are, of course, real risks in any devolution of power and authority. But the extent to which restraint or fear overcomes boldness and launching out in faith is regrettable, and highly detrimental to the work of the churches.

The current circumstances in the countries of continental Europe and in Britain cry out for greater and genuine lay participation. This is especially so when funding makes it impossible to supply what many would consider an adequate number of clergy and ministers. It is arguable that, at any time, but especially in the kind of situation that has developed in the West, the main and most valuable function of the professional priesthood and ministry is to mobilize, equip, empower and deploy the laity. The 'professionals' are uniquely placed to undertake such a task. By means of prayer, encouragement, training, cooperation on an equal footing with the laity in deciding upon ministerial policy and the possibility of new strategies, and by offering opportunities for uninhibited and satisfying service, they can enable a liberated laity to exercise their God-given talents to the full. This should apply to evangelism, pastoral care, help to the needy in their area, and almost every aspect of local church life. Such ministerial conduct and service to the laity should also assist lay people to meet their obligations as Christians in their all-important places of employment, in the midst of their families and in their friendship networks.

The full, unfettered exercise of such a role by clergy and ministers could transform many rather staid, and perhaps somewhat self-satisfied, congregations, which rest, rather too comfortably, on what the clergy or ministers can do for them, and could weld them into a powerful force for good and for the service of God. Of course, this would be an uneasy and in many respects disturbingly transformational process for all concerned, both ordained and lay. But it could revolutionize church life in a good and creative way. And, as a secondary consequence, it could immeasurably bolster the sense of worth of the clergy and ministers concerned, and enrich their own ministries. Such an outcome would almost certainly ensue as they worked together with the laity as equal partners in realizing something of the boundless scope for promoting the faith in their particular patch, as well as in the circles in which the laity move when not engaged in 'church' activities, as usually defined. Then, as a final potential fruit from such a reinvigorated, outward-looking church or chapel life, there could come a much fuller support for work in other parts of the world, by means of prayer, personal and church contact and friendliness, financial assistance, and perhaps in other practical ways.

Understandably, this approach to the very character and functioning of local churches will appear to many congregations as far too radical. And 'it would be a mistake to underestimate the staying power of old attitudes or the strength of conservatism within the churches'.[1] Changes that are taking place in various churches in mainland Europe and the United Kingdom along the lines just indicated are not widespread and common. They are scattered and exceptional, and the future trend is not clear. The introduction of such church-transforming principles and practices may largely depend on the degree to which the Western churches are prepared to listen to, and follow, the example being set by the generally far more flourishing churches in the Southern part of the globe.

A thorough unfreezing of the laity can and will only take place when the desirability of such an all-member approach is realized and earnestly pursued by the churches as a whole and by the ordained or set-apart leadership in particular. If it comes about merely because of expediency, or as a knee-jerk reaction to financial or other pressures, it is liable to be half-heartedly adopted, and to be insubstantial and short-lasting. There must be a widespread and passionate conviction of its rightness, and a deep and profound determination to embrace it, come what may, if true and permanent change is to be introduced.

Those parts of the world where the church has become weary, static and unadventurous and in urgent need of reinvigoration appear to be the very places where

> the laity have become marginalized and are in need of liberation from the systems which keep them there. The Christian faith and the practice of ministry have come to be the province of the clergy. That is an untenable position, inherently contradicting central teachings of the faith itself.[2]

It needs to be remedied as part of a programme of reform and renewal.

Allied to this devaluing and under use of the laity is a far too typical congregational mindset that is inward-looking. There is too often, in varying degrees, an unhealthy preoccupation with local church domestic matters, and a far from open and warm attitude towards strangers and visitors. All too frequently a church fellowship is regarded consciously or unconsciously by its members as a sort of closed club of long-familiar friends who obliquely, or very explicitly, resent the incursion of strangers, or at least give them a far from hearty welcome. Newcomers are not expected. The message conveyed is that the church is for the existing members, and additional men, women and children will only be admitted if they can break through the barriers erected. The misted-up glass case at the entrance announcing '8 a.m. HC BCP; 10.30 SE CW Order One', accompanied by a note that Jean would like names for this, and Joan requires helpers for that, together with an in-joke or two, transmits the feeling that the church is essentially a cosy cluster of friends who even resent and resist the possibility of additional members joining them. So often the response to a new face is at best surprise, at worse coolness or even hostility. In August 2006, a *Church Times* columnist attended a service in what was for him a new church. At its conclusion he handed in his hymn and service books and hovered near the coffee table. A woman approached him. 'I'm afraid coffee's only for regulars, dear,' she said.[3] What a contrast to the kind of friendliness of so many of the churches in areas of vibrant Christianity just about to be considered.

The dynamic church in the USA

The contrast between the church situation in general, and the place within it of the laity in particular, in many regions of Britain and continental Europe as just described, and that which prevails in most of the USA is astonishing and difficult to explain. The churches in the USA are not somewhat desperately holding on as they slither ever more downwards numerically, in terms of their quality of life and in regard to the influence they exert. Rather, they are remarkably alive, with the laity playing their part to a great extent. The churches command the loyalty and dedication of millions of Americans, and Christianity permeates the political and social life of the nation to a degree that seems incredible to many people in Europe and Britain.

The religion of the most fervent Evangelical Christians in the 'Bible Belt' of the South and elsewhere stresses personal faith, but it is not kept in a personalized, pietistic straightjacket. Conservative Protestants have been bolstered and greatly reinforced by the impact of Billy Graham, the campaigns of Jerry Falwell and his Moral Majority, and the countless and powerful ministries of pastors and other activists during the last half a century and more. And both Graham and Falwell have contributed to a well-balanced Evangelicalism that has encouraged engagement in social and political life at both local and national levels. Christians as a whole, and especially the Evangelicals, are currently sufficient in number and prominent enough to bring their opinions to bear in the public arena and to ensure that concerns they hold dear are given a full and thorough airing. Such a robust sector of the population cannot be ignored or by-passed by anyone wanting to win the hearts and minds of the people. This has been seen in the 2007 and 2008 programmes and pronouncements of the main contenders for Democratic and Republican nominations for the presidency of the USA.

It is of note that almost all the churches that exercise such undoubted sway, including the long-established Southern Baptists, the Lutherans, the Episcopalians, Methodists, Presbyterians and Congregationalists, together with numerous small sects and denominations, emphasize the importance of full lay involvement in their life and witness. The laity is to the fore. There are many charismatic and immensely influential pastors, but there is not an overwhelming and stifling clericalism. What is taking place in the USA, and in other pockets throughout the Western world, may well confirm the analysis and prediction of some sociologists that the future for Christianity in the West probably lies with the sects and with those denominations that are prepared to be flexible and innovative in their attitudes to church life, and which are able to enthuse and mobilize their lay members.

The USA demonstrates that enlivened and effective forms of Christianity are able to blossom in a highly developed and technologically sophisticated culture. Such vibrancy is not confined to the cultures of so-called 'developing countries'. Even so, it is necessary to look to the South to see examples of such Christian renewal and revival that embrace three continents, that are on a massive scale, and that show signs of probable persistence well into the future.

The laity in Southern territories where the churches are vibrant and growing

There are whole territories, as well as more localized regions of the world, where the vitality, alertness and seemingly boundless energy and unselfishness of the churches are exceptional. The high quality of their life should not be exaggerated or idealized; but, to an impressive degree, it is in so many cases expressed in the remarkable love and care of members for one another, in the enthusiasm to 'make the gospel known', and in a sacrificial offering of service to the poor and deprived outside the comfort zone of their own fellowship. A considerable number of widely dispersed outstanding churches in continental Europe, Britain, Canada, Australia and New Zealand display these marks of vitality, but they are not typical features of the Christianity in these countries and continents taken as a whole. Such distinguishing hallmarks are far more common in Latin America, sub-Saharan Africa and certain countries in Asia. And it is of note that in virtually all of these zones, wherever the types of local churches just briefly described are to be found, lay people make their own distinctive and incredibly powerful and significant contributions to what is going on.

With the exception of the USA, all the regions where the churches in great numbers are prospering most are in the Southern part of the globe. This is the outstanding new fact in the landscape of world Christianity.[4] As early as the 1970s, some observers identified this major shift in where the new and vast body of laity was to be found, and where they were conspicuously more integrated into the churches as dedicated and active members. Prominent among these perceptive analysts was Walbert Buhlmann. He expressed the view that 'the migration of the Church towards the southern hemisphere' offered scope for the emergence of what in effect constituted 'the Church of the future as well as the future of the Church'.[5]

The transfer of the focus of global Christianity from the North to the South means that 'the majority of the Christians in the world are now found living in contexts of poverty, even if all of them do not share in personal poverty'.[6] Such, mostly underprivileged territories represent two-thirds of the world, and 'Two-Thirds World' is a term the residents of these lands frequently prefer to other terms, such as 'underdeveloped' or even 'less developed'. In sub-Saharan Africa, as in Latin America and certain countries of Asia where some of the world's most enlivened and vibrant churches are located, it is to a great extent the poor who find salvation and consolation in the gospel. 'They can read the Bible and experience, in the midst of their poverty and powerlessness, the reality of the power of the Kingdom of God through faith in the Jesus who, in order to save the world, became poor.'[7]

Among such lay people, and indeed for others who are not yet committed Christians, Christianity is 'being seen increasingly as involving the participation of people who are not academic and professional theologians',[8] or indeed are not so evidently privileged materially, educationally and culturally as are so many of the church members in much of the Western world. The warmest and most winsome church fellowships are those that focus on basic human needs and deeply felt human aspirations, and that attempt to confront these and engage with them in the name of Christ, who was himself the friend of all, and not least of all the poor. And this approach to the ministry and nature of the local church helps to determine the whole outlook and lifestyle not only of individual Christians, but of church fellowships as well. It is also influential in moulding the Christian ideal for the type of society that most truly reflects Christian values. In the words of the Indian Samuel Rayan:

> It is likely that the greater the part played by the poor in insighting and articulating the meaning of the faith for today, the lesser will be the use of sophisticated scientific meditations and erudite language. Should not theology be expressed more and more in art forms – in dance and drama, in pictures and lines, in carving and sculptures? It should become embodied above all in new and beautiful relationships, in deeds of love, and finally in the new social order itself, in the beauty and shape of the just and free and equal fellowship of God's children and Christ's friends.[9]

The Pentecostal churches and the charismatic movement

Whatever reservations many people have about the Pentecostal and charismatic movements, with all their faults and failings, they have had an enormous impact on the thinking and on the lives of Christians worldwide, not least of all in the Western churches. And central to this has been at least the beginnings of a new look at the role and function of the laity. The movement

> has been one of the most prominent forces in fostering in wide swathes of Protestantism, especially evangelicalism, a broader participatory base in worship and ministry. Congregations admitting to no charismatic convictions sing charismatic songs. Fixation on spiritual gifts has rubbed off on mainliners in the form of heartier recognition of all- or multi-member ministry.[10]

For many non-Pentecostal churches, the challenge is not a call to slavish copying of Pentecostal or charismatic models, for that would be almost totally undesirable and unacceptable, and would be foolish and impracticable. But it is an invitation to non-Pentecostal churches to learn from them and, while being true to themselves, to seek in all earnestness to remedy some of their own shortcomings by taking on board transferable and applicable strengths, albeit in a modified form. The non-Pentecostal churches should be open to the possibility of being encouraged and stimulated by what their probably more exuberant brothers and sisters in the faith have to teach them.

And perhaps the greatest of all these lessons is the huge stress on the laity. The growth of the Pentecostal churches may have been due to many causes, but not least was the fact that they were predominantly lay in membership and in leadership.[11] All the Pentecostal churches rely heavily if not entirely on lay men and women for their very survival. They have ministries, but they are not hierarchies. Those designated as ministers quite typically undertake secular work and, in parallel with that, help to 'equip the saints for the work of service'. As a generalization, it is fair to say that the Pentecostal churches have evolved and revolved around the laity; whereas many of the non-Pentecostal churches have had an equivalent dependence on their ordained ministers quite often within a hierarchical structure.

The Reformation emphasis on the priesthood of all believers may have 'promised a reversal of the Roman Catholic conception of ministry and in principle laid the ground for it'.[12] But this has not been realized, or at least not been allowed to blossom to its full potential. In essence, clericalism has held sway in almost all the Protestant churches.

> Most Protestant denominations have been as priest-ridden as the Roman Catholics. It is the minister, vicar, or pastor who has dominated the whole proceedings. In other words, the clergy–laity divisions have continued in much the same way as in pre-Reformation times, and the doctrine of spiritual gifts and body ministry have been largely ignored.[13]

This may somewhat overstate the lack of change that has taken place in the last four hundred years, and many clergy and others may hotly contest what is asserted, but it surely resonates with many Protestants who are open to honest appraisals.

The Pentecostal and charismatic unwillingness to emphasize differences between lay and ordained Christians, the resultant great importance given to Christian community life and the obligation laid on all believers to play a full part in the life of the local church, have impacted on other denominations and on Christian thinking generally. Some Christians understandably, but unfortunately, view such revolutionary doctrines and practices as a threat to the special, but diminishing, role of the ordained priests and ministers in mainline non-Pentecostal denominations. Even so, regrettable as such defensiveness and such a feeling of having their status undermined may be, the new thinking, which owes much to the Pentecostals and charismatics, is well established and thriving in the Christian world of the early twenty-first century. And it does not look like going away, at least in the near future, but rather spreading and becoming more widely accepted. Such unfamiliar thinking and forms of church life should not be ignored or dismissed out of hand by churches that are locked into other Christian traditions.

For some decades now Christians from all over the world have questioned the respective roles of the ordained members of the church and the laity. The debate has become more intense as it has become more internationalized. Two responses to the WCC 1981 report *The Church is Charismatic* illustrate this readiness to consider new ideas and perspectives. The United Church of North India thought that basic issues should be honestly confronted:

> Should we not recognize that the celebration of the eucharist before it became the preserve of the ordained ministry was the legitimate and natural function of the layman and that structural hierarchical ordination bottled up the Holy Spirit with the laying-on-of-hands of ministers (order) with all the succeeding wrangles of 'apostolic succession' and the loss of charisma?[14]

The Church of the Czech Brethren, with equal forthrightness, declared that 'wherever the concept of the charismatically renewed congregation is thought of, the concept of the one-man leadership in the congregation is as well problematized'. Wherever the charismatic congregation prayed for the fullness of the gifts of the Holy Spirit, the problem of the one-man ministry came to the fore. 'In this new concept the pastor becomes only one of the many gifted members of the congregation.'[15]

For the churches in the areas where Christianity is flourishing, there is generally no great problem in such teaching. The leaders are generally not inordinately protective of their own 'rights' and status, and the members of local churches treat all-member participation in every aspect of church life as a desirable and normal *modus operandi* which in no way compromises or lessens the importance and value of what should be provided by the ordained leader, when there is such a person. But in areas such as continental Europe and Britain, where the churches are struggling to hold their own, the 'all-member' ministry notion is more severely questioned, and even tacitly, if not explicitly, discarded, or conveniently not addressed. This is in a way ironic, because such disregard of full lay involvement occurs in the very kind of situations where a new, imaginative and dynamic approach along these lines may be most dramatically effective.

In contrast to the prevailing situation in the West, it is in the Southern regions of the globe, where the churches have so successfully mobilized the laity, that countless poor and deprived people are joining the churches. These folk include marginalized members of underprivileged urban areas who are suffering from anomie and lack of community, who have few material possessions, and who have low self-esteem. Such self-confessed needy people are finding a sense of belonging, an awareness of being respected by others, and a thrilling sensation of personal liberation and life-enhancing personal endorsement as they a function within church groups. The very fact that such churches are lay-focused makes the outsider feel warmly welcomed.[16] It has rightly been said that 'the mission field for most Pentecostals is among the poor. According to existing studies, the areas of greatest growth among Pentecostals are urban shantytowns and, to a lesser extent, rural peasant communities.'[17]

Characteristics of the flourishing churches of all types

In order that less flourishing churches might benefit from the experiences and models of flourishing churches, it is critical to pinpoint the ways in which the laity are in practice making their contribution to local and regional church life.

Of supreme importance seems to be united as well as individual prayer. In almost all, if not all, the kind of churches so far identified that have the most abundant and fruitful ministries, prayer is given top priority. It is clear beyond any doubt that the Christians of Singapore 'believe that intercessory prayer is not meant to be . . . [their] last resort, but . . . [their] first response to any situation'.[18] The lay Christians in that not easy situation, where they are achieving so much, underpin all that they do with prayer. 'They encourage private prayer, *closet prayer* as they sometimes call it. They encourage *cluster prayer* as a small group gets together to intercede. This can include prayerwalking and prayer triplets.' In addition, 'they encourage *congregational prayer* – times when the congregation meets for intercession. And they make good use of *concerts of prayer*, bringing together churches from a variety of backgrounds to praise the Lord and pray for the city and the country.'[19] Many of the more reserved and more circumspect Western Christians may regard this as immoderate and excessively zealous, but it has to be acknowledged as a fact. In a way that it is difficult, if not impossible, to explain rationally and intellectually, there seems to be a close correlation between persistent and earnest prayer and thriving church life. The one may not simply produce the other, as day follows night, but prayer does seem to be a vital, if not indispensable, ingredient in the mix for churches with outstanding ministries.

Organizationally, a closer look at the cell arrangement is instructive. In Singapore it is 'the basic Christian community'.[20] Each cell, which comprises between seven and fifteen members, is viewed as a church, a vibrant and multiplying community of believers, set in a neighbourhood so that it can have an impact on that area. Each cell has a leader, who is regarded as a pastor, who always has an assistant. When the cell exceeds fifteen people, it divides into two, with the assistant leader taking responsibility for the new cell. The cells are not uniform – some are for children, some for business people, some for parents with children, others for particular occupational groups such as nurses, or for any group of people with a common feature that predominates in their life situation, whether that be age, their standing in the community, or some other factor. Some bridge any such categories, and consist of a cross-section of society. Usually they have in common a particular location, whether that is their place of residence, a hospital, school, business, army camp or whatever. The cell church pattern continues to be effective in promoting fellowship, teaching, leadership training and evangelism, and it is a stimulus for church planting.

Then, as a further component that characterizes those churches in the contemporary world that are on the march, and are healthy and progressive, is the presence within them of members who display 'vision', which is then translated into action. This God-given appreciation of the potential for a local church to exercise a full and abounding ministry that is relevant to the particular prevailing social context often emanates from the duly appointed leaders of the church; but it is not confined to them. In the type of prospering church under consideration, there is a notable openness to such perception, which might come from any member. It is not just a matter of giving consideration to 'good ideas'. Any insight regarding a possible way forward for the church is typically heard and received with respect, given careful and prayerful consideration, and then, perhaps after some quite long time lapse, acclaimed as acceptable and right and implemented.

Whatever its source, the subsequent putting into action of any suggestion becomes part of the 'mission statement' for that church. The working out in practice of the visionary declaration of good intent inevitably and indispensably for such churches entails the total and enthusiastic participation of all, or the vast majority, of the lay members. The stated goals of such churches are quite usually of a scale and type that both inspires and gains the enthusiastic confidence and cooperation of the entire church membership. And the goals are only achievable if there is a full and united effort in activating and realizing them. Most usually there is a vigorous and harmonious working together of leaders and members as they apply themselves to the fulfilment of their dream, and there is no clinging on to status as a barrier to unencumbered church-wide united action. All talents are needed and all abilities are harnessed and fully stretched in order to achieve what is believed to be the purposes of God for the church concerned.

Christian witness and conduct in 'the world'

In 1963, in the Introduction to *The Layman in Christian History*, Stephen Neill eloquently and pointedly commented on the need for the laity to exercise a Christian influence in the mundane world of family, friends, neighbourhood, employment and society at large. He wrote with conviction and passion about the role of the people of God in his day and generation:

> If the Church is ever again to penetrate this alienated world and to claim it in the name of Christ, its only resources are its convinced and converted laymen. There are vast areas, geographical and spiritual, which the ordained minister can hardly penetrate; the laymen are already there, and are there every day. What happens to society in the future will largely depend on the use they make of their opportunities, of their effectiveness as Christian witnesses in a new and as yet imperfectly charted ocean of being.[21]

In spite of the gender bias implied by the constant gender-specific term used both in the title of the book and in the text throughout, Neill admirably identifies some of the essential components in living out the Christian life in a 'secular' context. And these remain the same about half a century later.

As far as employment, or self-employment, is concerned, there are three essential ingredients. The Christian is first of all called upon to show 'simple personal integrity in all his doings'.[22] This includes carrying out the duties and demands of the work for which he or she receives a salary or wage, or which is undertaken in a voluntary capacity, as efficiently and competently as possible, for the sake of what is entailed and not with an eye to the resulting personal gain. The seeking of a just reward for services rendered is perfectly acceptable; but the concern for such a return must not, for the Christian, ever become more important than the conscientious carrying out of the work itself. Indeed, second, 'the Christian is called always to regard himself as the servant of society, and to estimate the quality of his work as service'.[23] Finally, 'the Christian layman is challenged to think out the Christian significance of his work'.[24] This entails Christians asking questions about the place of their work in the general economy of the society as a whole. It also directs a searchlight on the extent to which the standard of the work performed should be raised merely by virtue of it being performed by a Christian.

It is of relevance to note that around the mid-twentieth century, the churches in the USA started to give great emphasis to the laity. 'Not only the National Council of Churches, but increasingly the giant denominational headquarters' began 'allocating staggering quotas of manpower and magnificent sums of money for lay training of one kind or another.' There were countless 'retreats', lay institutes, lay academies, lay summer schools and other similar agencies for making the Christians more active and useful members of their churches. The trouble with 'so much of this admirably efficient lay programming' was that it was 'so much concerned with the duties of the layman in his local church, and so little concerned with his duties in the office and the plant and the supermarket and the down-town slum'.[25] A right balance needs to be struck.

It follows that the same basic principles with reference to paid or voluntary work should likewise motivate, direct and enrich every other aspect of life. And this raises the matter of the relationship between life within the institutional church, which has commanded much of the attention of this book so far, and the daily life of the laity amid the routines as well as the more important events that constitute the vast majority of their waking and sleeping hours. There should, ideally, be no disjunction. The two spheres of life should interact in a healthy wholeness, without the one being inconsistent with the other. But, more than that, the life within 'the church' should equip and empower the Christian for life outside the institutional church framework. In order to achieve a fruitful interlocking of personal witness 'in the world' and life in the church community, three things are necessary.

First, all lay men and women need to be fired with a concern to make the gospel known by bearing witness to it in their own lives by word as well as by behaviour. All Christians should willingly and joyfully, albeit with fear and trembling, engage sympathetically in discussions about the Christian faith with the people surrounding them who are outside the faith. By their friendship, their willingness to help in time of need, and their general consistency of conduct, but also by speaking out at appropriate times, all Christians should endeavour to communicate the 'good news' to others and attempt to bring them to faith.

Second, every Christian should not only be a member of a worshipping community, but should both receive rich and full spiritual nourishment from his or her church and should be able to invite any outsider to it with the full confidence that it will provide a warm welcome and a strong, attractive challenge to become a believer. The church services and any other church-based activities should be so manifestly genuine expressions of true worship and deep, sincere fellowship that Christians 'in the world' can depend on them to be helpful to any as yet uncommitted relative, friend or work colleague brought to them. They should offer a logical and powerful aid to reinforce, and even bring to a climax and resolution, the Christian testimony of the church member concerned who invited the guest. Dead or moribund churches, or those that do not present a deep sense of the presence of God, can do more harm than good to people who are in any case inclined to be critical. And this touches upon every part of the services of worship, including the friendship of the congregation to strangers in their midst, the awareness they convey of a sincere and deep fellowship that binds them together, as much as a well-conducted service and a sermon that is biblical and finely presented.

Finally, every Christian lay person also needs to be theologically literate. It is essential, if all members are prepared to give an account of their faith, are willing to present the gospel verbally when the opportunity arises, and are ready to answer sincere and intelligent, and often probing, questions, that they should themselves have a considered and balanced understanding of the Christian faith. This emphasizes the need for every church to have its own system for educating and training lay people, or access to such a resource. Of course, the sermons will be a prime means of providing such instruction and of fostering growth in the faith, but a well thought through and ordered supplement to this conventional way of conveying biblical knowledge is well worth considering by every church, or by a number of churches in combination in particular areas.

A neglected subject starts to receive attention

In the last fifty years or so, the importance of the laity appears gradually to have dawned on church historians and church leaders in a more forceful way than had been the case for a very long time. It is not that the laity had been unacknowledged as a vital component in the life of the churches in the past. Their importance could hardly be denied, even by the most bigoted and clerically minded of church people. The new focus was not a totally new thing. But the realization that the laity had to a great extent been placed in a straightjacket, or had at least not been fully engaged in the life of the churches, and that their full potential had not been released, has only recently surfaced. And it is only in the last few decades that such crucial issues have been openly and honestly discussed, with the implications being explored. For centuries the whole matter of an undervalued and underused laity had been more accepted in theory than in practice, and even in theory it had been given little attention. In the last fifty years or so there seems to have been a new awareness that the mobilized laity might be the obvious, readily available, God-given means to help in the revival of lagging churches, and to assist in sustaining thriving churches. The lay men and women are coming more into the limelight; slowly in some regions, but speedily in other places. The benefit to the churches of the full engagement of the laity in every aspect of ministry and outreach is starting to be appreciated more fully than for many centuries. The issue is being considered in a more serious and sustained way, and the theory is not infrequently being put into practice.

Hendrik Kraemer made an important, and indeed seminal, contribution to this process of reappraisal. In his 1958 book, *The Theology of the Laity*, he addressed the church all over the world, because he fervently believed that the theme he was considering cried out for attention. 'The laity or the body of lay-membership of the Church' had, he asserted, 'never in Church History enjoyed the distinction of being treated with care and thoroughness as a matter of specific theological importance or significance.' It had 'been dismissed in passing, by stray remarks or in generalities as e.g. the universal priesthood of believers'.[26] The subject had never been seriously or prominently on the agenda of theologians, church historians or church leaders.

He noted that in the ecumenical discussion that was going on quite vigorously at the time on the topic of the ministry of the church, in as far as it took place under the auspices and direction of 'Faith and Order', was quite patently restricted to comments on the clergy or the body of ordained ministers. This was, he observed, especially striking, because it appeared that that particular department was unaware of the thinking that was 'going on in its sister-department in the World Council of Churches, the Department of the Laity',[27] which had been created in 1954 by the Second (Evanston) Assembly of the Council. He condemned such 'subsidiary treatment or great neglect, by the professional theologians, of the laity as a distinct part of the full scope of the Church, as to its theological place or "locus"', as 'an inexcusable lack and an indication of a partly mis-orientated understanding of the Church in its wholeness'.[28] He conceded that in the preceding decades 'a steadily increasing amount of literature' had appeared and was appearing 'on the place, the significance and the responsibility of the lay-membership of the churches, as a concomitant of the growing appeal to the laity for their commitment to the task of the Church.'[29] Even so, most of such literature was primarily practical. Although some valuable theological comments had been interspersed, 'a systematic attempt at a theological foundation and motivation of the laity's place and meaning, as inherent in the nature and calling of the Church', had to that time not been undertaken.[30]

Kraemer acknowledged that in 1953 the Roman Catholic scholar Father Yves M. J. Congar had published a highly erudite work entitled *Jalons pour une théologie du laïcat*, of which an English translation appeared in 1957, under the title *Lay People in the Church*. But even he used the term *jalons*, that is to say, rough headings or first attempts, and made it clear that he regarded his work as novel and not as definitive. Kraemer made no greater claims for his more modest-sized book. But at least the two of them had fuelled a debate that was just beginning to gain some momentum. In the meantime, there were some commendably bold attempts to relate institutional church life more realistically and meaningfully to the marketplace. Together with the revived theological reflections on such topics, they helped to stimulate thought on how the laity might be usefully engaged in expressing and promoting the faith in the 'real world'.

Of primary and lasting importance in the rethinking of the role of the laity in the church and in the secular world has been the emergence of the new churches of the developing world. And it is well to remember that the missionary movement of the Western world that provided the modern roots for these churches was 'a singularly non-denominational function of international Protestantism of a rather lay and individualistic sort'.[31] Then, as already noted, the indigenous lay men and women of the countries to which the missionaries went were the ones who were largely responsible for propagating the faith. And it is providential for the long-term welfare of the churches in the developing world that it was so. It meant that by the time of the widespread achievement of independence in the middle of the twentieth century, there were large numbers of indigenous Christians to form the basis of lively churches. A measure of the extent to which these lay Christians progressed in their faith, and were able to take on responsibility for their own church life, became quite dramatically evident from about the 1970s onwards. One example will suffice.

The Lausanne International Congress on World Evangelisation in July 1974 was a landmark event. It has been said that to read the official account of it

> is to be transferred from a world of polemics into an international gathering of Christian leaders which can stand comparison with any of the great missionary conferences of the century, whether the Edinburgh conference of 1910, the Jerusalem Conference of 1928 or the Tambaram Conference of 1938.[32]

Half of those present, including 50 per cent of the key planning committee and of the speakers, were from developing world countries. The Congress put the developing world on the map of Evangelical Christianity in a new way. The Lambeth Conferences had, of course, brought together bishops from such countries, but here were more grass-roots leaders and participants, some of whom were lay people, and all of whom represented the laity. It was yet another acknowledgement that Western domination of the worldwide church was over. The event opened the eyes of many church people in the Western world to the thrilling developments that were taking place, especially, but not exclusively, in sub-Saharan Africa, in Latin America and in many countries of Asia.

The World Council of Churches was also deeply touched by what was going on in the developing world, and by the enormous part played in that huge surge forward for Christianity by lay people.[33] In October 1993, the Council's theological quarterly *The Ecumenical Review* devoted an entire issue to the topic of 'Re-opening the Ecumenical Discussion on the Laity'. This was followed up with a plenary session on the *laos* at the 1994 WCC central committee meeting in Johannesburg, South Africa. And, during 1995, there was a flurry of activity in which Harlan Stelmach drafted a discussion document preparatory to a cross-unit exploration on the subject, 'The Whole People of God'. Two papers on the laity by Barbara Schwahn were extensively discussed in 1996. As a consequence of these documents and gatherings, a consultation was convened on the theme 'Towards a Common Understanding of the Theological Concepts of Laity/Laos: The People of God'. Out of this came the publication in 1998 of *A Letter from God to the World: An exploration of the Role of the Laity in the Church Today*, edited by Nicholas Apostola.

Looking to the future

The prospect for further remarkable growth in the number of Christians is staggering (see Table 9.1).

What is perhaps most noticeable about these statistics is the fact that out of the ten countries with the anticipated largest Christian communities, only two are in the Western world. It is but one more indication that Christianity is not just due to survive in what is viewed by some as a post-Christian era, hanging on as it were by its finger nails, but is on the move. And this growth shows no sign of diminishing, but will most probably accelerate.

The trend will continue apace in coming years. Many of the fastest-growing countries in the world are either predominantly Christian or else have very sizeable Christian minorities. Even if Christians just maintain their present share of the population in countries like Nigeria and Kenya, Mexico and Ethiopia, Brazil and the Philippines, there are soon going to be several hundred million more Christians from those nations alone. Moreover, conversions will swell the Christian share of world population.[34]

In the face of many gigantic actual or unpredictable problems due to confront the churches in the future, of which there are plenty of indications, it would be unbelievably foolish if action was not taken on a global and massive scale to mobilize the laity more effectively as an army of witnesses and active church members. All local churches should engage every member in the battle. The present is arguably the most exciting and most promising age for Christian witness and growth ever, with limitless

Table 9.1 The Largest Christian Communities (populations in millions), 2000, 2025 and 2050[35]

Nation	Year		
	2000	2025	2050
USA	225	270	330
Brazil	164	190	195
Mexico	95	127	145
Philippines	77	116	145
Nigeria	50	83	123
Zaire/D. R. Congo	34	70	121
Ethiopia	36	65	79
Russia	90?	85	80
China	50?	60	60
Germany	58	61	57

opportunities for service in an incredibly needy world. It is a situation that demands the fullest possible involvement of the laity in every aspect of Christian life, both within the institutional church structure and beyond that in the daily round of home, work, leisure and neighbourhood life.

It would be a fitting climax to the history of the laity in Christian history if lay people in every quarter of the world in the twenty-first century were to play their full part in helping to renew, revive and re-energize the churches. It would be a worthy culmination of a chequered history if they were able to contribute in full to the work of the Kingdom of God. Perhaps the present age, and what is left of the history of the world and of the church on earth, could be their greatest and most glorious period of service and fruitfulness.

Notes

Preface

1 Stephen Neill and Hans-Ruedi Weber, 'Preface' in Neill and Weber (eds), *The Layman in Christian History*, p. 11.
2 Denis R. Janz (gen. ed.), *A People's History of Christianity*. Individual titles are listed in the bibliography.

Introduction

1 Jim Sharpe, 'History from below' in Burke (ed.), *New Perspectives on Historical Writing*, p. 26.
2 The comments in this section are greatly indebted to Peter Burke, 'Overture. The new history: its past and its future' in Burke (ed.), *New Perspectives*, pp. 1–24. For a review of the most significant landmarks in the emergence of the 'new' history, see Sharpe, 'History from below', pp. 25–42.
3 Vauchez et al., *The Laity in the Middle Ages*, p. xv.
4 Stephen Neill, 'Introduction' in Neill and Weber (eds), *The Layman in Christian History*, p. 15.
5 Neill, 'Introduction', p. 15.
6 Morris, *The Papal Monarchy*, pp. 496–7.

1 From apostolic times to AD 313

1 Floyd Filson, 'The significance of the early house churches', *JBL*, 58, 1939, 109, quoted in Malherbe, *Social Aspects of Early Christianity*, p. 61.
2 Martin Goodman, 'Judaism, the Roman Empire and Jesus. The emergence of the church' in Hastings (ed.), *A World History of Christianity*, p. 18.
3 The comments in this section are particularly indebted to Green, *Called to Serve*, pp. 18–29.
4 See Weber, *The Sociology of Religion*.
5 1 Corinthians 12.22.
6 For the discussion of these terms, see Barrett, *Church, Ministry and Sacraments*; Campbell, *The Elders*; Esler (ed.), *The Early Christian World*; Green, *Called to Serve*; and Lindsay, *The Church and the Ministry*.
7 The comments in this paragraph are indebted to Campbell, *The Elders*, pp. 204–5.
8 1 Thessalonians 5.12–13.
9 Osiek and Balch, *Families in the New Testament World*, p. 217.
10 Osiek and Balch, *Families in the New Testament World*, p. 217.
11 Gillian Cloke, 'Women, worship and mission: the church in the household' in Esler (ed.), *The Early Christian World*, vol. 1. p. 443.
12 Davidson, *The Birth of the Church*, p. 130.

13 Eisen, *Women Officeholders in Early Christianity*, p. 224.
14 Meeks, *The First Urban Christians*, p. 85.
15 Davidson, *The Birth of the Church*, p. 86.
16 Meeks, *The First Urban Christians*, p. 86.
17 1 Corinthians 1.26–29.
18 See Thomas M. Finn, 'Mission and expansion' in Esler (ed.), *The Early Christian World*, vol. 1, p. 298.
19 Bruce J. Malina, 'Social levels, morals and daily life' in Esler (ed.), *The Early Christian World*, vol. 1, p. 384.
20 Osiek and Balch, *Families in the New Testament World*, p. 97.
21 Davidson, *The Birth of the Church*, pp. 104–5.
22 Davidson, *The Birth of the Church*, p. 126.
23 Green, *Called to Serve*, p. 28.
24 See Finn, 'Mission and expansion', pp. 296–7.
25 See Patzia, *The Emergence of the Church*, p. 140.
26 Hengel, *Property and Riches in the Early Church*, p. 35.
27 Hengel, *Property and Riches in the Early Church*, p. 35.
28 For these figures, see Stark, *The Rise of Early Christianity*, pp. 131–2, and also Meeks, *The First Urban Christians*, pp. 10–16. The statistics are quoted in Patzia, *The Emergence of the Church*, p. 141.
29 Goodman, 'Judaism, the Roman Empire and Jesus', p. 22.
30 Adrian Hastings, '150–550' in Hastings (ed.), *A World History of Christianity*, p. 27.
31 Sordi, *The Christians and the Roman Empire*, p. 189.
32 The following brief summary of the life and teaching of Justin owes much to F. L. Cross and E. A. Livingstone (eds), *The Oxford Dictionary of the Christian Church* (Oxford, Oxford University Press, 1957, rev. edn, 1987), p. 770.
33 Eisen, *Women Officeholders in Early Christianity*, p. 70.
34 Davidson, *The Birth of the Church*, p. 297.
35 Lindsay, *The Church and the Ministry*, p. 199.
36 Davidson, *The Birth of the Church*, p. 386, points out that it survived longer in its original form in Ethiopia than anywhere else.
37 *Didache* 8.1.
38 *Didache* 11.10–11.
39 Irenaeus, *Contra Haereses*, III.xi.9 and IV.xxvi.2.
40 Lindsay, *The Church and the Ministry*, p. 213.
41 See Eusebius, *Ecclesiastical History*, V.xvii.3.
42 Eusebius, *Ecclesiastical History*, V.iii.2.
43 *Epistle to the Philadelphians*, 7.
44 See Lindsay, *The Church and the Ministry*, p. 236.
45 Davidson, *The Birth of the Church*, p. 184.
46 Davidson, *The Church and the Ministry*, pp. 197–8.
47 R. Merrifield, *The Archaeology of Ritual and Magic* (London, Batsford, 1987), p. 83.
48 Lane Fox, *Pagans and Christians*, p. 334.
49 Hastings, '150–550', p. 25.

50 Lane Fox, *Pagans and Christians*, p. 271.
51 The following statistics are culled from Thomas M. Finn, 'Mission and expansion' in Esler (ed.), *The Early Christian World*, vol. 1, p. 297.
52 Lane Fox, *Pagans and Christians*, p. 311.
53 Markus, *The End of Ancient Christianity*, p. 107.
54 Davidson, *The Birth of the Church*, p. 315.
55 Frend, *Martyrdom and Persecution in the Early Church*, p. 13.
56 Frend, *Martyrdom and Persecution in the Early Church*, p. 15.
57 For a useful commentary on saints, relics, miracles and pilgrims, see Finucane, *Miracles and Pilgrims*.
58 This section is greatly indebted to Lindsay, *The Church and the Ministry*, pp. 265–361. This is an old work, but still of great value.
59 Frend, *The Rise of Christianity*, p. 398.
60 Frend, *The Rise of Christianity*, p. 404.
61 Lane Fox, *Pagans and Christians*, p. 315.
62 Davidson, *A Public Faith*, p. 12. This is a work to which the present section owes much.
63 Winter, *Seek the Welfare of the City*, p. 202.

2 From AD 313 to the beginning of the medieval period

1 MacMullen, *Christianity and Paganism in the Fourth to Eighth Centuries*, p. 2. The present comments in this section are greatly indebted to this work.
2 Davidson, *A Public Faith*, p. 71.
3 Markus, *The End of Ancient Christianity*, inside cover.
4 MacMullen, *Christianity and Paganism*, p. 151.
5 Davidson, *A Public Faith*, p. 393.
6 MacMullen, *Christianity and Paganism*, p. 153.
7 Sordi, *The Christians and the Roman Empire*, pp. 191–2.
8 Davidson, *A Public Faith*, p. 284. This is a book to which this section is greatly indebted.
9 See Petts, *Christianity in Roman Britain*.
10 Davidson, *A Public Faith*, p. 256.
11 The comments in this section owe much to Davidson, *A Public Faith*, pp. 264–8.
12 P. Hunter Blair, *Northumbria in the Days of Bede* (London, Victor Gollancz, 1976), pp. 142–3.
13 Chadwick, *The Church in Ancient Society*, p. 684.
14 Chadwick, *The Church in Ancient Society*, p. 685. See also S. G. MacCormack, 'Loca Sancta, the organisation of sacred topography in late antiquity' in R. Ousterhout (ed.), *The Blessings of Pilgrimage* (Chicago, University of Illinois Press, 1990), pp. 7–40; and P. W. L. Walker, *Holy City, Holy Places? Christian Attitudes to Jerusalem and the Holy Land in the Fourth Century* (Oxford, Oxford University Press, 1990).
15 R. W. Southern, 'The church of the Dark Ages, 600–1000' in Neill and Weber (eds), *The Layman in Christian History*, p. 94.
16 Davidson, *A Public Faith*, p. 316.

17 The laity in the Orthodox Church will be considered in Chapter 8.
18 This account of the early years of the re-conversion of Britain is taken from Hylson-Smith, *Christianity in England from Roman Times to the Reformation*, vol. 1, *From Roman Times to 1066*.
19 For the origins of Kent and its early history, see Nicholas Brooks, 'The creation and early structure of the kingdom of Kent' in Steven Bassett (ed.), *The Origins of Anglo-Saxon Kingdoms* (Leicester, Leicester University Press, 1989), pp. 55–74.
20 For comments on St Martin's church, and generally on the early years of the Christian mission in Kent, see N. P. Brooks, *The Early History of the Church of Canterbury* (Leicester, Leicester University Press, 1984). This is a book to which this whole section is indebted.
21 Brooks, *The Early History of the Church of Canterbury*, p. 7.
22 Clare Stancliffe and Eric Cambridge (eds), *Oswald: Northumberland King to European Saint* (Stamford, Paul Watkins, 1995), p. 1.
23 B. Colgrave and R. A. B. Mynors (eds), *Bede's Ecclesiastical History of the English People* (Oxford, Clarendon Press, 1969), iii, 3, p. 218.
24 Clare Stancliffe, 'Oswald: Most Holy and Most Victorious King of the Northumbrians' in Stancliffe and Cambridge (eds), *Oswald*, p. 66.
25 Apparently Bede distinguished between the Middle Angles and the Mercians, although it is clear that by this time they were within the dominion of the Mercians. It is not certain where they resided, but it would have been in an area which included Leicestershire and Northamptonshire.
26 Southern, 'The church of the Dark Ages, 600–1000', p. 94.
27 1 Samuel 16.13.
28 Southern, 'The church of the Dark Ages, 600–1000', p. 94.
29 Southern, 'The church of the Dark Ages, 600–1000', p. 96.
30 John Godfrey, 'The place of the double monastery in the Anglo-Saxon minster system' in G. Bonner (ed.), *Famulus Christi: Essays in Commemoration of the Thirteenth Century of the Birth of the Venerable Bede* (London, SPCK, 1976), p. 344.
31 For the eighth-century continental missionary work, see especially George William Greenaway, *Saint Boniface: Three Biographical Studies for the Twelfth Century Festival* (London, Adam and Charles Black, 1955); W. Levison, *England and the Continent in the Eighth Century* (Oxford, Clarendon Press, 1946); and C. H. Talbot (trans.), *The Anglo-Saxon Missionaries in Germany* (London, Sheed and Ward, 1954). For the main primary sources, see Levison, *England and the Continent in the Eighth Century*, p. 2.
32 D. M. Wilson, 'The Vikings' relationship with Christianity in Northern England', *JBAA*, 3rd series, 30 (1967), 37–46.
33 Jolly, *Popular Religion*, p. 39. The whole of this present section owes much to this stimulating book.
34 R. Morris, *The Church in British Archaeology*, Council for British Archaeology, 47 (1983), p. 71.
35 Platt, *The Parish Churches of Medieval England*, p. 3. This is a book to which the present section is greatly indebted.

36 H. R. Loyn, *The Governance of Anglo-Saxon England 500–1087* (London, Edward Arnold, 1984), p. xiv.

3 From the eleventh century to the late fourteenth century

1 Morris, *The Papal Monarchy*, p. 287.
2 Morris, *The Papal Monarchy*, p. 293.
3 Deryck W. Lovegrove, 'Introduction' in Lovegrove (ed.), *The Rise of the Laity in Evangelical Protestantism*, p. 4.
4 See Lovegrove, 'Introduction'.
5 Quoted in Morris, *The Papal Monarchy*, p. 318.
6 Swanson, *Religion and Devotion in Europe*, p. 331.
7 A. Murray, 'Religion among the poor', p. 298, n. 70.
8 Crawford, *Women and Religion in England 1500–1720*, p. 25.
9 Dyer, 'The English medieval village community', 419.
10 Dyer, 'The English medieval village community', 419.
11 Sumption, *Pilgrimage*, p. 12.
12 Sumption, *Pilgrimage*, p. 11.
13 Sumption, *Pilgrimage*, p. 11.
14 See Kümin, *The Shaping of a Community*, pp. 14–15. This is a book to which the present section is greatly indebted.
15 See Blair (ed.), *Minsters and Parish Churches*.
16 Kümin, *The Shaping of a Community*, p. 14. For the context and source of these figures, see W. A. Christian Jr, *Local Religion in Sixteenth-Century Spain* (Princeton, Princeton University Press, 1981); Tanner, *The Church in Late Medieval Norwich*, pp. 2–3; and Brigden, *London and the Reformation*, pp. 24–5.
17 Kümin, *The Shaping of a Community*, p. 14. For the context and source of these figures, see Christian Jr, *Local Religion*, p. 14, and Swanson, *Church and Society*, p. 30.
18 This section is indebted to Morris, *The Papal Monarchy*, p. 295.
19 Beat Kümin, 'The European perspective' in French, Gibbs and Kümin (eds), *The Parish in English Life*, pp. 21–2.
20 The following comments are much indebted to Kümin, *The Shaping of a Community*, pp. 17f.
21 See Drew, *Early Parochial Organisation*.
22 Duffy, *The Stripping of the Altars*, p. 11.
23 Duffy, *The Stripping of the Altars*, p. 91.
24 Morris, *The Papal Monarchy*, p. 307.
25 Morris, *The Papal Monarchy*, p. 308.
26 Duffy, *The Stripping of the Altars*, p. 209.
27 Gervase Rosser, 'The Anglo-Saxon Gilds' in Blair (ed.), *Minsters and Parish Churches*, p. 31.
28 Rosser, 'The Anglo-Saxon Gilds', p. 32.
29 Southern, *The Making of the Middle Ages*, p. 155. This present section is greatly indebted to Southern, pp. 155–60.
30 Southern, *The Making of the Middle Ages*, p. 156.
31 See Geoffrey Chaucer, *Canterbury Tales*.

32 Morris, *The Papal Monarchy*, pp. 314–15.
33 Sumption, *Pilgrimage*, p. 103.
34 Sumption, *Pilgrimage*, p. 103.
35 Finucane, *Miracles and Pilgrims*, p. 196.
36 Duffy, *The Stripping of the Altars*, pp. 186–7. A useful comment on the saints in medieval church life can be found in Duffy's excellent book, pp. 155–205.
37 Finucane, *Miracles and Pilgrims*, p. 39.
38 Sumption, *Pilgrimage*, p. 137.
39 S. Runciman, *A History of the Crusades*, 3 vols (Cambridge, Cambridge University Press, 1951–54), vol. 1, pp. 106, 107.
40 For Urban II's address, in addition to the standard works on the crusades, see especially P. J. Cole, *The Preaching of the Crusades to the Holy Land 1095–1270* (Cambridge MA, Medieval Academy of America, 1991); and P. W. Edbury (ed.), *Crusade and Settlement* (Cardiff, Cardiff University Press, 1985).
41 There are very many modern works on the process of secularization. See especially P. L. Berger, *The Sacred Canopy* (New York, Doubleday, 1957), and *A Rumour of Angels* (New York, Doubleday, 1969); M. Hill, *A Sociology of Religion* (London, Heinemann Educational, 1973); David Martin, *The Religious and the Secular* (London, Routledge, 1969); E. Troeltsch, *The Social Teaching of the Christian Churches* (ET: London, George, Allen & Unwin, 1931); and B. Wilson, *Religion in Secular Society* (Harmondsworth, Penguin, 1966).
42 F. M. Powicke, *The Thirteenth Century 1216–1307*, 2nd edn (Oxford, Clarendon Press, 1962).
43 Moore, *The Origins of European Dissent*, p. 82.
44 Cohn, *The Pursuit of the Millennium*, p. xiii.
45 Cohn, *The Pursuit of the Millennium*, p. xv.
46 Moore, *The Origins of European Dissent*, p. 267. See J. B. Russell, 'Interpretations of the Origins of Medieval Heresy', *MS*, 25 (1963), 26–53, for a full survey of explanations which have been advanced from the mid-nineteenth century.
47 For the Cathars, see Barber, *The Cathars*.
48 See Brooke, *The Medieval Church and Society*, pp. 146–7.
49 For the Waldensians, see Strayer, *The Albigensian Crusades*.
50 Lambert, *Medieval Heresy*, p. 94.
51 See D. M. Stenton, *English Society in the Early Middle Ages* (Harmondsworth, Penguin, 1951; 4th edn 1965), p. 207.
52 Johan Huizinga, *The Waning of the Middle Ages* (London, Penguin, 1965), p. 134.
53 See Stenton, *English Society in the Early Middle Ages*, pp. 206, 207.
54 Duffy, *The Stripping of the Altars*, p. 338.
55 MacCulloch, *Reformation*, p. 6.
56 See P. Heath, *Church and Realm, 1272–1461* (London, Fontana Press, 1988), p. 165, on which these present comments are based.
57 See Heath, *Church and Realm*, p. 166.
58 See A. R. Myers, *England in the Late Middle Ages* (Oxford, Oxford University Press, 1961).

4 From the late fourteenth century to the mid-seventeenth century

1. M. McKisack, *The Fourteenth Century 1307–1399* (Oxford, Oxford University Press, 1959), p. 272.
2. Heinze, *Reform and Conflict*, p. 40.
3. Gerald Strauss (ed.), *Manifestations of Discontent in Germany on the Eve of the Reformation* (Bloomington, Indiana University Press, 1971), p. 219, quoted in Heinze, *Reform and Conflict*, p. 40.
4. Cross, *Church and People*, p. 14.
5. Cross, *Church and People*, p. 14.
6. For the life and teaching of John Wyclif, see H. B. Workman, *John Wyclif: A Study of the English Medieval Church* (Oxford, Oxford University Press, 1926), but also M. Aston, 'John Wycliffe's reformation reputation', *P&P*, 30 (1965), 127–48; A. Hudson, *The Premature Reformation: Wycliffite Texts and Lollard History* (Oxford, Clarendon Press, 1988); A. Hudson and M. Wilks, *From Ockham to Wyclif* (Oxford, Blackwell, 1987); Lambert, *Medieval Heresy*, pp. 247–65; M. Wilks, 'Predestination, property and power: Wyclif's theory of dominion and grace', *SCH*, 2 (1965), 220–36; and M. Wilks, '*Reformatio Regni*: Wyclif and Hus as leaders of religious protest movements', *SCH*, 9 (1972), 109–30.
7. Workman, *John Wyclif*, Bk 2, p. 149.
8. M. H. Keen, *England in the Late Middle Ages: A Political History* (London and New York, Methuen, 1973), p. 235.
9. E. C. Tatnall, 'John Wyclif and *Ecclesia Anglicana*', *JEH*, 20 (1969), 39.
10. For the history, teaching and influence of the Lollards, see M. Aston, 'Lollardy and sedition', *P&P*, 17 (1960), 1–44; M. Aston, 'Lollardy and Reformation: survival or revival?', *JEH*, 49 (1964), 149–70; M. Aston, 'Lollardy and literacy', *H*, 62 (1977), 347–71; M. Aston, *Lollards and Reformers: Images and Literacy in Late Medieval England* (London, The Hambledon Press, 1984); A. Hudson, *Lollards and Their Books* (London, The Hambledon Press, 1985); and Lambert, *Medieval Heresy*, pp. 266–305.
11. See MacCulloch, *Reformation*, p. 35.
12. M. Deanesly, *The Lollard Bible* (Cambridge, Cambridge University Press, 1920), p. 258.
13. Heath, *Church and Realm*, p. 181.
14. Crawford, *Women and Religion*, p. 25.
15. See works listed in n. 6.
16. For the history, teaching and influence of John Hus and the Hussites, see especially, Lambert, *Medieval Heresy*, pp. 306–82, and MacCulloch, *Reformation*.
17. Cohn, *The Pursuit of the Millennium*, p. 206.
18. Cohn, *The Pursuit of the Millennium*, p. 207.
19. The brief summary of the course of the Hussite revolution in Bohemia in this paragraph is greatly indebted to MacCulloch, *Reformation*, p. 37.
20. Brigden, *London and the Reformation*, p. 122.
21. Brigden, *London and the Reformation*, pp. 122–3.

22 See Watt, *Cheap Print and Popular Piety, 1550–1640*.
23 A. R. Myers, *England in the Late Middle Ages* (Harmondsworth, Penguin, 1952; 8th edn, 1971), p. 250.
24 Duffy, *The Stripping of the Altars*, pp. 77–8.
25 Heinze, *Reform and Conflict*, p. 59.
26 Heinze, *Reform and Conflict*, p. 59.
27 MacCulloch, *Reformation*, p. 22.
28 The so-called revisionist historians have been at pains to stress the essentially healthy state of traditional Catholicism on the eve of the Reformation. This interpretation has been presented in a number of important studies, including Duffy, *The Stripping of the Altars*; C. Haigh, *Reformation and Resistance in Tudor Lancashire* (Cambridge, Cambridge University Press, 1975); C. Haigh, 'The continuity of Catholicism in the English Reformation', *P&P*, 93 (1981), 37–69; C. Haigh (ed.), *The English Reformation Revised* (Cambridge, Cambridge University Press, 1987); C. Haigh, *English Reformations: Religion, Politics, and Society under the Tudors* (Oxford, Clarendon Press, 1993); C. Harper-Bill, *The Pre-Reformation Church in England 1400–1530* (London, Longman, 1989); and J. J. Scarisbrick, *The Reformation and the English People* (Oxford, Blackwell, 1984).
29 Scarisbrick, *The Reformation and the English People*, p. 16.
30 Beat Kümin, 'The English parish in European perspective' in French, Gibbs and Kümin (eds), *The Parish in English Life*, p. 22.
31 These examples are cited in Kümin, 'The English parish', p. 22.
32 Brigden, *London and the Reformation*, p. 13.
33 MacCulloch, 'Henry VIII and the reform of the church' in D. MacCulloch (ed.), *The Reign of Henry VIII: Politics, Policy and Piety* (Basingstoke, Macmillan, 1995), p. 160.
34 Tanner, *The Church in Late Medieval Norwich*, p. 167. This conclusion refers specifically to Norwich but also, by implication, to Christendom as a whole with, of course, great variations of detail for each region.
35 Lambert, *Medieval Heresy*, p. 383.
36 Stephen Neill, 'Britain, 1600–1780' in Neill and Weber (eds), *The Layman in Christian History*, p. 191.
37 M. Luther, 'To the Christian nobility of the German nation concerning the reform of the Christian estate' in J. Pelikan and H. T. Lehmann (eds), *Luther's Works*, 55 vols (St Louis, Concordia; Philadelphia, Fortress Press, 1955–86), vol. 44, pp. 127, 129.
38 MacCulloch, *Reformation*, p. 163.
39 E. Gordon Rupp, 'The age of the Reformation, 1500–1648' in Neill and Weber (eds), *The Layman in Church History*, p. 135.
40 For the 'evangelicals' of the period 1517 to about 1530, see especially Brigden, *London and the Reformation*; W. A. Clebsch, *England's Earliest Protestants 1520–1525* (New Haven CT, Yale University Press, 1964); D. Daniell, *William Tyndale: A Biography* (New Haven CT and London, Yale University Press, 1994); A. G. Dickens, *Lollards and Protestants in the Diocese of York 1509–1558* (Oxford, Oxford University Press, 1959; rev. edn, 1982); A. G. Dickens, *The English*

Reformation (London, Batsford, 1964; 2nd edn, 1989); D. MacCulloch, *Thomas Cranmer: A Life* (New Haven CT, Yale University Press, 1996); and MacCulloch, *Reformation*.
41 Brigden, *London and the Reformation*, p. 111.
42 Watt, *Cheap Print and Popular Piety*, p. 322.
43 Lawrence Stone, 'Review of W. K. Jordan, *The Charities of London*', EHR, 77 (1962), 328. See also M. M. Knappen, *Tudor Puritanism* (Gloucester MA, Peter Smith, 1963), p. 380, quoted in Thomas, *Religion and the Decline of Magic*, p. 204.
44 Thomas, *Religion and the Decline of Magic*, p. 204.
45 Brown, *Popular Piety*, p. 262. But also, see R. W. Scribner, *For the Sake of Simple Folk: Popular Propaganda for the German Reformation* (Cambridge, Cambridge University Press, 1981), pp. 3, 4; and Scarisbrick, *The Reformation and the English People*, pp. 164–5.
46 See Thomas, *Religion and the Decline of Magic*, p. 87.
47 Thomas, *Religion and the Decline of Magic*, pp. 327–8.
48 Thomas, *Religion and the Decline of Magic*, p. 88.
49 Brown, *Popular Piety*, p. 262.
50 Whiting, *The Blind Devotion*, p. 147.
51 Rupp, 'The Age of Reformation, 1500–1648', p. 146.
52 See Brigden, *London and the Reformation*, pp. 608–12.
53 For the life of Calvin, see Alister E. McGrath, *A Life of John Calvin: A Study in the Shaping of Western Culture* (Oxford, Blackwell, 1990), and Francois Wendel, *Calvin: Origins and Developments of his Religious Thought* (London, Collins, 1963).
54 See especially Thomas, *Religion and the Decline of Magic*, chs 8, 10, 11, 12, 14–18.
55 Handy, *A History of the Churches in the United States and Canada*, p. 19. This is a work to which the present section is greatly indebted.
56 Handy, *A History of the Churches in the United States and Canada*, p. 21.
57 Handy, *A History of the Churches in the United States and Canada*, p. 21.
58 See especially William C. Braithwaite, *The Beginnings of Quakerism* (London, Macmillan, 1912), and William C. Braithwaite, *The Second Period of Quakerism* (London, Macmillan, 1919).

5 The laity and the birth of the modern age

1 For an account of this historical development, see Jenkins, *The Next Christendom*; and Hylson-Smith, *To the Ends of the Earth*.
2 This section on the sixteenth-century spread of Christianity owes much to Jenkins, *The Next Christendom*.
3 Jenkins, *The Next Christendom*, p. 33.
4 John Walsh, 'Religious Societies: Methodist and Evangelical 1738–1800' in Sheils and Wood (eds), *Voluntary Religion*, p. 288.
5 Sheils and Wood (eds), *Voluntary Religion*, p. 300.
6 Church, *More about the Early Methodist People*, p. 141.

7 For the life and work of the Countess of Huntingdon, see Schlenther, *Queen of the Methodists*.
8 Handy, *A History of the Churches in the United States and Canada*, p. 138.
9 Handy, *A History of the Churches in the United States and Canada*, p. 139.
10 Handy, *A History of the Churches in the United States and Canada*, pp. 113–14.
11 Handy, *A History of the Churches in the United States and Canada*, p. 115.
12 For the life of Wilberforce, see especially Coupland, *William Wilberforce*; Furneaux, *William Wilberforce*; Hague, *William Wilberforce*; and Pollock, *Wilberforce*.
13 For an account of the Clapham Sect and the Saints, see especially James Stephen, *Essays in Ecclesiastical Biography* (London, 1860); and Howse, *Saints in Politics*. For a thorough analysis and critique, see in particular Ian C. Bradley, 'The politics of Godliness: Evangelicals in Parliament, 1784–1832', Oxford D.Phil 1974; Ian C. Bradley, *The Call to Seriousness: The Evangelical Impact on the Victorians* (London, Cape, 1976); and Ford K. Brown, *Fathers of the Victorians: The Age of Wilberforce* (Cambridge, Cambridge University Press, 1961).
14 For the life of Henry Thornton, see Standish Meacham, *Henry Thornton of Clapham 1760–1815* (Cambridge MA, Harvard University Press, 1964). For the life of John Shore, Lord Teignmouth, see Josiah Platt, *Sketch of the life of the late right Honourable Lord Teignmouth* (London, 1834); and Lord Teignmouth, *Memoir of the Life and Correspondence of John, Lord Teignmouth*, 2 vols (London, 1843). For the life of Zachary Macaulay, see Viscountess Knutsford, *Life and Letters of Zachary Macaulay* (London, 1900). For the life of James Stephen, see Caroline Stephen, *The Right Honourable Sir James Stephen, Bart, KCIS* (London, 1895). For the life of Charles Grant, see Thomas Fisher, *A Memoir of the Late C. Grant, Esq.* (London, 1833).
15 For the life and works of Hannah More, see P. Belham, 'The origins of elementary education in Somerset, with particular reference to the work of Hannah More in the Mendips', MA Bristol, 1953; M. J. Crossley-Evans (ed.), 'The curtain parted: four conversations with Hannah More, 1817–1818', *TBGAS*, 110 (1992), 181–211; Charles H. Ford, *Hannah More: A Critical Biography* (New York, Peter Lang, 1996); Robert Hole, 'Hannah More on literature and propaganda', *H*, 85 (2000), 623–33; M. G. Jones, *Hannah More* (Cambridge, Cambridge University Press, 1952); and Susan Pedersen, 'Hannah More meets Simple Simon: tracts, chapbooks, and popular culture in late eighteenth-century England', *JBS*, 25 (1986), 84–113.
16 Jones, *Hannah More*, p. 139.
17 The following comments owe much to Bradley, 'The politics of Godliness', and Bradley, *The Call to Seriousness*.
18 For the life of Thomas Fowell Buxton, see Charles Buxton (ed.), *Memoirs of Sir Thomas Fowell Buxton* (London, 1850).
19 David Hempton, 'Evangelicalism and reform c. 1780–1832' in Wolffe (ed.), *Evangelical Faith and Public Zeal*, p. 20.
20 Bradley, 'The politics of Godliness', p. iii.

21 Bradley, 'The politics of Godliness', p. iv.
22 *Edinburgh Review* (1838), p. 167, quoted in Howse, *Saints in Politics*, p. 131. The comments in this section owe much to Howse's book, pp. 129–31.
23 Nancy Uhlar Murray, 'The influence of the French Revolution on the Church of England and its rivals, 1789–1802', Oxford D.Phil 1975.
24 The following account of the life and work of Joshua Watson and the Hackney Phalanx is greatly indebted to A. B. Webster, *Joshua Watson: The Story of a Layman, 1771–1855* (London, SPCK, 1954). For the life of Joshua Watson, see also F. Churton, *Memoir of Joshua Watson*, 2 vols (Oxford, 1861).
25 Webster, *Joshua Watson*.
26 Webster, *Joshua Watson*.
27 Webster, *Joshua Watson*, ch. 5.
28 Stephen Neill, *A History of Christian Missions* (Harmondsworth, Penguin, 1964), p. 243.
29 Neill, *A History of Christian Missions*, pp. 243–4.
30 Bebbington, *Evangelicalism*, p. 41.
31 Elizabeth Elbourne, 'The foundation of the Church Missionary Society: the Anglican missionary impulse' in Walsh, Haydon and Taylor (eds), *The Church of England*, p. 247.
32 R. I. and Samuel Wilberforce, *Correspondence of William Wilberforce*, 2 vols (London, 1840), vol. II, p. 271, quoted in Howse, *Saints in Politics*, p. 94.
33 For the history of the early years of the Society, see Charles Hole, *The Early Years of the Church Missionary Society* (London, 1896); and Stock, *History of the Church Missionary Society*, 3 vols (London, Church Missionary Society, 1899), vol. 4 (1916).
34 See F. Pascoe, *Two Hundred Years of the SPG* (London, 1901), pp. 831, 832, referred to in Webster, *Joshua Watson*, p. 115.
35 The following comments owe much to E. A. Varley, *The Last of the Prince Bishops: William Van Mildert and the High Church Movement of the Early Nineteenth Century* (Cambridge, Cambridge University Press, 1992).
36 Noll, *A History of Christianity in the United States and Canada*, p. 167.
37 Handy, *A History of the Churches in the United States and Canada*, p. 163.
38 Handy, *A History of the Churches in the United States and Canada*, p. 158.
39 Handy, *A History of the Churches in the United States and Canada*, p. 158.

6 The laity in worldwide nineteenth-century Christianity

1 Heasman, *Evangelicals in Action*, p. 15. This is a book to which this present chapter is greatly indebted.
2 Anne Bentley, 'The transformation of the Evangelical party in the Church of England in the nineteenth century', PhD Durham (1971), p. 334.
3 For the life and work of Lord Shaftesbury, see Georgina Battiscombe, *Shaftesbury: A Biography of the Seventh Earl 1801–1885* (London, Constable, 1974); G. F. A. Best, *Shaftesbury* (London, Batsford, 1964); J. Wesley Bready, *Lord Shaftesbury and Social-Industrial Progress* (London, George Allen & Unwin, 1926); J. L. and Barbara Hammond, *Lord Shaftesbury* (Harmondsworth,

Penguin, 1923); Edwin Hodder, *The Life and Work of the Seventh Earl of Shaftesbury*, 3 vols (London, 1896); and John Pollock, *Shaftesbury: The Poor Man's Earl* (London, Hodder & Stoughton, 1985).

4 See especially Torben Christensen, *Origins and History of Socialism 1848–54* (Aarhus, 1962), P. D'A. Jones, *The Christian Socialist Revival, 1877–1914: Religion, Class and Social Conscience in Late-Victorian England* (Princeton, Princeton University Press, 1968); and also T. Christensen, 'F. D. Maurice and the contemporary religious world', *SCH*, 3 (1966), 69–90.

5 For the lives and work of William and Catherine Booth, see especially Hattersley, *Blood and Fire*.

6 For the life and work of Wilson Carlisle, see Sidney Dark, *Wilson Carlisle* (London, Eyre & Spottiswoode, 1945).

7 Prochaska, *Women and Philanthropy in Nineteenth-Century England*, p. 1. This is a book to which the present section owes much.

8 See *Periodical Accounts relative to the Baptist Missionary Society*, iii (1806), p. 138.

9 Elizabeth Elbourne, 'The foundation of the Church Missionary Society: the Anglican Missionary Impulse' in Walsh, Haydon and Taylor (eds), *The Church of England*, p. 247.

10 This whole section on the work of lay Christians in North America is greatly indebted to Noll, *A History of Christianity in the United States and Canada*.

11 Quoted from the Sunday School Union, *Sixth Annual Report* (1830), p. 3, to which reference is made in Handy, *A History of the Churches in the United States and Canada*, p. 180.

12 Handy, *A History of the Churches in the United States and Canada*, p. 180.

13 Handy, *A History of the Churches in the United States and Canada*, p. 181.

14 Handy, *A History of the Churches in the United States and Canada*, p. 181.

15 Noll, *A History of Christianity in the United States and Canada*, p. 296.

16 William Warren Sweet, *Revivalism in America* (New York, Charles Scribner's Sons, 1944), p. 154.

17 Handy, *A History of the Churches in the United States and Canada*, p. 185.

18 This section is much indebted to Sweet, *Revivalism in America*, pp. 156–9.

19 Noll, *A History of Christianity in the United States and Canada*, p. 314.

20 Handy, *A History of the Churches in the United States and Canada*, p. 208.

21 See E. Franklin Frazier, *The Negro Church in America* (New York, Schocken Books, 1964).

22 See Donald G. Matthews, *Slavery and Methodism: A Chapter in American Morality, 1780–1845* (Princeton, Princeton University Press, 1965).

23 Handy, *A History of the Churches in the United States and Canada*, p. 277.

24 Lewis French Stearns, *The Evidence of Christian Experience* (New York, 1890), p. 366, quoted in Handy, *A History of the Churches in the United States and Canada*, pp. 277–8.

25 Andrew Walls, *The Missionary Movement in Christian History: Studies in the Transmission of Faith* (Maryknoll NY, Orbis Books, 1996), p. 105. See also J. F. Ade Ajayi, *Christian Missions in Nigeria 1841–1891: The Making of a New Elite* (Evanston IL, Northwestern University Press, 1969), pp. 25 seq.

26 For Madagascar, see Bengt G. M. Sundkler and Christopher Steed, *A History of the Church in Africa* (Cambridge, Cambridge University Press, 2000), p. 491; and Stephen Neill, *A History of Christian Missions* (Harmondsworth, Penguin Books, 1964), p. 318.
27 Eugene Stock, *A History of the Church Missionary Society*, 4 vols (London, 1899–1916), p. 235.
28 Robert Hall Glover, *The Progress of World-Wide Mission*, rev. and enlarged by J. Herbert Kane (New York, Harper & Brothers, 1960), p. 152.
29 Glover, *The Progress of World-Wide Mission*, p. 152.
30 See Neill, *A History of Christian Missions*, p. 414.
31 Quoted in Neill, *A History of Christian Missions*, p. 321.

7 The laity in twentieth-century Christianity

1 For the history and characteristics of Pentecostalism, see Hollenweger, *The Pentecostals*; Nichol, *The Pentecostals*; Donald Gee, *The Pentecostal Movement: A Short History and Interpretation for British Readers* (London, Victory Press, 1941); N. Bloch-Hoell, *The Pentecostal Movement: Its Origin, Development, and Distinctive Character* (New York, Humanities Press, 1964); Williams, *Tongues of the Spirit*; and Scotland, *Charismatics and the New Millennium*.
2 Williams, *Tongues of the Spirit*, p. 51.
3 See T. N. Turnbull, *Brothers in Arms* (Bradford, Puritan Press, 1963), p. 90, figures quoted in Williams, *Tongues of the Spirit*, p. 65.
4 See S. Durasoff, *Bright Wind of the Spirit: Pentecostalism Today* (London, Hodder & Stoughton, 1972).
5 The following facts in this paragraph are culled from Williams, *Tongues of the Spirit*, pp. 66–7.
6 The details in this paragraph are culled from Glover, *The Progress of World-Wide Missions*, pp. 366–9.
7 Adrian Hastings, *A History of African Christianity 1950–75* (Cambridge, Cambridge University Press, 1979), p. 26.
8 See J. Massyngberde Ford, 'Neo-Pentecostalism within the Roman Catholic Church', *Dialog* 13/1 (1974), 45–50.
9 Scotland, *Charismatics and the New Millennium*, p. 15, n. 22.
10 Jenkins, *The Next Christendom*, p. 56.
11 Jenkins, *The Next Christendom*, p. 56.
12 These comments are based on Mariz, *Coping with Poverty*, p. 17.
13 Faustino Luiz Teixeira, 'Base communities in Brazil' in Enrique Dussel (ed.), *The Church in Latin America 1492–1992* (Tunbridge Wells, Burns & Oates; Maryknoll NY, 1992), p. 103.
14 Teixeira, 'Base communities in Brazil', p. 103.
15 Green, *Asian Tigers for Christ*, p. 14.
16 Matthew A. Ojo, 'Charismatic movements in Africa' in C. Fyfe and A. Walls (eds), *Christianity in Africa in the 1990s* (Edinburgh, University of Edinburgh Press, 1996), p. 93. This is an article to which the present section is greatly indebted.

17 Ojo, 'Charismatic movements in Africa', p. 94.
18 Aylward Shorter, 'The Roman Catholic Church in Africa today' in Fyfe and Walls (eds), *Christianity in Africa*, p. 23.
19 Hocken, *The Strategy of the Spirit?*, p. 124.
20 Shorter, 'The Roman Catholic Church in Africa today', p. 23.
21 The list is taken from J. and M. Hefley, *By their Blood*. This book, together with Dewar, *All for Christ*, and Craig, *Candles in the Dark*, gives some idea of the extent and range of twentieth-century martyrdoms.
22 John 7.17.
23 Gutiérrez, *Theology of Liberation*, pp. 26–7.
24 H. Assmann, *Practical Theology of Liberation* (London, Search Press, 1975), quoted in Yates, *Christian Mission in the Twentieth Century*.
25 Paul Freston, 'Charismatic Evangelicals in Latin America' in S. Hunt, M. Hamilton and T. Walter (eds), *Charismatic Christianity* (London, Macmillan, 1997), p. 189.

8 The laity in the Orthodox Church

1 This section, and indeed the whole of this chapter, is greatly indebted to Zernov, *Eastern Christendom*.
2 Nicholl, *Triumphs of the Spirit in Russia*, p. 1.
3 Ware, *The Orthodox Church*, p. 40.
4 D. M. Nicol, 'A layman's ministry in the Byzantine Church: the life of Athanasios of the Great Meteoron' in Sheils and Wood (eds), *The Ministry: Clerical and Lay*, p. 141. This is an article to which the present section is greatly indebted.
5 Nicol, 'A layman's ministry', p. 141.
6 Nicol, 'A layman's ministry', p. 141.
7 The following comments are indebted to Istavridis, 'The Orthodox World' in Neill and Weber (eds), *The Layman in Christian History*, p. 279.
8 Istavridis, 'The Orthodox World', p. 277.
9 Istavridis, 'The Orthodox World', p. 284.
10 Nicol, 'A layman's ministry', p. 142.
11 Hussey, *The Orthodox Church in the Byzantine Empire*, pp. 349–50.
12 The word 'liturgy' had, and retained, a double meaning, as it either referred to the eucharistic service or to the church services in general.
13 Istavridis, 'The Orthodox World', p. 282.
14 Nicholas Kabasilas, *The Life in Christ*, trans, C. J. de Catanzaro (Crestwood NY, St Vladimir's Seminary Press, 1974), quoted in Bishop Kallistos of Dioklea, 'The meaning of the Divine Liturgy for the Byzantine worshipper' in Morris (ed.), *Church and People in Byzantium*, p. 7. This is an article to which the present section is greatly indebted.
15 Prokopios, *Buildings*, trans. C. Mango in C. Mango (ed.), *The Art of the Byzantine Empire 312–1453: Sources and Documents* (Englewood Cliffs NJ, Prentice Hall, 1972), p. 76, quoted in Bishop Kallistos of Dioklea, 'The meaning of the Divine Liturgy', p. 8.
16 See Prokopios, *Buildings*, p. 76.

17 Mary B. Cunningham, 'Preaching and the community' in Morris (ed.), *Church and People in Byzantium*, p. 29. This is a work to which the present section owes much.
18 Morris (ed.), *Church and People in Byzantium*, p. 45. See also M. T. Clanchy, *From Memory to Written Record* (London, Edward Arnold, 1979); B. Stock, *The Implications of Literacy* (Princeton NJ, Princeton University Press, 1983); and R. Crosby, 'Oral delivery in the Middle Ages', *S*, 11 (1936), 88–110.
19 Cunningham, 'Preaching and the community', p. 46.
20 Both aspects are well portrayed in P. Hammond, *The Waters of Marah: The Present State of the Greek Church* (London, Rockliff, 1956), chs 5 and 6.
21 In epist. Primam ad Corinth, XXXVI, col. 313, quoted in Bishop Kallistos of Dioklea, 'The meaning of the Divine Liturgy', pp. 13–14.
22 Hussey, *The Orthodox Church in the Byzantine Empire*, p. 351.
23 Hussey, *The Orthodox Church in the Byzantine Empire*, p. 360.
24 Hussey, *The Orthodox Church in the Byzantine Empire*, p. 368.
25 Hussey, *The Orthodox Church in the Byzantine Empire*, p. 363.
26 Hussey, *The Orthodox Church in the Byzantine Empire*, p. 364.
27 Zernov, *Eastern Christendom*, pp. 139–40.
28 Quoted in Zernov, *Eastern Christendom*, p. 140.
29 Nicholl, *Triumphs of the Spirit*, p. 193.
30 Nicholl, *Triumphs of the Spirit*, p. 193.
31 For these examples, see Zernov, *Eastern Christendom*, pp. 202, 203.
32 The comments in the following paragraphs rest heavily on Keep, *Last of the Empires*, pp. 168–71, 304–6, 348–9.
33 Noll, *A History of Christianity in the United States and Canada*, p. 344. This is a book to which the present section is greatly indebted.

9 The contemporary lay scene in worldwide Christianity

1 Deryck W. Lovegrove, 'Introduction' in Lovegrove (ed.), *The Rise of the Laity in Evangelical Protestantism*, p. 11.
2 Crabtree, *The Empowering Church*, p. 45.
3 David Self, 'Church mislays its welcome mat', *Church Times*, 25 August 2006, p. 10.
4 For an account of this phenomenon, see Jenkins, *The Next Christendom*, and Hylson-Smith, *To the Ends of the Earth*.
5 Walbert Buhlmann, *The Coming of the Third Church: An Analysis of the Present and Future of the Church* (Slough, St Paul's Publications, 1976), p. 23, quoted in Kwame Bediako, *Christianity in Africa: The Renewal of a Non-Western Religion* (Edinburgh, Edinburgh University Press, 1995), pp. 127–8.
6 Bediako, *Christianity in Africa*, p. 128.
7 See, for instance, 2 Corinthians 8.9.
8 Bediako, *Christianity in Africa*, p. 186.
9 Samuel Rayan, 'Third World theology: where do we go from here?' in Leonardo Boff and Vergilio Elizondo (eds), *Theologies of the Third World: Convergences and Differences* (Edinburgh, T & T Clark, 1988), p. 138, quoted in Bediako, *Christianity in Africa*, p. 186.

10 David F. Wright, 'The charismatic movement' in Lovegrove (ed.), *The Rise of the Laity*, p. 260.
11 See Green, *Called to Serve*, p. 28.
12 Ogden, *The New Reformation*, pp. 50–1.
13 David Watson, *I Believe in the Church* (Grand Rapids MI, Eerdmans, 1978), p. 253.
14 A. Bittlinger (ed.), *The Church is Charismatic* (Geneva, World Council of Churches, 1981), p. 49, quoted in Wright, 'The charismatic movement', p. 256.
15 Wright, 'The charismatic movement'.
16 See Anna Adams, 'Brincando el Charco/Jumping the puddle: a case study of Pentecostalism's journey from Puerto Rico to New York to Allentown, Pennsylvania' in Cleary and Stewart-Gambino (eds), *Power, Politics and Pentecostals in Latin America*, p. 163.
17 Hannah W. Stewart-Gambino and Everett Wilson, 'Latin American Pentecostals' in Cleary and Stewart-Gambino (eds), *Power, Politics and Pentecostals*, p. 240.
18 Green, *Asian Tigers for Christ*, p. 30.
19 Green, *Asian Tigers for Christ*, p. 31.
20 Green, *Asian Tigers for Christ*, p. 43.
21 Stephen Neill, 'Introduction' in Neill and Weber (eds), *The Layman in Christian History*, p. 22.
22 Neill, 'Introduction', p. 22.
23 Neill, 'Introduction', p. 23.
24 Neill, 'Introduction', p. 23.
25 Gibbs and Morton, *God's Frozen People*, p. 181.
26 Kraemer, *A Theology of the Laity*, p. 9.
27 Kraemer, *A Theology of the Laity*, p. 10.
28 Kraemer, *A Theology of the Laity*, p. 10.
29 Kraemer, *A Theology of the Laity*, p. 10.
30 Kraemer, *A Theology of the Laity*, p. 10.
31 Hastings, *The Church in Africa 1450–1950*, p. 246.
32 Yates, *Christian Mission in the Twentieth Century*, p. 200.
33 This paragraph is greatly indebted to Nicholas Apostola, 'Introduction' in Apostola (ed.), *A Letter from Christ to the World*, pp. x–xi.
34 Jenkins, *The Next Christendom*, p. 2.
35 The information about religious affiliation in this table is based on US government statistics, found in the *Annual Report on International Religious Freedom*, and the CIA *World Fact Book*, and cited in Jenkins, *The Next Christendom*, p. 90.

Bibliography

Only those works particularly relevant to the subject matter of the book have been listed.

Anderson, O., 'Women preachers in mid-Victorian Britain: some reflections on feminism, popular religion and social change', *HJ*, 12 (1969), 476–84.
Apostola, Nicholas (ed.), *A Letter from Christ to the World*, Geneva, World Council of Churches, 1998.
Aston, M., 'Lollardy and sedition, 1381–1431', *P&P*, 17 (1960), 1–37.
Ault, W. O., 'The village church and the village community in medieval England', *S*, 45 (1970), 197–215.
Barber, Malcolm, *The Cathars: Dualist Heretics in Languedoc in the High Middle Ages*, London and New York, Longman, 2000.
Barrett, C. K., *Church, Ministry and Sacraments in the New Testament*, Carlisle, Paternoster Press, 1985.
Bebbington, D. W., *Evangelicalism in Modern Britain: A History from the 1730s to the 1980s*, London, Unwin Hyman, 1989.
Blair, W. J. (ed.), *Ministers and Parish Churches: The Local Church in Transition 950–1200*, Oxford, Oxford University Committee for Archaeology Monograph 17, 1988.
Blair, W. J. and Sharpe, R. (eds), *Pastoral Care Before the Parish*, Leicester, Leicester University Press, 1992.
Blumhofer, Edith L. and Balmer, Randall (eds), *Modern Christian Revivals*, Urbana and Chicago, University of Illinois Press, 1993.
Bready, J. Wesley, *England Before and After Wesley: The Evangelical Revival and Social Reform*, London, Hodder & Stoughton, 1939.
Brigden, Susan, *London and the Reformation*, Oxford, Clarendon Press, 1989.
Brooke, C. N. L., *The Medieval Church and Society*, London, Sidgwick & Jackson, 1971.
Brooke, C. N. L., 'Priest, deacon and layman, from St Peter Damian to St Francis' in Sheils and Wood (eds), *SCH* 26 (1989).
Brooke, R. B., *The Coming of the Friars*, London, HarperCollins, 1975.
Brooke, Rosalind and Christopher, *Popular Religion in the Middle Ages: Western Europe 1000–1300*, London, Thames & Hudson, 1984.
Brown, A. D., *Popular Piety in Late Medieval England*, Oxford, Clarendon Press, 1995.
Burke, P. (ed.), *New Perspectives on Historical Writing*, Cambridge, Polity Press, 1991.
Burrus, Virginia (ed.), *Late Ancient Christianity*, Minneapolis, Fortress Press, 2005.
Campbell, R. A., *The Elders: Seniority within Earliest Christianity*, Edinburgh, T & T Clark, 1994.

Carlson, Eric Josef (ed.), *Religion and the English People, 1500–1640: New Voices, New Perspectives*, New York, Jefferson University Press, 1998.

Chadwick, Henry, *The Church in Ancient Society: From Galilee to Gregory the Great*, Oxford, Clarendon Press, 2001.

Church, Leslie F., *The Early Methodist People*, London, Epworth Press, 1948.

Church, Leslie F., *More about the Early Methodist People*, London, Epworth Press, 1949.

Clark, G., *Women in Late Antiquity: Pagan and Christian Lifestyles*, Oxford, Oxford University Press, 1993.

Cleary, Edward L. and Stewart-Gambino, Hannah W. (eds), *Power, Politics and Pentecostals in Latin America*, Boulder CO and Oxford, Westview Press, 1997.

Cohn, Norman, *The Pursuit of the Millennium: Revolutionary Millenarians and Mystical Anarchists of the Middle Ages*, 1957, 3rd edn, London, Oxford University Press, 1970.

Collinson, P., *The Elizabethan Puritan Movement*, London, Cape, 1967.

Congar, Yves M. J., *Lay People in the Church: A Study for a Theology of the Laity*, trans. Donald Attwater, Westminster MD, Newman Press, 1985.

Coupland, R., *William Wilberforce*, Oxford, Clarendon Press, 1923.

Crabtree, D., *The Empowering Church*, Bethesda, Alban Institute, 1996.

Craig, Mary, *Candles in the Dark: Six Modern Martyrs*, London, Hodder & Stoughton, 1984.

Crawford, Patricia, *Women and Religion in England, 1500–1720*, London, Routledge, 1993.

Cross, Claire, *Church and People 1450–1660: The Triumph of the Laity in the English Church*, London, Fontana, 1976.

Cumming, G. J. and Backer, D. (eds), *Popular Belief and Practice*, SCH 8, Cambridge, Cambridge University Press, 1972.

Davidson, Ivor J., *The Birth of the Church: From Jesus to Constantine AD 30–312*, Oxford, Monarch; Grand Rapids, Baker Books, 2005.

Davidson, Ivor J., *A Public Faith: From Constantine to the Medieval World, AD 312–600*, Oxford, Monarch; Grand Rapids, Baker Books, 2005.

Davies, R. G., 'Lollardy and locality', *TRHS*, 6th series, 1 (1991), 191–212.

Dewar, Diana, *All for Christ: Some Twentieth-Century Martyrs*, Oxford, Oxford University Press, 1980.

Dozier, Verna (comp.), *The Calling of the Laity*, New York, Alban Institute, 1988.

Drew, C. E. S., *Early Parochial Organisation in England: The Origins of the Office of Churchwarden*, London, St Anthony's Hall Publications, 1954.

Duffy, Eamon, *The Stripping of the Altars: Traditional Religion in England c. 1400–1570*, New Haven and London, Yale University Press, 1992.

Dyer, Christopher, 'The English medieval village community and its decline', *JBS*, 33 (1994), 407–29.

Eastwood, Cyril, *The Priesthood of All Believers: An Examination of the Doctrine from the Reformation to the Present Day*, London, Epworth Press, 1967.

Eisen, U. E., *Women Officeholders in Early Christianity*, trans. L. M. Mahoney, Collegeville MN, The Liturgical Press, 2000.

Esler, P. F., *The Early Christian World*, 2 vols, London and New York, Routledge, 2000.
Finucane, R. C., *Miracles and Pilgrims: Popular Beliefs in Medieval England*, London and New York, Routledge, 1977.
Ford, Charles Howard, *Hannah More: A Critical Biography*, New York, Peter Lang, 1996.
Foxe, John, *The Acts and Monuments*, 8 vols, London, George Seeley, 1870.
France, R. T., *Women in the Church's Ministry: A Test-Case for Biblical Hermeneutics*, Carlisle, Paternoster Press, 1995.
French, K. L., 'To free them from binding: women in the late medieval parish', *JIH*, 27 (1996–97), 387–412.
French, K. L., *The People of the Parish: Community Life in a Late Medieval English Diocese*, Philadelphia, University of Pennsylvania Press, 2001.
French, K. L., Gibbs, G. G. and Kümin, B. A. (eds), *The Parish in English Life 1400–1600*, Manchester, Manchester University Press, 1997.
Frend, W. H. C., *Martyrdom and Persecution in the Early Church*, Oxford, Basil Blackwell, 1965.
Frend, W. H. C., *The Rise of Christianity*, London, Darton, Longman & Todd, 1984.
Frend, W. H. C., *Saints and Sinners in the Early Church*, London, Darton, Longman & Todd, 1985.
Furneaux, Robin, *William Wilberforce*, London, Hamilton, 1974.
Gibbs, Mark and Morten, T. Ralph, *God's Frozen People*, London, Fontana, 1964.
Glover, Robert H., *The Progress of World-Wide Missions*, 4th edn, London, Harper & Brothers, 1953.
Grant, R. M., *Early Christianity and Society*, New York, Harper & Row, 1977.
Green, E. M. B., *Called to Serve: Ministry and Ministers in the Church*, London, Hodder & Stoughton, 1964.
Green, Michael, *Asian Tigers for Christ: The Dynamic Growth of the Church in South-East Asia*, London, SPCK, 2001.
Greer, R. A., *Broken Lights and Mended Lives: Theology and Common Life in the Early Church*, reprint, Philadelphia, Pennsylvania University Press, 2001.
Hague, William, *William Wilberforce: The Life of the great Anti-Slave Trade Campaigner*, London, HarperPress, 2007.
Hall, S. G., *Doctrine and Practice in the Early Church*, London, SPCK, 1991.
Handy, Robert T., *A History of the Churches in the United States and Canada*, Oxford, Oxford University Press, 1976.
Hanson, R. P. C., *Christian Priesthood Examined*, London, Lutterworth Press, 1978.
Hastings, Adrian, *The Church in Africa 1450–1950*, Oxford, Oxford University Press, 1994.
Hastings, Adrian (ed.), *A World History of Christianity*, London, Cassell, 1999.
Hattersley, Roy, *Blood and Fire: William and Catherine Booth and Their Salvation Army*, London, Little, Brown & Co., 1999.
Heasman, Kathleen, *Evangelicals in Action*, London, Geoffrey Bles, 1962.
Hefley, J. and M., *By Their Blood: Christian Martyrs of the Twentieth Century*, London, Baker Book House, 1979.

Heinze, Rudolph W., *Reform and Conflict: From the Medieval World to the Wars of Religion,* AD *1350–1648*, Oxford, Lion, 2006.

Hempton, David (ed.), *The Religion of the People: Methodism and Popular Religion, c. 1750–1900*, London, Routledge, 1996.

Hengel, Martin, *Property and Riches in the Early Church: Aspects of a Social History of Early Christianity*, Philadelphia, Fortress Press, 1974.

Hill, Christopher, *The World Turned Upside Down: Radical Ideas During the English Revolution*, London, Temple Smith, 1972.

Hocken, Peter, *Streams of Renewal: The Origins and Development of the Charismatic Movement in Great Britain*, Exeter, Paternoster Press, 1986.

Hocken, Peter, *The Glory and the Shame: Reflections on the 20th-Century Outpouring of the Holy Spirit*, Guildford, Eagle, 1994.

Hocken, Peter, *The Strategy of the Spirit? Worldwide Renewal and Revival in the Established Church and Modern Movements*, London, Eagle, 1996.

Hollenweger, Walter J., *The Pentecostals: The Charismatic Movement in the Churches*, trans. R. A. Wilson, London, SCM Press, 1972.

Hollenweger, Walter J., *Pentecostalism: Origins and Development Worldwide*, Peabody MA, Hendrickson, 1997.

Horsley, Richard (ed.), *Christian Origins*, Minneapolis, Fortress Press, 2005.

Howse, Ernest Marshall, *Saints in Politics: The 'Clapham Sect' and the Growth of Freedom*, London, George Allen & Unwin, 1953.

Hussey, J. M., *The Orthodox Church in the Byzantine Empire*, Oxford, Clarendon Press, 1986.

Hylson-Smith, Kenneth, *The Evangelicals in the Church of England 1734–1984*, Edinburgh, T & T Clark, 1989.

Hylson-Smith, Kenneth, *High Churchmanship in the Church of England: From the Sixteenth Century to the Late Twentieth Century*, Edinburgh, T & T Clark, 1993.

Hylson-Smith, Kenneth, *The Churches in England from Elizabeth I to Elizabeth II*, 3 vols, London, SCM Press, 1996–98.

Hylson-Smith, Kenneth, *Christianity in England from Roman Times to the Reformation*, 3 vols, London, SCM Press, 1999–2001.

Hylson-Smith, Kenneth, *To the Ends of the Earth: The Globalization of Christianity*, London, Paternoster Press, 2007.

Inglis, K. S., *Churches and the Working Classes in Victorian England*, London, Routledge & Kegan Paul; Toronto, University of Toronto Press, 1963.

Jacob, W. M., *Lay People and Religion in the Early Eighteenth Century*, Cambridge, Cambridge University Press, 1996.

Jay, Elisabeth (ed.), *The Evangelical and Oxford Movements*, Cambridge, Cambridge University Press, 1983.

Jenkins, Philip, *The Next Christendom: The Coming of Global Christianity*, Oxford, Oxford University Press, 2002.

Jensen, A., *God's Self-Confident Daughters: Early Christianity and the Liberation of Women*, trans. O. C. Dean Jr, Louisville KY, Westminster John Knox Press, 1996.

John Paul II, *Christifideles Laici*, Homebush, NSW, St Paul Publications, 1989.

Jolly, Karen Louise, *Popular Religion in Late Saxon England: Elf Charms in Context*, North Carolina, University of North Carolina Press, 1996.
Kaufman, Peter Iver, *Thinking of the Laity in Late Tudor England*, Notre Dame IN, University of Notre Dame Press, 2004.
Keep, John L. H., *Last of the Empires: A History of the Soviet Union 1945–1991*, New York, Oxford University Press, 1995.
Kraemer, H., *A Theology of the Laity*, London, Lutterworth, 1958.
Krueger, Derek (ed.), *Byzantine Christianity*, Minneapolis, Fortress Press, 2006.
Krueger, Christine L., *The Reader's Repentance: Women Preachers, Women Writers and Nineteenth-Century Social Discourse*, Chicago, University of Chicago Press, 1992.
Kümin, Beat, *The Shaping of a Community: The Rise and Reformation of the English Parish c. 1400–1560*, Aldershot, Scolar Press, 1996.
Küng, Hans, *Women in Christianity*, London and New York, Continuum, 2001.
Lambert, M. D., *Medieval Heresy*, London, Edward Arnold, 1977.
Lampe, P., *The Christians of Rome in the First Two Centuries*, trans M. Steinhauser, ed. Marshall D. Johnson, Minneapolis, Fortress Press; Edinburgh, T & T Clark, 2003.
Lane Fox, R., *Pagans and Christians*, Harmondsworth, Penguin, 1986.
Latourette, Kenneth Scott, *Christianity in a Revolutionary Age*, 5 vols, Grand Rapids, Zondervan, 1962.
Latourette, Kenneth Scott, *A History of the Expansion of Christianity*, 7 vols, London, Faber & Faber, 1971.
Lindsay, T. M., *The Church and the Ministry in the Early Centuries*, London, Hodder & Stoughton, 1903.
Lovegrove, Deryck W. (ed.), *The Rise of the Laity in Evangelical Protestantism*, London, Routledge, 2002.
MacCulloch, Diarmaid, *Reformation: Europe's House Divided 1490–1700*, London, Penguin, 2003.
MacDonald, M. Y., *Early Christian Women and Pagan Opinion: The Power of the Hysterical Woman*, Cambridge, Cambridge University Press, 1996.
MacMullen, R., *Christianity and Paganism in the Fourth to Eighth Centuries*, New Haven and London, Yale University Press, 1997.
Macy, Gary, 'The ordination of women in the Early Middle Ages', *TS*, 61 (2000), 481–507.
Malherbe, A. J., *Social Aspects of Early Christianity*, 2nd edn, enlarged, Philadelphia, Fortress Press, 1983.
Malmgreen, Gail (ed.), *Religion in the Lives of English Women, 1760–1930*, London, Croom Helm, 1986.
Mantle, J., *Britain's First Worker-Priests: Radical Ministry in a Post-War Setting*, London, SCM Press, 2000.
Mariz, Cecilia, *Coping with Poverty*, Philadelphia, Temple University Press, 1994.
Markus, R. A., *The End of Ancient Christianity*, Cambridge, Cambridge University Press, 1990.
Mason, E., 'The role of the English parishioner 1100–1500', *JEH*, 27 (1976), 17–29.

Matheson, Peter (ed.), *Reformation Christianity*, Minneapolis, Fortress Press, 2006.
McFarlane, K. B., *John Wycliffe and the Beginnings of English Nonconformity*, 3rd edn, London, Penguin, 1972.
Meeks, Wayne A., *The First Urban Christians: The Social World of the Apostle Paul*, New Haven and London, Yale University Press, 1983.
Meeks, Wayne A., *The Moral World of the First Christians*, London, SPCK, 1987.
Meeks, Wayne A., *The Origins of Christian Morality: The First Two Centuries*, New Haven and London, Yale University Press, 1993.
Moore, R. I., *The Origins of European Dissent*, London, Allen Lane, 1977.
Morgan, Sue (ed.), *Women, Religion and Feminism in Britain 1750–1900*, Basingstoke, Palgrave Macmillan, 2002.
Morris, Colin, *The Papal Monarchy: The Western Church from 1050 to 1250*, Oxford, Clarendon Press, 1989.
Morris, Rosemary (ed.), *Church and People in Byzantium*, Society for the Promotion of Byzantine Studies, Twentieth Spring Symposium, Manchester, 1986.
Murray, A., 'Religion among the poor in thirteenth-century France: the testimony of Hubert de Romans', *Trad*, 30 (1974), 285–324.
Neill, Stephen and Weber, Hans-Ruedi (eds), *The Layman in Christian History*, London, SCM Press, 1963.
Nichol, J. T., *The Pentecostals*, Plainfield, Logos International, 1966.
Nicholl, Donald, *Triumphs of the Spirit in Russia*, London, Darton, Longman & Todd, 1997.
Noll, M. A., *A History of the Church in the United States and Canada*, London, SPCK, 1992.
Noll, M. A., Bebbington, D. W. and Rawlyk, G. A. (eds), *Evangelicalism: Comparative Studies of Popular Protestantism in North America, the British Isles, and Beyond, 1700–1900*, Oxford, Oxford University Press, 1994.
Norman, E. R., *Church and Society in England 1770–1970: A Historical Study*, Oxford, Oxford University Press, 1976.
Ogden, Greg, *The New Reformation: Returning the Ministry to the People of God*, Grand Rapid MI, Zondervan, 1990.
Osiek, C. and Balch, D. (eds), *Families in the New Testament World: Households and House Churches*, Louisville KY, Westminster John Knox Press, 1997.
Page, Patricia N., *All God's People are Ministers: Equipping Church Members for Ministry*, Minneapolis, Augsburg Fortress Press, 1993.
Patzia, A. G., *The Emergence of the Church: Context, Growth, Leadership and Worship*, Downers Grove IL, InterVarsity Press, 2001.
Pearson, Birger A. (ed.), *The Future of Early Christianity: Essays in Honor of Helmut Koester*, Minneapolis, Fortress Press, 1990.
Peck, G. and Hoffman, J. (eds), *The Laity in Ministry*, Valley Forge, Judson Press, 1984.
Petts, D., *Christianity in Roman Britain*, Stroud, Tempus, 2003.
Platt, Colin, *The Churches of Medieval England*, London, Secker & Warburg, 1981.
Pollock, John, *Wilberforce*, London, Constable, 1977.

Porterfield, Amanda (ed.), *Modern Christianity to 1900*, Minneapolis, Fortress Press, 2007.

Prochaska, F. K., *Women and Philanthropy in Nineteenth-Century England*, Oxford, Clarendon Press, 1980.

Rack, Henry D., 'Religious Societies and the origins of Methodism', *JEH*, 38 (1987), 582–9.

Rack, Henry D., *Reasonable Enthusiast: John Wesley and the Rise of Methodism*, London, Epworth, 1992, 3rd edn, 2002.

Reynolds, Susan, *Ideas and Solidarities of the Medieval Laity in England and Western Europe*, Aldershot, Variorum, 1995.

Sawyer, D. F., *Women and Religion in the First Christian Centuries*, London and New York, Routledge, 1996.

Schlenther, Boyd Stanley, *Queen of the Methodists: The Countess of Huntingdon and the Eighteenth-Century Crisis of Faith and Society*, Durham, Durham Academic, 1997.

Scotland, Nigel, *Charismatics and the New Millennium: The Impact of Charismatic Christianity from 1960 into the New Millennium*, Guildford, Eagle, 1995.

Shaw, Barry, 'The English Reformation and the laity: Gloucestershire, 1540–1580', *AJPH*, 45 (1999).

Sheils, W. J. and Wood, D. (eds), *Voluntary Religion*, SCH 23, Oxford, Basil Blackwell, 1986.

Sheils, W. J. and Wood, D. (eds), *The Ministry: Clerical and Lay*, SCH 26, Oxford, Basil Blackwell, 1989.

Smith, Mark, *Religion in Industrial Society: Oldham and Saddleworth 1740–1865*, Oxford, Oxford University Press, 1996.

Sordi, M., *The Christians and the Roman Empire*, trans. A. Bedini, London and Sydney, Croom Helm, 1983.

Southern, R. W., *The Making of the Middle Ages*, London, Folio Society, 1998.

Stark, R., *The Rise of Early Christianity: A Sociologist Reconsiders History*, Princeton, Princeton University Press, 1996.

Stevens, R. Paul, *The Equipper's Guide to Every-Member Ministry*, Leicester, InterVarsity Press, 1985.

Stott, John R. W., *One People*, Downers Grove IL, InterVarsity Press, 1968.

Strayer, J. R., *The Albigensian Crusades*, New York, Dial Press, 1971.

Sumption, J., *Pilgrimage: An Image of Medieval Religion*, London, Faber & Faber, 1975.

Swanson, R. N., *Church and Society in Late Medieval England*, Oxford, Basil Blackwell, 1989.

Swanson, R. N., *Religion and Devotion in Europe c. 1215–1515*, Cambridge, Cambridge University Press, 1995.

Swete, H. B. (ed.), *Essays on the Early History of the Church and Ministry: By Various Writers*, London, Macmillan & Co., 1921.

Tanner, N., *The Church in Late Medieval Norwich*, Toronto, Pontifical Institute for Medieval Studies, 1984.

Telford, John, *Wesley's Veterans: Lives of the Early Methodist Preachers Told by Themselves*, 7 vols, London, Robert Culley, 1912–14.

Theissen, G., *The First Followers of Jesus: A Sociological Analysis of the Earliest Christianity*, trans. J. Bowden, London, SCM Press, 1978.
Thomas, Keith, *Religion and the Decline of Magic: Studies in Popular Beliefs in Sixteenth- and Seventeenth-Century England*, Harmondsworth, Penguin Books 1978.
Thompson, E. P., *The Making of the English Working Class*, Harmondsworth, Penguin Books, 1968.
Thomson, J. A. F., *The Early Tudor Church and Society 1485–1529*, London and New York, Longman, 1993.
Thurston, B. B., *The Widows: A Women's Ministry in the Early Church*, Philadelphia, Fortress Press, 1989.
Tolley, Christopher, *Domestic Biography: The Legacy of Evangelicalism in Four Nineteenth-Century Families*, Oxford, Oxford University Press, 1997.
Torry, Malcolm (ed.), *Diverse Gifts: Varieties of Lay and Ordained Ministries in the Church and Community*, Norwich, Canterbury Press, 2006.
Valenze, Deborah, *Prophetic Sons and Daughters: Female Preaching and Popular Religion in Industrial England*, Princeton, Princeton University Press, 1985.
Vauchez, Andre, *The Laity in the Middle Ages: Religious Beliefs and Devotional Practices*, Notre Dame and London, University of Notre Dame Press, 1993.
Walsh, John, Haydon, Colin and Taylor, Stephen (eds), *The Church of England c. 1689–1833: From Toleration to Tractarianism*, Cambridge, Cambridge University Press, 1993.
Ward, W. R., 'Pastoral office and general priesthood in the Great Awakening' in Sheils and Wood (eds), *The Ministry: Clerical and Lay*, SCH 26 (1989), 303–27.
Ware, Timothy, *The Orthodox Church*, Harmondsworth, Penguin Books, 1963, rev. edn, 1993.
Watt, Tessa, *Cheap Print and Popular Piety, 1550–1640*, Cambridge, Cambridge University Press, 1994.
Watts, D., *Christians and Pagans in Roman Britain*, London and New York, Routledge, 1991.
Watts, Michael, *The Dissenters: From the Reformation to the French Revolution*, Oxford, Clarendon Press, 1978.
Watts, Michael, *The Dissenters: Vol. II, The Expansion of Evangelical Nonconformity*, Oxford, Clarendon Press, 1995.
Weber, Max, *The Sociology of Religion*, London, Methuen, 1965.
Webster, A. B., *Joshua Watson: The Story of a Layman, 1771–1855*, London, SPCK, 1954.
Whiting, R., *The Blind Devotion of the People*, Cambridge, Cambridge University Press, 1989.
Wilken, Robert L., *The Christians as the Romans Saw Them*, New Haven, Yale University Press, 1984.
Williams, Cyril G., *Tongues of the Spirit: A Study of Pentecostal Glossolalia and Related Phenomena*, Cardiff, University of Wales Press, 1981.
Winter, B., *Seek the Welfare of the City: Christians as Benefactors and Citizens*, Carlisle, Paternoster Press, 1994.

Bibliography

Witherington III, B., *Women in the Earliest Churches*, Cambridge, Cambridge University Press, 1988.
Wolffe, John, *The Protestant Crusade in Great Britain, 1829–1860*, Oxford, Clarendon Press, 1991.
Wolffe, John (ed.), *Evangelical Faith and Public Zeal: Evangelicals and Society in Britain, 1780–1980*, London, SPCK, 1995.
Wright, S. (ed.), *Parish, Church and People: Local Studies in Lay Religion*, London, Hutchinson, 1988.
Yates, Timothy, *Christian Mission in the Twentieth Century*, Cambridge, Cambridge University Press, 1994.
Zernov, Nicolas, *Eastern Christendom: A Study of the Origin and Development of the Eastern Orthodox Church*, London, Weidenfeld & Nicolson, 1961.

Index

acolytes 22
Additional Curates Society (1837) 100
Africa vii, 89, 90, 100, 102, 120, 129f., 136, 140–2, 163, 170, 171, 181; East-Central Africa 124f., 136, 140; West Africa 123, 142
African Association (1788) 102
African Methodist Episcopal Church 105
agnosticism 165
Aidan, St 35
Alaska 162
Alfred, king of England 40, 41
American and Foreign Anti-Slavery Society (1840) 121
American Anti-Saloon League (1895) 118
American Anti-Slavery Society (1833) 115, 121
American Bible Society (1816) 115
American Board of Commissioners (1810) 106, 115
American Civil War (1861–5) 117, 119, 121, 122
American Colonization Society (1817) 115, 120
American Education Society (1815) 115
American Home Missionary Society (1826) 115
American Peace Society (1828) 115
American Sunday School Union 115, 116
American Temperance Society (1826) 115, 117
American Tract Society (1825) 115
Ammia, prophet 16
Antioch 11
apatheia 154
apologists 11, 18
Apostola, Nicholas: *A Letter from God to the World* 181

Apostolic Canons 12
Apostolic Church 131, 132
Argentina 136
Asia 3, 7, 9, 16, 89, 90, 100, 101, 102, 127, 129f., 136, 163, 171, 181
Assemblies of God 131, 135
atheism 165
Athens 11
Athos, Mount 159
Augustine, St 33–5
Australia 170
Azusa Street, Los Angeles 131

Babylonian Captivity 68
Ban, Bishop Chiu 139
baptism: medieval 49; pre-medieval 28, 30; *see also* Orthodox Church: baptism
Baptist Missionary Society (1792) 101, 111
baptisteries *see* baptism
Baptists 104, 105, 117, 119, 120, 122, 135, 169
Base communities 137–9
Basle, Council of (1512–17) 78
Bede, the Venerable 34
Bellavin, Bishop Tikhon 162
Bengal 125
Benin 141
Bennett, David 134
bishops, early church 12, 13, 22
Bithynia 3, 9
Boehm, Hans 69
Boniface, St 36
Bowdler, John 100
Boxer uprising (1900) 127
Brazil 132, 136, 139, 145, 182
Brethren of the Common Life 75
Brethren, the 112
Britain *see* England/Britain
British and Foreign Bible Society 111, 112, 113
Buganda 124, 125
Buhlmann, Walbert 170
Buxton, Sir Thomas Fowell 96

Byzantium *see* Constantinople

Caesariani 23
Calvin, John 78, 84
Calvinism 84, 94
Cameroon 141
camp meetings 104
Canterbury 34, 46
Cape Comorin 125
Cappadocia 3, 9
Carey, William 101, 113, 125
Caribbean, the 128
Carter, Jimmy 135
catechumens 13, 28
Cathars 61–2, 72
Catholic Apostolic Church 112
Ceawlin, king of Wessex 34
Cedd, bishop 36
cell churches 175
Central America 89, 128
Ceylon (Sri Lanka) 113
chantries 64
charismatic movement 112, 129, 171f.; within Roman Catholic Church 133
charities 54–5
Chaucer, Geoffrey 66
Chile 89, 132
China 126, 131, 136, 182
Chinese Turkestan *see* Sinkiang
Christian drama 66
Christian Evangelical Social Movement (1977) 141
Christian Missionary Foundation (1981) 141
Christian Science 112
Christian Socialism 109–10
Chrysostom, John 152
church architecture, early 28
Church Missionary Society (1799) 102, 112, 113, 127
Church of the Czech Brethren 173
church ornaments/furnishings, early 30
church-scot 38
church services: medieval 45, 46, 51–4, 55, 56, 73; pre-medieval 14, 28, 30–1

Index

churches, flourishing, characteristics of 174–6
churches, witnessing 176–8
'Clapham Sect' 95–7, 101–3
Clapton Sect *see* Hackney Phalanx
Clement V 68
Clement VII 68
Clovis, king of the Franks 32
Cluny 44
Coke, Dr Thomas 92
Columba, St 35
Communism 157, 160
confraternities 54–5
Congar, Father Yves M. J. 180
Congregationalism 104, 117, 118, 123, 169
Constance, Council of (1414–39) 72, 78
Constans 26
Constantine I 25, 29, 30, 147
Constantinople: fall of (1453) 155; pre-medieval 32, 33, 36, 147
Constantius 26
Countess of Huntingdon Connexion 91
Cranmer, Thomas 78, 79
Cromwell, Oliver 79, 86
Crusades, the 58–60

Damascus 11
Danes *see* Vikings
Dante (Alighieri) 66
David, anointed by Samuel 36
deaconesses/deacons 2–6, 12, 22, 28–9
death, attitudes to 64–5
Deeper Life Bible Church, Lagos 140
Democratic Republic of Congo *see* Zaire
Denmark 114
Devotion Moderna 75
diakonos 2–4; *see also* deaconesses/deacons; sub-deacons
Didache 12, 13, 14, 15
Domesday Book 40
door-keepers 22
doulos 2
Drozdov, Philaret 156
Dunkers *see* German Baptist Brethren

Eckhart, Johannes 75
Edict of Milan (313) 25f., 29, 147, 151

Edward VI 79
Edwin, king of Northumberland 35
Egypt 9, 19, 113
elder 3–4, 12, 22
Elim Church 131
Elizabeth I 79
England/Britain 19, 29, 33–6, 38, 40, 41, 50–1, 69–72, 79–80, 81, 83, 84, 90f., 95–103, 109–13, 117, 123, 132, 134–5, 163, 170
Ephesus 7, 10
Episcopalians (North America) 117, 169
episcopos 3–4
Erasmus, Desiderius 74
Essenes 24
Ethelbert, king of Kent 33–4
Ethiopia 182
exorcists 22

Falwell, Jerry 135, 169
Finney, Charles 130
FMLN revolutionary army (El Salvador) 138–9
France/Gaul 19, 32–3, 36, 62, 63, 76, 77, 81–2, 84, 114
Francis of Assisi, St 56
Franciscans 45–6; *see also* Friars Minor
Freetown 123
French Revolution 94, 97
friars 45, 75
Friars Minor 56
Friedrich, Elector of Saxony 79
Friends of God, the 75
Friends of Humanity Association (1807) 120
Fukien province, China 127

Galatia 3, 7, 9
Gambia 141
Gardiner, Allen 127–8
Garrison, William Lloyd 120
Gaul *see* France/Gaul
German Baptist Brethren (Dunkers) 94
Germany 19, 63, 69, 77, 86, 114, 123, 182
glossolalia *see* speaking in tongues
Gorbachev, Mikhail 160
Gower, John 66
Graham, Billy 169
Grant, Charles 95
grave-diggers 22
Great Schism: (1378) 68; (1054) 147

Gregory I (the Great) 33, 34–5
Grey Friars *see* Friars Minor
Groote, Gerard 75
guilds 54–5
Gustavus Adolphus, king of Sweden 79
Guthrum, king of the Danish Vikings 40
Gutiérrez, Gustavo 144

Hackney Phalanx (Clapton Sect) 97–100, 102–3
Hadrian 11
Hagia Sophia 151, 155
Hannington, Bishop James 125
Henry VIII 79
Holiness Movement 131
Holland 114
Hopkins, Samuel 118
Hus, John 65, 69, 72
Hussites 65, 72–3, 75

Incorporated Church Building Society 100
India 125, 131, 132
Inquisition, the 62, 63
Irenaeus, bishop of Lyons 15
Ireland 35
Islam 136, 155
Italy 9, 19, 51, 62, 63, 68, 77, 88
Ivory Coast 141

Japan 132
Jehovah's Witnesses 112
Jerusalem 9, 57, 60
Jesuits 89
jihads 88
John of Leyden 83
John Paul II 141
Judaea 7
Julian, 'The Apostate' 26
Justin Martyr 11, 12
Justinian I 33

Kabalisas, St Nicholas 151
Kenya 140, 141, 182
Kerala 19
Korea 127, 136
Kraemer, Hendrik 179
Kucheng massacre 127

Langland, William 66
Langton, Stephen 70
laos of God xii–xiv
Lateran Council: Fifth (1512–17) 78; Fourth (1215) 48, 53

Index

Lausanne International Congress on World Evangelisation (1974) 181
laying on of hands 8
Lenin, Vladimir Ilyich 157
Letter from God to the World, A 181
Letters of Ignatius of Antioch 12
liberation theology 137, 143–4
Liberator, the (1831) 121
Liberia 120, 141
Lindisfarne, island of 35
literacy 63–7
Liuhard, Saxon bishop 34
Livingstone, David 124
Lollards 65, 70–2, 75
London Missionary Society (1795) 101, 113
Luther, Martin, 73, 78f.
Lutherans 169
Lydia 8

Macaulay, Zachary 95
Madagascar 124
Magdeburg, destruction of (1631) 86
Malta 7
martyrs 18, 21, 142–3, 157, 158
Marx, Karl 144
Marxism 156–7
matronae 23
Matthys, Jan (Mattijszoon) 83
Maurice of Saxony 79
Maximilla 16
Melanchthon, Philipp 78
Melchisedech 37
Mennonites 94
Metaxakes, Meletios 162
Methodists 104, 105, 117, 119, 122, 169
Mexico 182
minsters 38, 41, 49, 55
Missionary Society of Connecticut 105
monks/monasteries 55–6, 59; *see also* Orthodox Church: monasticism
Montanism 15–16
Monte Cassino 44
Moody, Dwight L. 122, 130
Moral Majority 135, 169
Moravians 90, 94
More, Hannah 96
More, Sir Thomas 76
Mormons 112
'mother' churches *see* minsters

Muntzer, Thomas 83
mysticism 75

Napoleonic Wars 97
National Society, The 99
nationhood 42–3
Nesterov, Mikhail 157
Netherlands 75, 84
New York Missionary Society 105
New Zealand 113, 170
Nigeria 136, 141, 182
Nisibis *see* Syria
nuns/nunneries 55–6
North Africa 19, 30
North America 85–6, 93–4, 98, 100, 101, 103–6, 114–23, 129ff., 163, 169–70, 177
Norway 114, 132
Nova Scotians 123
Nyanza Mission 124

occultism 156
Orthodox Church 84, 147–62; Archdiocese of North and South America 162; autocephalous churches 156, 160; baptism 150, 152; Brezhnev–Andropov era 160; church organization 149; Church and state 147, 148 151; 'Living Church Movement' 157–8; Metropolia 162; monasticism 149–50, 153; music 151, 153, 157; panegyria 155; Patriarchal Exarchate; patriarchs 148; perestroika 160; prayer 153–4, 158; rites of passage 152, 155; Russia 155–60; Russian revolution (1917) 156, 157, 162; sainthood 149, 154, 158; sermons 151, 152; visual art 153; worship 150–3, 158–9; writers and thinkers, twentieth-century 156–7; *see also* Communism
Oswald, king of Northumberland 35
Oswy, king of Northumberland 36
Ottheinrich of the Palatine 79

Paeda, king of the Middle Angles 36

Paine, Thomas 96
Palestine 9
Parham, Charles F. 131
Patarini 46
patriarchates, ancient 88
Peel, Sir Robert 97
penitential system: medieval 57, 73, 74; pre-medieval 23, 28
Pentecost, day of 1
Pentecostalism vii, 84, 112, 129–33, 163, 171f.
Pepuza 16
Persia 19
Peru 89
Philadelphia 16
Philippines 182
Philothey 156
Phoebe 4
Photios 151
Phrygia 9, 16
Pietism 90
pilgrimages: medieval 45, 56–8; pre-medieval 32
Pippin, king of the Franks 36
Pliny 8
Polycarp, Bishop of Smyrna 16
Poor People's Guerrilla Army (Guatemala) 139
Portugal 89
prayer 175; *see also* Orthodox Church: prayer; worship
presbuteros see elder
presbyter *see* elder
Presbyterians 104, 117, 119, 120, 169
Priscilla and Aquila 8
Priscilla, prophetess 16
Prokopios 151
prophecy: modern times 131; pre-medieval 3, 9, 15–16, 20
Puritans 93

Quadratus 16
Quakers 94

Ravenna 33
Rayan, Samuel 171
Readers, pre-medieval 12, 22
Reform Bill (1832) 99
Reformation, the 77, 78f.
Regan, Ronald 135
relics 21, 28, 45, 58
Religious Tract Society (1799) 113
Renaissance 73–4

Index

revival, eighteenth-century 90f.
Robertson, Pat 135
Romantic movement 94
Rome 9, 10, 22, 23, 28, 32, 57, 147
Romilly, Sir Samuel 97
Rouen, Council of (1335) 50
Russia 132, 182; *see also* Orthodox Church

Sabbath 14
saints, cult of: medieval 55, 57; pre-medieval 31
Salvation Army 110
Samaria 9
Samuel, Old Testament prophet 36
Sandinista government (Nicaragua) 138
Santiago de Compostela 45, 57
Schwahn, Barbara 181
Selina, Countess of Huntingdon 91
Serafim of Sarov 156
Seventh-Day Adventist Church 112
Seymour, William J. 131
Shaftesbury, seventh earl 108
Sharp, Granville 95, 102
Shore, John (Baron Teignmouth) 95
Sierra Leone 102, 113, 124
Sigbert, king of the East Saxons 36
Singapore 139–40, 174, 175
Sinkiang (Chinese Turkestan) 126
slavery: anti-slavery movements in England and Europe 95–7; in North America 118–22
Smith, William 71
social status, first-century Christians 6–8
Society for Promoting Christian Knowledge (SPCK) 102–3
Society for the Propagation of the Gospel (SPG) 102–3
soul-scot 38

South America 89, 90, 100, 127, 129, 132, 136, 144, 163, 170, 171, 181
South American Missionary Society 127, 128
Spain 19, 63, 88, 89
speaking in tongues (glossolalia) 3, 16, 130, 131
Sperou, Bishop Athenagoras 162
Speyer, Diet of (1526) 79
Spiritualist churches 112
Stanley, H. M. 124
Stelmach, Harlan 181
Stephen, James 95
Stowe, Harriet Beecher 121
Student Volunteer Movement for Foreign Missions (1888) 122
sub-deacons 22
Sunday, in early Church 14, 30
Sunday schools 108
Sweden 114, 132
Swithhelm, king of the East Saxons 36
Switzerland 75, 76, 114
Syria (Nisibis) 9, 19

Tanzania 140
Tarrant's Rules 120
Tauler, Johann 75
Tay, Bishop Moses 139
Taylor, James Hudson 126
Tertullian 22
theosophy 156
Therapeutai 24
Thirty Years' War 79
Thomas à Kempis 75
Thornton, Henry 95
Tibet 126
Tierra del Fuego 128
Torrey, R. A. 130
training, lay 176–7
Turner, Nat 121
'Two-Thirds World' 171

Uganda 141
Ukraine 160
United Church of North India 173
Urban VI 68

Vatican Council, Second (1962–5) 141, 144

Venn, John 95
Verona, Council of (1184) 62
Vikings 39, 40
Vindolanda, Hadrian's Wall 30

Waldensians 61–3, 72
Watson, Joshua 98f.
Wesley, John 91, 92, 94
West Indies 101
Westphalia, Peace of (24 October 1648) 86
Whitefield, George 91
Wilberforce, William 95–7, 101–2
women: in the medieval church 47, 71–2, 74, 78; in the pre-medieval church 4–6, 12, 28–9; Reformation to the present day 81, 82, 84, 91, 106, 110–12, 118, 121, 135, 141
Women's Christian Temperance Union 118
World Council of Churches 160, 173, 181; central committee meeting, Johannesburg (1994) 181; Department of the Laity 180; 'Faith and Order' 179; Second (Evanston) Assembly of the Council (1954) 180
World Missionary Conferences: Edinburgh (1910) 181; Jerusalem (1928) 181; Tambaram (1938) 181
Wyclif, John 65, 69–72

Yangtze valley 126
Yorubaland 124
Young Men's Christian Association (YMCA) 122
Young Women's Christian Association (YWCA) 122

Zaire (Democratic Republic of Congo) 182
Zambia 140
Zimbabwe 140, 141
Zwingli, Ulrich 78

Stitched in Ambition

Aria Townsend

Published by Aria Townsend, 2024.

This is a work of fiction. Similarities to real people, places, or events are entirely coincidental.

STITCHED IN AMBITION

First edition. October 8, 2024.

Copyright © 2024 Aria Townsend.

ISBN: 979-8224989331

Written by Aria Townsend.

Chapter 1: The Fashion Showdown

The bright lights of the New York City runway reflect the fervor in my heart as I stand backstage, adjusting the hem of my hand-sewn dress. My name is Mia Carter, a fashion blogger trying to carve my niche in a city that thrives on perfection. The fabric, a soft lilac with hints of gold threading, clings to my figure just right, but it's the intricate beadwork along the neckline—my late grandmother's vintage collection—that truly sets it apart. I'd stitched each bead on with care, imbuing my creation with fragments of family history and love, yet as the rhythmic claps of heels echo in the cavernous backstage, my heart thumps with a discordant melody of excitement and dread.

Watching the models glide down the runway is both exhilarating and agonizing. They float like ethereal beings, draped in designs that whisper of luxury and exclusivity. Each garment, kissed by the glow of strategically placed lights, appears to shimmer with its own aura of brilliance. I can practically feel the fabric's texture through the air—silks so smooth they could slip through your fingers, satins that catch the light in a flurry of soft movement. It's a visual symphony, and I'm merely a humble note in a grand composition, anxious to make my mark.

"Okay, breathe, Mia. You got this," I murmur under my breath, taking a deep inhale that does little to quell the storm of anxiety roiling in my stomach. My best friend and photographer, Ethan, is my lifeline, capturing moments through his lens with a precision that matches my sewing. I glance over at him, poised with his camera, his sandy hair tousled in a way that somehow makes him look effortlessly cool even amidst the chaos. He catches my eye and gives me a thumbs-up, his smile wide enough to melt away a few of my worries.

But then I see her. Lydia Hastings, a whirlwind of charisma and high-profile connections, strutting into the backstage area like she owns the runway itself. Her arrival is heralded by the gasps of stylists and whispers of admiration. Clad in a sleek black outfit that could easily pass for a couture creation, she oozes confidence and an air of superiority. It's hard not to feel overshadowed by her presence. The way she brushes past the models with a casual grace makes me feel like I'm drowning in a tidal wave of self-doubt.

"Mia! You should see Lydia's new collection! It's absolutely to die for," a voice chirps nearby, causing my stomach to clench. I turn to see Clara, a fellow fashionista with a penchant for gossip, her eyes sparkling with excitement. "I heard she's got an exclusive collaboration with one of the top luxury brands. Can you believe it?"

"Is that so?" I manage to say, forcing a smile that feels more like a grimace. "Good for her." The words taste bitter on my tongue. Lydia's success is like a cold gust of wind, whipping through the warmth of my aspirations, and I feel the weight of my ambitions pressing down harder with every passing moment.

As the final model exits the runway, applause erupts like a thunderstorm, resonating through the air. I can't help but feel a mixture of envy and admiration. These moments are fleeting yet monumental, and here I am, clinging to the hope that my own collection can spark even a flicker of the same reaction.

"Okay, showtime," Ethan says, slipping his camera strap over his shoulder and checking his settings. He strides over, and I can see the concern etched on his face. "You ready, Mia? Don't let Lydia get in your head. You've worked too hard for this."

I nod, though my heart betrays me with its erratic beating. "Right. I just—what if it's not enough? What if everyone loves her stuff and my designs just... fade into the background?"

"Mia, look at me." His voice is steady, and I lock my gaze with his. "You are not just 'enough.' You are brilliant. The pieces you've created have heart. They have a story. Lydia may have the glitz, but you've got something much deeper."

His words settle over me like a warm blanket, but the shadow of doubt looms large. Just as I'm about to reply, the backstage door swings open, and Lydia saunters in, flanked by a group of admirers, her laughter cutting through the tension like a knife. The way they hang on her every word is almost mesmerizing, and I can't help but feel like a background character in a story I desperately want to be the lead of.

"Hey, Mia!" she calls out, her voice dripping with feigned sweetness. "Still sewing away in the corner? I heard you're showcasing tonight! How quaint." The laughter that follows from her entourage feels like daggers.

"Yep," I reply, forcing a smile that I hope doesn't falter. "Just adding the final touches."

"Oh, that's adorable," she replies, her eyes twinkling with a mix of amusement and condescension. "You'll have to show me how to thread a needle sometime."

The laughter rings hollow, and I clench my fists, fighting back the urge to retort. Instead, I take a deep breath, reminding myself that my journey is mine alone. Lydia might have her spotlight, but I have my passion. As the clock ticks down to my moment, I refuse to be a mere footnote in someone else's story.

With each second that passes, the distance between us feels like a chasm, and yet I can't shake the feeling that it's not just her talent I'm up against, but my own insecurities. The reality is that the stakes are higher than ever. The struggle to stand out in a sea of talent has never felt so daunting, but somewhere within that storm of doubt, a flicker of determination ignites. This is my time. I'm ready to take center stage.

The murmurs of the crowd reach me like a distant tide as I stand nervously behind the curtain, mentally rehearsing every stitch of my presentation. Each passing second feels like an eternity, and the air is thick with the scent of hairspray and ambition. My heart flutters as if it wants to burst from my chest and join the parade of models on the runway, but I clamp a hand over my pounding heart, willing it to settle.

"Remember, you're not just a fashion blogger," Ethan's voice cuts through my thoughts, bringing me back to the present. "You're an artist. Let them see the soul of your work." He flashes me a grin that feels like a safety net, and I can't help but smile back, though my stomach still feels like it's doing acrobatics.

Just as the last model makes her exit, the audience erupts into applause, a wave of sound that crashes over me, thrilling and terrifying all at once. I can't let the fear of inadequacy pull me under. I take one last look at my creation, the lilac dress that has become an extension of myself, before stepping into the spotlight.

The instant I step onto the runway, the clapping morphs into an almost reverent hush. The world outside blurs into a hazy background; it's just me, the bright lights, and the sea of faces watching in anticipation. I stride forward, head held high, the fabric swirling around my legs like a soft cloud. Each step feels like a heartbeat, pulsing with the rhythm of my passion and perseverance.

And then, there she is again—Lydia. Her smirk is plastered across her face, her gaze piercing as if she's calculating my every move. Dressed in a dazzling outfit from her own collection, she appears every bit the queen of this domain. As I reach the center of the stage, her lips curve into a mock applause, the sound flat and sardonic.

"Bravo, Mia! How charming," she calls out, her voice carrying effortlessly across the space. "You look like you just stepped out of a DIY Pinterest board." Laughter erupts from her entourage, and the stabs of their mockery cut deeper than any sharp-edged critique.

I force a smile, but the heat of embarrassment creeps up my neck. "Thanks, Lydia! I appreciate your... unique perspective on craftsmanship," I reply, injecting as much sweetness into my voice as I can muster. The audience seems to shift, the tension rising, but I can feel Ethan's supportive gaze burning into me from the sidelines.

With every inch I cover on the runway, I channel the energy from my doubts into the fabric, allowing the grace of my movements to speak for me. The music shifts to a soft, whimsical tune, and I twirl, showcasing the intricate beadwork glinting under the lights. For a brief moment, I lose myself in the dance of fabric and rhythm, the world melting away until only I remain, infused with purpose.

As I turn back to face the audience, I catch a glimpse of Ethan, his camera snapping away, capturing the very essence of this moment. My heart swells, reminding me of why I'm here—to create, to express, and to share my vision with the world. Suddenly, I spot a familiar face in the crowd—a fashion editor I've long admired, her expression contemplative as she observes my every move. The knot in my stomach loosens slightly; perhaps I can do this after all.

Just as the last note of the music fades, I make my way to the edge of the runway, where I can finally take a breath. The applause washes over me, a warm tide that swells as I stand before the audience. I can't help but beam, soaking in the validation I'd been yearning for. But the triumph is short-lived.

From the shadows of backstage, Lydia steps forward, her demeanor shifting from playful to predatory. "Well, that was... unexpected. But we both know what really sells, don't we?" Her words drape over the moment like a cold veil, and I can see the gears turning in her mind, plotting her next move.

"What's that, Lydia?" I ask, the sharpness of my tone surprising even me. The crowd shifts, anticipation crackling in the air.

"Oh, come now. The audience loves drama as much as they love fashion. You've put on a lovely show, dear, but let's be honest—everyone's waiting to see how the real pros do it." Her smile is all teeth, and I sense the gears of the competition clicking into place, each turn a reminder of the stakes at play.

Just as I'm about to retort, I notice something flickering in the corner of my eye. A flash of movement, an unexpected stir. A model who should have left the stage suddenly steps forward, her face contorted in confusion. She looks ready to collapse, her heels wobbling dangerously beneath her.

"Help! I can't—" The words tumble out in a rush, and in an instant, the atmosphere transforms from one of competitive bravado to sheer chaos.

Ethan rushes to her side, his protective instincts kicking in. "Stay with us, you're going to be okay," he reassures, his voice steady as he helps steady her. The crowd gasps, the tension electrifying the air. In the blink of an eye, the focus shifts from fashion to the frantic moment unfolding on stage, a reminder that life has its own unpredictable designs.

"Do you want me to call for a medic?" I call out, my heart racing not just from the previous confrontation but from the urgency of the situation.

"No, no," the model gasps, shaking her head as she tries to regain her composure. "I just... I need to sit."

The crowd murmurs, and I can feel Lydia's eyes on me, weighing my response. The competitiveness of the night morphs into a shared humanity, reminding us all that behind the fabric and the fierce ambitions, we're still just people trying to navigate a complex world.

"Okay, let's get her off stage, everyone," I say, my voice ringing with authority. With Ethan by my side, I help guide the model toward the edge of the runway. The audience watches in a stunned silence, the moment's gravity hanging thick in the air.

In that chaotic instant, something shifts within me. The rivalry with Lydia suddenly feels distant, overshadowed by the reminder that while fashion is my passion, compassion is what truly defines us.

I'm here not just to compete but to connect, to create a community of dreamers and creators. And as I help the model down, I glance back at Lydia, her expression now unreadable.

Tonight may not go as planned, but as I embrace this unpredictable turn, I realize I'm more than just a contestant in this showdown. I'm Mia Carter, and I'm ready to make my mark, one stitch at a time.

With the model safely escorted off stage and the audience's chatter fading to a more subdued murmur, I take a moment to catch my breath. Adrenaline surges through me, mixing with the remnants of embarrassment, yet I feel a shift within. The night has taken an unexpected turn, and I can't help but wonder how it will affect my own showcase.

Ethan is still near the exit, crouched down to check on the model, who is now leaning against a wall, her breathing evening out. "You really scared us back there," I hear him say softly, a hint of relief in his voice. "You did great. Just needed a moment to breathe, right?"

She nods, gratitude flickering in her eyes. I can't help but admire Ethan's easy manner, the way he knows how to connect with people in a way that puts them at ease. It's a skill I've always envied; in a world that thrives on competition, he's the quiet hero behind the scenes, smoothing over the rough edges of chaos.

As the applause dies down and the crowd settles into casual conversations, I decide to step back out into the fray. The atmosphere has shifted; the earlier tension feels replaced by a sense of solidarity, even camaraderie. I scan the room, looking for familiar faces, people I've met during my journey in the industry, and those I hope to know better.

"Hey, Mia!" A voice breaks through my thoughts, and I turn to see Clara, her hair bouncing as she strides toward me, a drink in hand. "That was something else! I mean, the way you handled that moment? You were like a pro!"

"Thanks! It was... not what I expected, that's for sure." I can't help but chuckle, shaking my head at the absurdity of the night. "Just trying to keep it together."

"Please, you were practically born to be on that runway," she retorts, nudging me with her elbow. "So, what's next? Any plans for a post-show celebration?"

"Maybe a glass of wine and a Netflix binge?" I suggest, feeling the weight of exhaustion tugging at my limbs.

"You can't be serious! We need to celebrate this moment! It's your debut collection, Mia!" Clara's eyes sparkle with mischief. "And I know just the place."

Before I can protest, she grabs my arm and leads me toward a small group gathering by the bar. I spot a few industry veterans mingling, their laughter blending into the soundtrack of the night. It's both exhilarating and daunting; I feel like I'm standing at the edge of a cliff, ready to take the plunge.

As I join the group, the atmosphere buzzes with excitement and lighthearted banter. A few compliments are thrown my way, each one warming me from the inside out. It's a different kind of adrenaline than I experienced on the runway—this is the thrill of connection, of being part of something bigger than myself.

Then, just as I start to relax, I notice Lydia lingering near the bar, her gaze flickering over the group like a hawk assessing its prey. My stomach knots again as she saunters over, a predatory grace in her movements.

"Mind if I interrupt the party?" she asks, her tone deceptively sweet. "I couldn't help but overhear all this praise for Mia's 'brave' performance. It was certainly... entertaining."

"Wow, Lydia, I didn't know you were the queen of backhanded compliments," Clara shoots back, crossing her arms defiantly.

"Oh, please, I'm just admiring the creativity in trying to turn a near disaster into a fairy tale," she replies, her eyes sparkling with mischief. "But we all know that when it comes to real fashion, you need a little more than charm and a sewing machine."

I can feel the room tense, the laughter stifled by her words. Every bit of confidence I'd managed to muster begins to crumble like dry sand. "You know, Lydia, sometimes it's not just about the clothes. It's about the heart behind them," I counter, my voice steadier than I feel.

"Heart is nice and all, but heart doesn't pay the bills, darling," she retorts, her smile turning razor-sharp.

Just then, a loud crash resonates from across the room, breaking the tension and drawing everyone's attention. A waiter stumbles, a tray of champagne flutes cascading to the floor in a spectacular shower of crystal and bubbly. Laughter erupts from the crowd, and Lydia's momentary advantage slips away as she rolls her eyes in exasperation.

"Clumsy people," she huffs, before glancing back at me, her expression a mixture of annoyance and determination. "You might want to enjoy this moment, Mia. You never know when it could be your last in this cutthroat world."

The words linger in the air, heavy with implications, as she turns on her heel and strides away, the room buzzing with nervous chatter. I can feel Clara's hand on my arm, squeezing gently in reassurance. "Ignore her. She's just trying to rattle you. You know what you're capable of."

"Right. I just... it's hard to shake her off when she keeps showing up," I admit, feeling the weight of her disdain.

"Focus on the good, Mia," Clara insists, her voice firm yet supportive. "You've got talent, heart, and more than enough ambition to go around. If anyone's going to falter in this industry, it won't be you."

Her words resonate within me, a reminder that while the spotlight can be blinding, it's also an opportunity to shine. I take a deep breath, forcing my shoulders back. The evening may not have gone as planned, but I'm still standing, and I refuse to let Lydia's bitterness take root in my heart.

As the night unfolds, laughter and conversations swirl around me like a warm embrace. I feel lighter, buoyed by the support of friends and the thrill of possibility. But just as I begin to let myself enjoy the moment, I catch a glimpse of something—a flash of movement in the corner of my eye.

The crowd suddenly parts, and I see Ethan standing at the edge of the gathering, his expression shifting from casual to alarmed. My heart skips a beat as I follow his gaze, which lands on Lydia, who is now on her phone, speaking in hushed tones.

"Something's not right," he whispers to me, his brow furrowing. "I don't like the look on her face."

Before I can respond, the energy in the room changes again, the chatter dwindling as an unexpected figure enters the space. Tall and imposing, with an air of authority, he strides confidently toward Lydia. I feel my heart rate quicken as I try to piece together what's happening.

"Lydia," he says, his voice booming across the room, "we need to talk. Now."

The atmosphere crackles with tension, and a cold knot forms in my stomach. I exchange glances with Ethan, both of us silently questioning what this could mean for the night—and for me. Lydia's expression shifts from playful to something darker, and I can almost feel the storm brewing between them.

"Excuse me," I whisper to Clara, my heart pounding. "I need to see what's going on."

As I weave through the crowd, my instincts kick in. I have to find out what's unfolding, to understand what it could mean for my future in this industry. As I draw closer, the words become clearer, laden with urgency and implications that I can't ignore.

"You don't understand what's at stake," Lydia snaps, her voice low yet fierce.

I stop in my tracks, the tension wrapping around me like a tight grip. The world around me fades, and the realization hits—this night is far from over, and the stakes are higher than I ever imagined.

Just as I lean in to catch more of their conversation, Lydia's eyes flicker toward me, a mix of fury and something else—defiance? She shoots me a look that sends chills down my spine, and in that moment, I know that this encounter is just the beginning.

"Trust me, Mia," she warns, her voice barely above a whisper, "you're not ready for what's coming."

The words hang heavy in the air, resonating ominously as I stand frozen, the crowd swirling around me, the reality of the evening shattering like glass. I need to know what she's hiding, and what it means for everything I've worked for. In the distance, I hear the whispers grow louder, the room shifting in anticipation.

As I draw in a breath to confront Lydia, a sudden chill sweeps through the room. Before I can speak, the lights flicker, the music abruptly cutting off, plunging us into an uneasy silence. My heart races, and I can't shake the feeling that something monumental is about to unfold—something that could change everything.

And as Lydia's smirk returns, sharper than before, I realize I'm standing on the edge of a precipice, teetering between ambition and chaos. What lies ahead is anyone's guess, but one thing is clear: the fashion showdown has only just begun.

Chapter 2: A Chance Encounter

The doorbell jingled above me as I stepped into the café, the sound both familiar and oddly comforting, a gentle chime against the backdrop of the city's ceaseless hum. The rich aroma of freshly brewed coffee enveloped me like a soft embrace, mingling with the sweet notes of vanilla wafting from the pastry display. I glanced around, absorbing the eclectic décor: mismatched furniture, each piece telling its own story, and walls adorned with vibrant local art that breathed life into the otherwise unremarkable grayness of the Brooklyn streets outside.

I slid into a corner table, settling into the worn leather chair that creaked under my weight. My sketchbook lay open before me, its pages filled with swirling lines and bold splashes of color—fragments of dreams and inspirations fighting for attention amidst the chaos of my thoughts. The design world had been a whirlwind of glitz and glam, and I had been swept up in it, sometimes questioning if I was the one spinning or merely a spectator. Today, though, I craved stillness, a brief pause to breathe and find my center again.

With a half-hearted sip of my latte, I tried to concentrate on my sketches, the pencil gliding over the paper in a rhythmic dance. The café buzzed with conversation, laughter bubbling over from tables filled with friends and lovers, each moment punctuated by the sound of clinking mugs and the occasional whoosh of the espresso machine. I envied their ease, the way they navigated life with an effortless grace I often felt I lacked. My world was stitched together by threads of competition and ambition, each stitch tightening with every new collection I designed.

As I lost myself in my thoughts, the world around me faded. That's when it happened—a sudden collision that jolted me back to reality. I looked up to find myself staring into warm hazel eyes framed by tousled dark hair. The man towering above me exuded an air of both confidence and kindness, a blend that immediately disarmed me.

"Sorry about that," he said, his voice deep and smooth, like the dark chocolate I'd just spied on the counter. "Didn't see you there."

"No harm done," I replied, a hint of a smile dancing on my lips. There was something undeniably magnetic about him. "It's a crowded place, after all."

He chuckled, a rich sound that resonated deep within me. "I'm Alex, by the way. Alex Thompson. And you?"

"Eva," I managed, feeling a slight blush creep into my cheeks. "Eva Hartley."

He leaned against the table, casually, yet with a hint of curiosity that made my pulse quicken. "I've heard of you. The one who's making waves with those ethereal designs. It's nice to finally meet you in person."

I fought to suppress my surprise. Flattery came with the territory in our industry, but the sincerity in his gaze felt different. "And you're the avant-garde maestro everyone's been talking about. It's a pleasure." The words tumbled out before I could second-guess them, as if compelled by some invisible force.

As we dove into a conversation about our creative processes, my heart raced. We shared tales of inspiration found in the most unexpected places—an abandoned warehouse, a fleeting moment of sunlight illuminating a broken window, the laughter of strangers spilling into the streets. Our exchanges flowed easily, punctuated by laughter that echoed like music in the air. It was refreshing to meet someone who understood the relentless pursuit of art, someone who shared that burning passion beneath their surface.

"Are you in town for long?" I asked, attempting to steer the conversation into safer waters, the slight knot in my stomach tightening again as I remembered the showcase he'd mentioned.

"Just for a few days," he replied, his expression shifting slightly as he spoke. "I'm showcasing a new line at the Elmhurst Gallery this weekend. Should be interesting."

There it was again—the pang of jealousy. I had submitted my own designs for consideration at that very showcase, and while I was confident in my work, the thought of being pitted against someone as talented as Alex sent a shiver down my spine. What if I was merely a footnote in his story, a flicker of talent lost in the spotlight he commanded so effortlessly?

"Sounds exciting," I managed, forcing a smile even as my thoughts spiraled. "I'm sure it'll be a great success."

"Thanks, but honestly, it's all a bit nerve-wracking." He shifted in his seat, leaning closer, as if sharing a secret. "I feel like I'm on the brink of something monumental, but you know how it goes in this business. One minute you're the golden child, and the next... well, it's all gone."

I nodded, my heart aching at the vulnerability in his voice. "It's like walking a tightrope, isn't it? One misstep and everything crumbles. But then, that's what makes the moments of triumph so exhilarating."

Our eyes locked, and for a heartbeat, the world around us faded into insignificance. There was an understanding between us, an unspoken acknowledgment of the burdens we both carried. It was intoxicating, the way our conversation slipped into deeper waters, exploring not just our ambitions, but the fears that lurked beneath.

"You've got to take risks, though," he said, a playful glint in his eye. "Otherwise, what's the point? We might as well be painting by numbers."

I laughed, the sound bright and freeing. "You know, I've always thought of myself as a watercolor artist trapped in a world of oil painters. I want to blend and bleed, to create something that feels alive. But every now and then, I can't help but worry that my colors won't hold."

His expression softened, a hint of admiration mixed with something deeper. "You should never be afraid of your colors, Eva. They're what make you unique."

We sat in that café, two dreamers tethered by the invisible threads of ambition and fear, caught in a moment that felt both ephemeral and infinite. The chaos of the outside world slipped away, and I could almost imagine a life where competition didn't cast a shadow over our passions—a life where we could thrive without the constant pressure of comparison.

As the minutes turned into hours, I found myself laughing more, sharing stories that felt like whispers of my soul. I realized that Alex wasn't just a rival; he was a kindred spirit, someone who understood the delicate dance of creation. But even as I reveled in our connection, a nagging thought tugged at the back of my mind—was this budding friendship destined to be overshadowed by competition?

As the evening light poured through the café windows, casting golden hues across the hardwood floors, the energy between Alex and me thrummed with a peculiar intensity. Every laugh we shared felt like a thread weaving us closer together, a tapestry of unspoken words and glances that lingered just a second too long. I was entranced by his passion, the way his hands animatedly gestured as he spoke about fabric choices and the way color could evoke emotions. It was an intoxicating dance of creativity, one I hadn't realized I'd missed until that very moment.

"So, what's your latest project?" he asked, tilting his head slightly as if trying to unravel the mysteries I kept carefully guarded. "Are you working on something for the showcase?"

I hesitated, weighing my words. My latest collection was a deep dive into the fluidity of identity, inspired by the idea that we are all ever-evolving, yet tethered to our roots. "It's a bit of a departure from my previous work," I said, choosing my words with care. "I've been exploring themes of transformation and authenticity. You know, trying to capture that delicate balance between who we are and who we aspire to be."

He leaned in, intrigued. "That sounds incredible. I love the idea of blending those themes. Fashion is such a powerful medium for self-expression, isn't it? We wear our stories, sometimes without even realizing it."

His words resonated with me, pulling at the strings of my creative heart. "Exactly! It's like each piece holds a whisper of its creator's journey. But," I added, a slight frown creeping onto my face, "it's hard not to get caught up in the competitive side of things. I mean, we're all trying to carve our names into this relentless industry. It can feel like a game of survival."

A shadow flickered across his face, the warmth in his eyes dimming momentarily. "You're not wrong. Sometimes it feels like we're running a marathon with no finish line in sight. But if you're not careful, you end up losing the very essence of what you set out to create in the first place."

There it was, that raw honesty that kept drawing me in. I wanted to peel back the layers of his seemingly perfect exterior, uncovering the fears and dreams that pulsed beneath. The thought ignited something within me—an urge to forge a deeper connection, to dive into the tumultuous sea of shared aspirations and vulnerabilities.

"Have you ever thought about what you'd do if you weren't designing?" I asked, hoping to turn the tide of the conversation. "If all the pressure was lifted, and you could create just for the love of it?"

A grin broke across his face, and I felt my heart flutter like a wayward butterfly. "Oh, definitely. I'd probably open a bakery," he said, his eyes sparkling with mischief. "I'd trade in silk for soufflés and let my imagination run wild with flavors instead of fabrics. Can you picture it? 'Thompson's Tasty Threads.' All my pastries would be named after my favorite designs."

I burst into laughter, the sound bright and unabashed. "That's ridiculous! But I have to admit, I'd buy a cupcake named 'Avant-Garde Chocolate.' It sounds exquisite."

"Right?" He leaned back, folding his arms behind his head as if the mere thought of it had transported him to a utopia of confections. "And it would have this decadent layer of raspberry filling that explodes with every bite. An explosion of flavor, just like my designs!"

We both chuckled, the tension of the day dissipating in a sweet haze of camaraderie. But as the café's ambient noise swelled around us, a sense of reality crept back in. The showcase loomed like an ever-approaching storm cloud, reminding me of the uncharted waters we both navigated.

"I know it sounds silly," I said, the weight of the moment settling over me, "but I'm genuinely excited for your showcase. I hope it goes well. Really, I do."

"Thanks," he replied, his expression shifting to something more earnest. "But I have to admit, I'm equally excited about yours. I heard whispers about your collection, and they sound amazing."

I felt a flush of warmth creep into my cheeks, the compliment both uplifting and unnerving. "You think so? I mean, it's still a work in progress. I'm trying to balance my vision with what I think the judges will want."

"Don't do that," he interjected, his voice suddenly serious. "Design for yourself first. Trust your instincts. If you love it, someone else will too."

His fervor was infectious, and I found myself nodding, even as a lingering doubt tugged at my heart. "I appreciate that, really. But it's hard not to be consumed by what others expect. The pressure feels like a tidal wave sometimes."

He reached across the table, a subtle gesture that sent a jolt of electricity up my arm. "Eva, you've already made a name for yourself. Don't let fear dim your light. Your vision is valid, and you have every right to own it."

His words settled into my chest like a comforting weight. In that moment, I wished I could bottle his confidence, like a warm elixir to sip whenever insecurity threatened to drown me. But just as quickly as that thought arrived, the ever-present storm of competition loomed back in my mind. "But what if I fail?" I found myself asking, the vulnerability slipping out before I could reign it in.

"Failure is just a stepping stone," Alex replied, his voice steady. "It's how we learn. I've had my share of flops, trust me. Each one stung, but they've taught me more than any success ever could."

The sincerity in his tone struck a chord, making me realize how isolated I often felt in my own struggles. I hadn't expected to find a kindred spirit in Alex, someone who shared the weight of this chaotic world. "You make it sound so easy," I mused, the corners of my mouth lifting.

"Maybe it's not easy, but it's worth it," he said, a glimmer of hope in his hazel eyes. "We're in this together, right? Artists supporting artists. That's how we thrive."

A silence enveloped us, pregnant with possibilities and unspoken dreams. The bustling café faded into the background, and in that moment, I felt a shift within me. The competitive tension that had wrapped around my heart began to loosen, replaced by the warmth of newfound camaraderie.

But just as I opened my mouth to respond, a loud crash erupted from the entrance. A group of fashionistas burst in, their laughter echoing like a triumphant fanfare. They were draped in the latest trends, their presence commanding attention as they strolled toward the counter, oblivious to the world around them.

"Looks like we're not alone," Alex said, breaking the tension with a chuckle. I couldn't help but roll my eyes as one of the women, a striking figure with a mane of platinum blonde hair, strutted past our table.

"Ugh, there's a classic case of style over substance," I whispered to Alex, unable to stifle my amusement. "I wonder if she thinks those neon green shoes will distract from the fact that she looks like a walking fashion magazine ad."

"Right? Like, 'Look at me, I'm fabulous!'" Alex replied, his voice dipping into an exaggerated tone that had me snorting with laughter. "It's amazing how some people think a loud outfit makes them an artist."

We exchanged smirks, delighting in our shared disdain for the superficiality that often pervaded the fashion world. I felt lighter, as if the burdens I carried were momentarily lifted, transformed into laughter that danced between us.

As the clamor around us grew louder, I leaned back in my chair, the world feeling infinitely larger and more colorful than before. With Alex by my side, I found the courage to embrace the unpredictable chaos of our industry. Perhaps, just perhaps, the upcoming showcase wouldn't be a battleground after all, but a celebration of creativity, a canvas where two souls could flourish amid the madness.

The laughter of the fashionistas faded into the background, leaving a warm, comfortable silence between Alex and me. With each passing moment, the world outside the café felt increasingly distant. My focus sharpened on his every word, the lines of his face animated by the passion that fueled our conversation. I noticed the way the light danced in his hazel eyes, revealing layers of intrigue that beckoned me to explore deeper.

"What's your secret?" I asked, a playful lilt in my voice as I leaned in, intrigued by the man before me. "You seem to have this effortless charm. Is there some kind of avant-garde handbook I need to know about?"

He laughed, the sound bright and genuine, as if my question had caught him pleasantly off guard. "Oh, definitely. Chapter One: Always wear an oversized scarf and look vaguely aloof. Works every time."

I smirked, the tension in my shoulders relaxing. "I'll have to add that to my style guide. I'm sure the designers I've idolized for years would appreciate the tip."

"Ah, but you're doing just fine without it," he said, his gaze steady and earnest. "Your designs speak for themselves. You don't need a gimmick."

The compliment warmed me more than the coffee I sipped, stirring something deep within. "You really think so?" I ventured, feeling both flattered and exposed. "It's easy to get lost in this industry, you know? Sometimes I feel like I'm chasing after a shadow, trying to create something that's just as eye-catching as the next big thing."

"I get it. Trust me," Alex replied, his voice dropping to a more serious tone. "But don't forget why you started. It was never about being the loudest voice in the room; it's about being the most authentic. That's where the real beauty lies."

Our eyes met, and the connection between us intensified, pulsing with an energy that felt both exhilarating and terrifying. I wanted to dive into his mind, unravel the fabric of his experiences, and find out what made him tick.

"What made you want to become a designer?" I asked, curiosity bubbling over. "What's your story?"

He hesitated, his gaze drifting to the window where the sun began to dip behind the buildings, painting the sky in hues of orange and pink. "I grew up in a small town, surrounded by family who had their own dreams but never pursued them. I always felt this pull, this fire inside me to create. One day, I decided I wouldn't let that go unfulfilled. I packed my bags and headed for the city, ready to embrace whatever came my way."

I nodded, captivated by his honesty. "And have you found what you were looking for?"

"More or less," he replied, a hint of vulnerability creeping into his tone. "But the journey is messy. Sometimes I question everything I've built. You know how it is—every success brings a new wave of pressure. It's like climbing a mountain, only to discover a higher peak just beyond your reach."

His words resonated with me, mirroring my own doubts. "And do you ever feel like giving up?"

"More often than I'd like to admit." He let out a soft chuckle, his demeanor shifting back to lightheartedness. "But then I remind myself that life is too short to settle for mediocrity. And besides," he added with a playful smirk, "where's the fun in giving up?"

His grin was infectious, igniting a spark of determination within me. "You're right. It's all about embracing the chaos, isn't it?"

"Exactly," he said, raising his cup in a mock toast. "To the chaos, and the beautiful mess that comes with it."

As we clinked our mugs together, I felt an exhilarating sense of camaraderie envelop us. This was more than a chance encounter; it felt like fate conspiring to intertwine our paths. But just as I began to entertain thoughts of what could develop between us, the door swung open again, and the raucous laughter of the fashionistas broke the moment like a fragile bubble.

"Look who it is!" one of them screeched, spotting us in the back corner. The others turned, their gazes flitting over to Alex and me, wide-eyed and intrigued. "Did we interrupt something? A little café romance?"

The teasing tone was unmistakable, and I felt the heat rise to my cheeks. I shot Alex an apologetic glance, but he merely shrugged it off, his expression turning playful. "Just talking about soufflés," he quipped, earning a chorus of exaggerated "oohs" from the table.

"Good luck finding one in here," I replied, matching his tone. "You're better off with the cupcakes. They're clearly the real stars."

"Right? I'll take my chances," he said, grinning.

The group continued their playful banter, but I could sense the scrutiny in their gazes, and the atmosphere shifted. My earlier excitement was now tangled with uncertainty. I glanced at Alex, trying to gauge his reaction, and saw a flicker of something—was it discomfort?

"Anyway," one of the women piped up, tilting her head at me with a sly smile, "I hear you're both competing in the showcase this weekend. I can't wait to see who steals the spotlight."

The comment hung in the air like a guillotine, slicing through the levity of the moment. My heart raced, and I fought to maintain my composure. "Well, it'll be a fun event," I managed, forcing a smile that felt more like a grimace. "May the best designer win."

"Let's just hope it's not some amateur with a cupcake obsession," Alex added with a wink, trying to defuse the tension. The group erupted into laughter, but I felt the knot tighten in my stomach again, the impending competition looming larger than ever.

As the laughter echoed around us, I couldn't shake the feeling that my connection with Alex was now overshadowed by an unspoken rivalry. I watched as his easy charm flickered, the spark in his eyes dimming slightly under the weight of the spotlight the fashionistas had thrust upon us.

"Anyway, I should probably get back to work," I said, my voice barely above a whisper. "It was great chatting with you, Alex. Really."

"Yeah, you too," he replied, but the warmth was gone from his tone, replaced by a hint of disappointment.

I rose from my seat, my heart heavy as I gathered my things. As I turned to leave, I felt his gaze linger on my back, and I hesitated, a surge of emotion coursing through me. I wanted to say something, to bridge the chasm that had suddenly appeared between us, but words eluded me.

Just as I reached the door, I glanced back over my shoulder, catching his eye one last time. There was something unsaid hanging in the air, a promise of what could be if only we weren't bound by the invisible chains of competition.

And then, a shrill ring pierced the moment—the unmistakable sound of my phone vibrating against the wooden table. I hesitated, glancing down at the screen. It was my mentor, the renowned designer I'd worked for, her name flashing ominously. My heart raced. She never called unless it was important.

"Eva!" I heard her voice before I could even answer. "We need to talk. It's about the showcase."

The urgency in her tone pulled me back into the chaos I had tried to escape. "What's going on?" I asked, my pulse quickening as I stepped outside, the cool air hitting me like a splash of cold water.

"I need you to come to my office right away. We have an emergency situation regarding your collection."

"Emergency? What do you mean?" My stomach twisted with anxiety.

"Just get here, and I'll explain. You might need to make some last-minute adjustments."

I glanced back through the café window, where Alex sat with the fashionistas, laughter ringing out once more. But now, it felt like a distant echo, the thrill of our connection overshadowed by the weight of impending competition and the uncertainties that lay ahead.

"I'll be there," I managed, my heart racing not just from the unexpected call but from the flickering uncertainty of my future.

As I turned to leave, the world felt like it was shifting beneath me, the delicate threads I had begun to weave with Alex tangled in an intricate web of rivalry, ambition, and unexpected twists. I couldn't shake the feeling that the showcase was going to be more than just a display of talent; it would be a defining moment for both of us, one that could change everything.

Chapter 3: The Unlikely Partnership

The days unfurled like the soft fabric of my sketches, each one stitching together the tangled threads of anticipation and dread. The fashion showcase was a mere heartbeat away, and yet it felt like a lifetime, especially after receiving that last-minute call from Lydia. I had just settled into my routine of late-night sketching, coffee-fueled creativity, and the rhythmic buzz of inspiration when my phone buzzed like an angry hornet, pulling me from my reverie.

"Could you present alongside me?" Lydia's voice sliced through the static of the evening, her tone equal parts challenge and command. My heart thudded—a mixture of excitement and terror. Lydia was not just a designer; she was a titan in this world of fabrics and fantasies, and sharing the stage with her felt like stepping into the ring with a heavyweight champion. The butterflies in my stomach morphed into a full-blown avian colony, flapping furiously against my insides.

I had always known that my designs had potential, but the thought of standing next to someone as established as Lydia made me feel like a child playing dress-up in her mother's heels—wobbly and unsure, yet undeniably eager to be seen. As I pondered my predicament, I recalled the one person who could navigate this treacherous terrain: Alex.

We hadn't exactly started on the best footing, but the tension between us had morphed into something oddly familiar, like the quiet comfort of an old blanket. His sharp wit cut through my doubts, and I remembered how, beneath his cocky exterior, lay a genuine passion for fashion that mirrored my own. I texted him, my fingers hesitating over the screen, uncertainty bubbling up. Would he even want to help me?

The reply came swiftly. "Meet me at the café. Bring your sketches. We've got work to do."

It was a strange invitation—formal yet casual, like a business meeting wrapped in the guise of a date. I hurriedly gathered my sketches, the ink still drying in some places, as if they were nervous to meet their creator. When I arrived, the café was a microcosm of life, with the aroma of freshly brewed coffee mingling with the sweet scent of pastries, each note playing a melody of possibility.

Alex was already there, leaning against a chair with that familiar, infuriating smirk plastered across his face. He looked up as I approached, his expression shifting from playful to genuine as he noticed the anxious furrow in my brow. "You look like you're about to give a TED Talk on existential dread," he said, motioning for me to sit.

"Thanks, I'll add that to my resume," I shot back, feigning confidence while opening my sketches on the table between us.

The moment my designs spread out before us, the café faded into the background. I could feel the weight of my insecurities hanging over me like a storm cloud, but Alex leaned closer, examining the fabric swatches and intricate patterns I had worked tirelessly to create. "This is brilliant," he said, a hint of awe lacing his voice. "Why are you second-guessing yourself?"

I opened my mouth to respond, but the words caught in my throat. I wanted to explain the endless nights spent wondering if I was cut out for this world, the paralyzing fear of failure that loomed larger than the silhouettes of my designs. Instead, I shrugged. "I guess I just thought I'd have more time to prepare."

"Preparation is overrated," he countered, his voice playful yet sincere. "Sometimes, you just have to throw yourself into the fire and see if you come out unscathed."

His words struck a chord, igniting a flicker of courage within me. We dove into an intense brainstorming session, the air thick with ideas and laughter. I found myself sharing stories I had kept close to my chest—the reason I fell in love with design, the tiny moments of joy I found in fabric shops, and the nights I spent sketching under the faint glow of my desk lamp. He, in turn, revealed the sacrifices he had made, the family expectations that felt like a weight too heavy to bear.

"Everyone thinks it's all glitz and glam, but it's really just a series of late nights and questionable coffee," he said, running a hand through his hair in exasperation. "My parents wanted me to be a doctor. Can you imagine me in scrubs?"

I burst out laughing, the sound carrying a newfound ease. "Well, at least you wouldn't be surrounded by fabric swatches. You'd just be drowning in textbooks."

"Yeah, and I wouldn't be able to pull off this," he gestured to his outfit, a stylish ensemble that could only be described as effortlessly chic. "Doctors don't wear leather jackets and designer sneakers."

As we continued to exchange banter, the tension that had once defined our relationship began to unravel, revealing an unexpected friendship beneath. I discovered layers of vulnerability in Alex that made me feel less alone in this chaotic world of fashion. The pressure of the upcoming showcase faded, replaced by the realization that I wasn't just another designer lost in the sea of aspiring talents. I was building something real, and perhaps, with Alex's help, I could navigate the waters ahead.

As we finalized ideas for my collection, the shadows of doubt receded, replaced by a flicker of hope. It was in those late-night discussions and shared laughter that I realized this partnership was more than just a means to an end; it was a path toward rediscovering the joy that had initially drawn me to design. The dreams that had once felt distant and unattainable began to feel tangible, and I allowed myself to embrace the possibility of success—not just for the showcase, but for everything that lay beyond it.

The warmth of that evening lingered long after we left the café, casting a golden glow on the uncertainty that had wrapped itself around me. The world felt brighter, filled with potential, and for the first time in a long while, I felt grounded in my ambition. With Alex by my side, the once-daunting dream of showcasing my collection transformed into a shared adventure, one that promised to be filled with creativity, laughter, and perhaps a bit of chaos—a delightful chaos I was ready to embrace.

With the weight of our late-night brainstorming sessions pressing on me like a new coat of fabric, I found myself unexpectedly buoyed by the lightness of our collaboration. Each night, as we spread my sketches across the café table, Alex transformed my nervous chatter into focused determination. We tackled the chaos of ideas like seasoned seamstresses, snipping away the excess and stitching together a vision that felt fresh yet familiar.

One evening, after a particularly spirited session, we decided to celebrate our progress. Alex suggested we head to a nearby rooftop bar, a place known for its sweeping views of the city skyline and a cocktail menu that promised a mix of delightful disasters. "Trust me, the cocktails are as unpredictable as the weather," he quipped, nudging me playfully.

We climbed the narrow staircase that led to the rooftop, laughter echoing between us as we ascended. The city spread out below us, a tapestry of twinkling lights and sounds. The bar was alive with energy, music pulsing through the air, mingling with the laughter of patrons enjoying the cool evening. We found a small table at the edge, overlooking the vibrant expanse of the city.

"What's your drink of choice?" I asked, scanning the menu as if it held the secrets to the universe.

"Something strong enough to make me forget I have to face Lydia tomorrow," he replied with a mock-serious expression, and I couldn't help but laugh. "How about you? Trying to drown your insecurities?"

"Very funny. I'm just trying to fuel my creativity," I shot back, shaking my head. "I'll have whatever you're having. We need to celebrate our genius."

Our drinks arrived—colorful concoctions that glimmered under the string lights strung across the terrace. I raised my glass, the ice clinking like tiny bells. "To creativity, chaos, and conquering our fears!"

"To us," Alex added, his eyes twinkling as he clinked his glass against mine.

With the first sip, I felt the warmth of the drink bloom in my chest, mingling with the excitement swirling around us. We exchanged stories and dreams as the night deepened, our laughter weaving through the air like the delicate threads of my designs.

"So what's the dream?" he asked, a curious look crossing his face as he leaned forward. "Beyond this showcase, I mean."

"I guess I want to create pieces that tell a story, that make people feel something," I replied, my voice quieter now, as if revealing a secret. "It's not just about fabric and colors for me. I want to connect with people."

"I get that," he nodded, his expression thoughtful. "Fashion can be a language of its own."

"What about you? What's the end goal for the great Alex?" I teased, flicking a piece of ice at him from my glass.

His smile faltered for just a moment, and I saw a shadow cross his features. "Honestly? I want to be more than just 'the guy who can make a nice jacket.' I want to be known for something substantial, something that lasts."

Before I could delve deeper, the atmosphere shifted. A group of rowdy patrons nearby erupted into laughter, their voices rising above the music, momentarily drowning out our conversation. I watched Alex's gaze shift to them, his smile fading as he seemed to retreat into his thoughts. I recognized that look—the fleeting moment when someone hides their vulnerabilities behind a mask of indifference.

"Hey, you okay?" I asked, breaking through the raucous chatter.

He forced a chuckle, but it lacked the warmth it usually carried. "Yeah, just thinking. You know how it is. Everyone's always chasing something, right?"

"True," I said, feeling the weight of his unspoken thoughts lingering between us. "But sometimes, it's good to stop chasing and just... breathe."

"Easier said than done," he replied, a hint of a challenge in his voice.

Before I could respond, the evening took an unexpected turn. A figure stumbled into our space, clearly tipsy and unsteady. It was one of Lydia's associates, a woman I recognized from the showcases. She blinked at us, swaying slightly, and then fixed her gaze on Alex. "You! You're the one who thinks he can outshine Lydia, aren't you?"

The sudden tension crackled in the air, sharp as a fresh-cut hem. I glanced at Alex, who had stiffened, his posture shifting into something more defensive. "I wouldn't say that," he replied coolly, though his eyes darkened.

"Oh, please," she scoffed, her breath heavy with the scent of alcohol. "Everyone knows it's a competition. You think you're special because you've got those trendy little jackets? Newsflash: they're just clothes. You want to be in this industry? It's about who you know, not what you create."

I felt anger bubble inside me, a rush of protectiveness for Alex. "Actually, it's about passion and talent, something you clearly don't understand," I interjected, my voice steady despite the chaos around us.

The woman turned her gaze to me, momentarily surprised. "Oh look, it's the little designer trying to make a name for herself. How sweet."

With that, I saw the challenge ignited in Alex's eyes. "Sweet? Is that what you think it is? Passion is powerful, and so is creativity. Maybe you should try it sometime."

The tension was electric, crackling between the three of us as the woman opened her mouth to retaliate, but then she seemed to think better of it. With a flick of her wrist, she spun on her heels, stumbling away into the crowd, her laughter fading into the night.

Alex let out a breath he didn't realize he was holding, turning back to me. "Thanks for that," he said, his voice low. "I didn't think anyone would stand up for me."

"Someone has to," I replied, trying to lighten the mood, though my heart raced. "Besides, I can't let my collaborator be bullied."

He chuckled, but there was a flicker of something deeper in his gaze, a blend of gratitude and something I couldn't quite place. The moment passed, and we returned to our drinks, but the air felt charged with unspoken words, a new layer of understanding between us.

As the night wore on, we shared more than just our dreams; we navigated the complexities of this world together, forging a bond that felt both fragile and fierce. The vibrant city stretched out before us, a world filled with possibilities and the shadows of our insecurities. I could sense the chaos still swirling in the distance, but within that shared space, there was a flicker of hope—one that illuminated the unpredictable path we had begun to chart together.

The sun dipped below the skyline, casting the city in hues of amber and rose as I prepared for the showcase. My sketches lay sprawled across the floor of my tiny apartment, a chaotic mosaic of fabric swatches and ideas, each one a fragment of the story I yearned to tell. Days had blurred into a whirlwind of creativity and camaraderie with Alex, our late-night rendezvous fueling a fire within me that I hadn't realized had dimmed.

Yet, even as I immersed myself in preparations, the undercurrent of anxiety tugged at me. Each stitch I envisioned felt crucial, the pressure amplifying with every passing hour. Lydia's looming presence hung over me like a thundercloud, her sharp critique echoing in my mind. I had watched her navigate this world with a confidence I found daunting, but Alex was my anchor, his encouragement a lifeline in this sea of uncertainty.

"Breathe, designer extraordinaire," Alex said one afternoon as I wrestled with a particularly stubborn fabric that refused to drape the way I envisioned. He leaned against the doorframe, arms crossed, an amused glint in his eye. "It's just fabric, not the fate of the universe."

I shot him a mock glare, rolling my eyes as I tossed the offending swatch onto the pile of crumpled sketches. "Easy for you to say. You're not the one who has to impress the queen of couture."

He pushed off the door, stepping into my creative chaos. "That's the spirit! Now you're channeling your inner rebel. Let's turn that stress into something beautiful."

I watched as he sifted through my designs, picking up a sketch of a flowing gown adorned with intricate lace. "This one—what's the story behind it?" he asked, his tone shifting from playful to genuinely curious.

I paused, recalling the late-night inspiration that had sparked this particular design. "It's meant to evoke a sense of freedom. Like when you feel the wind rushing against you, and for a moment, nothing else matters."

Alex nodded, a thoughtful look crossing his face. "Then let's make it even more of a statement. If it's about freedom, let's make it something people can't ignore."

We delved into a spirited discussion, transforming my nervous energy into vibrant creativity. The laughter between us danced through the room, punctuated by the occasional exclamations of inspiration. Hours slipped away unnoticed, and as dusk settled, I felt a renewed sense of purpose.

That evening, I set up a makeshift workshop in my living room, determined to bring our ideas to life. Alex joined me, his fingers deftly manipulating fabric as he helped me sew and stitch. The warmth of his presence felt like home, and with each completed piece, the weight of my anxiety lightened.

"Do you ever wonder if we're too idealistic?" he mused, glancing at me between stitches. "Like, what if this all comes crashing down?"

"Maybe," I admitted, pausing to contemplate his words. "But isn't that part of the adventure? If everything worked out perfectly, wouldn't it be boring?"

"Fair point. Though I wouldn't mind a little less chaos in my life," he replied, a wry smile tugging at his lips.

I laughed, shaking my head. "Yeah, but then we wouldn't have stories to tell."

As we wrapped up our session, I felt a growing sense of excitement mixed with apprehension. Tomorrow was the showcase. Every piece felt like an extension of myself, the culmination of our late-night conversations, laughter, and unguarded moments.

Sleep eluded me that night, the city humming outside my window like a restless dream. My mind raced through the details—the lineup of models, the bright lights, and the eyes of critics poised to judge. I imagined Lydia's piercing gaze assessing every stitch, every color choice.

When morning arrived, I felt a mixture of exhilaration and dread. The day unfolded like a well-rehearsed choreography, and I found myself standing backstage, surrounded by the frenetic energy of the fashion world. Models in stunning outfits flitted by like ethereal beings, and the air buzzed with anticipation.

"Just remember to breathe," Alex whispered as he joined me, his presence a grounding force. "You've poured everything into this. Own it."

"Easy for you to say. You're not the one walking down that runway."

"I'd rather stick to behind-the-scenes chaos than risk tripping over my own ego," he replied, shooting me a conspiratorial grin that eased some of my tension.

As the show began, I felt my heart race, each beat echoing in my ears. The lights dimmed, and a hush fell over the crowd. My designs were up first, and as the first model stepped out, a surge of pride coursed through me. The gown flowed beautifully, the lace shimmering under the spotlight.

The applause washed over me, invigorating and terrifying all at once. I watched as each model showcased my creations, my vision taking flight in a world I had only ever dreamed of. But just as I allowed myself to bask in the moment, I spotted a familiar face in the front row—Lydia, her expression inscrutable.

She leaned in, whispering something to a colleague, and I felt a chill creep down my spine. Was it admiration or disdain? My breath quickened, the crowd's applause fading into a distant murmur as I focused solely on her.

When my final piece made its entrance, a dramatic gown with sweeping layers of fabric, the atmosphere shifted. The applause roared, but I could still sense Lydia's sharp gaze dissecting every detail.

Then, in the midst of my moment of triumph, I noticed something unexpected—my lead model faltered, a startled expression flickering across her face. In an instant, she stumbled, and I watched in horror as she lost her footing. The gown billowed around her like an angry wave, and for a heart-stopping second, time slowed.

"NO!" I gasped, the word escaping my lips as if it were an incantation against calamity. The audience collectively held its breath, eyes wide as they witnessed the chaos unfolding on stage.

In a flash, Alex dashed forward, leaping onto the runway with an agility I hadn't expected. "Hold on!" he shouted, arms outstretched. But as he reached her, a sudden silence enveloped the room, like the calm before a storm.

Just as he grasped her elbow, I felt the world tilt, my heart plummeting into a void of uncertainty. What would this mean for me, for my designs, for everything we had built together? The unexpected twist left a knot in my stomach, and as I stared at the scene unfolding before me, I could only wonder if this was the moment everything unraveled.

Chapter 4: The Show Must Go On

The gallery glows under the embrace of soft golden light, an intimate cocoon of warmth nestled within the bustling city. As I weave through clusters of guests, my heart thunders in rhythm with the buzz of conversations swirling around me like a heady perfume. Each laugh, every clink of champagne flutes, merges into an intoxicating symphony that both exhilarates and terrifies. Models, all long limbs and striking features, flit about in a controlled chaos, adjusting straps and smoothing out the fabric of the outfits I had poured my soul into. The vibrancy of my creations pops against the stark white walls, splashes of color that seem to breathe life into the space.

The air is thick with expectation, and I can almost taste the dreams I've stitched into the seams of every dress. It's the night of the showcase, the culmination of late nights and frayed nerves, yet as I glance at the seated audience—fashion moguls, critics, and potential investors—I feel as though the very air around me has conspired to weigh me down. My stomach somersaults, a traitorous reminder of my inexperience in this world of glitz and glam. Just as I prepare to step onto that stage, to watch my dreams come to life, I feel a sharp tug at my arm.

"Look who it is, the little designer who thinks she can make waves," Lydia sneers, her voice slicing through the ambient chatter like a knife. Her presence looms large, an unwelcome shadow at the brightest moment of my life. Her sleek black dress clings to her as if it were a second skin, the fabric glinting under the lights, but it's her words that pierce deeper than any fabric ever could. "What do you think this is, some sort of fairy tale? You're playing dress-up, sweetheart. You'll never measure up to the greats."

Her laughter dances on the edges of my consciousness, an echo of every self-doubt that has ever haunted me. I feel the color drain from my cheeks as the walls of the gallery close in, the laughter and chatter fading to a distant hum. "You're right, Lydia," I say, forcing the words out through the thickness in my throat, "this isn't a fairy tale. It's a nightmare, and you're the villain."

But her smirk only deepens, a wicked curve that reveals nothing but disdain. "Just remember, I'll be watching when you trip and fall flat on your face." With that, she flounces away, leaving behind an icy chill that settles in the pit of my stomach.

As I stand frozen, the weight of her words clinging to me like static electricity, I scan the gallery, desperate to find something, anything, to anchor me back to reality. And that's when I see him. Alex, with his easy smile and the kind of confidence that wraps around him like a well-tailored jacket, strides toward me, cutting through the oppressive atmosphere like a beacon of light. "Hey, there you are! I've been looking for you."

"Really?" I manage, forcing a smile even as I feel Lydia's taunts echoing in my mind. "You must have a death wish to find me before the biggest moment of my life."

He chuckles, the sound warm and grounding. "You're not going to let Lydia's toxicity ruin this night, are you? You've worked too hard for that."

I take a deep breath, trying to inhale his buoyant energy. "But what if she's right? What if I mess up? What if—"

"Stop." His voice is firm, yet gentle, cutting through my spiraling thoughts. "Remember why you're here. You didn't just wake up one morning and decide to become a designer. This is your dream. The sweat, the tears, the countless hours in the studio—it all led you to this moment. You're not playing dress-up; you're here to change the narrative."

His words swirl around me, each one wrapping me in warmth, stitching together the frayed edges of my confidence. "You really think I can do this?" I ask, vulnerability creeping into my voice, raw and unguarded.

"I know you can," he replies, eyes sparkling with sincerity. "You've created something beautiful, and tonight, the world gets to see it."

As he speaks, I feel the electric energy of the audience begin to ignite my spirit, flickering like the lights overhead. It pulls me from the depths of uncertainty, replacing fear with a fierce determination. I straighten my posture, shaking off the remnants of Lydia's venom. "You're right. I'm not just here to play it safe. I'm here to make a statement."

"Now that's the spirit!" He beams, and for a moment, everything else fades away. The chatter, the clinking glasses, the looming shadows of doubt dissolve into the background, leaving just the two of us standing in the heart of this beautiful chaos.

With a deep breath, I step back into the fray, ready to reclaim my narrative. The runway beckons, each step promising a little bit of magic and a whole lot of heart. As the music swells, I feel the rhythm echoing in my veins, harmonizing with my pulse. I won't just walk; I'll strut, each step a declaration of resilience, an embodiment of every fabric swatch and sketch that has shaped my journey.

When I finally take the stage, the spotlight floods over me like a warm embrace. It feels as if the entire universe is holding its breath, waiting for my next move. And in that moment, all I can think about is the passion that has driven me, the laughter shared over late-night design sessions, and the triumphs born from every failure. I glance out at the audience—there are Lydia's scornful eyes, but beyond her, there are faces lit with intrigue and appreciation.

With a fierce grin, I step forward, ready to claim my moment, my voice, and my dreams.

The spotlight envelops me like an electric cocoon, a swirling vortex of energy that thumps in time with my racing heart. I catch my breath, surrounded by a sea of expectant faces, each one a mosaic of curiosity and critique. The music pulses through the gallery, a vibrant anthem urging me forward, demanding that I reclaim every ounce of passion that had brought me here. I feel the cool wooden stage beneath my feet, a grounding reminder of the countless late nights spent sketching and sewing in my cramped studio, where dreams took form and color.

As the first model strides down the runway, my breath catches. She wears a flowing gown that dances like water over rocks, the fabric shimmering under the soft lights. It's one of my favorites, a piece inspired by the autumn leaves of my childhood—fiery oranges and deep reds blended into a tapestry of movement. The audience leans in, their interest piqued, and I can almost feel their admiration wrapping around me like a warm blanket. A soft murmur ripples through the crowd, the hushed tones blending with the rhythm of the music, creating a heartbeat that echoes my own.

I step further into the spotlight, allowing the vibrant energy of the room to engulf me. My eyes scan the audience, landing on familiar faces, each one a tether to my journey. There's Mia, my best friend, her wild curls bouncing as she whispers excitedly to the woman beside her. I can see the joy radiating from her, a lighthouse guiding me through the swirling fog of my anxiety. And then there's Alex, leaning casually against a column, a hint of pride dancing in his expression as he catches my gaze. His encouragement flickers in my mind, igniting a spark within me.

I take a deep breath, letting the moment wash over me. Each model that walks down the runway embodies not just my designs but the essence of who I am—an artist, a dreamer, and now, perhaps, a contender in this unpredictable world. The show unfolds like a beautifully choreographed dance, each piece revealing a new layer of creativity and inspiration. I can feel my earlier doubts beginning to dissolve, replaced by a sense of clarity that washes over me, igniting my purpose.

Then, just as I allow myself to bask in the warmth of the moment, I catch a flicker of movement out of the corner of my eye. Lydia, flanked by a couple of well-dressed friends, stands in the shadows, her arms crossed tightly against her chest. Her face is a mask of disdain, but I refuse to let her cast a shadow on my spotlight. Instead, I channel that energy into my performance, daring to push past the limitations she tried to impose on me.

The models continue to strut down the runway, and with each passing moment, I can feel the tension in the room shift. Whispers of admiration and surprise ripple through the audience, and I catch snippets of compliments—"Brilliant!" "Innovative!" "Where did she come from?"—each word a sweet balm against the sting of Lydia's earlier barbs. I let the momentum swell within me, propelling me into a realm where confidence and creativity intertwine.

"Who knew you had it in you?" a voice suddenly breaks through my thoughts, and I whip around to find Lydia standing beside me, her expression a curious mix of surprise and grudging admiration. "I mean, it's not terrible."

I arch an eyebrow, a smile tugging at my lips as I respond, "Thanks, coming from you, I'll take that as a compliment."

She smirks, but I can see the flicker of respect buried beneath her bravado. "Don't let it go to your head. It's still just one show."

"Oh, trust me, I'm only getting started." I can't help but relish the banter, a tiny victory that feels almost poetic amidst the chaos. "What's next? A fashion line titled How to Be Uninspired?"

The playful jab catches her off guard, and for a fleeting moment, I see a glimmer of something human in her eyes—perhaps even envy. She recovers quickly, tossing her hair back with an exaggerated flick. "Just remember, sweetie, fashion is brutal. It chews people up and spits them out. Don't get too comfortable."

As she walks away, I can't help but smile at her retreating figure. I turn back to the runway, where my creations are parading in front of an audience I had once deemed intimidating. With each model that walks by, I realize that I am not just showcasing clothes; I am unveiling a piece of my identity, stitched into every seam and hem.

The final model emerges, strutting confidently in a stunning ensemble that captures the essence of everything I had hoped to convey: strength, resilience, and beauty. The crowd bursts into applause, a thunderous wave of appreciation washing over me. I feel a sense of triumph swell in my chest, pushing away the remnants of doubt and fear that had once held me captive.

I step forward, the weight of their applause surging through me like an electric current. It's exhilarating, intoxicating even. And as I look out into the audience, I spot Alex once more. He's grinning, his hands clasped in front of him, utterly captivated. My heart skips a beat, and I can't help but feel that perhaps this night is not just about the showcase, but about more than I had initially imagined.

As the models take their final walk, I feel a rush of gratitude wash over me. Gratitude for the late nights, the moments of doubt that had pushed me to work harder, and for everyone who had believed in me—even Lydia, in her own twisted way. I may not have everything figured out yet, but this is my moment, and I am determined to own it.

When the final notes of music fade and the applause crescendos into a standing ovation, I take a deep breath, my heart full and my spirit soaring. The night is just beginning, and I know that whatever comes next, I am ready to face it head-on, with my head held high and a newfound sense of belonging.

The applause reverberates in my chest like the aftershock of a small earthquake, a potent reminder that I've just claimed my place in a world that once felt impossibly distant. As the final model exits the stage, I stand awash in the glow of a spotlight that feels warmer and more welcoming than it did moments ago. I take a deep breath, my heart still racing, but now it thrums with a sense of belonging, as if it has finally found its rhythm in this chaotic orchestra of creativity.

The room begins to shift, and I feel the weight of eyes on me, piercing yet oddly comforting. There's a dance floor-like atmosphere as people rise from their seats, clapping and calling out with genuine enthusiasm. "Amazing!" "Incredible work!" The words wash over me, soothing the remnants of self-doubt Lydia had inflicted. In that moment, I am no longer a fledgling designer in the shadows but a bright spark in a dazzling show.

As the applause dies down, the atmosphere thickens with possibility. I can hear snippets of conversation from the audience: fashion editors discussing potential features, influencers whispering about who they might collaborate with next. Each buzz wraps around me, weaving a tapestry of ambition and dreams that I'm eager to be a part of. I step off the stage, feeling light-headed yet invigorated, my body buzzing with adrenaline.

Mia rushes over, her eyes alight with excitement. "You were phenomenal! Did you see their faces? They were totally into it!"

"I did! I mean, I think I did. I can't be sure; I was too busy trying to keep my heart from exploding." I laugh, the sound bubbling out of me with an unexpected ease.

"And here I thought you'd faint right there in the spotlight!" she teases, her playful nudge a comforting reminder of the grounding friendships that have kept me sane in this whirlwind. "What's next? Paris Fashion Week?"

"Whoa, let's not get ahead of ourselves," I reply, trying to suppress a grin. "I'd be happy with a coffee shop showcase at this point."

Mia leans closer, her eyes narrowing in on something—or rather, someone—over my shoulder. "Speak of the devil, look who's making a beeline for you."

I turn just in time to see Alex approaching, his expression a mix of admiration and mischief, and my heart does that annoying little flutter again. "You were brilliant," he says, his voice low and smooth, almost conspiratorial. "I knew you had it in you, but you exceeded all my expectations."

"Did you think I'd trip over my own two feet?" I reply, feigning indignation, though I can't help but smile. "Lydia had me convinced I was going to implode on stage."

"Lydia's just a speed bump on the runway of your career. You took her detour and turned it into a victory lap." He glances around, his gaze assessing the crowd, and then leans closer, lowering his voice. "Let's grab a drink. I think it's time to celebrate your triumph."

I nod, unable to suppress my excitement. "Absolutely! But I should probably check in with a few people first."

As I move through the throng, I notice a small knot of attendees gathering near the entrance, their animated conversation cutting through the ambient noise of the gallery. I approach, curiosity piqued, and find them discussing a rather unexpected announcement.

"Have you heard? There's a new design competition launching next month," one woman exclaims, her eyes gleaming with enthusiasm. "The winner will have their collection featured at the next major fashion week!"

"What? No way!" another responds, her tone awash with disbelief and excitement. "Do you think it's going to be as cutthroat as the last one?"

My heart races. This could be my chance—a golden ticket to showcase my work on a grand stage. But as I contemplate the possibility, I feel an unsettling flutter in my stomach. The fashion world is a double-edged sword, after all, full of opportunities that can just as easily become traps. Lydia's words echo in my mind, her warnings whispering like a ghost in the corner of my thoughts.

"Are you okay?" Mia's voice breaks through my reverie, her brow furrowed with concern. "You look a bit pale. This is a good thing, right?"

"Yeah, I'm fine," I assure her, but the uncertainty lingers. "I just... it feels like the stakes keep getting higher."

"Good! High stakes mean high rewards. Besides, you've just proven that you can hold your own up there." She nudges me playfully, and the corners of my mouth twitch upward.

As I turn to find Alex again, I spot him near the bar, engaging in conversation with a group of well-dressed influencers. His presence radiates confidence, but I can't shake the strange unease creeping through me. Is this the moment I step into the limelight, or will it all crumble beneath the pressure?

The moment drags on, a tangible tension threading through the air. Suddenly, I catch Lydia's figure in the crowd, her dark dress an unmistakable silhouette. She's standing with a group of industry insiders, her voice rising above the others, animated and commanding. I strain to hear her words, an instinctual urge to understand what she's plotting.

"I'm telling you, it's a mistake to underestimate her," she insists, her tone dripping with faux sincerity. "But if you think about it, an inexperienced designer winning a prestigious competition could tarnish the integrity of the entire event. Don't you think?"

I feel a rush of anger bubble beneath my skin, heating my cheeks. How dare she manipulate the narrative around my dreams? The confidence I had just built feels threatened, slipping away as the audience listens to her poison-laced words.

I glance at Alex, who seems to sense my growing tension. He steps closer, his brow knitted in concern. "What's wrong?"

"Lydia's at it again. She's telling everyone I'm not qualified to compete in that new design competition." My voice quivers with frustration, and I can feel my hands tightening into fists.

Alex's expression hardens, his jaw tightening. "That's nonsense. You've just proven yourself tonight. Don't let her get to you."

As I prepare to respond, the room around me grows quiet. A hush settles as an unanticipated figure strides into the gallery—an esteemed judge from the fashion competition, her reputation looming like a dark cloud. She scans the crowd, her gaze sharp and discerning. The whispers of the attendees rise, punctuated by the sounds of glasses clinking and murmurs of intrigue.

I feel my breath catch in my throat, every muscle in my body tensing with a cocktail of excitement and dread. This is a pivotal moment, one that could shift the trajectory of my career forever. But as I step forward, a surge of determination floods through me, challenging the encroaching doubts that threaten to overwhelm.

Just as I summon the courage to approach the judge, I overhear Lydia one last time, her voice cutting through the air like a serrated knife. "You'll see, I'm right about her. She won't last. In this industry, we don't need more mediocrity."

I pause, the weight of her words pressing down on me. It's as if the universe has drawn a line in the sand, forcing me to choose between fighting for my place or letting her tarnish my hard-won success. The decision hangs heavy, a palpable tension that crackles around me.

With every ounce of courage, I decide to move forward. Just as I take a step, the judge's gaze locks onto mine, her expression unreadable.

In that charged moment, I hear Alex whisper behind me, "You got this. Just be yourself."

But before I can respond, I notice the judge's expression shift, her brows furrowing as she raises an eyebrow and leans closer, seemingly waiting for something—my next move, my next words.

The air thickens, and my heart pounds in my chest, teetering on the edge of an unseen precipice. As the silence stretches, the weight of the moment threatens to pull me under, leaving me suspended between fear and opportunity, poised on the brink of a life-changing decision that could catapult me into the spotlight or plunge me into darkness.

"Are you ready to show me what you're made of?" she asks, her voice cutting through the silence like a blade.

I open my mouth to respond, but no words come. Instead, a shocking realization grips me—this is my moment, and I have no idea how it will end.

Chapter 5: The Fall

The lights dimmed slightly, the rhythmic pulse of the music flooding the runway like a heartbeat, each beat an invitation to lose oneself in the art I had meticulously crafted. Models glided like ethereal beings, each step a testament to the hours spent pouring over fabric swatches, color palettes, and designs that felt like pieces of my soul stitched into existence. I stood backstage, my heart pounding with a mix of exhilaration and anxiety, ready to unleash my vision upon an audience that I hoped would embrace it.

As the first model stepped into the spotlight, the crowd erupted in applause. I caught glimpses of familiar faces: friends, colleagues, critics—all eyes trained on the runway. The fabric shimmered under the bright lights, catching the glances of every influencer and editor present. I had dared to break away from the conventional, to weave a narrative into my collection, one that celebrated not just fashion but also the resilience that comes with it. It was my statement against the tide of perfection that often suffocated creativity.

Just as I allowed myself to bask in the initial applause, the atmosphere shifted like a gust of wind before a storm. I watched, horrified, as one of my models, an exuberant girl named Mia, stumbled awkwardly, her ankle twisting just enough to send her tumbling toward the floor. Time slowed; the gasp from the audience echoed like a gunshot, the sudden silence almost suffocating. In that brief moment, I could almost hear the collective breath held in anticipation of the fallout.

The chaos that followed felt like a slap. Fabric ripped and twisted around her, transforming the elegant dress I had envisioned into a tangle of misfortune. Whispers cascaded through the audience, a tide of judgment that threatened to pull me under. "How could she let this happen?" I could hear Lydia's voice, sharp as glass, slicing through the tension. She stood on the sidelines, her smirk a cruel reminder of the stakes involved. I felt my heart sink, the heavy weight of embarrassment threatening to crush me.

But just then, I caught Alex's eye from the back of the room. He was leaning against the wall, arms crossed, a hint of a smile playing on his lips. That small gesture felt like a lifeline thrown into turbulent waters. I could feel the warmth of his gaze wrapping around me, urging me to rise above the chaos, to reclaim the narrative. It was as if he was saying, "You've got this. Don't let them see you falter." I inhaled sharply, the air filling my lungs with renewed determination.

The instinct to retreat into despair waged war with the fire ignited by Alex's encouragement. Instead of succumbing to embarrassment, I took a deep breath and stepped into the light. The music surged, and I let my mind race ahead, plotting an improvisation that could salvage not just my show but the message behind it. "Fashion is about resilience," I called out, my voice ringing through the dimness like a bell. "It's about embracing the imperfections."

With a flick of my wrist, I signaled the remaining models to pause. I stepped into the chaos, my heels clicking sharply against the runway, and faced the audience. "What you see here is not just a collection; it's a testament to how we rise from the unexpected." As I spoke, I gestured to Mia, who was struggling to her feet, her face flushed but her spirit unbroken. The audience shifted, the tension in the room gradually morphing into something different—curiosity mingled with admiration.

"Let this moment remind us that beauty lies not in perfection but in the strength to stand back up after a fall," I continued, feeling the energy of the room transform. The murmurs began to fade, replaced by intrigued whispers. The way I spoke seemed to weave a spell, pulling them into a shared understanding, a connection that transcended mere fabric and design.

Alex's smile widened as he straightened, his presence grounding me. I watched as the audience leaned forward, captivated. It was then that I realized I had turned a potential disaster into a statement—a conversation about resilience, about authenticity in a world obsessed with the flawless.

As the models resumed their walk, I joined Mia on the runway, my heart swelling with pride as we moved together. The applause began to swell, hesitant at first, but gaining momentum until it echoed off the walls like thunder. I felt the warmth of acceptance wash over me, mingling with the electric thrill of having turned a moment of despair into an affirmation of strength.

After the final model exited the stage, the air thick with applause and murmurs of appreciation, I took a moment to breathe. My heart raced, adrenaline still coursing through me, but amidst the noise, I felt an unmistakable shift. While the reviews that followed were mixed, the exhilaration of standing tall amidst chaos had ignited something deep within me—a fierce determination that would not waver.

Alex found me backstage, his eyes sparkling with pride. "You did it," he said, his voice warm like a familiar embrace. "You turned it around." I could see the sincerity in his gaze, and it filled me with an undeniable sense of hope. The chaos had not consumed me; instead, it had forged a new path, a brighter future woven with the threads of resilience. And as I stood there, my heart still racing from the performance, I knew I was ready for whatever came next.

The afterparty swelled with energy, a dazzling contrast to the turmoil of the runway. Glittering lights hung like stars overhead, illuminating the faces of those who had just witnessed my most chaotic moment. I stepped into the crowd, a refreshing cocktail in hand, but it was hard to shake off the remnants of anxiety that lingered in my chest. Every compliment felt like a lifeline, but whispers of criticism still loomed in the air, waiting to ensnare me like tendrils of smoke.

"Hey, look at you, the queen of resilience!" Alex's voice broke through the hum of conversation, smooth and playful. He leaned against a column, his presence commanding yet effortlessly casual. The way he said "queen" made it sound less like a title and more like an inside joke, as if we were sharing a secret that only we understood.

I smirked, tossing my hair over my shoulder, attempting to reclaim the confident persona I had exuded on the runway. "Yes, well, queens do have a flair for drama, don't they? I just didn't expect the stumble to be part of my royal debut."

"Let's be honest," he said, stepping closer, his eyes bright with mischief, "if the fabric hadn't ripped, I might have been worried about you. A little chaos adds character."

"Ah, so you're saying I need to embrace my inner disaster?" I laughed, swirling the drink in my hand. The ice clinked like tiny chimes, reminding me of the rhythmic cadence I'd found on the runway.

"Exactly," he replied, leaning in as if sharing a conspiratorial secret. "Think of it as fashion's way of keeping you humble. If it were too perfect, people would just assume you had a team of robots working behind the scenes."

"Robots?" I raised an eyebrow, intrigued. "What a boring fashion show that would be. Imagine the audience trying to clap for a bunch of metal arms. 'Oh, look at that perfectly stitched hem! Truly a marvel of engineering!'" I punctuated my mockery with a dramatic sigh.

"Right? Not even a single 'wow' moment," Alex said, laughing. "I, for one, prefer the unpredictability of human emotion over shiny robots. I'd take a fabric tear any day if it leads to a showstopper moment."

His encouragement was like an invisible thread stitching together the scattered pieces of my confidence. It was refreshing to talk with someone who didn't dwell on my stumbles but rather celebrated them. Just then, Lydia approached, her smirk slipping into a smile that didn't quite reach her eyes. "Congratulations on the show," she said, her tone laced with thinly veiled sarcasm. "Really bold to lean into a wardrobe malfunction like that. How avant-garde of you."

"Thanks, Lydia," I replied, matching her energy with a forced cheeriness. "I like to think of it as turning lemons into a fabulous cocktail dress."

She chuckled, but it didn't sound genuine. "You know, you might want to work on your model's coordination next time. A little practice could prevent such... dramatic falls."

"Or," I shot back, feeling a spark of defiance, "maybe I should teach my models how to embrace chaos. You never know when a spontaneous performance art piece might be just what the audience needs."

"Oh, darling, I can see it now: 'The Fall of Fashion.' A tragic tale of torn seams and broken dreams," she quipped, rolling her eyes. "Don't worry; I'm sure the critics will love it."

"Sure," I retorted, "as long as you remember to call me after the reviews come out. I'll need a good laugh."

Lydia narrowed her eyes, but before she could respond, Alex chimed in, "You know, Lydia, your critique might have more weight if you didn't sound like you were auditioning for a role in a Shakespearean tragedy. Have you considered comedy?"

"Maybe I should," she replied, her voice cold. "It's certainly more entertaining than your little drama, Alex."

As she flounced away, I leaned closer to Alex, lowering my voice. "Thanks for stepping in. Lydia's been particularly delightful tonight."

"Just doing my part to keep the trolls at bay," he said with a shrug, but I caught the underlying tension in his posture. "But honestly, don't let her get under your skin. You handled that whole thing like a pro. People are talking, and not just about the fall."

I glanced around the room, suddenly aware of the buzz that seemed to swirl around us. "You think?"

"Definitely," he said, his sincerity refreshing. "You've got the right blend of charm and tenacity. That's what people will remember—not the stumble, but how you turned it into a moment."

The warmth of his words wrapped around me, banishing the lingering shadows of doubt. I felt buoyed by a renewed sense of purpose, the fire inside me stoked by his belief. "You know," I said, glancing back at the crowd, "if I can survive Lydia's barbs and a fabric malfunction, I can handle anything. I'm practically invincible."

"Ah, but that's the danger," Alex replied, his eyes glinting with mischief. "Once you start believing you're invincible, the universe will throw a metaphorical piano at you just to prove you wrong."

"Thanks for the vote of confidence!" I shot back, pretending to roll my eyes. "So, should I start dodging pianos, or do you have any other catastrophes you'd like to warn me about?"

"Just stay on your toes. Fashion is a battlefield," he said, raising his glass in a toast. "Here's to surviving the chaos and coming out stronger."

"Cheers to that," I said, clinking my glass against his, the sound ringing out like a promise.

In that moment, amidst the laughter and chatter of the afterparty, I felt a shift within me. The night had transformed from a mere showcase into a celebration of resilience, a testament to the beauty of embracing the unexpected. I realized that I didn't just want to survive the chaos—I wanted to thrive in it, to mold it into something uniquely mine. The thought filled me with a sense of possibility, and as I stood there, surrounded by friends, laughter, and the lingering thrill of the runway, I understood that this was just the beginning.

The afterparty buzzed with an infectious energy that felt almost intoxicating. Laughter mingled with the sound of clinking glasses, and a kaleidoscope of colors danced before my eyes as guests moved through the room, their outfits a testament to the very creativity I sought to embody in my designs. I swirled my drink, the vibrant hue reflecting the lights like the remnants of a sunset, and felt the heady mix of pride and adrenaline coursing through me.

"You seem lost in thought," Alex remarked, slipping up beside me with that charming grin that always made my heart skip. "Plotting your next bold statement, or just enjoying the view?"

I turned to him, a smile tugging at my lips. "Maybe a bit of both. Or perhaps I'm just trying to figure out how to dodge the pianos you warned me about."

"Good thinking," he said, feigning seriousness. "If there's one thing I know about fashion, it's that you can never be too careful. I mean, who wants to be the designer known for a fatal fashion accident?"

"Right? I can hear it now: 'Tragic Fall Claims Aspiring Designer.' Not quite the headline I'm aiming for," I quipped, playfully rolling my eyes. "But seriously, the chaos had its silver lining. I didn't expect people to rally behind the whole 'embracing imperfection' theme."

"Sometimes, it takes a little chaos to reveal the brilliance beneath the surface," he replied, his gaze steady. "You're not just showcasing clothing; you're sharing a piece of yourself with them. That's what makes your work resonate."

"I hope so. There's always that nagging voice in the back of my head, saying I need to be perfect," I admitted, the weight of vulnerability spilling out before I could stop it. "But tonight, it felt liberating to just own it. To turn a disaster into something meaningful."

"Exactly!" he said, his enthusiasm infectious. "And let's be real: the fashion world is filled with disasters. It's how you handle them that defines you as a designer—and a person. You've got the talent and the passion. Just keep leaning into it."

As we laughed and chatted, I caught glimpses of familiar faces weaving through the crowd—some friendly, some not-so-friendly. Lydia hovered at the edge of the gathering, her presence as prickly as a thorn bush. She was engaged in conversation with a prominent fashion editor, her smile sharp and rehearsed. I couldn't help but wonder if she was weaving a narrative about me already, her favorite pastime.

"What's that look?" Alex asked, tilting his head slightly in the direction of Lydia. "You're not about to plot her downfall, are you?"

I chuckled, shaking my head. "No, but it wouldn't hurt to have a little fairy dust and a few well-aimed spells at my disposal. You know, just to keep her on her toes."

"Fairy dust is overrated," Alex said, leaning closer, his voice a conspiratorial whisper. "I'd suggest a well-placed critique about her last collection. I mean, the shades of beige she used were so dull they could have doubled as wallpaper."

I burst out laughing, the tension in my chest easing a bit more. "That's it! I'll just call it 'The Great Beige Dilemma' and watch her squirm."

"See? You're already thinking like a fashionista." He nudged me gently, a playful spark in his eyes. "Let's get you a drink and plot your witty comeback while we're at it."

As we made our way to the bar, I caught sight of a group of influencers who had just arrived, their phones out, recording every moment like it was some kind of reality show. They swarmed toward me, their excitement palpable. "That was epic!" one exclaimed, her voice barely audible over the cacophony. "How did you turn that fall into a statement piece? We need to capture this!"

STITCHED IN AMBITION

"Yeah, tell us everything!" another chimed in, her eyes wide with admiration.

I smiled, feeling a rush of adrenaline. "Honestly? I just decided to embrace the chaos. It's what fashion is about—surprise, spontaneity, and making a statement, even if it's not what you intended."

They hung on my every word, the realization hitting me that perhaps I was more than just a designer struggling for validation. I was a storyteller, weaving narratives that resonated with others.

But as I reveled in the attention, a shadow passed over my moment. Lydia approached, her expression hardening into something dangerously polite. "How charming," she said, her tone saccharine. "Turning a disaster into a marketing gimmick must be quite the talent."

"Glad you noticed," I replied, not bothering to hide my smirk. "Not everyone can pull off a wardrobe malfunction with such flair."

"True," she said, her smile unwavering. "But some of us prefer a more polished approach to our work. Perhaps you should consider investing in better craftsmanship next time."

"Or maybe I'll just stick to the art of improvisation. It's served me well tonight," I shot back, my confidence bubbling over.

She arched an eyebrow, and for a fleeting moment, I wondered if I'd gone too far. But the fire inside me was unrelenting. "Good luck with your next collection," she added, her tone dripping with faux sincerity. "I'm sure it'll be as... riveting as this one."

The moment hung in the air, a tension-filled silence slicing through the crowd like a knife. Just as I opened my mouth to respond, the lights flickered ominously, plunging us into near darkness. Gasps erupted as whispers spread like wildfire, and I felt the collective energy of the room shift dramatically.

"Uh-oh," Alex muttered, squinting into the shadows. "That can't be good."

Before I could react, a loud crash echoed through the venue. My heart raced as I whipped around, eyes wide, searching for the source of the chaos. The crowd began to stir, a mixture of curiosity and panic washing over us. A waiter rushed past, his tray of drinks scattering to the floor, a mosaic of glass and liquid glinting ominously in the dim light.

"What just happened?" I asked, my voice rising above the din, my pulse quickening as uncertainty enveloped me.

"Not sure, but it looks like the show isn't over yet," Alex said, scanning the room.

Just as I turned back to him, I spotted Lydia in the distance, a figure emerging from the chaos, her eyes narrowed and a mischievous grin splitting her face. Whatever had just happened, she seemed to be reveling in it, her fingers dancing in delight like she'd orchestrated the whole affair.

And then, with a swift movement, she pointed directly at me, her voice cutting through the noise. "Ladies and gentlemen! I think you're going to want to pay attention to what comes next!"

My breath caught in my throat, and as the lights flickered back on, revealing a shocking scene before me, I knew this was only the beginning.

Chapter 6: Unmasking Vulnerabilities

The aroma of freshly brewed coffee hung in the air like an old friend, wrapping around me as I hunched over my journal at the back corner of the café. Each sip felt like a brief hug, a comforting embrace against the chill of my thoughts. I had come here to escape, to drown out the chaos of the outside world, but as the pages of my journal filled with inked confessions, the noise inside my head only grew louder. The showcase had been a cacophony of applause and critique, and while the clamor had faded, its echoes lingered. I could still hear the whispers of doubt, sharp and cruel, gnawing at my confidence.

Why do I even try? I scrawled the question in loops, letting the ink spill like the tears I refused to shed. My mother would have loved to see me perform. I could picture her, her eyes gleaming with pride as she clapped, the light dancing in her hair as if the sun itself had decided to bless her presence. The thought of her made my chest tighten. I hadn't just lost a parent; I had lost my biggest cheerleader, my safe harbor. Those memories of her warmth were now tangled with the weight of expectations I felt from everyone else—friends, critics, and especially myself.

I paused, the pen hovering above the page. It was easier to bury those emotions, to build walls high enough that I couldn't even hear the echoes of my past. The grief had settled into a comfortable, heavy cloak around my shoulders, making me feel like I was carrying the weight of the world—one I had constructed brick by emotional brick. But today, in this little café where the chatter buzzed around me like a comforting hum, I realized I couldn't hide from it any longer.

Just as I was about to flip the page and distract myself with a fresh start, the bell above the door jingled, and Alex walked in. He looked like a breath of fresh air in his fitted navy jacket, tousled hair gleaming under the café lights. My heart did that annoying little flutter it had developed a habit of performing whenever he was near, and I quickly diverted my gaze back to my journal, hoping he wouldn't notice the embarrassment flooding my cheeks.

"Hey," he said, sliding into the seat across from me without an invitation. His eyes sparkled with mischief, but I could also see the weariness hiding just beneath the surface. "Still writing those secret novels?"

"Something like that," I replied, forcing a smile as I tried to keep my tone light. "It's more of a confessional than a novel, actually."

He arched an eyebrow, leaning closer, intrigued. "Ooh, secrets! I want in. What juicy drama are we talking about? Betrayal? Heartbreak?" His voice danced with playful intensity, coaxing me to spill my thoughts like a well-shaken soda.

I chuckled, unable to resist his charm. "More like existential dread and unrequited crushes." The honesty slipped out, and I winced inwardly, regretting my admission.

"Unrequited crushes, huh?" he mused, a smirk playing on his lips. "Sounds like the perfect basis for a tragic romance." He tilted his head, studying me. "What's the tragic part?"

"Probably the part where I can't bring myself to admit it," I said, biting my lip. The banter felt like a dance, light and teasing, but I could feel the gravity of my own truth pulling at me, begging to be released.

"Admitting it to whom? The crush?"

"Or myself," I murmured, the weight of those words feeling heavier than I expected. "Sometimes it's easier to pretend everything is fine when you're really just...lost."

A silence hung between us, thick and palpable, and for a moment, I could see the flicker of understanding in his gaze. "You're not lost," he said softly, and it felt like a promise rather than just a reassurance. "You're just...navigating. It's okay to not have it all figured out."

I looked down, tracing the lines of my journal with trembling fingers, the realization washing over me like a tide. This was the first time someone had seen through my carefully curated facade. "I've just been so afraid of failing," I confessed, the words spilling out like the raw, exposed nerves of my heart. "I thought I could bury my feelings and everything would be fine, but it's like I'm always standing at the edge of something I can't reach."

"Fear of failure can be paralyzing," he replied, his voice steady. "I get that. There are days when I wake up and wonder if I'm just chasing shadows. Like, is this all just a series of unfinished stories?"

The openness in his tone surprised me. It was as if he had peeled away layers of his own carefully constructed defenses. "You too?" I asked, meeting his eyes. "You feel that way?"

He nodded, a flicker of vulnerability passing over his features. "Yeah. Like everyone expects something from me, but what if I'm not enough?"

The weight of his confession hung between us, intimate and raw. In that moment, our shared insecurities became threads weaving us closer together. The café, once bustling and noisy, faded into a backdrop as we stood on the precipice of something profound.

"I thought I was alone in this," I admitted, my voice barely a whisper. "But knowing you feel the same..."

"It's a lot," he agreed, leaning back in his chair, running a hand through his hair. "But maybe it's about finding those moments that remind us why we started in the first place. You know?"

"Moments like this?" I said, a hint of teasing returning to my tone, hoping to lighten the mood again.

He laughed, and it was genuine, brightening his face in a way that made my heart swell. "Exactly. Like this. Or when you're up on stage, pouring your heart out."

The thought sent a shiver of excitement through me, the connection between us growing as we both recognized the importance of vulnerability. The shadows I had carried began to feel a little lighter, as if sharing my burden had made it easier to breathe.

"Maybe we can help each other," I suggested, my heart racing. "To navigate through the fears and the noise. You know, make it a team effort."

"I'd like that," he said, his smile turning softer, the warmth radiating between us undeniable. "Just as long as we don't get too lost along the way."

I laughed again, the sound bubbling up and spilling over, spilling light into the dark corners of my heart. "Deal. But just so you know, I'm terrible at directions."

"Perfect," he replied, leaning back, an amused glint in his eyes. "I'm pretty sure that makes you my perfect partner in crime."

As we sank into the comfortable rhythm of conversation, the café around us transformed from a mere backdrop into a cocoon of warmth and understanding. I could feel the beginnings of something beautiful unfurling, delicate yet vibrant, as if we were both shedding the weight of our pasts in the warm glow of the moment. And for the first time in a long while, I felt a flicker of hope—the kind that comes when you realize you might not be alone in your journey after all.

The sunlight streamed through the café windows, illuminating the dance of dust motes in the air like tiny stars caught in a perpetual twilight. I sat across from Alex, feeling as if we had crafted our own little universe where vulnerability was currency, and honesty sparkled like the coffee we sipped. Each shared word felt like a soft caress, a reassurance that we weren't merely actors playing our parts but co-authors of a narrative still being written.

"Okay, if we're unmasking vulnerabilities here, what's your biggest fear?" Alex leaned back, his arms crossed, a playful grin on his face that dared me to answer honestly.

I took a moment, letting the question hang between us. "I guess it's that I'll never be good enough. Not for the stage, not for my mom, and definitely not for myself. That I'll always be a half-finished painting, stuck in the gallery of my own mind."

His eyes widened, and the grin faded just slightly. "That's deep. I was expecting something more along the lines of spiders or heights."

"Oh please," I laughed, rolling my eyes. "I'm a performer. I've learned to embrace the drama."

"Fair point," he said, nodding. "But still, the idea of not measuring up... that's rough."

"And what about you?" I asked, leaning forward, eager to return the favor. "What haunts you?"

His expression shifted, and for a moment, I could see the shadows dance across his features. "I fear I'm just an echo, you know? Like, I've spent so long trying to live up to everyone else's dreams for me that I forgot to ask what my own are. It's like running on a treadmill but never going anywhere."

"That sounds exhausting," I said softly, the weight of his words settling in the space between us. "You should get off that treadmill, then."

"I'd love to," he replied, a laugh escaping his lips. "But it's surprisingly comfortable. Plus, my legs are in great shape."

"Always with the charm," I said, shaking my head. "But seriously, what would it take to figure out your own dreams?"

He looked thoughtful for a moment, then shrugged. "Maybe just a little courage. Or a map? I'm terrible with directions, after all."

"Right. You're a lost puppy on a treadmill," I teased, my heart swelling at the thought of his charmingly awkward self.

"Better than being a stray cat, I guess. They just knock things off the table and then stare at you like you did something wrong."

"Touché," I laughed, my eyes brightening with the ease of our conversation. There was something inherently comforting about our exchange, a sense that we were both grappling with our own inner chaos while simultaneously creating a little sanctuary together.

As we shared our fears, the walls I had built around my heart began to crack, allowing a glimpse of light in. Alex's presence felt grounding, a reminder that maybe I wasn't as alone as I thought. In turn, I could see the heaviness in his eyes lightening, if only just.

"Tell me," I said, suddenly serious, "what's something you've always wanted to do but haven't?"

His gaze dropped to the table, and for a moment, he seemed lost in thought. "I've always wanted to travel. There are so many places that exist beyond the confines of this town, beyond the expectations. I want to see the world—Paris, Tokyo, New York." He sighed, a wistful smile playing at the corners of his mouth. "But I keep telling myself it's not practical. What about work? Responsibilities?"

"Responsibilities? Who needs those?" I feigned a dramatic gasp. "We're too young for that! Imagine strolling through the streets of Paris, a baguette in hand, the Eiffel Tower towering above you."

"Right? But then reality hits, and I feel like I have to make a choice—stay safe or leap into the unknown."

"Why can't you do both?" I challenged, my heart racing with the thrill of the idea. "What if we make a pact? We can figure out how to chase our dreams together. You get to travel, and I get to perform without the weight of expectations suffocating me."

His eyes lit up with a spark of intrigue, and I could practically see the gears turning in his head. "A pact, huh? You're really going to hold me to that? What if I fail? What if I choose the treadmill again?"

"Then I'll drag you off it," I said, feigning seriousness. "No more running in circles."

"Deal," he said, a hint of laughter dancing in his voice. "But only if you promise to join me on my travels. Who else is going to keep me from getting lost?"

"Done. But only if I can pick the destinations."

"Fair enough. Where to first, oh wise one?"

I grinned, my excitement bubbling over. "Paris! We'll eat all the croissants, visit every art gallery, and I'll finally stand in front of the Mona Lisa and critique her smile. It'll be an adventure."

"Now you're talking!" he exclaimed, his enthusiasm infectious. "But what if she critiques you back?"

I couldn't help but laugh, the sound brightening the atmosphere around us. "Then I'll just remind her she's stuck behind glass, and I'm out here living my life!"

Our laughter echoed off the walls, weaving a thread of connection that felt as solid as the ground beneath us. It was exhilarating, this sudden plunge into the unknown. For the first time, I felt the flicker of excitement, a yearning to break free from the self-imposed confines I had wrapped around my heart.

But just as quickly as the thrill surged, a shadow crept back into my thoughts. What if I couldn't follow through? What if this was just another pipe dream destined to fade away like the wisps of steam rising from our cups? I glanced at Alex, his face illuminated with laughter and light, and I knew I had to try.

The conversation drifted into a comfortable rhythm, full of teasing jabs and playful challenges, and before I knew it, hours had slipped away. The café was bustling, the sun beginning to dip low in the sky, casting golden hues across the room.

"Look at us, wasting time with grand plans instead of getting back to reality," Alex said, mockingly serious.

"Ah, but this is reality," I replied, a spark of mischief in my eyes. "At least, it's our reality."

He raised his cup, a gesture of mock toast. "To our reality, then. May it be filled with croissants and questionable decisions."

"And unfiltered conversations," I added, clinking my cup against his with a flourish.

The moment felt momentous, like a threshold we had crossed into a world of possibilities. We had shared our fears, hopes, and dreams, and somehow, that felt like the beginning of something beautiful.

As we settled back into our chairs, a comfortable silence enveloped us, the warmth of our connection wrapping around us like a soft blanket. I couldn't help but wonder where this journey would take us, but for now, I was content to simply enjoy the moment, embracing the magic of possibility that crackled in the air around us.

The café hummed with the comforting buzz of conversation and clinking cups, an ambient backdrop to the flickering spark of something new that danced between Alex and me. We had both shed layers of ourselves, revealing vulnerabilities that felt as intimate as they were liberating. The laughter, the camaraderie, the shared dreams—all of it wove us together in a tapestry of newfound friendship that felt surprisingly sturdy.

"So, croissants in Paris, questionable decisions, and an ever-growing list of dreams," Alex said, leaning back in his chair, his fingers tracing the rim of his coffee cup. "What else should be on our itinerary? A romantic boat ride on the Seine?"

I couldn't help but roll my eyes, a smile tugging at my lips. "Oh please, I'm pretty sure that's just a cliché waiting to happen. How about we skip the romanticism and get straight to the adventure? Like, I don't know, eating our weight in pastries and trying to not get lost in the labyrinth of streets?"

"Ah, the true essence of travel," he replied with mock solemnity. "Food and a complete lack of direction."

"Exactly! We can post photos of ourselves looking bewildered with croissants half-eaten," I quipped, feeling lighter with each word.

"Now that's a travel blog I would read," he chuckled, and I noticed how his laughter had an effortless way of wrapping around me, disarming any lingering doubts I had.

But as we basked in our shared joy, a flicker of anxiety crept back in, tugging at the edges of my newfound enthusiasm. What if this moment was just a fleeting escape from the reality waiting for me outside these walls? What if the weight of my unresolved grief returned, heavier than before? My thoughts threatened to spiral, but I shook them off, refusing to let shadows dampen our laughter.

"So, what's the first thing you'd do when you get to Paris?" he asked, leaning forward, genuine curiosity shining in his eyes.

"Hmm, that's tough. Probably stop by a bakery first. I mean, you can't really claim to be in Paris without trying an authentic croissant, right?"

He nodded solemnly, as if we were discussing something of great importance. "Valid point. But after that?"

"Then I'd find a corner café, plop myself down with my journal, and scribble away like some tortured artist, all while sipping espresso. It's practically a rite of passage."

"Are you sure you wouldn't just sit there staring at the Eiffel Tower, too awed to write anything?" he challenged, his tone light yet teasing.

"Look, I can be profound and superficial all at once," I shot back, leaning in closer. "It's a talent."

His eyes sparkled with mirth. "I believe it. You could be a bestselling author in no time."

"And you could be my charming yet slightly obnoxious sidekick," I countered, raising an eyebrow playfully.

"Charming? I'll take that," he grinned, leaning back as if pleased with himself. "But I draw the line at being obnoxious."

"Really? You've set your standards that high?"

"Someone has to!" he declared with a mock heroism, gesturing grandly as if he were proclaiming a noble cause.

Our laughter melded with the clinking of cups and the murmur of voices around us, the atmosphere wrapped in warmth. For a moment, it felt like we had carved out our own little bubble, one free of judgment and expectations.

But just as I was beginning to lose myself in the moment, a figure entered the café, cutting through our laughter like a knife. It was Chloe, my former dance instructor and a name I hadn't heard in what felt like ages. Her presence sent an unexpected wave of tension rippling through the air.

"Oh great," I muttered under my breath, instinctively slumping in my seat. "The last person I wanted to see."

Alex's brow furrowed in concern. "What's wrong? Who is she?"

"She's... a bit of a legend around here," I explained, trying to sound casual as my heart raced. "But not the good kind. She's known for tearing apart performances like a shark with a feeding frenzy."

"Ah, the critic," he said, glancing over his shoulder at her. "Do you think she saw you?"

"Wouldn't surprise me," I replied, my stomach twisting in knots. "She has a way of making her presence felt. It's like she can smell fear."

"Then don't give her that satisfaction," he urged, his tone suddenly serious. "Stay in your moment. You've got this."

With a nod, I forced myself to breathe, concentrating on the warmth of the coffee cup in my hands, the softness of the moment we had created. But the instant the door swung open, Chloe's sharp gaze locked onto mine, and I could feel the weight of her scrutiny like a cold wind sweeping through the café.

"Look who we have here," she called, her voice dripping with feigned sweetness. "The star of the showcase, hiding in the shadows. How quaint."

My heart sank, and Alex shifted uneasily in his seat. "Ignore her," he whispered, but I could see the tension in his shoulders.

"Out of your element, are we?" Chloe continued, her smile predatory. "I heard your performance didn't quite meet expectations. I suppose that's what happens when you chase dreams that are a little too ambitious."

I bristled at her words, the familiar sting of self-doubt creeping back in. "What do you want, Chloe?" I managed to say, trying to keep my voice steady.

"I just thought I'd check in on my favorite underachiever," she retorted, her tone mocking. "After all, it's not every day I get to see someone with so much potential squander it."

The café suddenly felt too small, too suffocating, as I battled to maintain my composure. I could feel the warmth of Alex's presence next to me, a silent reminder that I wasn't entirely alone. "You really know how to make an entrance," he finally said, a hint of defiance in his voice. "Care to make a quick exit?"

Chloe raised an eyebrow, clearly unaccustomed to being challenged. "And who are you? Her guardian? This isn't a fairy tale, sweetheart."

"No, just a guy who thinks it's sad when someone has to belittle others to feel better about themselves," Alex shot back, his tone cool and unwavering.

The tension shifted, electrifying the air. Chloe's expression hardened, her eyes narrowing at Alex. "Cute. But you should know better than to interfere in matters that don't concern you."

"Actually, they concern me quite a bit," Alex said, unflinching. "She's not just an underachiever. She's a dreamer, and if you can't handle that, maybe you should take your negativity elsewhere."

I was torn between disbelief and gratitude. Here was this guy I'd only just started to connect with, standing up for me against someone who had loomed like a specter over my dreams. But would this confrontation embolden Chloe, or would it push her to strike harder?

"Watch yourself, darling," she hissed, her voice low and threatening. "Dreams are only as good as the talent that backs them up. I hope you've got the chops to match those ambitions."

As she turned on her heel and stalked away, I felt the weight of her words hanging in the air, taunting me. "Did you really just defend me?" I asked, astonished, my heart racing.

"I did," he replied, a mix of surprise and pride etched across his face. "But I think you owe me an explanation about her."

"I... I will," I stammered, the adrenaline still coursing through me. "But maybe I need a moment to collect my thoughts first."

"Take all the time you need," he said, his expression softening.

Yet just as I felt the safety of the moment return, my phone buzzed violently on the table, the screen lighting up with an incoming message. I glanced down, my heart dropping at the name displayed: my father.

The words were clear, cutting through the haze of the café like a cold wind: We need to talk. It's important.

A chill ran down my spine, and I could feel the world tilting beneath me. The warmth of the café faded, replaced by an icy grip of uncertainty that threatened to unravel everything.

"What's wrong?" Alex asked, concern etched into his features.

"Just... it's my dad," I whispered, dread coiling around my chest.

"What does he want?"

"I don't know," I admitted, the weight of the moment settling over me.

But even as I spoke, the lingering echo of Chloe's words haunted me, twisting in my mind like a dark melody. Was I really just a dreamer chasing shadows? And what could my father want that felt so urgent?

As Alex reached out, placing a reassuring hand on mine, the world around us seemed to fade into the background, leaving me standing on the precipice of the unknown, uncertainty looming ahead like a storm on the horizon. And just as I felt the pull of that storm beginning to gather, a sudden thought pierced through the chaos: what if this conversation with my father was the catalyst for everything I feared?

With my heart pounding, I braced myself for the unknown.

Chapter 7: Crossing Boundaries

The sun dipped low in the sky, casting a warm golden hue over the streets of Brooklyn. Alex and I meandered through the narrow lanes of Cobble Hill, the air thick with the scent of roasted coffee and fresh pastries wafting from a nearby café. Each step felt light, buoyed by the laughter that erupted between us, the kind that turns the mundane into something magical. I could barely remember the last time I felt so carefree, so completely present in the moment.

"Have you ever tried to take a perfect photo of a street vendor?" Alex asked, his voice playful, as we stopped near a bustling food truck. A long line of patrons awaited their turn for tacos, the sizzling sound of meat grilling punctuating the otherwise mellow afternoon.

"Are you kidding? It's like trying to capture the fleeting beauty of a sunset with a toaster," I replied, chuckling at the absurdity of it. "I've tried and failed more times than I can count. It's an art form, really."

He grinned, the kind of grin that crinkled the corners of his eyes and made my heart race in a way I wasn't quite ready to acknowledge. "Alright, Miss Toaster Photographer, let's give it a shot." He reached for my hand, and I felt the familiar flutter of warmth radiate up my arm.

We spent the next hour darting between the trucks, snapping pictures of messy tacos, colorful fruit cups, and smiling customers. Alex had a knack for capturing the essence of each moment, his camera clicking in sync with the beats of the city. I found myself enamored not just with his skill but with the way he saw the world, through a lens tinted with curiosity and a touch of mischief.

"You know, you could always try food photography if the whole modeling gig doesn't work out," he teased, leaning in closer to examine one of my shots.

"Ah, yes. Because who wouldn't want to be known as the 'Taco Whisperer'?" I shot back, shaking my head with laughter. But the playful banter masked an undercurrent of something more profound, something that thrummed between us like an unspoken promise.

As the sun set, casting long shadows that danced on the pavement, we found ourselves in the heart of DUMBO. The iconic view of the Manhattan skyline loomed before us, the city lights flickering to life, reflecting off the East River like a thousand stars fallen to earth. It was breathtaking, yet my attention was drawn elsewhere—toward the boy beside me.

"This is one of my favorite spots," I confessed, my voice barely a whisper as I took in the view, my heart thudding in my chest. "It feels like you can see the entire world from here, all its chaos and beauty."

"Just like us," he murmured, his gaze intense, as if he were reading the very pages of my soul. I felt my breath catch. "A little chaotic, but beautiful all the same."

In that moment, the world around us faded into a blur of colors and sounds, all reduced to the two of us standing on the edge of possibility. I could see the uncertainty in his eyes, mirroring my own. We both understood the implications of the feelings swirling between us, each of us cautiously aware of the stakes involved.

The first kiss came as a soft collision of fears and hopes, our lips brushing together under the glow of city lights. It tasted like the sweetness of vulnerability, a promise wrapped in the thrill of the unknown. But as quickly as it began, the fear of our professional lives intermingling with our personal ones crashed back over us like a cold wave.

"What does this mean for us?" I breathed, pulling back, the warmth of his presence now mingled with an icy dread.

"I don't know," he admitted, running a hand through his tousled hair, the moonlight catching the scattered curls. "But I know I don't want to hide this, whatever this is."

The tension hung between us, thick and palpable, as we navigated the jagged terrain of our budding relationship. Our laughter faded, replaced by the weight of reality, an unspoken agreement settling in. We both knew that Lydia's announcement of a new line, one that threatened to eclipse our own hard work, loomed over us like a dark cloud.

"What if it complicates everything?" I asked, trying to reconcile my heart's desire with the looming consequences. "What if people start to talk? It could ruin everything we've built."

"I'd rather risk it than pretend we're just friends," he said, his voice steady, yet there was a flicker of worry in his eyes. "But I don't want to jeopardize your career or mine."

With a sigh, I leaned against the cold, gritty surface of the building beside us. "I guess we keep it a secret for now? Just until we figure things out?"

His nod was slow, reluctant, but understanding. "Yeah, that seems best."

As we stood there, the city pulsing around us, I couldn't shake the feeling that we were standing on the precipice of something monumental. The lines between our professional lives and personal desires had blurred, and the path ahead felt fraught with uncertainty. Yet, despite the fear, there was a spark of exhilaration, an uncharted territory we were ready to explore together.

The moments that followed were filled with unspoken glances and accidental brushes of our hands, each touch igniting a warmth that belied our solemn agreement. We danced along the edge of friendship and something deeper, each interaction laced with a playful tension that made every shared smile feel electric.

The world felt alive with possibility, and as we wandered back through the vibrant streets of Brooklyn, I couldn't help but hope that whatever challenges lay ahead, we would face them together, one secret kiss at a time.

The next few weeks drifted by in a dreamy haze, the thrill of our secret burgeoning like the soft petals of a cherry blossom. The vibrancy of Brooklyn pulsed around us, each corner we turned a new canvas for our shared adventures. Alex and I navigated our dual lives with a delicate dance of stolen glances and hushed laughter, the thrill of our hidden relationship providing a spark that electrified the simplest moments.

One sunny Saturday afternoon, we found ourselves in Prospect Park, the lush greenery a stark contrast to the urban landscape we had come to know so well. The air was heavy with the scent of blooming flowers and the faint echoes of children's laughter, a backdrop to our clandestine escapade. We sprawled on a picnic blanket, an array of artisanal cheeses and freshly baked baguettes between us, remnants of a hurried stop at a local market.

"Why is it that every time I have brie, I can't help but feel like I'm indulging in the height of luxury?" I mused, slicing off another generous piece with a dramatic flourish.

Alex leaned back, propping himself on one elbow, his eyes sparkling with mischief. "It's the cheese-induced euphoria. Don't you know? Brie is the cheese equivalent of a cashmere sweater—soft, decadent, and utterly unnecessary."

I laughed, my heart swelling at the sound of his voice. "So, essentially, you're saying I'm living in a luxurious cheese fantasy? I'll take it."

The atmosphere around us hummed with life as we tucked into our spread, the chaos of the city far removed from our little sanctuary. We exchanged stories about our most embarrassing moments, each tale accompanied by animated gestures and bursts of laughter that seemed to echo off the trees surrounding us.

But as the sun dipped lower in the sky, the playful mood shifted ever so slightly. The weight of Lydia's impending line hovered over us, a silent specter that crept into our conversation with an unexpected seriousness.

"Have you thought any more about what she's planning?" Alex asked, his tone turning contemplative.

"Honestly? I'd rather not think about it," I admitted, shoving a piece of cheese into my mouth, as if somehow that could drown out the gnawing anxiety. "But it's hard to ignore, especially since I've been hearing whispers around the studio."

"I get it," he replied, reaching out to brush his fingers against mine. The warmth of his touch sent a shiver of something both thrilling and terrifying through me. "But you have to remember how talented you are. Whatever she launches, it won't change your vision."

I offered a weak smile, wishing his words carried more weight. "Easy for you to say. You're not the one whose work is about to be eclipsed by a new shiny collection. I feel like I'm standing on the edge of a cliff, and any moment, I'm going to topple over."

"Then let's take the leap together," he said, his eyes serious yet playful. "If we go down, we go down in style."

I chuckled at the absurdity of it. "So we're throwing ourselves off the cliff in matching outfits? What a fashion statement that would be."

"Absolutely," he grinned, and for a moment, the worry slipped away, replaced by the intoxicating warmth of our connection. But the reality of the situation loomed just beneath the surface, a constant reminder of the precarious balance we were trying to maintain.

The days rolled on, filled with whispered conversations and shared secrets. We would meet after work, exploring the nooks and crannies of the city, pretending the outside world didn't exist. On a particularly balmy evening, we found ourselves in a tucked-away speakeasy in Williamsburg, the dimly lit space buzzing with energy. The air was thick with the scent of bourbon and bitters, and the jazz band in the corner crooned a melody that wrapped around us like an embrace.

I leaned into Alex as we sipped our cocktails, his presence grounding me in a way I hadn't expected. "What would you do if you could create anything, no limits?" I asked, trying to pull him into a daydream, one where the pressures of our lives didn't exist.

He paused, contemplating, a glimmer of something faraway in his eyes. "I'd build a rooftop garden filled with every flower imaginable. A place where people could escape the chaos, even if just for a moment. You know, something to remind us all that beauty can bloom even in the darkest places."

"Sounds like a lot of maintenance," I replied, playfully raising an eyebrow. "And what if the flowers don't grow? Are we talking about a floral graveyard instead?"

He laughed, the sound rich and warm, sending butterflies dancing in my stomach. "Okay, so maybe I'd hire someone to take care of the flowers while I sip cocktails in the sun."

"Ah, the dream. How very unbothered of you," I teased, swirling the remnants of my drink.

"Hey, you're welcome to join me in my unbothered utopia anytime," he shot back, his gaze lingering on me with an intensity that made my breath hitch.

The moment felt electric, the air charged with possibilities, yet the harsh reality crept back in. I glanced around the room, momentarily haunted by the thought of Lydia and her new collection, the shadows of doubt threatening to eclipse the brightness of our evening.

"Do you think this will all catch up to us?" I asked, the weight of my worries spilling out into the air between us.

"Only if we let it," he replied, his voice steady. "We're allowed to enjoy this, to find joy amidst the chaos. We just have to keep moving forward."

His words resonated deep within me, a lifeline to hold onto as we traversed this uncharted territory together. But as the evening wore on, I couldn't shake the feeling that we were playing a dangerous game.

Later that night, as we strolled through the dimly lit streets, laughter dancing in the night air, I found my thoughts spiraling. I needed to channel the intensity of my feelings into my work. I could create something that would not only stand out but also be a reflection of who I was becoming.

But how could I do that while juggling this new layer of my relationship with Alex? It felt like a tightrope walk, and one misstep could send everything crashing down. Still, as I looked at him—his easy laughter and the way he made even the mundane feel exhilarating—I knew I wanted to take that risk.

And just as the weight of my thoughts threatened to pull me under, Alex reached for my hand, grounding me once again. I took a deep breath, willing myself to let the chaos of my mind settle.

"Let's just keep making memories," he said softly, and with that, I felt the tension ease, if only for a moment. Together, we stepped into the night, two souls entwined amidst the blooming uncertainty of the future, our laughter echoing off the walls of the city like a promise of what was yet to come.

As the days blurred into weeks, the weight of our secret loomed larger, like an intricate tapestry woven from both delight and anxiety. Alex and I found ourselves navigating a labyrinth of shared laughter and covert glances, each moment tinged with the sweetness of our budding romance and the bitter tang of competition lurking just out of sight. The chaos surrounding Lydia's new line threatened to overshadow everything we had been building, yet there was a comfort in our connection that offered a fleeting escape.

One particularly chilly evening, wrapped in layers of scarves and jackets, we decided to venture to an outdoor winter market in Union Square. The air was crisp, filled with the enticing aromas of spiced cider and roasted chestnuts, as twinkling lights adorned the stalls like stars scattered across a black canvas. We wandered through the market, stopping to admire handmade ornaments and artisan crafts, our fingers brushing together like whispers of something both new and familiar.

"Look at that," I said, pointing to a stall laden with hand-painted mugs. "That one looks like it's judging my life choices."

Alex laughed, a sound that warmed the chilly air. "I think it's judging the fact that you haven't bought it yet. That mug clearly has better taste than I do."

"I mean, who doesn't want a coffee mug that critiques their existence?" I replied, feigning a serious tone as I picked up the gaudy creation. "This is my new therapist. I'll call her 'Muggy McJudgerson.'"

We both cracked up, the sound of our laughter mingling with the festive atmosphere around us. But as I set down the mug, I noticed a few people eyeing me from a nearby booth. My stomach dropped as I recognized them as part of Lydia's team, and the laughter evaporated, replaced by a thick tension that twisted my stomach.

"Let's keep moving," I suggested, my voice suddenly tight.

"Everything okay?" Alex asked, sensing the shift in my demeanor.

"Just... business stuff," I muttered, the words feeling like a thin veil over the truth. I didn't want to shatter the evening with the weight of my worries.

As we weaved through the crowd, the warmth of our earlier banter dimmed, replaced by a growing awareness of the shadows that loomed over us. Just then, a blast of cold wind swept through the market, making me shiver despite my layers.

"Hot cider?" Alex offered, his eyes searching mine.

"Yes, please," I replied, grateful for the chance to retreat into something comforting.

We made our way to the stall, the inviting scent of cinnamon and cloves wrapping around us like a blanket. Alex ordered two steaming cups, and as he turned to pay, I felt my heart race at the thought of facing Lydia and her team. What if they said something? What if they connected the dots?

"Here you go, my dear hot beverage enthusiast," Alex said, handing me a cup adorned with a cheerful snowman.

"Thank you, my coffee mug critic," I said, lifting the cup to my lips. The warmth seeped into me, easing the chill that had settled in my bones.

But my moment of tranquility was short-lived. Just as I was beginning to relax, I caught a glimpse of Lydia's silhouette moving toward us, flanked by her ever-looming presence, Janice, her right-hand woman, who was known for her razor-sharp comments and even sharper judgment.

"Perfect. The universe hates me," I muttered under my breath.

"Don't look now, but your boss is coming over," Alex said, his voice low but edged with mischief.

"Thanks for the heads-up, Captain Obvious," I shot back, forcing a smile as I clutched the cup tighter.

"Darling, there you are!" Lydia's voice rang out, syrupy sweet yet tinged with a sharpness that made my stomach knot. "And Alex! What a surprise to see you here together."

"Just enjoying the market," I replied, injecting as much casualness as I could muster.

Lydia's gaze flickered between us, calculating and shrewd. "I love this time of year. So festive, don't you think?" Her smile was wide, but I sensed a darker undertone.

"Very festive," Alex echoed, his casual demeanor not quite hiding the tension in his shoulders.

"Speaking of festive, I'm thrilled to announce our new line will debut just in time for the holiday rush," Lydia continued, her eyes gleaming with ambition. "It's going to be magnificent."

I forced a smile, feeling the weight of her words settle like lead in my stomach. "I'm sure it will be," I managed, forcing a note of cheer into my voice.

"Are you two collaborating on anything special?" Janice chimed in, her eyes narrowing slightly, assessing us like a hawk.

The question hung in the air, a heavy, unwelcome presence. I exchanged a glance with Alex, the worry flickering between us like a candle about to be snuffed out. "Just some brainstorming," I replied, keeping my tone light. "You know, creative juices flowing and all that."

Lydia tilted her head, a sly smile forming. "Ah, brainstorming. I do love a good idea. Just remember, darling, the competition is fierce, and we have to stand out."

I felt a rush of irritation bubbling beneath the surface. "Of course, competition is what drives us," I replied, my voice steady despite the anger simmering inside. "But collaboration can be just as powerful."

"Oh, how charming," Lydia said, her tone dripping with sarcasm. "I look forward to seeing how you navigate that." With that, she turned to leave, her presence lingering like a storm cloud threatening to burst.

As she walked away, I let out a breath I hadn't realized I was holding. "That was... not subtle," Alex said, his expression reflecting my own discomfort.

"Not subtle at all," I agreed, taking a long sip of my cider to mask the tension brewing inside me. "This is getting out of hand. I can't keep hiding this."

"Maybe it's time we stop letting her dictate our lives," he said, a fierce determination in his voice.

The idea lingered in the air, a tantalizing prospect. But before I could respond, my phone buzzed in my pocket, interrupting the moment. I pulled it out, my heart racing as I saw the message from my colleague, Eva.

"Lydia's line is coming out sooner than expected. She's making big moves. We need to prepare."

The words felt like a punch to the gut, igniting a fire of urgency within me. "I need to go," I said, the weight of impending deadlines crashing down on my shoulders.

"Are you okay?" Alex asked, his eyes filled with concern.

"I don't know. I just—this is all too much," I admitted, frustration bubbling to the surface.

"Hey," he said gently, stepping closer. "We can handle this. Together. Just promise me you won't shut me out."

I nodded, though doubt gnawed at the edges of my mind. I wanted to believe we could weather this storm, but the thought of Lydia's looming threat sent shivers down my spine.

"Let's meet tomorrow, okay?" I said, trying to keep my voice steady. "We can figure out a plan."

"Absolutely," he agreed, a glimmer of hope in his eyes. "We'll come up with something brilliant."

With one last lingering look, I turned and began to walk away, my mind racing. I could feel Alex's gaze on me, grounding me in a way that felt both comforting and precarious. But just as I reached the edge of the market, my phone buzzed again.

This time, it was a call from Lydia.

I hesitated, the weight of the decision heavy in my hand. Should I answer? The ringing felt deafening against the backdrop of holiday cheer.

Taking a deep breath, I pressed the answer button, my heart racing. "Lydia?"

"Darling, we need to talk," she said, her voice smooth yet commanding, sending a chill down my spine. "And you might want to bring Alex."

In that moment, the world seemed to tilt on its axis, and I knew we were standing on the brink of something that could change everything.

Chapter 8: The Awakening

The sun hung low in the sky, casting a golden hue across the small, bustling town. I sat at my makeshift workspace, a cluttered corner of my apartment that doubled as a creative sanctuary. Every inch of the room was adorned with swatches of fabric, sketches pinned haphazardly to the walls, and piles of thread that seemed to multiply when I wasn't looking. The scent of fresh coffee wafted through the air, a constant companion in my quest for inspiration. This morning, however, the usual comfort of my caffeine fix was drowned out by an undercurrent of nervous excitement. I had made a decision, one that felt monumental, like the kind of decision that shifts the axis of your world ever so slightly, making everything tilt in unexpected ways.

As I pulled out a particularly vibrant piece of silk, its colors reminiscent of a sunset after a storm, I thought back to the nights Alex and I spent talking on my balcony. The way his eyes lit up when he spoke about his own dreams, how he painted vivid pictures of what could be. He believed in stories—believed that they had the power to heal. It was during one of those late-night chats, the stars winking above us like the universe was eavesdropping, that I realized I could weave our narratives together into something beautiful. Something that could transcend fabric and thread, transforming into a tapestry of our shared experiences, our highs and lows.

With each stitch I envisioned, I began to see the collection materialize in my mind. I pictured flowing gowns that danced like whispers in the wind, playful jumpsuits that encapsulated spontaneity, and tailored pieces that spoke of strength and resilience. I reached for a piece of paper, my heart racing as I sketched furiously. The pencil flew across the page, its lead capturing the contours of a design that blended elegance with an edge—a reflection of my journey. I could almost hear Alex's voice guiding me, urging me to dig deeper, to explore the rawness of our emotions.

Just then, a sharp knock on my door jolted me from my creative reverie. It was Alex, and my heart fluttered at the thought of him stepping into my world, bringing with him a spark that ignited my creativity. I opened the door, the sunlight streaming in, illuminating the playful tousle of his hair. He stood there, a familiar grin lighting up his face, holding two steaming mugs of coffee in one hand and a half-eaten croissant in the other. "I thought I'd bring breakfast to fuel your artistic genius," he said, his eyes twinkling with mischief.

I couldn't help but laugh. "You do realize I'm a coffee and croissant addict at this point, right? I'm practically a pastry away from being a walking bakery."

"Then consider this your emergency supply," he replied, stepping inside and placing the mugs down on my cluttered table. His casual presence seemed to brighten the chaotic atmosphere, and I felt the tension in my chest begin to ease.

"I've been working on something," I said, motioning toward the scattered sketches that filled the room. "I want to create a capsule collection that tells our story. Our journey of healing and love, and all the messiness that comes with it."

Alex raised an eyebrow, intrigued. "Are you saying you want to put our emotional baggage into fashion? Because I'm all for therapeutic dressmaking, but I'm not sure the world is ready for a line called 'Emotional Baggage.'"

I chuckled, shaking my head. "Not quite. More like a celebration of our experiences, the highs and lows, the colors of love and loss. Fashion is storytelling, and I want to blend our narratives into something that resonates with others."

His expression shifted, a mix of admiration and surprise washing over him. "That sounds incredible. But how do you plan to translate that into designs?"

With newfound fervor, I launched into my vision, explaining how each piece would embody different facets of our journey. "This silk dress here, for example—it represents the calm after the storm, a moment of peace amidst chaos. And this structured blazer symbolizes the strength we find in vulnerability."

Alex listened intently, nodding, a spark of inspiration igniting in his eyes. "You're onto something, you know. It's not just about fabric; it's about feeling. We need to infuse every piece with the emotions that brought us here."

I could see the gears turning in his mind, the possibilities unfurling like the fabric spread across my table. Together, we brainstormed, bouncing ideas back and forth, each suggestion building upon the last, creating a foundation for something extraordinary. As we delved deeper into our discussions, the laughter flowed easily, punctuating the serious moments with levity.

When I suggested we showcase the collection at the upcoming local market, the air between us crackled with excitement. It felt like a leap of faith, a chance to put our hearts on display. "What if we created a pop-up experience?" I proposed, my voice growing more animated. "A space where people can feel the collection, connect with it, and, in turn, connect with each other."

"That's genius!" Alex exclaimed, his eyes wide with enthusiasm. "We could create an interactive element—maybe a corner for people to share their own stories. Make it a community event."

The thought sent shivers down my spine, a tingle of exhilaration that raced through me. This wasn't just about showcasing designs; it was about building a community, fostering connections through shared experiences. The market would be our canvas, and we would paint it with threads of hope, resilience, and love.

As the afternoon sun began to dip, casting long shadows across my room, I couldn't shake the feeling that this was just the beginning. The world felt ripe with possibilities, and for the first time in a long time, I believed in the power of our story.

The days following our brainstorming session passed in a blur of creativity and adrenaline. Each morning, I awoke with an urgency that buzzed beneath my skin, a delightful itch that couldn't be scratched until I was back at my sewing machine. My apartment transformed into a vibrant workshop, cluttered yet inviting, as I pieced together the collection that had become my heart's work. Patterns sprawled across the floor, and threads danced like ribbons in the breeze of my open window. With every stitch I made, I could feel the weight of my past lifting, replaced by a burgeoning hope that painted the future in vibrant hues.

One evening, as I draped a cascade of soft lavender fabric over my dress form, I thought back to Alex's suggestion about community engagement. It struck me that our stories were not solitary but part of a broader tapestry. I wanted to encourage people to share their own narratives through art and fashion. The local market, with its eclectic mix of vendors and townsfolk, would be the perfect backdrop for this kind of exploration. I envisioned a space where visitors could contribute their thoughts, scribbling their own stories on fabric squares that we would later incorporate into our collection.

"Wouldn't that be an incredible way to involve the community?" I mused aloud, my voice echoing softly against the walls. I could almost hear Alex's laughter in my mind, the sound bright and infectious. Just then, my phone buzzed, breaking the tranquility. A message from Alex lit up the screen: "Ready for our first fitting? I hope you've made something fabulous because I'm wearing it."

I rolled my eyes playfully, but my heart leapt at the idea of seeing him in my designs. "Meet me at the park in an hour. You won't regret it," I typed back, my fingers dancing over the keys.

As I gathered my materials, the anticipation tingled in my stomach, a thrilling mix of nerves and excitement. I carefully selected a fitted blazer in a deep emerald green that shimmered like dew on morning grass, paired with a lightweight cream shirt that offered a perfect contrast. I hoped it would encapsulate the essence of both confidence and comfort, much like the relationship I was starting to build with Alex.

When I arrived at the park, I was struck by the vibrant colors of fall; the leaves glowed like fire, the air crisp with the promise of change. I spotted Alex lounging on a bench, scrolling through his phone, the golden light casting a halo around him. He looked up, and a smile broke across his face, lighting up his features.

"Wow, is that what you're wearing?" he teased, glancing at the ensemble I had on, a playful reminder of the creative process we'd embarked on together. "Did you steal that from a runway model?"

"Only the best for my favorite muse," I shot back, my confidence buoyed by his playful banter. "Are you ready to see how you'll look in a custom piece?"

He stood, stretching slightly before stepping into the sunlight, his posture radiating casual elegance. "I'm ready. But just a warning: if you've miscalculated my size, I'm going to need an emergency pizza as a consolation prize."

"Don't worry, your measurements are logged in my brain, along with your pizza preferences," I replied, waving him over to the fitting area I had set up among the trees. The soft rustling of leaves provided a comforting backdrop as I draped the blazer over his shoulders.

His eyes widened as he examined the fit in the small mirror I'd brought along. "This is nice! I mean, really nice. It feels like you've tailored it just for me. Well, I guess you did, but still!"

"You wear it well," I said, stepping back to admire my work. "It's amazing how clothing can transform a person's presence. This isn't just a blazer; it's armor. It's meant to make you feel powerful."

As he turned to examine himself from different angles, I felt a rush of pride. "What do you think? Is it ready for the market?"

He turned back to me, his expression softening. "It's definitely ready, but let's not forget about the emotional aspect. This needs to speak to people, not just look good."

I nodded, taking in his words. "That's what I'm aiming for. I want each piece to tell a story, not just ours but everyone's. I've been thinking about creating a space at the market where people can contribute their stories to fabric swatches. We can stitch them together and make something truly unique."

His eyes sparkled with enthusiasm. "That's brilliant! Imagine the tapestry we could create—a collective memory woven from the threads of everyone's experiences. It could be a beautiful representation of community."

Excitement bubbled between us, the kind that felt electric, and for a moment, the world outside our little bubble faded away. "We should brainstorm ways to present it," I suggested, my mind racing with possibilities.

But just as I was about to lose myself in the vision, a shout broke through our reverie. A group of children raced past us, laughter trailing behind them like confetti. It brought a warmth to the chilly air, reminding me of simpler times when my own laughter filled the air without reservations. Suddenly, I felt the weight of my worries creeping back, the fears of vulnerability and exposure hovering just out of reach.

"Hey," Alex said softly, pulling me from my thoughts. "What's going on in that beautiful mind of yours? You seem a million miles away."

I forced a smile, not wanting to dampen the mood. "Just thinking about how scary this all is. Putting ourselves out there. What if people don't connect with our story? What if it falls flat?"

"Then we try again," he said with a confidence that wrapped around me like a warm blanket. "But I have a feeling it won't. We're not just sharing our story; we're inviting others in. And that's where the magic happens."

His words resonated within me, a spark igniting a fire of determination. I took a deep breath, letting the crisp air fill my lungs. "You're right. It's not just about us anymore. It's about creating a safe space for others to share their truths, too."

With that, we began discussing our ideas for the market, laughter and creativity spilling forth like colors from a painter's brush. Each moment we spent planning felt like building a bridge between our dreams and reality. And amidst the laughter, I could feel the subtle shift inside me, a growing awareness that perhaps this journey was as much about Alex and me as it was about the stories waiting to be told.

The days melted into each other as we poured our hearts into the preparations for the market. Our makeshift workshop thrummed with energy, punctuated by bursts of laughter and the soft, rhythmic sound of the sewing machine. Each piece I crafted took on a life of its own, a story unfolding with every thread. I found myself dreaming of how it would all come together—the designs, the shared stories, the sense of belonging that we aimed to create within the community.

Alex became my steadfast companion in this whirlwind. He was relentless in his support, always pushing me to dig deeper into our narratives, to explore the layers of emotion beneath each design. "Think of it like layering flavors in a dish," he'd say, leaning against the doorframe as I stitched late into the night. "You don't want just one note; you want the whole symphony."

One evening, while we were finalizing the details of our pop-up space, I decided to introduce a more personal touch. "What if we create a wall of dreams?" I proposed, my excitement bubbling over. "We could hang fabric swatches where people can write their hopes and fears. It could serve as a visual representation of what connects us."

STITCHED IN AMBITION

He nodded, his eyes sparkling with enthusiasm. "That's perfect! A beautiful reminder that we're all intertwined in this chaotic dance called life. And maybe we can even offer a few prizes for the best stories submitted."

As the days ticked closer to the market, I felt a mixture of anticipation and anxiety. The fear of vulnerability lingered just beneath the surface, whispering doubts that tried to seep into my creativity. What if no one cared about our story? What if the designs I'd poured my soul into were met with indifference? But Alex was always there, a buoy in the turbulent waters of my mind, reminding me that this was more than just fashion. It was a celebration of our shared experiences.

The night before the market, I lay awake, my mind racing with thoughts and possibilities. The moonlight streamed through the window, casting delicate patterns across my floor. I thought about the journey that had led me here—the moments of heartbreak, the laughter, and the newfound strength I had discovered along the way. It was as if each piece I'd created was a fragment of my soul, woven into a larger narrative that held the potential to touch others.

When dawn broke, it came with a burst of colors, splashing the sky in hues of orange and pink. I rushed through my morning routine, excitement bubbling inside me. The market was a few hours away, and my heart raced as I set out to meet Alex at our designated spot. The air felt electric, charged with the thrill of the unknown.

As I approached the market, the sound of music and laughter enveloped me, a tapestry of joy that beckoned like a warm embrace. The vendors had set up their booths, each one bursting with local wares, the scent of fresh pastries wafting through the air. I spotted Alex near our designated space, his hands busily arranging the display. He looked up, his face brightening when he saw me.

"You made it! Look at this," he exclaimed, gesturing around us. The space had transformed into a vibrant oasis filled with our designs, interspersed with the fabric swatches ready for others to share their stories. "It's perfect! It's everything we dreamed of and more."

My heart swelled as I took in the sight. The colors danced together like a happy reunion, and I felt an overwhelming sense of gratitude wash over me. "We did this," I said, grinning. "Together."

As the market began to fill with visitors, my nerves tightened like a coiled spring. I stood behind our booth, a bundle of anticipation and hope. People trickled in, their curious eyes scanning our designs, their expressions shifting from intrigue to delight. I felt an electric current run through the air as we began to share our story, explaining how each piece represented a chapter in our journey of healing and discovery.

"Fashion is not just about what we wear; it's about what we feel," I told a woman admiring a flowing dress. "This one is inspired by the freedom we find when we let go of our past." She nodded, her eyes shining, and I felt a flicker of hope that perhaps we were creating connections, however small.

As the hours slipped by, I lost track of time, swept up in conversations and laughter. People began to engage with the wall of dreams, scribbling their hopes on swatches and pinning them up for others to see. A young girl approached, her eyes wide with curiosity. "Can I write something?" she asked, clutching a bright pink fabric square.

"Absolutely! What do you want to share?" I knelt beside her, eager to hear her thoughts.

"I want to be a princess," she declared, her voice full of conviction.

I smiled, the warmth spreading through me. "You can be anything you want, sweetheart. And you can dress like a princess every day if it makes you happy."

Just then, Alex called out, "Hey! We have a surprise for everyone!" He gestured to a small stage set up nearby, where a local musician was preparing to perform. The crowd shifted, drawn to the music, and I felt a ripple of excitement course through the air.

As the notes floated through the market, I caught a glimpse of a familiar face among the crowd—a figure I hadn't seen in years. My breath caught in my throat, my heart thudding loudly in my chest. It was Emma, my childhood friend, the one who had left town after everything had fallen apart. She stood there, her expression unreadable, her gaze fixed on me.

I swallowed hard, my mind racing. What was she doing here? After all these years? I thought I had closed that chapter of my life, only for it to swing wide open again in the most unexpected way.

"Is everything okay?" Alex asked, his voice laced with concern, pulling me from my thoughts.

I nodded, though my heart was pounding. "I think... I think someone I know just arrived," I managed to reply, my eyes locked on Emma as she moved closer, weaving through the crowd.

"Hey, I need a minute," I whispered to Alex, my voice barely steady. I stepped away from our booth, my heart racing as I made my way toward her, the music fading into a distant hum.

"Emma?" I called out, my voice trembling as I approached. She turned, surprise flickering across her face before she composed herself.

"Is that really you?" she asked, her tone a mix of disbelief and something else—was it regret?

Just as I was about to respond, a loud commotion erupted from the other side of the market, drawing our attention. The crowd surged, gasping and murmuring in confusion. My heart sank as I turned to see what was happening. There, amidst the chaos, stood a figure in a dark hoodie, the outline shrouded in mystery.

My instincts screamed at me that something was wrong, and I felt the ground beneath me shift as I searched for Alex in the crowd. The moment of reconnection with Emma faded into the background as anxiety twisted my gut, leaving me teetering on the edge of uncertainty. What was about to unfold? And how would it change everything we had worked for?

Chapter 9: The Tipping Point

The sun hung low in the sky, casting a warm, golden glow over the local market as the scent of baked goods and fresh produce mingled with the sharp tang of spices. Laughter echoed through the air, punctuated by the occasional cheer from vendors hawking their wares. My heart raced, a mix of excitement and anxiety fluttering like trapped butterflies in my stomach as I adjusted the tablecloth at our booth, its vibrant colors a reflection of the dreams I had stitched into each piece we were about to showcase.

Alex stood beside me, his fingers deftly arranging the handmade accessories that sparkled in the sunlight. His energy was infectious, each grin he flashed seeming to push me closer to the edge of my own potential. He was the embodiment of calm amidst the chaos, his presence like a buoy in a choppy sea. "Remember, this is just the beginning," he said, straightening up and flashing me a wink that was both reassuring and mischievous.

I took a deep breath, trying to savor the moment as the throng of people swelled around us, their laughter and chatter forming a backdrop of encouragement. This was our chance, the culmination of late nights filled with sketches and fabric swatches, of pouring my heart into every stitch. The vibrant booth, a chaotic symphony of colors and textures, beckoned passersby like an alluring siren.

Just as the first curious shoppers began to approach, the atmosphere shifted. The crowd parted as Lydia, draped in the latest high-fashion attire that practically screamed designer labels, strutted toward us like a storm cloud threatening rain. Her sharp gaze locked onto mine, and I felt the familiar flicker of competition ignite within me. It was as if she had orchestrated this moment, her presence amplifying the tension in the air.

"Nice booth," she said, her tone dripping with feigned sweetness. "But it seems a bit... basic, don't you think?"

The words hung heavy between us, a challenge wrapped in a velvet glove. I felt Alex stiffen beside me, ready to step in and defend our hard work, but I held up a hand to stop him. The look in Lydia's eyes promised something more than mere disdain; she wanted a fight, and I was not one to back down easily.

"What do you suggest, Lydia? Perhaps a live design duel?" I shot back, my voice steady despite the adrenaline coursing through my veins. The idea formed in my mind almost as quickly as I spoke it, a desperate gambit to reclaim the moment she threatened to steal.

The crowd buzzed with excitement at the notion, whispers swirling like leaves in the wind. Lydia's lips curved into a smirk, the corners of her mouth twitching with delight as if she had been waiting for this opportunity. "I thought you'd never ask. Let's make this interesting, shall we? A piece each, one hour. The crowd votes on the winner."

My heart pounded at the stakes she proposed. I glanced at Alex, who nodded, his expression a mix of encouragement and wariness. This wasn't just about fashion; it was about asserting my identity, about reclaiming my voice from the shadows of self-doubt Lydia often cast over me.

"Fine," I replied, my determination solidifying into something more formidable than just a retort. "One hour, and may the best designer win."

As we set the timer and gathered our materials, I felt the weight of the crowd's expectations settle on my shoulders. The vibrant fabric swatches I had chosen for this very moment suddenly felt like a lifeline. I could hear the murmur of excitement ripple through the spectators, and the tension became palpable, almost electric.

Lydia wasted no time, her fingers flying over the fabric as she expertly crafted a piece that oozed sophistication and high-end flair. The precision of her movements was both mesmerizing and infuriating. Meanwhile, I focused on my own creation, tapping into the vivid dreams that had inspired me from the start. I cut and stitched with fervor, channeling every ounce of my passion into a design that screamed authenticity.

The minutes ticked by like the frantic beats of a drum, the crowd's anticipation rising with each passing second. I could feel the weight of their eyes on me, a reminder that I was not just competing against Lydia but also against my own insecurities. With each passing moment, I pushed back against the whispers in my mind that told me I wasn't enough, that I would never measure up to Lydia's polished perfection.

"Looking good over there, Starla!" Alex shouted, his voice cutting through my swirling thoughts. "Just keep breathing! You've got this!"

His words were like a balm, soothing the frayed edges of my nerves. I let his encouragement wash over me, allowing it to propel me forward. I carefully draped a bold, floral fabric over my design, layering it with contrasting textures that danced together in a celebration of color.

With mere minutes remaining, I glanced at Lydia's piece, which was taking shape as an elegant dress that could grace the cover of a magazine. My heart sank momentarily, but I shook off the doubt. Instead, I leaned into my own style, channeling the raw, vibrant energy of the market around us.

The timer beeped, and I stepped back from my creation, breathless. The crowd erupted in applause, their enthusiasm washing over me like a wave. I stole a glance at Lydia, whose expression was a mixture of disbelief and irritation, and in that moment, I felt an unexpected surge of confidence.

This wasn't just a duel; it was a turning point. No matter the outcome, I had dared to stand up to the shadows of my past, to reclaim the space I occupied in this world. I wasn't just designing clothes; I was weaving together the threads of my identity, vibrant and unapologetic.

"Let's see what the crowd thinks," Lydia said, her voice tinged with a challenge. I knew she didn't truly believe I could win, but I was ready to prove her wrong. As we faced the crowd, I felt a newfound strength blossom within me, igniting a fire that I wouldn't let anyone extinguish.

The crowd's anticipation hung in the air, thick and electric, as I squared my shoulders, ready to face whatever Lydia threw my way. She had that glimmer in her eye, the kind that told me she was enjoying this far too much, but the applause and laughter from our audience ignited a spark of defiance within me. I took a deep breath, feeling the fabric beneath my fingers—my creation was more than just a dress; it was a tapestry of my journey, a collage of every moment that had led me to this vibrant marketplace.

"Alright, let's make this interesting," Lydia said, her voice dripping with faux sweetness. "I propose we add a little twist. Let's have a theme. Something spontaneous." Her gaze swept across the crowd, as if searching for inspiration. "How about... 'The Heart of the Market'? Create something that embodies the essence of this very place!"

The crowd erupted with cheers at her suggestion, and I could sense the excitement swelling. My mind raced. The heart of the market. What did that mean? It was easy to picture the chatter of friendly conversations, the laughter echoing between stalls, and the unmistakable vibrancy of life that defined this place. My heart hammered in my chest as I tried to focus, to translate those feelings into fabric and thread.

"Deal," I replied, forcing a smile that I hoped conveyed confidence. "But remember, Lydia, this is about more than just aesthetics. It's about connecting with the people." I couldn't help but inject a hint of sarcasm into my voice, something Lydia seemed blissfully unaware of.

"Oh, I'm counting on it," she said, flicking her hair over her shoulder as she turned back to her workspace. It felt like a challenge wrapped in a layer of disdain, a direct hit against my belief that fashion should be a language of emotion rather than mere visual spectacle.

I dove back into my materials, the vibrant fabrics swirling around me like a whirlwind of inspiration. I wanted to create something that captured not just the look of the market but its very soul. My fingers danced over the textures as I remembered the way people lit up when they found something special—the shared smiles, the spontaneous dance moves when a particularly lively band played, the scent of warm cinnamon rolls wafting through the air.

With newfound energy, I began to sketch ideas in the air, piecing together a vision that embodied all those moments. The bright oranges and deep greens of my fabrics became the colors of a sunset mingling with the laughter of children chasing one another around vendor stalls. As I cut and stitched, I allowed myself to envision the final piece—a flowing dress adorned with pockets to hold memories, an outfit that could dance as much as the wearer could.

I glanced over at Lydia. She was lost in her world, frowning in concentration as she worked on her creation, a structured piece that contrasted sharply with my vision. The way she controlled the fabric was mesmerizing, but I couldn't let myself be intimidated. After all, I was no stranger to hard work, to digging deep and finding that fire within myself.

"Your piece looks... very sophisticated," I called over, my tone playful, masking the tension that bubbled beneath the surface. "Is that what you're going for? A structured look to keep your emotions in check?"

She shot me a glare, eyes narrowing. "Better than an arts-and-crafts project," she shot back, voice sharp as a tack. "I just hope you can keep up."

The crowd buzzed with excitement, their energy palpable as they leaned closer, hanging on our every move. I felt the heat of the spotlight on my back, pushing me to dig deeper, to reach higher. As I added embellishments—a collection of hand-stitched flowers to mimic the market's bloom, a dash of glitter to reflect the twinkling lights strung overhead—I found myself lost in the joy of creation.

Moments before the timer was set to buzz, I caught sight of Alex from the corner of my eye. He was leaning against the table, arms crossed, a grin plastered on his face that radiated warmth and encouragement. His presence was like an anchor amidst the storm. "You're killing it, Starla!" he shouted, his voice slicing through the noise of the crowd. "Just keep going! Make them feel something!"

His words flowed through me like a gentle stream, urging me on as I turned back to my creation. The fabric billowed in the gentle breeze, a small mirror to the life surrounding us. I had only minutes left, but I was so close to manifesting everything I wanted to say through this piece. It was no longer just a competition; it had become my declaration of identity, a heartfelt tribute to the vibrant community that had embraced me.

The buzzer went off, cutting through the chaos like a knife, and I stepped back, breathless, taking in the sight of my creation. I had poured everything into it—the laughter, the joy, the struggles, and the triumphs of my journey. It was a reflection of me, and for the first time in a long time, I felt proud.

The crowd clapped, and I could hear snippets of conversation buzzing around me. "That's beautiful!" "Look at those details!" But as I turned to face Lydia, her expression was a study in annoyance, and I couldn't help but feel a spark of satisfaction at the sight.

"Let's showcase our pieces," I suggested, my heart racing with exhilaration. "Shall we?"

The crowd shifted as we turned to face them, and I felt a rush of adrenaline surge through me. Lydia's dress, while undoubtedly well-crafted, lacked the soul I had infused into my creation. I could see it in the crowd's eyes; they were leaning toward me, caught in the embrace of my work.

"Ladies and gentlemen," I announced, my voice strong and steady, "this isn't just a competition. It's a celebration of our community and the heart that drives us. Let's vote not just for a piece of clothing, but for what speaks to you!"

As I gestured to the vibrant creation that draped across the table, a chorus of cheers erupted. It felt like a triumph, a moment where I could finally stand tall amidst the shadows of self-doubt. The crowd was alive, a tapestry of voices, and in that moment, I knew I had reclaimed not just my voice but my spirit.

The votes were tallied, and as I caught Alex's encouraging smile, I felt ready for whatever came next. This duel had become more than just a test of skill; it was a testament to everything I was capable of achieving when I believed in myself. And as Lydia looked at me, her facade cracking for just a moment, I understood that perhaps the true victory wasn't in winning but in finding the strength to rise and shine in my own way.

The crowd's excitement swelled like the tide, and the vibrant energy buzzed in the air as Lydia and I stood shoulder to shoulder, ready for our creations to be unveiled. I could almost hear the collective heartbeat of the audience, their breaths held in anticipation, ready to respond to the artistry we had poured our souls into. The sun shone down, casting golden highlights on everything, illuminating the moments of creativity that had unfolded in the past hour.

Lydia stepped forward first, her confidence radiating like a force field. "Prepare to be dazzled, everyone," she announced, her voice smooth and practiced. "Behold the essence of sophistication and style!"

As she revealed her creation, a structured gown in muted colors that flowed like water over rocks, I felt a pang of envy mixed with admiration. The gown was impeccably crafted, its lines sharp and elegant, but something about it felt devoid of heart. It was like watching a high-budget movie devoid of plot—beautiful but lacking the emotional connection I craved in fashion.

The crowd clapped, impressed by her technical skill, but I felt my own excitement bubbling beneath the surface. It was my turn to speak. I took a deep breath, anchoring myself in the present, channeling the energy that had surrounded me since the market opened.

"And now," I said, stepping into the spotlight, "let me introduce you to a piece that embodies the spirit of this market." I paused, letting the crowd settle, their curiosity piqued. "I present to you... 'The Heart of the Market!'"

As I unveiled my creation, the dress cascaded down, vibrant and flowing, with splashes of color that danced in the light. It was a riot of hues—bright yellows, lush greens, and fiery reds—capturing the essence of the fresh produce and flowers that surrounded us. The pockets, a playful touch, were embroidered with tiny symbols representing everything from a dancing figure to a cinnamon roll, details meant to evoke joy and nostalgia.

Gasps echoed through the crowd, and I could feel the atmosphere shift. Laughter erupted as I gestured to the pockets. "Perfect for stashing your treasures—or snacks, if you're like me!"

The audience erupted in laughter, and the mood lifted. It was more than a dress; it was an invitation to share stories, to find delight in the everyday. I caught Alex's eye, and his proud smile sent a rush of warmth through me. It was clear that my piece had resonated, and for the first time that day, I felt like I was truly where I belonged.

As the crowd's enthusiasm grew, I turned back to Lydia, who was watching with narrowed eyes, calculating. "It's... colorful," she remarked, the edge in her voice unmistakable. "But can it stand up to a real design?"

"Guess we'll find out," I shot back, a playful grin on my face. "After all, it's not just about what looks good; it's about what feels good, too."

With the crowd buzzing with excitement, I knew the moment of truth was fast approaching. The murmurs escalated as we moved to the center stage, the makeshift runway of our little market, each person in the audience ready to cast their votes for the winner.

"Okay, everyone," the announcer called, his voice cutting through the noise. "It's time to vote! Please raise your hands for Lydia's design!"

Hands shot up, and I felt a tightness in my chest. Lydia's gown had its fans, but as I watched, I could see a significant number of hands hovering over the crowd, uncertain.

"And now for Starla's 'Heart of the Market!'"

More hands shot up than I could have hoped for, accompanied by enthusiastic cheers. The contrast was clear, and the applause was a melody that soared, wrapping around me like a warm embrace.

"And the winner is... Starla!" The announcer's voice rang out, and I barely registered the excitement spilling from the crowd, my mind still spinning from the victory. Cheers erupted, a symphony of approval that felt surreal, like I was floating above the ground.

But just as I turned to celebrate with Alex, a chill crawled down my spine. Lydia, her expression unreadable, stepped forward. "Well, it seems the crowd favors the colorful chaos. But let's not forget: fashion is a business, and I can assure you, this won't be the last time we meet on the runway."

Her words hung in the air, a dark cloud obscuring my joy. I forced a smile, but my heart raced. The implications were clear—she was not done with me.

"Don't worry, Lydia," I shot back, channeling every ounce of bravado I could muster. "I thrive on competition. Bring it on!"

But as I celebrated with Alex, I couldn't shake the feeling that this was only the beginning. Lydia's competitive spirit was a relentless beast, and I sensed she had more than just a rivalry in mind.

Suddenly, the atmosphere shifted again. The crowd began to disperse, their excitement fading like a summer sunset. Just then, I noticed something peculiar—a whispering from the back of the market that swirled through the throngs of people, a low murmur that felt oddly ominous.

Curiosity piqued, I turned to look, only to see a figure emerging from the shadows. A tall man, dressed sharply, his eyes concealed by sunglasses, seemed to be watching me intently. A flicker of recognition sparked in my mind, but before I could decipher it, he stepped forward, his voice smooth and confident.

"Congratulations on your win, Starla," he said, his tone laced with something I couldn't quite place. "But I think you're about to find out just how high the stakes really are in this business."

My stomach dropped. Was this another challenger? An ally of Lydia? Whatever he was, his presence sent a shiver of unease rippling through the crowd. As I met his gaze, a myriad of questions flooded my mind.

"Who are you?" I asked, my voice steadier than I felt.

He grinned, the corner of his mouth lifting in a way that sent a chill racing through me. "Just a friend. But I have a feeling we'll be seeing each other again soon. And let's just say the fashion world is about to get a lot more interesting."

As he turned to leave, the crowd continued to disperse, laughter fading into hushed conversations, but my heart raced with uncertainty. There was more to this day than a simple victory. I had entered a world rife with hidden dangers, and I realized that I wasn't just fighting for recognition in fashion. I was standing on the precipice of something much larger, with shadows lurking in the corners, waiting to disrupt the delicate balance I had just begun to establish.

In that moment, a single thought echoed in my mind, intertwining with the fading cheers of the crowd: the real battle had only just begun.

Chapter 10: The Showdown

The air thrummed with excitement, a palpable current that made the hairs on the back of my neck stand up. Lydia stood across from me, her arms crossed and a smirk tugging at the corners of her lips, her confidence radiating like an electric charge. She had always thrived on competition, and I knew she relished this moment, the way a cat might toy with a mouse before delivering the final blow. The challenge was simple: create a fashion look within an hour, using only the eclectic materials gathered from the buzzing market stalls around us. The clock ticked ominously, each second echoing my rising anxiety.

As the countdown began, I could feel the weight of the crowd pressing in around me, their eyes darting between us like spectators at a high-stakes duel. Their murmurs washed over me—a symphony of whispers, all wondering if I would rise to the occasion or crumble under the pressure. I stole a glance at Lydia, whose eyes glinted with mischief. She was ready to pounce, and I had to fight the urge to deflate under her watchful gaze.

I turned my back to the crowd, shielding myself from the judgment that threatened to swallow me whole. Taking a deep breath, I forced myself to focus. The market was a riot of colors, a feast for the senses that momentarily grounded me. Rolls of vibrant fabric lay sprawled across tables, shimmering metallic threads danced in the sunlight, and an array of eclectic accessories glinted invitingly. It was a chaotic paradise, and I needed to sift through the madness to find my inspiration.

A warm breeze tugged at my hair, carrying with it the scent of street food—spicy and sweet—and the distant laughter of children. As I moved from stall to stall, I gathered materials that spoke to me: a deep emerald silk that felt like liquid satin, a tangle of golden threads that shimmered like sunlight on water, and an assortment of buttons, each one a tiny work of art. My fingers brushed against each piece, feeling the textures come alive beneath my touch. Memories flooded back, images of my mother in her studio, the smell of fabric dye mingling with her laughter as she guided me through the basics of design. "Fashion isn't just about fabric; it's about storytelling," she would say, her eyes sparkling with passion.

With my heart pounding, I returned to my workstation, laying out my materials like a painter ready to create a masterpiece. The countdown clock loomed, and the pressure twisted in my stomach, but I pushed through, channeling my mother's voice, her encouragement a soothing balm against my nerves. I reached for my scissors, slicing through the fabric with precision, each cut echoing my determination. Lydia's shadow lingered nearby, her eyes narrowing as she assessed my choices, no doubt plotting her next move.

As the minutes ticked away, my initial hesitation transformed into a rhythmic dance. I wrapped the emerald silk around a form, draping it with care, envisioning how it would flow with the wearer's movements. The golden threads wove into my design, glimmering like a beacon of hope against the richness of the green. My fingers flew, each stitch a declaration of my intent. I could feel the energy of the crowd shifting, their focus sharpening, captivated by the unfolding spectacle.

"Is that all you've got?" Lydia's voice sliced through the air, sharp and taunting. She was draped in a striking ensemble of her own, colors clashing boldly, each element designed to scream for attention. I forced a smile, the kind that didn't reach my eyes, and replied, "Just wait and see, Lydia. You might be surprised." A flicker of doubt crossed her face, and I reveled in it, a flicker of triumph igniting within me.

As the clock counted down to the final minutes, I added the last embellishments, a flurry of golden buttons cascading down the front of the dress, each one telling its own story. I stepped back, my heart racing as I took in the complete picture. The design was bold yet graceful, a reflection of my journey—a tapestry of resilience woven through with threads of hope and rebirth.

The signal sounded, and the crowd erupted in applause, a wave of sound that crashed over me, thrilling and terrifying all at once. I could see the surprise in their eyes, the way they leaned in closer, captivated by my creation. I fought to suppress the flood of emotions that threatened to overwhelm me. This was more than a competition; it was a rediscovery of my passion, a reclamation of my voice that had long been silenced.

As I unveiled my design, the sun caught the fabric just right, sending ripples of light dancing across the emerald silk. The applause intensified, echoing around me, filling the hollow spaces in my heart. Lydia's expression shifted from smug satisfaction to something I couldn't quite place—was it admiration? Jealousy? Perhaps both? It didn't matter. In that moment, I felt powerful, my spirit soaring above the noise of the crowd. I had poured my heart into this dress, and in doing so, I had reignited a flame that had flickered dangerously low.

In the aftermath of the reveal, Lydia approached me, her demeanor a strange mix of respect and irritation. "I didn't expect that," she admitted, crossing her arms as if to shield herself from the vulnerability of complimenting me. "You really came through." I raised an eyebrow, a playful smirk creeping onto my face. "Don't worry, I won't let it go to my head. I wouldn't want to overshadow your glorious ensemble."

She laughed, a genuine sound that caught me off guard, and for a moment, the tension between us shifted. There was no animosity now, only the thrill of competition and the recognition of mutual talent. We were two forces of nature, unpredictable and full of life, carving our own paths in the world of fashion. In that chaotic marketplace, under the warm sun and the watchful eyes of our audience, I realized that this showdown was not just a test of skill—it was a celebration of our artistry, an acknowledgment that both of us had something valuable to offer.

The applause rang in my ears, a cacophony of excitement and relief that filled the air with an electric buzz. I turned to face Lydia, her earlier smirk replaced by a mixture of surprise and begrudging respect. "Not bad for a last-minute effort," she remarked, her tone dripping with faux nonchalance, but there was a glimmer of genuine admiration in her eyes. I couldn't help but smile back, feeling the adrenaline still coursing through my veins like a well-crafted cocktail, equal parts victory and validation.

"Thanks. Yours wasn't so shabby either," I shot back, maintaining eye contact. There was something almost refreshing about the tension that lingered, like a suspenseful movie plot twist that leaves you hanging on every word. With the crowd slowly dispersing, I felt a weight lift off my shoulders, the kind that comes with a newfound sense of purpose. It wasn't just about winning; it was about being true to myself, a truth I had been grappling with for far too long.

As we gathered our materials and prepared to leave the market, the vendors began packing up their colorful wares, their cheerful banter filling the air. The scent of spices and fresh produce swirled around us, mingling with the fragrance of fried dough from a nearby stall. "Care for a victory snack?" Lydia asked, gesturing toward the food vendor with a playful eyebrow raise.

"Only if you're buying," I replied, teasingly. "I'd hate to take advantage of your generosity."

She laughed, the sound light and genuine. "Alright, I'll treat you to a funnel cake, but only because I want to see how you tackle a deep-fried dessert. This should be interesting." We moved toward the stall, the atmosphere shifting from competitive tension to a camaraderie that felt almost surreal. I was grateful for this moment—sharing laughter and indulgence felt liberating after the pressure of our challenge.

As we waited in line, I caught a glimpse of a familiar face in the crowd. It was Sarah, my old friend from college, her curly hair bouncing as she waved enthusiastically. I hadn't seen her in ages, and the surprise of her presence sent a flutter of joy through me. "Sarah! Over here!" I called, waving her over.

She approached, a grin spreading across her face, her eyes sparkling with mischief. "Look at you! Winning challenges and making friends with your rivals? Who knew you had it in you?"

"Don't let her fool you," Lydia interjected, her tone playful yet sharp. "She's a softie beneath that competitive facade."

I shot Lydia a mock glare. "Thanks for the exposure. Just what I needed."

Sarah raised an eyebrow, her expression full of curiosity. "So, you two are friends now? This is news to me."

"Just a friendly rivalry," I explained, trying to sound nonchalant, but my heart raced at the thought of how we had transformed from adversaries to allies in the span of a single challenge. "We've agreed to set aside our differences for the sake of snacks."

Lydia rolled her eyes, but I could see her fighting a smile. "Yeah, and maybe even share fashion tips."

"Oh, I'd pay to see that," Sarah said, laughter spilling out as we moved to the front of the line. "One of you will emerge as the reigning queen of the runway, while the other becomes the court jester."

"Let's just hope I don't trip over my own dress on the way to the throne," I replied, nudging Lydia playfully.

"Don't worry, I'll catch you," Lydia shot back, her laughter blending with ours, the tension that once filled the air now transformed into a light-hearted banter that flowed effortlessly.

With our funnel cakes in hand, we stepped aside to enjoy our treats, the sweetness melting on my tongue as I took my first bite. The delicate crispness of the dough mixed with the powdered sugar created a delightful contrast to the whirlwind of the day. "Okay, this was worth it," I admitted, savoring the moment, the taste of victory mingling with the sugar rush.

"See? I knew you'd appreciate the finer things in life," Lydia said, leaning against the stall, a playful glint in her eyes.

"Alright, alright. You win this round," I conceded, raising my fork in a mock toast. "To unexpected friendships and deep-fried victories."

As we indulged in our sugary feast, I felt a surge of warmth from the connection that had blossomed between us, a strange alliance forged in competition and laughter. It was refreshing, and I could sense the potential for collaboration rather than conflict in the future.

But just as I was beginning to enjoy this newfound camaraderie, a loud voice cut through the air, shattering our moment. "Lydia! There you are!" A tall, imposing figure strode toward us, his presence commanding attention. It was Blake, Lydia's business partner, and I could instantly see the tension in her body language shift.

"Hey, Blake," she greeted, forcing a smile that didn't quite reach her eyes.

"What are you doing here?" he asked, his tone clipped. "I thought we were working on that project today."

Lydia hesitated, glancing at me before responding. "I needed a break, Blake. We've been at it for days."

His eyes flickered between us, assessing. "Looks more like you've been playing rather than working. Don't forget what's at stake."

The playful atmosphere instantly thickened, the air now tinged with unspoken tension. I felt my stomach knot as I realized the weight of Lydia's obligations pressing down on her. It was one thing to compete in a friendly rivalry; it was another to navigate the complicated dynamics of business and ambition.

"I'm capable of managing my time," Lydia retorted, a hint of defiance in her voice. "And this isn't just play; it's part of the process. Creativity doesn't thrive under pressure, Blake."

He crossed his arms, his expression unwavering. "I get that, but we have deadlines, and the last thing we need is for you to lose focus."

I could see the storm brewing behind Lydia's eyes, a whirlwind of frustration and determination. "I appreciate your concern, but I need to breathe every once in a while. If I can't enjoy the journey, then what's the point?"

The exchange hung in the air like a tightrope, teetering on the brink of something explosive. My heart raced, caught between the thrill of competition and the reality of ambition's toll. Just as I was about to interject, to ease the tension, Lydia stepped forward, her voice firm but not unkind. "I've got this, Blake. Let me do what I do best."

In that moment, I saw the fire in her, the passion that had driven her from the start. It was a reminder of the very thing we had both fought for today—the ability to express ourselves, to reclaim our passions, and to flourish in a world that often demands conformity.

The tension between Lydia and Blake crackled in the air, a silent challenge that flickered in their shared glances. I stood there, the half-eaten funnel cake in my hand suddenly feeling too sweet, almost sticky in the face of their brewing storm. Blake's expression was unyielding, a sharp contrast to Lydia's newfound resolve. It was fascinating and terrifying to witness her transformation from a competitive designer to a woman standing her ground, a warrior for her creativity.

"You know deadlines are important," Blake insisted, his voice low and firm, as if he were trying to coax a reluctant child to complete her homework. "We're on the brink of something big, and I can't have you distracted."

Lydia's chin lifted slightly, a gesture that spoke volumes of her determination. "I'm not distracted. I'm learning how to manage my time—and my life—better. What good is a project if it drains the joy out of it?"

Blake scoffed lightly, the sound almost dismissive. "Joy doesn't pay the bills, Lydia. Success does."

The words hung between us like a drawn bowstring, ready to snap. Lydia's face blanched for a moment, but then her fire returned. "And success without joy is just... well, an empty trophy case." She shifted her weight, standing taller, as if her very presence could deflect the pressure in the air.

"You think you're going to find joy in some random food market?" Blake's eyebrows knitted together, his skepticism palpable. "You're being naive."

"Naive?" Lydia echoed, her voice a soft yet piercing blade cutting through the tension. "Is it naive to believe that creativity is just as important as deadlines? That the spark of inspiration doesn't come from a boardroom but from life itself?"

Blake opened his mouth to respond, but I couldn't let this moment fester. "She has a point, you know. Sometimes you need to step back to move forward," I interjected, trying to diffuse the situation. "Creativity can be stifled by too much pressure."

Lydia shot me a grateful look, her expression softening for a brief second before she turned back to Blake. "See? Even my competitors recognize the value of balance."

Blake shook his head, a hint of frustration flickering in his eyes. "Balance doesn't build empires. It just allows for procrastination."

"Is that what you think I'm doing?" Lydia's voice hardened, a thundercloud brewing behind her words. "Playing around while you do the hard work?"

The confrontation reached a boiling point, the air electric with tension, and I felt as though I was on the precipice of something monumental. The world seemed to fade away, and it was just the three of us—their debate a charged wrestling match of wills.

"Maybe it's not about playing around. Maybe it's about rediscovering what you love." My voice trembled slightly as I spoke, but the conviction behind my words gave me courage. "You can't build a career on a foundation of burnout."

Blake opened his mouth, likely to argue, but before he could say anything, a loud crash resonated from behind the food stall. My heart jumped, and I spun around to see a vendor scrambling to catch a rogue table that had tipped over, scattering colorful jars and loose fabric everywhere.

"Watch it!" someone yelled, and the commotion drew the attention of everyone nearby, a wave of startled faces and shifting bodies.

"Let's help!" I exclaimed, my instincts kicking in. Without waiting for a response, I dashed over to assist. As I knelt to right the fallen table, my heart raced—not just from the surprise of the crash but from the way tension had hung so thickly moments before, like a storm cloud ready to unleash its fury.

Together with a few other onlookers, we helped the vendor gather their wares, my focus shifting from the fraught exchange between Lydia and Blake to the colorful chaos around me. The vibrant fabrics fluttered in the breeze, the sunlight catching on glass jars filled with an array of spices and beads, each glimmering like tiny treasures. The camaraderie among strangers who had come to help was refreshing, a reminder that sometimes, chaos brought people together.

As the vendor thanked us profusely, I returned to where Lydia and Blake were standing, but the air between them had shifted. Blake's shoulders had relaxed slightly, and Lydia looked less like a warrior ready for battle and more like someone who had just taken a breath of fresh air.

"I don't mean to downplay your passion," Blake said, his tone softer now, "but we're at a critical point in our business. I just want to ensure you're not losing sight of our goals."

Lydia nodded, a flicker of understanding passing between them. "I get that. And I want to build something amazing with you, Blake. But I can't do it if I'm only ever following orders. We have to find a way to mesh our visions."

"Okay," he conceded, the corners of his mouth twitching as if he was considering a smile. "But if you're going to take time for spontaneity, just make sure it's balanced with what needs to be done."

I watched the interaction unfold, a silent observer caught in a moment of potential reconciliation. It was like watching two characters finally find common ground in a tense scene of a romantic comedy. Just when I thought they might embrace this newfound understanding, Blake's phone buzzed insistently in his pocket, breaking the spell.

"Ugh, excuse me," he muttered, pulling out the device, his expression shifting back to business-like efficiency. He glanced at the screen, his brows furrowing as he swiped to answer. "What is it now?"

I turned back to Lydia, who was staring at Blake with a mixture of amusement and annoyance. "Typical," she muttered. "Right when it seems like we're making progress."

"Maybe this will be a good thing," I suggested, trying to maintain the positive momentum. "A little break can allow you both to regroup."

"Regrouping is code for ignoring the issues," she said with a sigh, but a playful smirk broke through. "Though I must admit, watching you try to diffuse my argument was entertaining."

"Hey, I'm just here for the funnel cakes and the drama," I replied, grinning.

Just then, Blake ended his call, his face pale. "We need to go. There's an emergency at the studio."

"What kind of emergency?" Lydia asked, her tone shifting back to serious.

"Funding issues. The investors are pulling out. If we don't act fast, we're going to lose everything," he replied, urgency lacing his voice.

"Wait, what?" My heart sank at the words. "Are you serious?"

"Completely. We need to get there now," he insisted, and I could see the wheels turning in Lydia's mind.

Her eyes darted between Blake and me, weighing her options as if caught in a whirlwind. "But I—"

"Lydia, you can't think about this. We need your input. You're not just an accessory; you're part of the foundation of this project!"

I watched as her resolve wavered, caught between two worlds—the one where she was free to explore her creativity and the one where her career and dreams hung in the balance.

"Let's go," she finally said, the decision solidifying her stance as she moved forward with purpose. But before she took a single step, I felt a chill run down my spine. My phone buzzed insistently in my pocket, an unfamiliar number flashing across the screen.

"Wait, I need to take this," I said, a sense of foreboding washing over me. I stepped aside, answering without a second thought, but as the voice on the other end spoke, my heart dropped.

"Is this you, Anna? You need to listen closely. It's about your mother."

Chapter 11: Ripples of Change

The sun dipped below the horizon, casting a warm glow that danced across the eclectic stalls of the market. Vibrant colors mingled like old friends, the rich hues of textiles and the glinting gold of handmade jewelry painting a scene that felt almost surreal. As I stood beside Alex, the buzz of excitement pulsing in the air wrapped around me like a soft embrace. I could see my design—a stunning, flowing dress that caught the light just right—capturing the attention of passersby. Each time someone stopped to admire it, a little thrill surged through me, a gentle reminder that all the late nights and relentless sketching hadn't been in vain.

Alex, tall and effortlessly charming, radiated pride. His dark curls caught the light, framing his face in a way that made my heart flutter unexpectedly. "You did it, Ava," he said, his voice laced with enthusiasm. "This is incredible. Look at how people are drawn to it."

I caught a glimpse of my reflection in a nearby vendor's mirror. The dress seemed to breathe with life, its flowing fabric echoing the way I felt—free and alive, bursting at the seams with possibility. It was more than just a piece of clothing; it was a manifestation of everything I had struggled to achieve, the culmination of dreams that felt so far away only weeks prior.

But just as my confidence began to swell, a familiar voice sliced through the warmth of the moment. "It's derivative, you know. Nothing original about it." Lydia stood there, arms crossed, her perfectly manicured nails tapping against her forearm as if conducting an invisible orchestra of disdain. The flicker of triumph in her eyes felt like a sudden chill in the warm evening air, and I braced myself against it, determined not to let her words unmoor me.

"Really, Lydia? Derivative? I thought we were past the whole 'this isn't new' routine." I couldn't help the sharpness that crept into my tone, my heart racing not just from the adrenaline of the day but from the very real frustration she stirred within me.

She stepped closer, her demeanor shifting slightly, revealing the vulnerability lurking beneath her polished exterior. "I just think it's a shame. You're talented, but this—" she gestured dismissively toward my dress, "—is just a rehash of what's been done before."

"Isn't that the point of design? To reinterpret what already exists?" I replied, my voice steady despite the simmering tension between us. "Or are you just mad that I actually did something?"

Alex shifted beside me, a mix of amusement and disbelief flickering across his face. I could feel his support like an anchor, steadying me amidst the storm of Lydia's critique. The market around us buzzed with life, vendors calling out to customers, the scent of roasted nuts mingling with the sweetness of caramel apples. It was a cacophony that normally soothed me, but Lydia's presence felt like a storm cloud threatening to rain on my parade.

"Oh please, Ava. You're not that special," she shot back, but beneath her bravado, I noticed a hint of something else—perhaps fear? Or was it jealousy? In that instant, I realized that Lydia's lashings were not merely a reflection of her opinion about my work but a window into her own insecurities.

"Why don't you come back when you can appreciate the hard work that goes into this?" I said, surprising even myself with the assertiveness of my words. "Because I don't need validation from someone who can't even accept their own flaws."

Her expression darkened, and for a moment, I feared I had gone too far. But then, a small, mischievous smile broke free on my lips. "Besides," I added with a playful tilt of my head, "I'd rather be derivative than downright miserable."

Lydia blinked, clearly taken aback by my unexpected jab, and in that moment, the intensity of our exchange faded, replaced by a strange sense of camaraderie—albeit a tenuous one.

"Fine. Just remember, the fashion world is unforgiving." She spun on her heel, her heels clicking defiantly against the pavement as she strode away. I watched her go, a curious mix of relief and exhilaration flooding through me.

Alex turned to me, his expression a delightful blend of admiration and mischief. "You really told her, didn't you? That was brilliant. I almost feel sorry for her."

"Almost?" I teased, nudging him playfully. "That's a little too generous. She could use a lesson in humility, I think."

"Or maybe she needs a new perspective." His tone shifted, suddenly thoughtful. "We all have our struggles, right? But it's how we choose to deal with them that defines us."

I tilted my head, pondering his words. "You might be right, but it's hard to extend kindness to someone who's consistently rude."

"True. But imagine if we all found a way to lift each other up instead of tearing each other down. That could change everything." He paused, glancing around at the vibrant market. "Look at this place. It thrives because everyone brings something different to the table. It's all about community."

As he spoke, I looked around at the colorful array of people—friends laughing, families exploring, and artists showcasing their creations. The atmosphere pulsed with camaraderie, a stark contrast to the earlier tension. I felt a shift within myself, as if I were stepping from the shadows into the spotlight, ready to embrace not just my journey but the journey of those around me.

"Alright, Mr. Philosopher," I said, a grin spreading across my face. "What do you suggest we do with this newfound perspective? Start a movement? Take over the world?"

He laughed, the sound rich and infectious. "Let's start with this market. We could host a fashion show, a celebration of all the talented designers here. Show them what real creativity looks like."

The idea sparkled in the air between us, igniting a sense of adventure that felt almost electric. "A fashion show? Here? I love it! We could highlight local talent, bring everyone together."

Alex nodded enthusiastically, his eyes alight with inspiration. "And we can include workshops, maybe even create a mentorship program. Let's empower others while showcasing your designs."

The possibilities unfolded before us like the intricate patterns of a well-crafted fabric. It was a moment of clarity—a turning point. I realized I didn't want to simply exist within the fashion world; I wanted to help shape it, to create a space where creativity flourished, where people could express themselves without fear of judgment.

As we talked about the logistics, the excitement bubbled over. The shadows of earlier confrontations faded, replaced by a sense of purpose that felt both thrilling and terrifying. I was no longer just a spectator in my life but a key player, ready to dive headfirst into this vibrant world of fashion and community.

The night wore on, and the market continued to hum with energy. I took a deep breath, inhaling the scents of street food and the sweet promise of change. I was ready for whatever came next, ready to embrace the beautiful chaos that was unfolding before me.

The scent of sizzling street food wafted through the air, mingling with the sweet tang of cotton candy as the sun dipped lower, painting the Brooklyn skyline in shades of pink and gold. Laughter erupted from nearby stalls where kids chased each other with sticky fingers and wide smiles, their carefree joy a stark contrast to the tension that had just sparked between Lydia and me. My heart still raced from our encounter, but now it pulsed with something more—a potent mix of determination and exhilaration.

"Okay, Mr. Philosopher, what's our next move?" I asked Alex, who was leaning against the vendor's stall, his arms crossed with a self-assured ease. The confidence he exuded was contagious, and I felt my spirits lift with every word that fell from his lips.

"Let's brainstorm ideas for the fashion show," he replied, his eyes dancing with enthusiasm. "We can draw in some local talent, and maybe even collaborate with other artists. This place is bursting with creativity; we just need to tap into it."

"Absolutely! I want to showcase not only my designs but the diverse styles and stories of everyone involved." I paused, my mind racing. "What if we made it a theme? Something like 'Roots and Wings'? A celebration of where we come from and where we're going."

"Brilliant!" Alex grinned, the enthusiasm radiating from him almost palpable. "We could incorporate different cultural elements, invite local musicians, maybe even have some spoken word artists. It could be a whole experience, not just a fashion show."

A spark of excitement ignited within me. The thought of mingling creativity with community made my heart race. "I can picture it now—the runway lined with vibrant designs, stories told through fabric and movement, music filling the air... it would be like magic."

"Right? And the best part? We can start planning right now." He straightened, his posture shifting from relaxed to determined. "Let's gather a group of designers, artists, and vendors who'd want to participate. We could use social media to get the word out, create a buzz before we even announce the date."

I couldn't help but chuckle at the image of our little venture exploding online. "You mean like a 'Save the Date' with my face on it, holding a dress, shouting, 'Join the revolution!'?"

"Exactly!" He threw his head back in laughter, the kind that was infectious. "But, you know, with a little more style."

As we brainstormed ideas, the energy of the market enveloped us, and I couldn't help but feel buoyed by the support I had from Alex and the excitement of the community surrounding us. But just as I felt the giddiness of possibility take flight, a familiar voice interrupted our reverie.

"Planning your little party, are you?" Lydia appeared again, her presence as unwelcome as a raincloud on a picnic day. Her arms were crossed, and her expression was a mix of disdain and curiosity.

"Actually, it's more than just a party," I replied, meeting her gaze with a newfound steadiness. "It's a celebration of creativity. You should join us. It might do you some good."

"Why would I join you?" she scoffed, her confidence faltering ever so slightly. "I'd rather stick to the serious stuff."

"Serious stuff?" Alex chimed in, a playful smirk forming on his lips. "You mean the kind of serious that stifles creativity? The world needs a little whimsy, Lydia. Why not embrace it?"

She hesitated, and for a moment, I saw a flicker of uncertainty in her eyes. "Look, I just think it's a waste of time. The fashion industry is cutthroat. You have to be sharp to survive."

"Right, but what if we don't just survive?" I pressed, leaning in slightly. "What if we thrive together? Imagine how powerful it could be to lift each other up instead of tearing each other down."

Lydia's brow furrowed as she considered my words. For a second, I thought I saw a crack in her armor, a moment where her bravado faltered. "You really think that's possible?"

"Absolutely," I said, the conviction in my voice surprising even me. "The more diverse perspectives we include, the richer our community becomes. It's about collaboration, not competition."

She opened her mouth to retort, but I could sense the shift. The intensity between us softened, the edges blurring into something almost hopeful. "I guess I could... consider it," she said slowly, her voice losing some of its bite.

"Great! Just think of all the interesting connections you could make," Alex said, his tone light, like he was coaxing a kitten out from under the bed. "It's a chance for growth, not just for Ava's designs but for everyone involved."

With a reluctant nod, Lydia turned and walked away, leaving us with an air of uncertainty hanging between us. "Did that just happen?" I whispered, half in disbelief.

"I think it did. You might have planted a seed of doubt in her mind about her whole 'lone wolf' persona," Alex replied, a bemused grin playing on his lips.

"Or it might have been the most fleeting moment of clarity she's ever had. Either way, I'll take it." I shrugged, feeling a mix of triumph and relief wash over me. The encounter had stirred something within me, a small reminder that even those who seemed most stubborn could be reached in unexpected ways.

The night continued to unfold around us, the market thrumming with life. As we discussed logistics and excitedly exchanged ideas for the upcoming fashion show, I felt a sense of purpose settling in my bones.

"We should start reaching out to potential collaborators," I suggested, the thought racing through my mind. "Maybe we can find a few emerging designers who are looking for exposure."

"Definitely! I can tap into some connections I have from the gallery circuit," he replied, his eyes lighting up. "I know a couple of artists who would jump at the chance to showcase their work alongside yours."

"Perfect! And we could include a section for local artisans too—jewelry, accessories... it would create a more immersive experience." The vision blossomed like a wildflower in my mind, vivid and alive.

Just then, my phone buzzed in my pocket, interrupting our flow. Pulling it out, I saw a notification from social media. A local influencer had posted a photo of my dress, tagging me in it with a glowing caption that could only be described as rapturous.

"Oh my God, Alex! Look at this!" I squealed, showing him the screen. His eyes widened in disbelief, a wide grin spreading across his face.

"Holy cow! This is huge! It's going to blow up!"

"I can't believe it. This could be the exposure we need for the show!" I could hardly contain my excitement as the realization sunk in. The world was suddenly feeling much more open, each opportunity like a new thread in the tapestry of my life, weaving together in unexpected patterns.

"Let's use this momentum," Alex said, his enthusiasm matching mine. "Let's plan a meeting with interested designers and artists for next week. We'll pitch the idea of the show, and I'll bring my connections. We can create a mini pitch deck to present to them."

"Mini pitch deck? Look at you, all business-like," I teased, nudging him with my shoulder.

"Hey, I can be professional when the occasion calls for it," he shot back, a playful glint in his eyes. "And trust me, this occasion calls for it."

As we discussed our plans, the market buzzed around us, the energy infectious and palpable. I felt as though I were standing at the precipice of something extraordinary, a sense of anticipation humming in the air. Everything was coming together, and for the first time in a long time, I felt that maybe—just maybe—my dreams were within reach.

The night wore on, laughter and excitement mingling with the evening air. It was clear: the ripples of change had begun to spread, and I was ready to ride the waves.

The vibrant pulse of the market continued to weave through the night, every stall and conversation vibrant with life, each moment a brushstroke on the canvas of the evening. As Alex and I bounced ideas back and forth, the thrill of possibility charged the air around us like static electricity. I could hardly keep my thoughts contained, my mind racing ahead with all the potential the fashion show could unleash.

"I'm thinking we should make a call to some local artists," I suggested, my excitement spilling over. "We could incorporate live art displays—maybe even have an artist create pieces in real-time during the show. It would be a fantastic way to blend different forms of creativity."

"That's a stellar idea!" Alex nodded, his eyes glinting with enthusiasm. "We could even stream it live to give it a broader audience. Imagine the engagement! Everyone loves a behind-the-scenes look, and it'll showcase the collaboration beautifully."

"Right? It's about showing that fashion isn't just fabric and thread; it's a living, breathing form of art." I glanced around, taking in the colorful market and the eclectic mix of people. "I want this event to reflect the spirit of Brooklyn—a melting pot of cultures and creativity."

As we continued to brainstorm, the night took on a life of its own, laughter and excitement spilling from our lips like confetti. The challenges ahead felt tangible but surmountable, and I reveled in the notion that I wasn't facing them alone.

Suddenly, the air around us shifted, and I felt the familiar weight of scrutiny bearing down on me. I turned just in time to see Lydia hovering at the edge of our conversation, arms crossed and lips pressed together in a tight line, an expression of irritation etched across her face.

"Are you two done planning your little utopia?" she said, her voice dripping with sarcasm.

"Actually, we were just discussing how you might want to join us," I replied, forcing a smile. "You know, in the spirit of collaboration?"

"Collaboration? How quaint," she shot back, rolling her eyes. "But if you're asking me to be part of this... amateur circus, then you can forget it. I don't need to waste my time on something that's unlikely to succeed."

Alex shot me a look, a mix of disbelief and amusement. "You know, Lydia, it's a shame you can't see the value in supporting the local community. Not everything has to be a competition."

Her face twisted, disbelief flickering in her eyes. "What do you know about the fashion industry? You're just a guy with pretty words."

"And you're just a girl stuck in the past," I shot back before I could stop myself. "We're trying to forge a new path here, one that includes everyone. But if you want to be a lone wolf, that's your choice. Just know that it doesn't have to be this way."

For a brief moment, she looked taken aback, and I felt a rush of satisfaction. Maybe there was more to her than just the bravado she wore like armor. Yet, before I could savor the small victory, her expression hardened.

"I'll be watching," she said coolly, and then she turned and stalked away, her high heels clicking ominously against the pavement.

"Wow," Alex remarked, raising an eyebrow. "That was... intense. But I have to say, you held your ground beautifully."

"Thanks, but I still feel like we're not done with her," I replied, glancing back in the direction Lydia had vanished. The tension felt like a loose thread waiting to unravel. "I'm not sure if she's really going to let this go."

"Maybe not," he said, his expression thoughtful. "But that's not our problem. We have bigger things to focus on."

And he was right. We dove back into our planning, tossing around ideas like confetti. We jotted down potential vendors, brainstormed a guest list, and even came up with a hashtag for the event. I was lost in the excitement, my worries momentarily forgotten.

But as we wrapped up the night, the vibe shifted. The lively chatter of the market seemed to fade into the background, the lights flickering like fireflies caught in a sudden breeze. I felt a strange prickle at the back of my neck, the sensation of being watched.

"Hey, do you feel that?" I asked, glancing around.

"Feel what?" Alex replied, brow furrowing as he followed my gaze.

"That... heaviness in the air. Like something's about to happen."

Just then, I spotted a figure lingering near the edge of the market, shrouded in shadows. My heart raced as recognition struck me. It was Nathan, a designer I had met at a previous event—a man with an eye for talent and an uncanny knack for stirring the pot. He was notorious for his sharp critiques and ruthless ambition.

"Uh-oh," I murmured. "Looks like the storm clouds are gathering."

"What do you mean?" Alex asked, squinting in Nathan's direction.

"That's Nathan. He's... intense," I replied, watching as Nathan's gaze locked onto ours, a predatory glint flashing in his eyes. "He's known for his cutting remarks and high expectations."

"Great. Just what we need—another critic."

I felt a rush of uncertainty as Nathan sauntered closer, his presence commanding and electric. "Ava," he called out, his voice smooth yet sharp as a knife. "Fancy seeing you here."

"Hey, Nathan," I replied, trying to keep my tone light even as my insides twisted. "What brings you to this little gathering?"

He stepped closer, a slow, assessing smile spreading across his face. "I heard whispers about your upcoming show. Thought I'd come to see what all the fuss is about."

"Whispers, huh? Sounds ominous," I quipped, crossing my arms defensively.

"Oh, you know me," he said, feigning innocence. "I'm just a simple admirer of the art, eager to see if you can back up the buzz." His gaze flicked to Alex, sizing him up, an unspoken challenge hanging in the air.

"You'll just have to wait and see," I replied, my voice steady despite the storm brewing in my gut.

He chuckled softly, but there was no warmth in it. "I look forward to it. Just remember, not everyone will be as forgiving as your little market crowd. The real world can be... unkind."

"Isn't that the truth?" Alex interjected, his tone cool. "But kindness is a choice, isn't it? Maybe you should consider it."

Nathan turned his gaze back to me, his expression unreadable. "I'll keep that in mind, Alex. But don't get too comfortable, Ava. It's a jungle out there, and I'd hate to see you get eaten alive."

With that, he pivoted and strode away, leaving behind a palpable tension that settled like a stone in my stomach.

"What was that about?" Alex asked, his brow furrowing in concern.

"I have no idea. But I have a feeling he's going to stir the pot before this is all over," I replied, my heart pounding.

As we stood there, the weight of the encounter settled over me like a shroud, my excitement from earlier dimming. The challenges ahead felt more daunting now, and with Nathan lurking in the shadows, it seemed the path we were forging was about to get a lot more complicated.

Suddenly, my phone buzzed again, this time a notification from a fashion blog I followed. My heart sank as I read the headline: "Rising Star or Flash in the Pan? Ava's Designs Under Scrutiny."

"What's wrong?" Alex asked, concern etching lines on his forehead.

"Nathan's already at it," I whispered, my voice barely above a breath. "The storm's already brewing, and we're right in its path."

Before I could respond, my phone buzzed again. This time, it was a direct message. I glanced at the screen, my heart racing as I read the name attached to it. "It's Lydia," I said, eyes widening. "She wants to meet."

"What? Now? Why?"

"I have no idea," I replied, my heart pounding as I hit the button to read more.

The message read simply: "We need to talk. It's important. Meet me at The Diner."

The air grew thick with tension, my pulse racing as I looked at Alex. "Should I go?"

His eyes darkened, a mix of concern and defiance. "It could be a trap. Or it could be something else entirely. Either way, it sounds serious."

I hesitated, the choice hanging heavy before me like a pendulum swaying in the dark. The possibilities raced through my mind, but as I glanced back at the market—alive and buzzing with excitement—I knew one thing for sure: I couldn't ignore this.

"Whatever happens next," I said, resolve hardening in my chest, "I have to face it. No matter the outcome."

And just like that, I turned on my heel, ready to confront whatever lay ahead, my heart pounding with a mix of dread and anticipation. The path was unclear, but one thing was certain—change was coming, and I was right in the thick of it.

Chapter 12: Shadows from the Past

The market buzzed with life, a chaotic symphony of laughter, chatter, and the tantalizing aroma of street food wafting through the air. I stood at a stall draped in vibrant fabrics, the colors a riot against the drabness of my thoughts. Each bolt of material whispered possibilities, yet my heart felt heavy, weighed down by shadows from my past. The thrill of the crowd, the bright smiles around me—everything felt like a mask I could wear but never truly own.

As I ran my fingers over a particularly luxurious shade of emerald silk, a familiar guilt settled in my chest like a stone. It was almost as if I could hear my mother's laughter, a melodic sound that used to fill our home, weaving through our lives like a favorite song. But now, the melody was broken, a haunting refrain that echoed my sense of loss. I had spent so long shoving my grief into the dark corners of my mind, burying it beneath layers of ambition and distraction, but it never quite stayed buried.

The chatter of the market faded as I stepped away, seeking refuge in the quiet of my small apartment. It was here, in the stillness, that the memories rushed back like the tide, relentless and overwhelming. I stumbled upon an old box tucked away in the back of my closet, dust gathering like secrets on its surface. Inside lay my mother's journal, its pages filled with delicate sketches of dresses that seemed to dance across the paper. She had a way of capturing the essence of a fabric, a movement, a moment.

I opened the journal gingerly, the scent of old paper wafting up, mixed with something that smelled faintly of her favorite perfume, a hint of jasmine. Each page revealed a world she had imagined, a world she had poured her dreams into—dreams she had once passed on to me. "You have the talent, my darling," she would say, her voice lilting with encouragement. "Fashion is not just about the clothes; it's about the stories we tell."

My heart constricted as I traced the lines of her sketches. They were vibrant, filled with life and possibility, and yet here I was, stuck in a cycle of self-doubt. I could almost hear her voice urging me to do more than just survive in this world; she had always believed I could thrive. I squeezed my eyes shut, willing the tears to stay at bay, but they came unbidden, slipping down my cheeks like rain on a windowpane.

It was late, shadows creeping into the corners of my room, when I reached for my phone, my fingers shaking as I scrolled through my contacts. I hesitated before hitting Alex's name. He had been my rock through the ups and downs, always able to slice through my anxiety with his sharp wit and unwavering support. "You're not alone in this," he would remind me, as if saying it could make it true.

When he answered, his voice was a warm blanket, wrapping around me in my chill of despair. "Hey, everything okay?" he asked, his tone instantly shifting to concern.

"I... I found something," I said, my voice cracking. "It's Mom's journal. The sketches and notes she made about fashion."

"Are you at home?" he asked, and I could almost see him running a hand through his hair, trying to gauge the situation.

"Yeah," I replied, feeling the tremor in my words.

"I'll be right there."

The urgency in his voice was soothing, a promise that I wouldn't have to face this alone. As I waited, I reflected on how much Alex had changed my life. He was my lighthouse, guiding me through the stormy seas of grief and regret, yet I had never fully let him in on the depth of my struggles.

When he arrived, his presence filled the room with an energy that pushed the shadows away, even if just for a moment. "Okay, show me what you've got," he said, a teasing grin dancing on his lips.

I handed him the journal, and as he flipped through the pages, his expression shifted from playful curiosity to deep reverence. "This is incredible," he murmured, scanning the sketches. "Your mom had talent. You can see where you get yours from."

I wanted to tell him how much her loss hurt, how the weight of expectation felt like a noose around my creativity, but the words tangled in my throat. Instead, I took a deep breath, summoning the courage he always seemed to inspire in me. "I don't know if I can do this without her," I confessed, my voice barely above a whisper.

"Of course you can," he replied, his eyes serious now. "Art is about channeling pain, joy, everything. You need to honor her legacy, but you also need to own your own voice. What if you took these sketches and turned them into something? A collection, maybe?"

I felt a spark ignite inside me at his words. It was a flicker of hope amidst the lingering darkness, a reminder that my pain could be transformed into something beautiful. "You really think so?" I asked, my voice trembling with possibility.

"Absolutely," he insisted, leaning closer, his enthusiasm contagious. "This is your chance to tell your story through her eyes and your own. Think of it as a collaboration between you two. The past and the present merging into something new."

His words resonated deeply, a melody weaving its way through my grief. I could envision a collection inspired by her sketches, each piece a tribute, a dialogue between generations. I felt the tide of despair begin to ebb, replaced by a burgeoning excitement.

"Okay," I said, the determination rising within me like a phoenix from the ashes. "I'll do it. I'll create something that honors her."

Alex grinned, and for the first time in days, I felt the heaviness lift just a bit. In that moment, surrounded by memories and dreams, I found the strength to weave my past into the fabric of my future. The shadows might still linger, but they no longer held dominion over me.

With a newfound determination bubbling inside me, I set to work immediately. The sketches became my compass, guiding me through a labyrinth of creativity and emotion. I transformed my living room into a makeshift studio, cluttering it with swaths of fabric, sketchbooks, and the scattered remnants of my mother's legacy. The air hummed with possibility, each thread I pulled and snipped felt like a step toward reclaiming a part of myself that had been lost in grief.

As the sun dipped below the horizon, painting the sky in hues of orange and purple, I immersed myself in the world of design. I listened to the soft crackle of the radio, the melody mingling with the rhythm of my heartbeat, each note an encouragement to create. I could almost hear my mother's laughter in the background, a soft whisper reminding me of the countless nights we had spent together, her guiding hand over mine as we explored the magic of fabric and thread.

"Do you think I can pull this off?" I mumbled aloud, holding up a vibrant blue satin, its sheen reflecting the dying light. The question hung in the air, a challenge I was desperate to answer.

Just then, the door creaked open, and Alex stepped in, arms laden with snacks. "I come bearing sustenance! Because nothing fuels creativity like chips and dip," he announced, a playful grin stretching across his face.

"Chips? Really?" I arched an eyebrow, my hands buried in a heap of sketches. "I was hoping for something more... sophisticated."

"Look, haute couture doesn't have to mean haute cuisine," he shot back, plopping down next to me. "Besides, when was the last time you indulged in something that wasn't a kale smoothie?"

I couldn't help but laugh, the sound breaking the tension that had coiled tightly around me. "Fair point. But the chips better be worth it." I took one, savoring the crunch, allowing the salty flavor to invigorate my senses.

"Now, what's the master plan?" he asked, diving into the mountain of sketches spread across the coffee table. He flipped through them, his brow furrowing in concentration. "These are beautiful. You're really channeling her, aren't you?"

"I hope so," I replied, biting my lip as a wave of uncertainty crashed over me. "I just want to do her justice. It feels like I'm carrying the weight of her dreams on my shoulders."

Alex nodded, his expression serious. "But those dreams don't have to be a burden. They can be your wings. What's the first piece you're thinking of creating?"

I looked down at the sketches, my fingers tracing the lines of a gown adorned with delicate lace and cascading layers. "I think I want to start with this one. It's inspired by the last dress she wore before... well, before everything changed."

He tilted his head, clearly intrigued. "What made that dress special?"

"It was a simple design, but it captured her spirit perfectly," I said, my voice barely above a whisper. "Every time she wore it, she lit up the room. It was like she brought the sun with her. I want to evoke that same feeling."

"Then let's do it!" Alex's enthusiasm was contagious, and I could feel the weight lifting. "Let's start with fabric swatches. You need to feel the texture in your hands, let it inspire you."

We dove into the chaos, sorting through piles of fabric. The thrill of discovery surged through me with each new piece. I held up a deep crimson silk, and Alex raised an eyebrow. "Are you sure you want to go with that? Red can be a bit... intense."

"Intense is exactly what I need," I retorted, a playful smile tugging at my lips. "It's bold and powerful, just like her."

The evening flew by in a whirlwind of laughter and creativity. We bickered over colors, traded quips about fabric choices, and fueled each other's enthusiasm with ridiculous ideas that ranged from the absurd to the brilliant. I marveled at how easily the conversation flowed, how the tension that had clung to me for so long began to dissolve like mist under the morning sun.

As we worked, I felt a shift within myself. Each stitch I envisioned seemed to unravel threads of grief, weaving them into something vibrant and alive. Alex, ever the instigator of chaos, proposed a midnight design session. "We're too close to stop now. What if we pull an all-nighter? Who needs sleep when you can design?"

"Sounds like a recipe for disaster," I replied, but the glimmer of mischief in his eyes was hard to resist. "Fine! Let's do it."

Hours passed like whispers, our laughter and conversations filling the room with warmth. The moonlight spilled through the window, illuminating our makeshift studio, casting playful shadows against the walls. It felt magical, like we had entered a world of our own creation where anything was possible.

As dawn broke, painting the sky in soft pastels, I sat back and surveyed the chaos around us—discarded fabric scraps, crumpled sketches, and the remains of our snack feast scattered like confetti. In the midst of it all, I felt a flicker of hope blossom within me, mingling with the lingering sadness. I had poured my heart into these designs, crafting each stitch with both joy and sorrow, and for the first time in a long while, I felt a sense of purpose.

"Okay, what's next?" Alex asked, his voice slightly hoarse but filled with enthusiasm. "I think we should set a timeline for your collection launch. You can't just keep working in this bubble forever."

I stared at him, the thought daunting yet exhilarating. "You really think I'm ready to share this with the world?"

"Absolutely," he replied, his expression unwavering. "Your mom would be so proud. And you're more than ready. Let's make a plan, and I'll help you every step of the way."

His support was a balm to my anxious thoughts, and I felt the corners of my mouth twitch into a smile. It was in that moment, amidst the chaos and uncertainty, that I realized the shadows of my past no longer held the same power over me. They had transformed into a wellspring of inspiration, propelling me forward into a future I was eager to embrace.

With Alex by my side, I could almost hear my mother's laughter echoing in my ears, urging me to take the leap. It was time to step into the light, to celebrate the stories woven into each design, and to honor the legacy that was now mine to carry.

The sunlight streamed through my window, filtering in like a warm embrace, casting a golden glow on the scattered remnants of our all-nighter. I sat at my kitchen table, my fingers stained with ink and the remnants of yesterday's chaos, surrounded by sketches that felt like whispers from my past, urging me forward. The excitement of creating something tangible from my mother's dreams kept bubbling within me, a sweet effervescence that sparked ideas faster than I could jot them down.

As I began to sketch, the strokes of my pencil transformed into fluid lines, a dance of creativity that felt both invigorating and terrifying. Each curve and contour of the designs was a conversation with my mother, and I could almost hear her voice guiding me through the process. "Design with passion, darling. Let the fabric tell your story." The words echoed in my mind, and for the first time, I allowed myself to envision a full collection—something that celebrated her legacy while showcasing my own voice.

"Alright, Picasso," Alex said, sauntering into the room, a steaming cup of coffee in hand. "What genius is brewing this morning?" He leaned over my shoulder, peering at the sketches sprawled across the table. "Wow, you've really outdone yourself. This one looks like it belongs on a runway in Paris."

"Or maybe just on a mannequin at the local thrift shop," I teased, a playful smirk tugging at my lips. "But hey, it's a start. I think I'm finally starting to find my style, my voice."

"Exactly! And speaking of style, you need to start gathering materials. We can hit the fabric store later. I'll be your personal shopping assistant," he declared with a mock bow, causing me to chuckle.

I watched as he made his way to the fridge, rummaging for breakfast. He was like a whirlwind, brightening the space with his infectious energy. "What about you? Are you planning to wear your pajamas all day?" he called over his shoulder, pulling out a container of leftover pizza.

"Who are you kidding? This is fashion!" I gestured to my baggy sweats and oversized hoodie. "I'm embodying the 'creative genius' aesthetic."

"Sure, if by 'creative genius' you mean 'I just rolled out of bed and forgot to brush my hair,'" he shot back, laughter dancing in his eyes.

"Touché." I couldn't help but laugh, the sound echoing in the cozy apartment. As we shared playful banter, a sense of camaraderie enveloped us, a bond forged through late-night conversations and shared dreams.

"Okay, so what's the plan for the collection launch?" Alex asked, his tone shifting to seriousness as he took a seat across from me. "I think you should aim for something big—like a fashion show."

"A fashion show?" My heart raced at the idea. "That's... ambitious."

"Ambitious is what you need right now," he replied, leaning in closer. "It's the perfect way to debut your collection, to let people see not just the clothes, but the story behind them. And we can make it a tribute to your mom, to everything she meant to you."

I bit my lip, excitement and fear clashing within me. "But what if no one shows up? What if it flops?"

"Then we'll turn it into an epic disaster movie," he said, his eyes sparkling with mischief. "I'll be the hero who rescues you with ice cream. But seriously, you won't know unless you try. You have to believe in yourself, even if it's hard."

I took a deep breath, feeling the weight of his words sink in. The idea of hosting a fashion show felt like standing on the edge of a precipice, ready to leap. "Alright, let's do it!" I declared, newfound determination washing over me.

We spent the next few hours mapping out the details—setting a date, reaching out to local venues, and compiling a list of potential models who could bring my designs to life. Each detail was a step closer to making my dreams a reality, and for the first time in a long time, the shadows that had loomed over me began to dissipate.

By the time we were done, the sun hung low in the sky, casting a warm golden hue across the room. "I can't believe how much we accomplished in just a few hours," I said, glancing around at the organized chaos we'd created.

"Who knew planning a fashion show could be this fun?" Alex replied, stretching his arms overhead. "You're going to crush this, just you wait."

As if on cue, my phone buzzed on the table, interrupting our moment. I picked it up, glancing at the screen to see a message from an unknown number.

"Hey, I know this is random, but I have something of your mother's that I think you'd want back."

I stared at the screen, my heart pounding in my chest. "What is it?" I mumbled, my mind racing with possibilities.

"Meet me at the café on 5th in one hour. It's important."

"What does it say?" Alex leaned over, trying to catch a glimpse of my phone.

"It's from someone I don't know," I replied, my voice trembling slightly. "They have something of my mom's."

"Sounds mysterious," he said, his curiosity piqued. "Are you going to meet them?"

"I don't know. It feels... risky," I admitted, uncertainty creeping into my mind.

"Look, if you want to go, I'll go with you. You shouldn't face this alone," he said, a reassuring hand on my shoulder.

I hesitated, my thoughts a whirlpool of confusion. Part of me wanted to dismiss it as a prank, while another part felt a magnetic pull toward the café, an urge to uncover whatever was hidden in the shadows of my past. "Okay, let's go," I finally said, determination igniting within me.

As we made our way to the café, the air thickened with anticipation, each step drawing me closer to something I couldn't quite grasp. What could this person want? And what did they mean by having something of my mother's?

The café buzzed with life, the smell of coffee mingling with the sweet scent of pastries. I scanned the room, searching for the sender. A figure sat at a small table in the corner, their back to me. Anxiety coiled in my stomach as I approached, Alex at my side, his presence a comforting anchor.

"Excuse me?" I said, my voice shaky as I neared the table. The figure turned slowly, and my breath caught in my throat.

The face that looked back at me was familiar, yet time had etched lines of worry around her eyes. "I'm sorry to reach out like this," she said, her voice barely above a whisper. "But I have something to tell you about your mother."

In that moment, the world around us faded, leaving only the weight of her words hanging in the air, heavy with secrets waiting to be unveiled.

Chapter 13: New Beginnings

Each day, the sun crested the skyline with a riot of colors that made the city feel like an artist's canvas, ready to be splashed with imagination. I had always been drawn to the way light filtered through the buildings, casting whimsical shadows that danced on the pavement. Today, as I settled into my small but vibrant studio, I took a moment to soak it all in. The walls, painted a soothing shade of teal, were adorned with sketches and swatches—each piece a fragment of my soul, infused with hopes, dreams, and a sprinkle of anxiety.

The aroma of coffee wafted through the air, mingling with the scent of fabric dye and the crispness of freshly unwrapped textiles. I turned my attention to the bolts of fabric lying across my drafting table. I'd chosen colors reminiscent of a sunrise: soft corals, delicate golds, and serene blues, each hue whispering the promise of new beginnings. It was a palette that spoke of resilience, of the beauty that could arise from chaos, and it made my heart race with possibility.

"Ready for another round of inspiration?" Alex's voice broke through my reverie, rich and warm like the coffee he was holding. His eyes sparkled with that mischievous glint that always made me feel like we were conspirators in a delightful game.

"Always," I replied, a smile spreading across my face. "What do you have for me today?"

He stepped closer, placing the steaming cup beside my sketchpad. "I thought we could try something different. What about mixing textures? We could layer that silk with some linen and see how it drapes."

"Textures are the unsung heroes of fashion," I said, picking up a piece of luxurious silk that shimmered like sunlight on water. "Let's do it."

Our evenings often flowed like this, a comfortable back-and-forth of ideas and laughter. Alex had a knack for pulling the best out of me, his enthusiasm infectious as he shared wild concepts that made my imagination soar. As we draped the silk over a mannequin, I found myself lost in the rhythm of our collaboration, the fabric falling in soft waves that evoked the gentleness of a summer breeze.

"I love how this feels," I said, running my fingers along the fabric's smooth surface. "It's like... it's embracing me."

"Then let it embrace everyone who wears it," he replied, a teasing smirk on his lips. "What's a capsule collection without a little bit of love?"

The air buzzed with creativity, our laughter echoing off the walls, yet I could sense an undercurrent of tension in my gut. The stakes felt higher than ever. This collection was my heart laid bare, and as our bond deepened, I couldn't ignore the growing fear that our dreams might be a precarious balancing act. The fashion industry was a fierce battleground, and I was well aware that the competition could turn friendships into rivalries in the blink of an eye.

As we worked late into the evening, the city outside transformed into a shimmering sea of lights. It was intoxicating, the way the world seemed to pulsate with energy, mirroring the urgency in my heart. I glanced at Alex, his brow furrowed in concentration as he meticulously pinned a hem. He looked so focused, so absorbed, and I realized how much I cherished these moments.

"You know," I began, attempting to lighten the mood, "if we keep this up, we might just become the next big thing in fashion. Can you imagine? We'll have our faces plastered all over magazines, sipping champagne at runway shows."

He chuckled, looking up from his work. "Or we could just end up as a pair of stressed-out designers in a cramped studio, fighting over who forgot to buy more thread."

I laughed, shaking my head. "Let's aim for the champagne, shall we?"

Our banter flowed effortlessly, but as the night wore on, I found myself torn. My heart swelled with affection for Alex, yet the reality of our ambitions hovered like a storm cloud. What if my dream threatened his? What if the world I longed to belong to swallowed him whole, leaving only shadows in its wake?

The following morning brought with it a stark reminder of those looming pressures. I woke to a flurry of notifications on my phone, each one a reminder of the impending fashion showcase that had been the talk of the industry. Invitations had been sent, and the whispers of competition echoed through my mind. It was exhilarating and terrifying all at once.

"Are you ready for this?" Alex asked, peering over the edge of his own phone as we met for coffee at our favorite café. The cozy atmosphere buzzed with chatter and the hiss of the espresso machine, but my mind was elsewhere.

"Ready?" I echoed, the weight of the world suddenly feeling heavier. "I don't know, Alex. What if we're not good enough?"

He reached across the table, his hand warm and steady against mine. "We are good enough. More than good enough. You've poured your heart into this collection, and that's what matters."

I met his gaze, and for a moment, the world around us faded. In his eyes, I saw a reflection of my own fears and aspirations, and a flicker of something deeper—something that made my heart race and my palms sweat. It was as if he could read my mind, peeling back the layers of my uncertainty, exposing the raw truth beneath.

But just as quickly, the weight of reality crashed back down, a reminder that dreams were often accompanied by sacrifice. The showcase was a chance to shine, but the pressure could just as easily extinguish the very spark we were trying to ignite.

"What if the collection doesn't resonate?" I asked, my voice barely above a whisper.

"Then we'll learn from it," he replied with unwavering confidence. "We'll adapt, and we'll come back stronger. But I believe in you, and I believe in us."

The warmth of his hand lingered long after I withdrew, and as we returned to our creative haven, I couldn't shake the feeling that we were teetering on the edge of something monumental. Every stitch we made brought us closer to unveiling a piece of our souls to the world. But with each passing moment, I wondered if our newfound connection could withstand the challenges ahead.

The week unfurled like a delicate silk scarf, each day bringing a fresh set of challenges and a subtle thrill that kept me on my toes. As the showcase approached, my mind became a kaleidoscope of fabric swatches and sketch ideas, a swirling vortex of creativity and dread. The hours spent with Alex felt both exhilarating and nerve-wracking, a bittersweet cocktail of collaboration and burgeoning emotions.

One evening, after a particularly long day of experimenting with a new draping technique, we found ourselves sprawled across the floor of the studio, surrounded by a colorful chaos of fabrics, sketches, and the remnants of a hastily devoured dinner of takeout Thai. My head rested against the cool wood, and I stared at the ceiling, watching the shadows shift as the evening light waned.

"You know, if we don't get this right, we'll probably end up as that couple in the corner of a café, bitterly reminiscing about our 'glorious fashion days,'" I said, my voice tinged with mock gravity.

Alex laughed, the sound rich and warm. "You mean the couple who insists on ordering the cheapest wine while loudly critiquing the fashion choices of passersby? I can totally see us in that role."

"Exactly! 'Look at that poor soul—doesn't she know stripes and polka dots are a fashion crime?'" I added, dramatically gesturing with my hands, sending a stray napkin fluttering across the floor.

His laughter was contagious, wrapping around me like a comforting blanket, but as the mirth faded, I felt the weight of reality creeping back in. "But seriously," I said, straightening up, "what if we really do fail? What if all of this—this connection, this creativity—isn't enough?"

"Failure is just a stepping stone," he replied, his expression shifting to one of earnestness. "Besides, we won't know unless we try. And I'm not letting you drown in self-doubt while we're this close to achieving something amazing."

His words hung in the air, a potent blend of encouragement and challenge. I smiled at him, grateful for the unwavering support he offered. There was something undeniably magnetic about his passion—every time he spoke, it felt like the universe conspired to weave our destinies closer together. Yet, beneath that warmth lingered a flicker of uncertainty, a whisper that gnawed at my insides.

We continued to work late into the night, our creativity igniting with each new idea. But as I shifted my focus to the sketches, I couldn't help but notice how our artistic dance felt increasingly choreographed. Each laugh, each shared glance, seemed imbued with a tension that hinted at something more than just friendship. And while I reveled in our connection, it felt like walking a tightrope without a safety net beneath me.

The following morning dawned crisp and clear, the sun casting golden rays that filtered through my studio windows. But the beauty of the day did little to ease my anxiety. The showcase loomed on the horizon, an approaching storm that threatened to disrupt the serene landscape we had created together. As I arranged my sketches for review, the excitement in my chest twisted with nerves, a potent cocktail that left me breathless.

"Do you have everything you need?" Alex asked, peeking through the doorway, a cup of steaming coffee in hand. He wore that same disarming smile, and for a moment, my heart skipped.

"Yeah, just some last-minute touches," I replied, forcing a smile despite the gnawing unease. "But can we talk about our presentation? I mean, what if the judges don't like our concept? What if they think we're just two starry-eyed dreamers with more ambition than skill?"

"Then we'll impress them with our charm," he declared, winking at me as he sauntered in. "We'll dazzle them with our passion. And if that doesn't work, we'll resort to bribery—cookies, perhaps?"

"You think cookies will sway seasoned fashion judges?" I laughed, feeling the tension in my shoulders ease just a fraction. "I'd say they're more likely to appreciate our aesthetics than our baked goods."

"Ah, but what if we combine the two? A taste of our creative process paired with a slice of sweet nostalgia. Imagine the judges tasting our cookies while admiring the collection!" His eyes gleamed with excitement, and I couldn't help but feel a rush of adrenaline.

"Okay, I'll admit it: that's not the worst idea I've ever heard. But what if they end up hating both? What if our aesthetic is the equivalent of serving burnt toast?"

Alex leaned against the wall, arms crossed, a mischievous grin on his face. "Then we'll simply say it's an avant-garde statement piece. 'Burnt toast' is just a metaphor for raw creativity, right?"

I chuckled, shaking my head. His lighthearted banter was like a balm for my frayed nerves, but I couldn't ignore the growing sense of competition. The whispers of doubt loomed larger, threatening to drown out the warmth of our camaraderie.

"Hey, can I ask you something serious?" I ventured, my tone shifting as I glanced at him, vulnerability creeping in.

"Of course," he replied, his voice suddenly serious. "What's on your mind?"

"What if we don't make it? What if all this—us, our work, everything—falls apart? I don't know how to navigate this and keep you in my life. I don't want to lose what we have, but this industry... it can be brutal."

He stepped closer, his expression earnest and attentive. "I get it. But you need to understand that this isn't just about winning or losing. It's about us finding our voice together, regardless of what happens next. We can't control the outcome, but we can control how we approach it."

His words washed over me like a cool breeze on a sweltering day, calming the storm in my heart. Yet, even as I nodded, I couldn't shake the nagging feeling that our journey might lead us down separate paths.

As the days rolled on, the pressure mounted. The anticipation of the showcase felt like a balloon swelling inside me, ready to burst at any moment. And just when I thought I had a handle on my emotions, the unthinkable happened. The night before our presentation, I received a call from an old friend from fashion school. She'd secured a spot as one of the judges, and her words were a double-edged sword, cutting through my already frayed nerves.

"Just wanted to give you a heads-up. The competition is fierce this year. Everyone is gunning for the spotlight, and they're not playing nice," she said, her voice laced with a mix of concern and excitement. "You've got to bring your A-game."

"Thanks for the warning," I replied, my stomach twisting in knots. "But can I ask you something? Do you think it's really about winning, or is there something more? Because I'm not sure what that even looks like anymore."

"Sometimes it's about the journey," she said, a hint of nostalgia creeping into her tone. "But let's be real. In this industry, it's mostly about winning. Just remember to stay true to yourself. That's the only way you'll survive."

The call ended, but the lingering anxiety settled like a heavy blanket over my heart. The next morning, as I prepared for the showcase, I felt like I was stepping into a ring, ready to face whatever the judges—and the industry—might throw at me. With Alex by my side, I was determined to face it head-on, even as the shadows of doubt danced around the edges of my resolve.

The day of the showcase dawned with a chill in the air, the kind that made you want to bundle up in your favorite sweater and sip hot cocoa while gazing out at a snowy landscape. Instead, I found myself standing in front of a mirror in my studio, my heart thundering in my chest like a jackhammer as I adjusted the collar of my crisp white shirt. It felt like an armor, but it was also a fragile shell that could crack under pressure at any moment.

"Breathe," I muttered to myself, forcing a steadying inhalation, but it barely calmed the storm swirling inside. As I glanced around the studio, the remnants of our late-night work sessions lay scattered about—crumpled sketches, fabric remnants, and the faint scent of coffee clinging to the air like an old friend reluctant to leave.

Alex entered the room, his expression a mix of concern and encouragement. "You look incredible," he said, offering a soft smile that melted some of the ice encasing my heart. His outfit—a perfectly tailored blazer over a vibrant shirt—made him look both polished and effortlessly cool. "Let's get this show on the road, shall we? Remember, you're a force of nature."

"Easier said than done," I replied, rolling my eyes playfully, though my stomach twisted with nerves. "It's not like we're walking a dog at the park, Alex. We're about to parade our creations in front of a panel of industry titans. No pressure!"

"Hey, remember what we said? It's about the journey, not just the destination," he replied, flashing that charming grin that made me weak in the knees. "And besides, even titans need to be dazzled by brilliance. And we? We're the embodiment of brilliance!"

"Brilliantly anxious, maybe," I retorted, trying to mask the flutter of fear with humor.

As we made our way to the venue, I stole glances at the streets bustling with people, each immersed in their own lives. It struck me how surreal it felt to be on the verge of presenting my heart and soul to the world while everyone else remained blissfully unaware. The venue, an old theater transformed into a fashion show space, loomed ahead—grand and intimidating.

Once inside, the atmosphere buzzed with excitement and anxiety. Models flitted about, adjusting their hair and checking their outfits, while stylists scurried like ants on a mission. The air was electric, crackling with the promise of what was to come. I could feel my heart pounding, each thud echoing in my ears like a drumroll heralding an impending explosion.

"Okay, showtime," Alex said, squeezing my hand as we navigated through the crowd. "Let's do this together. Just like we practiced."

"Together," I echoed, but the word felt heavy, weighed down by the reality of competition. As we took our places behind the curtain, I caught sight of our models, the vibrant fabrics draping elegantly over their forms, each piece a testament to our late nights and shared dreams.

"Are you ready?" Alex asked, his voice low, yet steady.

"As ready as I'll ever be," I replied, though I could feel the knot in my stomach tightening.

The music swelled, a perfect backdrop to the unfolding drama, and as the curtain lifted, the stage flooded with light, illuminating our creations in a way that made them shimmer with life. The audience was a sea of faces—critics, influencers, and hopeful dreamers—each pair of eyes trained on the models gliding down the runway.

"Look at them," I whispered, my breath hitching. "They're stunning."

"They're wearing your vision," Alex said, pride radiating from him like sunlight. "Now let it shine."

The first model stepped onto the runway, and I felt my heart leap as the audience erupted in applause. My collection—a blend of textures and colors—danced under the lights, each piece telling a story of rebirth and transformation. With each passing model, the excitement in the room grew, a palpable energy that ignited my own creativity.

But just as I began to savor the moment, a figure caught my eye in the audience. It was a familiar face, one I hadn't expected to see—the very person I thought I'd left behind. In a sleek black dress, her demeanor exuded confidence, but her eyes were piercing, scanning the runway as if hunting for flaws. My heart sank, a heavy stone settling in my gut.

"Do you know her?" Alex asked, his gaze following mine.

"Yeah, that's my former mentor, Lisa," I replied, my voice barely above a whisper. "She's... well, she's everything I'm trying to escape."

"Then maybe she's exactly what you need," Alex suggested, a spark of mischief lighting his eyes. "Channel that energy into your work."

As the models continued to walk, I tried to focus on the beauty of the moment, but the presence of Lisa loomed like a dark cloud, casting shadows over my joy. When the final model took her turn, the applause erupted into a thunderous roar. My heart swelled with pride, yet anxiety clawed at me, intertwining with the remnants of doubt.

Once the show concluded, we stepped backstage, the air buzzing with excitement and chatter. Alex turned to me, his expression a mix of euphoria and relief. "We did it! They loved it!"

"Yeah, but..." I trailed off, my eyes wandering back to where I'd seen Lisa. "I can't shake the feeling she'll say something to ruin this."

"You can't control what others think. But you can control how you respond. Focus on us, not her," Alex said, his voice a steady anchor amid the chaos.

Suddenly, a voice cut through the noise, sharp and pointed. "Well, well, if it isn't the prodigal designer making her grand return. Did you think you could simply repackage your insecurities as art?"

I froze, recognizing Lisa's voice, the way it sliced through the crowd like a knife. My breath caught, the joy of the moment dimming as I turned to face her.

"Nice collection, but don't let the applause fool you," she continued, her eyes narrowing. "You're still just a girl playing dress-up, hoping to impress everyone with your whimsical fantasies."

The air thickened, and I felt the world tilt beneath my feet. Alex stepped closer, his body a shield between me and the venom of Lisa's words. "That's not how it works, Lisa. She's poured her heart into this."

"And yet, hearts alone won't save you in this industry," Lisa shot back, dismissive. "It's cutthroat. You'd do well to remember that."

"Maybe so," I managed, summoning all my courage. "But I'm not playing dress-up. I'm creating a new narrative."

"Good luck with that," she sneered, her gaze flicking dismissively. "But I've seen it all before. The industry chews people up and spits them out. Don't say I didn't warn you."

As she walked away, the crowd continued to swirl around us, the excitement of the showcase lingering, but I felt as though I were trapped in a whirlwind of self-doubt. The very foundations of my dreams trembled as I faced the implications of her words.

"What do you think?" I whispered, turning to Alex, seeking reassurance in his eyes.

But before he could respond, the sound of clattering heels echoed down the hall, and suddenly a voice I didn't expect called out my name. I turned, and my breath hitched in my throat as a figure emerged from the shadows—someone from my past who I thought was long gone, someone whose presence could change everything.

"Surprise!" they shouted, their eyes alight with mischief and a hint of something darker. "I've come to see your grand debut."

The air around me shifted, tension coiling tightly in my chest as I prepared to confront the unexpected arrival, my heart racing with questions I hadn't dared to ask. And in that moment, the ground beneath me felt unsteady, the stakes higher than I ever imagined, the path ahead obscured by uncertainty.

Chapter 14: A Twist of Fate

The warm aroma of freshly brewed coffee enveloped us as I nestled into the plush corner of our favorite café, a sanctuary from the relentless clamor of the city. The air was thick with the laughter and chatter of patrons, mingling with the soft jazz melodies that played in the background, creating a cocoon of familiarity and comfort. I could hardly believe the day had finally arrived—the eve of my capsule collection showcase, an event I had envisioned for months, meticulously crafting each piece as if they were extensions of my very soul.

Across the table, Alex leaned back, his chair creaking in protest as he sipped his espresso, a small smile curling at the corners of his mouth. His eyes sparkled with a mixture of pride and excitement that made my heart flutter. "I can't believe we're finally here," he said, his voice warm and teasing, a perfect counterpoint to the crisp autumn air outside. "You, a rising star, and me... well, just a guy trying not to trip over his own shoelaces at a fashion gala."

I chuckled, shaking my head. "You're more than just 'a guy.' You're going to blow everyone away with your presentation tomorrow. I'm convinced of it." The truth was, I meant it. I had watched him toil away, sketching and sewing, pouring every ounce of his heart into his designs. His ambition was as palpable as the steam rising from our cups.

Yet, beneath my excitement lay a simmering unease. Our aspirations were tangled together like threads in a tapestry, vibrant and interconnected, yet potentially frayed. The gala where he would showcase his line was the same night as my event, and while I wanted nothing more than to cheer him on, a pang of fear gripped me. What if our paths were indeed diverging? What if this competition, however unintentional, created a chasm between us?

"Do you ever think about what happens when we're both on our own paths?" I asked, my voice softer now, more tentative, as if I were testing the waters of a particularly deep pool. I held my breath, feeling the weight of my question hang between us.

He paused, his brow furrowing slightly, and I could almost see the gears turning in his mind. "You mean, like, what if one of us makes it big while the other is still trying to catch up?" His tone was light, but I could sense the undercurrent of seriousness.

"Exactly," I replied, my fingers tracing the rim of my cup, feeling the warmth seep into my skin. "What if... I don't know, we become rivals instead of partners?"

He leaned in, his expression shifting into something more earnest, a flicker of concern igniting in his eyes. "But why would we let that happen? We're on the same team, right? I'll always be in your corner, and you'll be in mine. We just need to support each other, no matter what."

I smiled, trying to absorb the reassurance he offered, but the knot in my stomach remained, tightening with each beat of my heart. I wanted to believe him, but the specter of competition loomed over us, casting a shadow on our dreams.

"So, what are you going to wear tomorrow?" he asked, attempting to lighten the mood. "Something fabulous, I hope. You know, something that says 'I'm ready to take on the world!'"

I laughed, relieved for the shift in conversation. "Well, I've been thinking about a bold red dress that's fitted at the waist and flares out at the hips. It has this dramatic neckline that feels both powerful and feminine." My eyes sparkled with enthusiasm as I imagined the way the fabric would sway around me, accentuating every curve, making me feel invincible.

"I can already see it," he said, his tone teasing yet sincere. "You'll walk in and everyone will be like, 'Who is that goddess?'"

"And you'll strut into your gala looking like a fashion overlord," I countered, the playful banter lightening the atmosphere once more. "With all your little minions trailing behind, hanging on your every word."

We both burst into laughter, the kind that bubbles up from deep within, spilling over into the space around us. The ease of our camaraderie melted away the tension, if only for a moment. I allowed myself to forget about the looming uncertainties, to savor the warmth of his presence, the comfort of knowing we had each other, no matter what.

As the evening drew to a close, the café began to empty out, the soft jazz fading into a distant hum. I glanced at the clock, realizing how much time had slipped away, and my heart sank a little at the thought of parting ways. "I should probably head home and get some rest. Tomorrow's going to be a whirlwind," I said, my voice tinged with a mixture of anticipation and dread.

"Yeah, me too," he replied, a hint of reluctance threading through his words. "But remember, no matter what happens tomorrow, I'll be cheering you on from the sidelines. And I expect a full report on every detail later."

I nodded, feeling a warmth spread through me at his words, yet I couldn't shake the unease that danced at the edges of my mind. As we rose from the table, I wrapped my arms around him, inhaling the comforting scent of his cologne, a mix of cedar and something citrusy. It felt like home, like a promise that our bond was stronger than any competitive spirit that might arise.

"Good luck," I whispered, holding on just a moment longer, wishing desperately to bottle this feeling of unity and love before stepping into the uncertainties of tomorrow. As we pulled away, I caught a glimpse of his expression—determined, hopeful, but shadowed with the same fears that had plagued me all night.

STITCHED IN AMBITION

The morning light filtered through my window, casting soft, golden hues across my room, and for a fleeting moment, it felt like magic. I lay in bed, cocooned in my blankets, my heart racing with a blend of excitement and trepidation. Today was the day my capsule collection would finally take its first steps into the world, yet the thrill of it all was shadowed by the knowledge that Alex was preparing for his own big moment. The clock ticked steadily, each second a reminder that I couldn't hide from the collision of our dreams any longer.

Pushing the covers away, I swung my legs over the side of the bed, my feet touching the cool hardwood floor. A shiver raced up my spine as I contemplated the outfit I had so painstakingly crafted for the showcase. The red dress hung on the back of my door, its vibrant fabric shimmering under the soft light, waiting to transform me into someone fierce and formidable. I could almost hear its call, urging me to take my place on that stage, but an echo of doubt lingered, whispering that maybe I was about to step into a battleground instead of a platform for my creativity.

After a shower, I stood in front of the mirror, tugging at my unruly hair and attempting to tame it into submission. The reflection staring back at me looked every bit the part of a designer on the brink of recognition, yet beneath the surface, I felt more like a house of cards, teetering dangerously close to collapse. I practiced my smile—confident yet warm—before stepping into the dress. As I slipped it on, the sensation of the fabric hugging my curves ignited a flicker of empowerment within me.

Once I was fully dressed, I grabbed my clutch, taking a moment to admire the confident woman I had become—or at least the one I hoped to be tonight. Stepping outside, the crisp autumn air filled my lungs, grounding me as I navigated the bustling streets of the city. The world was alive with color: the leaves painted in shades of amber and crimson, couples walking hand in hand, and children laughing as they dashed past.

Reaching the venue, I was greeted by the familiar faces of friends and fellow designers, all of whom buzzed with the kind of energy that both thrilled and terrified me. As I entered, the scent of fresh flowers and polished wood wrapped around me, a stark contrast to the frenetic energy pulsing just beneath the surface. Each corner was adorned with intricate displays of fabric swatches and sketchbooks, visions of creativity laid bare for the world to admire.

"Look who's here!" a voice chimed from across the room, pulling me from my reverie. It was Mia, my best friend and the unyielding cheerleader of my life. Her hair danced like a halo around her face as she rushed over, pulling me into a fierce hug. "You look absolutely stunning. That dress was made for you!"

"Thanks, Mia," I replied, my smile broadening despite the flutter of nerves in my stomach. "I just hope it doesn't fall apart on stage."

Mia waved her hand dismissively, her confidence radiating like sunshine. "Please, you're going to be amazing! Just remember, this is your moment. The world is waiting to see what you've created." Her words were like a balm, easing the tightness in my chest, if only temporarily.

As the hour approached, I found myself pacing near the back of the venue, clutching my clutch like a lifeline. The murmur of voices melded with the rustle of fabric as everyone prepared for their presentations. I could see glimpses of other designers, their collections vibrant and varied, each telling a different story. But every time my gaze flickered to the door, my heart raced.

It was then that I caught sight of Alex across the room, his presence commanding yet comforting. He looked dashing in his tailored suit, the kind of outfit that screamed ambition and style. I felt a surge of pride, mingled with a gnawing fear. We were both about to showcase our dreams, yet the night felt like a balancing act on a tightrope strung high above an uncertain abyss.

"Hey!" he called, striding toward me with that warm, familiar grin that melted away my worries, if only for a moment. "You look incredible. Just... wow."

"Thanks, you too," I said, glancing down at his ensemble, which he pulled off effortlessly. "I'm sure you'll wow them tonight. Just remember to breathe. And don't forget to take notes for me."

"Only if you promise to do the same." His laughter bubbled up, a joyful sound amidst the tension. But I could see the uncertainty dancing in his eyes as well. "Seriously, if you need someone to carry your bags or hold your drinks, I'm your guy."

I chuckled, appreciating his effort to lighten the mood. "Yeah, right. You'll be too busy charming the judges and dazzling the crowd."

As we shared a brief moment of connection, I felt the weight of my concerns lift slightly. But soon, the moment was broken by the organizer calling everyone to attention, and the room fell into a hushed excitement. The air thickened with anticipation, a palpable energy that surged through the crowd.

One by one, designers took their turns at the front, presenting their collections with fervor, their voices a mixture of pride and anxiety. I found myself clapping enthusiastically, but my heart raced with each presentation, caught in a cycle of hope and anxiety. What if my designs didn't resonate? What if Alex stole the spotlight?

Finally, it was my turn. I stepped into the spotlight, the fabric of my dress swirling around my legs like a gentle reminder of the artistry I had poured into every stitch. The audience's eyes were on me, a sea of expectation, and I felt as if the weight of my dreams rested squarely on my shoulders. I took a deep breath, summoning every ounce of courage within me.

"Hello, everyone. Thank you for being here tonight," I began, my voice steady despite the tremor of my heart. As I spoke, sharing the inspiration behind my collection—the stories woven into each piece, the colors reflecting the changing seasons—I noticed Alex in the front row, nodding encouragingly. He was a beacon of support, even in the tumult of the moment.

But just as I was about to unveil the centerpiece of my collection, an unexpected voice broke through the atmosphere, slicing through my confidence like a cold breeze. "What's so special about this collection? Everyone's doing the same thing." A figure from the back scoffed, their tone dripping with condescension.

A silence fell over the room, and my heart skipped a beat. The sudden jab took me off guard, and I felt heat rush to my cheeks. I had anticipated criticism, of course, but not so abruptly. For a moment, doubt gnawed at me, threatening to unravel everything I had worked for. But then I caught Alex's eye again, and a flicker of determination ignited within me.

"Perhaps you're right," I replied, my voice gaining strength. "But art is subjective, and if I can touch even one person's heart with my designs, then I've succeeded." The words flowed from me, fueled by a mix of passion and the support I felt surrounding me. I could see some nodding in agreement, and it was enough to propel me forward.

The presentation continued, and as I showcased each piece, the initial tension began to dissolve. My confidence grew, allowing me to flourish in my vulnerability. I could feel the pulse of my dreams beating alongside those of others in the room. And though uncertainty still lingered, it was slowly overshadowed by the warmth of shared creativity.

As I finished my presentation, the applause rang out, filling me with a sense of triumph and relief. I caught Alex's gaze again, his smile bright and proud, and I knew that whatever came next, we were still on this journey together, woven into the fabric of each other's aspirations.

The applause rang in my ears like the beating of a drum, a rhythm that filled me with exhilaration and disbelief. I had just unveiled my collection, and while I stood there basking in the moment, the exhilaration quickly morphed into a heady cocktail of anticipation and fear. My heart raced, and as I stepped off the stage, I was met with a flurry of congratulatory smiles and eager faces.

"Honestly, you were incredible!" Mia squealed, enveloping me in a tight hug. "I told you everyone would love it! The way you spoke about each piece—it was like watching a masterclass in passion."

"Thanks, Mia." I laughed, still trying to catch my breath. "I can't believe I didn't trip over my own feet."

"Believe it," she grinned, her eyes shining. "You were a star."

But as the evening wore on, I felt a knot tightening in my stomach again. Despite the success of my showcase, Alex's gala was looming like a specter at the back of my mind. I couldn't shake the feeling that the night wasn't just about me. I turned to look for him, scanning the crowd, but all I saw were faces—many smiling, some eager, and a few bored. The room buzzed with excitement, yet I felt an undertow pulling me away from the moment.

"Where's Alex?" I asked Mia, trying to keep the tremor from my voice.

"He should be here any minute. He's probably still basking in his own glory," she said, waving off my concern. "You know how he is. The world revolves around him, and he loves to remind us of that."

I rolled my eyes but couldn't help but smile at the affection woven through her sarcasm. Just then, a familiar silhouette caught my eye. Alex burst through the crowd, his smile brightening the room like a spotlight. The way he carried himself exuded confidence, and I couldn't help but feel a rush of pride. Yet, as he approached, the tension in my stomach twisted tighter, squeezing the joy out of the moment.

"Sorry I'm late," he said, wrapping me in a warm embrace, the kind that sent a shiver down my spine. "I was trapped in a discussion about fabric weights with someone who clearly needs a lesson in light versus heavy." He laughed, a sound that had always made my heart skip. "How did it go?"

I stepped back, forcing a smile that felt too wide, a mask over my swirling emotions. "It was great! I think they really liked it." I hesitated, sensing the unspoken words hanging between us, laden with the weight of our competition. "What about you? How was your gala?"

"Crazy, honestly. But so exhilarating. I didn't expect the feedback to be so positive," he replied, his eyes sparkling with enthusiasm. "But I kept thinking about you up here. How you'd feel."

"Really?" I asked, a flutter of warmth spreading through me. "I thought you'd be too busy charming the crowd to think about anything else."

He chuckled, shaking his head. "Not a chance. I was cheering you on in my head the whole time."

We exchanged a brief moment of connection, but just as the air seemed to clear, the fabric of the evening began to fray. I could sense it; an electric charge pulsed through the room as whispers spread like wildfire.

"Did you hear?" someone said, their voice barely above a whisper but sharp enough to slice through the cheerful chatter. "A major buyer from Paris is here tonight."

At first, the news washed over me like a gentle tide, exciting yet distant. But as I glanced at Alex, I could see the way his expression shifted. The opportunity hung in the air like a ripe fruit, tantalizing yet just out of reach.

"Who?" I asked, my curiosity piqued.

"Luc Renard," the same voice chimed in, eyes wide with disbelief. "He's looking for new talent for his spring collection. They say he's making decisions tonight."

Alex's gaze darkened, a shadow flickering across his face as he digested the information. "That's... big," he murmured, rubbing the back of his neck, a nervous habit I had come to recognize. "I didn't know he'd be here."

I felt a pang of empathy for him, realizing that while I was trying to celebrate my success, he was faced with the possibility of losing out on a dream he'd nurtured just as fiercely as I had.

"Do you want to go talk to him?" I offered, the words tumbling out before I had a chance to think.

"What? No! I mean, yes, but..." he hesitated, a flicker of vulnerability crossing his features. "I'm not sure I'm ready."

"Why not? You're amazing! Your collection deserves to be seen."

He gave me a wry smile, but there was something uneasy behind it. "What if he doesn't like it? What if he thinks I'm a joke?"

I frowned, stepping closer to him. "You're not a joke, Alex. You're incredibly talented, and you've worked so hard. This could be your shot."

As I spoke, I could see the gears in his mind turning, the weight of ambition wrestling with the fear of failure. He was a brilliant designer, yet the pressure of potential success was a heavy shroud. Just then, a commotion erupted across the room, snapping us both from our moment of contemplation.

The crowd parted, revealing a tall man with a commanding presence. His tailored suit hugged his frame perfectly, exuding an air of authority that sent a wave of excitement rippling through the room. Murmurs rippled among the guests, and I felt Alex stiffen beside me.

"Is that him?" I whispered, my breath catching as the man scanned the room, his gaze cutting through the crowd like a laser.

"Yeah," Alex said, his voice low. "That's Luc Renard."

The moment stretched, time seeming to warp as Luc approached, flanked by admirers and other designers hoping to catch his eye. He was a force of nature, commanding attention effortlessly, and I could see the way everyone around him buzzed with nervous energy.

"Alex," I said, breaking the tension that had settled between us. "You need to go. Now."

He hesitated, glancing at Luc as if the man were a great chasm he couldn't quite bring himself to cross. "But what if—"

"No more 'what ifs.' You've got this. Don't let this opportunity slip away." I reached out, squeezing his hand reassuringly, feeling the warmth of his skin beneath my fingers.

He took a deep breath, and for a moment, I could see the resolve building within him, pushing aside the doubts. "Okay. Okay, I'll go."

But just as he stepped away, a familiar voice cut through the crowd. "Alex! I need to talk to you!"

It was Jenna, one of our fiercest rivals, striding toward us with purpose, her eyes glinting with a competitive spark. I watched as Alex's confidence faltered, the glimmer of ambition dimmed by the sudden twist in the evening's fate.

"Not now, Jenna," he said, a note of frustration creeping into his voice.

But she wasn't listening. "It's important. I think you need to hear this."

I watched helplessly as Jenna's presence created a rift between us, the opportunity slipping away just as quickly as it had arrived. My heart raced, torn between wanting to push him forward and the sense that something was about to unravel.

"I'll be right back," Alex promised, his gaze flicking between me and Jenna, uncertainty etched across his features. He took a step toward her, and I felt a sinking sensation in my chest.

As I stood there, the chaos of the evening swirling around me, the realization hit hard: ambition had a way of complicating everything, even the purest of connections.

The crowd surged, and I caught snippets of conversation, the atmosphere thick with tension. My heart thudded in my chest as I watched Alex and Jenna speak, her animated gestures casting a shadow over his fading confidence. Suddenly, a voice cut through the noise, the unmistakable sound of Luc Renard addressing the crowd.

"Ladies and gentlemen, thank you for your patience. I've decided to make an announcement tonight..."

I held my breath, the world narrowing to that singular moment. I could feel the anticipation in the air, like a coiled spring ready to snap.

And then, just as he prepared to reveal what everyone had been waiting for, my phone buzzed in my pocket. I fished it out, my heart racing as I glanced at the screen.

It was a message from my mentor, a single line that froze me in place: "We need to talk. It's urgent."

A chill crept down my spine, and as I looked back up, Luc's voice cut through the tension, the words heavy with the promise of change. "Tonight, I will be choosing a new talent to mentor..."

The room faded into a blur as my world tilted on its axis, the weight of uncertainty crashing down on me. I was about to discover not only the fate of our dreams but the very foundation of what I thought we were building together. And just like that, everything began to unravel.

Chapter 15: The Night of Reckoning

The rooftop garden sprawls beneath a canvas of twilight, the sky painted in deep purples and blues, the city below glittering like a sea of stars. Twinkling lights hang from delicate strings, casting a soft glow on the vibrant foliage that sways gently in the evening breeze. The scent of jasmine and rosemary intertwines in the air, an intoxicating blend that fills my lungs and fuels my anticipation. My fingers brush against the fabric of my creations, each stitch a testament to sleepless nights and endless revisions, a labor of love that has brought me to this moment.

Backstage is a whirlwind of chaos and beauty. Models flit around in an array of colors and patterns, each one a canvas painted with my dreams. I catch snippets of their conversations—laughter mingling with nervous energy, the sound like music to my ears. But amidst the joyous clamor, a gnawing anxiety festers within me, a shadow lurking at the edges of my excitement. I can't help but glance at my phone, hoping for a text, a glimpse of the familiar name that has been my anchor and my muse. But the screen remains stubbornly dark, and with it, my heart sinks deeper into uncertainty.

"Hey, you're going to be great!" Lena, my best friend and unofficial cheerleader, snaps me out of my reverie. She adjusts the collar of my dress shirt, her hands steady even as her eyes gleam with the thrill of the moment. "You've worked too hard to let some last-minute jitters take over. Just breathe." Her enthusiasm is infectious, and I manage a shaky smile in response. It's reassuring to have her here, yet the absence of Alex—a silent specter hovering over my thoughts—shrouds the night in a veil of doubt.

As the minutes trickle by like melting ice, I try to focus on the present, on the voices around me, the way the garden buzzes with anticipation. My heart races in rhythm with the pulsating energy of the crowd below, a sea of unfamiliar faces waiting to witness the culmination of my hard work. With each model who steps onto the stage, my anxiety morphs into exhilaration. They glide effortlessly, adorned in my designs that mirror the beauty of the night: flowing fabrics that catch the breeze, colors that resonate with the vibrancy of the cityscape. Applause erupts with each presentation, and I can feel the collective breath of the audience as they lean forward, drawn into the world I've created.

But each burst of applause feels like a weight on my chest. I look out at the crowd, searching for a familiar face among the sea of strangers, but I see only shadows and silhouettes. Where is he? The thought cuts deeper than I'd like to admit. This moment was supposed to be ours—his laughter mingling with my triumph, his pride my guiding light. But instead, I stand alone, my success tainted by a sense of loss. I remind myself that this is what I wanted, what I dreamed of since I was a little girl sketching dresses on napkins during family dinners. But dreams have a way of twisting, don't they? They often demand sacrifices, and sometimes those sacrifices feel heavier than the prize.

Lena's voice brings me back, her laughter cutting through my thoughts like a knife. "Look at you! You're shining brighter than those lights!" She winks, nudging me playfully as the last model takes her turn. I can't help but beam, the pride swelling in my chest as I catch the tail end of their applause. I step into the spotlight, heart racing as the warmth of the lights washes over me. I take a deep breath, the air thick with expectation and the scent of blooming flowers.

"Thank you all for being here tonight," I begin, my voice steady despite the chaos within. "This collection is not just a reflection of my designs; it's a piece of my journey. Each fabric tells a story, each seam weaves together my dreams and fears. It's a celebration of the path I've traveled to get here." I pause, letting my words linger in the air, hoping to forge a connection with the audience. "But it's also a reminder of the people who have supported me, who have pushed me to be better—even when I didn't believe in myself."

As I speak, I search the crowd once more, a part of me unwilling to let go of the hope that he might be here, hidden among the faces. Just then, a voice shouts from the back, slicing through my thoughts. "You're amazing! Your work is stunning!" It's a compliment, but the voice feels distant, like a warm breeze that brushes past me without truly touching my heart. I can't focus on it, not when the silence left by Alex's absence looms larger than the applause.

The moment stretches on, and I feel the weight of every eye on me. "I hope this collection inspires you to embrace your own journeys, to take risks and chase your dreams," I conclude, allowing my heart to pour into my final words. "Because at the end of the day, what matters most is not just the destination, but the people we meet along the way."

The applause roars to life again, and I bow my head, a mixture of gratitude and grief swirling within me. I step off the stage, my mind racing, a whirlwind of elation and despair. The night is supposed to be a celebration, yet the emptiness in my chest feels as vast as the city skyline, illuminated but distant. As the crowd mingles, I scan the faces again, but deep down, I know that the absence I feel isn't just physical. It's a reminder of everything that has shifted, everything that has changed. And in this moment of triumph, I'm left questioning whether I'm truly ready for the sacrifices that success demands.

The applause fades, leaving a lingering hum in my ears as I retreat into the dimly lit backstage. The vibrant colors of my collection still flicker in my mind like fireworks, each explosion of fabric and design a testament to my hard work and ambition. But with each step away from the spotlight, the reality of Alex's absence presses down like a heavy blanket, smothering the exhilaration that should accompany my success. I lean against the cool, metal wall, taking a moment to catch my breath, and my heart flutters with a mix of triumph and unresolved ache.

"Look at you, superstar!" Lena bursts into the space, her energy a bright contrast to the shadows swirling in my mind. She's flushed from the excitement, her cheeks pink, and I can't help but smile at her infectious spirit. "You were phenomenal out there! I swear I saw a few people in the front row actually tear up."

I chuckle softly, shaking my head. "They were probably crying for my sanity, watching me fumble my words on stage."

"Please. You were a vision, and those designs were pure magic. Who needs a boyfriend when you can have a fashion show like that?" she quips, but her laughter doesn't reach my heart.

The tension inside me tightens, a cord drawn taut. "Yeah, but it feels a little hollow, you know? I mean, I imagined this moment so differently." I push off the wall, shoving my hands into the pockets of my tailored trousers. "I thought I'd feel elated, but instead, I just feel... empty."

"Okay, well, maybe you should channel that energy into a post-show celebration," she suggests, her voice brightening with enthusiasm. "There's a bar down the street known for its creative cocktails. We could totally hit it up! I need to see you embrace this moment properly, like the fierce designer queen you are!"

I hesitate, the idea of mingling with crowds and vibrant laughter feeling overwhelming when all I want to do is curl up in my blanket fort and binge-watch terrible rom-coms. But Lena's hopeful expression softens my resolve. "Okay, fine. But only if we can get a table by the window so I can pretend I'm people-watching for inspiration."

"Deal!" she chirps, practically bouncing on her toes.

As we make our way down from the rooftop, the cool night air washes over me, and the city sprawls before us, alive with energy. The sounds of laughter and music spill from nearby streets, mingling with the intoxicating scent of street food that wafts through the air. The city, usually so daunting in its vastness, feels like a cozy blanket of familiarity tonight.

The bar, a trendy spot with an ambiance of eclectic charm, is buzzing with life. We slide into a table by the window, and I can't help but admire the kaleidoscope of faces passing by, each person wrapped in their own story. Lena orders us drinks—something pink and sparkling for her and something dark and mysterious for me.

"Cheers to your brilliance and to avoiding romantic entanglements," she declares, raising her glass high. I clink mine against hers, the sound sharp and clear, momentarily slicing through my melancholy.

"Here's to designs that don't need an audience to validate them," I say, though the words taste bittersweet on my tongue.

As the night unfolds, laughter bubbles between us, each sip of our drinks melting away the tension knotting my stomach. But just as I begin to relax, the door swings open, and in walks a familiar silhouette. My heart stutters as I lock eyes with Alex. He stands there, framed by the light spilling in from the street, an uncertainty etched across his face that mirrors my own inner turmoil.

He's dressed casually, jeans hugging his form in all the right places, his signature leather jacket hanging effortlessly over his shoulders. The bar's noise fades to a dull roar as we share a moment—his eyes searching for me amidst the crowd, my heart battling between anger and longing. I thought I had prepared myself for this encounter, but the reality of seeing him again leaves me breathless.

"Wow, that's awkward," Lena mutters, her gaze darting between us like a ping-pong ball.

I roll my eyes but can't tear my gaze away from him. "I should have known he'd show up here. It's practically his second home."

"Maybe he's come to apologize for ghosting you," she whispers, trying to keep her voice low.

"Or to give me a lecture on how I'm not cut out for this," I retort, bitterness creeping into my tone.

Just then, Alex spots me and approaches our table, his expression shifting from uncertainty to determination. "Hey," he says, his voice warm but laced with hesitation. "Can we talk?"

The room seems to shrink as Lena instinctively moves her glass to the edge of the table, a silent invitation for me to decide. "You're not actually going to have a heart-to-heart with him in front of me, are you?" she hisses.

"Why not? It's a free country." I shoot back, feigning bravado.

Alex watches us, the tension in the air thick enough to slice through. "Please, just a minute? I won't take long."

Against my better judgment, I nod, and he pulls out a chair, sitting down across from me. The space between us feels electric, a magnetic pull that sends shivers racing down my spine.

"I'm really sorry for not being there tonight," he starts, his voice earnest, cutting through the noise of the bar. "I should have been at your show. You deserve that support, and I..." He falters, running a hand through his hair, and suddenly, I'm confronted with the raw vulnerability etched on his face.

"What? You didn't have time?" I bite back, trying to keep the hurt from seeping into my tone.

"No, it's not that. It's just—things got complicated," he admits, and in that moment, I see the conflict swirling in his eyes, an honest admission that he's grappling with something deeper.

"Complicated how? You've been my best friend for years. I thought we shared everything," I reply, feeling the heat rise in my cheeks, a mix of frustration and longing.

He leans forward, lowering his voice. "I wanted to be there. I did. But I was scared. I didn't want to take away from your moment.

You've worked so hard, and I didn't want my... my feelings to complicate everything."

The honesty in his words stirs something within me, a potent blend of anger and affection. "So, you just decided to disappear? That's your solution?"

"I thought it would help. I thought you'd be better off without the baggage."

"Baggage? Since when did friendship become a burden?"

His eyes darken, and I can see the conflict dancing behind them. "When the line between friends and something more blurs, it can become messy. And I didn't want to add more chaos to your life when you were trying to shine."

For a moment, we sit in silence, the air thick with unsaid words, our emotions swirling like a tornado, threatening to pull us both in. The familiar warmth that once felt comforting now feels like an anchor, holding me down in an ocean of uncertainty.

The silence stretches between us, palpable and heavy, laden with all the unsaid words that have built up over the months. My heart thuds against my ribcage, a drumbeat of confusion and longing. "So, you thought going radio silent would keep me from realizing how much I needed you?" I ask, my voice barely above a whisper, yet the intensity behind it crackles like electricity.

Alex's gaze falters, but he steadies himself, his expression shifting from uncertainty to a determination I hadn't seen before. "I thought it would be easier for both of us. I didn't want to distract you from your dreams. You're on the verge of something incredible, and I didn't want to make it about me."

I can't help but roll my eyes, a mixture of irritation and amusement bubbling up. "Look, I appreciate the thought, but that's the problem, Alex. You always overthink things. You're not a distraction; you're part of my dream. You've always been part of it."

The honesty in my own words surprises me. I hadn't fully realized until now just how much his absence had left a void in my life, a hollow echo where his laughter and support used to reside.

He shifts in his seat, and for a moment, I think he's going to say something profound, something that will bridge the gap between us. Instead, he hesitates, glancing down at the table as if searching for the right words buried beneath the wood grain. "I didn't want to ruin everything," he finally murmurs, his voice thick with unspoken fears. "I thought if I just stepped back, you'd be free to soar."

"Ruin? You think being honest with me would ruin things?" I lean forward, feeling the warmth of his presence envelop me like a blanket. "What's ruining things is not being honest. You left me to guess why you vanished, and that hurt more than I can say."

His eyes meet mine, and there's a flicker of vulnerability that ignites a spark in my chest. "I know. And I'm sorry. I was scared of what I felt, scared of losing you in a way I couldn't predict. But seeing you up there tonight, shining like you were meant to, made me realize how wrong I was."

I can feel the tension in the air shift, a crackle of electricity mixed with an undercurrent of something deeper—something that pulls at the edges of my heart. "So what now? We just pretend everything's okay and go back to being friends?"

His brow furrows, and a hint of frustration crosses his features. "I don't want to pretend. But I also don't want to ruin the best thing in my life. It's complicated."

"Complicated is my middle name," I shoot back, unable to mask the playful edge in my voice. "But seriously, if we don't address this, it'll linger like a bad smell in the fridge. And I can't stand the idea of having to avoid you because of some weird tension."

He laughs, a genuine sound that ripples through the air, easing some of the heaviness between us. "I guess we could air it out, like old laundry. But where do we even start?"

"Why don't you try telling me how you feel?" I challenge, leaning back in my chair, a teasing smile dancing on my lips. "Or is that too terrifying?"

Alex narrows his eyes, the playful glint in his expression returning. "Terrifying doesn't even begin to cover it. But you're right. If I'm going to say anything, it's best to just blurt it out."

"Great! I'm all ears, so lay it on me."

He takes a deep breath, his gaze steadying on mine. "Okay, here goes. I miss you. I miss the way we used to be—always joking around, sharing our dreams, and just being ourselves. When I distanced myself, I thought I could protect you from whatever this is. But now, seeing you like this... I can't ignore it any longer."

My heart stutters, caught between relief and apprehension. "You mean... you want us to be more than friends?"

"It's more than just wanting; it's about needing. I've realized that the way I feel about you has shifted into something deeper, something I can't shake off. And it scares the hell out of me because I don't want to mess this up."

For a heartbeat, time freezes, the weight of his confession hanging in the air. It's a moment suspended between possibility and fear, two worlds colliding in a dizzying spiral. "And if I told you I feel the same?" I ask, my voice barely above a whisper.

His eyes widen, hope igniting in their depths. "You do?"

"Honestly, I've been trying to ignore it," I admit, feeling a rush of vulnerability seep through my defenses. "But here we are, sitting across from each other, and it's hard to pretend I don't feel this insane connection."

His lips curve into a smile, but it's quickly shadowed by a flicker of uncertainty. "But what if we mess it up? What if it changes everything?"

"Life's messy. Relationships are messy," I reply, unable to suppress the warmth that floods my heart at his admission. "But I'd rather take that risk with you than live in a world where we're just friends, tiptoeing around what we could be."

"I like that idea," he says, his voice dropping lower, a conspiratorial edge taking over. "But what happens if it doesn't work out? What if we end up hating each other?"

"Then we'll just have to stage a fabulous fashion show, pull out our best smiles, and pretend we're the best of friends. I'm not above dramatics."

His laughter fills the space between us, a sound I've missed more than I realized. "Okay, fair point. I can handle that. But I'd rather us not reach that point."

"Neither would I," I reply, feeling a wave of courage wash over me. "But maybe we could take this one step at a time? Start with being honest about what we want?"

He nods, the weight of our shared emotions hanging heavily yet beautifully in the air. "I'd like that."

Just then, as we share a moment laden with unspoken promises, the door swings open again, and a commotion rises from the entrance. A group of rowdy patrons enters, laughter and loud voices spilling into the bar, momentarily breaking our bubble. Among them is someone I recognize—an acquaintance from the fashion scene, her presence sharp and magnetic. She strides in with confidence, her long hair shimmering under the bar lights.

"Is that who I think it is?" Alex leans closer, squinting to get a better look.

I'm too busy assessing the new arrivals to respond, my heart sinking when I catch sight of the woman standing at the bar. Her expression is fierce, her gaze sweeping over the crowd as if searching for someone—or something. And as she locks eyes with me, the confidence drains from her face, replaced by a scowl that sends a chill down my spine.

"What is she doing here?" I mutter under my breath, tension tightening in the pit of my stomach.

Before Alex can answer, the woman strides over, her heels clicking sharply against the wooden floor, each step echoing like a warning bell. "Well, well, if it isn't the shining star of the fashion world," she sneers, her voice dripping with sarcasm. "I heard you had a little showcase tonight. How quaint."

The atmosphere shifts, heavy with the tension of an impending storm. I can feel Alex tense beside me, his presence an anchor I desperately need. "What do you want?" I manage, trying to hold my ground.

"Oh, just came to see the spectacle for myself," she replies, her lips curving into a smile that doesn't reach her eyes. "And to remind you that in this world, success doesn't come without consequences."

The words hang in the air, thick with foreboding, and my heart races. "What do you mean?"

Her smile widens, an unsettling glint in her eyes. "Let's just say, not everyone is pleased with your sudden rise. And I'm afraid you're about to find out just how high the stakes really are."

The threat lingers in the air like smoke, suffocating and relentless. I glance at Alex, his expression a mixture of concern and determination. But before I can process the gravity of her words, the bar door swings shut, sealing our fate—and whatever lies ahead in this unpredictable world.

Chapter 16: The Broken Connection

The air was thick with celebration, the kind that lingers long after the last guest has left and the echoes of laughter dissipate into the walls. My showcase had been a symphony of vibrant colors and exquisite creations, each piece carefully crafted to resonate with my vision. As I basked in the afterglow, the clinking of glasses and the murmur of excited voices surrounded me like a warm embrace. But amid the revelry, an unsettling chill brushed against my skin, whispering reminders of an absence I couldn't shake.

Alex's absence was a shadow that loomed over the festivities, a palpable void that swallowed my joy. We had been inseparable, a duo of dreamers, but somewhere along the path of ambition, the connection that tethered us seemed to fray. I sent him a flurry of messages—bright emojis and enthusiastic exclamations about my night—but his responses were akin to faint echoes, barely there and lacking the usual vibrancy. Each reply felt like an invitation to a party where I was the only guest, one where the music played but nobody danced.

In a desperate bid to rekindle what we had, I arranged a post-show celebration. It felt like the perfect solution, a chance for us to reconnect over laughter and late-night tacos, our shared love language. I envisioned us nestled in a booth at our favorite diner, the soft glow of neon lights illuminating the contours of his face as he animatedly recounted his experiences. But as I awaited his arrival, my stomach twisted with anticipation and anxiety, my heart fluttering like a trapped bird.

When he finally walked in, I could hardly recognize him. The casual confidence he usually wore like a second skin seemed to have slipped away. His eyes, once bright and filled with mischief, now carried an unfamiliar weight. He smiled, but it didn't reach his eyes, leaving an unsettling emptiness in its wake. As he settled into the booth across from me, the world around us faded into a blur of color and sound. My heart sank as I struggled to pinpoint the shift in our dynamic, the moment when we had drifted into separate orbits.

"Congratulations on the showcase, by the way," he said, his voice steady but lacking the warmth I longed for. "I heard it was incredible."

"Thanks! It was everything I hoped for and more," I replied, forcing enthusiasm into my tone, the words tumbling out like the last drops of champagne from a bottle. "You should have been there. I missed you so much."

He shifted in his seat, the fabric of the booth creaking under the weight of unspoken words. "I had my gala," he murmured, tracing the rim of his glass with a finger, the clink a jarring reminder of the distance between us. "It was... different this year."

"Different how?" I pressed, eager for the banter we once shared, the playful teasing that felt like a dance.

His gaze flickered away, and in that moment, I felt like a juggler with too many balls in the air, teetering on the edge of disaster. "Just more serious, I guess. Everyone's focused on the next big thing. It's like they forgot how to enjoy themselves." He chuckled softly, but it was hollow, devoid of the joy we used to share.

I took a deep breath, determined to steer the conversation toward familiar waters, where our laughter once flowed like a river, unimpeded and joyful. "Remember the first time we went to that gala? We spent half the night pretending to know what wine we were drinking, just so we could giggle about it later."

His lips curved slightly, a flicker of the old Alex surfacing. "And you spilled red wine all over that poor woman's white dress. I thought you'd die of embarrassment."

"I thought I would too, but instead, we ended up dancing on the tables. Who knew that wine stains could lead to such a memorable night?" I laughed, hoping to coax more warmth into his eyes, to reignite the spark that once danced between us like the stars above a clear night sky.

But his smile faltered, and he leaned back, crossing his arms. "I wish I could say things are the same, but it feels like we're both caught up in different worlds now. I'm drowning in deadlines and expectations, and it's suffocating."

A silence enveloped us, heavy and suffocating. My heart raced, a wild horse trying to escape the confines of my ribcage. I had sensed the shift, the ever-widening chasm that lay between us, but hearing him articulate it was like a punch to the gut. "But we can't let that happen, Alex. We're supposed to be each other's lifelines."

His eyes flicked up to meet mine, a storm brewing beneath the surface. "Are we? Or have we just become two people pursuing dreams that don't overlap anymore?"

I leaned forward, desperation clawing at me. "We can make it work. We've always found a way before. It just takes a little effort, right? We can't let the world pull us apart."

"Effort?" He scoffed, the sound bitter on his tongue. "Sometimes it feels like we're the ones who need to change, and I don't know if I'm ready for that. You're on this incredible path, and I'm just trying to keep my head above water."

I felt the heat of his words sting like a slap. "And what about the path we carved together? I refuse to believe that the dreams we have can't coexist. We just need to remind ourselves what it felt like before everything got so complicated."

His gaze softened for a fleeting moment, and I could almost feel the memories swirling between us—lazy Sunday mornings filled with pancakes, nights spent plotting our futures under a blanket of stars. But just as quickly, the wall between us rose again, thick and unyielding. The shared dreams of our youth felt like ghosts, haunting a past that slipped through our fingers like sand.

The waitress arrived with our order, a colorful array of tacos that I had ordered without thinking, the kind we used to devour late at night. I watched him pick at the food, each bite accompanied by a silence that gnawed at my heart. "So, what's next for you?" I ventured, trying to recapture the thread of connection that seemed to fray with every passing moment.

He sighed, the weight of his ambitions pressing down on him like a leaden cloak. "I don't know. I thought I did, but it feels like I'm just chasing shadows now."

And there it was—the chasm between us widened, echoing with unfulfilled promises and unsaid words. I wanted to reach across the table, to bridge the gap that seemed insurmountable, but how do you mend something that feels irrevocably broken? The uncertainty loomed, an invisible fog wrapping around us, thickening with every shared moment of silence. The night stretched on, filled with laughter that felt borrowed, memories that lingered like the taste of tequila on the tongue, and the aching question that haunted my every thought: could we find our way back to each other, or were we destined to drift apart, two ships lost in the dark, vast sea of our ambitions?

The vibrant ambiance of the diner buzzed around us, the hum of conversation punctuated by the sizzle of frying bacon and the clatter of plates. My gaze flitted between the neon lights and Alex's expression, which remained inscrutable, a canvas painted in shades of distant contemplation. I could almost hear the ticking clock in the corner, counting down the moments of connection slipping through my fingers like grains of sand. As he toyed with the remnants of his untouched taco, I felt a familiar pang of frustration mixed with longing.

"You know," I said, forcing a lightness into my voice, "if we keep this up, I'll have to start charging you for emotional support. It's like pulling teeth getting you to share your thoughts these days."

He chuckled, but it was more of a reflex than a genuine laugh, like a pre-programmed response. "You're right; I'm a bit of a buzzkill tonight."

"Just a bit?" I quipped, raising an eyebrow. "I was expecting a full-on rave, complete with confetti cannons and dancing. Instead, I feel like I'm dining with a wall."

He leaned back, the booth creaking in protest. "I guess I'm just not in the party mood. I'm sorry."

"It's okay to feel that way," I replied, my tone softer. "Life's a rollercoaster, right? Sometimes it's exhilarating, and sometimes it feels like you're just hanging on for dear life, praying not to hurl."

His gaze flickered to the window, where the night sky stretched like a velvet blanket dotted with stars. "It's more like the rollercoaster is stuck upside down," he murmured, the hint of a smile playing at the corners of his mouth. "But at least there's good food here."

I couldn't help but laugh. "True. Tacos can solve a multitude of problems. If only they could solve existential crises."

"Maybe I should add them to my gala menu. 'Tacos: because nobody's ever sad while eating tacos.'"

"Exactly! You could create a whole theme around it. Call it 'Taco Therapy' or 'Guilt-Free Taco Tuesdays.'"

The corner of his mouth lifted slightly, and for a fleeting moment, the warmth between us felt tangible again. "I'd hire you as the marketing director. Your enthusiasm could sell ice to an Eskimo."

I leaned in, emboldened by the spark igniting between us. "Just promise me you'll keep the margaritas flowing at this taco therapy session. I'll bring the good vibes."

"Deal. And maybe a little salsa dancing while we're at it."

The playful banter hung in the air, a delicate thread woven between us. I seized the moment, my heart racing as I leaned forward, elbows on the table. "What's really going on with you,

Alex? I can see you're trying to put on a brave face, but I know you better than that. Talk to me."

He hesitated, the mask of humor slipping as he considered my question. "Honestly? I'm feeling lost. I thought I had everything figured out, but now it just feels like I'm treading water. My dreams are starting to feel more like weights, and I can't tell if I'm drowning or just too exhausted to keep swimming."

A heaviness settled in my chest. I reached out, my hand brushing against his. "I get it. I really do. I've been feeling the pressure too. But we're in this together, right? We can figure it out. We just need to communicate. Don't shut me out."

He looked down at our hands, the connection barely sparking as he pulled away, his brow furrowing. "It's hard, though. I don't want to drag you down with me. You're flying high, and I'm... well, I'm floundering. I can't be the anchor that keeps you from soaring."

"Alex," I said, my voice firm yet tender, "you're not an anchor. You're a part of my sky. And every great flight has its turbulence. I want to be here for you. Just as you've always been there for me."

The vulnerability hung between us, thick and intoxicating. He studied me, his expression shifting like the shifting winds of a storm brewing on the horizon. "It just feels like we're both so busy trying to chase these dreams, we forgot what it means to just be us."

"Then let's make a plan. Not just for the dreams, but for us. Let's have a taco night every week or something. No pressure. Just us, talking and laughing—no expectations."

His eyes softened, and for a moment, I thought I saw the spark I'd been longing for. "I like that idea. I miss just hanging out with you. We were good at that."

"See? The good times aren't gone; they're just hiding. All we have to do is coax them out." I grinned, my heart swelling with hope.

He chuckled, shaking his head. "You always did have a knack for optimism."

"Someone has to balance out your brooding," I teased, enjoying the way his laughter eased some of the tension that had been coiling in the air like a spring.

The warmth of our shared laughter felt like a lifeline, but as the minutes slipped by, I sensed a shift again. His gaze wandered, a flicker of uncertainty dancing across his features. "Can I ask you something?"

"Of course. Shoot."

"What if we can't make it work? What if the things we're passionate about pull us in different directions?"

I took a deep breath, the weight of his question settling into the pit of my stomach. "Then we find a way to make it work. We've been through too much to let a little distance come between us."

"Sometimes it feels insurmountable, you know? Like the closer we get to our dreams, the further apart we drift."

"Maybe," I said, my voice steadying, "but we're not just dreams. We're people with hearts that want connection, and that's worth fighting for."

He nodded, though his brow remained furrowed. "I want to believe that. I do. But I can't shake this feeling that we're running out of time."

"Time is relative," I said, unable to mask the apprehension in my voice. "And right now, we have time. Let's use it. Let's make the most of every moment."

A silence stretched between us, thick and heavy, yet it held a glimmer of hope. "So what's next? What are you going to do with this newfound fame and success?"

"Honestly? I want to create pieces that speak to the journey, to the struggles, to the laughter and the heartache. I want my art to resonate with people, to tell stories that matter."

He leaned forward, intrigue brightening his eyes. "That sounds incredible. Your passion always had a way of pulling people in."

I felt my cheeks warm at his compliment, and the familiar thrill of inspiration coursed through me. "What about you? What do you want to achieve?"

Alex took a deep breath, a flicker of determination igniting in his gaze. "I want to create experiences, moments that people will remember long after the gala lights have dimmed. I want to build a legacy, something that connects people in ways that matter."

I smiled, my heart swelling with pride. "Then let's do it. Let's support each other in making those dreams a reality."

His lips twitched into a smile, and for the first time that night, I saw a glimmer of the old Alex—the one who believed in the impossible. As we delved deeper into our dreams, the world outside faded into a blur, and I could almost feel the boundaries of our connection shifting, stretching to accommodate the weight of our aspirations. The night still felt electric, and though the path ahead was uncertain, the light of possibility flickered between us, waiting for us to reach out and grasp it.

The night wrapped itself around us like a cocoon, shielding our little booth from the chaos of the diner, but it did little to dissolve the tension that still hung in the air like a thick fog. Our laughter faded into moments of quiet introspection, where words became fragile and the spaces between them weighed heavy. I found myself watching him, the way he traced the rim of his glass with a pensive finger, lost in thought. I yearned to reach into that storm of emotions swirling behind his eyes, to pull him out and remind him of the joy we once shared.

"Okay," I said, breaking the silence like a fragile egg, "how about a challenge? Something to shake off the cobwebs and remind us why we started this crazy journey in the first place."

His brow arched, curiosity piqued. "A challenge? I'm intrigued. What do you have in mind?"

"Let's each create something new, something that embodies where we are right now. It could be art, music, a poem, whatever speaks to you. Then we'll share it next week over tacos."

"Are we trying to bring back the old 'creative sessions' vibe?" he asked, a hint of a smile flickering across his face.

"Exactly! And you have to promise not to overthink it. Just let it flow, no pressure. I'll even bring the glitter."

"Now you're just playing dirty," he said with mock seriousness. "You know I can't resist glitter. It's like my kryptonite."

"Good! Then it's settled. I expect to see a masterpiece that'll blow my mind."

"Challenge accepted," he said, finally leaning forward, a glimmer of excitement sparking in his eyes. The atmosphere shifted again, the weight on our shoulders beginning to lift. "But if you're bringing glitter, you'd better watch out. I might make a mess that'll rival a toddler's art project."

"Bring it on, Picasso!" I laughed, feeling the warmth returning between us, the laughter weaving a thread of connection I thought we had lost.

As the night wore on, we moved from memories to dreams, our conversation flowing like a well-loved playlist. It was exhilarating and exhausting, as if we were both drinking from the same cup of inspiration, the words spilling over in a colorful cascade. We talked about our hopes, our fears, and the winding paths we envisioned for ourselves. For the first time in weeks, I felt as if we were navigating the same map, our dreams and aspirations intertwining like the branches of a tree reaching for the sun.

But as I watched him, I sensed that his enthusiasm, while genuine, was still tempered by something deeper—an undercurrent of doubt and fear. The laughter was a mask, a band-aid over a wound that hadn't fully healed. And I couldn't help but wonder if I had done enough to help him through it, or if we were both just putting on a show, playing roles in a drama that felt increasingly real.

As we finished our meal, the conversation took a more serious turn. "What happens if we don't achieve our dreams?" he asked suddenly, his tone shifting, the weight of the world resting on his shoulders again.

I hesitated, the question hanging heavy in the air. "That's a tough one. I guess... I guess we find new dreams. Or we redefine what success looks like for us."

"Redefine, huh? You make it sound so easy," he said, a wry smile tugging at his lips. "What if my new dream is to become a professional taco critic?"

"If that's what makes you happy, then yes! I'll be your first fan, and I'll help you craft a winning résumé. 'Expert in taco textures and flavors, with an emphasis on guacamole.'"

He chuckled, the tension in his shoulders easing a bit. "I can see the tagline now: 'Taco Alex—when life gives you lemons, make tacos.'"

"Exactly! See, that's the spirit. We can pivot when life throws us curveballs."

"But what if," he paused, his eyes searching mine, "what if it's not just about the dreams anymore? What if it's about finding a way to keep the people we care about close while we chase them?"

I felt a rush of vulnerability at his words, an urge to pull him closer and share every fear that lurked in the corners of my heart. "I want us to keep each other close, Alex. I do. But it takes work. We have to be willing to fight for it."

His gaze softened, and in that moment, I saw a flicker of hope—a tiny ember of understanding igniting between us. "I'm willing to fight," he said quietly. "Just... don't give up on me, okay?"

"I could never give up on you."

As we walked out of the diner, the crisp air nipped at our cheeks, and the night sky glittered above us, a canvas of stars reflecting the possibility of new beginnings. I felt buoyant, as if we had just carved out a slice of happiness amidst the chaos of our lives. With each step, I savored the idea that we were on the brink of rekindling something beautiful, something worth nurturing.

"Let's take a detour," I suggested, pointing down a side street lined with twinkling fairy lights and charming storefronts. "I want to show you something."

"Lead the way," he replied, his spirits noticeably lighter.

We meandered through the streets, the laughter echoing off the brick walls like music. I led him to a small art installation—a temporary mural splashed with color, a vibrant display of the community's heartbeat. "Look at this," I said, gesturing toward the art, my voice bursting with excitement. "Isn't it amazing?"

"Wow. This is incredible," he said, his eyes wide with wonder as he took in the swirling patterns and the explosion of hues that told stories of love, struggle, and resilience. "It's like every stroke of paint has its own heartbeat."

"Exactly! Art can be so powerful, you know? It speaks when words fail."

He turned to me, his expression shifting to something deeper. "You know, I can't help but think of you when I see this. You put your heart into everything you create."

My heart raced at his compliment, warmth blooming in my chest. "Thank you. That means a lot, especially coming from you. But it's not just me. This mural is a reminder that we're all connected, that every dream and struggle is part of something bigger."

As we stepped closer, the soft glow of the lights cast a halo around us, a protective bubble where the outside world faded away. "So, what if we painted our own mural?" he mused, his eyes sparkling with ideas. "Something that tells our story—our struggles and triumphs. It could be our joint masterpiece."

"Now that sounds like a plan," I said, my heart soaring at the thought. "A celebration of us, of everything we've been through together."

But just as the warmth of possibility enveloped us, the atmosphere shifted again. A distant shout echoed through the streets, cutting through our moment like a knife. We turned to see a commotion a few blocks down, a group of people gathered, their voices rising in agitation.

"Should we check it out?" I asked, instinctively taking a step toward the crowd.

"I don't know. It might be nothing," he replied, his brow furrowing with concern.

But curiosity tugged at me. "Come on. What if it's something amazing? Maybe it's another art installation or a surprise performance."

Reluctantly, he nodded, and we made our way toward the gathering crowd. As we approached, I could see people pointing, their faces a mixture of excitement and fear. My heart raced as we squeezed through the throng, the air thick with tension.

And then, just as we reached the front, I froze. My breath caught in my throat as I took in the scene before us.

"Is that...?" I whispered, a chill running down my spine.

Alex's hand tightened around mine, his expression shifting from curiosity to alarm. "Oh no. It can't be."

The crowd parted slightly, revealing a figure at the center, cloaked in shadow but unmistakable. As the light flickered, illuminating a familiar face, a wave of realization crashed over me, leaving me reeling.

The unexpected twist felt like a punch to the gut, a sudden shift in the narrative that threatened to unravel everything we had just built. My heart raced, panic mingling with disbelief as I struggled to comprehend the scene unfolding before us, each moment stretching like a taut wire about to snap.

Chapter 17: Searching for Answers

The studio was alive with the chaotic energy of creation, the air thick with the scent of fabric dye and fresh pencil shavings. As I stepped inside, the familiar hum of a sewing machine greeted me like an old friend. Sunlight streamed through large windows, illuminating the vibrant sketches that adorned the walls, each one a window into Alex's imagination. Yet, despite the burst of colors and shapes, a somber shadow loomed over the space. The fluttering fabric swayed gently, almost mournfully, as if echoing the weight in my chest. I hesitated, uncertain how to bridge the distance that had crept between us.

"Hey," I called softly, stepping further into the room, my voice barely rising above the whir of the machine. Alex looked up, his brow furrowing slightly as he pushed a stray lock of hair from his face. There was a moment, just a flicker, where our eyes met, and the world around us seemed to pause. But then, as quickly as it came, that moment dissipated, replaced by the awkward silence of unacknowledged tension.

"Hey," he replied, his tone casual but lacking its usual spark. He turned back to his work, the fabric slipping through his fingers like water, but I noticed how his movements lacked their usual grace. I cleared my throat, a tentative attempt to break the fragile ice between us.

"Wow, these are incredible," I said, gesturing to the sketches that lined the walls. Each one was a testament to his talent, a kaleidoscope of potential and imagination. Yet, as I admired his work, I couldn't shake the feeling that the vibrant colors didn't quite match the shadows dancing in his eyes.

"Thanks," he muttered, still focused on the fabric. There was an edge to his voice, a clippedness that suggested he wasn't entirely present. I took a step closer, the warmth of his presence pulling me in, but I hesitated, afraid of shattering the delicate balance between us.

"Alex," I began, searching for the right words, the ones that could untangle the knot of misunderstanding that had formed between us. "I've been thinking... about us. About everything." His shoulders stiffened at my words, and I felt a rush of urgency to explain. "I know I've been wrapped up in my own world lately, chasing my dreams. I didn't consider how that might affect you."

He paused, finally looking up from his work, his expression a mixture of surprise and something else—something more vulnerable. "You don't need to apologize for your success, you know. I should be happy for you." His voice was steady, but there was a tremor in his gaze that betrayed him. "It's just... hard sometimes."

"Hard?" The word hung between us like a thick fog. "Hard how?" I pressed, unable to mask the concern in my voice.

Alex sighed, a sound that seemed to carry the weight of the world. "I guess I didn't expect to feel so... overshadowed. You've been killing it, and I've just been—" he gestured vaguely, as if the words eluded him. "I've been in the background."

The revelation struck me with unexpected force. I had been so focused on my own victories that I had failed to see the toll it had taken on him. My heart twisted painfully, a sharp reminder that relationships require more than ambition—they require attention, care, and sometimes a little vulnerability. "Oh, Alex..." I whispered, stepping closer, drawn to him as if by an invisible thread. "I never wanted to make you feel that way."

He met my gaze, and for a moment, the world outside faded away, leaving just the two of us suspended in our unspoken truths. "I didn't think it would bother me, honestly," he admitted, a hint of frustration creeping into his voice. "But it does. I thought I'd be proud of you, and I am, but it feels like I'm still stuck here while you're out there living your dreams."

"You're not stuck," I insisted, my heart racing as I reached out, lightly touching the fabric he was working on. "You're incredibly talented. I've always admired that about you." The warmth of his skin radiated through the layers of fabric, igniting a spark of courage within me. "Maybe we've both been chasing different dreams, but that doesn't mean we can't chase them together."

His eyes softened, a flicker of hope igniting within them. "What do you mean?"

I took a deep breath, willing my heart to speak freely. "Let's support each other. I want to help you find your voice again, Alex. We can inspire each other. Your work deserves to shine as brightly as mine."

The corners of his mouth quirked up in the faintest smile, and I felt a rush of warmth. "You really mean that?" he asked, his voice barely above a whisper.

"Of course," I said, a fierce determination settling in my chest. "We're a team. We always have been. And besides," I added with a teasing glint in my eye, "how could I let you hog all the success?"

His laughter broke the tension, a sound that melted the heaviness in the air. "Fine. But if you want to be a team, we're going to have to work on your sketching skills."

I feigned offense, placing a hand over my heart. "Excuse me? My sketches are masterpieces!"

"Right, masterpieces from the Picasso of stick figures," he countered, a playful glint in his eye.

"Touché," I replied, laughing as I leaned into the banter, grateful for the ease that was beginning to weave its way back into our interaction. The shadows began to lift, replaced by a warm glow of connection. It was as if, in that moment, we were both reminded of the unbreakable bond that had drawn us together in the first place, the shared laughter and the countless late-night conversations that had defined our friendship.

"I promise I won't just be your cheerleader," I continued, my voice steadying as the moment turned earnest. "I'll be in the trenches with you. We can take on this crazy world together."

His gaze softened, and I could see the gratitude reflecting in his eyes. "You really think we can do that?" he asked, vulnerability creeping back in.

"I know we can." The words tumbled out, infused with sincerity and hope. The weight of uncertainty began to lift, revealing a clear path forward, one where we could both flourish, side by side.

The days that followed our heartfelt conversation at the studio unfolded like a patchwork quilt, each piece vibrant yet slightly frayed at the edges. There was a newfound energy buzzing between Alex and me, a delicate dance of mutual encouragement, but with each step forward came a reminder of the hurdles still to overcome. I had made a promise to be there for him, and I intended to keep it. Yet, as much as I believed in us, doubt lingered like an uninvited guest at a party—quietly watching, waiting to be acknowledged.

One crisp autumn afternoon, the kind that bathed the world in golden hues and crispness, I found myself pacing the park near my apartment. The crunch of leaves underfoot mirrored the disquiet in my mind, each step drawing me deeper into thought. My phone buzzed in my pocket, a lifeline to the outside world, and I pulled it out to see a message from Alex.

"Got a new idea brewing. Want to come over?"

I paused, a smile tugging at my lips. It was the kind of text that felt like a warm invitation to a cozy fire on a chilly night. I quickly replied, my fingers dancing over the screen.

"Absolutely! Bring on the genius."

A minute later, I was on my way, the chill in the air invigorating my spirit. The sun began its slow descent, painting the sky in brilliant strokes of orange and pink. I knocked on his door, heart racing in anticipation. The familiar sound of his footsteps echoed before the door swung open, revealing Alex in a well-worn flannel shirt and jeans, looking both relaxed and disheveled in that perfectly charming way he always did.

"Welcome to my lair," he said, gesturing with a flourish, as if I were entering a grand gallery. "Prepare to be amazed."

"By your ability to attract chaos?" I quipped, stepping over a few scattered sketches that had decided to take a stroll across the floor.

He feigned offense, hand on his chest. "These are masterpieces in progress, thank you very much."

"Sure they are. If 'masterpiece' means an explosion of creativity that has gotten completely out of control," I teased, picking up a half-drawn figure and raising an eyebrow.

"Hey! That one has feelings," he protested, snatching the sketch from my hands and carefully setting it back down. "Now, let's get to business. I need your opinion on something."

He led me to his worktable, cluttered with an array of colored pencils, fabric swatches, and coffee-stained sketches. In the center was a new design—bold, daring, and undeniably him. I leaned in closer, tracing the lines with my finger. "This is amazing, Alex. It feels... alive."

His eyes lit up, a spark of the artist I adored. "Really? You think so?"

"Absolutely. It's got personality. It's almost like it's shouting, 'Look at me! I'm fabulous!'"

He chuckled, the tension from earlier dissipating like steam from a freshly brewed cup of coffee. "I wanted to push boundaries. I've been trying to break out of my comfort zone, you know?"

"I get it," I said, feeling the weight of my own ambitions pressing against my chest. "But remember, it's not just about pushing boundaries; it's about feeling good while you do it."

His expression shifted slightly, contemplative. "That's the tricky part, isn't it? It's so easy to get caught up in the noise of what everyone else is doing. Sometimes I wonder if I'm just chasing shadows."

"Shadows can be tricky," I acknowledged, leaning against the table. "But it's in the pursuit of light that we find clarity. We need to shine together, not just individually."

He smiled softly, nodding as if my words were a warm blanket wrapping around him. "You always have a way of putting things that makes it feel possible."

"Just doing my part," I said with a wink, shifting the conversation to lighter ground. "Now, are you going to tell me what the design is for, or are we playing a game of charades?"

Alex laughed, the sound brightening the room. "I'm designing a collection for a local fashion show next month. Thought I'd take a leap and enter it."

"Wait, that's huge! Why didn't you tell me sooner?" I exclaimed, suddenly caught up in the excitement. "You have to let me help! We can brainstorm, and I can help with the logistics."

He hesitated, a shadow passing over his features. "I don't want you to feel obligated. You've got your own projects to focus on."

I stepped closer, locking my eyes on his. "And that's exactly why I want to be involved. You're not just my friend; you're my inspiration. I want to see you succeed."

He held my gaze for a moment, and I could see the walls he had built around himself beginning to crack. "Okay, then. Let's do this. But if we're teaming up, we're going all in. I expect late-night sketch sessions and maybe a few terrible puns."

"Bring them on!" I replied, feeling invigorated by the thought of us working together. The air around us felt charged, like electricity before a storm, each spark promising new adventures. "I can handle terrible puns."

With renewed enthusiasm, we dove into planning. We bounced ideas off each other, laughter punctuating our brainstorming sessions. As we shifted between fabric choices and color palettes, the atmosphere lightened, transforming the space into a haven of creativity and camaraderie. Hours slipped away unnoticed, lost in a world that felt rich with possibility.

Just as we were starting to finalize the first design, a loud knock echoed through the studio, jolting us from our creative bubble. Alex's face dropped, and he glanced at the clock. "I wasn't expecting anyone."

Before I could comment, the door swung open to reveal his older sister, Mia, her expression a mix of excitement and urgency. "There you are! I've been looking everywhere for you."

"What's up?" he asked, rising to greet her, the warmth from our earlier conversation evaporating into the sudden chill of her arrival.

"I need to talk to you about the fashion show," she said, her tone serious. "It's more important than you realize."

"Uh-oh," I whispered to Alex, a grin tugging at my lips. "Sounds like trouble."

"Just a little," he replied dryly, but I could see the tension creeping back into his shoulders as he turned his attention to his sister.

Mia stepped further into the room, her presence commanding and assertive. "I've been hearing rumors about some heavy competition this year. You need to be prepared."

"Is it really that bad?" Alex's voice held a hint of apprehension, and I felt my heart tighten in response.

"Let's just say there are some big names entering this time around. I didn't want to scare you, but I thought you should know," she said, scanning the sketches scattered across the table. "Are you still planning to submit?"

He exchanged a glance with me, uncertainty flickering between us. "Of course. But I have a plan."

"Good," she replied, her gaze softening slightly. "Just remember, you're not in this alone. You've got support."

Mia's words hung in the air, a reminder that even when the shadows threatened to overtake us, we didn't have to face them alone. As she continued to discuss strategies with Alex, I felt a swell of determination rise within me. We had a chance—one that we would seize together, no matter the competition or the chaos that loomed ahead.

And as the sun dipped below the horizon, casting the studio in a soft glow, I knew we were just beginning to write our story.

The atmosphere in the studio buzzed with a mixture of excitement and anxiety as Mia's words settled over us. I watched as Alex's expression shifted, a whirlwind of determination battling against a shadow of uncertainty. He straightened up, shoulders squared as if preparing for battle, but I could see the flicker of doubt lingering just beneath the surface.

"I appreciate you looking out for me, Mia," he said, his voice steady but tinged with a hint of defensiveness. "I'm not just going to fold under pressure. I've got a plan."

"Oh, I know you do," she replied, crossing her arms as she studied him, a glimmer of pride mingling with concern in her gaze. "But you need to be realistic. These designers are fierce, and they won't pull any punches."

"You know I thrive under pressure," he shot back, his playful edge returning. "Just like you thrive under your coffee addiction."

"Touché," she said, a teasing smile breaking through her serious demeanor. "Just remember, caffeine can only get you so far. When was the last time you slept, anyway?"

"Who needs sleep when you have creative genius?" he quipped, casting a quick glance at me, and I couldn't help but smile at the banter. The tension from earlier seemed to dissipate like steam from a fresh cup of coffee, leaving behind a warmth that reminded us all why we cared so deeply for one another.

Mia took a step closer, her demeanor shifting to something more serious. "Just don't underestimate your competition, Alex. You've got talent, but so do they. Make sure you're not just designing for yourself; you need to think about the audience."

"I'm aware," he said, a hint of irritation creeping into his tone. "It's not like I'm entering this blindly. I want to create something authentic—something that reflects who I am. If it doesn't resonate with people, what's the point?"

"Exactly!" she exclaimed, her hands gesturing animatedly. "But that means you need to tap into what people want and need. Fashion isn't just art; it's about connection. You have to weave your story into the fabric."

I watched as Alex nodded slowly, absorbing her words, and for a moment, I felt a swell of admiration for both of them. They were like fire and ice—her practicality balancing his dreaminess in a way that could spark real magic.

"Okay, I get it," Alex finally said, his voice softening. "I'll figure it out. But I'm also going to stay true to myself. That's non-negotiable."

Mia seemed satisfied, her expression softening into one of approval. "Good. Just remember, I'm here if you need me. And if all else fails, I can bribe the judges with baked goods."

"Is that your secret plan?" I chimed in, laughing. "It all makes sense now! You're the mastermind behind the whole operation."

She shot me a wink. "I'd say it's a strong backup plan."

As they continued to exchange playful jabs, I couldn't help but feel a sense of belonging wash over me. The studio, once filled with shadows and insecurities, now felt like a cocoon of warmth and creativity. However, beneath the laughter, an underlying tension remained, a reminder that the road ahead was still riddled with challenges.

With newfound determination, Alex returned to the sketches, flipping through his ideas as if they were the keys to a new kingdom. "Let's take Mia's advice seriously. I want to focus on a collection that's not just about me but resonates with others. How do we start?"

"I could help with some market research," I offered, feeling a rush of excitement. "We can analyze trends and see what's buzzing right now. Maybe even tap into what people are longing for."

"Sounds good," he replied, leaning closer as the three of us gathered around the table, pouring over sketches and swatches, the chaotic energy transforming into focused enthusiasm. The air crackled with ideas as we bounced concepts back and forth, each suggestion met with laughter or a cheeky retort.

Suddenly, Mia glanced at her phone, a frown knitting her brow. "Oh no. I have to go. Something came up at work," she said, her voice laced with regret. "But you two keep going. I want to see where this leads."

"Sure thing," Alex replied, though a hint of disappointment slipped through. "We'll keep the creative fire burning."

As she hurried out the door, I caught the look of determination that flared in Alex's eyes, and I felt my own resolve strengthen. We were in this together, facing the storm like two ships tethered to the same anchor. The thrill of collaboration coursed through me, and I was eager to see where this journey would lead us.

As the hours slipped by, the studio filled with the clattering of sketches and the aroma of coffee, a steady rhythm emerging as we worked side by side. I could feel the stress melting away, replaced by a sense of purpose that surged through us like electricity. We were shaping something real, something that felt significant. But just as I began to relax into the flow of creativity, my phone buzzed again.

It was a text from Mia. "Change of plans! I need you at the venue tonight. Bring Alex. Urgent."

My heart raced as I read the words. "What's going on?" I asked Alex, glancing up from the sketches.

He frowned, tension creeping back into his posture. "I don't know, but it sounds serious."

Before I could reply, my phone buzzed again, and I quickly scanned the message. Mia had sent a follow-up: "We might have a problem with one of the designers. You'll want to see this."

"Do you think it's about the competition?" Alex's eyes were wide, a mixture of curiosity and dread.

"Only one way to find out." I grabbed my bag, adrenaline surging through me. "Let's go. We can't ignore this."

As we hurried out of the studio, I felt the weight of uncertainty settling in once more. The streets outside were alive with the pulse of the city, yet the energy felt charged, almost ominous. Each step echoed my growing apprehension.

"What could it possibly be?" Alex mused, glancing at me. "Do you think someone's trying to sabotage the show?"

"I don't know," I replied, my heart racing with every word. "But whatever it is, it feels like it's going to change everything."

The venue loomed ahead, a sleek modern building with glass facades reflecting the darkening sky. As we entered, the atmosphere was thick with tension, and the usual hum of excitement was replaced by hushed whispers and concerned glances.

Mia spotted us immediately, rushing over, her face pale. "You're here. Good."

"What's going on?" Alex asked, his voice steady but laced with concern.

"There's been a... incident," she replied, glancing around as if to ensure no one was listening too closely. "One of the designers was found... sabotaging the others' work. It's chaos in there."

A chill crept down my spine. "Who?"

Before she could respond, the doors swung open, revealing the backstage area teeming with frantic energy. Designers rushed around, clutching sketches and swatches, voices rising in panic.

"Whatever is happening, we need to get to the bottom of it," I said, glancing at Alex. His expression mirrored my concern, a fierce determination igniting in his gaze.

"Let's go find out what's really going on."

We stepped into the fray, the chaos swirling around us as we navigated through clusters of people. Each moment felt like a heartbeat, quickening with every step toward the unknown. I could feel the weight of the impending reveal hanging in the air, like a storm on the horizon.

And then, just as we reached the main stage, a scream pierced through the noise, cutting through the tension like a knife. We turned to see a figure collapse on the floor, surrounded by a crowd that gasped in horror.

My heart stopped, the world around me narrowing to a single point of focus. Something was terribly wrong, and we were about to uncover a truth that could shatter everything we had been building.

"Stay close," I whispered to Alex, the adrenaline coursing through my veins. "Whatever this is, we're in it together."

As we pressed forward, determination battling the rising fear, I couldn't shake the feeling that this night was about to change everything we thought we knew. The storm was upon us, and the real fight was just beginning.

Chapter 18: The Unexpected Catalyst

The air in the studio crackled with the tension of unspoken words, the kind that hung like dust motes in the golden shafts of afternoon sunlight streaming through the high windows. Fabrics lay scattered across the floor—swathes of silk in vivid emerald and deep cerulean, and crumpled cotton that whispered of summer days. I brushed my fingers across the textures, feeling the coolness of the materials seep into my skin, a reminder of what we were about to create, or perhaps what we were trying to salvage.

"You know, if we're going to merge our styles, we might as well throw in some sequins," I quipped, breaking the silence that had settled between us like a well-worn blanket. My gaze shifted to Clara, her brow furrowed in concentration as she scrutinized a sketch pinned to the wall. Her hair, a riot of auburn curls, framed her face like a wild halo, and in this moment, she looked impossibly beautiful, almost ethereal.

"Sequins?" she echoed, arching an eyebrow, the corner of her mouth curling into a smirk. "And what, pray tell, do you think sequins say about our collaboration? That we're aiming for disco ball chic?"

I laughed, the sound bubbling up from somewhere deep inside, surprising even me. "Well, they could add a touch of whimsy. Besides, I thought whimsy was your forte." I leaned against the table, crossing my arms in a playful gesture of defiance. "Or have you gone all serious on me since the last collection?"

Her laughter chimed in response, filling the space around us with warmth, and for a moment, the weight of our past seemed lighter, almost manageable. "Oh, please. The last collection was just a slight detour. I'll have you know, I can be very whimsical when the mood strikes," she replied, her tone a delightful mix of mock indignation and genuine affection.

It was these exchanges that made the long hours in the studio worth it, those flickers of laughter that reminded me why we had decided to work together again. We were like a pair of mismatched socks—surprisingly complementary, always a little chaotic, yet undeniably unique.

"Okay then, whimsy it is!" I declared, twirling back to the swatches, my mind buzzing with ideas. "We'll need some patterns that clash beautifully—like a catwalk in the middle of a carnival. Think bold florals paired with geometric prints."

"Now you're talking," she agreed, her voice rich with excitement. She moved to my side, her fingers brushing mine as she reached for a bright pink fabric. "And let's add this pop of color to the palette. It'll be the cherry on top of our sundae."

Just then, the door swung open, and in walked Julian, our mutual friend and the unintentional catalyst of our recent tumult. He was a whirlwind of energy, his entrance as flamboyant as his personality. "Ladies, what fresh madness are we concocting today?" he asked, hands on his hips, surveying our chaotic landscape of fabrics and sketches.

"Just the usual—fighting the good fight against drabness," I replied, gesturing to the colorful explosion around us.

"Drabness, beware! We are armed with sequins and whimsical prints!" Clara added, a twinkle in her eye.

Julian clapped his hands together, a grin splitting his face. "This is exactly the energy I needed to see! I mean, who wouldn't want to wear a dress that's basically a party in fabric form?"

Our laughter echoed off the walls, and I felt the initial tension dissolve, leaving behind only the thrill of creativity. Julian was infectious that way, his enthusiasm like a jolt of caffeine, and in his presence, the looming specter of our past seemed to retreat, allowing us to focus on the present.

The three of us dove into the project, brainstorming ideas that danced around the room. Inspiration flowed like an uncontrollable tide, and for the first time in weeks, I felt a sense of purpose solidifying within me. Clara and I sketched furiously, our ideas melding together seamlessly.

As the days passed, our collaboration became a sanctuary. Late-night brainstorming sessions turned into coffee-fueled marathons where we sketched and laughed until our sides hurt. The quiet intensity of our previous arguments gave way to an easy camaraderie, and it felt like the cracks in our partnership were slowly mending.

But as the excitement built, so did a gnawing unease in the pit of my stomach. Each time we gained traction, every mention of our upcoming fashion show in the local press, I felt the ghost of our past lurking at the edges. We had both made sacrifices, faced disappointment, and lived through misunderstandings that could easily bubble to the surface.

I caught Clara's eye one afternoon as we stood in front of a wall plastered with our ideas. "Are we really ready for this?" I asked, a trace of hesitation creeping into my voice. "What if it all falls apart again?"

She turned to me, her expression earnest. "It's different this time. We've built something together, and we're stronger now. I can feel it. This project—it's not just about the clothes; it's about us."

Her words hung in the air, shimmering like the fabrics we had chosen. I wanted to believe her, to drown out the doubt that wrapped around my heart like a vice. But as our launch date approached, that feeling of impending doom returned, sneaking in through the cracks of my bravado, whispering insidiously that the past had a way of resurfacing when least expected.

And just like that, the vibrant world we were building seemed to teeter on the edge of chaos, a precarious balance of hope and anxiety, with each moment offering the tantalizing promise of either triumph or collapse.

The days melted into a frenetic blur as Clara and I flung ourselves into our project, fueled by an unquenchable energy that transformed our small studio into a riot of color and creativity. Each morning brought a new set of challenges—how to incorporate Clara's sharp, architectural lines with my softer, fluid designs, all while keeping our shared vision intact. Our styles collided and danced around each other like fireflies in the twilight, illuminating fresh ideas that took flight on the wings of our laughter.

"Okay, but what if we do a dress that's half structured and half draped?" I suggested one afternoon, tossing a bright yellow fabric onto the table like a culinary chef presenting a secret ingredient. "We could call it 'The Identity Crisis.' It'll be a metaphor for fashion as a personal journey!"

"Identity Crisis? Brilliant. And so relatable," Clara shot back, her lips curving into a teasing smile. "Let's be honest; we've all been there at some point. But tell me, will it come with a complimentary therapy session?"

"Only if you promise not to charge me for it," I replied, leaning in closer, my eyes sparkling with mischief. "I can't afford your rates, and you know my emotional baggage isn't covered under insurance."

Our playful banter flowed effortlessly, each quip a thread weaving us tighter together. The walls echoed with our creativity, but underneath the surface, a subtle undercurrent of anxiety persisted. The press had started to notice our collaboration, which meant the fashion world's keen gaze was upon us.

One afternoon, while adjusting a particularly stubborn bolt of taffeta, I glanced at Clara, who was meticulously pinning a hem. "Have you ever thought about what might happen if we really pull this off?" I asked, a tremor of excitement creeping into my voice.

"Like, what if we become the next big thing? Could you handle the fame?"

Her eyes sparkled with the challenge. "I'm not too worried about fame. It's the judgment that terrifies me."

"Judgment is just praise in disguise," I said, lifting my chin defiantly. "Well, most of the time."

Clara snorted, the sound bubbling from her like effervescent champagne. "Ah yes, the 'most of the time' is the catch, isn't it? But let's face it, it's the critics that can turn a masterpiece into a dumpster fire with a single review."

As we navigated our creative journey, we also began to face the scrutiny of those around us. Our friends were a double-edged sword, their excitement tinged with the weight of expectation. At a gathering one evening, Julian, ever the instigator, leaned against the bar with a cocktail in hand, eyeing us like a hawk.

"So, when do I get to see the 'next big thing' in action?" he asked, his tone laced with playful sarcasm.

"Soon, very soon," Clara replied, crossing her arms with a confidence that made my heart swell. "We're just making sure it's a solid foundation first. You know, before we explode onto the scene."

"Or implode," I chimed in, feigning innocence. "I'm really not sure which would be more entertaining."

Julian shook his head, a teasing grin plastered across his face. "You two are like a sitcom waiting to happen. I'd binge it if you threw in a few more melodramatic plot twists."

The night wore on, filled with laughter and jabs at one another's expense, but beneath the surface, I felt the pressure mounting like a rubber band stretched to its limit. Clara and I exchanged glances throughout the evening, a shared understanding simmering between us, an acknowledgment that we were walking a tightrope suspended above a chasm of uncertainty.

As the days turned into a countdown to our show, the excitement was palpable, but so was the tension. Clara had begun to stay late, pouring over the designs with a fervor that was both inspiring and worrying. I found her most evenings hunched over a sketchpad, her brow furrowed in concentration, the light from her desk lamp casting long shadows that danced along the walls.

"Hey, you're going to burn out at this rate," I said one evening, my voice a gentle chime amidst the stillness. "We're supposed to be enjoying this process, remember?"

She looked up, her eyes wide and frantic. "Enjoying? I'm trying to make sure we don't crash and burn! The stakes are high, and we can't afford to mess this up."

Her urgency sent a jolt through me. "You're right, but remember why we started this in the first place. It was about fun, about rediscovering what we loved. Let's not lose sight of that."

For a moment, her fierce gaze softened, and I saw a flicker of the joy we had found amidst the chaos. "You're right. But let's make sure our fun doesn't end up as a punchline," she replied, the corners of her mouth curving upward slightly.

As we settled back into a rhythm, a knock at the studio door disrupted our flow. Julian entered, his face lit with enthusiasm, but it quickly dimmed when he saw the expression on our faces.

"I come bearing news!" he announced dramatically, but the weight of his words lingered in the air, heavy and unyielding. "You two have been getting some buzz in the industry. People are talking, and I heard whispers of a potential sponsorship deal."

My heart raced. A sponsorship? The opportunity sounded incredible, but a knot formed in my stomach. "That's amazing! But... is it what we want?" I asked, glancing at Clara, who wore an expression that mirrored my uncertainty.

"Is it what we need?" Clara added, her voice steady yet cautious. "We're just starting to find our footing. I don't want us to lose our vision amidst the glitz."

Julian shrugged, his playful demeanor still intact. "That's the thing about success—it has a way of complicating everything, doesn't it? It can be a blessing or a curse. Just ask the last few fashion icons to try and make a comeback."

The weight of his words settled between us, the thrill of potential success entangled with the fear of losing ourselves in the process. Each of us had once harbored dreams that had turned into ghosts haunting our past, and the specter of failure loomed just as large as the tantalizing promise of triumph.

I inhaled sharply, my heart racing at the crossroads we faced, the stark choice laid out before us like a runway. It was a moment suspended in time, charged with possibility, yet shadowed by the question that lingered at the edge of my mind—would this journey we were embarking on lead us to salvation, or would it ultimately unravel everything we had worked so hard to rebuild?

The morning of the show dawned with a bittersweet blend of excitement and dread, the air in the studio crackling with an energy that felt almost electric. As I pushed open the heavy door, the familiar scent of freshly unwrapped fabric swirled around me, mingling with the fragrance of strong coffee brewing in the corner. Clara was already there, a blur of movement as she darted around, her auburn curls bouncing with a life of their own.

"Coffee?" she called out without looking up, her voice muffled under the cacophony of our final preparations.

"Black as my soul!" I replied, chuckling as I poured myself a steaming cup. The humor was a thin veil over the nerves twisting in my stomach. "Is it too late to run away and open a bakery instead?"

"Only if you want to live a life of frosting and regret," she shot back, finally turning to face me. Her eyes sparkled with mischief.

"Besides, have you seen how much fun it is to put sequins on everything? A bakery can't compare!"

She held up a dazzling fabric adorned with tiny, shimmering disks, and I had to admit she was right. The thought of indulging in cakes and pastries seemed painfully mundane in comparison to the whirlwind of creativity and chaos that had consumed our lives for the past few months.

"Okay, fair point," I conceded, setting my cup down and diving back into the piles of dresses and designs. We had spent countless nights perfecting our collection, the ebb and flow of our ideas blending like vibrant brushstrokes on a canvas. But as the clock ticked ever closer to showtime, I could feel the tension building—a pressure cooker about to blow.

As Clara and I hustled to finish the final touches, I caught her glancing at her phone, her expression shifting from excitement to unease. "What's up?" I asked, trying to mask the concern creeping into my voice.

"Nothing," she said quickly, but her fingers tightened around the device. "Just... a message from Julian."

The mention of Julian's name sent a jolt through me. Despite his lively antics and infectious energy, he had recently taken on the role of an unwanted harbinger of reality. "Is he bringing bad news? Because I'm pretty sure I can't handle it right now."

"Not exactly bad news," she replied, biting her lip. "He just mentioned something about a potential investor wanting to meet us after the show."

"Investors? On the day of our show?" The words felt like a balloon being punctured, the air rushing out in a loud whoosh. "You're joking, right?"

Clara shook her head, the gleam of excitement now dulled by uncertainty. "I don't know if it's a good idea. What if they try to change everything we've built?"

"Or worse, what if they want to exploit us?" I added, the taste of dread washing over me. "We've worked too hard for this, Clara. We can't let someone else dictate our vision."

"I know. But it could be a great opportunity. We could have the funding to take this even further," she said, her tone wavering between hope and fear.

"Funding," I echoed, the word hanging between us like a guillotine. "Or strings attached."

We stood in silence, the weight of our ambitions crashing over us like waves against a rocky shore. I could feel the familiar tension creeping back in, a reminder of the ghosts that had haunted us before. The past lingered like a shadow, casting doubts that threatened to unravel the vibrant tapestry we had woven.

With the hours slipping by, we put the nagging thoughts aside, pushing forward with a shared determination. As models began to trickle in for fittings, the energy in the studio shifted, buzzing with anticipation. I caught snippets of chatter, laughter intertwining with the sound of zippers and rustling fabric, igniting a flicker of hope within me. Perhaps we could do this; maybe we could rise above the chaos and create something truly extraordinary.

"Time to shine, my dear!" Clara exclaimed, clapping her hands together with enthusiasm as the final model stepped into the dress we had crafted together. "You look stunning!"

The model twirled, the fabric swirling around her like a whirlpool of color, and I felt a swell of pride. The show was not just about the clothes; it was about the story we were telling, a narrative of collaboration, resilience, and a fierce love for fashion.

The venue was alive with energy as the first guests filtered in, their murmurs vibrating through the air like a crescendo building toward a grand symphony. I could see the flashes of cameras, the bright lights capturing every moment. As I adjusted the final details backstage, I stole glances at the audience, their expressions ranging from curiosity to intrigue.

And then, with the kind of flair only Julian could muster, he burst onto the scene. "Ladies and gentlemen, welcome to the unveiling of something spectacular!" he declared, his voice booming through the venue like a proud rooster announcing the dawn.

I felt Clara's hand clutch mine, a mixture of excitement and apprehension coursing between us. This was it—the moment we had been building toward. "You ready?" she asked, her eyes wide with a mixture of fear and exhilaration.

"Ready or not, here we go," I said, forcing a smile. We exchanged a glance that spoke volumes—an unbreakable bond forged through chaos, laughter, and a shared dream.

The show began, each model gliding down the runway in our creations, the energy in the room rising with every step. I felt alive, exhilarated by the sight of our dreams unfurling before us, the designs we had envisioned and crafted together coming to life under the spotlight.

But just as I began to bask in the glow of our success, a figure emerged from the crowd, a presence that sent a chill rippling through me. It was Miranda, the fierce critic whose words could build or destroy in a single breath. Her sharp gaze cut through the festive atmosphere, and I felt my stomach twist into knots.

"What is she doing here?" I hissed to Clara, my voice barely a whisper.

"I have no idea," Clara replied, her brows knitting together.

Miranda made her way closer, her expression unreadable, and the tension in the air thickened, heavy with the weight of our hopes and fears. I could almost hear the collective gasp of the crowd as she approached, every moment stretching out like an elastic band, ready to snap.

With the show in full swing, a sense of inevitability enveloped me. As the last model stepped onto the stage, the audience erupted into applause, but my heart raced with uncertainty. Would this be a celebration or the harbinger of criticism?

Then, just as Clara and I shared a victorious grin, my phone buzzed in my pocket. Pulling it out, I glanced at the message, my breath hitching in my throat.

Julian: They're here. The investors. They want to talk NOW.

The words hit me like a freight train, slamming into my chest with enough force to knock the breath from my lungs.

I looked at Clara, who was still lost in the applause, her joy radiating like a beacon. But as the reality of the message sank in, I felt the ground beneath me shift, the walls we had built starting to tremble. The investors were here, and just when I thought our dream was finally taking flight, I realized the next moment could shatter everything we had worked so hard to create.

And then, out of the corner of my eye, I saw Miranda approaching the stage, a predatory gleam in her eye, as if she were ready to pounce. The room felt smaller, the stakes impossibly high, and the looming question loomed larger than life: Would this be our moment of triumph or the beginning of our unraveling?

Chapter 19: The Storm Within

The air crackled with an energy that felt electric, the kind of tension that coiled tight in my stomach as I stared at the cluttered table in front of me. Stacks of papers teetered dangerously close to the edge, adorned with half-erased notes and colorful markers that had morphed into a chaotic collage of our ideas. Every scribble was a testament to the late nights and caffeine-fueled brainstorming sessions Alex and I had embraced in our quest to reinvent our shared dream. We had danced around the edges of our emotions for too long, and this was our moment—a chance to reclaim what we'd almost lost.

But just as we began to weave our plans into something tangible, the looming shadow of Lydia reared its ugly head. Her name hung in the air like a dark cloud, and with it came the whispers, subtle yet insidious, wrapping themselves around our minds like a vine that suffocated the life out of the roses it consumed. I could see it in Alex's furrowed brow, the way he tapped his fingers against the table, each rhythmic thump a countdown to an eruption that seemed inevitable. It was inescapable—the rumors that our collaboration was a desperate attempt to overshadow her felt like shards of glass, cutting through the fabric of our hard work and trust.

"You can't let her get to you," I said, attempting to infuse my voice with optimism, but the quiver betrayed me. "We're stronger than her games, right?" I tried to sound convincing, yet doubt crept in like an unwelcome guest.

"Easier said than done," he muttered, eyes darting to the window as if he could will the storm outside to answer his silent plea. "It's like she's taken a match to everything we've built." The rain pounded against the glass, each droplet mimicking the weight that had settled in my chest. "What are we even doing here if all we're doing is playing into her hands?"

The desperation in his tone sliced through me, and I felt a pang of empathy as I reached out to place my hand on his arm. The warmth radiating from him was like a soothing balm, a reminder of the camaraderie that had initially sparked between us. "We're not playing into anything. We're trying to create something that matters. Something real."

He glanced at me, a flicker of vulnerability breaking through the frustration, his dark eyes softening momentarily. "And what if it doesn't matter to anyone else?"

That question loomed over us like the looming storm clouds outside, thick and oppressive. What if all our efforts were in vain? I swallowed hard, forcing a smile that felt more like a grimace. "Then we'll make it matter. Together."

A silence enveloped us, charged with a mix of uncertainty and hope. I could feel the invisible thread that tethered us tightening, a bond both fragile and fierce. But just as I thought we might bridge the gap, the unmistakable sound of a notification chimed on his phone, slicing through the moment like a razor. He picked it up, his expression shifting from confusion to dread, and my heart plummeted.

"What now?" I asked, half-dreading the answer.

"It's from Lydia," he said, jaw clenched as he scrolled through her message. "She's... she's claiming our ideas as her own on social media."

I could almost hear the collective gasp of disbelief around us, as if the world had paused to take in the audacity of her claim. My gut churned, the anger bubbling up like lava threatening to spill over. "What kind of person does that? We're not even in competition!"

He sighed heavily, tossing the phone onto the table as if it were a grenade. "I don't know how much longer I can keep pretending this doesn't bother me."

The truth was, it bothered me too. The passion we'd poured into this project felt like it was slipping through my fingers, a sandcastle eroded by the relentless tide of her envy. "So what do we do? Just let her bully us into silence?"

"Maybe we should call her out," Alex said, his voice low but laced with defiance. "Expose her for what she is."

"Or we could rise above it," I countered, the fight igniting a fire within me. "Show the world what we're capable of without her shadow looming over us."

He studied me, a mix of admiration and uncertainty reflected in his gaze. "You really believe we can do this? Create something that outshines her?"

"I do," I asserted, the conviction taking root in my heart. "But it has to be on our terms. We can't let her define our success."

The rain began to taper off, and for a moment, the sun broke through the clouds, casting a warm glow across the room. I felt a rush of clarity, like a weight lifting from my shoulders. "Let's get back to work. We can make our project undeniable. Let's drown out the noise with brilliance."

His lips twitched, a hint of a smile breaking through the storm of frustration. "You're right. Let's show her what we've got."

As we dove back into our plans, the energy shifted, crackling with the fervor of our renewed determination. Together, we could face Lydia and the whirlwind of emotions swirling between us. The road ahead was fraught with uncertainty, but as I glanced at Alex, I felt the storm within me begin to subside. Whatever challenges awaited us, we would face them side by side, armed with passion and creativity, ready to rise above the chaos.

The next morning dawned gray and drizzly, the kind of weather that invites introspection but simultaneously wraps you in a thick layer of gloom. I sat at my kitchen table, cradling a steaming mug of coffee that barely warmed my fingers. The scent of rich, dark roast filled the air, mingling with the muted sound of rain drumming against the window. It should have felt cozy, but the knot in my stomach refused to loosen. I glanced at my phone, half-expecting a message from Alex, a spark of brilliance that would dispel the clouds hovering over our partnership. Instead, I was met with silence, the digital stillness echoing the tension that had settled between us.

As the day dragged on, I found myself drifting between bursts of productivity and endless spirals of worry. The project we were working on had started to feel like a delicate origami creation, beautiful yet painfully easy to tear apart. Lydia's influence loomed larger than life, her whispers ricocheting in my mind like unwelcome echoes. I couldn't shake the feeling that we were teetering on the edge of something monumental—or catastrophic.

Determined to reclaim the narrative, I decided to pay a visit to the local art supply store. The vibrant chaos of paint tubes, sketchbooks, and brushes always had a way of invigorating my spirit. Plus, I figured I could pick up a few supplies to revamp our presentation, hoping the fresh materials might ignite a new wave of inspiration.

The shop was a riot of color, the shelves overflowing with possibilities. I wandered through the aisles, my fingers grazing the spines of sketchbooks, feeling the textured covers beneath my fingertips. The smell of fresh paint and paper was intoxicating, drawing me deeper into a world where imagination reigned supreme. Just as I was losing myself in the potential of our project, a voice interrupted my reverie.

"Is that you hiding in here, or just a particularly bright paint palette?"

I turned to find Mia, my favorite barista from the café down the street, her auburn hair pulled into a messy bun, paint-streaked overalls giving her a whimsical air. "Mia! What are you doing here?"

"Picking up some supplies for my latest masterpiece," she said, her eyes sparkling with enthusiasm. "You know how it is—gotta feed the muse. What about you? Are you here to drown your sorrows in glitter and glue?"

I let out a laugh that felt foreign, almost hollow, but Mia's infectious energy was hard to resist. "Something like that. Trying to turn a sad situation into art."

"Let me guess, it's about that jerk Lydia?"

I sighed, the mere mention of her name a bitter taste on my tongue. "You've heard the rumors, then?"

"Oh, please. It's practically the town gossip at this point. But I wouldn't let her get to you," she said, her brows knitting together in concern. "She's like a mosquito—annoying, but ultimately insignificant if you don't give her the time of day."

I chuckled again, grateful for her perspective. "You make it sound so easy. I wish I could just swat her away."

"Swatting is too passive. Why not set a trap instead?" she suggested, a mischievous grin spreading across her face. "Show her that you and Alex are a force to be reckoned with."

"Now you're talking," I said, feeling the weight in my chest lighten just a bit. "Maybe we can create something that showcases not just our talent but our resilience. Something that says, 'Look at us, thriving despite your best efforts!'"

"Exactly! Let's make it a statement piece—bold colors, daring designs. Just like you two!"

Mia's enthusiasm was contagious, and as we wandered through the aisles, brainstorming ideas, I could feel my creative juices flowing again. I picked up a handful of vibrant paints, their colors so striking they practically sang. "We'll make her regret ever crossing us," I declared, buoyed by the adrenaline of inspiration.

When I returned home, I found myself surrounded by a sea of art supplies, the chaos invigorating rather than overwhelming. I set to work, each brushstroke a cathartic release, a declaration of defiance against the looming storm that was Lydia. Hours melted away as I poured my heart onto the canvas, colors clashing and blending in a beautiful riot, each layer a testament to our struggle and ambition.

As the sun dipped below the horizon, painting the sky with strokes of orange and purple, my phone buzzed, breaking the trance I had fallen into. It was a message from Alex: Can we meet? I need to talk.

My heart raced at the urgency of his words. Had Lydia pulled another stunt? I quickly texted back, agreeing to meet at our usual spot, the small bistro nestled at the edge of the park.

The atmosphere buzzed with the chatter of evening diners as I settled into a booth, glancing at the door every few seconds. When he finally walked in, drenched from the rain and looking like a walking storm himself, the air shifted. The tension that had once felt thick as molasses now crackled with an electricity that sent my heart racing.

"Hey," I said, gesturing for him to sit.

"Hey," he replied, his voice low and rough. The weight of whatever he was carrying hung heavily between us, and I could almost see the invisible chains binding him to his frustration. "I've been thinking about what you said. About rising above."

"Good," I replied, trying to inject some lightness into the mood. "Because I have a plan, and it's going to involve a lot of paint and maybe even a few sparkles."

His lips twitched at my enthusiasm, but the moment of levity faded as he shook his head. "Lydia's not just going to back down. She's threatening to take this public."

My heart plummeted, the world around me blurring into a haze. "What does that mean? What is she planning?"

He leaned forward, the urgency in his gaze piercing through the tension. "She's talking about how she can destroy our careers if we don't back off. It's not just rumors anymore; it's a full-blown war."

For a moment, everything felt impossibly heavy, like the universe had pressed down upon my chest, making it hard to breathe. The warmth of my creative spark dimmed, suffocated by the harsh reality of our situation. But as I looked into Alex's eyes, I saw something else—fire, determination, a fierce resolve that echoed my own.

"We're not backing down," I said, the words tumbling from my lips with unexpected ferocity. "We're going to show her that we're not afraid. If she wants a fight, then let's give her one she won't forget."

Alex's gaze sharpened, a glimmer of something fierce igniting in his expression. "Then let's do it together. No more running away."

In that moment, the storm brewing outside mirrored the tempest within us, and I knew we were about to step into a battleground. But with our combined strength, I felt an inkling of hope. Whatever came next, we would face it side by side, ready to reclaim not just our project, but our very identities in the process.

The bistro was alive with the clinking of glasses and the soft murmur of conversations, yet for Alex and me, the air felt thick with an urgency that drowned out the world. We sat in a cozy booth, a dim light illuminating the space between us, casting shadows that danced like the doubts swirling in my mind. Alex leaned forward, his elbows resting on the table, his eyes boring into mine with an intensity that made my heart race.

"We need to strategize," he said, his voice low but steady, as if the gravity of our situation demanded a military precision. "Lydia's not going to go quietly. She thrives on chaos. If she senses weakness, she'll pounce."

I nodded, the fire in me rekindled by his resolve. "We have to be two steps ahead. If we're going to fight back, we need to make sure we're prepared. What do you think her next move will be?"

"Public statements, maybe even a social media campaign," he said, his fingers drumming against the table. "She'll twist the narrative to make it seem like we're the villains here."

A sharp laugh escaped my lips, surprising both of us. "Villains? Oh, that's rich. We should just get matching capes and call ourselves the 'Dynamic Duo of Disruption.'"

A smile tugged at the corners of his mouth, a momentary reprieve from the storm brewing between us. "I'd rather not have to wear a cape, but I see your point. We need to flip the script. Instead of responding to her, let's take the lead. Let's create something so compelling that it demands attention."

The idea hung in the air, buzzing with possibility. "What if we held a showcase? An unveiling of our project, front and center, with our own narrative woven in?"

"Exactly," he replied, leaning back as excitement sparked in his eyes. "We can invite key figures from the industry, make it an event they can't ignore. If Lydia tries to attack us then, she'll only reveal herself as petty."

The more we talked, the more I felt the fear that had gripped me loosen its hold, replaced by a bubbling excitement. Planning a showcase was an ambitious move, but it felt right—a defiance against Lydia's petty games. "We could create a theme that highlights our journey," I suggested, enthusiasm swelling within me. "Something that tells our story, the struggles we've faced, and how we've turned them into something beautiful."

"Beautiful," he echoed, a soft smile dancing on his lips. "Like the chaos of a thunderstorm leading to a rainbow."

"Or a flaming phoenix rising from the ashes," I added, the imagery filling my mind with vivid colors. "A celebration of resilience."

We spent the next hour brainstorming every detail, from the venue to the guest list, sketching ideas on napkins like two kids plotting their summer adventure. The laughter came easily, the tension that had once seemed insurmountable evaporating in the warm glow of our camaraderie. For the first time in days, I felt light, as if we were carving our own path amidst the darkness Lydia had cast over us.

As the sun dipped below the horizon, painting the sky with hues of lavender and gold, I felt a surge of optimism. I reached across the table, taking his hand in mine, the warmth of his skin igniting something deep within me. "This is it, Alex. This is our moment. We're going to take back our narrative."

He squeezed my hand, his gaze lingering on mine, a mix of determination and something more—something that sent a thrill racing through me. "Together," he said, his voice steady, the promise hanging between us like a spark waiting to ignite.

Just then, a loud crash shattered the intimate atmosphere, making both of us jump. We turned to see a group of patrons huddled near the entrance, eyes wide with shock. A figure was standing in the doorway, drenched and shivering, a hood obscuring their face. The tension in the bistro shifted, murmurs rippling through the crowd as they stared.

"Who is that?" I asked, my heart racing for an entirely different reason now.

Alex's eyes narrowed as he rose to his feet, instinctively protecting me as he moved toward the entrance. "Stay here," he whispered, though I could see the urgency in his stance.

As he approached the figure, I could make out a sliver of rain-soaked hair peeking from beneath the hood, a shock of red against the gray of the evening. My heart dropped as recognition hit me like a punch to the gut. "Mia?"

Alex turned slightly, his expression shifting from concern to confusion. "You know her?"

"Yeah," I called out, moving to catch up with him. "She's my friend from the café."

Mia lifted her head, her eyes wide with panic and something else I couldn't quite place. "I'm so sorry to barge in like this," she gasped, shaking the water from her hair as she stepped forward. "But I heard some things—about Lydia."

"What about Lydia?" I pressed, dread pooling in my stomach.

"Lydia's planning something big. Something that involves both of you, and it's not good." Her voice trembled, the urgency palpable as she glanced around, as if sensing the weight of unseen eyes watching us. "You need to be careful. I thought you should know."

Alex's brow furrowed as he stepped closer, concern deepening in his eyes. "What do you mean, 'not good'?"

Mia hesitated, glancing back at the gathering crowd. "She's not just spreading rumors anymore. She's got something concrete—something that could ruin both of your careers."

"Like what?" I asked, my pulse quickening.

Before she could answer, the door swung open again, and the atmosphere shifted as Lydia stepped inside, dripping wet but radiating confidence. She scanned the room until her eyes landed on us, a sly smile creeping onto her face. "Well, well, if it isn't my favorite duo. I hear you've been busy."

The color drained from Mia's face as she took a step back, but Alex and I stood our ground, adrenaline coursing through us. Lydia leaned against the doorframe, arms crossed, her gaze flickering with amusement, as if she held all the cards.

"Are you ready for a little surprise?" she purred, her voice dripping with false sweetness.

The tension in the air snapped like a taut wire, a storm of confrontation gathering around us, and I realized in that moment that whatever plans we had crafted were about to be thrown into chaos. With Lydia here, the stakes had just been raised, and the next move was uncertain.

Chapter 20: The Winding Path

The sun dipped low in the sky, casting a golden hue over Central Park, as if the universe had decided to sprinkle a bit of magic on the mundane. I could hear the laughter of children somewhere in the distance, their shrieks punctuating the soft rustle of leaves. The air was cool against my skin, crisp enough to evoke memories of sweater weather and pumpkin spice lattes, yet not so cold that it numbed my thoughts. My boots crunched over the tapestry of fallen leaves, each step a reminder that the vibrant chaos of autumn mirrored the turmoil brewing in my heart.

Lydia's latest whispers echoed in my mind, taunting me like an overzealous child hiding behind a tree, ready to leap out and startle me. I had tried to shake them off, but the tendrils of her words clung stubbornly. Each rumor felt like a sharp stone lodged in my shoe, one I couldn't simply ignore. I wrapped my arms around myself, pulling my coat tighter, as if it could shield me from the chill of her malice. Lydia was an artist in her own right, crafting narratives that twisted the truth until it became something unrecognizable. And I? I was just a canvas, marred by her brush strokes.

But I wouldn't let her control the colors of my life. I had learned that much, at least. A deep breath filled my lungs with the scent of wet earth and decaying leaves, grounding me in the moment. I was determined to paint my own narrative, one that would leave her words trailing far behind. As I ambled deeper into the park, the serenity of the landscape was interrupted by my racing thoughts, all weaving back to Alex.

He had always been a burst of color in my otherwise muted palette. His laughter was like a melody that played softly in my ears, brightening even the dullest of days. Yet lately, there had been a strain in our conversations, an unspoken tension that filled the air between us. It was frustrating; we were two artists who had once painted together so effortlessly, but now we stood on opposite banks of a turbulent river, shouting across the divide without truly hearing one another. I longed to bridge that gap, to dive into the whirlpool of our emotions and emerge on the other side, stronger and more united.

With each step, I imagined our conversation, shaping the words like clay in my hands. I pictured myself standing before him, the light catching his tousled hair, and how his blue eyes would reflect a mixture of frustration and longing. I could almost hear him asking, "Why can't you just trust me?" My heart clenched at the thought, because deep down, I knew the answer wasn't easy. Trust had become a fragile thread, frayed by the weight of unspoken fears.

As I rounded a bend, I came upon a small pond, its surface reflecting the fiery hues of the trees surrounding it. A few ducks paddled lazily, their gentle quacking a soothing balm to my frayed nerves. I decided to take a seat on a nearby bench, the worn wood warm beneath me despite the cool air. I leaned back, letting the serenity of the scene wash over me as I mulled over the next steps.

"Isn't it beautiful?" A voice interrupted my reverie, breaking the spell of tranquility. I turned to see an older woman sitting on the opposite end of the bench, her silver hair gleaming like a crown in the fading light. She wore a scarf that swirled with shades of orange and red, a vibrant testament to the season.

"It really is," I replied, a smile breaking across my face. "There's something magical about this time of year, don't you think?"

She chuckled softly, her laughter like the tinkling of wind chimes. "Ah, magic indeed. But it's also the time when everything seems to fall apart, isn't it? The leaves, the warmth of summer. It's all so... fleeting."

Her words struck a chord deep within me. "Yeah, it can feel like that. Especially when you're trying to hold onto something that feels just out of reach." I glanced back at the pond, the gentle ripples distorting the reflections of the trees. It felt all too fitting.

The woman tilted her head, her eyes glinting with understanding. "Is it love, then? Or perhaps friendship? Sometimes the hardest things to grasp are the very things that mean the most to us." Her gaze turned thoughtful, and I could see the memories flickering behind her eyes, a tapestry of joys and heartaches woven together.

"It's both, really," I admitted, feeling a warmth spread through my chest as I shared my burden with this stranger. "I'm afraid of losing my best friend, and the fear of losing something more is suffocating."

"Fear can be a heavy cloak," she replied, her tone soothing. "But remember, even in the most chaotic moments, there's beauty to be found. Embrace the chaos. Sometimes, it's in those unpredictable storms that we discover who we really are." She smiled, a knowing twinkle in her eyes, and I felt as if I were sitting across from a sage rather than a stranger.

I pondered her words, the weight of them sinking in. The chaos I had been trying to flee from might just be the very path I needed to traverse. I could no longer dance around the edges of my fears, hoping they would simply vanish. I had to confront them head-on, both with Alex and with Lydia.

As the sun dipped below the horizon, casting a deep indigo over the park, I rose from the bench with newfound resolve. The chill in the air wrapped around me, invigorating and alive, urging me to take my next steps boldly. I felt lighter, as if the conversation with the woman had peeled away a layer of doubt, exposing a heart ready to embrace the tumult.

With each crunch of leaves beneath my feet, I felt the anticipation build, the thrill of possibility coursing through my veins. The winding path ahead was unknown, yes, but it was also filled with potential. I would face Alex, Lydia, and whatever else lay in wait, not as a victim of circumstance, but as an artist ready to reclaim my narrative.

The city seemed to hum with a peculiar energy as I made my way towards the small café nestled on the corner of the park, its warm lights spilling onto the sidewalk like a promise of comfort. The autumn air was electric, alive with the mingling scents of spiced cider and freshly baked pastries wafting through the open doors. It felt like a sanctuary amidst the chaos, a place where I could gather my thoughts and perhaps fortify myself for the conversation that loomed ahead.

Pushing through the door, a bell chimed softly, and I was greeted by the cozy ambiance of the café. The walls were adorned with local artwork, splashes of color that spoke to the creativity brewing within. I spotted Alex in a corner, his dark curls tousled as he scribbled notes into a well-loved notebook. The sight of him made my heart flutter, a contradiction to the heaviness that had settled in my chest. I hesitated for a moment, feeling as if I were about to step onto a stage where the spotlight would illuminate our every flaw.

"Hey, I ordered you a hot chocolate," he said, looking up with a sheepish smile that could melt any lingering tension. "Extra marshmallows, just the way you like it."

I chuckled softly, the familiar warmth of our shared moments creeping back in. "You do know the way to my heart." As I slid into the chair opposite him, I could see the shadows of frustration still etched in his features, mingling with the spark of hope in his eyes.

"I figured you'd need it," he replied, his tone light but underscored by a seriousness that sent my heart racing. "How was your walk?"

"Let's just say it was enlightening." I took a sip of the rich, velvety hot chocolate, allowing the warmth to spread through me, a temporary shield against the storm brewing beneath the surface.

"You know, I ran into a wise woman who told me that sometimes we just have to embrace the chaos."

He raised an eyebrow, amusement flickering across his face. "You ran into a wise woman? Are we talking fortune teller or a rogue philosopher who just happened to be wandering through the park?"

"Definitely the latter," I said, leaning in as if sharing a juicy secret. "She had silver hair and a scarf that could probably double as a magic carpet."

"Sounds like a character from a children's book." He chuckled, the sound lightening the atmosphere around us. "What else did she say? Did she tell you to abandon all worldly possessions and follow your dreams?"

"Something like that," I replied, biting my lip to suppress a grin. "She suggested I stop being so afraid of losing the things that matter. You know, embrace the chaos. Maybe we should both take her advice."

His smile faltered slightly, and the light-hearted banter faded as quickly as it had appeared. "I wish it were that easy," he said quietly, his gaze dropping to the table. "It feels like everything is unraveling. Lydia is relentless, and it's hard not to feel trapped in this whirlwind."

"Believe me, I know," I said softly, the gravity of our situation weighing heavily in the air between us. "But I refuse to let her dictate our lives. We have to confront this head-on."

"Confront it? What does that even mean? I feel like every time I try to address it, it blows up in my face," he retorted, a hint of exasperation creeping into his voice. "I just want us to go back to the way things were. When it was easy."

The pang of nostalgia hit me like a wave, threatening to drown out my resolve. "But maybe that's the problem. We can't go back. We have to figure out how to move forward."

A beat of silence stretched between us, heavy with unspoken words. "What if we can't?" he asked, vulnerability breaking through the surface of his frustration.

I reached across the table, my fingers brushing against his in a moment that felt electric, grounding. "We can. But we need to be honest. About everything."

His gaze held mine, the intensity of our connection sparking a flicker of hope. "Okay, then let's be honest. You know Lydia is saying things that aren't true. But it's hard not to let it seep into my head."

"I get it. And trust me, her words hurt." I could feel my heart racing as I continued, "But we can't let her define who we are or what we mean to each other. We've built something beautiful in the midst of chaos. Isn't that worth fighting for?"

The tension in his posture seemed to shift, the weight of uncertainty giving way to a spark of determination. "You're right," he said slowly, his voice gaining strength. "We've always been better together. I guess I just needed to hear that from you."

"Good, because I'm not going anywhere," I replied, unable to hide my smile. "We'll tackle this together, marshmallows and all."

As our conversation flowed, the room around us faded into the background. The laughter of the patrons, the clinking of mugs, even the rustling of the barista behind the counter melded into a comforting hum. We spoke openly about our fears, our frustrations, and even the wild dreams that felt so close yet so far away. Each revelation was a brushstroke in our shared canvas, colors blending and brightening with every word.

But just as the mood began to shift towards the light, my phone buzzed on the table, shattering the fragile moment. I glanced down, my heart sinking as I saw Lydia's name flash across the screen. "Speak of the devil," I muttered, the air growing thick with tension once again.

"Are you going to answer it?" Alex asked, his tone cautious.

"I... I don't know." I hesitated, the weight of her presence heavy in the air. "What if it's just another jab?"

"Then let it go to voicemail," he suggested, his brow furrowing. "You have every right to protect your peace."

Taking a deep breath, I silenced the phone, the decision both liberating and terrifying. "You're right. I won't let her control this moment."

Alex's expression softened, his eyes shimmering with understanding. "Exactly. We've got enough chaos without adding her drama."

In that instant, I realized that the fight wasn't just against Lydia; it was a fight for our bond. For the laughter that came so easily, for the dreams we shared in late-night conversations, and for the unshakeable belief that we could weather any storm—together.

With that clarity, the unease that had hovered over us began to dissipate, leaving space for possibility. We resumed our conversation, each word laced with renewed determination. The chaos outside faded into a distant echo as we crafted our own narrative, one rooted in honesty, resilience, and a hint of rebellion. Whatever came next, we would face it together, our hearts entwined like the leaves swirling in the autumn breeze.

A light laugh escaped my lips, lingering in the air between us like the fading notes of a sweet melody. The warmth of Alex's presence grounded me, a soft anchor amidst the chaotic storm brewing outside. Our conversation flowed seamlessly, thoughts and feelings spilling forth as we delved deeper into the heart of our struggles. Yet, with every shared truth, I could feel a tremor of uncertainty curling in my stomach—a lingering question that hung between us like a stubborn fog refusing to lift.

"So," I began, breaking the comfortable rhythm of our dialogue, "what do you think we should do about Lydia? Should we confront her directly?" The very mention of her name felt like calling forth a tempest, and I braced myself for Alex's reaction.

He leaned back in his chair, his fingers tracing the rim of his mug, his brow furrowing in thought. "Confrontation could lead to more chaos. You know how she thrives on drama. Maybe we should just let her dig her own grave. She's bound to trip over her own lies eventually."

I nodded, appreciating his instinct to avoid the fray, but something stirred in me—a deep-seated desire to reclaim control. "But what if that just lets her keep spinning these tales? I don't want us to be the side characters in her twisted narrative. We deserve to be the protagonists in our own story."

"Protagonists, huh?" he said, a teasing lilt in his voice. "So, we're going full Shakespearean drama now? I can see it now: 'To confront or not to confront, that is the question.'"

I rolled my eyes but couldn't help but smile. "You know, the best stories often come from conflict. Maybe it's time we start writing our own."

As our laughter subsided, the weight of my words settled in the air. What had started as playful banter transformed into something more potent, a rallying cry for both of us to take a stand. I could feel the energy shifting, an invisible thread weaving our fates closer together.

"We've dealt with enough of her nonsense," Alex said, his voice firm now, conviction threading through his words. "I'm all in if you want to confront her. But we need to do it strategically. We can't let her see us sweat."

"Strategic sounds good," I replied, leaning in with a conspiratorial grin. "Let's think like the architects of our own destiny—creative and cunning."

Just as the mood began to brighten, the café door swung open with a sharp chime, slicing through our shared moment. Lydia strutted in, her confidence radiating like an unwelcome spotlight. Her auburn hair danced around her shoulders, framing her face with an air of superiority that sent a jolt through me. I froze, the laughter dying on my lips as I caught sight of her smug expression.

"What a coincidence!" she exclaimed, her voice dripping with feigned cheerfulness. "I didn't expect to see you two together." She turned her gaze toward Alex, an exaggerated smile plastered across her face. "You must be having quite the love affair. How romantic!"

I clenched my jaw, fighting the urge to roll my eyes. Alex's hand moved subtly across the table, brushing against mine, grounding me as I resisted the urge to engage in her game.

"Funny, isn't it? How people can make up stories?" he replied coolly, his demeanor shifting into a defensive stance. "But we prefer the truth around here."

Lydia feigned surprise, her eyes widening in mock innocence. "Oh, I wouldn't dream of spreading rumors! That would be entirely beneath me." She leaned in closer, her voice dropping to a conspiratorial whisper. "But you have to admit, the drama does make things interesting, doesn't it?"

"Lydia, if you're looking for a stage, I suggest you check your reflection," I shot back, the words escaping before I could filter them. I couldn't help it; her presence ignited a fire within me, pushing me to reclaim my narrative. "We've moved on from your high school theatrics. This isn't a production, and you aren't the director."

Her expression darkened, a flicker of irritation sparking in her eyes. "Careful now. You wouldn't want to cross me."

"And you wouldn't want to underestimate us," Alex added, his voice steady and resolute. "We've been through the wringer, and we're still standing. You don't scare us."

For a moment, time hung suspended as tension crackled in the air like electricity. Lydia's lips curled into a dangerous smile, her eyes narrowing as if she were sizing us up, weighing our resolve against her own power. "We'll see about that," she said, a chilling note underscoring her playful tone.

As she turned on her heel and swept toward the counter, I could feel my heart racing, adrenaline pulsing through my veins. I locked eyes with Alex, both of us recognizing the shift in the atmosphere. This was no longer just about her rumors; it had morphed into a full-blown clash, a battle for our lives and our truth.

"I don't want her to get under our skin," I said quietly, my heart pounding in response to the confrontation. "We can't let her control the narrative."

Alex nodded, his gaze sharp and focused. "Then we do what we planned—keep moving forward, stay united. Let her do her worst. We'll be ready for whatever she throws at us."

I felt a surge of adrenaline course through me, a wild exhilaration as I realized we were finally taking control. "Together, then," I said, a firm determination settling within me. "We're stronger together. Let's keep pushing back."

"Together," he echoed, his voice steady, eyes gleaming with determination.

The café around us began to buzz again as Lydia ordered her drink, the atmosphere returning to its familiar hum. But the tension remained, a tightrope stretched between us and her. I felt an urgency, a sense of impending confrontation.

"Are you ready for this?" Alex asked, the gravity of the moment settling into our shared space once more.

"I've never been more ready," I replied, my heart thundering with the weight of my words.

Just then, Lydia sauntered back, a triumphant smile on her face as she cradled her drink like a trophy. "You know, I can't help but think how delightful it is to have friends like you."

I opened my mouth to respond, but before I could muster a witty retort, a loud crash erupted from outside, echoing through the café like a warning bell. The door burst open, and a figure stumbled inside, a disheveled young man with wild eyes and an expression of sheer panic. "Help! Someone's been hurt! There's been an accident!"

The café fell silent, the warmth of our confrontation instantly replaced by confusion and concern. I looked to Alex, our conversation abruptly halted, a new kind of tension brewing in the air.

"What just happened?" he whispered, the words barely escaping his lips.

Lydia's expression shifted from annoyance to intrigue, her gaze locked on the newcomer. "Looks like we've got a real-life drama unfolding, folks," she quipped, but the edge in her voice betrayed her own concern.

I stood, the sudden urgency in the air igniting something primal within me. "Let's go see," I said, my heart racing with both fear and adrenaline.

But as I moved toward the door, a voice within me warned that this was only the beginning. Whatever chaos awaited us outside was sure to ripple through our lives, intertwining with our confrontation with Lydia in ways we could never have predicted.

Chapter 21: The Heart of the Matter

The bistro was alive with the kind of energy that felt both electric and warm, like a hug from an old friend. Twinkling fairy lights draped across the exposed beams cast a golden hue over the rustic wooden tables, each adorned with flickering candles that danced in rhythm to the soft jazz wafting through the air. I sat there, nervously toying with the edge of my napkin, the cloth soft against my fingertips. The aroma of garlic and fresh basil intertwined with the scent of roasted tomatoes, enticing my senses and momentarily distracting me from the weight in my chest.

Alex arrived a few minutes late, his usual charm slightly dimmed as he stepped inside, shaking off the chill of the evening air. He looked disheveled in that artistically deliberate way—his tousled hair, the worn leather jacket, and those jeans that somehow always managed to look stylish yet effortless. My heart did a little flip, but the uncertainty in his eyes felt like a slow drip of water, a reminder of the conversation that loomed ahead of us.

As he slid into the chair opposite mine, the small table felt impossibly intimate, a fortress for our fragile truths. "Sorry I'm late," he said, his voice tinged with a weariness that made my heart ache. "The subway was a nightmare."

"It's okay. I just ordered us some wine," I replied, my voice a little too bright, a thin veneer over the anxiety bubbling beneath. I raised my glass, the crystalline clink punctuating the silence that stretched between us. "To... us?"

"To us," he echoed, but his smile didn't quite reach his eyes. We both took a sip, the rich, velvety notes swirling on my palate, yet they did little to soothe the tightness in my throat.

"Alex, we need to talk." I finally said, the words tumbling out like marbles off a table. I felt the way my heart thudded against my ribs, a rhythmic reminder of the vulnerability I was about to lay bare. "About Lydia. About everything."

He stiffened slightly, his brow furrowing as he leaned back in his chair. "Is she really still bothering you?"

"I don't think it's just her," I replied, the heat of frustration rising within me. "I feel like we're caught in this whirlwind, and I'm not sure we're facing it together. It's like she's this shadow hanging over us, and I'm terrified of what that means for... us."

"Shadow?" He scoffed lightly, a flicker of defensiveness flashing in his eyes. "I thought we had it under control. You know I'm always in your corner."

"Are you?" The question slipped out before I could rein it back in, and I winced at the edge of bitterness in my tone. "Because sometimes it feels like I'm competing with her for your attention. Like I'm just another project in your busy life."

His eyes widened, and for a moment, I could see the gears turning in his mind, the internal struggle reflected in the way he ran a hand through his hair. "That's not how I see it at all. I care about you, Zoe. But I can't help feeling... overshadowed, too."

"By me? You?" My laughter was a brittle sound, a glass shattering at a birthday party. "I'm just trying to keep my head above water while you're off chasing your dreams."

He leaned forward, and the space between us pulsed with tension. "But what if I'm not sure I want to chase those dreams anymore? What if I just want to be here? With you?"

The raw honesty in his words settled like a weight in the air, both heavy and liberating. "Then let's talk about that," I urged, my heart racing anew at the thought of laying everything bare. "Let's redefine this. I want to be your partner, not just your girlfriend or a distraction. I want us to be allies, navigating this chaotic world together."

"Is it really that simple?" he asked, the skepticism clear in his voice, though the edges softened as he gazed into my eyes. "I feel like every time I think I understand what you need, it changes."

"Because we're not the same people we were when we first met. We've grown, and that's okay," I said, searching for the right words to encapsulate the whirlwind of emotions swirling in my chest. "But we need to communicate, to express our fears and desires instead of bottling them up."

He nodded slowly, his gaze piercing into mine as if seeking a truth hidden within the depths of my soul. "I'm scared, Zoe. Scared of losing you, scared of what comes next. But I'm here, and I want to figure this out with you."

"Then let's do it," I urged, a fire igniting within me as my heart filled with hope. "Let's be honest with each other, no more pretending. No more shadows."

The tension between us slowly dissipated, replaced by a shared understanding, a sense of purpose binding us closer. As we began to navigate our fears and uncertainties, the conversations flowed, wrapping around us like the warmth of the bistro. We explored the depths of our aspirations, revealing not just our dreams but the underlying fears that threatened to tear us apart.

With each word exchanged, the heaviness lifted, the unspoken anxieties fading into the background. I realized that within this fragile cocoon of vulnerability, we were both discovering pieces of ourselves we had long neglected. I could almost hear the soft symphony of our hopes intermingling, crafting a melody that sang of resilience and love, a tune that I was beginning to believe could carry us through whatever storms lay ahead.

As the evening unfolded, the candlelight flickered, casting playful shadows that danced across the walls, almost as if they were echoing the turmoil in my heart. Alex leaned back in his chair, the weight of our conversation settling between us like a tangible entity.

I noticed the way he absently traced the rim of his glass, his brow furrowed in thought, as if he were constructing an intricate puzzle from the fragments of our words. I took a deep breath, wishing for the right blend of humor and sincerity to lighten the atmosphere.

"So, if we're redefining our partnership, does that mean I get to take the lead on taco night?" I joked, hoping to ease the tension. "Because if there's anything I'm certain of, it's that my guacamole skills are unmatched."

He chuckled, the sound like a balm to my frayed nerves. "Only if you promise not to drown it in sour cream this time. You do realize that's sacrilege, right?"

"Sacrilege? Please, have you seen how much of a cooking disaster I am? Sour cream is basically a culinary safety net," I replied, feigning indignation. "But you know, I could also bring in some of your famous empanadas. You know, the ones I had to practically bribe you for?"

A smile crept onto his face, a warmth spreading through me at the sight. "Ah, yes, the infamous empanadas of my childhood. You have to earn them, you know. A simple 'please' won't cut it."

"Fine," I said, raising an eyebrow playfully. "I'll bring a whole team of cheering fans, if that's what it takes."

We shared a laugh, the air between us lightening momentarily, but underneath the humor lingered the tension of our earlier revelations. I could see it in the way Alex's smile faltered when he thought I wasn't looking, like he was still grappling with the gravity of our discussion.

"Zoe," he said, his voice low and serious, pulling me back to the heart of our conversation, "I want to be clear about something. I don't want you to feel like you're competing with anyone, especially not Lydia. You're not just my girlfriend; you're my inspiration."

I swallowed hard, the sincerity of his words warming my chest. "And you're my favorite chaos. But what happens when the chaos gets too loud? When it drowns out everything else?"

He shifted in his seat, his eyes meeting mine with an intensity that sent shivers down my spine. "I don't know. But maybe we need to set some boundaries—both with Lydia and with each other. We can't let external pressures dictate what we have."

"Boundaries," I mused, tapping my fingers on the table as if contemplating the very meaning of life. "Like saying 'no' to dinner invitations that make my skin crawl?"

"Exactly," he said, a smirk tugging at his lips. "Like saying no to endless discussions about my latest gallery show with people who wouldn't know a brushstroke from a breakfast menu."

"Or standing up to my mother when she insists on introducing me to every eligible bachelor within a five-block radius?"

"Definitely. If they're anything like the last one, you should start crafting those polite but firm 'thank you for your interest' texts."

Our banter swirled around us, a reassuring layer of familiarity and affection. But beneath the laughter lingered the unresolved questions that lingered like a shadow. What would these boundaries look like? Would they bring us closer or push us apart?

As we finished our meal, the waitress approached, a mischievous grin on her face. "You two are adorable. Would you like to share dessert or just gaze into each other's eyes for another hour?"

I felt the heat creep up my cheeks, and Alex's laughter filled the space like a warm embrace. "We'll take dessert, thanks," he said, not breaking eye contact with me.

When the chocolate lava cake arrived, I couldn't resist leaning in to take a bite straight from his fork. "That's the benefit of sharing dessert," I declared, grinning. "Double the calories, double the fun."

"Let's just hope it's not another case of 'Zoe tries to take the whole fork and fails miserably,'" he teased, his eyes sparkling.

"Hey, it's not my fault I have an adventurous spirit when it comes to food," I shot back, but there was an underlying tension in my chest. Every bite of the rich, gooey chocolate reminded me of how quickly things could shift—sweet and indulgent, yet heavy and dark.

As we indulged, I glanced around the bistro, taking in the cozy ambiance and the sound of laughter mingling with the music. There was a couple in the corner sharing whispered secrets, and I could see a group of friends toasting to their latest escapades. It was all so vibrant, so alive, and yet here we were, navigating our own quiet storm.

"Do you think we're being too dramatic?" I asked suddenly, the question hanging in the air between us. "Like, should we really be worried about this? I mean, relationships are hard, right?"

He considered my words, a furrow appearing on his brow. "It's not dramatic to care about what happens to us. If anything, it's brave. But maybe we're overthinking it? It's like we're staring at the painting up close, and all we see are the brushstrokes. We need to step back, see the bigger picture."

"True," I nodded, digesting the metaphor. "But stepping back is hard when the paint is splattering everywhere. It's messy."

"Life is messy," he said softly, reaching across the table to take my hand. The warmth of his skin against mine felt like an anchor in the swirling sea of uncertainty. "But that's part of what makes it beautiful. And I want to create a masterpiece with you, even if it gets chaotic."

"Then let's embrace the chaos, shall we?" I replied, squeezing his hand, the thrill of excitement rushing through me. "And if we need to wipe some paint off our faces along the way, we can do that too."

His eyes sparkled with mischief, and I could see the weight of doubt slowly dissipating. "You know what? I think I like that plan."

Just then, the bistro door swung open, a gust of chilly air sweeping through the warm space. A figure stepped inside, shaking off the cold, and as they turned toward us, my heart dropped. It was Lydia.

She spotted us almost immediately, her gaze landing on our intertwined hands with a look of smug satisfaction. My stomach twisted in knots, and for a moment, the playful banter evaporated, replaced by an all-consuming tension that threatened to strangle the laughter from the air.

The moment Lydia walked in, the cozy atmosphere of the bistro shifted, the warmth replaced by a chill that curled around my spine like an unwelcome vine. She swept through the door with an air of confidence, her designer coat trailing behind her like an extravagant cape, and I could almost hear the ominous soundtrack of a soap opera playing in the background. My heart raced not with excitement, but with a familiar sense of dread, as if I were suddenly thrust onto a stage with no script.

"Fancy seeing you two here," Lydia purred, her voice smooth like honey, but with an underlying edge that was anything but sweet. She leaned against the doorframe, surveying us with a bemused smile, her eyes flickering between our hands entwined on the table and our startled expressions.

"Lydia," I managed, forcing the word out as if it were a foreign concept. "What a surprise."

"Surprise is one word for it," she said, a smirk tugging at her lips. "I didn't realize you were back from the 'artsy' side of town." She made air quotes with her fingers, as if our lives were little more than a whimsical charade.

Alex stiffened beside me, and I could feel the tension crackling in the air, a silent challenge igniting between Lydia and him. "We were just having dinner," he replied, his voice steady but laced with an unmistakable edge. "How was your evening?"

"Oh, just the usual—networking, planning my next big move. You know how it is." Her gaze flickered to me, a calculated look that spoke volumes. "It must be exhausting being so... creative without a solid plan."

I felt my cheeks heat, a mixture of anger and embarrassment washing over me. "We were just discussing our plans, actually. You know, redefining our partnership," I said, injecting as much confidence as I could muster. "Something you wouldn't understand."

She chuckled softly, tilting her head, eyes sparkling with mischief. "Oh, I understand plenty. Partnerships can be so tricky, can't they? Especially when one half feels... neglected."

The air in the room thickened with unspoken tension, and Alex's grip tightened on my hand, grounding me against the surge of vulnerability that threatened to engulf me. "Lydia, this isn't about you," he said, his voice low but firm. "Zoe and I are figuring things out for ourselves. We don't need your commentary."

"Figuring it out?" she echoed, the laughter in her voice tinged with disbelief. "How quaint. I'd say it sounds more like grasping at straws."

I opened my mouth to respond, to throw back a witty retort, but the words tangled in my throat. Was that how it appeared to her? A desperate flailing in the face of an impending storm?

Lydia stepped forward, invading our space, her presence overpowering. "You're playing a dangerous game, Alex," she warned, her tone dropping an octave, a velvet glove hiding iron underneath. "Don't let her lead you down a path you can't come back from."

"Not everything is a competition, Lydia," he shot back, his voice strong. "We're not in a race, and I won't let you turn our relationship into some kind of reality show."

Lydia's lips curled into a smile that felt like a trap. "Oh, sweetie, relationships are always a competition. You just have to choose whether you want to win or lose."

With that, she turned on her heel, gliding toward the bar as if she owned the place, leaving a ripple of tension in her wake. My heart raced, and I felt like I was both a spectator and a participant in a drama I never signed up for.

"What just happened?" I whispered, bewildered by the whirlwind of emotions swirling around us. "Did we really just get steamrolled?"

"I think we need to regroup," he replied, his voice steady but laced with uncertainty. "Lydia has a way of twisting everything into her narrative, and I don't want her to come between us."

"You don't think she's right, do you?" I asked, the question hanging in the air, heavy with implications. "About us?"

"No!" His response was immediate, fervent. "You mean too much to me for her to dictate anything. But we have to be careful. She won't give up easily."

"Careful, huh? Is that code for playing it safe?" I challenged, my voice tinged with frustration. "Because I don't want to live in fear of what she might do. I want to be bold. I want to take risks."

"Taking risks is one thing; making reckless decisions is another," he countered, his expression serious. "This is our relationship. We need to protect it."

As we navigated the swirling emotions, I caught a glimpse of Lydia in the reflection of a nearby mirror, her eyes trained on us, a knowing smirk dancing across her lips. My pulse quickened, the walls of the bistro suddenly feeling as if they were closing in, the atmosphere suffocating.

"I need to say something," I blurted, heart pounding. "We can't keep letting her interfere. If we want to make this work, we have to confront her. Set some ground rules."

"Zoe, that's not a good idea. She's unpredictable," Alex warned, concern etched on his face. "What if she retaliates? We could end up in a bigger mess."

"Retaliation is inevitable if we don't stand our ground," I insisted, leaning forward, driven by a sudden surge of determination. "I refuse to let her dictate how we live our lives. I want to fight for us, Alex. Whatever it takes."

He stared at me, uncertainty warring with admiration in his eyes. "You're incredibly brave," he said softly, a note of respect in his voice. "But what if we lose?"

"Then we lose together," I replied, my voice fierce and resolute. "At least we tried."

Just then, Lydia reappeared at our table, a gleam of triumph in her eyes that set my teeth on edge. "I couldn't help but overhear your little strategy session," she said, her tone sugary sweet. "And I must say, I admire your spirit. It's like watching a soap opera unfold."

"Thanks for your unsolicited commentary," I replied, my voice steady despite the butterflies swirling in my stomach. "But we're not here to entertain you."

She leaned closer, her breath tinged with the sweet scent of her perfume. "Oh, sweet Zoe, you have no idea how entertaining you truly are. But if you think you can take me on, I wish you the best of luck. This game is just getting started."

With a wicked smile, she turned away, leaving a chilling silence in her wake. I felt the heat of Alex's hand on mine, grounding me, but the uncertainty hung between us like a storm cloud.

"Zoe, are you sure about this?" he asked, his voice low, concern coloring his words.

"I have to be," I replied, heart racing. "This isn't just about us anymore. This is about standing up for what's right."

The door swung open again, a burst of cool air slicing through the tension, and in walked someone I hadn't expected to see—my mother, her eyes scanning the room, searching. When they locked onto mine, I froze, realizing the storm I had been trying to navigate was only just beginning.

Chapter 22: Rekindling the Flame

The sun dipped behind the jagged peaks of the Catskills, painting the sky in strokes of lavender and burnt orange, a canvas that seemed to echo the intricate tapestry of emotions woven through my heart. I inhaled deeply, the crisp mountain air tinged with the earthy aroma of fallen leaves and distant pine, each breath revitalizing my spirit. Alex was nearby, his silhouette framed against the twilight, casting a long shadow that danced with the flickering firelight. The world felt vast and open, a perfect metaphor for the hopes we had stowed away like neglected canvases, ready to be splashed with color once more.

We had arrived at the retreat earlier that afternoon, a charming cabin nestled among towering trees, its wooden beams worn and inviting, whispering stories of warmth and camaraderie. I'd watched Alex unload our bags, his brow furrowed in concentration, but when he caught my eye, his face softened. A flicker of the spark we had so desperately sought to reignite glimmered in the depths of his hazel eyes. I couldn't help but smile, a quiet thrill coursing through me at the prospect of rediscovering the camaraderie that had once felt so effortless between us.

Our first evening unfolded with the simple pleasure of preparing dinner together, the cabin filled with the comforting sounds of sizzling and chopping, punctuated by laughter that echoed against the rustic walls. Alex had insisted on making his famous pasta, a dish I had come to cherish, the way he mixed the ingredients as if creating a symphony. I stirred the pot while he diced fresh basil with meticulous precision, our conversation flowing as naturally as the bubbling sauce.

"Remember the last time we attempted a cooking experiment?" I teased, leaning against the counter. "I still find it hard to believe that we didn't burn the place down."

Alex chuckled, his laughter warm and infectious. "Hey, that was a learning experience. We were ambitious, if nothing else. I'd say we're due for another culinary adventure."

"Oh sure," I said, rolling my eyes with playful sarcasm. "Let's not just stop at pasta. Maybe we can attempt soufflés next. That'll end well."

As he tossed the basil into the pot, the aroma wafted toward me, mingling with the rich scent of tomatoes and garlic. It was intoxicating, reminding me that, like our cooking attempts, our journey together had its share of missteps and victories. I glanced at him, the shadows playing across his features, revealing lines of determination that seemed more pronounced than I remembered. In that moment, I realized how much I had missed sharing these everyday joys with him.

After dinner, we gathered by the fire pit outside, the flames crackling and casting an amber glow on our faces. The night sky unfurled above us, a velvety tapestry of stars that twinkled like scattered diamonds. I wrapped my arms around my knees, feeling the warmth of the fire seep into my skin. As we sat in companionable silence, I couldn't help but feel a burgeoning sense of hope blossom between us, like the first hints of spring after a long winter.

"Do you ever wonder if we've lost our way?" Alex asked suddenly, breaking the tranquil stillness. His voice was low, almost hesitant, as if he were afraid the night might swallow his words.

I turned to him, sensing the weight of the question hanging in the air. "All the time," I admitted, my heart fluttering at the vulnerability of the moment. "It's like we've been so caught up in trying to be everything to everyone that we forgot how to be just... us."

He nodded, a flicker of understanding passing between us. "I miss that. The spontaneity, the laughter. Remember how we used to dream about the future? No limits, just wild aspirations."

"Of course," I said, recalling nights spent stargazing, crafting plans as if the universe were ours to shape. "We had it all figured out then. It felt so simple."

"Maybe it's still simple," he mused, leaning forward, his elbows resting on his knees. "What if we just let go of the expectations? What if we created for the sake of creating?"

The idea resonated within me, a gentle urging to strip away the layers of doubt that had begun to suffocate our creative spirits. "You're right. We've let the pressure of success cloud our passion. We need to find joy in the process again, not just the end result."

As we sat by the fire, our dreams began to unfurl like the flames before us—wild and unpredictable yet mesmerizing. The conversation flowed effortlessly, shifting from our shared love of art to the wild ambition of embarking on projects that excited us, reigniting that playful spirit we had both once cherished.

"Let's do something crazy," Alex suggested, his voice filled with excitement. "Let's collaborate on a piece together. No pressure, just... what we feel."

I laughed, the sound bubbling forth like champagne. "Crazy sounds good. But what if it's terrible?"

"Then it'll be our terrible masterpiece," he said, grinning. "We'll make it a tradition: every time we get stuck, we create something utterly absurd. Like a giant canvas of splatters or a sculpture made from pinecones and glitter."

"Now you're just being ridiculous," I teased, but I felt the thrill of the idea. "You're on."

The fire crackled and popped, punctuating our laughter as we imagined the outrageous possibilities that lay ahead. It felt as if we were reclaiming pieces of ourselves that had been lost in the shuffle of expectations and pressures. Each shared dream, every burst of laughter, built a bridge over the chasm of uncertainty that had threatened to pull us apart.

As the night deepened, I felt the tension that had hung between us dissipate, replaced by a palpable warmth and connection. In that sacred space, illuminated by the flickering firelight and the shimmering stars above, I realized that we were not just rekindling a flame; we were forging a new fire, one fueled by resilience, laughter, and a renewed commitment to our craft—and to each other.

The next morning dawned with a symphony of sounds—birds chattering excitedly, leaves rustling in the gentle breeze, and the distant gurgle of a stream as it wove its way through the woods. Sunlight poured into our cabin, spilling across the wooden floors and bathing the space in a warm, golden hue. I stirred awake, blinking against the brightness, and turned to see Alex sprawled on the couch, his hair tousled and a faint smile dancing on his lips even in sleep. It was a sight so familiar yet somehow comforting, like the first sip of coffee on a cold morning.

I quietly slipped out of bed, careful not to wake him, and made my way to the kitchen. The space felt inviting, filled with the lingering scents of last night's dinner, now replaced by the rich aroma of brewing coffee. As I poured myself a steaming mug, I couldn't help but feel a surge of gratitude for this moment—a tranquil morning in the mountains with the promise of a fresh start hovering in the air.

After a few moments, I heard the soft shuffle of feet behind me. Alex emerged from the living room, rubbing his eyes, a sleepy grin spreading across his face when he caught sight of me.

"Is that the smell of coffee or just my imagination coaxing me back to life?" he asked, his voice still thick with sleep.

"Definitely coffee, but you'll have to fight me for it," I teased, holding the mug just out of reach.

He chuckled, stretching like a cat before he grabbed a second mug and joined me at the counter. "I'm not sure I'm ready for a battle yet. Perhaps a truce over breakfast instead?"

"Smart choice," I said, relenting and sliding him the coffee. "I'm feeling particularly generous this morning. How about a hearty breakfast to fuel our creative ventures?"

"Now you're speaking my language." He took a sip of coffee, his eyes lighting up. "But let's make it an adventure. How about pancakes with whatever weird ingredients we can find in this place?"

I raised an eyebrow, a grin creeping onto my face. "Pancakes with weird ingredients? You're on. Let's see how adventurous we can get. I think there's some maple syrup in the cabinet, but the rest is up to us."

After rummaging through the pantry, we unearthed flour, eggs, and a can of pumpkin puree. "Pumpkin pancakes it is!" I declared, my excitement bubbling over as we set to work.

As we whisked the ingredients together, our playful banter filled the kitchen. "This is definitely going to be the breakfast of champions," Alex said, pouring batter onto the griddle. "Or the breakfast of disasters, depending on how this goes."

"Why not both? It's a multifaceted meal," I replied, flipping a pancake with newfound skill. The golden brown discs stacked up, becoming a fluffy tower that somehow managed to capture the essence of our newfound enthusiasm.

Once breakfast was served, we settled outside on the porch, the morning sun warming our faces as we dug in. Each bite was a delicious reminder that sometimes the simplest moments held the most profound joy.

"Okay, what's next on our agenda?" I asked between mouthfuls, my heart racing with excitement. "We could hike to that waterfall I saw on the map, or we could just get lost in the woods and see what happens."

Alex leaned back, considering. "What if we mix both ideas? We can hike to the waterfall but take the unmarked trail and let ourselves get sidetracked by whatever we find. It could lead us to something unexpected."

"Or to a bear," I countered, but I couldn't help the smile that spread across my face. "But I like the idea of unexpected. It feels fitting for us right now."

After breakfast, we packed a small bag with water, snacks, and a sketchbook for our artistic impulses. The world outside the cabin beckoned us like an open book, each leaf rustling a new story waiting to be discovered. As we ventured onto the winding trail, the air was rich with the scent of damp earth and pine needles, and I felt my worries lift like the mist around us.

We walked in comfortable silence, the forest surrounding us alive with color. The trees wore their fall attire—a patchwork of reds, oranges, and yellows—each leaf a tiny work of art in itself. Sunbeams broke through the canopy above, casting playful shadows that danced at our feet, illuminating the path ahead.

"Tell me about your dream project," Alex said suddenly, breaking the tranquility with a question that had been lurking beneath the surface. "You know, the one you've been afraid to start."

I paused, the thought catching me off guard. "Honestly? I've been toying with the idea of a graphic novel," I admitted, the words spilling out with a mix of excitement and trepidation. "Something that combines my art with storytelling—sort of a love letter to the chaos of life."

Alex nodded, his interest piqued. "That sounds incredible! What's been holding you back?"

"Fear, mostly. I worry it won't be good enough. Or that I'll get stuck halfway through and lose the drive."

He looked at me with a sincerity that made my heart flutter. "You can't let fear dictate your creativity. Besides, you know I'll be your biggest cheerleader, no matter how many drafts it takes."

STITCHED IN AMBITION

I smiled, buoyed by his words. "And what about you? What's your dream project? The one you've been too busy to explore?"

He took a deep breath, the kind that spoke volumes. "I've always wanted to delve deeper into abstract art, to explore emotions in a more visceral way. But I've been stuck in my own head, afraid to step away from what's safe."

"That sounds fascinating! Why not start with a series of pieces inspired by this weekend?" I suggested, the idea igniting something within me. "We can use the landscapes, the feelings we've been talking about. Let nature guide us."

"Now that's a plan." He grinned, his eyes sparkling with newfound determination. "Let's allow the mountains to spill their secrets onto the canvas."

With each step further down the trail, I felt a renewed sense of purpose and creativity, the tension and fear that had once held us captive slowly unraveling. This weekend had transformed into a sanctuary, a place where the world outside faded away, leaving only the two of us—bold, messy, and entirely unafraid to dream.

As we continued our hike, laughter echoed through the trees, mingling with the whispers of the wind. I could feel the weight of expectations begin to lift, replaced by the exhilarating freedom of possibility. We were on the brink of something beautiful, a rekindling of not just our artistic passions but also the connection that had once felt so effortless.

Then, just as I felt we were moving forward, the path before us forked unexpectedly. I hesitated, glancing at Alex. "So, left or right? Which direction do we trust to lead us to our inspiration?"

He chuckled, his expression playful. "If we end up lost, we can blame it on the pancakes. But I say we go left. It feels like an adventure waiting to happen."

"Left it is, then." I nodded, my heart racing with anticipation. I stepped forward, ready to dive deeper into the unknown, the promise of discovery lighting a fire within me that I was no longer afraid to embrace.

We ventured left, the path narrowing into a delightful tapestry of moss and scattered stones. The sun, now higher in the sky, filtered through the leaves above, creating a dappled pattern on the ground that danced beneath our feet. The air buzzed with the sound of nature awakening—squirrels scurrying up trees, birds flitting between branches, and the ever-present rustle of leaves that seemed to whisper secrets just out of reach.

As we walked, I let the tranquility seep into my bones, feeling lighter with every step. Alex kept pace beside me, his casual banter transforming the hike into an adventure rather than a mere trek through the woods.

"So, what would you say if I told you I had a brilliant idea for our art project?" he quipped, a mischievous glint in his eye.

"I'd say you've been reading too much of those 'creative thinking' books again," I shot back, suppressing a laugh. "But I'm intrigued. Spill it."

He grinned, pulling at a stray leaf that had tangled in his hair. "How about we create an interactive piece? Like a community art installation where people can contribute their stories on canvas. We can leave it at the cabin for anyone who passes by."

I paused, taken aback by the spontaneity of the idea. "That's actually brilliant. It opens up our work to a wider audience, and we could gather so many different perspectives!"

"Exactly! We could set up a small space right outside where people can add their thoughts, sketches, or anything they want. It'll become this living piece of art, a reflection of everyone who stops to share."

I could feel my heart racing, excitement bubbling just below the surface. "And we could document it! Each contribution could spark a new story or inspire a new piece of our own. It could really bring our art to life."

We continued down the path, enthusiasm weaving a vibrant thread between us, the idea blossoming like wildflowers in spring. But as the trail twisted and turned, I began to notice the familiar weight of uncertainty creeping back in, a nagging voice whispering doubts.

"What if no one stops? What if we're just sitting here, staring at a blank canvas?" I muttered, a hint of apprehension threading through my excitement.

"Then we'll fill it ourselves," Alex replied, a confident lilt to his voice. "We're not just waiting for people to come to us. We're creating the space for connection. Trust the process."

"Trust the process." I echoed, the words swirling in my mind. "I suppose that's true for art, and for us as well."

"Exactly!" he exclaimed, taking my hand as we climbed over a fallen log. "Life's about the messiness, the unpredictability. If we fail, at least we'll fail together."

I squeezed his hand, feeling a warmth spread through me, like sunlight breaking through the clouds. "Okay, let's do it. Let's create something that reflects our journey—and everyone else's."

We pushed forward, invigorated by our newfound resolve, each step feeling more purposeful. Just as we rounded a bend in the trail, an unexpected sight stopped us in our tracks.

Before us stood a small clearing, and in the center was an enormous, gnarled tree—its trunk twisted and thick, as if it had survived a thousand storms. Branches arched overhead, forming a natural canopy that filtered the sunlight into a magical glow. But it wasn't the beauty of the tree that caught my attention. It was the collection of art strewn at its base.

"What in the world?" I whispered, stepping closer.

Alex followed, his eyes wide with surprise. As we neared, I realized that nestled among the roots were colorful stones, each painted with intricate designs, words, and messages. There were small canvases, too—some with brush strokes that seemed to tell stories, others with playful doodles that expressed pure joy.

"Did people really stop here to create?" Alex marveled, kneeling to inspect one of the stones. "This is incredible!"

"Look at this one!" I exclaimed, picking up a rock adorned with swirling colors that seemed to come alive in my hands. "It says, 'Embrace the chaos.'"

"Perfect," he said, laughing softly. "It's like we've stumbled upon a treasure trove of inspiration."

Together, we wandered the clearing, marveling at the contributions from unknown artists, each piece resonating with its own unique story. It was a reminder of the beauty of community, of voices that intertwined to form a rich tapestry of life experiences.

"This is exactly what we want to create," I said, a wave of excitement washing over me. "Imagine if we could add our own stories to this."

"Absolutely. This is the spark we needed," Alex agreed, his face lit up with inspiration.

As we explored, I noticed a slightly larger canvas leaning against the tree, its surface still blank. An idea struck me, one that sent a shiver of thrill through my spine. "What if we leave our mark here? Something to represent us?"

"Now you're talking!" Alex's eyes gleamed with enthusiasm. "What do you want to create?"

I bit my lip, considering. "Let's not overthink it. Let's just let our hands and hearts guide us. How about a mural of the mountain landscape, but we blend in the stories we want to tell?"

"Sounds perfect," he said, and without another moment's hesitation, we began gathering supplies from our packs—brushes, paints, and a few markers. The moment felt electric, a shared anticipation hanging between us as we prepared to bring our vision to life.

We worked in joyful silence, our brushes moving in unison, the colors melding together like the stories waiting to be told. Each stroke was an expression of our journey, a celebration of the creativity we had once feared to embrace.

Time slipped away, our laughter and the soft rustling of the leaves forming a soundtrack to our labor of love. I felt a sense of liberation wash over me, a weight lifted as I poured myself into the canvas. I had forgotten how exhilarating it was to create without bounds, to allow the world around us to seep into our art.

Then, as the sun dipped low on the horizon, casting a golden glow around us, the air grew still. I paused, stepping back to admire our progress, the mural now an explosion of color that seemed to pulse with life. Just as I was about to call out to Alex, a sound interrupted the moment—a sudden rustling in the bushes nearby.

We both froze, our brushes poised midair. "Did you hear that?" I whispered, my heart racing.

"Yeah," he replied, his voice barely above a murmur. "What was that?"

The rustling grew louder, more insistent, a chaotic burst of movement that sent a flurry of leaves cascading to the ground. We exchanged a glance, uncertainty flashing between us.

"Maybe it's just a deer," I suggested, though my instincts told me otherwise.

"I think I'd prefer a deer right now," he said, chuckling nervously. "Or a squirrel. Something less... ominous."

Before we could analyze it further, the bushes parted, and a figure emerged, silhouetted against the waning light. My breath caught in my throat as recognition washed over me.

Standing there, with a look of disbelief and curiosity, was someone I never expected to see—a face from my past that had once brought both joy and heartache, now framed by the fading sunlight and uncertainty.

Chapter 23: The Fashion Fusion

The city buzzed with life, a heartbeat thrumming through the concrete veins that held us captive. The lights glimmered against the backdrop of twilight, creating a mosaic of colors that spilled into the apartment we shared. It was a sanctuary, an unlikely haven crafted from mismatched furniture and the eclectic remnants of our lives. The scent of coffee lingered in the air, mingling with the faint whiff of fabric softener from the piles of textiles we had strewn across the living room. We had transformed it into our creative battleground, a chaotic tapestry of sketches, swatches, and half-finished prototypes. It was here that I felt most alive, surrounded by the cacophony of our laughter and the shared dream that fueled our ambition.

I leaned over the table, my fingers tracing the edge of a vibrant turquoise silk, its sheen catching the light in a way that made my heart race. "What if we combined this with that graphic print you love?" I suggested, glancing at Tessa, my partner in both crime and creativity. She looked up, her curly hair bouncing with enthusiasm. "You mean the one with the abstract flowers? I thought it was too loud, but maybe... if we layered it right?"

"Yes!" I exclaimed, a grin spreading across my face as I envisioned our designs coming to life on the runway. The ideas flowed between us like a dance, each thought building upon the last until the room pulsed with energy. This fusion show wasn't just a showcase of our talents; it was a testament to everything we had fought for, an expression of our shared journey through heartbreak and self-discovery. Each fabric we selected told a story, and every sketch we crafted was a step closer to our dreams.

As the evening wore on, our brainstorming sessions often devolved into playful banter. Tessa had an uncanny knack for making me laugh, her dry wit cutting through my moments of self-doubt like a hot knife through butter. "If we manage to pull this off," she teased, her voice laced with mock seriousness, "I might just consider entering the witness protection program to avoid all the fame and fortune."

"Right, because the world needs another fashion fugitive," I shot back, feigning seriousness while my heart fluttered with the thrill of the impossible. We were dreamers, both of us, lost in a world where reality often felt too mundane to handle. As we flitted from one idea to another, I momentarily forgot about the lurking shadow that was Lydia, our former classmate whose talent was only rivaled by her penchant for sabotage. The thought crept into my mind like an unwelcome guest, but I quickly shooed it away, focusing instead on the bright future we were forging together.

But as the days slipped away, the weight of anticipation settled upon my shoulders like a heavy cloak. The date of the show was fast approaching, and with it came a surge of expectation that felt almost suffocating. I couldn't shake the feeling that Lydia was biding her time, waiting for a chink in our armor, a crack in our confidence. The thought was as unwelcome as a summer storm, dark and ominous, but I had made a vow to myself: I wouldn't let her dampen our spirits.

One evening, as I fiddled with a particularly stubborn zipper on a jacket we were designing, the door creaked open, and in walked Tessa, her cheeks flushed with excitement. "You won't believe this," she gasped, nearly tripping over a pile of fabric scraps. "I just got off the phone with that influencer, the one we sent our sketches to!"

I dropped the zipper, my heart pounding. "What did they say?"

"They love our concept! They want to feature us on their channel before the show!" Tessa bounced on her toes, and for a moment, the clouds of doubt parted, revealing a sunbeam of possibility.

"Seriously?" I laughed, a thrill coursing through me. This was it. This was the affirmation we needed, the push that could propel us into the spotlight we had dreamed of.

"Seriously!" Tessa replied, her eyes sparkling with mischief. "I told them we'd need to do a fitting, and they're all in for a little behind-the-scenes action."

"Behind-the-scenes action?" I repeated, my mind racing with the implications. "Do we look cute in sweatpants and paint-stained aprons?"

She chuckled, "I don't think that's the vibe they're going for, but we could try. Or we could clean ourselves up a bit and show them how fabulous we are."

With the rush of excitement coursing through us, we dove back into our designs, pouring our energy into crafting a collection that was vibrant and bold, echoing the city's pulse outside. Fabric swirled around us as we breathed life into our creations, the lines blurring between who we were and who we wanted to be.

But just as I started to feel a flicker of confidence rekindle within me, the shadows began to loom again. I spotted Lydia's name popping up in my social media feed, her latest posts dripping with thinly veiled critiques of "authenticity" in fashion. My stomach tightened, a gnawing fear clawing at the edges of my mind. She was coming for us, and I could feel the tension creeping back in, wrapping around me like a vise.

"Let's not let her get into our heads," Tessa said, noticing my distraction. "We're not here to please anyone but ourselves. And remember, every good show needs a little drama."

I offered her a small smile, but the tightness in my chest remained. "Drama, sure, but let's make it our drama," I countered, shaking off the lingering unease. With every swatch we cut, every seam we stitched, we were weaving not just clothing, but a tapestry of resilience, stitched together by laughter and a shared dream that refused to die. The world outside continued to spin, but within our little sanctuary, the magic of creation flourished, a testament to the power of hope amidst uncertainty.

Days bled into nights, each moment punctuated by bursts of inspiration that surged through our apartment like electric currents. We became architects of a dream, carefully constructing an experience that was both a culmination of our individuality and a celebration of our partnership. The living room transformed into a chaotic studio, a gallery of possibilities where fabric swatches hung like a colorful tapestry on the walls, and sketches littered the floor like fallen leaves. It was here, in this whirlwind of creativity, that I discovered the joy of creation anew, the exhilarating pulse of adrenaline fueling our every decision.

As we sifted through piles of textiles, I couldn't help but marvel at Tessa's unwavering enthusiasm. She had a way of turning even the most mundane tasks into an adventure. "Look at this plaid! It's like a picnic blanket went rogue," she quipped, holding up a vibrant green and blue checkered fabric, her eyes sparkling with mischief.

"Or like it's auditioning for a role in a 90s rom-com," I replied, unable to suppress a laugh. "It's charmingly chaotic—perfect for a line that screams 'look at me!'"

Tessa grinned, her expression shifting to one of mock seriousness. "You know, if this fashion thing doesn't pan out, we could always become fabric critics. We'd go viral for our over-the-top reviews. 'This polyester is so stiff, it could stand up and walk out of the store by itself!'"

We fell into a fit of laughter, the sound echoing through the apartment, mingling with the distant hum of the city outside. Yet, beneath our playful banter lay a current of anxiety, a silent acknowledgment of the stakes we were juggling. We were stepping onto a stage that felt precariously high, with both excitement and fear gripping us as the date of the show loomed closer.

Despite the laughter, my thoughts often drifted to Lydia, her presence hanging over us like a storm cloud, threatening to unleash chaos at any moment. I could almost feel her watching from the shadows, her ambition sharp and calculating. The very idea of her undermining our efforts gnawed at my resolve, making it difficult to focus on our designs.

One evening, as we meticulously crafted a daring gown that paired blush satin with bold black leather, Tessa broke the silence that had settled like a heavy fog. "You know, for a show that's supposed to be a celebration of our styles, it feels a bit... tense."

I looked up, meeting her gaze. "Yeah, well, I can't help but think about Lydia. She's like a hawk circling its prey, waiting for the right moment to swoop in."

Tessa rolled her eyes, her frustration bubbling to the surface. "Honestly, we need to stop letting her live rent-free in our heads. It's exhausting."

"Agreed," I said, pushing my hair back in a futile attempt to clear my mind. "But how do we shake her off? It feels like she has this weird sixth sense for knowing when we're feeling good about our work."

"Maybe we need to show her that we're not afraid," Tessa suggested, a fire igniting in her eyes. "Let's turn her negativity into fuel. We'll create something so fabulous that it leaves her speechless!"

With renewed determination, we poured our energy into the gown, draping the satin over the leather with a flair that felt like a dance, each movement intentional and powerful. The fabric slipped through my fingers, whispering promises of grandeur. As we worked late into the night, Tessa pulled out her phone, scrolling through social media until she stumbled upon a post that made her gasp.

"Look at this!" she exclaimed, her eyes wide. The screen illuminated her face as she showed me Lydia's latest post, a photograph of herself draped in an opulent gown that shimmered under the studio lights. The caption read, "All about authentic expression in fashion—something to think about for the upcoming show."

A bitter taste filled my mouth. "She's definitely throwing shade."

"Let's not give her the satisfaction of knowing she's getting to us," Tessa said, her tone steady and resolute. "Instead, let's make sure our pieces shine even brighter."

The next few days became a whirlwind of activity. We worked tirelessly, fueled by our shared mission to outshine Lydia's dark clouds. Mornings turned into afternoons, and afternoons melted into sleepless nights as we immersed ourselves in our designs. Every stitch was imbued with our hopes and fears, each fabric a canvas for our creativity.

On the day of the show, the energy in the air was electric. The venue buzzed with anticipation, a thrumming heartbeat that resonated within my chest. As I stood backstage, the cacophony of voices and the clattering of heels on the polished floor felt surreal. I could hear the murmur of the crowd, a sea of faces eager for the spectacle that was about to unfold.

Tessa stood beside me, her hands clasped tightly. "This is it," she said, her voice barely above a whisper. "We've come so far, and now it's time to let the world see what we've created."

The lights dimmed, and a hush fell over the audience, the kind of silence that crackled with potential. My heart raced as I looked at our designs hanging on the racks, each piece a testament to our labor and love. The first model stepped onto the runway, and I held my breath, watching as our creation flowed gracefully with each movement, a dance of fabric and form.

With every model that walked, our vision took shape, the crowd responding with enthusiastic applause. I caught glimpses of Lydia in the front row, her expression a mix of admiration and surprise. The knot in my stomach began to loosen, replaced by a swell of pride as I realized we had transformed our insecurities into something beautiful.

But as the final model strutted down the runway, wearing a show-stopping ensemble that seamlessly blended our distinct styles, I felt an undeniable shift in the atmosphere. The audience erupted into cheers, but there was something else lurking beneath the surface, an undercurrent of tension that prickled at my skin. I turned to Tessa, her eyes wide with excitement, but I couldn't shake the feeling that our moment of triumph was only the beginning of something far more complex. The applause felt like a curtain rising, revealing not just our achievements, but the looming specter of competition that had yet to reveal its true form.

The applause roared like a wave crashing against the shore, and I felt my heart swell with an overwhelming mix of relief and exhilaration. Tessa and I stood at the edge of the runway, our hands gripping each other tightly as we exchanged wide-eyed glances, unable to fully absorb the magnitude of our accomplishment. Our designs had taken flight, swirling around the runway like dandelion seeds caught in a summer breeze. The colors we had chosen, vibrant and alive, shimmered under the lights as they danced to the rhythm of our hopes and dreams.

The final model, a tall woman with striking features, turned at the end of the runway, striking a pose that seemed to encapsulate everything we had worked toward. As she raised her arm, showcasing the intricate details of our creation, the audience erupted into a cacophony of cheers. I felt a giddy rush of joy, a heady cocktail of adrenaline and pride. "We did it!" I whispered to Tessa, unable to contain the grin that split my face.

"Can you believe this?" she replied, her voice a mix of disbelief and elation. "They love us! They really love us!"

But just as the euphoria began to settle, the weight of Lydia's presence seeped into the air like a cold draft. I caught her eyes in the front row, and despite the bright lights and the applause, her gaze was sharp, slicing through the moment with a glimmer of disdain that was hard to ignore. It was like a cloud passing over the sun, casting a shadow that threatened to dim our joy.

As the show wrapped up, we rushed backstage, adrenaline still coursing through our veins. The atmosphere buzzed with excitement and chaos, models unzipping their outfits and stylists fussing with hair and makeup. Tessa and I exchanged breathless laughter as we made our way through the throng of people, but my gaze kept drifting back to Lydia, who was still hovering at the edge of the stage like a storm waiting to unleash its fury.

"Okay, we need to celebrate!" Tessa declared, her eyes sparkling with enthusiasm. "I'm thinking champagne, maybe some overpriced appetizers? Nothing says success like tiny food!"

I laughed, trying to shake off the unease Lydia had stirred within me. "Absolutely! But first, let's get through this crowd without losing a limb."

As we maneuvered our way toward the exit, I felt a presence behind me. I turned to find Lydia gliding through the crowd with the grace of a predatory bird. She approached us with a smile that felt all too practiced, her red lipstick perfectly applied, her confidence radiating like a heatwave. "Well, well, if it isn't the dynamic duo," she said, her voice dripping with sweetness that could only be described as venomous. "Congratulations on your little show."

"Thanks, Lydia! It was a lot of work, but totally worth it," I replied, forcing a smile that felt more like a grimace.

"Worth it, indeed," she echoed, glancing at the models as they walked by. "But, you know, I can't help but wonder how well your designs will hold up under the scrutiny of actual critics."

Tessa's eyes narrowed, and I felt her grip tighten on my arm. "Our designs held up just fine. Did you see the audience? They loved it!"

"Oh, I did. They love a good spectacle," Lydia shot back, her gaze icy. "But a few pretty dresses don't guarantee success. You'll need more than that to survive in this industry."

Her words hung in the air like smoke, tainting the high we had just experienced. I opened my mouth to respond, to tell her that our work was more than just pretty dresses, but before I could utter a word, she leaned closer, her voice dropping to a conspiratorial whisper. "You should be careful. Fashion can be a cruel mistress. Just ask anyone who's ever fallen from grace."

With that, she turned on her heel and sauntered away, leaving a chill in her wake. I stood there, rooted to the spot, the excitement of the evening evaporating as doubt began to seep back in. "What was that about?" Tessa asked, her brows knitted together in confusion.

"I don't know, but it felt ominous," I muttered, frustration bubbling beneath the surface. "She thinks she can intimidate us. But we won't let her."

Tessa nodded, though I could see the unease flickering in her eyes. "Let's not let her spoil our night. We've earned this moment."

As we stepped outside, the cool night air wrapped around us, and I inhaled deeply, trying to ground myself. The streets were alive with energy, a vibrant pulse that mirrored the excitement still buzzing within me. The city lights twinkled like stars, a perfect backdrop for our celebration.

We headed to a nearby bar, the atmosphere buzzing with laughter and the clinking of glasses. The moment we stepped inside, we were enveloped in warmth, the air rich with the scent of aged whiskey and freshly tapped beer. We found a cozy corner and ordered our drinks, the anticipation of toasting to our success lifting my spirits.

"Here's to us!" Tessa declared, raising her glass high. "To conquering the runway and to all the fabulous things to come!"

"To us!" I echoed, clinking my glass against hers, the sound ringing clear in the bustling bar.

But just as we began to relax, the door swung open, and in walked a familiar face—Lydia, flanked by a group of equally polished individuals, each wearing expressions that mirrored her air of superiority. My stomach dropped as I recognized one of them as a well-known fashion blogger, her presence a potent reminder that the industry was a web of connections and rivalries.

"Of course she'd show up here," I muttered under my breath, my earlier enthusiasm evaporating like a mirage.

Tessa shot me a concerned look. "Let's ignore her. This is our night!"

As the evening wore on, the tension between us and Lydia's group became palpable. Lydia seemed to revel in it, casting sidelong glances our way, her laughter cutting through the air like a knife. Each time she glanced in our direction, I felt a knot form in my stomach, the weight of her words echoing in my mind.

But it was when a waitress approached with a sly grin that the atmosphere shifted dramatically. "Excuse me, ladies," she said, her tone casual, "but someone sent over these champagne cocktails for you."

My heart raced as I looked at the glasses, glistening with a hint of gold and topped with what appeared to be edible glitter. A small card rested beside them, and I reached for it, my fingers trembling slightly. The handwriting was unmistakable: "Cheers to a fabulous show and an even more fabulous downfall."

Panic surged through me, and I glanced at Tessa, whose expression mirrored my shock. "This is from Lydia," I breathed, anger bubbling up from within.

Before I could process it fully, Lydia's laughter rang out again, this time accompanied by her friends, the sound a cruel melody that twisted the knife deeper. "You ladies look a bit pale! Hope you enjoy the drinks."

The bartender glanced over, concern etching his brow as he spotted the tension simmering at our table. "Everything okay?" he asked, stepping closer, sensing the shift in the atmosphere.

"No, it's not," I snapped, anger surging like a tidal wave. "It's not okay at all."

Just as I opened my mouth to confront Lydia, she caught my eye and raised her glass, her smile infuriatingly smug. "To fresh starts and new beginnings, girls! Just remember—fashion isn't just about the clothes. It's a game."

And in that moment, I realized that Lydia wasn't just an obstacle; she was the embodiment of the challenges we would have to face in this industry, a reminder that not everyone played fair. I took a deep breath, my heart racing as I steeled myself for what was to come.

Just as I was about to respond, the world spun on its axis, and the bar door flew open again, this time revealing a figure that made my heart stop. Standing in the doorway was an unexpected visitor, a face from my past that sent shockwaves through the very foundation of my newfound confidence.

Chapter 24: The Great Reveal

The vibrant glow of the city lights filtered through the tall glass windows, casting a warm, golden hue over the venue. The air was thick with the scent of fresh flowers and the soft murmur of hushed conversations swirled around me like a comforting blanket. I stood at the edge of the runway, my pulse racing as models began to glide past in a kaleidoscope of colors and textures. Each outfit we had crafted together whispered stories of resilience, of late nights fueled by coffee and laughter, and of the unexpected twists that had brought Alex and me to this moment.

"Do you see that?" I nudged Alex, pointing toward a model draped in a breathtaking teal gown, its flowing fabric catching the light in waves. "That was the one we almost scrapped! Remember how I thought it was too bold?"

He chuckled softly, a sound that sent a ripple of warmth through me. "And I insisted it was going to steal the show. You doubted my vision, but look at it now." His eyes sparkled with pride as they followed the model's every step, a smile tugging at the corners of his mouth. In that moment, I felt invincible, our creative energies entwined in a way that felt almost ethereal.

But as the show progressed, my gaze darted toward the front row, where Lydia sat with her perfectly manicured nails and an expression that could curdle milk. It was as if she was the only dark cloud in this otherwise perfect evening, a reminder that success could often bring with it a swarm of wasps buzzing at your heels. She leaned back in her seat, arms crossed defiantly, her lips pressed into a thin line. Just like that, the vibrant atmosphere shifted slightly; the air turned dense with unspoken tension.

"Don't let her ruin this for you," Alex whispered, his voice steady, a calming presence amid my swirling thoughts. He reached for my hand, squeezing it gently, and I felt a rush of affection for him. In the chaos of the evening, he remained my anchor, grounding me in the face of uncertainty. "Remember why we're here. It's about us, not her."

I nodded, taking a deep breath and allowing the warmth of his words to wash over me. The applause thundered like a heartbeat, the audience captivated by the collection we had poured our souls into. The designs, vibrant and daring, reflected not only our individual styles but also the transformation of our partnership—a fusion of dreams and ideas that had once felt so unattainable.

With each model that passed, I felt the thrill of validation. This was our moment, an exclamation point at the end of a long, tumultuous sentence. But the knot of anxiety in my stomach refused to dissolve completely. Lydia's presence was a shadow that loomed large, and with every clap of the audience, I could almost hear her seething beneath her composed exterior.

"Do you think she's going to make a scene?" I asked Alex, my voice barely above a whisper. I could imagine the headlines, the scandalous whispers that would undoubtedly follow if she chose to make an entrance of her own.

"Let her try. We've worked too hard to let her take this away from us," he said firmly, but there was a hint of concern in his eyes. I could sense that he shared my apprehension about Lydia, a former ally turned adversary.

As the final model took her turn, showcasing a daring ensemble that brought gasps from the audience, I felt a surge of adrenaline. The applause was deafening, a tidal wave of appreciation that washed over us and drowned out my doubts. I turned to Alex, and we shared a moment of triumph, our eyes locking in a silent understanding of all we had faced to reach this pinnacle.

"Get ready," he said, his voice low and conspiratorial. "They're going to want to meet the masterminds behind this show."

The moment had arrived. The lights dimmed slightly, and the spotlight shifted to us. I felt like I was floating as we stepped forward, hand in hand, into the blinding glow. The audience rose to their feet, clapping with such fervor that it echoed in my ears like a love song. I soaked it in, the sense of belonging and achievement blooming within me like a long-awaited spring.

Then, just as we began to bask in our well-deserved glory, Lydia stood up, her movements sharp and deliberate. I could practically feel the temperature drop as the spotlight flickered to her. She cleared her throat, an almost imperceptible smile tugging at her lips as she prepared to deliver whatever venomous statement she had concocted.

"Isn't this charming?" she began, her voice dripping with sarcasm. "A lovely little fairy tale where the once-fallen are suddenly the stars of the show." The audience's applause faltered, and a murmur rippled through the crowd like a stone tossed into a still pond.

I braced myself, adrenaline flooding my veins as I clenched Alex's hand tighter. This was it—the great reveal I had dreaded. The air around us thickened, and I could almost hear my heartbeat echoing in the silence that enveloped us.

"Just remember," Lydia continued, her eyes narrowing as they settled on me. "Every fairy tale has its wicked witch. And I'm not finished with you yet."

A collective gasp arose from the audience, and I felt the weight of her words settle over me, cold and suffocating.

Lydia's words hung in the air like a storm cloud, dark and oppressive, threatening to swallow the bright energy of the evening whole. As she stood there, poised and self-satisfied, I could feel the collective breath of the audience catch in their throats. The applause faded, replaced by a tense silence, punctuated only by the faint sound of fabric rustling as models exited the runway. The spotlight that had moments ago celebrated our achievements now felt like a blaring siren, a spotlight drawing attention to a dark chapter I'd hoped was closed.

"Are you seriously going to stand there and act like you're some kind of fairy tale princess?" Lydia continued, her voice dripping with sarcasm. "This isn't a happy ending, sweetheart. You're still in the story." She leaned forward, her perfectly manicured finger jabbing toward me like a lightning bolt, igniting the tension in the room.

I could feel Alex stiffen beside me, a low growl of protectiveness emanating from him. "Lydia," he started, his voice low but steady, the warmth of his hand squeezing mine grounding me against the chaos unfolding. "This isn't the time or the place."

"Isn't it, though?" she shot back, turning her gaze on him. "This is the moment everyone gets to see how desperate you both are. Selling your sad little story of triumph while you pretend I'm not here. How quaint." Her smile was sharp, like broken glass reflecting the dim lights of the venue.

"Desperate? Us?" I found my voice, surprising myself. It emerged stronger than I expected, buoyed by adrenaline. "What's truly desperate is someone who can't stand to see others succeed. You're clinging to a narrative that's all but finished." The words tumbled out of me like confetti, colorful and chaotic, scattering the tense atmosphere just a little.

The audience gasped collectively, a tide of disbelief that surged through the crowd. Lydia's eyes narrowed, the smile faltering for just a moment before she regained her composure. "Nice try, but the ending's not yours to write. Not yet."

With a flick of her wrist, she dismissed me, turning her attention back to the audience. "Ladies and gentlemen, it's a classic story: the young upstarts against the reigning queen. Only, you see, I'm not going anywhere." Her voice dripped with confidence, but beneath it,

I sensed a tremor of insecurity. Was that fear? Did she really believe she could disrupt everything we'd built together?

"Look around you," I shot back, stepping forward despite Alex's grip tightening on my arm. "This isn't about you anymore. This show is about unity, collaboration, and moving forward. You're just the ghost of a chapter we've already closed."

The audience buzzed, some murmurs erupting into laughter at Lydia's expense. I felt a swell of triumph. I wasn't just defending our work; I was reclaiming my narrative, one I had spent too long allowing her to dictate.

For a moment, it seemed like I might win this battle. But Lydia, always the skilled performer, didn't skip a beat. "Unity? Is that what you call it? Your little alliance is built on borrowed confidence and secondhand ideas. Let's not pretend you didn't need me to launch your careers in the first place."

The air thickened with tension, and I could feel the weight of those words pressing down on my shoulders. Was it true? Had I truly relied on her more than I cared to admit? The questions spiraled in my mind, a chaotic dance threatening to drown out my resolve.

"Remember," Lydia continued, her eyes gleaming with triumph. "You're only as strong as your connections. And I'm still here, waiting for my next move."

At that moment, Alex stepped in front of me, a wall of strength and determination. "You can't just waltz back in and try to rewrite history, Lydia. We've fought too hard for this moment, and you're not going to undermine it." His voice rose, steady and unyielding.

The crowd's tension began to shift, a palpable energy swirling around us, filled with the need for resolution. I watched as some of the audience members nodded in agreement, as if they were realizing the truth of our journey—a shared story that extended far beyond Lydia's petty sabotage.

"You think this is over?" Lydia's voice dropped to a whisper, laced with menace. "You think you've won? I have connections. I can ruin you both with a single phone call."

"Ruin us?" I laughed, the sound escaping me, surprising even myself. "How charming! But here's the thing: we're not afraid of you anymore. You may have been our storm, but look around. We're the rainbows that come after, and we're not hiding."

The audience erupted in applause, a wave of support that washed over me, igniting a fierce determination within. It was as if their energy rekindled my confidence, illuminating the path ahead.

Lydia's face twisted into a mask of disbelief, her carefully crafted persona beginning to crack. For a brief moment, she faltered, and I could see the unraveling threads of her façade.

"Good luck with that, darling," she shot back, but there was an edge of desperation in her voice now. "Just remember that fairy tales have a way of becoming nightmares."

With a flourish, she turned on her heel, strutting away like a peacock denied its time in the spotlight. Her retreat felt more like a defeat, and the tension in the room began to dissipate, replaced by a newfound excitement.

As the applause crescendoed, Alex and I shared a triumphant glance, the electric current of victory coursing between us. "You were incredible," he breathed, his eyes sparkling with admiration.

"We were incredible," I corrected, a grin breaking across my face. "Together."

With each clap echoing in the venue, it became clear that the night belonged to us. Our designs had resonated, and despite Lydia's attempted sabotage, the truth of our work had shone through. And in that moment, as the audience continued to celebrate, I realized that we had not only won this battle but had also emerged stronger, united in our mission to redefine our story.

"Let's go out there and enjoy it," I said, my heart soaring with the realization that we were ready to take on whatever came next. The world was our runway, and I felt ready to strut down it, hand in hand with Alex, unafraid of the shadows that lingered behind us.

The applause swelled like a tide, a visceral echo of the excitement that wrapped around us, a shield against the lingering shadows Lydia had cast. I felt lightheaded, not just from the thrill of success but from the sudden realization that this was it—our moment had arrived. As we stood at the edge of the runway, the bright lights illuminating our faces, a soft breeze from an unseen fan sent a shiver down my spine, a gentle reminder that this was a world of fashion, where appearances danced like whispers on the edge of a secret.

"Ready to bask in our glory?" Alex asked, his voice teasing, but I could see the genuine excitement gleaming in his eyes.

"Only if you promise not to trip on the runway. I can't have you stealing my spotlight." I nudged him playfully, feeling the warmth of camaraderie bloom between us.

"Tripping is part of my charm. But it's hard to fall when you're standing next to greatness." His wink was disarming, and I felt the familiar flutter of affection that had grown into something solid and unshakeable.

With the show winding down, we stepped off the stage and made our way to the backstage area, where a vibrant cacophony of chatter erupted around us. Stylists buzzed like busy bees, adjusting last-minute details, while models high-fived each other, their spirits buoyed by the collective energy that filled the space.

"Can you believe it?" I said, my heart racing with exhilaration. "We did it!"

Before Alex could respond, a sharp voice sliced through the jubilant atmosphere. "Well, well, if it isn't the dynamic duo, back from the brink." Lydia had returned, her earlier bravado seemingly revived, but now there was a glint of something darker in her eyes.

"Didn't you have somewhere to be?" I shot back, crossing my arms defiantly. "Somewhere far away from us?"

Her laughter rang hollow, like a brittle glass shattering on a concrete floor. "Why would I miss the chance to watch your little fairy tale unravel? After all, you're the ones who invited me into your story."

"Not anymore," Alex interjected, positioning himself protectively beside me. "You're not part of this chapter."

"Oh, but that's where you're wrong." Lydia stepped closer, her expression a mask of feigned innocence. "I'm still the one holding the pen, and you both are just characters dancing along the edges."

I clenched my jaw, refusing to let her words penetrate the buoyancy of the evening. "You think we need you? That you can control our narrative? You're living in a fantasy, Lydia."

"Am I?" she challenged, a sharp smile playing on her lips. "Or am I merely showing you the truth? You might have everyone eating out of your hands right now, but the fashion world is fickle. Today's darlings can easily become tomorrow's has-beens."

Before I could respond, a sudden commotion erupted behind us. A group of stylists clustered around a model who had just stepped off the runway, her eyes wide with shock. "The dress! It's torn!" she cried, holding the fabric up like a battle flag.

Lydia's smile widened. "Oops, looks like someone's not as perfect as they think."

I felt my stomach drop. "That was one of our best pieces!" I shot back, but deep down, I could feel a seed of panic sprouting. How could this happen now, after everything?

Alex's eyes narrowed, his focus shifting back to Lydia. "You're behind this, aren't you?"

"Me? Why, I'm just a spectator, darling. Besides, a little wear and tear can happen to anyone."

But the sharpness in her tone betrayed her. The subtle satisfaction in her eyes was all too telling. It was as if she thrived on chaos, her energy crackling with malicious delight.

"Look, whatever you're trying to do, it's not going to work," I said, my voice rising above the noise of the backstage frenzy. "We've built this together, and you're not going to tear it down."

"Oh, but I'm already inside, sweetheart," she replied, her voice low and smooth, like silk concealing a blade. "You can't control what happens next."

Before I could formulate a response, a loud crash echoed from the side of the stage. Everyone turned, their faces a mixture of surprise and concern. A backdrop had fallen, narrowly missing one of the crew members, sending everyone scrambling.

"What the hell?" I exclaimed, my heart racing as I surveyed the chaos.

"Looks like luck isn't on your side tonight," Lydia said, a hint of triumph dancing in her voice.

I felt a surge of anger rising in me, fueled by the adrenaline coursing through my veins. "This isn't luck; this is sabotage!"

As the crew worked to rectify the situation, I caught Alex's eye. He was shaking his head, a mix of disbelief and frustration etched on his features. "We need to go," he said, urgency lacing his words. "This could spiral out of control."

"Not without addressing this first." I gestured to Lydia, who stood there, basking in the turmoil she had unleashed.

"Why don't we make this interesting?" she proposed, her eyes sparkling with mischief. "How about a little wager? If you can survive the next round of fashion critiques, I'll step aside. But if you falter, you're out of the game. Permanently."

"Why would we ever agree to that?" I shot back, but even as I said it, I could feel a part of me tempted by the challenge.

"Because I have the power to make or break you, and you know it." Her confidence radiated like a dark force. "You want to play with the big leagues? Then play the game."

I could feel the weight of her challenge pressing down on me, and despite the chaos around us, my resolve began to solidify. This was not just about the fashion show anymore; it was about proving that we belonged in this world, regardless of the obstacles Lydia tossed our way.

"Fine," I said, surprising myself with my own conviction. "We accept your challenge."

A smug smile spread across Lydia's face. "Oh, this is going to be delicious. Let's see how you fare when the critics come for you."

Before I could say anything else, she turned on her heel, slipping away into the swirling chaos. The moment she vanished, the atmosphere shifted, the energy crackling with newfound tension.

"Are we really going to let her get under our skin?" Alex asked, concern etched across his features.

"We have to stand firm," I replied, determination hardening my voice. "We're not going to let her sabotage what we've built."

But as we braced ourselves for the coming storm, I couldn't shake the feeling that this was just the beginning. The stakes had risen, and with each passing moment, I sensed that Lydia was more than just a thorn in our side—she was the specter of a nightmare I couldn't escape.

And just as I turned to look at Alex, the lights flickered ominously, casting shadows that danced around us. My heart raced at the ominous signs, a chill creeping down my spine as I realized that whatever happened next could change everything.

Chapter 25: A Shattering Blow

The hum of anticipation vibrated through the dimly lit backstage area, an electric current buzzing between the flickering light bulbs that cast a warm, golden glow across the chaos. The air was thick with the scent of hairspray and faint perfume, a concoction that usually felt comforting but now suffocated me. I stood amidst a whirlwind of fabric, heels clicking, and frantic whispers, all swirled into a chaotic ballet. Just moments before, everything had felt perfect, a well-rehearsed routine of models strutting down the runway in stunning designs that spoke of elegance and artistry. But the delicate balance had shattered like glass.

It began innocuously enough, a model named Jasmine, poised to grace the stage in a breathtaking gown made of cascading layers that shimmered like liquid silver. The moment she turned, the sound of tearing fabric sliced through the ambient noise, and time seemed to stop. Her face contorted in a mix of shock and horror as she clutched the remnants of what had just moments ago been a masterpiece. Panic rippled through the crew like a pebble dropped in a pond, its effects spreading far and wide, creating waves of anxiety.

"Help! Someone! I need—" Jasmine's voice cut through the rising clamor, desperation echoing in the space. I could see her distress mirrored in the frantic eyes of our stage manager, Carla, who was already diving into the fray, her ponytail bouncing like a metronome keeping time with the mounting chaos. The tension in the room thickened, a living thing that wrapped around us, squeezing tighter with every second.

Without a second thought, I dashed toward Jasmine, adrenaline flooding my veins. The fabric flapped awkwardly, the delicate threads seemingly mocking her misfortune as she struggled to maintain her composure. I reached her just as another model rushed past, their shoulder colliding with mine, sending me stumbling. "Hold on," I murmured, my voice steadier than my heartbeat. "We'll fix this. Just breathe."

The scene spiraled into pandemonium as I fumbled with safety pins, trying to piece together the gown while chaos erupted around me. Lydia, our head designer, stood nearby, her hands on her hips, a sneer plastered on her face. "This is what happens when you don't prepare properly," she barked, her voice laced with venom. "If you can't handle a little pressure, maybe you should reconsider your role here."

I swallowed hard, biting back the retort that surged to my lips. The last thing I needed was to engage in a battle of wits with Lydia when Jasmine's dignity hung in the balance. But as I caught a glimpse of Alex across the room, trying to coordinate the crew with a calm that seemed superhuman, an unsettling sense of vulnerability washed over me. It wasn't just about the dress; it was about our passion, our art—everything we had worked so hard to create teetered on the edge of collapse.

"Just a little tighter," Jasmine urged, her voice quivering as I struggled to keep the gown from slipping any further. My hands worked deftly, but I could feel the weight of Lydia's derision pressing down on me. It was suffocating. Every snicker, every dismissive glance she shot in my direction felt like a slap, igniting a fire within me that I wasn't sure how to contain.

In a single moment, my focus shattered when I heard a shout. It came from Alex, his voice slicing through the confusion. "Watch out!" Panic painted his features, and before I could turn, bodies collided with a force that sent Jasmine stumbling backward. The world around me twisted into a blur of limbs and chaos, and my heart plummeted as I saw Alex caught in the crossfire, arms raised as he attempted to defuse the situation.

"Alex!" I screamed, the sound raw and laced with fear. I rushed toward him, but it felt like wading through molasses as I pushed past the frantic crew and models, each person wrapped in their own chaos. It felt surreal, a nightmare where the world around me twisted and turned, leaving me powerless to change the outcome.

Then, as if in a cruel twist of fate, Lydia stepped into the fray. "This is embarrassing," she declared, her voice dripping with disdain, casting a look around as if surveying a crumbling set rather than a team in distress. "And it's all because of your incompetence."

A fierce anger flared within me, igniting a determination I hadn't known I possessed. "You don't get to belittle us," I shot back, my words sharper than I intended. "We are here pouring our hearts into this, and you mock us?"

Her laughter echoed through the chaos, chilling and dismissive. "Please, darling. You think this is passion? It's just a job." The disdain in her tone felt like a blade against my skin, cutting deeper than I'd like to admit. In that moment, vulnerability morphed into a shield of defiance, and I took a step closer, my chin tilted up.

"This isn't just a job," I retorted, each word dripping with conviction. "This is our dream, our craft, and you will treat it with the respect it deserves."

In the space that followed, time seemed to stretch as the tension thickened. The chaos around us faded into the background, and I could see the flicker of surprise in Lydia's eyes, a crack in her façade of superiority. Just as I thought she might respond, a loud crash reverberated through the room. I turned, heart racing as I watched a rack of dresses topple to the floor, cascading like dominos in a tragic design.

In that surreal instant, I realized that beneath the surface of our art, we were all standing on the edge of something vast—fear, vulnerability, and the burning desire to be seen. I wasn't just defending my passion; I was standing for all of us, for every moment we had poured into this show, and the raw, undeniable beauty of creation itself.

The aftermath of chaos clung to the air like smoke, thick and palpable. As the last of the dresses were scooped up from the floor, I stood in the eye of a storm, my heart still pounding against my ribs. The dim lights cast erratic shadows around us, reflecting the disarray that had unfolded moments before. I could still feel the remnants of adrenaline coursing through my veins, a volatile mixture of anger and indignation battling for dominance.

Jasmine, now steadied by a pair of quick-thinking assistants, brushed her hair back, eyes wide with a blend of disbelief and embarrassment. "I swear I'm going to cry," she said, laughter bubbling nervously in her throat. "I don't think I've ever been so mortified in my life. I just wanted to be a sparkly princess for one night!" Her humor, even in the midst of disaster, was a bright thread woven through the fabric of tension that gripped the room.

"Forget the sparkly princess; you're a warrior," I replied, a smile breaking through my worry. "You handled that like a pro. Who else could turn a wardrobe malfunction into an impromptu drama?" I reached out to squeeze her hand, anchoring us both in the absurdity of the moment. The camaraderie felt like a warm blanket, wrapping around us as the reality of our situation began to settle.

But the shadows of Lydia's disdain loomed larger. She was not just a person; she was an institution—a strict enforcer of perfection, and I could feel her eyes darting between Jasmine and me, taking in our moment of levity with the sort of disdain reserved for a botched painting. "Keep it together, ladies," she quipped, her voice cutting through our shared laughter like a knife. "This isn't a charity event; it's a runway show."

Rolling my eyes, I couldn't help but shoot back, "Funny, I thought we were all here to showcase talent and creativity, not just be your puppets." My voice dripped with a bravado I didn't entirely feel, yet there it was, leaping from my lips as if it had been waiting for the right moment to pounce.

Jasmine snorted, and a few crew members exchanged glances, their eyes wide with surprise at my audacity. Lydia's lips curled into a smirk that could have been charming if it hadn't been so laced with contempt. "You really think you can challenge me?" she taunted, leaning closer, her tone laced with condescension. "It's cute, really."

But it was not cute; it was infuriating. The hair on my arms stood at attention, a visceral reaction to her derision. "You don't get it, do you?" I found myself saying, the defiance in my chest swelling. "This is about more than just a show. It's about us. Our dreams, our art—everything we put on the line every time we step onto this runway."

The shift in Lydia's expression was subtle but noticeable; a flicker of something—was it doubt?—passed through her features. But before I could cling to that fleeting hope, a loud crash echoed through the backstage area. We turned to find one of the lighting rigs teetering dangerously on its stand, the crew scrambling to catch it before it fell. In a split second, I was propelled back into the fray, instinctively moving toward the sound, my heart pounding like a drumbeat in my ears.

"Watch out!" I shouted, my voice rising above the chaos, but it was too late. The rig tipped, and a frantic scramble ensued. I ducked instinctively as the crew dove for safety, adrenaline coursing through my veins once again. Somehow, amidst the madness, Alex's voice rang out—steady and reassuring. "I've got this! Just stay calm!" His presence was a lighthouse in the storm, guiding everyone back to sanity.

I skidded to a halt, nearly colliding with him as he righted the equipment with an expert flick of his wrist, managing to stabilize it before it could cause further chaos. The sheer calmness radiating from him was intoxicating. "You're amazing," I said, breathless with relief. "I don't know how you keep your cool."

His eyes sparkled with mischief, the tension easing slightly as he replied, "Years of practice. Or maybe I'm just too stubborn to let chaos win." The brief levity offered a momentary reprieve, the laughter hanging in the air, lifting our spirits ever so slightly.

But Lydia, lurking like a storm cloud, remained resolute. "If you all spent more time focusing on the show instead of running around like headless chickens, maybe we wouldn't have these issues." Her voice was sharp, cutting through the camaraderie like a blade.

"Right, because panic is totally the best approach to artistry," I shot back, unable to hold my tongue. "We need flexibility and creativity, not just a stiff routine."

"Flexibility?" she scoffed, eyes narrowing. "You mean chaos."

"Chaos is a part of creativity!" I countered, my pulse racing with the thrill of standing my ground. "Art doesn't flourish in sterile conditions. It breathes in spontaneity!"

"Maybe that's why your designs aren't ready for the runway," Lydia retorted, her voice slick with malice.

In that moment, I felt the weight of her words—sharp, like ice piercing through the protective shell I had been trying to build. My breath hitched, but before I could respond, Jasmine chimed in, her voice steady. "Actually, I think her designs are brilliant. They have heart, and that's something you wouldn't know anything about."

The air shifted, a palpable change sparking through the room. Lydia's lips pressed into a thin line, the challenge hanging in the air between us like a taut string. For the first time, she seemed to recognize the strength of the team standing against her, the tide slowly turning.

Just then, another assistant scurried up, hair wild and eyes wide. "We need everyone at the front! It's almost time!" The urgency in her tone snapped us back to reality. The show was about to begin, and despite the chaos, we were still on the cusp of something beautiful.

"Let's finish this," Alex said, his voice steady, igniting a spark of determination in my chest. I could feel the energy shifting, a sense of unity blooming amidst the fragments of earlier tension. Lydia could scoff all she wanted; we were going to prove her wrong.

As we hurried to our positions, I caught Alex's eye. "No matter what happens out there, let's make sure it's unforgettable." His nod felt like an unspoken promise, and as I took a deep breath, a newfound resolve settled within me. The stage was set, the lights glimmered, and we were ready to step into the spotlight.

The tension in the air thickened as the final moments before the show felt both exhilarating and terrifying. We moved like a well-rehearsed dance, each of us slipping into our roles with an urgency born from chaos. I could feel my heart thumping in rhythm with the last-minute preparations, a wild drumbeat that underscored our frantic energy. The previously looming shadows of doubt seemed to dissipate, replaced by a fierce camaraderie and a shared determination to turn this evening into something unforgettable.

As the lights dimmed, a hush fell over the backstage area. It was a moment suspended in time, a brief interlude before the world outside took center stage. The clamor of voices quieted to whispers, and for a heartbeat, I felt a profound connection with everyone around me—an unspoken promise that we were in this together, no matter what Lydia said or thought.

Alex leaned closer, his breath warm against my ear. "You ready?" His eyes sparkled with a mischievous confidence that sent a thrill of excitement coursing through me. I nodded, a smile breaking through the last remnants of anxiety that clung to me.

"Ready as I'll ever be. Just let me know when to step aside so you can swoop in and save the day again."

"Always," he grinned, a flash of determination lighting up his features.

As the music swelled, the energy in the room shifted. Models began to line up, their excitement palpable, laughter mingling with last-minute touch-ups. I watched as Jasmine, now fully composed, slipped into her gown, the silver fabric sparkling under the soft lights like a cascade of stars. She caught my eye and gave a quick thumbs-up, a silent communication of solidarity.

"Alright, everyone!" Carla shouted, her voice slicing through the air with authority. "Positions! Let's make this the show of a lifetime!"

The models filed out, and as the first one stepped onto the runway, the applause erupted from the audience, a roaring wave that surged through the air. My heart raced alongside the claps and cheers, every sound a reminder of why we did this—to create, to inspire, to evoke emotion.

I took my place near the edge of the stage, adrenaline coursing through me, fueled by the palpable energy of the crowd. The lights bathed everything in a warm glow, illuminating the hard work and passion we had poured into every detail of the show. Each model glided down the runway, showcasing the intricate designs that were more than just clothing; they were expressions of dreams and creativity.

The moments passed in a flurry, each model making their mark on the runway, and with each step, my confidence grew. I caught glimpses of Alex moving gracefully among the crew, ensuring everything was executed flawlessly. He caught my eye several times, each glance exchanged sending a silent affirmation of support that filled me with courage.

But just as I began to relax into the rhythm of the night, a sudden gasp echoed through the audience. A model, her face pale with shock, stood frozen at the end of the runway. Her gown, a vivid floral creation, had snagged on a stray piece of equipment, leaving her teetering precariously. A collective inhale swept through the crowd, an unspoken fear that mirrored my own.

"Not again," I breathed, my stomach tightening as I watched Alex spring into action. He moved with purpose, a sleek panther weaving through the chaos, determination etched into every line of his face. "Just breathe, you got this!" he shouted, a lifeline thrown to the model who looked ready to bolt.

But Lydia's voice cut through the air, her tone sharp and derisive. "Fix it! This is unacceptable!" She glared, her frustration visible, as if the success of the show depended solely on this one moment.

The model's eyes widened, and for a heartbeat, everything felt suspended—time itself holding its breath as the audience leaned forward, their collective anticipation palpable. I could see Alex's jaw set, determination mixing with a flicker of exasperation, and I knew he would not let her down.

With a swift motion, he closed the distance, whispering quick instructions to the model while delicately working the fabric free. I could almost see the invisible thread connecting him to her—a silent exchange of trust that somehow transcended the chaos around us.

Then, as if the universe conspired to test us further, the lights flickered ominously, plunging the room into momentary darkness. A collective gasp rippled through the audience, and my heart dropped as I fumbled to catch the edge of the stage for balance. Just as suddenly, the emergency lights flickered on, casting an eerie glow that made everything feel surreal.

In that moment of confusion, a shadow moved in the periphery of my vision. Lydia's silhouette darted toward the circuit panel, her movements frantic, panic replacing her usual icy demeanor. "What are you doing?" I yelled, my voice straining against the chaos.

"Fixing this!" she shot back, her voice taut with frustration.

The audience was restless, a murmur of concern rippling through the crowd. I turned my attention back to Alex and the model, who still teetered at the end of the runway, hope mixed with despair in her eyes.

And then, just when it seemed like we might regain control, a loud pop reverberated through the air, followed by the shattering sound of glass breaking. My heart raced as I glanced toward the direction of the noise, only to see one of the overhead lights had burst, raining shards down like shooting stars.

"Everyone, get back!" I shouted, panic lacing my words as I rushed toward Alex, who was still bent over the model, shielding her from the chaos erupting around us. The glinting shards fell like confetti, and in that moment, a sense of dread unfurled within me, twisting tightly around my gut.

As I reached them, I felt a sharp pain slice through my arm, and a gasp escaped my lips. Blood trickled down, warm and vivid against my skin. I glanced down, shock coursing through me as I registered the source—a shard had caught me.

"Are you okay?" Alex's voice broke through the tumult, full of concern, but his gaze flickered to the chaos around us, a growing anxiety surfacing in his eyes.

Before I could respond, Lydia shouted something incomprehensible, her voice rising above the chaos. I could see her, frantically waving her arms as if orchestrating a mad symphony.

And then, as I caught Alex's worried gaze, everything shifted again. The audience was on their feet, a sea of faces contorted in alarm, and it dawned on me—the night we had fought so hard to salvage was slipping through our fingers like sand.

"Get ready!" I yelled to Alex, adrenaline pushing me forward as I reached for the microphone, hoping to calm the rising panic. "We're not done yet!"

But as I opened my mouth to speak, the lights flickered one last time before plunging us into darkness again. The collective gasp of the audience echoed in the void, and just as my pulse quickened with fear, I heard a voice—low and menacing—cutting through the panic.

"Let's see just how well you handle this."

The darkness swallowed everything, and a shiver raced down my spine. As my heart thundered in my chest, I realized that the night was far from over, and the true test of our resilience had only just begun.

Chapter 26: Unraveling Threads

The air in my studio is thick with the scent of fresh fabric, each bolt unspooling like my thoughts. Swatches of silk and cotton are strewn across the room, vivid colors fighting for attention amid the chaos of my sketchbook, where ideas overlap in a frenzied dance. Each line I draw feels like a whisper of hope against the cacophony of doubt that has nested itself in the corners of my mind. I stand in front of my latest creation, a dress that mirrors the tumult within me—a riot of colors, swirling patterns, and delicate lace accents that clash beautifully in a way that somehow feels right.

The night of the show still plays in my head like a broken record. Moments flash through my memory: the applause ringing in my ears, Lydia's icy stare piercing through the crowd, and Alex's strained smile that felt more like a grimace. It's maddening how a single event could unravel so many threads—my confidence, our connection, the dream we built together. I glance at the unfinished dress hanging in the corner, an echo of my inner turmoil. I long to pour every feeling into it, to stitch my emotions into the seams and create something magnificent from the wreckage.

"Hey, you," Alex's voice breaks through my reverie, smooth and warm as ever, but I sense a hesitation behind his words. He leans against the doorframe, arms crossed, and I can't help but notice how the lines of worry crease his brow. "You've been holed up in here for days."

"Just trying to bring my visions to life," I reply, trying to keep my tone light, but it comes out sharper than I intended. "You know how it is."

He steps inside, the weight of his presence somehow grounding yet disconcerting. "I get it, but you're avoiding me."

The accusation hangs in the air, a tension so palpable it almost crackles. I turn away, my fingers brushing over the swatches as if they could provide comfort. "I'm not avoiding you. I just—" I pause, searching for the right words. "I'm trying to sort through everything."

"Everything? Or just what happened with Lydia?" He approaches, concern replacing the tension in his posture. "You can't let her get under your skin like this."

I spin around to face him, frustration bubbling over. "It's not just Lydia, Alex! It's the pressure, the expectations, and what happened on stage. I don't know how to be both a designer and a person in this industry."

He watches me, his eyes softening. "You are both. You just need to find a balance. We can figure this out together." His voice is steady, reassuring, but it feels like a fragile promise, teetering on the edge of a precipice.

"Together," I repeat, the word feeling foreign on my tongue. I want to believe it, yet doubt lingers like an unwelcome guest. "But what if we can't?"

"Then we'll fight to make it work." He steps closer, and I can see the sincerity in his gaze, yet something still feels off. "That's what partners do, right?"

A flicker of warmth ignites in my chest, but the shadows of uncertainty dampen it. "What if we're too caught up in our own worlds to really see each other anymore?" The words slip out, raw and unfiltered.

His expression falters, and for a moment, I wonder if I've crossed an invisible line. "I don't want that. I don't want to lose you, Amelia." His voice drops to a whisper, heavy with vulnerability.

I want to reach out, to bridge the growing chasm between us, but fear coils in my stomach like a serpent. "I don't want to lose you either."

A silence stretches between us, thick and unyielding. It's as if the walls of the studio are closing in, and I can feel the weight of the unspoken truths hanging in the air like a dark cloud. The joy we once shared now feels like a distant memory, overshadowed by the chaos that surrounds us.

"Can we go somewhere?" he finally suggests, breaking the tension with a spark of spontaneity. "Just for a bit? Get out of our heads."

I contemplate the idea, the thought of leaving the sanctuary of my studio appealing yet daunting. The outside world is loud and chaotic, a stark contrast to the cocoon I've built here. But perhaps it's time to step out, to breathe in the air of possibility instead of the suffocating stillness of doubt. "Okay," I agree slowly, letting the decision wash over me like a gentle tide.

He grins, and in that moment, the tension between us seems to dissolve, if only for an instant. "Let's grab coffee at that little place by the waterfront. I've been meaning to take you there."

The thought of a warm drink and a change of scenery fills me with a flicker of excitement. "Sounds perfect."

We step outside into the bright daylight, the sun casting long shadows on the pavement. The world is alive, bustling with people and sounds, a stark reminder of the life waiting beyond my fabric-strewn sanctuary. As we walk side by side, I steal glances at him, trying to memorize the way the light plays in his hair, the lines of his smile that make my heart race despite the weight of uncertainty still hanging between us.

"I hope the coffee's good," he muses, breaking the comfortable silence. "Or else I'm going to regret dragging you out."

"Oh please, it's coffee. It's practically a universal truth that coffee is good, even when it's bad," I reply with a playful smirk, feeling the familiar banter ease the tension.

He chuckles, a sound that feels like a balm against the lingering worries. "I'll hold you to that. If it's terrible, we're getting pastries to make up for it."

"Deal," I say, the promise of indulgence adding a sweetness to the air.

Yet as we approach the café, my heart beats a little faster, caught between the hope of rekindling our connection and the fear of what lies ahead. What if this outing doesn't solve anything? What if we're merely delaying the inevitable? The thought nags at me like a persistent itch, but I shake it off. For now, I choose to savor this moment, this fragile space between doubt and possibility, where laughter can still weave a thread through the chaos.

The café buzzes with life as we step inside, the air thick with the rich aroma of coffee and the hum of chatter. It's a small, eclectic place adorned with mismatched furniture and local art plastered on the walls—a warm embrace against the chill of uncertainty that has crept into my heart. I scan the room, noting the intimate corners where couples lean in close, sharing secrets over steaming mugs, and a group of friends erupting into laughter, their joy a stark contrast to my internal turmoil.

"Okay, what's your go-to order?" Alex asks, glancing at the chalkboard menu above the counter, his brow furrowing as if it holds the secrets of the universe.

"I'm a simple girl," I reply, nudging him playfully. "A caramel macchiato, no extra foam. And maybe a slice of that chocolate cake. It's basically a requirement."

"Chocolate cake for breakfast? You're living the dream." He chuckles, shaking his head as he steps up to the counter, his expression lightening. "I'll have what she's having, minus the cake, unless you want to share."

The barista, a bright-eyed woman with a colorful sleeve of tattoos, nods enthusiastically as she takes our orders. I watch her deft hands as she measures out the coffee, and for a moment, I'm lost in the rhythm of her movements. It's mesmerizing, almost like the art of sewing—each gesture precise, each ingredient vital.

When our drinks are ready, we find a small table near the window, sunlight spilling across the worn wooden surface, illuminating the creases in Alex's shirt. He looks different here, more relaxed, his usual tension ebbing away like a tide pulling back from the shore.

"Cheers to new beginnings," he raises his cup, and I can't help but smile at his earnestness.

"Cheers," I echo, clinking my cup against his, the sound bright and clear, slicing through the residual shadows of the past few days.

We take a sip, and I close my eyes, allowing the warm caramel to coat my tongue. "Okay, you were right. This is good. I'm glad you dragged me out."

He grins, a flash of mischief sparking in his eyes. "See? I do have my moments."

"So, tell me—what's been going on with you? I feel like I've been buried under fabric and fears, and I barely even know what you're thinking."

He leans back in his chair, the smile fading as he seems to sift through his thoughts. "It's just... the show threw me off. Lydia's comments, the way she undermined your work, it made me realize how cutthroat this world can be."

I nod, understanding his frustration but wishing I could ease the tension knotting in his shoulders. "I'm still processing everything. I know Lydia's always been tough, but I didn't expect her to go for the jugular."

Alex looks out the window, a thoughtful expression washing over his face. "You're so talented, Amelia. It's infuriating to see someone trying to dim your light. You deserve the accolades, not her petty attempts to knock you down."

"Thanks," I say, warmth blooming in my chest at his words. "It means a lot to hear you say that, especially when I'm feeling so... unmoored."

He meets my gaze, his eyes piercing through the haze of self-doubt. "You're not unmoored; you're just navigating rough waters. And I'm here with you. We'll chart our course together."

Just then, a loud laugh draws our attention to a nearby table where a group of friends are animatedly discussing their weekend plans. One of them, a tall woman with bright red hair and a contagious smile, catches my eye and winks at me. I can't help but smile back, and the moment feels refreshing, a reminder of the world beyond my worries.

"What?" Alex asks, following my gaze.

"Nothing," I say, though the corners of my mouth lift involuntarily. "Just reminded me that life exists outside of stress and deadlines."

"Right? I think we need to embrace more of that," he muses, his own smile returning. "Like maybe planning a spontaneous getaway. Just us."

The suggestion hangs in the air, tantalizing and almost too good to be true. "A getaway? Where would we even go?" I ask, my heart quickening at the thought.

"Anywhere. Somewhere we can breathe, explore, and forget about the pressure for a little while."

The notion is intoxicating—a heady mix of excitement and fear. "But what about work? The collection? It's due soon."

"Sometimes you have to step back to step forward," he replies, his voice steady. "I know it feels like everything is riding on this, but creativity can't thrive in a vacuum. We need to recharge."

I take a deep breath, the weight of his words sinking in. Maybe he's right. Perhaps this moment of escape could lead to clarity, inspiration, or at the very least, a brief respite from the turmoil swirling around us. "Okay, let's do it," I find myself saying before I can overthink the decision.

"Really?" His eyes widen in delight. "You're not just saying that to humor me?"

"No, I mean it," I say, a grin spreading across my face. "But you have to promise me we won't talk about work the whole time. I want to relax, enjoy some sunsets, maybe even get a little lost."

"Deal," he laughs, the sound brightening the dim corners of the café. "I'll be the best adventure partner you could ask for. We'll get lost, eat questionable food, and make bad decisions. You know, the usual."

"Great," I tease, raising an eyebrow. "As long as none of those decisions involve jumping out of an airplane."

"Noted. Grounded adventures only," he says, holding up his hands in mock surrender.

As we exchange playful banter, I feel the tension easing between us, the fabric of our relationship slowly stitching itself back together. Yet just beneath the surface, I can't shake the feeling that this newfound connection is fragile, like a delicate piece of lace threatened by the slightest breeze.

Then, without warning, the café door swings open, and a familiar figure strides in—Lydia, the very embodiment of elegance and poise, dressed in a tailored blazer that screams authority. My heart sinks, the air turning heavy with apprehension as she scans the room, her eyes landing on us with a predatory glint.

"Amelia," she calls out, her voice syrupy sweet yet laced with something sharp. "What a delightful surprise to see you here."

I glance at Alex, whose expression shifts instantly, the lightness of our moment evaporating. He meets my gaze, an unspoken agreement passing between us—this isn't over. Not yet.

The warmth of the café is swiftly overshadowed by Lydia's presence, as if a storm has rolled in, blocking out the sun. Her perfectly coiffed hair bounces with each step, a vivid contrast to the lively ambiance, and her sharp gaze slices through the laughter and chatter, landing squarely on us. There's a flash of something akin to triumph in her eyes, and my heart sinks.

"Amelia," she calls out again, her voice dripping with that sickly-sweet tone I've come to loathe. "What a delightful surprise to see you here."

I can feel Alex tense beside me, the jovial atmosphere evaporating like steam from a freshly brewed cup. He straightens, the easy banter we were just sharing replaced by a palpable unease.

"Lydia," I manage, trying to keep my voice steady, though it quivers slightly at the edges. "What brings you here?"

"Just stopping in for a quick coffee before another meeting," she replies, glancing at Alex with a smirk that makes my skin crawl. "I hope you're not distracting him from more important things."

Alex's jaw tightens, and I can see him wrestling with the urge to defend me. "We're just catching up, Lydia. There's nothing wrong with that."

"Oh, but there is," she counters, her smile never reaching her eyes. "You two are quite the little duo, aren't you? I would hate to see your ambitions hindered by... frivolous distractions."

I want to retort, to launch into a witty comeback that would leave her speechless, but the words fizzle in my throat. Instead, I feel like I'm caught in a net, unable to break free. "We're handling things just fine, thanks," I say, mustering a hint of defiance.

Her laugh is high and sharp, like the crack of a whip. "Oh, sweet Amelia, your naïveté is almost charming. But in this industry, appearances can be deceiving. You need to be careful who you align yourself with."

I glance at Alex, his brows furrowed in frustration. "I think Amelia is doing just fine on her own," he retorts, an edge to his voice that surprises me. It's nice to see him stand up for me, but I can also feel the tension escalating like a balloon ready to burst.

"Is she?" Lydia replies, leaning forward slightly, her voice dripping with faux concern. "I thought her designs were a bit too... pedestrian for the show. I'm surprised you haven't realized that, Alex."

The jab feels like a punch to the gut. I can't tell if Lydia is genuinely concerned or just relishing in the power she holds over us. "You know, you should really consider taking a step back and letting others shine," I shoot back, surprising myself with the boldness of my words.

Lydia raises an eyebrow, clearly unaccustomed to being challenged. "Oh, sweetie, you're cute when you're feisty. But we both know that in this game, cute doesn't cut it."

"Maybe you should try being cute instead of catty," I snap, the heat rising in my cheeks. Alex shifts in his seat, clearly caught between admiration and worry.

"Amelia," he begins, but I wave him off, determined to stand my ground.

"Lydia, you're the queen of undermining. If you spent as much time promoting others as you do tearing them down, maybe you'd actually help someone for once."

The silence that follows feels charged, the tension so thick it could be sliced with a knife. Lydia's expression shifts, a flicker of anger passing through her carefully constructed facade. "I'll give you credit for bravery, Amelia," she says, her voice low and dangerous. "But be careful. Bravery in this business can be just as dangerous as stupidity."

With that, she turns on her heel, striding out of the café as if she owns the place. The door swings shut behind her with a definitive thud, leaving us in a stunned silence.

"Well, that was delightful," I say, attempting to lighten the mood, though my heart races in my chest. "Who knew she had such a flair for the dramatic?"

Alex chuckles, though it's tinged with concern. "You really stood your ground back there. I'm proud of you."

"Thanks," I reply, though I can feel the unease creeping back. "But I'm also terrified of what she'll do next."

"Don't let her get to you," he insists, leaning forward with a fierce intensity. "You're better than her. You don't need her approval."

"I know," I say, but the words sound hollow. It's easy to say that when you're not the one facing her wrath. "But this is more than just a petty feud. It's my career on the line."

"Then let's use that fire," he urges, a spark of inspiration lighting his eyes. "What if we took the idea of a getaway and made it a working retreat? We can brainstorm and recharge, but also come back stronger. We can push back against Lydia's negativity together."

The notion sends a jolt of energy through me. "You mean, like a creative boot camp?"

"Exactly," he nods, enthusiasm pouring from him like the coffee we'd just downed. "We find a quiet place, immerse ourselves in nature, and just—create. No distractions, no Lydia looming over us."

It sounds enticing, almost like a dreamscape where we can regain our footing. "Okay, I'm in. But I still want cake for breakfast."

Alex laughs, the tension in his shoulders relaxing just a fraction. "Of course, cake for breakfast is non-negotiable."

As we share a moment of laughter, the door swings open again, and I glance over my shoulder, half-expecting Lydia to storm back in. Instead, a man walks in, his presence immediately commanding attention. Tall and broad-shouldered, with tousled dark hair and an easy smile, he exudes a confidence that feels almost magnetic.

He strides toward us, an unmistakable glint of recognition in his eyes. "Amelia? Is that you?"

"Uh, yes?" I reply, confusion knitting my brows together. "Do I know you?"

His smile widens, and he reaches our table. "It's Ethan—Ethan Greene. We met at the last design expo, remember? I was with the team that showcased the sustainable fabrics?"

A rush of memory floods back, and I nod, recalling his friendly demeanor and infectious enthusiasm for eco-friendly design. "Oh! Yes, I remember now. How are you?"

"Doing great! I just moved back to the city and was actually hoping to connect with you again. I saw your collection at the show, and it was incredible."

"Thanks," I say, a swell of pride rising within me. "I'm still recovering from it, to be honest."

Alex watches the exchange, an unreadable expression on his face as Ethan leans against the table. "Any chance you're free to discuss a collaboration? I think we could create something amazing together."

The offer hangs in the air, tempting and thrilling. My heart races with possibilities, but my mind spins with the weight of everything else happening around me. "Wow, that's... unexpected. I'd love to hear more."

"Great!" Ethan replies, his enthusiasm palpable. "Let's grab a drink sometime this week. I can share my ideas, and maybe we can brainstorm some innovative designs."

Before I can respond, Alex clears his throat, his voice cutting through the excitement. "Actually, Amelia has a full plate right now."

Ethan's smile falters for a moment, his gaze flickering between us, the shift in dynamics palpable. "Oh, really? I didn't mean to intrude."

"It's not an intrusion," I interject, sensing the tension rising. "I'm definitely interested, but I also have a lot on my mind right now."

"Sure, no pressure," Ethan says, though I can see the disappointment shadowing his features. "I just thought it might be a good opportunity."

As he takes a step back, the weight of the moment settles in. I want to explore this potential collaboration, but the thought of

Lydia's looming presence, combined with my complicated feelings about Alex, pulls me in different directions.

"Let me think it over, and I'll get back to you," I say, trying to keep my voice steady.

Ethan nods, his smile returning, though it doesn't quite reach his eyes. "Absolutely. Just let me know!" With a final wave, he turns and exits the café, leaving me in a whirlwind of emotions.

Alex shifts in his seat, a deep breath escaping his lips. "That was unexpected."

"Yeah," I reply, my heart racing as I process what just happened. "But now I have to figure out how to navigate all of this."

"Do you think you'll take him up on the offer?" he asks, a hint of concern creeping into his voice.

"I don't know," I admit, glancing out the window where Ethan's figure disappears into the bustling street. "But it feels like another complication I didn't need right now."

Just as I'm about to voice my uncertainty, the café door swings open again, and the world seems to come crashing back in. The sound of muffled conversation rises like an unseen wave, crashing into the fragile moment we've been trying to build.

But it's not just the noise that pulls me back—it's the figure that steps through the doorway. Lydia, again, this time flanked by two

Chapter 27: Fractured Bonds

A gray haze settled over the city like an unwelcome blanket, casting everything in muted shades as I sat on the worn leather couch of our shared apartment. The coffee table was cluttered with half-finished sketches and crumpled pages filled with frantic notes, remnants of late-night brainstorming sessions turned silent standoffs. I could hear the scratch of Alex's pencil against paper, each stroke punctuating the air with tension. It was a familiar rhythm, one I had come to find both comforting and maddening, like the distant roar of traffic muffled by thick walls.

I stole a glance at him, his brow furrowed in concentration, a lone strand of dark hair falling across his forehead. He had always been a picture of focus, his eyes lighting up whenever he dove into a new project. But today, the spark felt dimmed, replaced by an unease that hung between us like a forgotten promise. The easy camaraderie we once shared was buried under layers of unresolved emotions, each of us too stubborn to reach out, yet too aware of the fracture that had begun to spread.

"Hey," I ventured, my voice barely breaking through the oppressive silence. He looked up, the light in his eyes flickering briefly before he returned to his work. My heart sank; this wasn't how I envisioned our partnership. We had dreamed of creating together, not this awkward dance of avoidance. "Do you think we should talk about... everything?"

He sighed, setting his pencil down with a deliberation that felt heavy with unspoken words. "What's there to talk about? It's pretty clear we're both busy." His tone was sharp, like a knife slipping through the delicate fabric of our connection.

I felt the words welling up, a tidal wave of frustration and hurt. "Busy? Is that all this is to you? Just... work?" I took a breath, trying to keep my voice steady. "It feels like we're both just pretending everything is fine while it's falling apart."

"Pretending? You think I'm pretending?" His voice rose, echoing in the small space, and I could see the muscles in his jaw tense. "What do you want from me, then? A heartfelt discussion about our feelings while we're both knee-deep in deadlines?"

I opened my mouth to respond, but nothing came out. My stomach twisted. He was right; the deadlines loomed over us like storm clouds, threatening to unleash a deluge if we didn't find a way to navigate this. Yet, the heart of the matter was buried beneath our projects, like the twisted roots of a tree hidden under the earth.

"Look," I said, forcing calm into my voice, "I don't want to fight. But it feels like we're drifting apart, and I don't know how to fix it."

His eyes softened for a moment, a flicker of vulnerability breaking through his defensive wall. "I don't know either," he admitted, his voice lowering. "I just... I don't want to mess things up more than they already are."

The admission hung in the air, heavy and raw, but before I could respond, a sudden burst of frustration welled up in me. "Then let's stop dancing around it! We're not just co-workers; we're partners! When did we stop caring about each other?"

The word "partners" echoed between us, a bittersweet reminder of all we had built together. I could see the internal struggle flickering across Alex's face, a storm of emotion brewing behind his usually calm demeanor. "Maybe we need a break," he said finally, each word laden with the weight of finality.

A chill ran through me at his suggestion. "A break? From what? From each other?" My heart raced, a cacophony of panic and disbelief. "Is that really what you want?"

He looked away, a shadow crossing his features as he struggled with the implications of his own words. "I don't know what I want right now. Everything feels so... overwhelming."

In that moment, a familiar voice echoed in my head—Ethan's calm reassurance, urging me to confront the issues before they spiraled out of control. Yet here I was, facing the man I loved, and all I could muster was a sense of impending loss. "I can't believe you'd rather walk away than face this with me."

"Walking away isn't the answer!" he snapped, frustration spilling over. "I'm just saying... maybe space is what we need."

The words struck me like a slap, sending a pulse of hurt through my chest. "Space? So you can just avoid everything?" I stood up abruptly, feeling the heat of anger surge through me. "You're running away, Alex! We're in this together!"

He stood up too, the tension in the room thickening like smoke. "I'm not running away! I'm trying to figure out how to breathe without suffocating under the weight of it all."

"Breathing isn't the problem; it's the ignoring!" I shouted, my voice rising as I gestured wildly to the scattered papers, the remnants of our dreams now gathering dust. "We can't just ignore the reality of what we've built!"

"Maybe we should have thought about that before everything fell apart!" His voice cracked, each word laced with frustration and sorrow, and suddenly the argument felt like an avalanche, too big to stop.

I could feel my heart pounding in my chest, the suffocating weight of our unresolved issues bearing down on me. "I can't keep pretending everything is fine when it isn't!" I was breathless, caught in a whirlwind of emotion. "Maybe I should just go."

Before he could respond, I turned on my heel, the door swinging shut behind me with a resounding finality. As I stepped into the cool air, I felt the sting of tears threatening to spill over. The world outside seemed oblivious to the chaos that churned within me, the streets bustling with life while I felt utterly alone.

Each step away from the apartment felt like I was shedding pieces of myself, the connection I had with Alex unraveling thread by thread. I needed to escape the weight of it all, to find solace in the vibrant chaos of the city. I didn't know where I was going, only that I had to keep moving—away from the silence that had taken root in our hearts, away from the uncertainty that lingered like a dark cloud.

The city was a living organism, a blend of color and chaos that enveloped me as I stepped into the evening air. I wandered aimlessly, my heart racing like the traffic that whizzed past. Each car seemed to embody the frantic rhythm of my thoughts, blurring together as I fought against the wave of emotions threatening to drown me. The streets pulsed with life; laughter spilled out of nearby cafes, the aroma of food wafted through the air, but I felt like a ghost, haunting a world that had suddenly become foreign.

With each step, I tried to shake off the weight of the argument, the raw edges of our disagreement still stinging like fresh cuts. I needed a distraction, something to pull me out of my spiraling thoughts. As I turned a corner, I found myself drawn to a small art gallery tucked away between two larger buildings. Its warm light spilled onto the sidewalk, illuminating a sign that read "Opening Night: Local Artists." The invitation felt like a siren call, promising a reprieve from the internal storm brewing inside me.

Inside, the gallery was filled with vibrant canvases that screamed for attention. I could feel the pulse of creativity in the air, a stark contrast to the suffocating silence of my apartment. I wandered through the exhibits, letting the colors wash over me, hoping to lose myself in someone else's vision. Each piece told a story—wild brush strokes captured emotions I could barely articulate, and surreal images seemed to mirror my own tangled thoughts.

As I meandered deeper into the gallery, I bumped into a familiar face. Ethan stood there, an uncharacteristically serious expression on his face as he admired a piece that depicted a stormy sea. "Hey,

I didn't expect to see you here," he said, his tone lightening as he recognized me. "This is a little different from your usual escape, isn't it?"

"Yeah, well, I needed a change of scenery," I replied, forcing a smile that didn't quite reach my eyes. "Also, my usual escape was a bit too... complicated."

"Ah, the complexities of adult relationships," he said, rolling his eyes with an exaggerated flair. "Like trying to assemble IKEA furniture without the instructions—nobody really knows what they're doing."

His humor was a balm, easing the tension in my chest. "Right? One moment you're all excited about building something together, and the next, you're just staring at a pile of screws, wondering where it all went wrong."

Ethan chuckled, but then his expression softened. "You want to talk about it? I mean, you're here, so it must be serious."

I sighed, torn between wanting to vent and fearing that spilling my heart would only lead to more complications. "It's just... Alex and I had a fight. A big one. Like, the kind that makes you wonder if you've even known the person for as long as you thought."

"Those moments can be brutal. You start questioning everything," he said, his tone shifting to one of understanding. "But maybe those fights are necessary. They can force you to confront the real issues, like peeling back the layers of an onion—painful, but sometimes worth it."

I nodded, contemplating his analogy. "Peeling back layers... right. But what if you peel back too much and end up with nothing but a mushy mess?"

"Then you grab some chips and make salsa," he replied, a mischievous glint in his eye. "Life's too short to get bogged down by mushiness. Besides, sometimes the mess is where the best flavors are."

His wry wit made me laugh, easing some of the tightness in my chest. But as the laughter faded, the weight of my situation returned. "What if the mess is too much for him to handle? What if he decides he'd rather walk away than deal with the chaos?"

"Then he's not the right person for you," Ethan said, his gaze steady and firm. "You deserve someone who wants to weather the storm with you, not someone who runs for cover at the first sign of rain."

His words settled into my mind like the brush of a gentle breeze, carrying a sense of clarity I desperately needed. "But what if I'm the one causing the storm? What if I'm too much?"

"Too much is a compliment in my book," Ethan quipped, crossing his arms. "Life is too short to be anything less than fully yourself. And if he can't handle that, then he doesn't deserve the amazing person you are."

Just then, a loud laugh erupted from the corner of the gallery, drawing our attention. A group of artists was huddled around a particularly outrageous piece that seemed to depict an octopus playing poker. The absurdity made my heart flutter with a mix of disbelief and delight, reminding me that life continued to unfold, artfully chaotic and unpredictable.

"See?" Ethan said, gesturing to the painting. "If they can put a poker-playing octopus on display and still find joy, I think you can muster up the courage to confront your own emotional mess."

"Is that your way of saying I should go back and talk to Alex?" I asked, arching an eyebrow.

"Only if you want to," he replied, shrugging. "But you seem like you need closure. You know where you stand with him, right? This is just a bump in the road, not the end of the journey."

The thought of returning to our apartment filled me with dread, yet something deep inside urged me to confront the silence that lay between us. Maybe Ethan was right. Maybe it was time to peel back those layers and face the storm instead of running from it.

"Okay," I finally said, the decision crystallizing in my mind. "I think I'll head back. Thanks for being my emotional lighthouse in this messy sea."

"Anytime," he replied, grinning. "Just promise me you won't leave him stranded if he's floundering. Love is messy, but it's worth the effort."

With a last look at the vibrant chaos of the gallery, I turned to leave. As I stepped out into the bustling streets once more, the sounds of the city wrapped around me—a cacophony of life that somehow felt comforting. My heart beat a little faster with purpose, and I knew I had to face the chaos head-on.

Each step toward our apartment felt like reclaiming a part of myself that had been lost in the silence. The evening sky darkened overhead, stars flickering to life as if cheering me on, and I realized that whatever awaited me within those four walls, I was ready to confront it. No more running, no more avoiding. Just the messy, chaotic truth of love, waiting for me to dive in.

As I approached our apartment, my heart raced with a mixture of apprehension and determination. The familiar front door loomed ahead, a barrier between the chaotic emotions swirling within me and the silence that had become a palpable presence inside. I paused for a moment, taking a deep breath and steeling myself for the conversation that awaited. The city buzzed around me, life continuing unabated while I felt like I was stepping into an alternate universe, one filled with tension and unresolved feelings.

With a trembling hand, I pushed open the door. The familiar scent of coffee mixed with the faint trace of paint greeted me, a reminder of our shared moments and the dreams we had built together. But now, it felt heavy, burdened by the weight of our last argument. The soft light in the living room highlighted the chaotic mess we'd created in our work, papers strewn about like fragments of our fractured bond.

"Alex?" I called, my voice tentative, unsure if I would be met with silence or the warmth of his presence. The silence stretched, pulling at my nerves. Just as I began to think he might not be home, I heard the faint clatter of something being set down.

"I'm in here," he replied from the kitchen, his voice flat, devoid of its usual warmth.

I stepped further into the apartment, my heart pounding. He emerged from the kitchen, holding a mug of coffee that he didn't seem to want, the steam curling up into the air like ghosts of our past laughter. The tension crackled like electricity between us, and I felt the urge to break the silence before it could solidify into something even more insurmountable.

"I think we need to talk," I said, my voice steadier than I felt. "I don't want to ignore what happened earlier."

He met my gaze, the expression in his eyes a mix of wariness and something deeper—something that felt like regret. "Do we really? I thought we were just going to let it simmer for a while."

"Simmering hasn't worked out so well for us, has it?" I replied, crossing my arms defensively. "Look, I'm not asking for a grand confession or anything, just... some honesty."

He sighed, rubbing the back of his neck as if the weight of the world rested on his shoulders. "Fine. I guess honesty is all we have left, right?"

I took a seat on the edge of the couch, trying to project calm even as my heart raced. "What's really bothering you, Alex? Because I feel like there's something underneath all of this that we haven't addressed."

"Everything," he said, a flicker of frustration igniting in his tone. "It feels like we're both drowning in our projects, and in all this noise, we've lost sight of what we started out to do together."

The sting of his words cut deeper than I expected. "So, you're saying it's my fault? That I'm dragging you down?"

"Not dragging, more like... diverging paths," he replied, a hint of desperation seeping through his calm facade. "I feel like I'm chasing after something, and you're not even sure what you want anymore."

The truth of his statement echoed in my mind, but I didn't want to admit it out loud. "Maybe I'm still figuring it out, but that doesn't mean I want to lose you in the process."

He shook his head, frustration mounting. "And what if losing me is what's best for you? You're talented, passionate. You should be out there, creating something amazing without being tethered to my uncertainty."

His words cut deep, igniting a fire within me. "I'm not here to be your safety net, Alex! I want to support you, but I also need you to meet me halfway. This feels like a battle instead of a partnership."

The air thickened with tension as he stepped closer, and for a moment, I thought he might finally see the heart of the matter. "Do you even want this anymore?" he asked, his voice dropping to a whisper, almost afraid to voice the question.

My breath caught in my throat. "Of course I do! But it feels like we're constantly on the edge, like one wrong word will send us both tumbling over."

"Maybe we're already tumbling," he said, his eyes searching mine, a vulnerability cracking through the bravado. "Maybe this is just the reality of who we are now."

I felt the ground shift beneath me, as if the very foundation of what we had built was teetering on the brink of collapse. "And what if I refuse to accept that?" I shot back, my voice fierce. "What if I want to fight for what we have, even if it's messy and complicated?"

He stepped back, his expression unreadable. "Then fight, but know that I might not be here when the dust settles."

His words landed like a heavy weight between us, and I could feel the tremors of fear echoing in my chest. I opened my mouth to respond, but a sudden crash from the living room interrupted us, jolting us both into action.

"What was that?" I exclaimed, my pulse racing again, but this time it was a mixture of dread and confusion.

"I don't know," he replied, his eyes wide with surprise. "It sounded like it came from your work area."

Without thinking, I dashed down the hall toward the sound, Alex following close behind. My heart raced, an odd mix of anxiety and curiosity propelling me forward. When I reached my workspace, the sight that greeted me made my stomach drop.

Papers were strewn everywhere, the weight of the fallen shelf clearly visible. But more alarming was the figure standing in the middle of the chaos, a familiar face framed by the dim light of the setting sun filtering through the window.

"Ethan?" I blurted, incredulity flooding my voice. "What are you doing here?"

He turned, a sheepish grin on his face that did little to ease the tension in the air. "Uh, just trying to check on you two lovebirds. Looks like I stumbled into a bit of a situation."

Before I could respond, he motioned behind him, and I felt my heart plummet as I saw what lay in his hands. "I thought I could help clear some space, but, um, I think I might have accidentally broken the shelf."

I glanced at Alex, whose expression had shifted from frustration to shock. "You came here to help? You didn't think to text first?"

Ethan shrugged, the grin slipping slightly. "I thought it was more of a 'show, don't tell' moment."

"Show? You mean break?" I interjected, feeling the tension morph into something lighter, yet still heavy with the weight of unspoken words.

Suddenly, a knock echoed from the door, startling all of us. I glanced at Alex, our eyes wide with a mix of dread and curiosity. "Who else could it be?" he murmured, a hint of anxiety creeping back into his tone.

Before I could voice my own concerns, I crossed the room to answer the door, my heart pounding with a mix of trepidation and anticipation. I opened it slowly, the cool air brushing against my face, and stared into the eyes of an unexpected visitor whose presence would send ripples through everything we thought we knew.

"Hey, I know this is a bad time," the figure said, their voice low and tense, "but we need to talk. Now."

As they stepped into the light, the truth of their words hung heavy in the air, the potential for upheaval brewing just beneath the surface. In that moment, with the three of us standing in a room laden with unfinished conversations and precarious emotions, I knew that nothing would ever be the same again.

Chapter 28: Finding My Voice

The sunlight filtered through the wide-open window of my studio, dancing off the bolts of fabric scattered around like a technicolor explosion. The scent of freshly cut cotton mingled with the faint aroma of coffee brewing in the corner, creating an intoxicating blend that settled into my bones like a warm hug. I perched on the edge of my well-loved sewing machine, fingers itching to bring my visions to life. Each thread that slipped through my fingers felt like an extension of my very being, a way to weave my emotions into something tangible, something beautiful. The fight with Jonah still echoed in my mind, but as I began to stitch, the world around me started to blur, the noise fading to a comforting hum.

"Okay, you dramatic piece of fabric," I murmured to a vibrant emerald silk that lay before me, "let's see what kind of magic we can create together." I pressed the foot pedal, and the machine whirred to life, the rhythmic sound quickly becoming a soothing mantra. With every stitch, I felt myself shedding the heaviness of that confrontation, the shadows of doubt lifting with each pass of the needle.

The designs began to flow naturally, shapes and colors emerging like an abstract painting coming to life. I envisioned a collection that was both bold and delicate, much like my journey. Each piece told a story—one of resilience, of transformation. I pulled a piece of fabric closer, its texture whispering promises of elegance and strength. It was time to create something that spoke of my past while celebrating the woman I was becoming. I wanted each design to shimmer with authenticity, a snapshot of my evolution.

Hours passed, my studio turning into a whirlwind of creativity. I layered fabrics, mixing textures and patterns, crafting pieces that felt like extensions of myself. I channeled my hurt and confusion into each cut and seam, feeling the catharsis wash over me like a gentle tide. The outside world faded into oblivion as I was lost in my creation. The memory of Jonah's angry words lingered, but they became less of a burden and more of a catalyst, pushing me to explore what I truly wanted.

When I stepped back to survey my work, a sense of pride swelled within me. I could see the collection taking shape—a symphony of colors and emotions that perfectly encapsulated my journey. With a lightness in my heart, I grabbed my sketchbook, eager to plan the pop-up event that would unveil my creations to the world. The idea fluttered in my mind like a firefly in the dark, illuminating the path ahead. It wouldn't just be an event; it would be a celebration of growth, a testament to my resilience.

As I scribbled down ideas, the sound of footsteps approaching pulled me from my thoughts. I glanced up to see my best friend, Tara, hovering in the doorway, her arms crossed and a knowing smirk on her face. She had that uncanny ability to read my moods, to see beyond the surface.

"Diving deep into the creative abyss again, are we?" she teased, stepping inside and gesturing at the chaos surrounding me. "You're going to need a life raft soon if you keep this up."

"More like a flotation device," I shot back, laughing as I tossed a scrap of fabric her way. "You know me, all or nothing. If I don't drown in my art, what else am I going to do?"

Tara rolled her eyes, picking up a shimmering piece of satin. "You could always try having a normal social life, you know. Or maybe actually talk to Jonah about what happened."

The mention of his name sent a wave of unease through me. Jonah and I had been like fireworks—explosive, vibrant, but inevitably fleeting. Our fight had cut deeper than I had expected, leaving behind a tangle of unresolved feelings. "I don't know, Tara," I replied slowly, feeling the familiar tension grip my chest. "Every time I think about it, I just... I don't know if we can come back from this."

Tara softened, her expression shifting to one of understanding. "You don't always have to come back, you know. Sometimes moving forward is what really counts."

She moved closer, picking up my sketchbook and flipping through the pages. "These are incredible," she said, her eyes lighting up with excitement. "You've really captured something special here. This pop-up idea, it's genius. You have to do it."

Her enthusiasm was infectious, and as she continued to flip through my designs, I felt a swell of determination rising within me. "You're right. I'm going to do this, and I'm going to do it my way. No distractions, no regrets."

"Now that's the spirit!" Tara beamed, her smile wide enough to light up the entire room. "Let's turn this studio into a runway. I'll help you plan, and we'll make sure everyone knows it's your time to shine."

The thought sent a thrill through me. My heart raced at the idea of showcasing my work, sharing my story with the world. I could almost envision the lights dimming, the excitement of the crowd, the whispers of admiration as they took in my creations. It was a far cry from the fear and doubt that had once plagued me.

The two of us spent the next few hours brainstorming, laughter punctuating our ideas as we fleshed out the details. The tension of my earlier confrontation began to melt away, replaced by a sense of purpose. The fear that had held me captive now became a flicker of motivation, a reminder that my journey was only just beginning. I wasn't ready to fade into the background, not when I had so much to say, so much to create.

With each plan we set in motion, the light inside me grew brighter, illuminating the shadows that had lingered for far too long. The world was waiting, and I was ready to make my mark, stitch by stitch, heart and soul.

The days drifted by in a kaleidoscope of creativity, each sunrise bringing with it fresh ideas and a renewed sense of purpose. Tara and I worked side by side, our laughter echoing against the walls of my studio as we transformed it into a sanctuary of color and ambition. The fabric swatches grew more vibrant, each choice reflecting a piece of my heart.

"Okay, so what about the name?" Tara asked one afternoon, her brow furrowed in thought as she balanced a stack of sketches in one hand while rummaging through a bag of buttons with the other. "You can't just call it 'Stuff I Made.' That's like the least inspiring title ever. It needs pizzazz!"

"Pizzazz, huh?" I leaned back, crossing my arms and feigning a contemplative look. "How about 'The Art of Fabrication'? No, wait—'Sewn from the Soul'? Too pretentious?"

Tara rolled her eyes, tossing a button at my forehead. "If you keep naming things like that, you'll have a collection full of phrases that sound like they belong on a motivational poster. Let's keep it relatable, not like you're giving a TED Talk on fabric."

I chuckled, the absurdity of it all lifting my spirits further. "Fine, fine. How about 'Stitching My Truth'? It hints at my journey without being too on-the-nose."

"Now we're cooking!" Tara clapped her hands together, the sound echoing like a victory cheer. "It's catchy and personal. Perfect."

Once we settled on a name, it felt like a weight had been lifted, and I poured all my energy into finalizing the designs for the event. With each piece, I was telling a story, weaving my experiences into the fabric. There were dresses that flared like wildflowers in spring, playful and unrestrained, and more structured pieces that mirrored the strength I had cultivated within myself.

As the event date loomed closer, I felt a mixture of excitement and apprehension bubbling within me. I hadn't shown my work to anyone beyond Tara, and the thought of unveiling my creations to the world felt like standing on the edge of a diving board, peering into the deep unknown.

One evening, I decided to step away from my sewing machine and take a walk to clear my mind. The streets were alive with the sounds of chatter and laughter, the city bustling in a way that made my heart swell with hope. I passed by a small café, its outdoor seating filled with friends sharing stories and cups of steaming coffee. The warm light spilling from the windows created a cozy ambiance, inviting me in.

I settled at a table in the corner, ordering a mocha that arrived adorned with a heart in the froth, a sweet touch that made me smile. As I took a sip, the rich chocolate danced across my palate, and I felt a sudden pang of nostalgia for simpler times. Back when my biggest worry was whether my favorite band would drop a new album. Now, the stakes felt higher, the world's expectations pressing down on my shoulders.

Just as I was beginning to lose myself in thought, the familiar sound of a deep voice broke through my reverie. "Fancy seeing you here."

I looked up to find Jonah standing at the entrance, the light framing him like a cinematic moment I had seen in a film. My heart skipped a beat, a cocktail of emotions swirling in my chest.

"Uh, hey," I managed, setting my mug down with a slight tremor. "I didn't expect to run into you."

"Clearly, I'm not the only one trying to escape reality," he said, a playful smile tugging at the corners of his mouth. He gestured to the empty seat across from me. "Mind if I join?"

I hesitated, a storm of thoughts crashing around in my head. We had left things unresolved, the tension still crackling like static in the air. But the part of me that longed for closure couldn't resist the opportunity. "Sure, why not?"

He slid into the chair, and for a moment, we were simply two people sharing a space, the past swirling around us like a lingering fog. "So, how's the world of fashion treating you?" Jonah asked, a hint of genuine curiosity in his eyes.

"It's been a whirlwind, to be honest," I replied, trying to maintain a light tone. "I'm actually preparing for a pop-up event. It's been a bit chaotic, but exciting."

"Really? That's amazing!" He leaned forward, interest sparkling in his gaze. "What's it called?"

"'Stitching My Truth,'" I said, watching as his expression shifted from surprise to admiration. "It's about my journey, my growth, everything I've been through."

"Sounds powerful," he said softly, his tone turning more serious. "I'd love to see it."

The sincerity in his voice sent a wave of warmth through me, but it was quickly overshadowed by the recollection of our fight. I took a deep breath, willing myself to focus on the moment. "Well, I guess you'll have to come. It's in a couple of weeks."

He nodded, and for a brief moment, our eyes locked, an unspoken understanding passing between us. But just as quickly, I felt the air thicken with unaddressed tension. "I'm sorry for what happened between us," he said finally, the weight of his words hanging in the air like a fragile promise. "I never meant to hurt you."

I opened my mouth to respond but hesitated, a whirlwind of emotions bubbling to the surface. "We both said things we didn't mean," I managed, choosing my words carefully. "But I need you to know that I'm working on finding my voice again. That fight was just... one moment in time. I'm moving forward."

Jonah nodded slowly, his eyes filled with something that looked almost like regret. "I want to support you in that. I've been thinking about what I said, and I realize now that I let my fears get in the way. You deserve to shine."

The sincerity in his voice made my heart race, but a part of me remained guarded. "Support is great, but I need to do this for myself. I can't rely on anyone else to validate my journey."

He smiled, a hint of admiration in his expression. "I get that. You're stronger than you realize."

We continued talking, laughter easing the tension as we shared stories and updates about our lives. With each moment, the distance that had formed between us began to dissolve, replaced by a tentative camaraderie. But just when I felt like we were navigating toward solid ground, Jonah's phone buzzed, interrupting the moment.

He glanced at the screen, and the light in his eyes dimmed slightly. "Sorry, I need to take this."

As he stepped away to take the call, I couldn't help but feel a pang of unease. This newfound connection felt delicate, like a spun sugar web that could shatter with a single wrong move. When he returned, his expression was contemplative, and I sensed a shift, as if the air between us had thickened again.

"Everything okay?" I asked, my heart racing slightly.

"Yeah, just work stuff," he replied, but the shadows that flickered across his face betrayed him.

We fell into a comfortable silence, sipping our drinks and watching the world go by. But as I glanced at him, I realized that the conversation we had been dancing around was still very much unresolved. Just as I opened my mouth to say something, the door swung open, and a whirlwind of energy burst in, a group of friends laughing and exclaiming over a cake that looked far too big for the tiny café. The moment shattered, and I felt a sense of loss, like a curtain had fallen on our little play.

Jonah glanced at the commotion and then back at me, a wry smile forming. "Guess this place is a popular spot today."

I chuckled, grateful for the distraction. "Seems like it. Not that I'm complaining—cake makes everything better."

"Right? Who doesn't love cake?" He grinned, a glimmer of the old Jonah returning. "So, do you think you'll be offering cake at your pop-up?"

"Not quite the vibe I'm going for, but it's an interesting thought," I quipped, feeling the weight lift a bit more.

The energy in the café shifted, and it dawned on me that while there were still unanswered questions lingering between us, we were forging a path forward, one stitch at a time. And even if the future felt uncertain, I was ready to embrace it, hand in hand with my art and perhaps with Jonah too—if we could navigate the complexities that lay ahead.

The days melted into each other like colors on a painter's palette, the excitement of my upcoming pop-up event enveloping me in a warm embrace. Tara and I had transformed my studio into a vibrant wonderland, fabric swatches hanging from the ceiling like oversized petals, and sketches plastered on the walls like confetti celebrating a grand occasion. The atmosphere buzzed with creativity, and I thrived in it, feeling alive in a way I hadn't in a long time.

As the event drew nearer, my nerves began to dance in my stomach. I spent hours perfecting each piece, pouring my heart into every stitch. But the thought of exposing my work to the world was a double-edged sword; it was exhilarating yet terrifying. I knew I was inviting judgment, opening the door to opinions that could either uplift or devastate me.

One afternoon, while I was sewing a delicate lace overlay onto a flowing dress, my phone buzzed on the table. It was a text from Jonah, a simple message that sent a jolt of electricity through my veins: "Hey, how about we grab coffee later? I want to talk more about the pop-up."

A flurry of emotions rushed through me—anticipation, anxiety, and a hint of excitement. I glanced at Tara, who was diligently organizing buttons into a rainbow of colors. "Jonah wants to meet for coffee," I said, trying to keep my voice casual despite the butterflies tumbling around in my stomach.

Her head snapped up, eyes gleaming with mischief. "Oh, this is perfect! A little coffee rendezvous to discuss your artistic brilliance and rekindle old flames. Who knew he'd come crawling back so soon?"

I shot her a playful glare. "I wouldn't say it's about rekindling anything. We're just talking about the event." But deep down, the notion of old flames made my heart race in a way that both thrilled and terrified me.

"Right. Just casual coffee," she replied, smirking as she returned to her task. "Don't forget your 'I'm a Strong, Independent Woman' mug for extra flair. You know, in case he forgets just how fabulous you are."

I rolled my eyes, but the corners of my mouth twitched upwards. Maybe she was onto something. The thought of wearing my "fabulous" mug made me chuckle. "I'll consider it. But if I drink too much caffeine, I might just start hyperventilating about my collection."

"Perfectly reasonable. Nothing like a little existential crisis over lattes to get the creative juices flowing."

The playful banter helped ease my nerves as I responded to Jonah, suggesting a time and place for our meeting. I found myself counting down the hours, each tick of the clock amplifying my anticipation. As I prepared to meet him, I put on my favorite dress—an ensemble I had created with the very emotions I was trying to express, an embodiment of both strength and vulnerability.

When I arrived at the café, the familiar scent of roasted coffee beans wrapped around me like a warm blanket. I spotted Jonah at a corner table, a casual air about him as he scrolled through his phone. He looked up when I approached, and the warm smile that spread across his face melted away the remnants of my anxiety.

"Hey there, fashionista," he said, his tone teasing yet soft. "You look incredible."

"Thanks! I figured I should wear something that embodies my artistic soul," I replied, settling into the chair opposite him. "How's the real world treating you?"

"Busy, as always," he replied with a hint of exhaustion in his voice. "But seeing your work in progress has been inspiring. I can't wait for your pop-up. I think it's going to be amazing."

His genuine enthusiasm was infectious, and I felt my cheeks warm with a mix of pride and nerves. "I really hope so. I'm pouring everything into it—every stitch, every idea."

He nodded, his eyes intent on mine, as if searching for something deeper beneath the surface. "That's what it takes, right? Real art comes from a place of vulnerability."

"Exactly. It's scary, but it's also liberating," I said, feeling the walls I had built slowly begin to crumble. "Speaking of vulnerability, I've been thinking about what happened between us..."

Jonah's expression shifted slightly, tension creeping into the space between us. "Me too. I'm sorry for the way I reacted. I let my insecurities cloud my judgment."

"I understand," I said, my voice softening. "But I don't want that to be our story, you know? We both have so much to learn and grow from."

He leaned in, his gaze piercing as he searched for the right words. "You're right. I want to be part of your journey, if you'll have me."

My heart raced, and I felt the weight of his words settle around us like a fragile truce. Just as I was about to respond, the door swung open, letting in a gust of cool air and an unexpected figure. A tall woman with striking features and an air of confidence walked in, her presence demanding attention like a spotlight.

I recognized her instantly—Maya, the designer whose work had dominated the fashion scene for years. She had a reputation for cutting-edge designs and a knack for spotting talent before it even emerged. I had admired her from a distance, a pillar of success that felt both inspiring and intimidating.

"Is that a ghost I see?" Jonah's voice was low, barely a whisper as Maya approached our table, her sharp gaze sweeping over me before settling on him. "Jonah, darling, it's been a while."

"Hey, Maya," he replied, his demeanor shifting into something more guarded. "What brings you here?"

"Just passing through. Thought I'd stop by for a quick caffeine fix." Her eyes flickered to me, curiosity dancing in them. "And who is this?"

I felt the urge to shrink back under her scrutiny, but something inside me pushed back. "I'm a designer too, preparing for my pop-up event. Nice to meet you."

Her lips curled into a sly smile, her interest piqued. "A pop-up? How exciting! I hope it goes well for you. Just remember, in this industry, it's all about making an impression. Don't let the noise drown you out."

Her words were laced with an intensity that sent shivers down my spine, and I couldn't help but feel the weight of her presence.

"Thanks, I'll keep that in mind," I said, trying to sound confident despite the swirling uncertainty in my chest.

"Good. Remember, I'll be watching." With that, she turned on her heel, leaving us at the table with a silence that felt heavier than before.

I looked at Jonah, whose expression mirrored my unease. "What was that about?"

"I don't know, but she has a reputation for being both brilliant and ruthless. You just caught her eye," he said, his voice a mixture of awe and caution.

A flicker of anxiety curled in my stomach. "Why do I feel like she just dropped a gauntlet at our feet?"

Jonah chuckled, though it lacked the warmth of earlier. "Welcome to the world of fashion. Just remember, you're not alone in this. You have a vision, and that counts for everything."

His words offered a sliver of comfort, yet the weight of Maya's encounter lingered, gnawing at my thoughts. As we resumed our conversation, I couldn't shake the feeling that the real challenge was only beginning. I had poured my heart into my art, but with Maya's presence looming over me, I wondered if I was ready for the scrutiny that would come with it.

The café buzzed with life around us, but my mind raced as I pondered the implications of Maya's interest. Would I rise to the occasion, or would her words haunt me as I stepped into the spotlight? As we finished our coffees, a sense of determination ignited within me, a flicker of hope that maybe, just maybe, I could navigate this unpredictable landscape.

But just as I was about to voice my thoughts, my phone buzzed on the table. I glanced at the screen, my heart dropping as I read the message. "We need to talk. It's important."

The sender's name was one I hadn't expected to see, sending a jolt of panic through me. My mind raced, the uncertainty creeping back in like an unwelcome shadow. I looked at Jonah, who was watching me intently, his expression shifting from curiosity to concern.

"What is it?" he asked, leaning forward.

I opened my mouth to respond, but the words felt stuck in my throat, the air thick with unspoken tension. And just like that, the fragile truce we had built began to unravel, leaving us on the precipice of something far more complicated than I could have ever anticipated.

Chapter 29: The Turning Point

The morning sun poured through my apartment window, illuminating the chaos that had become my life. Fabric swatches draped over every surface like the aftermath of an explosion in a craft store. I darted between the remnants of my designs, a kaleidoscope of color and texture, trying to make sense of it all. My heart raced as the pop-up event loomed closer, an exhilarating beacon of hope nestled between the creases of my anxiety. Each day felt like a countdown, my calendar filled with reminders and scrawled notes that had turned into an indecipherable code of self-encouragement.

The scent of freshly brewed coffee wafted through the air, mingling with the faint notes of lavender from the essential oil diffuser I'd turned on in a moment of desperation. I took a deep breath, allowing the aroma to wrap around me, grounding me in the moment. This was more than just a pop-up; it was a manifestation of my resilience, a testament to every late night spent stitching and unpicking, to every tear shed over failed designs. My fingers brushed over the smooth silk of a dress I had poured my heart into, and I could almost hear its whisper, urging me to push through the discomfort and embrace the vulnerability of sharing my creations with the world.

I glanced at my phone, my pulse quickening as I noticed a message from Alex. It was a simple invitation, a suggestion to grab coffee, but the implications were electric. Since the fallout that had left us both reeling, I had avoided him like he was the ghost of a bad decision. But now, I found myself responding with a shaky finger, typing out a hesitant invitation to the pop-up. It was more than just a casual ask; it was a bridge, and I was hoping he'd take the first step to cross it. When his reply came, almost instantaneously, I felt an unexpected warmth wash over me. "I'd love to come," he had written.

Just like that, my heart shifted gears, racing toward possibilities I had long shelved away.

The day arrived, and with it, a whirlwind of emotions. My venue was transformed into a vibrant sanctuary, a celebration of creativity and community. The walls, once bare, now boasted my designs, each piece telling a story that was uniquely mine. Bright splashes of fabric hung from the ceiling, and fairy lights twinkled like stars, casting a soft glow that made everything feel intimate and inviting. The air buzzed with laughter and conversation as friends and family mingled with local influencers and industry professionals, all eager to witness what I had crafted in the face of adversity.

As I stood behind a makeshift booth adorned with my creations, the familiar sensation of imposter syndrome crawled up my spine. Was I really deserving of this? But as familiar faces approached, their expressions filled with pride and support, a rush of warmth flooded my cheeks. I could feel the love and encouragement pulsing through the crowd, creating an invisible shield against my self-doubt. I engaged with guests, sharing the inspirations behind my pieces, each story like a thread weaving through the fabric of my journey. Laughter erupted between exchanges, the kind that felt like music, sweet and intoxicating, as I realized that I was not just presenting my work but sharing a piece of myself.

Then, there he was—Alex. He strode in, a burst of warmth in the cool atmosphere. The sight of him ignited a whirlpool of emotions I thought I had tucked away. His eyes scanned the room before landing on me, and in that moment, the world around us faded, leaving only the thrum of unspoken words hanging between us. I could see the tension in his posture, the slight frown of concentration as he took in the scene before him. When he finally approached, a hesitant smile played on his lips, and I felt a ripple of nostalgia wash over me.

"Wow, this is incredible," he said, his voice low but filled with sincerity. "You've really outdone yourself."

"Thanks," I replied, attempting to keep my tone light. "I figured it was time to let the world see what I can do."

Our eyes locked for a heartbeat, and in that split second, I could almost hear the echoes of our past. The laughter, the shared dreams, the weight of our last conversation hung in the air like a delicate thread ready to snap. "So, what do you think?" I asked, gesturing toward a particularly bold piece—a vibrant, flowy jumpsuit with intricate patterns that mirrored my chaotic yet colorful emotions.

"Honestly? It's stunning. You've always had an eye for detail, but this... this feels like you've unlocked something new," he said, stepping closer, his voice laced with admiration.

A flush crept up my cheeks, but I quickly deflected the attention. "It's all just fabric and thread," I quipped, a nervous laugh escaping my lips. "But it does feel like I'm finally back in the driver's seat."

His smile widened, and for a moment, we were two stars in the same orbit, gravity pulling us closer despite the distance that had formed. "I think you're ready to take the wheel," he replied, his gaze unwavering. "And maybe even take a few scenic routes along the way."

Just as I was about to respond, a loud cheer erupted from the crowd, snapping us back into the reality of the moment. Friends were clapping, the air thick with excitement as I turned to see the centerpiece of the event—my designs showcased in a mini runway. My heart soared as I realized that, despite everything, this was not just a turning point for my career, but a possible rebirth for us as well. The day stretched out before me like a canvas, and I was ready to paint my story anew.

The atmosphere was electric, a palpable energy that buzzed in the air like static electricity before a storm. My heart raced as I mingled among the crowd, buoyed by the waves of chatter and laughter that washed over me. The pop-up had turned into a vibrant celebration, an explosion of color and creativity that mirrored the designs I had painstakingly crafted. I watched as friends and acquaintances admired my pieces, fingers grazing the fabrics like lovers whispering sweet nothings. The pride swelling within me felt almost tangible, a warm glow that spread from my chest to my fingertips.

Then there was Alex, weaving through the throng like a ship cutting through waves. I caught glimpses of him engaging with others, his laughter ringing out above the din, and each time, it felt like a magnet pulling my attention away from everything else. I wanted to be mad at him for the way he effortlessly drew people in, for the way he seemed to carry a light with him, illuminating the corners of the room. But the truth was, I was drawn to him, too, like a moth to a flame, a part of me yearning to rekindle the spark we had once shared.

"Are you going to introduce me, or am I just going to stand here like a lost puppy?" he joked, sidling up to me with an exaggerated pout. The corners of his mouth twitched, fighting the grin threatening to spill over.

"Maybe a lost puppy is exactly what I need to attract attention," I shot back, unable to suppress my own smile. "But sure, let's tell everyone that the puppy's name is Alex."

He chuckled, his eyes sparkling with mischief. "You're lucky you're cute when you're snarky. If I didn't know better, I'd say you were trying to flirt with me."

"Oh, please. Flirting is overrated," I replied, feigning nonchalance as I waved him off. But even as I said it, the fluttering in my stomach contradicted my words, like a secret I wasn't ready to admit.

We fell into a rhythm, darting from one group to another, exchanging pleasantries with friends and industry professionals alike.

Each shared laugh, every lingering gaze, felt like a step toward rebuilding what had been lost between us. It was refreshing, yet terrifying, this new dynamic, as though we were both navigating uncharted waters in a small boat, the waves unpredictable and turbulent.

"Tell me," he said, leaning closer as we paused by a particularly striking ensemble—a midnight blue gown adorned with intricate beadwork that reflected the dim lights like stars. "What was the inspiration behind this one?"

"Ah, that," I replied, pretending to ponder deeply. "It's an homage to those nights when you feel the weight of the world pressing down, yet somehow, you still manage to twirl like you're the only person in the universe."

He raised an eyebrow, clearly amused. "So, it's a 'party in the front, existential crisis in the back' kind of dress?"

I burst into laughter, my cheeks warming. "Exactly! You've captured my creative essence perfectly."

Just then, a hush fell over the crowd, and I turned to see what had drawn their attention. A group of models was making their way down the mini runway I had set up, each showcasing a piece from my collection. The fabric flowed like water, catching the light in waves, and as they strutted past, I felt my heart swell with a mix of pride and disbelief. This was real. I was actually doing it.

The applause was thunderous, echoing through the room, and I caught sight of Alex clapping enthusiastically, his smile wide and genuine. I felt buoyed by the energy, swept up in the applause that felt more like a wave than mere sound. My cheeks hurt from smiling, but the sensation was intoxicating, a high I didn't want to come down from.

But just as I began to bask in the afterglow of my success, an unexpected figure appeared at the edge of the crowd. My heart sank as I recognized Marissa, the woman who had once been my mentor, now a shadow from my past. She stood with arms crossed, a cool, assessing gaze sweeping over the scene like a searchlight. The air around her seemed to thicken, the warmth I had felt moments before suddenly replaced by an icy grip of uncertainty.

I steeled myself, determined not to let her presence dampen my spirit. She was here, and I needed to face her, if only to show her that I had risen from the ashes of her dismissal.

"Look who it is," I muttered under my breath, trying to keep the bitterness at bay.

Alex leaned closer, his brow furrowing. "You okay?"

"Yeah, just peachy," I replied, forcing a grin that felt more like a grimace. "Just my former mentor showing up to rain on my parade."

"Want me to go distract her while you escape through a window?" he offered, a playful glint in his eye.

I snorted, the tension easing slightly. "As tempting as that sounds, I think I'll face her head-on. You know, like a brave warrior or something equally dramatic."

"Alright, brave warrior. Just remember, you've got an army behind you." He gestured to the crowd, his voice low and serious. "You've built this, and it's incredible."

With a deep breath, I squared my shoulders and made my way toward Marissa. As I approached, she regarded me with an expression that was difficult to read—a mixture of surprise and something else, perhaps begrudging admiration.

"I see you've managed to create quite the spectacle," she said, her tone sharp but layered with a hint of acknowledgment.

"Thanks, Marissa," I replied, surprising myself with the steadiness of my voice. "It's nice to see you, too."

She arched an eyebrow, the hint of a smile playing at the corners of her lips. "It seems you've found your voice again. I must admit, I didn't think you had it in you."

"Looks like I've proven you wrong," I shot back, unable to resist the urge to push back against her skepticism.

She studied me, her gaze unwavering, and for a moment, I felt exposed under the weight of her scrutiny. "Perhaps there's hope for you yet," she finally said, her tone softening just a fraction.

Before I could respond, a chorus of cheers erupted from the crowd, drawing our attention back to the runway. The models took their final turns, and I couldn't help but smile as the applause crescendoed. In that moment, I realized that I wasn't just reclaiming my place in the industry; I was reclaiming myself.

"Go on," Marissa said, a rare flicker of encouragement shining in her eyes. "You belong out there."

As I turned back to the crowd, the warmth of their applause wrapped around me like a cozy blanket, and I felt ready to embrace whatever came next—whether it was the thrill of success or the challenges that loomed ahead. With Alex by my side and a newfound sense of purpose, I was ready to weave my story into the tapestry of my life, one stitch at a time.

The applause continued to echo in my ears as the final model strutted down the makeshift runway, her silhouette framed by the warm glow of the fairy lights. I felt as though I were floating, the ground beneath me a mere suggestion. The crowd erupted into cheers, their faces lit up with joy, and for a moment, the weight of the past felt impossibly light. Yet, amid the celebration, my eyes kept darting back to Marissa, still hovering at the edge of the crowd, an enigmatic smile lingering on her lips like a riddle waiting to be solved.

"Hey, Warrior Princess," Alex said, his voice breaking through my reverie. He leaned closer, a teasing glint in his eye. "You're not planning to start a cult with those fans, are you? Because I'm already convinced you're the high priestess of fabulous."

"Only if you promise to be my loyal follower," I replied, smirking back. "But the initiation rites include some questionable dance moves, so be prepared."

He laughed, the sound rich and warm. "I'll practice in front of a mirror. You'll be amazed at my interpretive skills."

Just then, a sharp gasp pierced the atmosphere, drawing everyone's attention. I turned to see Marissa, her expression suddenly tight, eyes fixed on something—or someone—behind me. My stomach dropped as I instinctively followed her gaze, my heart pounding like a drum. Standing at the entrance was a figure I hadn't expected to see: Julia, my former business partner, the very embodiment of everything that had gone wrong in my life. She looked like she had just stepped out of a glossy magazine, impeccably dressed in a sleek black suit, her hair pulled back in a perfect bun that screamed authority.

"Ah, the prodigal partner returns," I murmured, barely able to keep the bitterness out of my voice.

"Should I be worried?" Alex asked, his brow furrowed in concern.

"Only if she brings a team of lawyers and a cake with hidden daggers," I joked, though the humor fell flat. My pulse raced as Julia strolled toward us, confidence radiating from her like heat from a flame.

"Nice show you've put on here," she said, her tone slick and polished. "I see you've managed to turn your little hobby into a spectacle."

"Thanks, Julia. Nice to see you, too. Did you come to help me prepare my acceptance speech for 'Most Dramatic Comeback'?" I shot back, the words dripping with sarcasm.

Her smile tightened, but I could see the wheels turning in her mind. "I'm here for business, actually. I heard whispers about your little event and thought it might be the perfect time to discuss future opportunities."

"Is that what you're calling it? Future opportunities? Because it looks more like you're eyeing my designs like a vulture waiting for dinner," I replied, crossing my arms defiantly.

"Don't be naive, darling. We both know you can't handle this alone. It's only a matter of time before you crash and burn again."

"Thanks for the encouragement, Julia," I said, the edge in my voice sharper than I intended. "But I think I'll take my chances. At least this time, I'm surrounded by people who actually care about me."

The air thickened with tension, and I could feel the crowd's curiosity turning toward us. Alex shifted closer, a protective stance forming as he shot Julia a look that could wither flowers.

"Why don't you step back?" he said, voice low and firm. "She's worked hard for this. No need to undermine her just because you're jealous."

"Jealous? Oh, please." Julia laughed, a sound that lacked any real humor. "I'm more concerned about your safety, sweetie. This business can chew you up and spit you out without a second thought."

"Then I guess I'm lucky I've got teeth," I snapped back, feeling the embers of my courage flare up.

"Are we really going to do this now?" Marissa interjected, stepping in closer to my side, her presence a reassuring anchor. "This is a celebration, not a battlefield."

But Julia wasn't deterred. "A celebration, yes, but one that won't last. It's time you faced reality. This moment in the spotlight will fade, and soon you'll be scrambling again."

"I'm not afraid of a little hard work," I retorted, fighting to keep my voice steady. "And I certainly won't let you dictate my future."

The intensity of Julia's gaze didn't waver, and I could sense a storm brewing behind her carefully curated exterior. "You think you can just erase everything that happened? You're deluding yourself. I won't let you forget what you did."

As her words hung in the air, a chill swept through the crowd. It felt as though the very fabric of the evening was fraying at the seams. My breath caught in my throat as the weight of her accusation settled in. Memories flashed through my mind—mistakes I had made, betrayals I had endured, and the fiery fallout that had driven us apart.

"Are you really going to bring up the past here?" I managed, my voice softer now, laced with vulnerability. "This isn't about what happened before; it's about what I'm building now. You can't keep holding onto a grudge."

"Maybe I'm not the one holding onto anything," she countered, her eyes narrowing. "Maybe I'm just reminding you of the lessons you so conveniently forget."

At that moment, the air shifted, and the crowd seemed to hold its breath, anticipation crackling like electricity. My hands trembled at my sides, the adrenaline coursing through me. I could feel Alex's presence beside me, an unspoken promise of support.

"I've learned a lot, Julia," I said, my voice gaining strength. "I've learned that I can stand on my own two feet. That I don't need to cling to the past to create something beautiful."

"You think you've learned?" she replied, her smile now sinister. "I'd hate for you to discover just how wrong you are. Just when you think you're soaring, I can assure you there's always a way to bring you back down."

Before I could respond, the lights flickered, casting an unsettling shadow over the room. Gasps erupted from the crowd, and I felt the world around me tilt dangerously. Just as I was about to dismiss Julia's veiled threat, a loud crash echoed through the venue, making everyone jump. The sound was followed by a resounding silence, broken only by the hushed whispers of the crowd.

"What was that?" I murmured, instinctively leaning closer to Alex.

His brow furrowed, and he stepped slightly in front of me, scanning the room for the source of the disturbance. "Stay close," he whispered, concern etched in his features.

And then it hit me—the realization that this night, which had started as a celebration of resilience, might just spiral into something darker, something I couldn't control. A sinking feeling twisted in my stomach as I turned back to Julia, her expression inscrutable, eyes glinting with a mix of triumph and malice.

Suddenly, another crash shattered the air, this one louder and closer, followed by the distant sound of glass shattering. My heart raced as I felt the unmistakable sense that something was about to change irreversibly. I barely had time to process it when the lights flickered again, and I caught a glimpse of a shadow moving behind Julia, a figure hidden in the chaos.

And just like that, the atmosphere shifted from one of celebration to something unsettlingly sinister, the uncertainty hanging in the air like an uninvited guest. I could feel the tension thickening, could sense the eyes of the crowd darting around in confusion, each breath heavy with unanswered questions.

"Alex, what's happening?" I whispered, my heart pounding as panic clawed at the edges of my mind.

"I don't know, but we need to—"

Before he could finish, the shadow stepped forward, and the room held its breath, the atmosphere thick with anticipation and dread. My instincts screamed for me to run, to get away from the gathering storm, but I was rooted in place, my gaze locked on the figure emerging from the darkness.

Then, everything shifted again. The lights went out entirely, plunging the room into darkness, and I felt a rush of fear grip me, the kind that clawed at my throat and left me breathless. A distant laugh echoed through the void, chilling me to my core, and I was left standing on the precipice of uncertainty, unsure of what—or who—would emerge when the lights returned.

Milton Keynes UK
Ingram Content Group UK Ltd.
UKHW030746221024
449869UK00001B/48

9 798224 989331